Croatia

timeout.com/croatia

Croatia

Major sight or landmark ....
Hospital or college ....
Railway station ....
Parks ....
River ....
Motorway ....
Main road ....
Main road tunnel ....
Pedestrian road ....
Airport .... ✈
Church .... ✚
Area name .... PILE

Time Out Guides Ltd
Universal House
251 Tottenham Court Road
London W1T 7AB
United Kingdom
Tel: +44 (0)20 7813 3000
Fax: +44 (0)20 7813 6001
Email: guides@timeout.com
www.timeout.com

Published by Time Out Guides Ltd, a wholly owned subsidiary of Time Out Group Ltd.
Time Out and the Time Out logo are trademarks of Time Out Group Ltd.

© Time Out Group Ltd 2009
Previous edition 2006.

10 9 8 7 6 5 4 3 2 1

This edition first published in Great Britain in 2009 by Ebury Publishing.
A Random House Group Company
20 Vauxhall Bridge Road, London SW1V 2SA

Random House Australia Pty Ltd 20 Alfred Street, Milsons Point, Sydney, New South Wales 2061, Australia

Random House New Zealand Ltd 18 Poland Road, Glenfield, Auckland 10, New Zealand

Random House South Africa (Pty) Ltd Isle of Houghton, Corner Boundary Road & Carse O'Gowrie, Houghton 2198, South Africa

Random House UK Limited Reg. No. 954009

For further distribution details, see www.timeout.com.

ISBN: 978-1-84670-061-3

A CIP catalogue record for this book is available from the British Library.

Printed and bound by Firmengruppe APPL, aprinta druck, Wemding, Germany.

The Random House Group Limited supports The Forest Stewardship Council (FSC), the leading international forest certification organisation. All our titles that are printed on Greenpeace approved FSC certified paper carry the FSC logo. Our paper procurement policy can be found at http://www.rbooks.co.uk/environment.

Time Out carbon-offsets its flights with Trees for Cities (www.treesforcities.org).

While every effort has been made to ensure the accuracy of the information contained within this guide, the publishers cannot accept responsibility for any errors it may contain.

All rights reserved. No part of this publication may be reproduced, stored in a retrieval system, or transmitted in any form or by any means, electronic, mechanical, photocopying, recording or otherwise, without prior permission from the copyright owners.

Contents

Introduction

By now, everybody knows about Croatia. The most successful modern-day turnaround in tourism has seen this thinly populated, natural wonder of a country boom with five-star luxury hotels, quality contemporary restaurants and coast-to-coast motorways. The key to the country's success is the coast, a stretch of nearly 2,000 kilometres and 1,200 islands. Apart from a few pockets of package resorts and the odd port, the coast and its waters are as pure now as they were in Roman times.

Only Rijeka and Split significantly sully Croatia's sliver-thin littoral with industrial clutter. These are the ports from which the sleek, white Jadrolinija fleet of catamarans, hydrofoils and liners head out for the islands, short hops for a foot-passenger price equivalent to a Zone 1 tube fare in London.

And what islands! Naturist islands, islands with just deer and naturists feeding them, islands with cocktail bars for the VIP set, islands for windsurfers, islands for sculptors, islands for Tito's political prisoners, islands for Tito's collection of safari animals, islands so remote they're nearer to Italy, islands called home by a family of 120 dolphins, islands of age-old fishing traditions, islands with a particular cave in which the sunlight turns a brilliant blue for an hour each day, islands known for their wine, cheese or anchovy pasties... More than 80 per cent of Croatia's islands have no people on them at all.

All of them dot a transparent Adriatic, the smooth stones of its seabed rippling through it at each of the thousands of indents from Rijeka in the Kvarner Gulf down to Croatia's tapering tip past Dubrovnik at Montenegro. A variety of water sports – sailing, especially, but also windsurfing and kayaking – are practised down the coast. The crystal-clear sea contains amphorae from the ancient world, shipwrecks from century-old conflicts and crashed planes from World War II. This is perfect diving territory.

Local history – Greek, Roman, early Slav, Venetian, Napoleonic, Habsburg, Yugoslav, Nazi, Communist – is easier to appreciate on land. The Roman centres of Pula and Zadar, the masterpiece in stone that is Dubrovnik, the Habsburg grandeur and symmetry of Zagreb, all testify to the invasions and divisions that define the history of the nation.

Despite all the hoo-hah about the coast, much of Croatia is mountainous, with a quarter of it forested. Eight national parks and ten nature parks contain waterfalls, lakes and, in the case of Kornati, a string of 140 islands. Running wild around them are bears, lynx, wolves, chamois, wild cats and wild boar. The lesser known Velebit National Park alone has more than 2,500 species of plant life. Some 126 bird types have been found in Plitvice and the marshes of the Kopački Rit Nature Park contain rare black storks, white-tailed eagles and thousands of cormorants. Brijuni has elephants, zebras and authentic dinosaur footprints, remnants of the Tito era and prehistoric times. In the Kvarner Gulf, griffon vultures and dolphins both have conservation centres open to the public.

As for the humans, your hosts, there are four and a half million of them. All the men are huge, big, broad-shouldered Slavs, some descended from a rather ill-defined tribe known as Illyrians. The women make a show of being chic, and no one of either sex goes anywhere without a fashionable pair of sunglasses. Many social customs, though no Croat will admit this, are shared with Italy. Most spend an entire lifetime talking over coffee.

This being the Balkans, social interaction is very direct. Croats don't mumble and they don't beat about the bush. They are, as a general rule, delightfully hospitable, and not just because their economy depends on tourism. Nearly everyone in the service industry speaks basic English at worst, decent English in the main, the result of a classical education system and the fact that Western TV shows are subtitled, not dubbed. All grow up with popular culture and most Croats are music-savvy. As well as the music scene in Zagreb, a city blessed with many mid-sized venues, the most prestigious clubs on the (mainly northern) Dalmatian coast attract big-name international DJs every summer.

Which brings us back, inevitably, to the coast. Spain's is ruined, Italy's privatised or industrialised, France's is too exclusive. In Croatia, you see the sea as something close to how nature intended. For once, the local PR soundbite is right: the Mediterranean as it once was. No wonder they found it easy to turn their tourist industry around so quickly.
Peterjon Cresswell, Editor

Around Croatia

ZAGREB
Croatia's capital is more than worthy of a city break in its own right. The town is pretty and compact enough to walk around easily, with enough museums, restaurants and nightlife to warrant an extended stay.

Built during the 19th-century heyday of the Habsburg empire, Zagreb was constructed in the style of a Vienna or a Budapest. Zagreb will soon boast a new Museum of Contemporary Art, the city's most significant cultural attraction to open in decades and one that should transform the otherwise underused residential expanse of New Zagreb on the other side of the Sava river. The surrounding countryside at the foot of the Medvednica highlands has plenty of skiing, wildlife and hiking on offer.
► For more, see pp67-94.

CONTINENTAL CROATIA
Known for its historic castles and fertile vineyards, the mainly agricultural territory between Istria and Serbia is known as Continental Croatia. Comprising hilly Zagorje, the regional hub of Varazdin, and Slavonia, Continental Croatia has its main towns dotted in a landscape of wheatfields and wine cellars: Osijek, the capital; the cathedral town of Djakovo; Ilok; Vinkovci; and Vukovar. Less attractive but with more cultural firepower, Slavonski Brod is a frontier town beside the Bosnian border.
► For more, see pp95-108.

ISTRIA
Geographically, culturally and often historically separate from Croatia, the compact triangular peninsula of Istria relates to Italy in many ways. Pula, the largest town, is the gateway to the sporty, seaside hubs of Medulin and Premantura. Further up the west coast are lined the tourist resort of Porec, fashionable Rovinj and secluded Novigrad. Between them, by Vrsar, the Limski kanal cuts a fjord-like slice of pretty green water. The lesser known east coast contains Rabac and its sister settlement of Labin.
► For more, see pp109-143.

KVARNER & ISLANDS

The deep Kvarner gulf contains the largest islands in the Adriatic: busy Krk; Rab, for beach holidays; unspoiled, rural Cres; and Losinj, containing the area's largest town of Mali Losinj. On the mainland, transport hub Rijeka, classic spa resort Opatija and Lovran are connected by Lungomare promenade, established in the Habsburg days.

► *For more, see pp145-188.*

ZADAR & ŠIBENIK

Northern Dalmatia's main towns offer plenty of appeal. Zadar's waterfront has been transformed by Nikola Basic's wave-controlled installation, while Šibenik offers enough variety to warrant a weekend stay. Pretty Primošten is within easy reach, as are the area's national parks: remarkable Kornati, a string of uninhabited islands; and Krka, with its waterfalls and abbey.

► *For more, see pp189-220.*

SPLIT & ISLANDS

A port city with a ruined Roman centre, Split gives access to Croatia's three most popular islands: five-star Hvar; family-friendly Brač and unspoiled Vis. The mainland coast, with Trogir and Kaštela to the north and Omiš, Dugi Rat and the Makarska Riviera to the south, is gearing up to compete with spa hotels and a marina complex.

► *For more, see pp221-276.*

DUBROVNIK & ISLANDS

The jewel in the crown, historic Dubrovnik attracts tourists year-round with its pristine Old Town enclosed within stark white fortifications and lapped by a blue Adriatic. Croatia's biggest cultural event, the Dubrovnik Summer Festival, takes place here. Two minutes from the main square, boats set off for the uninhabited island of Lokrum and the waterside retreat of Cavtat. From the ferry terminal, you can reach the island national park of Mljet, home of mongooses and lagooned monasteries, and Venetian Korčula. Its main namesake town faces the tip of Pelješac, a peninsula of wine cellars and oyster beds with windsurfing at Orebić.

► *For more, see pp277-318.*

Partner network in Croatia

vodafone

out of sight,
but close to mind

Stay connected with the best quality mobile network!

Enjoy your stay in Croatia, and enjoy feeling of connection with the whole world that Vip roaming services provide to you.

Tourist info enables you to get information about destinations, accommodation, events and other travel information in Croatia. Just dial 7799 anytime and anyplace.

Tourist guide is a simple way to discover everything you want to know about cultural heritage of Croatia. When you find a site that interests you, dial 7766 and you'll get the right information.

Prepaid Roaming Top-up for Vodafone user enables you to top-up your account by buying Vipme prepaid vouchers, anywhere in Croatia. This service is valid only for customers of certain Vodafone networks.

For further information visit www.vipnet.hr

The Best of Croatia

SAILING

Sailing allows visitors to see Croatia at its most magical: hidden coves, sheltered bays, restaurants accessible only to sailors, so much of this fabulous coastline is there to discover. And you don't need to be rich or experienced. Novices can hire a boat and a captain, then take to the relatively safe, calm sea.

Croatia has a modern, well equipped network of marinas, charter bases and any number of picturesque anchorages and village harbours. Berthing at the local harbour gives you more privacy – just walk off the boat and into the nearest restaurant. Boats themselves offer surprising luxury, with comfortable cabins and room on deck to eat, drink, sunbathe and make merry. Lap it up – this is once-in-a-lifetime stuff.

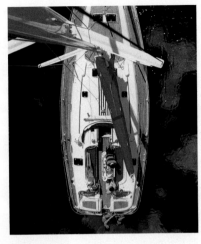

DINING

The Adriatic provides Croatia with its famously fresh seafood, prepared and served in the classic Mediterranean manner or, increasingly, used in imaginative, new cuisine, particularly in Istria. Improvements in service now make this one of Europe's most enjoyable and surprising dining experiences, but it would all go to waste without the quality of the produce involved – here a tomato tastes like a tomato. A sea view completes a perfect picture.

LUXURY HOTELS

Nowhere is the revolution in Croatian tourism more apparent than in the rapid expansion of five-star hotels. It started in Dubrovnik, where Goran Štrok almost single-handedly kickstarted the post-war recovery with jaw-dropping venues such as the Hotel Dubrovnik Palace (*see p297*), the Hotel Bellevue (*see p297*) and the Hotel Excelsior (*see p297*). Others have followed suit, among them the Hilton Imperial (*see p297*), the Hotel Grand Villa Argentina (*see p297*) and the Rixos Libertas (*see p302*). All offer the best in mod cons, but their USP is that awesome view of Adriatic blue. With the opening of Le Méridien Grand Hotel Lav (*see p238*), Split is not left behind, while Istrian pearl Rovinj can now boast the Hotel Monte Mulini (*see p127*) and the Hotel Villa Angelo d'Oro (*see p127*).

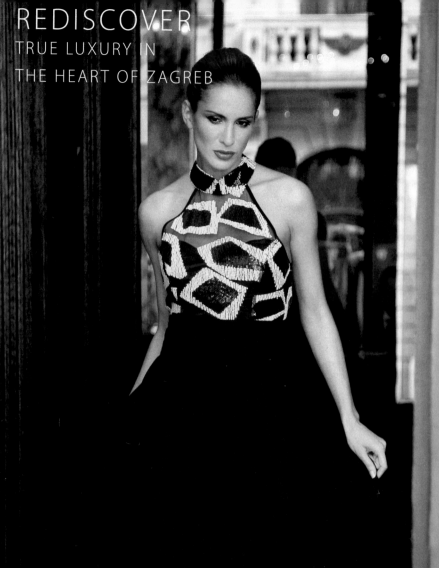

REDISCOVER
TRUE LUXURY IN
THE HEART OF ZAGREB

LIVE THE LUXURY℠

THE
Regent
ESPLANADE ZAGREB

BEIJING   SINGAPORE   TAIPEI   BERLIN   BORDEAUX   ZAGREB   BAL HARBOUR   TURKS AND CAICOS

Mihanovićeva 1   10000 Zagreb   Croatia   T.+385(0)1 45 66 666   F.+385(0)1 45 66 020
Info.Zagreb@RezidorRegent.com   www.regenthotels.com

WINE REGIONS

Little known outside Croatia, the country's deep reds and golden whites – Vugava, Pošip, Grk foremost among them – are winning over international wine experts, who are more than pleasantly surprised by their quality. The key terroir is Pelješac, where age-old techniques combine with calcified, rocky soil and long months of Dalmatian sun to create Dingač, the label to look out for. In the north, amid the wheatfields of Slavonia and the hillsides of Istria, wine cellars open to the visiting public.

FESTIVALS

From the overnight success of the Garden Festival of DJ music and seaside raving outside Zadar (*see p63*) to the venerable, 60-year-old highbrow Dubrovnik Summer Festival (*see p63*), set around the historic open-air spaces of the Old Town, cultural events in Croatia span the complete range of locations and artistic disciplines. Choice is all, and is best exemplified by the many different locations in which you can catch a film festival: a Roman amphitheatre in Pula (*see p65*), atop a medieval hilltop village (Motovun; *see p65*), alongside partying students in Zagreb (*see p65*) or by the Danube in the recovering war zone of Vukovar (*see p63*). For music, you couldn't ask for a better line-up than Zagreb's InMusic (*see p63*) in June, although organisers at the Radar (*see p63*) in Varaždin may well be challenging them for top-draw business.

GETTING AWAY FROM IT ALL

When it gets too crowded on the coast, Croatia offers more chances than most to get away from the sound of clinking glasses and idiotic laughter. It isn't only the islands, islets and peninsulas of Europe's most celebrated coastline – it's what's not on them. People. For example, nearly all of the 140 islands of the Kornati archipelago, which is a protected national park, are uninhabited. You might see the occasional sheep or small votive chapel built by a grateful sailor saved from a storm. Best of all are the clumps of rock stuck out halfway to Italy with nothing but a lighthouse (*see p311*) on them – the perfect recipe for a tranquil getaway.

Time Out Croatia

Editorial
Editor Peterjon Cresswell
Deputy Editor Edoardo Albert
Proofreader Mandy Martinez
Indexer Jonathan Cox

Managing Director Peter Fiennes
Editorial Director Ruth Jarvis
Series Editor Will Fulford-Jones
Business Manager Dan Allen
Editorial Manager Holly Pick
Assistant Management Accountant Ija Krasnikova

Design
Art Director Scott Moore
Art Editor Pinelope Kourmouzoglou
Senior Designer Henry Elphick
Graphic Designers Kei Ishimaru, Nicola Wilson
Advertising Designer Jodi Sher

Picture Desk
Picture Editor Jael Marschner
Deputy Picture Editor Lynn Chambers
Picture Researcher Gemma Walters
Picture Desk Assistant Marzena Zoladz
Picture Librarian Christina Theisen

Advertising
Commercial Director Mark Phillips
International Advertising Manager Kasimir Berger
International Sales Executive Charlie Sokol

Marketing
Marketing Manager Yvonne Poon
Sales & Marketing Director, North America
  & Latin America Lisa Levinson
Senior Publishing Brand Manager Luthfa Begum
Marketing Designer Anthony Huggins

Production
Group Production Director Mark Lamond
Production Manager Brendan McKeown
Production Controller Damian Bennett
Production Coordinator Kelly Fenlon

Time Out Group
Chairman Tony Elliott
Chief Executive Officer David King
Group General Manager/Director Nichola Coulthard
Time Out Communications Ltd MD David Pepper
Time Out International Ltd MD Cathy Runciman
Group IT Director Simon Chappell
Marketing & Circulation Director Catherine Demajo

Produced in association with Time Out Croatia
Directors David Plant, Vanda Vucicevic

Contributors
Introduction Peterjon Cresswell. **History** Reuben Fowkes, Marcus Tanner. **Croatia Today** Reuben Fowkes. **Food & Drink** Alison Radovanović (*Traditional Konobas* Matt Field; *Zembo on Fish* Deniz Zembo). **Nature & Wildlife** Alex Crevar (*Falconry for Beginners* Jane Cody). **Sailing** Jane Cody. **Children** Tom Popper (*Child-Friendly Lodging* Jane Cody). **Festivals** Peterjon Cresswell. **Zagreb** Peterjon Cresswell, Alex Dragaš, Maja & Reuben Fowkes, Matt Field, Jane Cody, Anja Mutić. **Continental Croatia** Maja & Reuben Fowkes, Alex Crevar, Jane Cody, Matt Field. **Istria** Alison Radovanović, Tom Popper, Peterjon Cresswell, David Plant. **Kvarner & Islands** Tom Popper, Peterjon Cresswell, Alex Crevar, Vanda Vukadinović, Alex Dragaš. **Zadar & Šibenik** Jane Cody, Alex Crevar, Maja & Reuben Fowkes, Peterjon Cresswell, Anja Mutić. **Split & Islands** Jane Cody, Alex Crevar, Tom Popper, Peterjon Cresswell. **Dubrovnik & Islands** Peterjon Cresswell, Alex Crevar, Tania Unsworth, Bob Cohen, Vesna Marić. **Directory** Peterjon Cresswell, Brian Gallagher, Marcus Tanner.

Maps JS Graphics Ltd (john@jsgraphics.co.uk), based on material supplied by Netmaps.

Photography Carly Calhoun, except: pages 20, 23, 34, 77, 79, 85, 86, 89, 90, 91, 122, 129, 241, 253, 318 Matt Field; pages 20, 21 Krumrovec Museum; page 24 Zagreb Tourist Board; pages 29 Fumie Suzuki; pages 32, 43, 69, 70, 71, 75, 81, 82, 90, 93, 111, 120, 126, 128 (top), 137, 139, 147, 159, 225, 227, 248, 261 (top, middle left), 262, 275, 279, 286, 291, 294, 295, 307 Vanda Vucicevic; page 39 Konoba Molorran; pages 47, 213 Sibenik Falconry Centre; page 48 Griffin Vulture Centre Cres.; page 49 Hidden Croatia; pages 53, 205 Sail Croatia; pages 56, 154 Rijeka Karneval PR; page 59 Pula Aquarium; page 60 Falkensteiner Hotels; page 61 Monotum Film Festival; page 66 Dubrovnik Summer Festival; page 66 Garden PR; page 76 Museum of Contemporary Art PR; pages 87, 88 Nikola Fox; page 92 Sheriff & Cherry; page 101 Hotel Osijek; page 105 Vukovar Tourist Board; page 106 Ilok Tourist Board; pages 108, 214, 243, 245 Jane Cody; pages 111, 112, 118, 131, 132, 168 Dave Jepson; page 116 Valasabbion PR; page 119 Brijuni National Park; pages 125, 128, 129, 143, 148, 150, 157, 161, 283, 284, 287, 289, 293, 296, Rajko Radovanovic; pages 135, 158 Eni Nurkollari; page 165 Tom Popper; pages 178, 179 Bozo Vukicevic; page 187 Aquarius PR; page 195 Nikola Basic; page 198 Arsenal Multimedia Centre; page 201 Bastion PR; page 203 Rupert Baby; page 209 Ilivija Group PR; pages 216, 250 Etnoland PR; page 217 Pelegrini PR; page 237 Le Meridien Grand PR; page 244 Klapa Libar; page 246 Omis; page 299 Hotel Argentina; pages 300, 301 Adriatic Luxury Hotels; page 302 Marc van Bloemen; page 304 Konave Tourist Board; page 313 Dino Centivic; pages 315, 316 Hotel Odisej.

The Editor would like to thank all contributors to the previous edition of *Time Out Croatia*, whose work forms the basis for this book.

© **Copyright Time Out Group Ltd**
All rights reserved

About the Guide

GETTING STARTED

The seven sections in this guide are arranged in a rough north-to-south order; each one begins with an introduction and a map of the region. All the individual areas start with background history and sightseeing highlights, followed by details on the best places to eat, drink and stay (in the bigger towns, these venues have been marked on detailed street maps with coloured bullets: ❶ for hotels, ❶ for restaurants, and ❶ for bars and cafés), and tourist information. We also give travel directions; however, note that public transport options around inland rural areas are very limited.

THE ESSENTIALS

For practical information, including visas, disabled access, emergency numbers, useful websites and local transport, please see the Directory. It begins on page 319.

THE LISTINGS

All listings were checked and correct at press time. However, arrangements can alter at any time, and economic conditions can cause prices to change rapidly.

The very best venues, the must-sees and must-dos, have been marked with a red star (★). We've also marked sights that offer free admission with a FREE symbol, and budget restaurants with a **Kn** symbol.

THE LANGUAGE

A few basic Croatian phrases go a long way. You'll find a primer on page 326.

PHONE NUMBERS

The national code for all numbers in this guide is 385. From outside Croatia, dial your country's international access code (00 from the UK, 011 from the US), followed by 385, then the number listed in the guide but omitting the initial 0. Within Croatia, dial the whole number given in the guide. Mobile numbers – most commonly starting with 091 and 098 – are expensive to dial from abroad or with a foreign mobile.

FEEDBACK

We welcome feedback on this guide, both on the venues we've included and on any other locations that you'd like to see featured in future editions. Please email us at guides@timeout.com.

Time Out Guides

Founded in August 1968, Time Out has grown from humble beginnings into the leading resource for anyone wanting to know what's happening in the world's greatest cities. Alongside our influential what's-on weeklies in London, New York and Chicago, we publish more than 20 magazines in cities as varied as Beijing and Beirut, and a range of travel books that includes more than 50 City Guides and the newer Shortlist series. The company remains proudly independent, still owned by Tony Elliott four decades after he launched *Time Out London*.

Written by local experts and illustrated with original photography, our books also retain their independence. No business has been featured because it has advertised, and all restaurants and bars are visited and reviewed anonymously.

ABOUT THE EDITOR

Peterjon Cresswell edited the first *Time Out Croatia Guide*, and has edited and written many other guidebooks to the region. He has lived and worked in this part of the world since 1990.

A full list of the book's contributors can be found opposite. Note that we have also included details of our writers in selected chapters spread throughout the guide.

BOAT TRIP FOR TWO: 200 KN
SCUBA DIVING FOR TWO: 360 KN
NIGHT IN FISHERMAN'S COTTAGE: 500 KN

ARRIVING: PRICELESS™

Accepted in over 28 million locations
worldwide and all over Croatia.

In Context

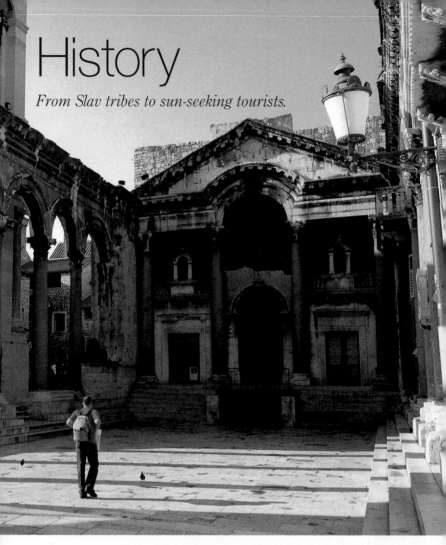

History

From Slav tribes to sun-seeking tourists.

Scholars have yet to resolve the etymology and meaning of the word Croat, with clues as to its origins sought variously in the Greek words for 'people who have a lot of land', 'tree', 'a dance', and the inhabitants of the island of Krk. The word has also been taken as evidence of distant Iranian roots, with an original meaning of 'friend' or 'protector'. Arriving at the shores of the Adriatic at the start of the seventh century, the Croats were among a wave of Slav invaders that reached their most western point of conquest in Istria at the gates of Italy. At the same time, the Slav tribes also pressed south, destroying Salona in AD 614, the magnificent capital of Roman Dalmatia.

ISLAND LIFE

In the face of the barbarian onslaught, the Romans, and other Romanised peoples of Illyria, moved to the islands, later returning to their cities on the mainland when it became clear that the Slavs were not interested at this stage in urban living. This resulted in an interesting situation, in which two quite different civilisations co-existed in close proximity during the seventh century. The Romans kept to the towns of Zadar, Trogir and Split, while in the Dalmatian hinterland, tribes of Slavs maintained their own social systems, religion and language. There was a pragmatic exchange between the two societies, with the Romans ready to exchange craftwork and commercial services for the livestock and agricultural products of the Slavs. Over time, the two cultures intermixed. Rulers of the pagan Slavs came under the influence of the Christian civilisation of the cities, and the urban population became progressively less distinct from the more numerous ethnic Slavs living in the surrounding countryside.

In a pattern that was to be repeated again and again over the centuries, the ups and downs of distant empires gradually changed the political constellation on the Adriatic coast. The struggle between the Franks and the Byzantines in the age of Charlemagne, crowned Emperor of the Holy Roman Empire in 800, had direct repercussions for Dalmatia. When Charlemagne and the Byzantine Emperor made peace in Aachen in 812, the Byzantines were allotted the Roman cities, while the Franks got the rural hinterland, founding a dukedom that was centred on Sisak.

LATIN OR GLAGOLICA?

The first historical document referring to Croatian state institutions dates from 852, when Trpimir (845-864) styled himself 'Dux Croatorum'. The small territory of this Croatian dukedom extended across the hinterlands of Zadar, Trogir and Split, but did not include the coastal cities themselves. Interestingly, there was also a fledgling Pannonian Croatian state, positioned along the river Drava, in an area that in the Middle Ages became known as Slavonia. Cautious progress by the Croat rulers was suggested by an agreement made between Byzantium and the Croatian state, according to which the cities on the Adriatic seaboard would pay a fee to the Croatians in exchange for the right to work their own fields. The Venetians also paid the Croats for the right of their ships to pass through.

The Croat ruler Tomislav (910-928) succeeded by 925 in becoming a full-blown *rex*. The Byzantine empire allowed him to rule the cities of the Adriatic as the Emperor's pro-consul. During his rule, there were two Church assemblies in Split in which vital questions facing the early medieval Church were discussed. Militarily, Tomislav kept the Hungarians in the north at bay and stopped Bulgarian Emperor Symeon's attempt to conquer the country. He was an administrative innovator, bringing the machinery of feudal government up to date, with the division of Croatia into 11 administrative districts.

Culture and religion in the kingdom were marked by the division between the users of Latin and the users of the Slavic alphabet, *Glagolica*. In the early years, inland Croatian priests knew no Latin, could marry, and wore their hair long like the Byzantine clergy, but by the 12th century, the papal authorities and the mostly Latin-speaking coastal nobility had brought the Croatian Church firmly within the established order of Roman Catholicism. Glagolitic survived as the secular alphabet for Croatian literature from the 14th to 16th centuries, and was to enjoy a partial revival in the 19th century, thanks to the influence of Romantic literary nationalists.

In a fateful accident of royal marriage and inheritance, the Croatian crown passed in 1102 to King Kálmán of Hungary. He assumed the Croatian throne under a joint agreement that was to guarantee the separate but unequal existence of Croatia within the Hungarian kingdom until 1918. According to the *Pacta conventa* the Croatian nobility kept their Sabor (assembly) and local authority in the country. While Croatia continued to exist as a separate political entity, the process of state building was blocked for almost 900 years by the interests and competing sovereignties of the Ottomans, the Venetians, the Hungarians and the Habsburg empire.

IN CONTEXT

Remembering Tito

Croatia's uneasy relationship with its old overlord.

Born in 1892 in the village of Kumrovec, Josip Broz Tito, ruler of Yugoslavia from 1945 to his death in 1980, remains a paradoxical figure in contemporary Croatian culture. He is seen as a Communist dictator, who kept Croatia in Yugoslavia, crushed the Croatian Spring independence movement in 1971 and built the notorious Goli Otok island prison camp to punish his enemies. He was also a Croatian hero from the hilly region of Zagorje, the only World War II resistance leader who managed to liberate his own country and tread a difficult third way between Stalin and the West. At home, he was the preserver of Brotherhood and Unity.

A wave of Tito nostalgia has seen a best-selling cookery book of his favourite recipes; the marketing of the Tito cult on Brijuni; several new films about his life; a photo exhibition about his travels, and the planned restoration of his yacht *Galeb* as a tourist attraction in Rijeka.

Over the border in Serbia, an optimistic entrepreneur is setting up a Yugoland theme park in Subotica. In Bosnia, there's a Tito Café in the Sarajevo History Museum, full of memorabilia.

Tito's life story is an extraordinary one. Raised on the Slovene-Croatian border, he left his peasant background to become an engineering worker, ending up in Vienna. In World War I he was taken prisoner by the Russians but freed after the Bolshevik Revolution, staying on as a Red Guard during the Civil War. After returning home, he worked in a flour mill, shipyard and foundry, and was made head of the Zagreb Communist Party in 1928. He was then arrested and spent six years in prison, debating Marxist theories with fellow prisoners. After his release he went to Moscow and became a leading Communist functionary under the name Comrade Walter. Avoiding the Stalinist purges, he was appointed leader of the Yugoslav Communist Party in 1939. The origins of his new name, Tito, lie either in his abrupt style of giving orders 'Ti...to' ('You...that.') or in the initials of a Soviet-made pistol, the TT-30.

From 1941 he led the Yugoslav partisan resistance against the Nazi invasion, narrowly escaping death or capture on several occasions. He

IN CONTEXT

secured the support of both the RAF Balkan Air Force, thanks to the efforts of Churchill's special envoy Fitzroy Maclean, as well as Stalin's Red Army, whose pincer movement north tied up the Nazis and opened the way for the Partisans to liberate first Belgrade then Zagreb.

Head of a new six-republic Yugoslavia from 1945, Tito indulged his taste for palaces and conspicuous expenditure. He wore a gold-edged uniform with a belt buckle of pure gold, he dyed his hair and he changed his clothes several times a day. He had Brijuni transformed into an elite residence and playground, where he entertained world leaders, film stars and other celebrities. Constantly on the move, he stayed in luxurious residencies across Yugoslavia, on *Galeb* ('Seagull') and his specially kitted-out Blue Train. As the economy gradually ground to a halt, Tito strutted the world stage as a leading figure of the non-aligned movement.

When the news of Tito's death broke on 4 May 1980 a football match in Split between Red Star Belgrade and Hadjuk was abandoned and the players left the playing field in tears. His funeral drew delegations from 128 countries while huge crowds packed the stations between Ljubljana where he died and Belgrade where he was buried to watch the funeral train go past. It was the end of an era for the country.

Today, the towns that bore his name have been renamed, but many street signs remain. All the wealth and property he amassed, in accordance with the principles of the Communist system, reverted to the state on his death. The presidents of independent Croatia have found themselves sleeping in his bedrooms, from the official Zagreb residency of Pantovčak to Brijuni.

The village of Kumrovec is now an ethnographic museum and a visitor attraction. Forty houses from the old village have been restored, each featuring staged scenes of traditional rural culture, such as a Zagorje-style wedding, the blacksmith's forge and the wheelmaker's workshop, though the main attraction remains the birth house of Josip Broz.

IN CONTEXT

VILLAS FORUM

PROPERTIES & SERVICES

THE LEADING PROVIDER OF LUXURY VILLAS IN ISTRIA AND DALMATIA

VILLA FLOTILLA
Skippered Yacht by Day, Luxury
Farmhouse by Night.
This unique service allows you
to cruise the Adriatic Sea by day
with your own private skipper
then be chauffeur driven to a
different idyllic villa ever night!

PERSONAL CHEF
Perfect for the gourmet enthusiast,
a tantalising feast of fresh local
specialities prepared in the
intimate atmosphere and privacy
of your own villa. Relax by the
pool and wait to be served at your
beautifully laid dining table.

TAILOR MADE ACTIVITIES
A morning experiencing local life
first hand with a personal guide.
An afternoon on a yacht with
our captain – swim, fish, snorkel,
whatever you wish. An evening
having a relaxing back, shoulder
and neck massage in your villa.

OTHER POSSIBILITIES INCLUDE:
Venice, tickets to local concerts and events, child care, chauffeurs, truffle hunting, hot air ballooning
To find out more or to book call +385 52 375 600 or email contact@villasforum.com, www.villasforum.com

Josip Jelačić. *See p25.*

THE TURKS ARE ATTACKING

The decline of the medieval Croatian kingdom was hastened by the rise of Venice, which in the 14th century consolidated its hold on Dalmatia. One low point was the sale of Dalmatia to the Venetians for 100,000 ducats, with the result that the Venetians ruled both the cities and islands of Dalmatia, with only the rump of Croatia in Slavonia left. After the fall of Bosnia in 1463, Croatian lands were more vulnerable to Turkish attacks, and defeat at the Battle of Krbavsko Polje, in Lika, in 1493 ushered in a century of chaos and destruction. The situation was just as serious for the Habsburgs, who trembled as the Turks drew nearer and nearer to Vienna, crushing the Hungarians at the Battle of Mohács in 1526. With the King of Hungary killed at Mohács, the following year the Croatian nobility chose to put their faith in the Habsburg ruler King Ferdinand, in the hope that he would protect them from the depredations of the Turks.

PIRATES AND PEASANTS

Croatian trust in the Habsburgs was not very generously rewarded. The Emperor Ferdinand I carved another slice off what was left of the Kingdom of Croatia with the establishment of a broad military zone, controlled from Vienna, along the border with the Ottoman empire. This was the 'Vojna Krajina', or Military Border. After the fort at Bihać fell in 1592, only small parts of Croatia remained unconquered. The remaining 16,800 square kilometres (6,486 square miles) were referred to as the 'remnants of the remnants of the once great Croatian kingdom'. The 16th century in Croatia was also the era of Matija Gubec's bloodily suppressed peasant uprising, and the Uskok pirate state in Senj, which had managed to harass the Venetians, Habsburgs and the Turks from its stronghold on the inhospitable coastline around Senj.

An exception in this story of hardship and imperial domination is provided by Dubrovnik. Known as Ragusa, and recognised as a sovereign republic, the city was the main Mediterranean centre for trade with the Ottoman empire by the 16th century, and maintained its independence until the Napoleonic Wars. Despite the difficult political situation, Dalmatia in the 15th and 16th centuries was something of a mecca for Renaissance culture. In this period, hundreds of Croat humanists studied at universities

Zagreb.

ZAGREB. (Croatie) Ilica.

abroad, such as Padua. The strong cultural identity of the coastal cities of Dalmatia was as much connected to their sense of belonging to a cultural heritage going back to the Romans and Greeks, as to their Latin scholarship and the development of Croat vernacular literature. Italian humanists, along with painters, sculptors and architects, who came to work on the magnificent building projects of Renaissance Dalmatia, must have felt very much at home here.

THE TURKS ARE RETREATING

The eventual reversal of Ottoman fortunes followed their defeat at the Battle of Sisak in 1593. But instead of relaxing Habsburg control of the country, Ferdinand II consolidated the imperial organisation of the Military Border, taking it completely out of the hands of the Croatian Parliament. The noble Zrinski and Frankopan families plotted to eject the Habsburgs from Croatia, in an unlikely and desperate-sounding coalition with Louis XIV of France, the King of Poland, the Venetians and even the Turks. Unfortunately, word of the plot leaked out, and Peter Zrinski and his brother-in-law Franjo Frankopan were beheaded in Vienna Neustadt in 1671. The 17th and 18th centuries saw the power of the Croatian nobles in the Habsburg lands decline, with the Croatian Sabor in an increasingly weak position relative to the Vienna-appointed Governor, or Ban.

Following the Ottoman retreat after their second failed advance on Vienna in 1683, southern Slavonia was also brought into the Vojna Krajina. From the mid-16th century onwards, the Habsburgs had attracted border guards to the area with offers of free land without manorial obligations and by allowing freedom for Serbs to practise the Orthodox religion. Consequently, according to the first census of 1819 over half the population of the Military Border were Serbs, whose large presence in historic Croatia was to become a source of tension. The economy of the Military Border stagnated thanks to bureaucratic restrictions on the size and transfer of agricultural holdings, a complex customs regime and the fact that all men of military age had to spend much of the year on exercises.

'Cheated of all hopes of uniting Croat lands into one autonomous unit within the empire, Croat loyalty to the Habsburgs declined.'

When the Hungarians tried under Ferenc Rákóczi to rid themselves of the Habsburgs, the Croatian nobility opted to collaborate with Vienna, signing the 'pragmatic sanction' that made possible Maria Teresa's accesion to the throne in 1740. This turned out to be a mistake, as during her 40-year rule she further centralised power, shutting down the Croatian Sabor. Her son, the enlightened despot Joseph II, made some small improvements in the conditions of the peasantry, but was even more determined than his mother to carry out the Germanisation of the Habsburg empire.

CROATS FOR THE CORSICAN

After Venice fell to revolutionary France in 1797, her possessions in Dalmatia also fell under French control. French rule brought a number of advanced but short-lived administrative reforms, which included Napoleon's innovative establishment of an Illyrian kingdom, embracing Dalmatia and much of modern Slovenia. After Napoleon's defeat, Dalmatia passed into the control of the Habsburgs. At the same time, the growing strength of nationalism in Hungary was felt in Croatia, which many Hungarians treated as a province and attempted to 'magyarise'. It was against this background that a new direction in Croatian politics was defined, with the emergence of the Illyrian movement.

CROATS FOR THEMSELVES

The fragmentation of the lands of the medieval Kingdom of Croatia had long been bemoaned, triggering calls for the 'Triune Kingdom of Croatia, Slavonia and Dalmatia' to be reunited under the House of Habsburg. However, the Slav activists of the early 19th century, fearing the term 'Croat' was too narrow, and following the example of the writer Ljudevit Gaj, instead described themselves as Illyrians, thereby hoping to bring under one umbrella the Habsburg empire's Croat, Slovene and Serb inhabitants.

Political Illyrianism ended after 1848. Although the Croatian Ban, Josip Jelačić, had helped the Habsburg monarchy suppress the Hungarian uprising, it earned him no favours from Vienna. Instead, during the authoritarian backlash against national independence movements between 1849 and 1860, the Sabor was not allowed to meet, and the Austrians ruled Croatia even more directly than before. Jelačić died a bitter man.

In the latter half of the 19th century, the Illyrian movement split. Ljudevit Gaj's heirs continued to champion a broad alliance with other Slavs, notably the Serbs. Now describing themselves as Jugoslavs (South Slavs) rather than Illyrians, their leader for many decades was the redoubtable scholar-Bishop of Djakovo, Josip Strossmayer. Their opponents, under Ante Starčević, rejecting the pan-Slav alliance with the Serbs as unworkable and as detrimental to Croat interest, gathered under the banner of the Party of Rights. A struggle between Strossmayer and Starčević for hearts and minds dominated Croat politics in the late 19th century.

While the political situation resembled stalemate, the economic development of the country advanced apace. The ejection of the Ottomans from Bosnia in 1878 removed the purpose of having a Military Border, and opened up new opportunities for both trade and mineral exploitation. The building of strategic railways made possible the industrial development of Slavonian cities such as Osijek and Slavonski Brod. The inland towns, which had stagnated for centuries, enjoyed an urban renaissance, with the transformation of Zagreb a case in point. A major earthquake provided an opportunity to remodel the city according to the civic ideals of the fin de siècle, creating a distinctive green horseshoe of squares and parks.

IN CONTEXT

INDEPENDENCE – OF SORTS

Not surprisingly, the beginning and, even more, the long continuation of World War I tested the Croats' loyalty to the old order to its limits. At first most Croats fought loyally for the octogenarian Emperor Francis Joseph but, as the fighting dragged on and the prospect of defeat loomed, many Croats began pondering their future without the Habsburgs. The leaking of the terms of the secret London Treaty of 1915, by which the Entente Powers promised Italy most of Dalmatia if it were to come into the war on their side, shocked Croats into action. Alarmed by the possibility of partition between Italy in the west and Serbia in the east, opinion swung towards the establishment of a South Slav state embracing Serbia and Montenegro in order to guarantee the integrity of Croat lands. The first Croats to advance this programme were three Dalmatians, Supilo, Trumbić and the sculptor and architect Ivan Meštrović, who set up the Yugoslav Committee for this purpose in 1915.

The campaigners for Yugoslavia envisaged Croatian autonomy and equality within the new framework. But the state formed in 1918, after Austria-Hungary collapsed, disappointed them. It became clear that Yugoslavia's Serbian rulers saw Yugoslavia as an extension of Serbia and the imposition of a centralised constitution in 1921 discredited the Yugoslav cause in Croatia.

Opinion now rallied to the separatist Stjepan Radić, leader of the Croat Republican Peasant Party, who had never supported the Yugoslav project. Having warned the Croats that 'they were rushing into union with Serbia like a band of drunken geese in a fog', he campaigned for an independent Croatian republic. The young Yugoslav state was immediately faced with fierce opposition from Radić's party, which only became more radical and intransigent following his assassination in the Belgrade Parliament in 1928. His successor as leader was Vladko Maček, who maintained the Peasant Party's policy of non-violent struggle against Serb domination. Alongside this popular movement, which usually won the elections in Croatia, a more extremist opposition movement grew up on the far right under Ante Pavelić. His Ustashe movement traced its descent from Starčević's Party of Rights. But unlike the latter, it was prepared to engage in violence to achieve the goal of independence. An extreme solution on the left was offered by the Communist Party, destined to take control of the country later on, but in the 1920s and '30s a minority group.

IN CONTEXT

Diocletian Palace, Split.

PAUL OVERRULES PETER

While in politics, the Kingdom of Yugoslavia drifted in the 1930s towards authoritarianism, in the cultural sphere there was a resurgence of opposition to parochialism and right-wing politics. The leading figure in Croatian literature in this
period was Miroslav Krleža, who opposed the clerical right and the political dominance of the Peasant Party. He was aligned politically with the underground Communist Party, but in cultural matters he struggled against the confines of Socialist Realism.

The assassination of Yugoslavia's authoritarian King Alexander in Marseille in 1934 put an end to the political stalemate. Because the new King Peter was a minor, power passed to a regent, Prince Paul, an Anglophile liberal who was bent on solving Croat grievances without, however, conceding independence. Maček was brought in from the cold and after tortuous negotiations over borders and competencies, an autonomous Croat unit – the Banovina – was established within Yugoslavia in 1939. Dismissed as a façade by Pavelić's now-exiled Ustashe, the Banovina managed to alleviate Croat frustration – a necessity for the whole of Yugoslavia now that Nazi Germany and Fascist Italy were threatening the balance of power within Europe.

However, the Banovina had no time to establish itself. After a pro-British faction in the Yugoslav army overthrew Prince Paul in 1941, Hitler invaded Yugoslavia and rapidly conquered the country. In Zagreb, Mussolini hurriedly installed Pavelić and his Ustashe cronies as lords of the new Independent State of Croatia (NDH), a name that belied its real status as an Italian dependency.

CIVIL WAR

The NDH co-operated wholeheartedly with Nazi plans to exterminate the Jews and other minorities. Its agenda also included forcing Serbs to convert to Catholicism or be killed; many simply fled. As the Axis powers awarded the NDH the whole of Bosnia-Herzegovina, where Serbs made up the single largest ethnic group, the NDH was locked into civil war from the moment it was established in April 1941.

As World War II intensified, a frightful three-cornered conflict developed over Croatia between Communists, Serbian royalists, known as jetniks, and the Ustashe, who claimed the support of Nazi Germany and Fascist Italy. In reality, Italy was an ambivalent godparent of the NDH, making no secret of its eventual ambition to annex Dalmatia and realise Mussolini's goal of turning the Adriatic Sea into an Italian lake. Pavelić's poorly equipped army was no match for its opponents, and especially the well-organised Communist Partisans, led by Josip 'Tito' Broz (*see p20* **Remembering Tito**). The Partisans showed their strength by holding two congresses inside the NDH in 1942 and '43 at Bihać and Jajce, where they sketched out the foundations of a new Yugoslav state. This was to be a truly federal arrangement, with Serbs sharing power not only with Croats and Slovenes but with Macedonians, Montenegrins and Bosnians.

TITO'S YUGOSLAVIA – AND AFTER

With the defeat of the Nazis in 1945, Ustashe leader Ante Pavelić fled and it was the turn of the Communists to rule Croatia. Once more, Croatia was back inside Yugoslavia as one of six federal units. Its borders were smaller than those of the Banovina, owing to the Communists' decision to resurrect Bosnia as a federal unit. Those losses were partially offset by the inclusion in Croatia of the cities of Rijeka and Zadar and of most of Istria, which Italy had obtained from the Habsburg empire after 1918.

While there was little nostalgia for the bloodstained rule of Pavelić, now in exile in Argentina, the imposition of full-blown Soviet-style Communism grated on Croats, most of whom resented the persecution of the Catholic Church, symbolised by the trial and imprisonment of the Archbishop of Zagreb, Alojzije Stepinac, in 1946. A hate figure to Serbs for his initial colloboration with the NDH, Stepinac was correspondingly admired by Croats, especially in the countryside, and an official campaign against him merely fuelled a cult of Stepinac as a national martyr.

IN CONTEXT

The tense atmosphere felt in Croatia lessened after Stepinac's death in 1960, which Tito cleverly exploited to bring about a rapprochement with the Church, allowing Stepinac a grand funeral in Zagreb to which foreign diplomats were invited. The Church took the proffered olive branch at face value and under Stepinac's successor, Cardinal Šeper, church-state relations lost their bitterness.

COSTA DEL CROATIA

The development of mass tourism in the '60s also brought new life to the Croatian economy, especially in Dalmatia and Istria. It was helped by market reforms, accompanied by a considerable degree of local autonomy, allowing Croatia to become the second-most prosperous republic within Yugoslavia. Domestic production and Western imports led to an improved supply of both food and consumer goods. And Croatians took advantage of going to work abroad as 'guest workers', bringing back their hard-earned Deutschmarks to fuel a boom in Communist consumerism.

In several republics and provinces, including Macedonia and Kosovo, the post-war generation of leaders was challenged by relative youngsters offering a heady mix of liberalism and local nationalism. In Croatia, the standard bearer for change was the Croatian Spring, or Maspok, short for *masovni pokret*, mass movement. Its broad aims were economic and political reforms to secure Croatia a greater share of the wealth it generated and to increase Croatia's autonomy – and that of the other republics – within Yugoslavia. It was seen by many Serbs as a device to reduce their influence as an ethnic group in Yugoslavia, as well as to marginalise the role of the Communist Party.

The most pressing economic issues included the fact that although Croatia brought half the foreign capital into the country, it disposed of only 15 per cent of it. The centralisation of decision-making and budgetary considerations in Belgrade worked to the disadvantage of Croatia, and led to the widespread perception that Croatia was being economically exploited within the federation.

THE SILENT REPUBLIC

The crunch came in 1971, as the demands of the Croatian nationalists became increasingly radical, with calls for a separate Croatian currency and seat at the UN, as well as frontier changes with Bosnia. Croatia's 12 per cent Serb minority were concentrated in the old Military Border region. That December, Tito moved to crush the Croatian Spring. With tanks revving ominously at their army barracks, he summoned the leaders of the Croatian Party to his hunting lodge at Karadjordjevo, in Serbia, and ordered them to resign. They duly quit without demur, though their quiet exit did not save Croatia from a wide-ranging purge. The cultural organisation, Matica Hrvatska, was closed, hundreds of prison sentences were handed out and thousands of Party members were expelled. It was the end of an experiment in a democratic form of Communism and its failure led to a great silence falling over Croatia, which gave rise to its new nickname in the late 1980s – 'the silent republic'.

The mute discontent of Tito's last years was alleviated by rising living standards based largely on foreign credits. But after Tito's death in 1980, the credits dried up and the economic situation worsened rapidly. As foreign debts spiralled and inflation spun out of control, the Communists rapidly lost prestige and the power to successfully suppress criticism. The old ideology of 'Brotherhood and Unity' became an object of general ridicule as the six republics fought openly over economic policy.

New Communist leader Slobodan Milošević began to tear up the ground rules that had existed in Yugoslavia since 1945, openly promoting a violent and aggressive brand of Serb nationalism that paid no heed to the rights of Croats, Albanians, Bosnians or anyone else.

Milošević's first target was Kosovo, the Albanian-dominated province in southern Yugoslavia that Serbs regarded as the cradle of their medieval state. With the army behind him in 1989 Milošević quelled Kosovo, gunning down dozens of Albanian protesters in the streets. An internal coup then delivered Montenegro peacefully into his hands.

St Mark's Church, Zagreb.

CIVIL WAR AGAIN

The rise of Milošević forced other Communist leaders to look to their constituencies and concede democratic reforms. A plethora of parties appeared on the political scene, and with that, the prospect of multi-party elections. In Croatia the Communist Party leader Ivica Račan called a poll in April 1990 but he profoundly miscalculated the depth of Croat resentment against Communist rule and the prize went instead to the nationalist Croatian Democratic Union (HDZ) whose leader, a former general, Franjo Tudjman, had served prison terms after the Croatian Spring.

Tudjman at first confined himself to arguing for a confederation and greater Croatian self-rule. But growing violence dictated its own course of events. No sooner was the election over than armed Serbs based in the hilly north Dalmatian town of Knin threw up roadblocks and proclaimed a separate Serb state within Croatia – the Republic of Serbian Krajina (RSK).

With Milošević's energetic backing and Yugoslav tanks, the RSK rapidly annexed as much of the republic as possible. Facing a clamour from a panicked population, Tudjman edged towards proclaiming total independence – risking the threat of open war. The Croats also had to march in step with their Slovene neighbours, who were also busily proceeding towards independence anyway. The two republics agreed to jump ship together on 25 June 1991. But whereas Slovenia shrugged off Yugoslav control without effort, after a ten-day shoot-out with the Yugoslav army, Croatia faced determined opposition from Milošević, the army and the 600,000 Croatian Serbs.

SERBIA INTERVENES

In the summer and autumn of '91, the RSK mopped up one district after another, at its highpoint controlling one-third of the republic, including most of northern Dalmatia, eastern Lika, Kordun and Banija, parts of western Slavonia and the regions of Baranja and Srijem in eastern Slavonia. The eastern border town of Vukovar came under especially prolonged joint RSK and army siege, reducing the graceful baroque streets to rubble. When the town fell on 17 November, the victorious Serbs committed one of the worst atrocities of the conflict, butchering more than 200 wounded soldiers lying in Vukovar hospital. With less success, hundreds of miles away, the army pounded away at the historic city of Dubrovnik. However, the blaze of international publicity intimidated them from repeating the tactics in Vukovar and the town stayed in Croat hands.

The horrific scenes screened all over the world fed a clamour to punish Belgrade through recognising Croatian independence. France and Britain, Serbia's traditional allies, held out to the end but bowed to the inevitable after Germany – the destination of many Croat refugees – threatened to recognise Slovenia and Croatia unilaterally, if need be. Fearing an ugly open rupture in the European Union, its member states agreed jointly to recognise the two states at Christmas 1991, a decision that took effect in January 1992.

Tudjman perceived recognition as an historic victory and the fulfilment of what he called the '1,000-year-old dream' of a Croat state. Nevertheless, at first the victory seemed hollow. The war had cost thousands of lives and inflicted massive infrastructural damage. Towns, railways and factories lay in ruins, hundreds of thousands of people had been made homeless and the once lucrative tourist industry had collapsed. The RSK was also still in control of one-third of Croatia's territory, its gains seemingly cemented by a UN-brokered peace plan and by the deployment of peacekeepers along the frontline. Problems worsened in 1993-94, when Tudjman hurled the infant Croatian army on to the side of the ethnic Croats in Bosnia's own messy civil war – a fateful decision that led to Croatia's virtual international isolation. Under strong pressure from the US in 1994, Tudjman executed a humiliating retreat from the Bosnian arena.

By 1995, the US was desperate to roll back the Serb juggernaut in Bosnia, end the war there and rescue the hard-pressed Muslim-led government in Sarajevo. Croatia was brought in from the cold as the US gave the green light for armament supplies, which made the Croatian army a significant regional force. Thus reinvigorated, Tudjman

IN CONTEXT

'As Bosnia appealed for foreign aid, Tudjman sent his army racing over the border, where they rapidly routed the supposedly invincible Serbs.'

determined to reverse Serb gains in Croatia at the same time as doing US bidding in Bosnia. A *casus belli* presented itself in July when the Bosnian Serbs threatened to overrun the large but isolated Bosnian city of Bihać, near the Croatian border. As Bosnia appealed for foreign aid, Tudjman obligingly sent his army racing over the border, where, much to the outside world's surprise, they rapidly routed the supposedly invincible Serbs, relieving Bihać before doubling back south to sever the RSK's supply lines through Bosnia to Serbia. In Knin, Tudjman ordered an all-out attack on the RSK, Operation Storm. The RSK crumbled and the next morning Croat soldiers were hosting their red-and-white flag over the battlements of Knin whose inhabitants, along with about 150,000 other Serb inhabitants of the RSK, fled to Serbia in a long column. Victory was complete. The remaining Serbian-controlled territories in eastern Slavonia, including Vukovar, were returned to Croatia in 1998 under UN supervision. Tudjman had only a short time to savour these triumphs, succumbing to cancer in December 1999.

Thousands attended Tudjman's cold funeral in Zagreb, though few international leaders joined the throng. While most Croats mourned the man, they did not mourn the HDZ's increasingly corrupt and authoritarian style of government, turfing out Tudjman's henchmen at the next elections and putting back in the driving seat Ivica Račan, the old Communist leader recast as a Social Democrat.

TOURISM, STABILITY AND PROGRESS

The Račan government acted fast to mend fences with Europe. The President's almost monarchical powers were massively trimmed, state interference with the media was curbed by law, the path was cleared for exiled Serbs to reclaim property and return, and Zagreb pledged never again to meddle in Bosnia.

The progress was not all plain sailing, as Europe made any serious rapprochement conditional on Croatia's absolute co-operation with The Hague war crimes tribunal. And the court's demand for the extradition of key military figures was deeply unpopular in a country still not recovered from the trauma of what was called the Homeland War.

Yet, with Tudjman and Milošević now gone, there was a distinct feeling that Croatia had turned a corner and passed key tests. The war had not delivered political extremism nor the return from the grave of the Ustashe. The tourists were back in bigger numbers than ever and – much to the shock of locals – now buying up holiday homes. In 2005 the arrest of alleged war criminal Ante Gotovina, after years on the run, won brownie points with the West – although the event polarised the locals.

At the same time, the Zagreb-Split motorway opened, linking the capital to Dalmatia. It is due to be extended as far as Dubrovnik by 2011. With routes opened from the UK and Germany, the airports of Split, Dubrovnik and Zadar saw busy traffic and Croatia became the destination of the moment – 'the Mediterranean as it once was', went the line from the tourist office. New luxury hotels were built, particularly on Hvar and in Dubrovnik, which saw the regular arrival of A-list celebrities. Shopping malls sprang up around Zagreb.

Compulsory military service ended in 2007. A year later, Croatia became a member of the UN Security Council on a two-year term and NATO membership is expected in 2009. The much talked-about EU accession may happen in 2012 – although a border dispute with Slovenia will need to be sorted well beforehand.

At home, the parliamentary elections of 2007 passed almost unnoticed. The leadership of Stipe Mesić as President and Ivo Sanader as Prime Minister seem to be steering a stable ship until the next presidential elections due for 2010.

IN CONTEXT

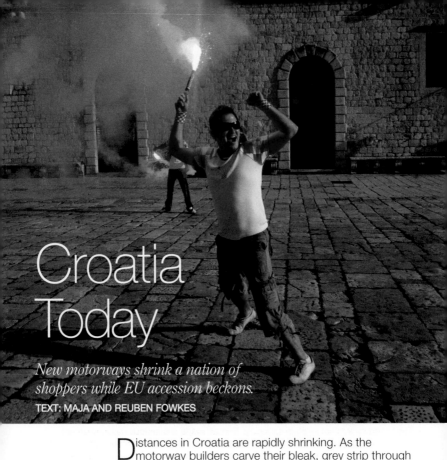

Croatia Today

New motorways shrink a nation of shoppers while EU accession beckons.

TEXT: MAJA AND REUBEN FOWKES

Maja and Reuben Fowkes are curators and art historians who work between Croatia, Hungary and the UK. They publish their joint work on www. translocal.org.

Distances in Croatia are rapidly shrinking. As the motorway builders carve their bleak, grey strip through the Dalmatian hinterland, blasting tunnels and laying bridges towards the final frontier of Dubrovnik, technological progress is putting an end to centuries of glorious isolation. While the citizens of Europe's most picturesque medieval walled-town will welcome the practical benefits of getting connected to the rest of the continent, from cheaper food and a wider choice of consumer goods to safer and faster road travel, they may well miss the special status and strong sense of local identity that remoteness brings. Historical separateness and the claustrophobic intensity of life within the city walls gave rise to a 'Dubrovnik syndrome' of deep local patriotism combined with the nagging fear of being left behind as the rest of the country modernised. As communication of all kinds becomes easier, outlying places such as Dubrovnik are getting more accessible and thus less particular, and as a result the personality of whole communities is changing with the broadening of horizons and the weakening of local identities.

'Possessing the latest mobile has overtaken wearing designer sunglasses as the ultimate signifier of Croatian chic.'

A similar phenomenon is at work on the national level. The arrival of budget airlines has made it much easier for everyone else to get to Croatia, relieving holidaymakers of the necessity of making the arduous and hair-raising odyssey across treacherous mountain passes, which was for decades the only low-cost option to reach the promised land of the Adriatic. However, cheap flights have also changed the travel habits of the Croatians, with implications for geo-politics, European culture and the nation's favourite pastime: shopping.

During the long night of the Yugoslav Socialist experiment, Croatians took advantage of the freedom to travel that citizens of non-aligned Yugoslavia enjoyed – and the hard-earned currency brought home by a generation of *Gastarbeiteri* – to become, until recently, the most loyal victims of the Italian fashion industry. Although in the 1990s Croatian buses still plied the motorways of North Italy en route to strategically-located shopping centres, today the situation has completely changed. Why brave the Slovenian and Croatian border guards to bring back last year's Gucci bag from an '80s shopping mall in an industrial park near Trieste, when you could buy this year's model at the state-of-the-art shopping and leisure complex a short drive from your home? Today dedicated followers of fashion, a category which includes most of the adult population, find it increasingly hard to get excited about shopping in Trieste or Vienna, when it's quicker and cheaper to fly to London, the fashion capital of Europe.

TRACKIE TOPS AND TELEPHONES

At the other end of the shopping spectrum, the onward march of globalisation has also changed consumer behaviour, and with it a whole range of social attitudes and opinions. Whereas until a few years ago people would queue for hours at the border to cross into Hungary to buy everything from fizzy drinks to tractor tyres, today even medium-sized towns are ringed with out-of-town supermarkets, DIY wholesalers and brash new shopping centres with virtually the same choice of outlets as anywhere else in Europe.

The culture of visiting the lawless *Korridor* between Croatia and Bosnia to buy poor quality imitations of global brands is also in decline, and with it goes the spirit of adventure and sense of humour necessary to forage in no man's land for an abrasive tracksuit with 'adidas' misspelt down the sides. From a national economic perspective, it is presumably better that people spend their money in Croatian shops rather than abroad, and this is evidence of the wider process of bringing this ex-Socialist, ex-war torn country into harmony with European norms. The last straw will come in 2010 when Croatia finally gets its own IKEA, and, to the chagrin of Austrian business interests and IKEA Graz, the last piece of the local consumerist puzzle falls smoothly into place.

The most visible symbol of the widespread desire for connectivity in an increasingly globalised Croatia is the mobile phone, which has in recent years become an essential marker of social status. Every second advertisement on television and on roadside billboards seems to be for one of the three competing foreign-owned networks, which rival each other in promising unbelievably low tariffs and keeping quiet about the hidden catch in the small print. Consumers are constantly bombarded with detailed technical specifications of the latest handheld devices, so it's no wonder that possessing the latest mobile has overtaken wearing designer sunglasses as the ultimate signifier of Croatian chic. In the interests of full network coverage transmitters are even going up in the uninhabited national park of the Kornati archipelago, threatening to disturb one of the last remaining ringtone-free zones in the country.

COAST AND CORRUPTION

The extension of the motorway network, the explosion in new retail parks, and the general economic upswing is raising urgent questions about environmental sustainability. One of the main fronts in the battle to slow the spread of concrete is the campaign to preserve Croatia's unique coastline, which is still remarkable for the relative scarcity of high-rise hotel complexes, intact eco-systems, abundance of shoreline views without a single sign of human habitation, and the gloriously clear blue waters of the Adriatic Sea. Most citizens have applauded the government's willingness to take on the scourge of illegal building by sending in teams of bulldozers to remove dozens of unsightly seaside villas that were brazenly constructed without planning permission.

The Ministry of Tourism tries to promote Croatia as an exclusive and specialised travel destination for aficionados of yachting, medieval architecture and fine dining, both because the infrastructure for Mediterranean-style mass tourism is lacking and because no one wants to repeat the mistakes of Italy and Spain during the 1970s and '80s when they devastated much of their coastlines with tacky tourist resorts. Croatia still has some quite extensive areas of virtual wilderness, such as along the inhospitable coastline of Konavle north of Dubrovnik, in the dramatic Velebit mountain reserve, or on the many uninhabited islands of the Adriatic, as well as along the eastern borders to Bosnia.

The overwhelming majority of Croatian politicians firmly believe that the path to fulfilling the nation's European destiny passes through membership of the European Union and NATO. The process of accession, as in other transitional countries, involves a complex set of negotiations covering virtually all aspects of legal, political and economic life. One of the most serious stumbling blocks has proved to be reform of the judicial system and finding the political will to tackle the widespread culture of corruption and bribery. The ugliest face of this problem is the power of the mafia, which shocked the whole nation in autumn 2008

'The police appear powerless to stop the wave of murder and the intimidation of investigative journalists.'

with the assassination of Ivo Pukanić, the high-profile editor of a political weekly. The police appear powerless to stop the wave of murder and the intimidation of investigative journalists and the legal system unable to keep convicted members of criminal gangs behind bars for long. Those of a conspiratorial frame of mind suspect that key figures in the trans-Balkan mafia may enjoy high-level political protection.

The other main hurdle to joining the EU comes from fellow ex-Yugoslav nation Slovenia, which is threatening to block Croatian's membership application pending resolution of a smouldering border dispute. International arbitration may be needed to sort out the rival territorial claims over the Gulf of Piran's 7.3 square miles, which hinge on hitherto irreconcilable interpretations of legal and historical arguments. If good relations with neighbouring Slovenia can be restored, and if Croatia succeeds in expeditiously closing the remaining chapters of the accession process, then full membership of the European Union is possible by 2012.

NEW EUROPE OR BANANA REPUBLIC?

Change in Croatia is reflected in national politics, with the fading away of the era of presidents Franjo Tudjman, who ruled the country from independence until his death in 1999, and Stipe Mesić, whose final term in office runs out in 2010. While Mesić thrives on memories of World War II and hankers after Tito's role in the Non-Aligned Movement (recently causing a scandal in neighbouring Slovenia with a tactless reminder that were it not for the bravery of Croatian partisans, 'Slovenians would be looking at the sea from a distance of 20 km'), a younger generation of politicians is transforming the local terrain.

Mesić's counterpart in the current political cohabitation is Prime Minister Ivo Sanader, who cuts a more cosmopolitan line, speaks five languages, and has a PhD in Comparative Literature from an Austrian university. His most famous political gaffe was to joke, when asked by a journalist about the effects of the global economic crisis on Croatia, that '*Hrvatska je u banani*' ('Croatia is in bananas'). Sanader's greatest political achievement has been to transform the HDZ from a catch-all right-wing party for the country's unruly nationalist and populist tendencies, into a respectable, fairly liberal, moderate-conservative political machine. Ivo Banac, a leading historian and the best-known voice of Croatia's liberal conscience, significantly changed his tune from the 1990s, when he famously dubbed the HDZ 'Frankenstein', to praising Sanader, the current HDZ leader, for his 'liberal economic politics, liquidation of right-wing influences and policy on minorities.'

The European orientation of Croatia is most visible in the interests and activities of young people. It is easier than ever for students from Zagreb University to spend a semester in another European capital as part of the Erasmus scheme; there are also more opportunities for young artists to apply for European scholarships and residencies; and visa-free travel, combined with cheap flights, makes city-hopping around the continent a regular reality for Croatians as much as anyone else. National feeling swells when Croatia excels at international sporting events, as it does so often in football, handball, athletics, skiing and tennis, and the papers are full of gossip about the exploits of Croatian celebrities in Cannes, Hollywood, or on the catwalks of Milan.

Although the Tourist Board continues to promise visitors 'the Mediterranean the way it used to be', they might be tempted soon to change their advertising slogan ('Europe the way it could be?'), to reflect the outward-looking and future-oriented reality of contemporary Croatia.

Food & Drink

As fresh as it gets – and diverse with it too.

TEXT: ALISON RADOVANOVIC

The landscape, climate and history of Croatia dictate what's put on the dinner table. In a space less than half the size of England, you've got alluvial plains formed from ancient sea beds, high mountain ranges and 2,000km (1,240 miles) of coastline (including islands), as well as the two major rivers of the Danube and the Sava. Add in three distinct climatic regions – Continental, Alpine and Mediterranean – plus cultural and political incursions by Turks, Venetians, Austrians, French and Hungarians, and it's no wonder that Croatia's cuisine is so varied.

Many visitors miss out on much of this diversity, being served standard dishes in bland ways, a hangover from the package-travel days of the 1980s. Dalmatia – Dubrovnik in particular – can disappoint. In its Old Town, buildings, and thus storage space, are small, so farmed and frozen fish are often the norm.

Elsewhere, notably but not exclusively in Istria and mainland Kvarner, there has been a revolution in the kitchen. A new generation of Croatian chefs are using imaginative and advanced cooking techniques to create something truly special – with the use of wonderfully fresh seafood from the Adriatic and universally organic vegetables.

Domestic wines, too, have improved enormously over the last five years. Although little is exported, there is much to enjoy in situ, particularly from Pelješac and Slavonia.

Alison Radovanovic is the director of Ravnica Center for Cultural Exchange.

Croatian cuisine can be divided between the Central European tradition and that of the Central Mediterranean. For centuries the region was ruled by the Austro-Hungarian empire and the Venetian Republic and both cultures have left their culinary mark. Each region of Croatia contributes its own specialities but it should be borne in mind that these are regarded as national dishes and can therefore be found all over the country.

Istria is considered Croatia's culinary temple, its peasant traditions, fresh, seasonal ingredients and inventive chefs combining to make this small peninsula the destination of choice for gastronomes. Italians flood across the border on Sundays to sample the best of it. The celebrated use of truffles, to season steaks or added to chocolate cake, is only one example of the sophisticated dishes on offer. Dalmatia does the simple things right, relying on the high quality of the local olive oil, wine, garlic, tomatoes – and freshness of its seafood. The only true demarcation derives from Croatia's love of fresh ingredients, whether meat-based or piscine cuisine.

FISH AND SEAFOOD

The Adriatic boasts more than 400 species of fish, but with limited quantities of each kind. This is different from the North Sea, where some of the same species can be found in abundance, whereas others are not found at all, such as the renowned *zubatac* (dentex).

Dalmatia has a culinary tradition dating back to Greek, Roman and Byzantine times of preparing fish and seafood. Its waters are famously clean, producing fresh fish and seafood. Oysters from Mali Ston were first farmed by the Romans after Augustus conquered the Illyrian tribes. These days Dalmatian tuna is highly prized by the Japanese.

Mass tourism has seen some types become rare. Sea dates (*prstaci*), once commonplace, are now a protected species in Croatia, and are smuggled in from the adjoining tiny coastline of Bosnia and Hercegovina. Cooked in white wine and garlic, they are a delicacy beyond compare. Fish farms for striped sea bass (*lubin* or *brancin*) and gilthead sea bream (*orada*) have been set up in Ston and on Brač.

Seafood is prepared in a few set, simple ways, the most common being *buzara*, gently poached in a tomato-based sauce. Fish is often just cooked on the grill, *na žaru*. Red mullet (*trilja*) is considered perfect for this. *Brodet*, fish stew, is also popular. Seafood risottos are another standard feature, especially *crni rižot* using dark squid ink. If there is any made *od sipe*, from cuttlefish, it has stronger, tastier ink.

Don't be afraid to ask if the fish on offer is fresh, frozen or farmed. You will usually be shown the fresh fish on offer for you to choose from. Fish is priced by the kilo, often in the 300kn-350kn range. About half a kilo should be enough for one person. You can ask how much it weighs, or have it weighed.

Škrpina, scorpion fish, has deliciously tender meat but it's the devil's own job to pick through the bones. John Dory (*kovač*), golden grey mullet (*cipal*) and the bream family (*pagar*, *arbun* and *pic*) are also common – just ask what's fresh. Dentex is usually excellent.

You'll find grilled squid (*lignje na žaru*) on almost every menu. Octopus (*hobotnica*) is often used as a salad, chopped portions mixed with onion and herbs. The most popular shellfish are scampi (*škampi*), served in their shells, and invariably *buzara* style. Warn children that it won't be neatly packaged in breadcrumbs. Use your fingers and expect it be pretty messy. Lobster (*jastog*) is invariably the dearest item on the menu, 500kn a kilo.

Continental Croatia is well known for its freshwater fish, including *šaran* (carp) and *štuka* (pike). *Fiš paprikaš*, freshwater fish stewed in a paprika broth, is another favourite. If you're inland but don't want fish, then *čobanac*, a meaty, paprika goulash, is also a regular find.

The classic accompaniment to fish is *blitva*, a local kale mixed with potatoes. A simple side salad also goes well.

GRILLED MEAT AND GAME

Croatians love their meat. Prime cuts such as *ombolo* (medallion of pork) and beefsteak are cooked quickly, often over an open fire, and served very simply. A favourite is a mixed grill, Balkan *ćevapčići* (minced meatballs) and kebabs together with typical Central

When the sea doesn't want You...

...we are there for You

D⌀LLAR®

RENT A CAR

BRANCH OFFICES WITHIN CROATIA

reservation@subrosa.hr

DOWNTOWN OFFICES
Split
Tel.: +385 (0)21 398 800
Split Harbour
Tel.: +385 (0)21 398 800
Zagreb
Tel.: +385 (0)1 4836 004
Zadar
Tel.: +385 (0)23 311 360
Rijeka
Tel.: +385 (0)51 325 901

AIRPORT OFFICES
Split Airport
Tel.: +385 (0)21 203 179
Zagreb Airport
Tel.: +385 (0)1 6265 444
Zadar Airport
Tel.: +385 (0)23 311 360
Dubrovnik Airport
Tel.: +385 (0)20 773 589
Rijeka Airport
Tel.: +385 (0)51 337 917

BRANCH OFFICES IN SLOVENIA
Ljubljana Airport
Tel.: +386 (0)4 236 5751
BRANCH OFFICES IN B & H
Sarajevo Airport
Tel.: +387 (0)33 760 646
BRANCH OFFICES IN SERBIA
Belgrade Airport
Tel.: +381 (0)11 228 6499

Seasick? Or just sick of the sea?
Take a break, see the sites...
Explore the land, Thrifty way!

BRANCH OFFICES WITHIN CROATIA

AIRPORT OFFICES
Split Airport
Tel.: +385 (0)21 895 320
Zagreb Airport
Tel.: +385 (0)1 6265 333
Zadar Airport
Tel.: +385 (0)23 315 733
Dubrovnik Airport
Tel.: +385 (0)20 773 588
Rijeka Airport
Tel.: +385 (0)51 337 917

DOWNTOWN OFFICES
Split
Tel.: +385 (0)21 399 000
Split Harbour
Tel.: +385 (0)21 399 000
Zagreb
Tel.: +385 (0)1 4836 466
Zadar
Tel.: +385 (0)23 315 733
Rijeka
Tel.: +385 (0)51 325 900

BRANCH OFFICES IN SLOVENIA
Ljubljana Airport
Tel.: +386 (0)4 236 5750

BRANCH OFFICES IN B & H
Sarajevo Airport
Tel.: +387 (0)33 760 645

BRANCH OFFICES IN SERBIA
Belgrade Airport
Tel.: +381 (0)11 228 6499

reservation@subrosa.hr

Traditional Konobas

The authentic tastes of Croatia.

The traditional konoba is defined by its rustic atmosphere and authentic approach. Before these popular venues became public, konobas were private cellars with wine barrels, hams hung out to dry, vats of pickled vegetables and fireplaces for preparing food. Today, konobas are the cornerstone of the Adriatic dining experience, old stone houses with heavy wooden tables, fishing nets and perhaps a few traditional implements on display. It feels like dining in someone's living room. Rather than an elaborate menu, konobas offer no-frills, freshly prepared dishes and a selection of well preserved products. Everything offered should be home-made or locally

sourced. The table wine will be universally acceptable – Croatians wouldn't go there otherwise – and various kinds of rakija brandy, made with herbs, flowers or fruits, will also be on offer.

European sausages and cutlets. *Pljeskavica* is like a Balkan hamburger. Dishes, such as *Zagrebački odrezak*, a schnitzel stuffed with cheese and ham, reflects a strong Austrian influence, while the hot, spicy *kulen* is a superb salami liberally permeated with paprika, showing the influence of Hungarian cuisine. Cured meats are a great tradition, with each region producing their own slightly different versions. *Pršut*, air-cured ham, is a delicacy in Istria and Dalmatia.

Look for the little jars of Ajvar, a paprika and aubergine relish, to garnish your grilled meat on any restaurant table.

You may see roadside spits, roasting whole lambs or pigs, placed outside restaurants as an enticement to passers-by. This is typical of the mountainous Gorski Kotar region, which produces some of the finest lamb in Croatia. Beef is also used in a slow-cooked stew, *pašticada*. The real deal you often must order a day in advance: *peka* or *od peke*, the cast-iron dome used to cover meat slow-roasted with hot coals. Octopus can also be prepared like this. The saline climate of Pag and Cres produces exquisite lamb, raised on salty wild herbs, and *paški sir*, sharp sheep's cheese from Pag, dried, matured and prepared with olive oil.

More than 30 per cent of Croatia is covered in forest and hunting is a national pastime. The game widely available is mostly venison and wild boar. This meat is normally slow cooked either by braising on top of the stove or in rich, meaty goulashes. They are frequently served with Italian-style gnocchi or polenta.

GRAPE AND GRAPPA

Wine is either red (*crno*), white (*bijelo*) or rosé (*crveno*), dry (*suho*) or sweet (*slatko*). In Dalmatia, the deep reds are mixed with water as a *bevanda*, the whites in the north with mineral water (*gemišt*). Of the coastal reds, the most renowned (and most expensive) is **Dingač**. Deep ruby red in colour, and a superb accompaniment to grilled fish (the tradition in Dalmatia), Dingač is produced in the restricted area of the same name on the steep south slopes of the Pelješac peninsula. The grape variety there is Plavac Mali, a cousin of Zinfandel. Native Croatian wine maker Miljenko Grgić, who gained his reputation in Napa Valley, California, came back to his homeland to produce quality wines of the Plavac Mali

IN CONTEXT

Enjoy your stay

and save money with

ZAGREB CARD

ZAGREB CARD offers you unlimited travel on public transport, discounts at virtually all of the city museums, reduced prices at many restaurants, shops, and much more that makes Zagreb Card an irreplaceable travel companion in Zagreb.

Zagreb Card is valid for 72 hours and it costs 90 kn or if you prefer 24 hours then it costs **only 60 kn!** Zagreb Card is available online at **www.zagrebcard.fivestars.hr** or in most Zagreb hotels as well as Tourist Information Centres.

ZAGREB TOURIST BOARD | www.zagreb-touristinfo.hr

'A Wine Roads trail makes it easy for visitors to find the best cellars and taste these wines first-hand.'

variety. **Postup**, also from Pelješac, is equally reputed. **Babić** from Šibenik is a popular and reasonably priced alternative.

Because of the rocky, limestone soil, southern white wines are mostly dry, such as the golden yellow **Pošip**, strong in alcohol from the jara vineyards on Korčula. **Grk,** its name ('Greek') echoing its ancient tradition, is another white from Korčula, from Lumbarda. Vis is known for **Vugava**, from the grape of the same name, Krk for Vrbnička Žlahtina. Inland, whites are dominated by the lightweight **Graševina**.

The primary wine of Istria is **Malvasia**. Possibly one of the oldest types in Europe, this white grape is grown in over two-thirds of Istria's vineyards. Malvasia is usually dry and it is best drunk young. Because Istria has two distinctive soil types, Malvasia produced near the coast tends to be more robust; grapes from the hinterland provide a more delicate bouquet. Istria's indigenous red wine is **Teran**, a rich red tipple with a strong, fruity flavour.

Many of Istria's best wines are being produced by a new generation of vintners, who formed Vin Istra (www.vinistra.hr), dedicated to improving the quality of local production and to the promotion of Istrian wines. A Wine Roads trail makes it easy for visitors to find the best cellars and taste these wines first-hand.

Clear fruit brandy (*rakija*) is the common spirit, and is akin to grappa. Grape brandy is *loza*. Regional varieties include mistletoe, *biska*, from Istria. If it grows then some Istrian will have popped it into grappa. Fruits, berries, nuts, herbs, even truffles, the range is staggering. *Orahovac* (walnut) grappa and any number of fruit brandies are sold from small, roadside stalls. In most restaurants you will be offered a complimentary shot on settling your bill.

WHERE AND HOW TO CHOOSE

Dining venues fall into general categories of a standard *restoran*, a more informal, often family-run *gostionica* and, best of all, a *konoba*.

The *jelovnik*, menu, is divided rather differently from its British counterpart. First on the list will probably be *hladna jela* (cold food), the starter or antipasti. Typical dishes might be thin slices of *pršut*, *ovčiji sir* (sheep's cheese) or *kozji sir* (goat's cheese) or perhaps a carpaccio of meat or fish. Then there are the soups, *juhe*, such as *riblja juha* (fish) or *govdja juha* (beef). *Mineštra/manistra* is a hearty pulse soup, based on pork stock.

Gotova jela, finished food, are the dishes that are pre-prepared in quantity and therefore fast. *Gulaš*, goulash, would be a typical example, a rich stew usually served with pasta, gnocchi or polenta. Local *fuži*, pasta twists, are a popular form. *Divljač gulaš* is game, quite often *crna* (venison) or *svinja* (wild boar).

Jela sa roštilja is grilled meat (*meso*) or fish (*riba*), also rendered as *na žaru*. *Jela po narudžbi* are the house specialities, also known as *specijaliteti*. These are main courses and the ingredients will depend on which region of Croatia you are dining in. Istria will inevitably offer *tartufi* (truffles), while in Dalmatia it's likely to be a form of *buzara* sauce.

Prilozi i salate are side dishes and salads. This will include *krumpir* (potatoes), *blitva* (local kale), *mješana salata* (mixed salad), *rajčica* (tomato), *zelena* (green salad) and *rokula* (rocket). *Kruh* (bread) may also feature on the menu.

Kolači means cakes and this section of the menu covers puddings in general. As well as pancakes, there's *pita od jabuka*, apple strudel, and *kroštuli*, which are tiny, deep-fried doughnuts without the jam. *Sladoled* is ice-cream. The better establishments offer a digestif, perhaps a herb grappa (*travarica*) or fruit brandy (*rakija*). Coffee (*kava*) is always strong. For all menu vocabulary, *see p327*.

IN CONTEXT

Reach new horizons

How will you see the city?
What will your memories look like?
Visit The Westin Zagreb hotel,
where discovering the city is only
half the experience.

For more information or to make a reservation,
please call + 385 1 4892 058 or visit westin.com/zagreb

This is how it should feel.^{SM}

THE WESTIN
ZAGREB

STARWOOD PREFERRED GUEST®

© 2009 Starwood Hotels & Resorts Worldwide, Inc. All rights reserved. Westin is the registered trademark o

Zembo on Fish

Croatia prides itself on its seafood. One of its most accomplished and adventurous chefs, Deniz Zembo of Le Mandrać in Volosko, shares some tips, new and old.

'More often than not, fish is overcooked in Croatian restaurants. This is partly due to the lack of trained chefs but also the seasonality of the restaurant business in the coastal parts of the country. For restaurants that only open in summer, freezing fish and using farmed fish are necessities. This is particularly true of the bigger fish. If you're keen to only enjoy fish caught that day, stick to a restaurant open year-round. When shown a platter selection of fish by the waiter, some wily local diners score or chop off the tail of the fish they choose so that they know it's the same one coming cooked out of the kitchen.

'The traditional cooking methods are stewing (for shells and scampi) called *buzara*; chargrilled, *gradele*; and baked in salt crust (*u soli*). The best fish for baking are sea bass, sea bream or dentex of a larger size, usually more than 1.5kg. Fish can also be boiled (*lešo*); and certain small oily fish (anchovies, sardines) and squid can be fried, *frigano*.

'One popular way to prepare fish, particularly red scorpion, is to braise it in the oven (*in forno*) with potatoes, white wine and local fresh herbs.

'Croatians prefer chargrilled, although some fish (turbot, sole, John Dory) are better grilled on a flat surface. The fish most suitable for chargrilling are sea bass, sea bream, dentex, monkfish and tuna but you can also chargrill squid, shell fish, scampi and lobster. Boiling fish produces a very light Mediterranean dish. The best fish to boil are red scorpion, turbot, sea ray and John Dory. In many standard restaurants, the method of cooking will be on a simple grill, *na žaru*.

'A new generation here are using more advanced cooking techniques such as "sous vide" or vacuum cooking in water, a kind of contemporary *lešo*. Fish cooked this way are very delicate and usually temperatures never exceed 55C, so it may appear as if the fish is not quite cooked enough. The technique is very difficult and it requires a skilful chef to accomplish it properly. Cooking times are given in seconds rather than minutes. Only a handful of venues are up to the task.'

Nature & Wildlife

Rare creatures, diverse birdlife and outstanding beauty.
TEXT: ALEX CREVAR

Alex Crevar lives in and writes about the countries of the former Yugoslavia. His work has appeared in the New York Times, *the* Washington Post, National Geographic Traveler, National Geographic Adventure, Outside *and* SKI.

Croatia is blessed with 20 National Parks and nature parks, from **Kopački rit** at the country's far eastern border down to **Mljet** at its southern tip. They take in spectacular waterfalls, challenging mountain climbs and an archipelago of 140 deserted islands.

Equally impressive is the wildlife they contain – hundreds of species of birds, bats, plants and reptiles, not to mention brown bears, lynx, wild boars, snow voles, water shrews and a happy little community of mongooses that are as much a part of Mljet's identity as its tranquil saltwater lakes or abandoned medieval monastery.

On top of this, Croatia's unspoilt landscape and surrounding waters attract an exotic range of creatures whose activities are protected as part of a conservation project or reserve. Dolphins at **Blue World** in **Veli Lošinj** (*see p182*) and rare griffon vultures on **Cres** (*see p176*) are cared for and monitored in their natural habitat. Visitors may observe them while volunteers can gain experience working close to them. Visitors may also spend a day with falcons at the **Dubrava Centre** near **Šibenik** or go on a five-day course in falconry.

*'Plitvice Lakes, an easy drive from the coast, are
the crown jewel of Croatia's National Parks, the
oldest, most visited and most spectacular.'*

Since 1949, Croatia has created eight National Parks and a dozen nature parks. The
oldest, Plitvice, is perhaps the most spectacular, with 16 lakes connected by waterfalls.
Krka National Park has waterfalls too, as well as plunging rapids and a collection of remote
villages. The nature park of Kopački rit contains the most prolific birdlife in the region,
while **Kornati** (*see p204*), **Mljet** (*see p315*) and **Brijuni** (*see p118*) all offer away-from-it-all
diversion. At Brijuni you can even see footprints of creatures who came before: dinosaurs.

PLITVICE

Just off the motorway between Zagreb and Split, an easy drive from the coast, Plitvice
Lakes are the crown jewel of Croatia's National Parks, the oldest, most visited and most
spectacular. Every year, upwards of a million tourists head past the road sign marked
'NP Plitvicka Jezera' – but don't let this deter you.

Set in the Lika region, known for its recent war-time hardships and fantastic lamb,
Plitvice is home to 1,146 species of plants, 140 types of birds and more than 50 mammals.
Most of all, though, people flock here for the series of 16 continually changing, cascading,
crystal-clear lakes. The dimensions of these lakes have been created from centuries of
calcium carbonate deposits, which find home in and on algae, moss and bacteria. This
deposit-and-plant combination creates a travertine barrier, a natural dam, which is
growing by a couple of centimetres a year. This process, a singular occurrence and
the reason Plitvice is included on UNESCO's World Heritage List, means the bodies
of water and the waterfalls linking them are always evolving.

Atop these morphing conditions, boardwalks – tasteful enough to appear natural –
follow the contours of and criss-cross over the fantastically turquoise water. These
walkways, set amid the surrounding beech, spruce and fir forests, give you a fish-eye view
of the lakes and falls. Regular trams travel the length of the most visited part of the park, a
two-sq km (0.8sq mile) fraction of its near 300sq km (115sq miles), from the upper lakes to
the lower ones, and the Veliki slap, or big waterfall. If you start early, you can easily see the
area in a day. There are also electric-powered boats to transport visitors across the larger
lakes above. Although the water looks divine, swimming is strictly forbidden.

A handful of tourist-friendly eateries dot the park. The best known is **Lička kuća**
(Entrance 1, 053 751 024), open April to October, a sprawling terrace offering the house
speciality of *Lička juha* sausage stew. Three hotels stand near Entrance 2, including the
three-star **Jezero** (Velika poljana, 053 751 015), with doubles around 100 euros. Cheaper
still is the nearby **Plitvice** (same phone number), renovated after the Yugoslav war whose
first victim worked here at the park headquarters.

The lake area has two entrances, with parking a few kilometres apart on the old main
road between Zagreb and Dalmatia, the E59/E71. The A1 motorway running parallel to it
has turn-offs at Otočač and Gorna Ploča. Buses from Zagreb or Zadar take about three
hours and cost about 70kn.

KRKA

Continuing south towards Split brings you to the beautiful town of **Skradin**, near
Šibenik. This is the entrance to the Krka National Park and the site of its **Visitor Centre**
which opened in 2007. The park is so-named because it encompasses the majority of the
75km-long Krka river. Within its confines there are seven waterfalls and the park's calling-
card attraction: **Skradinski buk**, a 17-step series of cascades, surrounded by boardwalks.
Under the 45-metre-high, 800-metre-long waterfall, you can take a dip in the pure pools

beneath the rushing water, giving onlookers a Niagara-like sensation. Visitors can also drop in on the stone houses of an ethno-village, its mills, traditional and working weaving looms, and the not-so-traditional souvenir shop.

Krka, like Plitvice, is awash in the marvel and miracle of natural travertine. Where the two differ is the degree of interaction with nature. Where Plitvice has sheer wow power, Krka offers hands-on adventure. To find out, take the riverboat four-hour tour to **Roški slap** waterfall. Backdropped by three towns on the riverbanks, 222 bird species, 19 types of reptiles, 18 species of bats and 860 plant types, and rushing tributaries leading to the Krka estuary and the Adriatic, give Krka its flavour. On the way you can visit the park's strange treasure: **Visovac**. This man-made isle is home to a Franciscan monastery where monks still reside and where novices spend a year enjoying occasional games of basketball and greeting tourists.

As you arrive back on land, majestic swans swimming past local fishermen in threadbare sweaters and rubber waders, you realise that Krka isn't just one thing but many at once. It's a river, a gorge, a monastery, a collection of villages and a place from which people still feed their families. 'Krka differs from other National Parks because people live here,' says guide Marija Gundić, as she stands on the side of the boat while a flock of cormorants bob and weave just over the water. 'People work the land. Visitors can feel the power in this place. We all feel at one with nature.'

Opened in 2008 near the park's main entrance, the **Hotel Vrata Krke** (Lozovac, 022 778 091, www.vrata-krke.hr) offers 50 comfortable, three-star rooms, as well as a large restaurant and bar.

Regular buses run to Krka from Šibenik. Various agencies offer day trips by boat for about 300kn, including transport, a guide and entrance fees.

KOPAČKI RIT

Ten kilometres north-east of Osijek is the Kopački rit nature reserve, one of the biggest areas of wetland in Europe and home to more than 200 species of birds. This 23,000-hectare (57-acre) site is a natural maze of interconnected lakes, reeds, woodland and pasture, with a swamp-like atmosphere. The park is at its most spectacular during the spring and autumn floods, when a vast area remains under water for weeks at a time, creating a uniquely soggy habitat for birds and small animals. The lakes support a large population of carp, pike, catfish and perch, alongside an abundance of frogs, snails and insects, preyed on by those higher up the food chain, notably herons and cormorants.

Krka.

Falconry for Beginners

Learn about Croatia's magnificent birds of prey.

The **Sokolarski Centar** is unique to Croatia. As you drive through the small village of **Dubrava**, ten minutes from Šibenik, and along the track to get there, you're met by an orderly arrangement of small garden areas, a café, stone walls and outhouses, and the ready smile of Emilio Mendjušić, the centre's founder. The Sokolarski Centar embraces everything to do with falconry and wild birds of prey in Croatia. As well as continuing a 5,000-year-old tradition of falconry, the Sokolarski's team of 20 falconers also provide the best substitute for parental coaching for orphaned or injured young birds hoping to stand a chance of surviving back in the wild. Each year some 150 injured birds are brought in to the centre to be treated.

The centre made world news in October 2008 for the rescue of an eagle owl with 30 damaged feathers. In an ancient falconry process known as imping, carried out under anaesthetic, the owl's feather shafts were implanted with new feathers from the centre's feather bank and the bird was released back into the wild in time to re-establish

his territory. Conservation work with birds of prey is just part of the centre's work which includes educational programmes and falconry courses.

Each falconer undergoes specific training and is required to become a member of a local rescue team. Here, helping out a bird of prey in the wild is considered a duty. It is illegal to capture and train a wild bird – those used for falconry must be bred in captivity.

Visitors may visit for the day or take part in a five-day course in falconry. The single visit involves time with trained birds, a tour and a chance to see the regular flying demonstrations. The more dedicated can learn about ornithology over a week.

Emilio has a vision of a number of centres, readily accessible for members of the public who find injured wild birds. Equally important is the research being carried out into the conservation status of native breeds.

Sokolarski Centar
Dubrava Skugori, Šibenik (091 506 7610 mobile/www.sokolarskicentar.com). **Open** 10am-7pm Mon-Sat. **Admission** 20kn.

Griffon vulture.

The main entrance is at the **Visitor's Centre** outside the village of **Kopačevo**, in a traditional thatched hut. Reaching it is difficult without your own transport – it's a good 4km walk from the nearest bus stop in **Bilje**. From the entrance, there's a pleasant 2km walk to the first dyke, from which you can see a partially sunken forest – you half-expect to see a crocodile hiding in the marshes. This is also the start of the boat trip on Eagle One around the park that leaves from a well-signposted jetty (enquire at the entrance for departure times). Other attractions accessible by bike, jeep tour or car include the **Tikveš Hunting Lodge**. This was built for the Archduke Franz Ferdinand, then taken over by Serbian royalty between the wars, before becoming the favourite hunting resort of Tito.

Back in Kopačevo, the **Zeleni zabac** restaurant (Ribarska 3, 031 752 212) has a view of the park. In the park itself, **Kormoran** (031 753 099) is the best known of the eateries. Perch, carp and *fis paprikas* are the local specialities. Accommodation options nearby are a small number of bed & breakfasts in traditional peasant houses. **Vas** (Ribarska 82, 031 752 179) in Kopačevo has two rooms for rent in a scenic courtyard. The owner Tibor is also happy to take you on an unofficial boat tour of the nature reserve, which is right outside the bedroom window, and to lay on home-made food for his guests.

Kopački rit is 10km (six miles) north-east of Osijek. Most tour agencies in town can arrange trips. **Generalturist** (Kapucinska 39, 031 211 500, www.generalturist.com) and **Cetratour** (Ružina 16, 372 921, www.cetratour.hr) are two of them.

Kopački rit
031 752 320/www.kopacki-rit.hr. **Open** varies. **Admission** *Mon-Sat* 60kn; *Sun* 45kn; 45kn reductions.
Krka National Park
022 201 777/www.npkrka.hr. **Open** varies. **Admission** *Jan, Feb, Nov, Dec* 30kn; 20kn 7s-14s. *Mar-May, Oct* 80kn; 60kn 7s-14s. *June-Sept* 95kn; 70kn 7s-14s. Free under 7s.
Plitvice Lakes National Park
053 751 015/www.np-plitvice-jezera.hr. **Open** 8am-7pm daily. **Admission** 50kn-95kn; 25kn-55kn 7-18s; free under 7s.

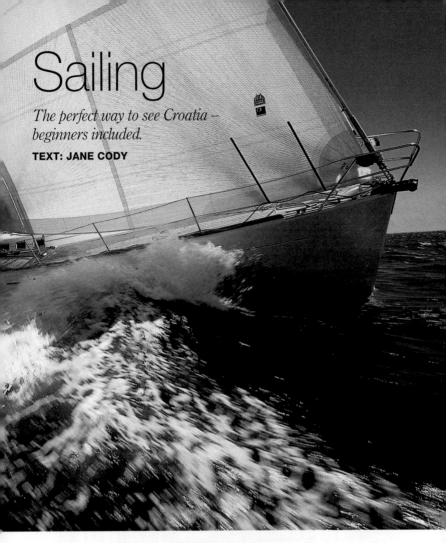

Sailing

*The perfect way to see Croatia –
beginners included.*

TEXT: JANE CODY

*Jane Cody is
the author of* The
Croatia Cruising
Companion *(www.
wileynautical.com),
one of the few
guide books to
include onshore
information. She
can be contacted
via her website,
www.croatiaonline.
blogspot.com.*

To explore Croatia by sea is to reveal its true secrets
and, despite what you might think, you don't need vast
amounts of sailing experience or piles of money to do it.
That said, it certainly doesn't hurt if you're a Russian
billionaire. But whatever your financial situation, Croatia
has it all – the range of sailing options, the spectacular
scenery, the unspoiled bays, the myriad islands and, most
important of all, the clear, calm and clean waters around
them. Europe's finest sailing playground is a little over two
hours from London. It's affordable, relatively safe (at sea
and on shore) and contains a diversity of destinations for
sailing routes amenable to all.

Get the local experience

Over 50 of the world's top destinations available.

**TIME OUT GUIDES
WRITTEN BY
LOCAL EXPERTS**
visit timeout.com/shop

> *'After partying all night in Hvar, relax at the neighbouring Pakleni islands, the perfect anchorage to soothe the spirits.'*

Novice sailors can charter a boat with a qualified skipper, potter round the islands, and find out as much, or as little, about sailing as they'd like. Those who are serious about learning to sail, or improving their skills, can take a course at one of the sailing schools. Sailors of varying abilities, wanting the security and bonhomie of a group can join a flotilla holiday. If your party includes someone with a skipper's ticket there's a multitude of bareboat charter options (yachts and motor boats); high rollers can take a fully crewed luxury yacht, classic or contemporary, and cruise the party hotspots.

WHEN AND WHERE TO GO

Avoid late July and August if you can. Italians sail over en masse at the beginning of August and popular marinas and ports can be hard to access in the evening. Charter prices are at their peak and most marinas add on ten per cent to their mooring fees. May and June can be warm and sunny, with relatively calm weather; however the sea is still warming up so can be a little bracing at times. September is great for sea temperatures but, as with May and June, you may well find that some of the restaurants in the more remote destinations are closed. Serious sailors may prefer the more challenging weather conditions in April and October or perhaps want to join in a winter sailing regatta.

It's surprising how much you can see in a week. The diverse appeal of Croatia's 2,000 islands, islets and reefs, together with the varied mainland ports and anchorages, will leave you wanting to come back for more.

In the north, the Istrian peninsula and the Kvarner Bay have a high concentration of marinas and a more cosmopolitan feel than Dalmatia due to the pervasive Italian influence. If gastronomy and culture are important, this may be your cruising area. Stunning and newly popular islands such as Lošinj, Rab and Brijuni are a magnet for luxury yachts. What is lacking is the diversity and number of islands that Dalmatia can offer. Exploration by boat reveals fewer surprises than down south.

Kornati is easily reached from the marinas at Zadar, Biograd and Murter. For tranquil wilderness, start from here. With its 152 islands, islets and rocks, Kornati archipelago is the densest group of islands in the Med. It can be tricky sailing, and the navigator will be working hard counting off the islands and watching out for rocks, but for peace and quiet, it's hard to beat the rugged lunar landscape and deserted bays. It's also something of a gourmet's paradise, with some notable restaurants geared towards passing sailors and others that serve up a perfectly good grilled sea bass or a steak. The islands around Šibenik are pretty special too – less barren and remote but still largely undiscovered.

On the mainland, Skradin's ACI marina, 5km (eight miles) upstream from Šibenik, on the river Krka, is a favourite for sailors who want to explore the waterfalls. Tribunj Marina near Vodice and Marina Frapa are two of Croatia's classier marinas, situated in a quiet fishing village. NCP (Nautical Center Prgin) has just announced the development of Croatia's first dedicated superyacht marina and resort area around its existing facilities in Mandalina. This could make Šibenik the new destination for luxury yachts.

Central Dalmatia meets most holidaymakers' requirements, starting with the marinas and charter bases within easy reach of Split airport. Brač and Hvar are an easy sail away from Split. Scores of picturesque anchorages and village harbours lie peacefully between the busier and more discovered towns. For a longer stay there's the more remote but gentile island of Vis, and for a Dalmatian time warp try Šolta. High rollers should head to Trogir and Hvar town. After partying all night in Hvar, relax at the neighbouring Pakleni islands, the perfect anchorage to soothe the spirits.

IN CONTEXT

For your perfect holidays

Experience Avis quality service and reliability in Croatia.
Enjoy the best rates and widest selection of vehicles
with over 30 branch offices at your service.

AVIS

We try
harder.

+385 1 4673 603 or 062 222 226 (for domestic calls only)
www.avis.com.hr

Further south towards Montenegro, Cavtat, on the mainland close to Dubrovnik airport is another regular superyacht destination. Pelješac is a favourite with experienced sailors for its weather conditions. Picturesque Korčula town is a popular land-based tourist destination but the island has plenty more to offer. Mljet has its salt water lakes and large bays which make for popular anchorages in summer; remote Lastovo has good berthing facilities for passing yachts, and a number of restaurants. Close to Dubrovnik, Lopud and Šipan are islands to escape from the metropolis – for both sailors and ferry passengers.

MARINAS AND ANCHORAGES

Most boats are surprisingly luxurious, providing toilets, showers, electricity, gas, usually ample kitchen/diner space, comfortable cabins and plenty of room on deck to eat, drink, sunbathe and be merry. But where do you park? Do you choose marinas, village harbours or anchorages? Most people opt for a mixture.

There are more than 50 marinas in Croatia, of which 21 are state-owned, recognisable by the acronym ACI. Planned and built ahead of its time, the ACI network ensured you could always find a safe haven almost wherever you were in the Croatian Adriatic. Now you're spoiled for choice but the demand for space is still high. Overnighting in a marina is great for improving the confidence of inexperienced crew and for a little extra comfort. You'll be moored on lazy lines (*see below*) and protected by a breakwater that reduces the motion of the boat to a very gentle sway. You'll always have access to toilets, showers, shore power and water, though the electricity and water supply may be restricted on the more remote islands. Often there'll be a restaurant, shop and café, and sometimes you'll find nightclubs, swimming pools and other entertainment. Comfort costs money and most of the marinas have hiked their prices over the past three years by between five and 15 per cent. That said, Croatia is still good value compared with Greece and Turkey. The intangible cost is the change in atmosphere: one minute the waves are lapping against the sides of the boat, the wind is blowing out the sails and there's no one in sight; the next the skipper is wedging your floating hotel into a tight space between two loud boats full of partygoers. Be prepared.

There's nothing like being lulled to sleep by nature and waking up in the morning in glorious sunshine to have a quick dip, off the back of the diving platform, in your own bay. Your charter boat will have a tender (a rubber dinghy) to get you to the shop or restaurant ashore without getting wet. You'll have the choice of paying extra for an outboard motor if you don't have the energy to row. Anchoring can be idyllic but occasionally novices find it hard to get used to. A local skipper will know the best bays given the prevailing conditions and your preferences. Otherwise, consult a good cruising guide and check out the charts. In some anchorages, particularly Kornati and the Zadar area, someone will come round and collect a fee. Very occasionally, a local entrepreneur may also try and charge for anchoring, so politely check credentials.

'The mighty Bura wind from the north-east is usually only a problem in winter but deserves respect year round.'

Berthing in a village or town harbour can give you the best of both worlds. You'll normally pay less than at a marina, many have shore power and water, some have toilets and showers, and you'll generally get the protection of a breakwater and the stability of lazy-line moorings. Depending on location, you probably won't be berthed like sardines, as in a marina, and you'll be able to walk off the boat to the nearest restaurant. Some restaurants in otherwise deserted bays also have lazy-line berthing on pontoons, sometimes with electricity and water.

TIPS AND CONDITIONS

Croatia has practically no tidal differences to worry about and only occasional strong currents, in channels or at the mouths of rivers. Summer weather is normally calm and sunny though you will get the odd thunderstorm that can rough up the seas. The Croatian Meteorological and Hydrological site (http://meteo.hr/index_en.php) has detailed weather forecasts on the Adriatic in English. The mighty Bura wind from the north-east is usually only a problem in winter but deserves respect year round. Weather forecasts in English are easily available at marinas, from the harbourmaster or on the radio, and locals are always happy to fill you in on climate tips. The cooling Maestral wind is predominant in summer but you may end up motor sailing over a few days if winds are light.

At most marinas and ports and in many bays with piers, using the lazy line is the standard method of berthing. Normally, when you approach a destination with lazy-line berths, someone comes to meet you on the quay or pontoon and holds up a rope. Heading in forwards allows for a little more privacy on deck but most prefer reversing in – it's easier to get on and off for a start. So, heading in backwards, someone stands at the back with a boat hook (normally supplied), picks up the raised rope, walks with it along to the front of the boat, pulls it in and secures it to the cleat on the front. Simultaneously, two other members of crew should be ready at the back of the boat with coiled ropes, already tied to the cleats on both sides of the back end. The ropes should be passed under the bottom rail and back over the top rail towards you so that when you throw the rope, it pulls directly on the cleat and not over or under a rail. As the boat reverses in, throw one rope to the person on land who's helping you berth and he will secure it; then throw the other rope. It's worth practising the throw a little to measure the weight of the ropes and to avoid hitting anyone in the face or chucking the ropes straight in the water. Don't worry though if you make a mistake – the locals have seen it all.

HOW MUCH?

Book early, shop around and avoid the peak months of July and August. Check the charter company small print for extras – final clean, outboard motor for the dinghy, extra sails, towels, etc - and make absolutely sure your boat has a bimini, a cockpit cover for protection against the sun. You also need to budget for fuel, onboard provisions, flights, transfers, eating out and the odd night at a hotel if you can't get your flights to coincide with the charter period, which normally runs from Saturday to Friday.

For novices, a basic one week's charter of a Bavaria 44, from Bavadria Charter (www.bavadria.com), with plenty of room for four people and a skipper, will cost around 2,500 euros in late September and around 3,550 euros in late July/early August. A skipper will cost 125 euros per day plus food and if you stay in a marina every night, allow around 70 euros per day (double for a catamaran), though some of the town and village ports are well equipped and considerably cheaper. Only some anchorages charge a fee.

RYA-approved Sailing School Croatia (www.sailingschoolcroatia.com) offer practical courses from their base near Split airport and cater for singles as well as families and groups. Depending on the level and the time of year, the price per person per week starts from around 600 euros. Flights, transfers and evening meals are excluded but you won't need to dig into your wallet for much else.

Sailing Holidays (www.sailingholidays.com) and Sunsail (www.sunsail.com) organise regular flotilla getaways. Sailing Holidays give a price guide of 1,300 euros to 2,200 euros per person per week, including flights, transfers and fuel, for sharing a Bavadria 33 with one other person on any of their flotilla holidays. The price goes up or down according to the size of yacht and how many are sharing it.

If you don't need a skipper, take your pick from the yachts and motorboats. An Elan 333, just over ten metres in length, provides ample space for two and is relatively easy to manage. A week in early September, chartering from Feral Tours (www.feral-tours. com) in Zadar, costs around 1,250 euros before discounts; in August it's 1,600 euros.

For jet setters there's even more choice, with many charter companies offering larger yachts and motorboats. Blue Yachts (www.blue-yachts.com) can charter you a Sunseeker Predator 95 for 84,560 euros for an all-inclusive weekly package with transfers, a skipper, a stewardess, a daily fuel allowance of up to 40 nautical miles, marina fees, use of jet skis and watersports equipment, and all on-board food and drink. For yacht and crew only, it's 61,500 euros. A classic Galatea yacht is around 40,000 euros a week in peak season from Exclusive Travel (www.exclusivetravelcroatia.com). Dalmatian Destinations (www. dalmatiandestinations.com) claims to have the largest yacht in Croatia for charter – the 41-metre boat, based in Split, has 16 double en-suite cabins and the base weekly charter price starts from 29,000 euros.

Modern yachts and motorboats are designed to maximise storage space but leave your rigid suitcases behind and pack everything in bags that fold away. Sunscreen, sunglasses and a hat are essential; long sleeved shirts and a warm jumper are advisable; waterproofs hopefully won't be necessary but can be a godsend if you're unlucky with the weather. Plastic, rubber or jelly shoes protect against stony beaches and sea urchins, whose spikes are painful but not life-threatening. Charts and guides are provided but check if snorkelling gear is on board. Most charter boats will have a CD player. Lifejackets and other essential safety equipment are supplied as are kitchen essentials.

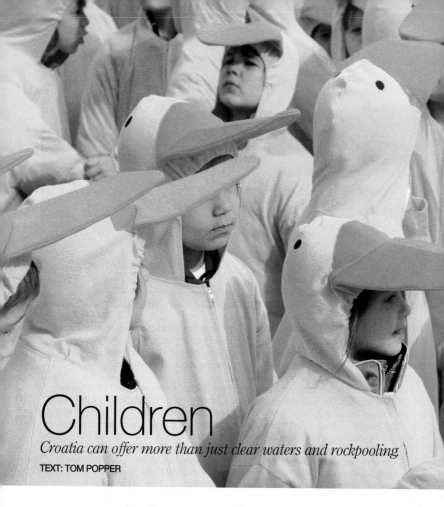

Children
Croatia can offer more than just clear waters and rockpooling

TEXT: TOM POPPER

Tom Popper
is editor of Time
Out Budapest
*and has worked
extensively around
Central and
Eastern Europe.*

Sure, sun, sea and splashing about on the beach are fun, but how much fun can a child take? Croatian beaches aren't like Spanish ones, man-made and groaning with gaudy attractions to weasel more euros out of poor parents. Stony shore, clear sea, a little snorkelling – and that's it. By day three, youngsters may need some kind of alternative diversion, and Croatia can oblige.

Many resort hotels offer structured activities for children, but they can feel a little too structured, almost like summer camp. One immediate solution is a visit to the nearest aquarium (there are a few good ones) for an hour of indoor diversion. Other child-oriented activities include nature trails, a donkey reserve, go-karting and a museum of old PCs. And then there are events such as the Rijeka Carnival and the Children's Festival.

THE INTERNATIONAL CHILDREN'S FESTIVAL

For two weeks every summer in **Šibenik**, the International Children's Festival takes over. For this 49th consecutive year, the 2009 event runs from mid June to early July, and has become a major celebration for Croatian families. The whole town is given over to puppet shows, theatre, dance and music performances for children. Often, children are the performers, such as for some of the folk-music and dance groups. Kids are also the stars in the art shows, with drawings and paintings based around a theme, or just more general exhibitions. You can look for a programme and find specific venues, or just stroll the Old Town of this less touristy seaside settlement, and see what you can find. Sibenik also contains the child-friendly **Bunari Museum**, designed by UK team JANVS, real hands-on stuff, due to open in 2010. If events in town get to be too much, the **Krka National Park** nearby is a great day trip, with trails leading through gorgeous forests and lakes. *See p45*. For more information about the festival, contact the organising office at Kralja Zvonimira 1, Šibenik (022 21 31 23, www.mdf-si.org).

FISH

Taking children to an aquarium provides a fun break from the beach, and it can even be an educational reminder that the sea is not only a place for people to play. Just being near the shore, you'll usually spot some fish darting around, but even with scuba gear, you probably won't get the kind of close-up view of marine life that an aquarium offers.

Don't expect all-singing, all-dancing whale enclosures or trained dolphin shows in Croatia. The government here has a policy of keeping dolphins in the sea, so larger themed establishments of the Sea World variety are not been permitted. Families may care to visit **Blue World** (*see p182*) in Veli Lošinj, a research and protection centre, with a modest exhibition centre. The organisation does not organise boat trips to see the resident colony of bottlenose dolphins, but will recommend a couple of tour companies who do. Blue World is at pains to stress that at no time should visitors touch the dolphins, let alone swim with them – but if you go out in spring or autumn you're as likely as not to see the creatures swimming near your boat.

Aquariums in Croatia tend to be rather small. A hyperactive child could whip through one – and start reminding you about that ice-cream you promised – in five minutes. You should set a reasonable pace at the beginning, and get everyone to linger at the various tanks for a couple of minutes, or at least to go back and see the fish they ran past. Once you get into enjoying the fish, you could spend from 30 minutes to an hour in any typical Croatian aquarium, which usually has about 25 tanks and/or pools.

Some of the aquariums are located at places of interest to tourists. In **Dubrovnik** and **Pula**, they're in fortifications; and the **Poreč** and **Rovinj** aquariums are in grand, aged structures in their respective old towns. These are places where Mum and Dad might want to do a little sightseeing but the children can get bored. A tour through a dark room full of funny looking fish can be a nice way to calm down youngsters who don't always appreciate the charms of antiquated architecture.

MORE FISH

One of the older establishments in Croatia, and the only sizeable one on the Dalmatian coast, is the **Dubrovnik Aquarium & Maritime Museum** (Damjana Jude 2, in St. John's Fortress, 021 427 937; 20kn adults, 10kn children). Here you can find 27 tanks, with many indigenous fish, giving the visitor some idea of the incredibly diverse life they're sharing the beach with – as well as an appreciation of the need to protect the sea. There are also a number of ocean-dwelling species that you wouldn't necessarily spot in the Adriatic. The attached maritime museum features charts, documents, boat models and other artefacts of the seafaring tradition.

Further north and west, up near Krk Island, in the Kvarner town of Crikvenica, is the **Crikvenica Aquarium** (Vinodolska 8, 051 241 006, www.raviko.hr/aquarium). This modest facility, with 24 tanks, was the first in Croatia to dedicate serious space to tropical fish. It

IN CONTEXT

'Plitvice's trails are fun: walkways made of wood carry you over swamps and streams, and you cross the lakes via charming covered ferryboats.'

boasts 100 varieties indigenous to the Adriatic – moray eels, sea horses and an octopus – along with 50 types of tropical fish, including the stunning butterfly fish and scorpion fish.

Going north to Istria, you'll find four aquariums lining the west coast of the peninsula, starting with Pula at the southern tip and reaching up to Umag near the Italian border. The largest of them is the **Pula Aquarium** (Verudela, 091 568 2986 mobile, http://aquarium.hr/eng; open summer 10am-10pm daily; 25kn adults, 15kn under-7s). This attraction, opened in 2002, is located inside the old Verudela Fort, with a nice garden for running around afterwards. There are 30 exhibits, including a touching pool, an open-topped basin where visitors can pet the scary shark-shaped dogfish, a turtle, a crab and other sea creatures. A tunnel through the back of the fortress leads to a freshwater pond, which holds the fish native to Croatia's lakes and rivers. Other exhibits include fishermen's nets and traps, and underwater photography.

The Pula Aquarium is also the home of the **Marine Turtle Rescue Centre** (www.aquarium.hr/mtrc/index-eng.htm), which treats injured specimens from this endangered species. Sea turtles swim in the Adriatic but they do not go ashore there unless they are sick or wounded – they are often damaged by fishing nets. Those rescued are brought here to be healed and eventually set free. You can usually get a look at the centre and check on the turtles under treatment.

EVEN MORE FISH

One of Croatia's oldest aquariums is in Rovinj, at the **Rudjer Bošković Institute's Centre for Maritime Research** (Giordano Paliaga 5, 052 804 700; open summer 9am-9pm daily; 10kn). Founded in 1891, Rovinj's aquarium is in a pretty stone house near the outskirts of the Old Town. The lobby area is promising, with a two-headed dogfish in a jar of formaldehyde. Inside, the fish are less freaky, but there is a good selection of local aquatic life.

Poreč Aquarium (F Glavinića 4, 052 428 720; open summer 10am-5pm daily) was opened recently. Near the harbour, in the heart of the Old Town – announced by at least a half-dozen billboards – the venue is certainly well-located. It contains 25 tanks displaying fish, flora and fauna from the Adriatic. Most of the fish on show were donated by local fishermen.

Not to be left behind by its neighbours, Umag, on the northern edge of Istria, has Croatia's newest facility. The **Umag Aquarium** (1.svibnja, 052 721 041; open April-Oct 9pm-9am daily; Nov-Dec, March 10am-5pm daily; 25kn), opened in 2005, is set in a shopping centre near the Old Town, easily accessible from the resorts by the Marina. Here you'll find 25 tanks, all with species from the Adriatic, including one open-topped pool.

ANIMALS WITH FUR

There's more to the local wildlife than what you'll find underwater. Horse riding, a donkey sanctuary and the **Plitvice Lakes National Park** offer a chance to get away from the sea.

Beginners and serious riders can enjoy horseback treks through beautiful countryside 20km from Pula and the coast at the **Barba Tone Ranch** (Manjadvorci 60, Manjadvorci, 052 580 446, www.barbatone.com). There are a variety of trails to choose from, and you can stay overnight at the ranch and take weekend-long trips. The most serious day-long excursion (500kn) includes an Istrian-style lunch and a trek down into caves, leaving the horses tethered outside. But there are also short hour-long trips or you can put a toddler on a pony for a few laps around the paddock. The ranch also has licensed physical therapists, trained to help disabled children and adults enjoy horse riding.

IN CONTEXT

Elsewhere in Istria, the shorter relatives of horses run riderless and unencumbered. Although the donkey is a domesticated animal, certain types are considered to be in danger of extinction, including many breeds that are indigenous to Croatia. Concerned Croatians have set up the **Liburna Reservation** (office Ulica Slobode 3, Labin, 052 857 706, www.rezervatliburna.hr). Call ahead to arrange a visit. The reservation is in Raša, by Labin near Istria's east coast. It provides a sanctuary for donkeys and an entertaining afternoon for kids. The donkeys roam wild in a large patch of green surrounded by a river, and visitors can get a chance to observe, and feed, them. Visitors can also take a nature walk, on a path with educational signs, or visit an ethnographic museum of farm implements, not all donkey-related.

LAKE LIFE

Another fun way to get close to nature is the Plitvice Lakes (*see p45*), Croatia's most popular National Park. The natural wonder of a series of waterfalls connecting a string of lakes make for stunning viewing, and the shady forests and cascading water keep things cool while you hike around. Best of all, Plitvice's trails are fun: walkways made of wood carry you over swamps and streams, and in certain sections you cross the lakes via charming covered ferryboats, designed for viewing the scenery. Those who want to lose the crowds can head out into wilder trails, but the well marked boardwalks are a perfect length for letting kids roam without getting exhausted. Using the maps provided at the entrance, you can choose trails that take much of the day to cover, or just an afternoon's jaunt.

PETROL POWER

If that's a bit too much like hard work, older kids and Dads may prefer to burn energy vicariously – through a go-kart engine. Croatia has many tracks, most requiring under-tens to be accompanied by an adult. Tracks are not all are well advertised and you may want to check with the tourist office. Some are near the beach. In Split, the go-kart track is right on Bačvice, the city beach, beside the children's play area which also includes trampolines and bouncy castles. In Pula, there is year-round racing at the **Green Garden Karting Race Track** (Šijana Forest, 052 535 639, www.karting.hr); and there is a well-established track in Poreč, the **Istra Motodrom** (052 456 100, www.istra-kart.com).

Child-Friendly Lodging

Hotels offering more than small food portions for their younger guests.

Croatian children mostly thrive without the gadgets that seem essential for the amusement of their Western European peers. A day on the beach provides all they need, and that's also how the family resorts and hotels have developed – around beach activities. Heritage destinations, such as Dubrovnik and Korčula, tend to focus on upscale adult-orientated hotels, but the established resort destinations, with those long stretches of mostly pebble beaches, offer many activities and facilities for all ages. You just have to accept the odd reminder of the package holiday era of old – decor and furniture for example.

The **Borik** area of **Zadar** is a prime example and is led in quality by **Falkensteiner's Club Funimation**. In 2009, their **Family Hotel Diadora**, in the new Punta Skala resort in nearby Petrčane, with its adventure park and Game Heaven, may just provide the ultimate in luxury family holidays (*see p201*). In **Biograd**, the **Ilirija Group** (*see p210*) has achieved something similar, albeit on a smaller scale, with their three hotels and a vast, activity-packed, beach and woodland area which includes a large tennis centre and pool area. **Olympia** in **Vodice** (*see p211*) and **Hotel Zora** in **Primošten** (*see p220*) and are also good Dalmatian options, as is Blue Sun's **Hotel Elaphusa**, in Bol on **Brač** (*see p255*), which has the advantage of one of Croatia's best beaches on its doorstep.

Istria is perhaps the most established family resort destination in Croatia. In **Poreč**, Plava Laguna's **Hotel Laguna Park** and Valamar's **Hotel Club Tamaris** lead the way (*see p132*; in **Rovinj** it's the **Maistra** group (*see p127*) and in **Rabac** there's **Valamar Bellevue Hotel & Residence** (*see p143*).

Most of the above offer modern four-star facilities. On a tighter budget there is the **Solaris** complex near **Šibenik** (*see p218*), for example, and a number along the **Makarska Riviera** in **Vrsar** and **Medulin** in Istria. Wherever you go, it pays to check beforehand that the Children's Clubs and activities are conducted in English rather than German or Italian. Also beware of confusing 'family hotels' with 'family run hotels' when doing your research. The latter is a government-led initiative to encourage the development of small independent hotels. They may also be good for families, but not by definition.

IN CONTEXT

THE OLD COMPUTER CLUB

If the great outdoors gets to be too much, there's always the great indoors. There are hundreds of museums around, but not all of them are that enticing to young ones. In Rijeka, kids can have some hands-on time with old computers at **Club PEEK&POKE** (Ivana Grohovca 2, 091 780 5709 mobile, www.peekpoke.hr; open 5-8pm Mon-Fri, 10am-2pm Sat; 10kn). Old Commodore 64s, the first generation of Macs (with two five-and-a-half inch floppy drives!) and a working game of Pong stand alongside scores of other old computers and computer games, most still working, preserved and collated in this quirky, interactive museum. Enthusiastic, English-speaking guides take children's groups or drop-in tourists for a tour of machinery that is ancient history for the very young, but a reminder of how time flies for the rest of us. An upstairs internet café is going online this summer.

Festivals

Cultural and traditional bashes from January to December.

From Rijeka's **Carnival** at Mardi Gras to revellers seeing in **New Year** in the streets of Dubrovnik's Old Town, Croatia likes to celebrate. Culturally, Dubrovnik's **Summer Festival** (60 in 2009!) packs the most oomph, while Zadar's **Garden Festival** and the **Motovun Film Festival** are characterised by a Glastonbury-like devotion to partying and hedonism.

Genre-wise, Croatia excels in festivals of film (Motovun, Pula, Zagreb, Split, Dubrovnik and now Vukovar) although the live music scene is increasingly strong. Zagreb's **INMusic** and **Radar** in Varaždin have attracted the likes of Bob Dylan, Nick Cave and Kraftwerk in the last two years. For theatre, **Eurokaz** in Zagreb is always adventurous, also embracing dance, circus and body art.

Then there are events of niche interest and even outright oddities, such as the festivals of street performance (**Cest is d'Best**, Zagreb), extreme sports (**Sutivan**, Brač) and cartoons (**Animafest**, Zagreb).

Most of Croatia's national holidays and celebrations are either religious and family-based (Easter, Christmas) or tied in with the recent war and independence. Some cities (Dubrovnik's **St Blaise's Day**; **Zagreb City Day**) hold major annual urban celebrations, otherwise the best time to visit is for New Year's Eve.

OPENING
autumn2009

MUSEUM of
Contemporary
Art Zagreb

www.msu.hr

MSU MUZEJ SUVREMENE UMJETNOSTI ZAGREB
MUSEUM OF CONTEMPORARY ART

INFORMATION

There is no one-stop information resource for Croatia's major festivals. The website of the national tourist office (www.croatia.hr) has a search engine for events but tends to focus on minor local food festivals. Zagreb's own site (www.zagreb-touristinfo.hr) has an excellent event directory by theme and date.

SPRING

Contemporary Dance Week
Zagreb/Rijeka (www.danceweekfestival.com).
Date Late May.
Founded in 1983, this international event showcases a wide range of European choreographers – part of the programme is geared towards those under 27. Venues across the capital, plus a couple in Rijeka.

FREE Zagreb City Day
Zagreb (www.zagreb-touristinfo.hr). **Date** 31 May.
Shows, concerts and exhibitions across a flower-strewn town centre mark Zagreb City Day.

Animafest
Zagreb (www.animafest.hr). **Date** Late May-early June.
Approaching its 20th anniversary, this festival of animated films has screenings all over the city, particularly at the Europa Cinema, Varšavska 3.

SUMMER

Strossmartre
Zagreb (www.kraljeviulice.com). **Date** June.
This month-long outdoor event stages free films, concerts and unusual happenings (best mongrel dog show; best wine-and-soda spritzer competition) in the leafy setting of Zagreb's Strossmayerovo Šetalište.

FREE Cest is d'Best
Zagreb (www.kraljeviulice.com). **Date** June.
This popular celebration of street entertainment is set in the streets and squares of Zagreb city centre. Performers come from far and wide.

INMusic Festival
Lake Jarun, Zagreb (www.inmusicfestival.com).
Date June.
This high-profile, four-stage, two-day music festival is set on an island in Lake Jarun. Recent acts have included Nick Cave and Iggy Pop. For 2009 the line-up features Kraftwerk, Moby and Franz Ferdinand.

Radar Festival
Gradski stadion, Varaždin (www.radar-festival.com). **Date** June.
The real highlight of 2008 – when Bob Dylan did Varaždin – hopes to keep the big names coming in 2009 and beyond.

Histria Festival
Amphitheatre, Pula (www.histriafestival.com).
Date June-September.
Ten performances are spread over the summer at this annual series of events in Pula's open-air arena. Dance, classical, opera and pop are the genres represented – Manu Chao played in 2008.

FREE International Children's Festival
Šibenik (www.mdf-si.org). **Date** Late June-early July.
Taking place in theatres and on open-air stages, this annual children's festival features puppeteers, actors, musicians and sundry performers in bright clothes and silly costumes. Tickets are available from the main Šibenik Theatre box office (Kralja Zvonimira 1, 022 213 145) but many events are free.

Eurokaz International Festival of New Theatre
Zagreb (www.eurokaz.hr). **Date** Late June-early July.
Since 1987, Eurokaz has presented hundreds of artists and companies from around the world, in disciplines ranging from theatre to contemporary dance, and body art to new circus. There are also multimedia presentations and visual arts.

Libertas International Film Festival
Dubrovnik (www.libertasfilmfestival.com).
Date Late June-early July.
Now the leading celebration of celluloid in Dubrovnik, Libertas shows arthouse and mainstream movies. It attracts many big names to town – recent celebs snapped here have included Owen Wilson and Woody Harrelson.

The Garden Festival
Petrčane, Zadar (www.thegardenzadar.com).
Date Early July.
Biggest DJ and live music fest in Croatia. *See p66.*

Vukovar Film Festival
Vukovar (www.vukovarfilmfestival.com).
Date July.
Inaugurated in 2008, this event aims to revitalise a town still devastated by the Yugoslav war. Screenings take place on a cargo barge moored on the Danube, a treat for local and visitor alike.

Dubrovnik Summer Festival
Dubrovnik (www.dubrovnik-festival.hr).
Date 10 July-25 Aug.
The grandaddy of them all, Croatia's most prestigious cultural event celebrates its 60th anniversary in 2009. Inaugurated by director Marko Fotez in 1950, this mainly high-brow happening concentrates on theatre (mainly Shakespeare and his Croatian equivalent, Marin Držić), classical music and dance.

IN CONTEXT

TimeOut

timeout.com/travel
Get the local experience

Dream deli counter at Franchi, in the Prati district, **Rome**

© Gianluca Moggi

All kinds of venues are used, indoors and out, most famously the Lovrijenac fortress for theatre. Many events sell out but there will be any number of street performances, side shows, signings, exhibitions, and so on. Hotels fill up, so plan well ahead.

Split Summer

Split (www.splitsko-ljeto.hr). **Date** mid July-mid Aug.
Split Summer comprises a month of theatre, opera, music and dance, much of it taking place in open-air settings around the Diocletian's Palace. The National Theatre is used for prestigious shows.

FREE Extreme Sports

Sutivan, Brač (www.sutivan.hr). **Date** mid July.
Otherwise known as Vanka Regule, this week-long event takes place in and around Sutivan, close to Supetar, a ferry hop from Split. Now in its tenth year, Extreme Sports involves free diving, windsurfing, skateboarding, climbing and bike events.

Pula Film Festival

Amphitheatre, Pula (www.pulafilmfestival.hr). **Date** July.
Pula's famous cinematic event is mainly staged in the historic setting of the Roman arena. Although not as prestigious as when Tito hobnobbed with Sophia Loren here, the PFF is slowly regaining its profile. The first three days are dedicated to international films, the rest to Croatian works.

FREE Motovun Film Festival

Motovun (www.motovunfilmfestival.com). **Date** late July.
Croatia's liveliest and most enjoyable filmfest features the international arthouse and independent cinema. More than that, it's a week-long party in this idyllic Istrian hilltop village.

FREE Street Art Festival

Poreč (052 887 216/www.poup.hr/saf2). **Date** early Aug.
The streets and squares of Poreč Old Town play host to visual art projects, music, acrobatics and outdoor entertainment of all kinds. A few days earlier, nearby Rovinj hosts Grisia, a week-long art festival in the gallery-lined street of the same name.

Špancirfest

Varaždin (www.spancirfest.com). **Date** late Aug.
Street festivities, concerts, craft and food stalls are set up around this pretty Baroque town.

PIF

Zagreb (http://public.carnet.hr/pif-festival). **Date** early Sept.
Zagreb's International Festival of Puppetry is now in its fifth decade, a week-long series of performances for children and adults in theatres and open-air venues across the capital.

Dubrovnik Summer Festival. *See p63.*

Split Film Festival

Split (www.splitfilmfestival.hr). **Date** mid Sept.
Movies, videos, installations, workshops and various types of new media across the city.

AUTUMN

Zagreb Film Festival

Zagreb (www.zagrebfilmfestival.com). **Date** Oct.
A week-long celebration of celluloid that has become one of the biggest cultural events in the capital's calendar. Thousands descend on the main venue, the Student Centre, to watch films and party.

International Jazz Days

Zagreb (www.jazz.hr). **Date** Oct.
One of two major jazz festivals to take place in the capital, mainly at the prestigious city-centre BP Club (Teslina 7, www.bpclub.hr). The other is in March, same web details.

Nebo World Music Festival

Zagreb (www.nebofestzagreb.com). **Date** Oct.
Acts from Mongolia to Zambia come to Zagreb to perform at a number of venues across the city.

FREE St Martin's

Zagreb (www.kraljeviulice.com). **Date** Nov.
The capital's annual celebration of wine and roast goose involves music shows and food stalls set up across the city. Major acts play as well.

IN CONTEXT

WINTER

FREE New Year's Eve
Dubrovnik. **Date** 31 Dec.
Of all the public celebrations of the new year across Croatia, Dubrovnik's is usually the most intimate and enjoyable. Locals stride down Stradun, bars and restaurants fill to bursting, and the city's luxury hotels cater to moneyed guests with slap-up meals. It's crowded but without the claustrophobic festivities of Zagreb or Split.

FREE St Blaise's Day
Dubrovnik. **Date** 2-3 Feb.

Dubrovnik's patron saint is honoured with a procession, street entertainment and communal dancing.

FREE Rijeka International Carnival
Rijeka. **Date** Sunday before Shrove Tuesday.
Croatia's main Mardi Gras carnival is a series of pre-Lent pageants, including a Children's Parade. The big event is the mass costumed procession on the Sunday.

FREE Zagreb Wine Gourmet Festival
Zagreb (www.1001delicija.com). **Date** late Feb.
Some 400 types of wine and many gastronomic delicacies are presented at a venue in the capital.

Garden Party

Music and dance under the trees and on the waves.

Croatia's biggest dance music event takes place at a secluded seaside spot just outside Zadar: the **Garden Festival** in Petrčane. Named after the club, the Garden Festival is a natural development of the quality music venue from city to seaside. It began in 2006, with a few hundred people gathered over a rainy weekend. But now it's a big deal – numbers reached 3,000 in 2008 and will be limited to 2,000 for 2009 and probably beyond. The key to its success is not only the high standard of the music on offer – UK music producer Nick Colgan takes care of that – but the site itself.

Petrčane is a peninsula carpeted with pine trees, both intimate and isolated. Festival goers party without causing any disturbance, but don't feel part of an uncomfortable multitude. Since the Garden team reconfigured the main indoor venue, a '70s building now called Barbarella's, the festival has four hubs: a main stage; Barbarella's; the Tiki Bar and Dance Terrace, and, a stroke of genius, this, the Argonaughty party boat. Another innovation is to make the Garden Festival a ten-dayer – under the heading 'Double Whammy', the 2009 bash takes place over two weekends. *See p63.*

Zagreb

Trg bana
Jospipa
Jelačića.
See p69.

Zagreb

Newly swish and chic, the Croatian capital retains its Habsburg charm.

Set, as it is, nearer to Vienna than Dubrovnik, visitors will find that this pocket-sized metropolis is also closer in character to its Central European cousins. An ecclesiastical and political hub in medieval times, under the Habsburgs Zagreb expanded greatly, with pretty parks and elegant façades providing a suitable environment for its inhabitants. Now as capital of an independent Croatia, this pretty, relaxed city has become a regional business and conference centre, as well as a pleasant destination for tourists investigating one of Europe's less-known destinations.

INTRODUCING THE CITY

Set by Mount Medvednica, where the last foothills of the Alps meet the Pannonian plain, Zagreb still lacks the urban gravitas of a Vienna or a Budapest but this is part of its charm. It's small enough for you to be able to walk to most places. If not, most of its 16 tram routes pass through **Trg bana Josipa Jelačića**, the main square where you might start your day over a slow coffee at one of the city's many terrace cafés. Everyone in Zagreb meets over coffee. The communal, post-shop sip, or *spica*, is a Saturday tradition. During the week, once you've browsed around the nearby market, **Dolac** (*see p90* **Profile**), and established that much of downtown Zagreb has hardly changed since Tito, you should be in time for *gableci*, cheap lunches for locals.

INSIDE TRACK
ZAGREB CARD

Like many other cities, the Croatian capital produces a discount card for tourists, allowing them free public transport, discounts or free entry to most museums, plus reduced prices at many shops, restaurants and service providers. The **Zagreb Card** comes in 24-hour (60kn) or 72-hour (90kn) versions and is available online (www.zagrebcard.five stars.hr) or at several outlets in town, including the tourist office (*see p94*).

Everything here has a time and place, and an underlying order common to German-speaking Europe but with a Balkan sense of fun and, after dark, hedonism.

Light sightseeing duties may involve a hike around the cobbled **Upper Town**, a stroll of the landscaped greenery and grid-patterned streets of the **Lower Town**, and, as of spring 2009, a hop over the Sava river to **Novi Zagreb** and the key attraction of the **Museum of Contemporary Art**, *see p76* **Profile**.

Tourism and business travellers have been encouraged by a crop of new hotels (the local authorities have set their sights on hosting conferences and conventions). The introduction of a budget air link with the UK has increased visitor figures, as has a handful of high-profile festivals in the summer.

HISTORY

Zagreb grew up on the north bank of the Sava. It comprised two rival hilltop settlements, **Gradec** and **Kaptol**, the site of today's **Sabor**, or Croatian Parliament, and the **Cathedral**. After Hungarian King Ladislas founded a diocese here in 1094, it remained under the archbishopric of Hungary until 1852. Kaptol and Gradec fought for most of that millennium. A testament to their animosity can be found in the naming of **Krvavi most**, Bloody Bridge, the alley at the western end of Skalinska and scene of battles between churches.

By the 17th century, with the Governor (Ban) of Croatia and the Sabor based here, Zagreb's importance overshadowed the local rivalry. By the 19th, its development reflected a growing search for a Croatian identity. Prestigious buildings such as the **Academy of Arts and Sciences** and the **National Theatre** centrepieced a neat spread of grid-patterned streets and squares between the Upper Town (Gornji Grad) of Kaptol and Gradec, and the new railway station. Habsburgian in appearance, it gained the name of Lower Town (Donji Grad). A main square, Harmica, was laid out where the Upper and Lower Towns met.

But power still rested in the twin Habsburg capitals of Vienna and Budapest. With the clamour for reform, in 1848, the Croatian Ban, Josip Jelačić, led an army into Hungary. His bid failed and Jelačić died a broken man. He was honoured with a statue on Harmica, on his horse, his sword pointed in defiance. Tito had it taken down and the square named Trg republike. With the fall of Communist rule in 1990, the statue was reassembled and the square renamed Trg bana Josipa Jelačića.

Across the Sava, Tito built the Socialist-style housing estate of Novi Zagreb. Zagreb, as the second city of Yugoslavia, acquired an industrial edge. Many Socialist-era shopfronts can still be seen around the Lower Town. At the same time, an underground rock and art scene flourished and a Zagreb spirit emerged, distinct from the bourgeois atmosphere between the two world wars. It was savvy, independent, liberal, certainly not supportive of rule from Belgrade,

but neither comfortable with the nationalist undercurrents of Tudjman and his cronies. Apart from an audacious rocket attack in 1991 on the Ban's Palace and one on citizens in 1995, Zagreb was spared the worst of the war. Its population swelled by refugees from Bosnia and the countryside, Zagreb and its outskirts did see a significant political shift to the right. This has been dissipated with the need for post-war recovery. Zagreb, in the mid-point between Mitteleuropa and the Mediterreanean, knows its future lies with Europe.

The war and the economic struggle after independence froze the city in its two seminal points in time, 19th-century Habsburg and 20th-century Socialist. Recently, shiny malls, fashionable shops and gleaming office blocks have sprung up, as well as a bar quarter on the pedestrianised streets around **Preradovićeva**, and a commercial district along **Savska**, south-west of the Lower Town.

SIGHTSEEING

All journeys start and begin with Trg bana Josipa Jelačića main square, often referred to as Jelačić plac. Nearly everything in the city centre is walkable – and parking is a nightmare.

For serious sightseeing, invest in a three-day **Zagreb Card** (www.zagrebcard.fivestars.hr, 90kn) from the main **tourist office** (*see p94*) on Jelačić plac.

Upper Town.

ZAGREB

The city centre

Close on the map to Jelačić plac, a short, steep climb away, is the well-stocked and always busy daily market, Dolac, and **Zagreb Cathedral**. Further over on Gradac, the other side of Bloody Bridge, is a cluster of sights around the main one of **St Mark's Church**.

This group of churches and galleries is best accessed from a funicular (Tomićeva, every 10mins, 6.30am-9pm daily; 4kn) by Ilica, a gentrifying commercial street running west from Jelačić. The short ride takes you to the **Lotrščak Tower** (Strossmayerovo šetalište 9, 01 48 51 768, open 11am-8pm Tue-Sun, 10kn), a lookout tower built in the 13th century, reached by climbing a winding wooden staircase. It has since housed a sweet shop and, on the first floor, Zagreb's first pool hall. Every day since 1877, a couple of loud cannon blasts from here signal noon sharp.

Leafy Strossmayerovo šetalište runs by the tower giving a lovely view of the rooftops. Nearby stands **St Catherine's Church** (Katarinski trg, 01 48 51 950, open 10am-1pm daily), built by the Jesuits in the 17th century, with a beautiful baroque interior of pink-and-white stucco. Clustered around it are the **Croatian Museum of Naive Art** and **Klovićevi Dvori**. Just north of Klovićevi Dvori stands the Stone Gate (Kamenita Vrata), the only remaining medieval entrance to the Upper Town. It's more of a short, bendy tunnel than a gate, and is a shrine to mark a fire, in 1731, that consumed everything here but a painting of the Virgin Mary. Prayers are whispered, flowers laid and candles lit.

Passing through it, you wander around the cobbled streets of Gradec, looking into little squares, perhaps popping into the **Croatian History Museum** (Matoševa 9, 01 48 51 900, www.hismus.hr; open 10am-6pm Mon-Fri, 10am-1pm Sat, Sun; 10kn), a lovely baroque mansion with a collection of photographs, furniture, paintings and weapons thematically relating to Croatia's development.

At the heart of Gradec stands **St Mark's Church** on Markov trg, a square housing the Croatian Parliament and the Ban's Palace. North, edging towards the verdant slopes of Mount Medvednica, are the **Meštrović Atelijer**, the **Natural History Museum** (Demetrova 1, 01 48 51 700, www.hpm.hr; 10am-5pm Tue-Fri, 10am-1pm Sat, Sun; 15kn) and the **Zagreb City Museum**.

Walking back through the Stone Gate, you come into Radićeva and, crossing back over Bloody Bridge, to one of the most atmospheric and lively streets in Zagreb, **Tkalčićeva**. Pastel-shaded low-rise old houses accommodate galleries, bars and boutiques. The parallel street

Tkalčićeva Street.

of Opatovina, once a legendary bar hub, has long lost its verve and is now lined with display cases of cheap clothes.

Crossing the market square, your eyes are drawn towards the spires of the cathedral, surrounded on three sides by the ivy walls of the Archbishop's Palace. Around it runs Vlaška, which brings you up to the park of **Ribnjak**, pleasant by day, filled with amorous teenagers after dark at weekends.

The Lower Town begins at Jelačić. A criss-cross of streets starts with a pedestrianised zone around Preradovićeva flower market, by the new bar quarter of **Gajeva**, Preradovićeva and **Margaretska**. Stern, grey Habsburg façades run down to the train station, some with shopfronts that have remained virtually unchanged since 1965. Parallel to them are two neatly planned rectangles of green public space stretching north-south as far as the train station, bookended by the **Botanical Gardens**. This is the so-called Horseshoe, an attempt by 19th-century urban designer Milan Lenuci to create a city in the Austrian mode. Each park is parcelled up into three parts, centrepieced by grandiose landmark buildings of prominent institutions: the Academy of Arts and Sciences; the National Theatre, and the **Mimara Museum** alongside. **Zrinjevac**, the northernmost section, features tree-lined paths, a gazebo and a fountain designed by Herman Bollé, responsible for many of Zagreb's major architectural works, including the cathedral.

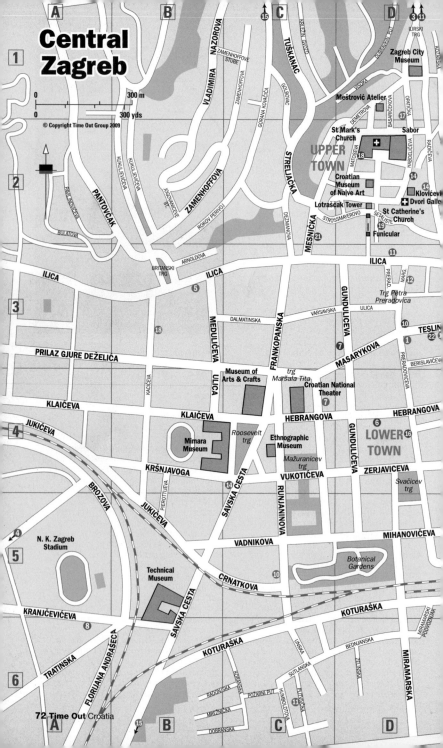

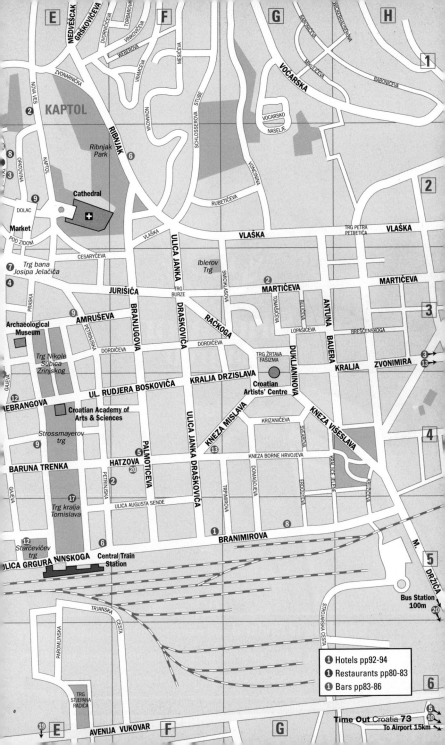

MEDVEŠČAK

E GRŠKOVIĆEVA F G H

DVORNIČKOVA
VINKOVIĆEVA
TORBAROVA

ZVONARNIČKA VRAMČEVA MESIĆEVA

VOĆARSKA

NOVA VES

KAPTOL

NOVAKOVA

SCHLOSSEROVA STUBE

VOĆARSKO NASELJE

BABONIĆEVA
MIKLOUŠIĆEVA
VICKERHAUSEROVA

❷

Ribnjak Park ❻

OPATOVIČKA

KAPTOL

❽

❾

VONČINNINA

RUBETIĆEVA

❶

❷

Cathedral

DOLAC

Market

POD ZIDOM

VLAŠKA VLAŠKA TRG PETRA PETRETIĆA VLAŠKA

CESARYČEVA

Trg bana ❼
Josipa Jelačića
❹

PRAŠKA

JURIŠIĆA

ULICA JANKA

Iblerov Trg

SMIČIKLASOVA

TRG BURZE

MARTIĆEVA MARTIĆEVA

❷

TOMAŠIĆEVA
BULIČEVA
ANTUNA
BAUERA

❸

AMRUŠEVA ❾

BRANJUGOVA

DRAŠKOVIĆA

RAČKOGA

PETRINJSKA DORDIČEVA

DORDIČEVA

LOPAŠIĆEVA

BREŠĆENSKOGA

Archaeological Museum

Trg Nikole Šubiča Zrinjskog

UL. RUDJERA BOSKOVIĆA

KRALJA DRZISLAVA

DUKLJANINOVA

KRALJA ZVONIMIRA

❸
❸

GAJEVA

ŠEBRANGOVA ❷

Croatian Academy of Arts & Sciences

ULICA JANKA DRAŠKOVIĆA

KNEZA MISLAVA

TRG ŽRTAVA FAŠIZMA

Croatian Artists' Centre

KRIŽANIĆEVA

SIVERNOVA

KNEZA VIŠESLAVA

Strossmayerov trg
❾

BARUNA TRENKA

PALMOTIĆEVA

HATZOVA
❷❺
❷⓿

KNEZA BORNE HRVOJEVA

DOMAGOJEVA

KRALJICE JELENE

ERDODYEVA

KRUŽIĆEVA

GAJEVA

PETRINJSKA

Trg kralja Tomislava ⓰

ULICA AUGUSTA SENOE

TRIPIMIROVA

❽

❻

❶

BRANIMIROVA

❷
Starčevićev trg

ULICA GRGURA NINSKOGA

Central Train Station

Bus Station 100m

M. DRŽIĆA

❺

TRJANSKA CESTA

STROJARSKA CESTA

PAROMLINSKA

❻

❶ Hotels pp92-94
❶ Restaurants pp80-83
❶ Bars pp83-86

TRG STJEPANA RADIĆA

❺
❿

❶⓽

E AVENIJA VUKOVAR F G

Cathedral.

Linked to Jelačić by Masarykova, Trg Maršala Tita is notable not only for the neo-baroque **Croatian National Theatre** but also for the fact that the square has kept its name, Tito. In front of the theatre stands one of the most famous works by sculptor Ivan Meštrović, *The Well of Life*.

The Lower Town ends at the railtracks and another fin-de-siècle façade, the neo-classical train station, Glavni kolodvor. A major stop on the Orient Express, it echoes another era, when arrival by train was the norm. Next to it was built one of Europe's great railway hotels, the **Regent Esplanade**, surrounded by a pedestrianised square of fountains and an underground shopping mall. The main railway lines still run to Vienna and Budapest – the domestic network is extremely limited.

Art Pavilion

Trg kralja Tomislava 22 (01 48 76 487/www. umjetnicki-paviljon.hr). **Open** 11am-7pm Mon-Sat; 10am-1pm Sun. **Admission** 20kn; 10kn reductions. **No credit cards. Map** p73 E5.
Created for the Millennial exhibition in Budapest in 1896, this impressive, iron-framed building was then shipped back to Zagreb, where it centrepieces Tomislav square facing the train station. It still hosts major events and exhibitions.

▶ *At the front of the building is one of central Zagreb's most convivial restaurants, the Paviljon; see p83.*

FREE Botanical Gardens

Marulićev trg 9a (01 48 44 002). **Open** Apr-Nov 9am-2.30pm Mon, Tue; 9am-dusk Wed-Sun. **Admission** free. **Map** p72 D5.
These lovely gardens, founded in 1889, contain giant trees, lily-pad-covered ponds, an English-style arboretum, symmetrical French-inspired flower beds and ten glasshouses, the latter closed to the public. Around 10,000 plant species come mainly from Croatia, some from as far as Asia. It's a shaded spot in summer, with plenty of benches.
▶ *For more green space close to the city centre, head to the Maksimir Park & Zoo; see p79.*

★ FREE Cathedral

Kaptol 31 (01 48 14 727). **Open** 10am-5pm Mon-Sat; 1-5pm Sun. **Admission** free. **Map** p73 E2.
The Cathedral is Zagreb's main attraction and most visible presence, its neo-Gothic twin towers being visible right across the city. It's had a troubled life, however. The original church was destroyed by the Tatars in 1242 and the later reconstructions were damaged by fire. After the earthquake of 1880, Viennese architect Hermann Bollé added the 105m-high (345-foot) belltowers. The interior contains medieval frescoes, a Renaissance triptych altar attributed to Albrecht Dürer and an Ivan Meštrović relief that marks the resting place of controversial Croatian Archbishop Alojzije Stepinac.

Croatian Artists' Centre

Trg žrtava fašizma (01 46 11 818/www.hdlu.hr). **Open** 11am-7pm Tue-Fri; 10am-2pm Sat, Sun. **Admission** 15kn. **No credit cards. Map** p73 G4.
This Ivan Meštrović-designed 1930s masterpiece is among Zagreb's most striking sights. Classical columns support a white circular structure made of stone from Brač. In 1941, to attract Muslims to the Fascist regime, the building became a mosque. The three minarets were demolished in 1949. Since 2003 it has housed the Croatian Association of Artists, serving as its main exhibition space.

Croatian Museum of Naive Art

Ćirilometodska ulica 3 (01 48 51 911/www.hmnu.org). **Open** 10am-6pm Tue-Fri; 10am-1pm Sat, Sun. **Admission** 20kn; 10kn concs. **Credit** AmEx, V. **Map** p72 D2.
This collection of 50 or so paintings is a decent introduction to Croatia's naive art movement. Housed on the second floor of the 18th-century Raffay Palace, the permanent exhibit focuses on the Hlebine School, with works by Ivan Generalić, Franjo Mraz, Mijo Kovačič and Ivan Lacković Croata. There are a further 1,600 works still in storage.

ZAGREB

Profile Museum of Contemporary Art

Croatia's most prominent new museum opens in Zagreb.

ZAGREB

At the corner of Avenija Dubrovnik and Avenija Većeslava Holjevca, the new Museum of Contemporary Art comprises nearly 5,000sq m of exhibition space, a library, a multi-media room, a boutique and children's workshop. It is the first museum to be built in Zagreb for 125 years and it will be the largest ever built in Croatia – when it opens.

The unwritten law of building, which states that a) the work will invariably last longer than intended and b) it will always cost more than intended, has proved to be true in the case of the Zagreb Museum of Contemporary Art. Its foundation was laid in 2003 and its original finishing date was late 2006 – but the MSU, to give it its local acronym, will only reach completion in late 2009. The original construction budget of 350 million kuna has also been exceeded by 100 million.

As the palace that hosted the MSU in the Upper Town proved to be inadequate, solutions were sought for a new location and purpose-built building. The new museum is across the river Sava in Novi Zagreb, on the axis of the famous green horseshoe that stretches from Zrinjevac Park via Strossmayer's Gallery of Old Masters and the Art Pavilion in the Lower Town, to the Lisinski Concert Hall and the National Library.

Igor Franić, the Croatian architect who designed the building in the spirit of the functionalist tradition, was inspired by the shape of the meander. This snake-like form has special significance in Croatian art. In his Gorgona period in the 1960s, the influential Julije Knifer stayed devoted to this single motif, painting it over and over again in black and white.

As part of the preparations for their eventual move, the MSU published a complete catalogue of its collection, which consists of more than 4,000 works by 900 artists. The highlights of the new display include EXAT 51, New Tendencies, the experimental films of Ivan Ladislav Galeta and Tomislav Gotovac and artists such as Goran Trbuljak, Sanja Iveković and Dalibor Martinis.

The long delays and poor communication between the City of Zagreb and the Ministry, the main financiers of the project, have also provoked the art scene to engage. Croatian artist Željko Badurina decided that the only way to help the new museum out of its impasse was to turn to a higher power, so he decided to pay for a mass in the Church of St Catherine, close to the museum's old building. The Minister of Culture and the Mayor of Zagreb failed to turn up, although several curators from the museum did. The priest led a prayer for the swift completion of the building and its new role in the cultural life of the city, and so did the artists present. Reportedly there was a terrible storm during the mass, all of which was interpreted by the artist as a promising sign from above.

MORE ART
Right in the city centre, the **Nova Galerija** (Nikole Tesle 7, 01 487 25 82) hosts the works of WHW, an all-girl Croatian foursome invited to curate for the prestigious Istanbul Biennial in 2009.

Ethnographic Museum

Trg Ivana Mažuranića 14 (01 48 26 220/www. emz.hr). **Open** 10am-6pm Tue-Thur; 10am-1pm Fri-Sun. **Admission** 15kn; 10kn reductions. Free Thur. **No credit cards. Map** p72 C4.

This two-floor collection of folk artefacts is set inside a Secessionist palace. Downstairs, the permanent collection includes traditional costumes from all over Croatia and overseas items brought home by Croatian explorers – ritual masks from the Congo, tree-bark paintings from Australia and Chinese ceremonial dresses. Temporary shows on the second floor are organised around local and global themes.

Galerija Klovićevi Dvori

Jezuitski trg 4 (01 48 51 926/www.galerija klovic.hr). **Open** 10am-8pm Tue, Wed, Fri-Sun. 10am-10pm Thur. **Admission** 20kn; 10kn concs. **No credit cards. Map** p72 D2.

This high-profile gallery, set in the stunning space of a former Jesuit monastery in Gornji Grad, is known for curating first-rate temporary exhibits of big-name local and international artists.

★ Meštrović Atelijer

Mletačka 8 (01 48 51 123/www.mdc.hr/ mestrovic). **Open** 10am-6pm Tue-Fri; 10am-2pm Sat, Sun. **Admission** 20kn; 10kn reductions. **Credit** *50kn min* AmEx, DC, MC, V. **Map** p72 D1.

Croatia's most internationally renowned sculptor, Ivan Meštrović, lived and worked in this restored trio of adjoining 17th-century mansions between 1923 and 1942. The collection here – marble, stone, wood and bronze sculptures, reliefs, drawings and graphics – grace two floors of the house, the front atrium and his atelier off the ivy-covered courtyard.
► *For more Meštrović, head to Split and his major gallery/studio; see p226.*

★ Mimara Museum

Rooseveltov trg 5 (01 48 28 100). **Open** 10am-5pm Tue, Wed, Fri, Sat; 10am-7pm Thur; 10am-2pm Sun. **Admission** 20kn; 10kn reductions. **No credit cards. Map** p72 B4.

Zagreb's finest art collection was given to the city by shady dealer Ante Topić Mimara. Despite their dubious origins, the 1,700 artefacts housed in 42 exhibition rooms are undeniably impressive. Paintings, statues and historical items, organised chronologically and thematically, include medieval icons, Chinese porcelain, plus paintings by Spanish and Flemish masters.

Museum of Arts & Crafts

Trg maršala Tita 3 (01 48 82 111/www.muo.hr). **Open** 10am-7pm Tue, Wed, Fri, Sat; 10am-10pm Thur; 10am-2pm Sun. **Admission** 30kn; 20kn reductions. **No credit cards. Map** p72 C4.

Inside this grand Hermann Bollé-designed palace opposite the National Theatre are 160,000 items, 3,000 on permanent display. Exhibits, presented in a series of halls around a galleried atrium, span the 14th and 20th centuries – Gothic to art deco – and include furniture, pottery, glass and ivory, plus musical instruments, clothes and photo equipment.

ZAGREB

Mimara Museum.

Strossmayer's Gallery of Old Masters.

★ Technical Museum

Savska 18 (01 48 44 050/www.mdc.hr/tehnicki).
Tram 12 to Tehnički muzej. **Open** 9am-5pm
Tue-Fri; 9am-1pm Sat, Sun. **Admission** 15kn
for permanent collection; 10kn reductions. Free
under-7s. 15kn for planetarium; 10kn reductions.
Free under-7s. Tram rides free. **No credit
cards. Map** p72 B5.

The city's quirkiest museum contains 19th-century
fire engines, 1930s locomotives, a Dubrovnik tram
from 1912, a 1930s diving suit, old Yugoslav planes
and a World War II Italian submarine that you can
climb into. Accessed by guided tour are re-creations
of inventor Nikola Tesla's devices, and a planetarium. On Sundays, a 1924 tram does a city tour to
Maksimir and back.

★ Zagreb City Museum

*Opatička ulica 20 (01 48 51 361/www.mdc.hr/
mgz).* **Open** 10am-6pm Tue, Wed, Fri; 10am-
10pm Thur; 10am-2pm Sat, Sun. **Admission**
20kn; 10kn reductions. Free under-7s. **No
credit cards. Map** p72 D1.

Occupying the 17th-century Convent of the Clares,
the City Museum contains a worthwhile collection
of 4,500 objects tracing Zagreb's history from prehistoric times. Themed sections include Iron Age
finds, walk-through reconstructions of 19th-century
Ilica shops and study rooms of famous Croatian
artists. Other items include old packaging and auto-
matic music machines. Many exhibits are interactive and it's all well documented in English. The
sundial in the courtyard still shows the right time.

Over the Sava & beyond the centre

Across the Sava river spread the suburbs
of Novi Zagreb, Socialist-era housing blocks
without the charm of the city's Habsburg hub.
Traffic whizzes down multi-laned boulevards,
such as Vukovarska, where Orson Welles
filmed his version of Kafka's *The Trial* in 1962.
With downtown gridlocked almost all day, the
city authorities are encouraging businesses to
set up here and residents to relocate, most
notably with the long-awaited opening of the
Museum of Contemporary Art, due for
completion 2009/2010 (*see p76* Profile). Along
with the **National Library** and the prestigious
Lisinski Concert Hall on this side of the
river, a multiplex cinema is soon expected.

Further afield, three main attractions are
accessible on public transport from the city
centre. **Jarun** is a recreational lake by the Sava,
on tram route No.17 south-west of Jelačić. Built
for the World Student Games in 1987, it's a
haven for cyclists and rowers. It also houses
several nightclubs, including the landmark
Aquarius. Another easy tram hop is to
Maksimir, the city's main park, with public
gardens, the zoo and, across the main road, the

![FREE] St Mark's Church

Trg sv Marka 5 (01 48 51 611). **Open** 9am-noon,
5-5.45pm daily. **Admission** free. **Map** p72 D2.

Two coats of arms grace the red-white-and-blue che-
quered roof of this emblematic church: Zagreb's and
Croatia's. Since the 1200s when the Romanesque
original was built, the church has gone through
many architectural styles – note the Gothic south
portal and baroque, copper-covered belltower. Inside
are hand-painted walls by Jozo Kljaković and a crucifix by Meštrović. The square outside, housing the
Ban's Palace and the Croatian Parliament, has been
the hub of political activity since the 1500s.

★ Strossmayer's Gallery
of Old Masters

*Trg NŠ Zrinskog 11 (01 48 95 117/www.mdc.
hr/strossmayer).* **Open** 10am-1pm, 5-7pm Tue;
10am-1pm Wed-Sun. **Admission** 10kn; 5kn
reductions. **No credit cards. Map** p73 E3.

Built in 1884 to accommodate Bishop Strossmayer's
European masterpieces, this neo-Renaissance palace
showcases works spanning the 14th to 19th centuries. Of the 4,000 items in the permanent collection, only 400 are displayed at one time, in ten rooms
on the second floor. Italians, including Tintoretto,
feature in the first six, followed by Flemish, Dutch
and German (Albrect Dürer among them) painters.
French and Spanish artists, with Delacroix and El
Greco foremost, complete the collection.

national football stadium, home of Dinamo
Zagreb. North-east of the city, the beautiful tree-
lined cemetery of **Mirogoj** (open dawn-sunset
daily), designed by Herman Bollé, is filled with
ivy-strewn cupolas and pavilions. The motley
gravestones include five-pointed stars, Cyrillic
inscriptions, Stars of David and Islamic half-
moons, pointing at Croatia's ethnic tapestry.
Works by renowned Croatian sculptors line the
neo-Renaissance arcades. From the cathedral,
take bus No.106.

Maksimir Park & Zoo

*Maksimirski perivoj (01 23 02 198/www.zoo.hr).
Trams 11, 12 to Bukovačka.* **Open** *Park* 8am-
sunset daily. *Zoo* summer 9am-7pm daily; spring
& autumn 9am-6pm daily; winter 9am-4pm daily.
Ticket office closes 1hr before closing time.
Admission *Park* free. *Zoo* 30kn; 20kn
reductions. Free under-7s. **No credit cards**.
Map p72 A6.
A ten-minute tram ride east of the centre, 18 hectares
(45 acres) of green were opened to the public in 1794,
with what was termed English landscaping of
woods, meadows and lakes. At the far eastern end
is the City Zoo with a modest collection of creatures
and daily feeding times of seals, sea lions and otters.
Opposite stands Croatia's main football stadium and
home of Dinamo Zagreb, also called the Maksimir.

Museum of Contemporary Art

*Avenija Dubrovnik/Avenija Većeslava Holjevca
(01 48 51 930/www.mdc.hr/msu).* **Open**
2009/2010.

The most significant attraction to open in Zagreb for
many a decade. *See p76* **Profile**.

Around Zagreb

The forested slopes of **Mount Medvednica**
beckon nature lovers for a hike, or a cablecar
ride above the trees to the highest peak of
Sljeme. More than half of Medvednica, Bear
Mountain, is covered in trees, featuring forests
of beech, oak, fir and maple, with extensive
flora that includes 14 endemic and 93
endangered plant species. In spring and
autumn, the area is at its most beautiful,
with colourful flowers – from saffron to
dog-tooth violets – and clear crisp horizons.
Sljeme (www.sljeme.hr) offers stellar vistas
of Zagreb and the Zagorje countryside. This
is where four-time Olympic champion Janica
Kostelić learned to ski. Thanks to her success,
Sljeme has been developed into a ski centre of
international standard. It can be reached by one
of the many well-marked paths leading up from
the foothills of Medvednica – when we went to
press the cablecar from Gračanski Bliznec was
still under repair.
The most popular day trip from Zagreb
is **Samobor**, 23km (14 miles) west of the city,
on the eastern slopes of the Samobor Hills. With
medieval origins and baroque architecture,
this charming village centres on Trg kralja
Tomislava, a square lined with pastel-coloured
19th-century townhouses, traditional cafés and
a clutch of churches. On one side stands the

ZAGREB

Mirogoj Cemetery.

town museum (Livadičeva 7, 01 33 61 014; open 9am-3pm Tue-Fri, 9am-1pm Sat, Sun) whose archaeological and ethnological items include furniture and pottery – there's also a section on Croatian mountaineering. Just off the square is Little Venice, where wooden bridges criss-cross the Gradna brook. Try and see the collection at the **Marton Museum** (Jurjevska 7, 01 33 26 426, www.muzej-marton.hr; open 10am-1pm Sat, Sun; 15kn) showcasing 1,000 exhibits from Biedermeier furniture to 19th-century silverware and Russian porcelain. That aside, the reason why so many locals come here is for the famous Samobor *kremšnite*, the trademark cream pie available at central cafés such as **U prolazu** and **Livadić**.

For the region's best hiking and biking, head to **Žumberak-Samobor Mountains Nature Park**, starting 5km (3 miles) west of Samobor and extending a further 30km (19 miles). The area is hard to reach by public transport, but if you do find your way here, you'll be treated to hilltop hamlets, extensive vineyards, karst canyons with waterfalls and old-fashioned watermills. Information and eco centers are located at **Slani Dol** 6km (3.5 miles) west of Samobor and in the village of **Budinjak** 35km (22 miles) from town.

The Zagreb County Tourist Board (Preradovićeva 42, www.tzzz.hr) offers information and maps of the region's biking routes (www.pedala.hr). Samobor is a 45-minute ride by frequent buses from Zagreb's main bus station or from the Črnomerec bus terminal.

WHERE TO EAT

Agava

Tkalčićeva 39 (01 48 23 806). **Open** 11am-11pm daily. **Credit** AmEx, MC, V. **Map** p73 E2 **❶**

Bright Agava offers cosmopolitan dining on this gentrifying thoroughfare. Warm focaccia bread precedes starters such as swordfish carpaccio or snails Bourgoignon-style; mains include beefsteak with seven kinds of mushroom and truffles. Istrian or Slavonian wine may complement your meal; plums in red wine may conclude it.

▶ *For something more traditional on the same bar strip, Atlanta at No.65 is a reliable choice.*

Baltazar

Nova Ves 4 (01 46 66 808). **Open** noon-midnight Mon-Sat. **Credit** AmEx, DC, MC, V. **Map** p73 E1 **❷**

In a little Kaptol courtyard, this rustic restaurant attracts an upmarket clientele with its traditional grills from Zagorje and Slavonia. Service and presentation are impeccable. In summer a pretty terrace of similarly rustic character comes into its own.

★ Bistro Apetit

Jurjevska 65A (01 46 77 335). **Open** 9am-midnight Tue-Sun. **Credit** AmEx, DC, MC, V. **Map** p72 D1 **❸**

Ignore the complete twaddle on the menu – Austrian chef-owner Christian Cabalier's Apetit offers impressive contemporary dishes. It's not cheap but worth the outlay and a summer terrace allows for a couple of peaceful hours just outside the city bustle.

Kerempuh.

Kn Boban

Gajeva 9 (01 48 11 549). **Open** 10am-midnight daily. **Credit** AmEx, DC, MC, V. **Map** p73 E3 ❹
Named after its owner, local football hero Zvonimir Boban, this popular two-storey operation is set just off Jelačić. Upstairs is a café, downstairs a mainly Italian restaurant. Carlo Conforti's kitchen turns out pastas at giveaway prices – portions are staggering.

Kn Čiho

Pavla Hatza 15 (01 48 17 060). **Open** 9am-midnight Mon-Sat; noon-midnight Sun. **Credit** MC. V. **Map** p73 F4 ❺
This homely spot near the Sheraton Hotel offers Dalmatian standards in traditional surroundings – downstairs is big on rustic decor. Fish and *rakija* brandy come in multiple varieties. Old-school staff, old-school prices.
▶ *For more Dalmatian delights, try Korčula; see right.*

★ Gallo

Hebrangova 34 (01 48 14 014). **Open** noon-11pm daily. **Credit** AmEx, DC, MC, V. **Map** p72 D4 ❻
Posh but relaxed, Gallo offers seasonal and organic Med cuisine. Outside is a herb garden; sheets of pasta hang in the classic interior. Truffles are sprinkled wherever possible and the risotto with porcini mushrooms is worth a return visit alone. A choice of 70 Croatian and global wines may accompany.

Kn Gostionica Tip-Top

Gundulićeva 18 (01 48 30 349). **Open** 7am-10pm Mon-Sat. **Credit** AmEx, DC, MC, V. **Map** p72 D3 ❼
Locals know this age-old eaterie as Blato as it's run by restaurateurs from Korčula. Little has changed here since Tin Ujević and his literary gang were regulars in the 1940s – their pictures and an outline of Tin's iconic hat provide decoration. The daily special may include an outstanding octopus goulash but you can also opt for red mullet, sole or sea bass. Plenty of Korčula varieties on the wine list.

Kn Ivica i Marica

Tkalčićeva 70 (01 48 28 999). **Open** noon-11pm Tue-Sun. **Credit** AmEx, DC, MC, V. **Map** p73 E2 ❽
Named after Hansel and Gretel, this venue by the bakery of the same name, decorated in fairy-tale style, is Zagreb's leading health-food restaurant. It serves national staples with no preservatives, artificial colouring or GM ingredients.

★ Kerempuh

Kaptol 3 (01 48 19 000/www.kerempuh.hr). **Open** 9am-3pm, 7-11pm Mon-Sat. **Credit** AmEx, DC, MC, V. **Map** p73 E2 ❾
The Kerempuh earned its considerable reputation when TV chef Anna Ugarković worked here. Then,

as now, the adjoining Dolac market provides fresh ingredients on the daily changing menu. Quality vegetarian options in a relaxing atmosphere.

Korčula

Teslina 17 (01 48 72 159). **Open** *Mid Aug-mid July* 9am-10pm Mon-Sat; 9am-4pm Sun. Closed mid July-mid Aug. **Credit** AmEx, DC, MC. V. **Map** p72 D3 ❿
As traditional as it gets, this fish restaurant was here long before the trendy bars set up nearby. The kitchen turns out top-quality seafood standards, plus specialities like baked octopus with potatoes.
▶ *For more authentic food from Dalmatia, try Čiho; see left.*

★ Marcellino

Jurjevska 71 (01 46 77 111). **Open** *Sept-July* noon-11pm Mon-Sat. Closed Aug. **Credit** AmEx, MC, V. **Map** p72 D1 ⓫
For interesting, ambitious international food, at a price, go no further. Owner and head chef Mario oversees each ordered, symmetrical and delicate plate, such as venison with blueberries, chestnuts, pears and wine, or prawns with orange juice and olive oil. This is a place to impress, surrounded by embassy staff and local celebrities. *Photo p82.*

INSIDE TRACK ŠTRUKLI

Zagreb's local dish, *štrukli* are delicately prepared parcels of filo pastry, usually filled with cottage cheese and covered with cream. They are quite versatile, savoury or sweet, boiled or baked, and can be filled with stuffings as varied as cod, spinach or apple. Each housewife in Zagreb and around the Zagorje region has her own method of rolling, baking and filling her *štrukli*. Despite these differences, the Croatian Ministry of Culture has managed to give the dish protected status should the bureaucrats of Brussels come sniffing after Croatia's accession to the European Union.

ZAGREB

ZAGREB

INSIDE TRACK
FRESH BREAKFASTS

Daily Fresh Gourmet Food & Coffee
(www.dailyfreshgroup.com) has seven
spots around Zagreb. Each offers fresh
juices, decent coffee and croissant
or granola, ideal for the city's young
professionals on the move; just as well,
since seating is limited. DFGF&C is also
worth considering as a lunch refuel stop
while sightseeing – there's lasagne,
salads and sushi as well as more local
specialities such as pitta and *štrukli*.
Prices won't trouble you.

★ Mašklin i lata
Hebrangova 11A (01 48 18 273/www.
masklinilata.hr). **Open** noon-11pm Mon-Sat.
Credit AmEx, DC, MC, V. **Map** p73 E4 ⑫
In case you're wondering, Mašklin is named after
traditional Dalmatian wine-making tools. A wine-
cellar restaurant, it also offers a taste of the sea.
Lobster, cod, monkfish, squid, prawns or octopus
can be combined with home-made pasta, gnocchi,
risotto, wild asparagus, Istrian truffles, or turned
into stews. Thoroughly recommended.

mú
Vukovarska 72 (01 63 10 090). **Open** 8am-
11.30pm Mon-Sat; 10am-5pm Sun. **Credit**
AmEx, DC, MC, V. **Map** p73 H3 ⑬

Mú is a sleek, efficient, open-plan operation, buzzy
and busy with groups of twenty- and thirtysomethings on weekend evenings. If you want steak, it's
one of the best in town. Book ahead.

★ Noce
Kamenica 5 (01 48 51 343). **Open** 10am-
midnight Mon-Thur; 10am-1am Fri, Sat; 10am-
6pm Sun. **Credit** MC, V. **Map** p72 D2 ⑭
A change of name has done little to alter the quality
of the fresh, Italian-influenced fare on offer here. A
weekly-changing menu features one fish, one meat
and one meat-free choice as a main. Brunches are
also offered, as is a fine range of world wines.

Okrugljak
Mlinovi 28 (01 46 74 112/www.okrugljak.hr).
Tram 14 to Mihaljevac then a 300m walk.
Open 10am-1am daily. **Credit** AmEx, DC,
MC, V. **Map** p72 C1 ⑮
The grande dame of Zagreb restaurants is worth the
hike to reach it. Its cachet attracts old money and
new jet set, munching and mingling in the two high-
ceilinged wooden-clad dining halls near Sljeme. Top
traditional dishes from inland Croatia and the coast
are prepared with due care. Reserve at weekends.

Kn Pauza
Preradovićeva 34 (01 48 54 598). **Open** 9am-
11pm Mon-Sat. **Credit** AmEx, DC, MC, V.
Map p72 D4 ⑯
Actors, creatives and thirtysomethings come here
for home-made food with an interesting touch.
Generous tuna steak is served raw if you want, a rar-

Marcellino. *See p81.*

ity in a nation that seems to delight in cooking tuna until it's dry. Also popular are the spicy tomato soup and pastas with chunks of salmon and broccoli. Several wines by the glass and the draught beer are equally affordable .

★ Paviljon
Trg kralja Tomislava 22 (01 48 13 066). **Open** noon-midnight Mon-Sat. **Credit** AmEx, DC, MC, V. **Map** p73 E5 ⑰
Within the Art Pavilion, the Paviljon treats diners in a manner fitting to the ornate surroundings. Choose from a list of Stanko Erceg's well conceived dishes laden with healthy vegetables. Appetisers include swordfish carpaccio, and shrimp and fennel salad, mains grilled swordfish with fennel seeds and pork medallions in truffle sauce with polenta.

Prasac
Vraničanijeva 6 (01 48 51 411). **Open** 7-11pm Mon; noon-3pm, 7-11pm Tue-Sat. **Credit** AmEx, DC, MC, V. **Map** p72 D2 ⑱
The Croatian chef here worked in Michelin-star restaurants in Italy as well as preparing menus for the local Sheraton Hotel – the food here is great but pricey. It's intimate too; some 20 diners gather in a cosy, Old-Town location. Recommended are the tuna and most meat dishes, as well as the Japanese citrus fruit dessert. The name is a peasant term for pig.

Pod Gričkim Topom
Zakmardijeve stube 5 (01 48 33 607). **Open** *July, Aug* 11am-11pm Mon-Sat. *Sept-June* 11am-11pm Mon-Sat; 11am-5pm Sun. **Credit** AmEx, DC, MC, V. **Map** p72 D2 ⑲
This leafy enclave, beneath the Grič cannon, is a summer evening favourite. On offer are dishes from different regions of Croatia such as Dalmatian *pašticada* stew or Zagreb steak. Portions are well sized, the service good and the clientele chatty.

Sofra
I gardijske brigade Tigrovi 27 (01 61 31 026). **Open** 9am-midnight Tue-Sat; 11am-10pm Sun. **Credit** AmEx, DC, MC, V. **Map** p73 H5 ⑳
The best Bosnian in town is popular despite its hidden location – take a taxi. Grilled meats are the order of the day here – *pljeskavica* and *ćevapi*, served with traditional bread. Dishes are designed to be shared and enjoyed slowly – allow a good two hours for your meal. Make sure you reserve.
► *If Sofra is booked, Mitnica (Črnomerec 37, 01 37 78 640) is a popular destination for authentic Balkan grilled delights.*

Kn Stari Fijaker
Mesnička 6 (01 48 33 829). **Open** 9am-11pm Mon-Sat; 10am-10pm Sun. **Credit** DC, MC, V. **Map** p72 C2 ㉑
The Old Coach has been a restaurant for a century or more, hence the sepia pictures of old Zagreb.

Traditional dishes, many from Zagorje, number 50 in all. The waiter will be happy to talk you through the chef's recommendations, all hearty, all cheap.
► *In a similar vein, on the other side of the main square Purger (Petrinjska 33, 01 48 73 394) offers reasonably priced local standards.*

Vinodol
Teslina 10 (01 48 11 427/www.vinodol-zg.hr). **Open** 10am-midnight daily. **Credit** AmEx, DC, MC, V. **Map** p72 D3 ㉒
You can dine on the covered patio terrace accessed through an ivy-clad passageway off Teslina; the cold weather alternative is the massive dining hall with vaulted stone ceilings. The service is swift, the cuisine heavy on meat. A popular lunchtime spot, so be prepared to wait.

WHERE TO DRINK

Apartman
Preradovićeva 7 (01 48 72 168). **Open** 9am-midnight Mon-Wed, Sun; 9am-1am Thur-Sat. **No credit cards. Map** p72 D3 ❶
Located in bar central near the flower market, Apartman is a funky first-floor spot where the young clientele intertwines on big bright cushions. Incongruously, this was also once the headquarters of the local scouts' association, its past function indicated by a plaque and an outdoor scene covering one wall. DJs spin after dark.
► *If this venue is too full, the Pif and Golf bars diagonally opposite are of similar ilk.*

Booksa
Martićeva 14D (01 46 16 124/www.booksa.hr). *Trams 1 & 17 to Trg žrtava fašizma.* **Open** 9am-11pm Tue-Sun. **No credit cards. Map** p73 G3 ❷

INSIDE TRACK GABLECI

Loosely but somewhat misleadingly rendered as 'elevenses', *gableci* are a late-morning or early afternoon snack, something far less fancy than a brunch, but more hearty and substantial than just tea and biscuits. As the local workers tend to start their day at least an hour earlier than their UK counterparts, 'cheap lunches' gives the visitor a better idea of the concept. Most modest downtown eateries will offer a weekday dish for around 30kn-40kn, perhaps even a choice. An ideal spot is in and around the Dolac market, where you'll find the early-rising traders tucking into stuffed cabbage or bean stew from around 10am onwards.

Zagreb's first literary club doubles as a café, a collective run by three women. The books are Croatian only, but the music is good, the atmosphere laid-back and regular events include exhibits, concerts and readings, some by visiting English speakers.

★ Cica Bar
Tkalčićeva 18 (no phone). **Open** 9am-11pm Mon-Sat. **No credit cards. Map** p73 E2 ❸
This narrow 'grapperia, cafeteria and galleria' is the funkiest place you'll find on the tatty Tkalčićeva strip. Cica is famed for its home-made *rakija* brandy: blueberry, honey, nut, fig, anis or mixed herbs. Hedonism and random DJ sounds abound.

Dobar Zvuk
Gajeva 18 (01 48 72 222). **Open** noon-11pm Mon-Sat. **No credit cards. Map** p73 E4 ❹
Suitably set in an old hi-fi store, this superior music bar is a lively and popular rendezvous for younger, spiky-haired locals and older rockers.

Eli's Caffè
Ilica 63 (091 527 9990 mobile). **Open** 8am-9pm Mon-Sat; 9am-3pm Sun. **No credit cards. Map** p72 B3 ❺
This contemporary café is a busy little spot a stroll down Ilica from Jelačić. A foxy young professional clientele gather to gossip and guzzle cups of Illy coffee, produced just over the border in Trieste, where staff are trained. A capo triestino is one of 30 plus coffee varieties here. No smoking.

Fanatik
Ribnjak 26 (no phone). **Open** 8pm-4am Tue-Sat. **No credit cards. Map** p73 F2 ❻
On the Ribnjak slope, this red-lit, zebra-striped room attracts a gay/straight mix. A busy bar-club since the mid 1990s, the Fanatik suffered a fire in 2008, reopening with a new look in the spring of 2009.

Hemingway Lounge Bar
Trg Maršala Tita (www.hemingway.hr). **Open** 7am-3am daily. **Credit** AmEx, DC, MC, V. **Map** p72 C4 ❼
Hemingway is a chain of upmarket cocktail bars throughout Croatia. This one is the most popular, set opposite the National Theatre. Three stylish rooms contain crystal chandeliers and photos of Papa. In summer pavement tables pack with the pretty set posing over cocochinos and finger food by day, Mai Tais and Long Island Ice Teas at night.
► *Private parties and special events are held at Hemingway, Tuškanac 1 (01 48 34 958).*

Hop Devil
Branimirova 29 (01 38 76 343). **Open** noon-midnight daily. **Credit** AmEx, DC, MC, V. **Map** p73 G5 ❽
This Belgian bar, which is done out in a Gothic style, has an attractive buzz despite being located in a

INSIDE TRACK SPICA

Spica is a concept peculiar to Zagreb and impossible to translate with one word or sentence. If you drop in to one of the terrace cafés around the Flower Market around noon every Saturday, you'll find fashionable young professionals, ideally couples, posing and chatting over an improbably slow coffee, gossiping and comparing purchases, ideally from the Dolac market. Some may be interviewed for a local TV programme dedicated to the concept, or sundry journalists covering the lifestyle beat – a number of local celebrities show their face during Spica. Combining the communality of the Italian *passeggiata* with urban flair, the social ritual of coffee and the Saturday urge to shop, Spica sums up modern-day Zagreb to a tee. Don't even think about turning up without sunglasses.

shopping mall. Each of the many bottled beers – fruity, colourful, malty – from the Benelux comes with its branded glass and beermat.

Kolaž
Amruševa 11 (no phone). **Open** 7am-11pm Mon-Sat. **No credit cards. Map** p73 E3 ❾
Owned by a one-time staff member at Limb (*see below*), this small red-brick basement bar offers draught Starobrno and (unusually) dark Gösser, with Belgian varieties (Kriek, Chimay) by the bottle. It's a good spot for breakfast and by dusk a well-chosen music backdrop (Velvets, indie) kicks in.

★ Krivi Put
Runjaninova (no phone). **Open** 6pm-1am Mon-Sat. **No credit cards. Map** p72 C5 ❿
Wrong Way comes to you from the people behind the Melin (*see p85*). Naked lightbulbs, sparse art and Stefan Lupino photographs provide minimal decor in a large, otherwise bare interior. At one end is a sturdy bar counter; at the other, a small stage. The boho crowd fills the courtyard in summer.

Limb
Plitvička 16 (01 61 71 683). **Open** 9am-1am Mon-Sat. **No credit cards. Map** p72 C6 ⓫
Back in the day, Limb was *the* spot in town for music fans. It's since lost some of its edge, though older musos still occupy three tiny colourful rooms and the glass-enclosed terrace centrepieced by a tree. Chatty Francophile owner Selma sorts out the *chansons* on the stereo.
► *For somewhere similar closer to the city centre, Kolaž is run by an ex-Limb barman; see above.*

Maraschino

Margaretska 1 (01 48 12 612). **Open** 8am-1am Mon-Sat; 9am-1am Sun. **No credit cards**. **Map** p72 D3 ⑫
Named for the sweet cherry liqueur from Zadar, Maraska, this two-floor spot in trendy bar central is packed to the rafters in the evenings. Decked out in old Maraska posters, it offers Maraska-infused coffee, long drinks, and decent local wines.
▶ *To find out more about Zadar's famous export of Maraska; see p199.*

Melin

Tkalčićeva 47 (01 48 28 966). **Open** 9am-1am daily. **No credit cards**. **Map** p73 E2 ⑬
The spirit of old Zagreb, Melin is a cult spot set back from Tkalčićeva, scruffy but with bags of character. The two-space interior is grungy, the air thick with smoke and the music loud. At weekends drunken teenagers spill on to the terrace or the playground outside – the nearby Portal bar is a handy refuge.

MK Bar

Radićeva 7 (no phone). **Open** 7am-midnight Mon-Sat; 9am-1pm Sun. **No credit cards**. **Map** p72 D2 ⑭
Known as by all as 'Krolo' after the writer Miroslav Krleža who lived here, this beautiful old wooden bar near Jelačić gives a flavour of pre-1991 Zagreb. An older clientele, many in trilbies, religiously scan the day's newspapers while younger regulars talk with reverential quiet around the circular seating. Timeless is the word you're looking for.

Movie Pub

Savska 141 (01 60 55 045). **Open** 7am-2am Mon-Wed; 7am-3am Thur; 7am-4am Fri, Sat; 6pm-2am Sun. **No credit cards**. **Map** p72 B6 ⑮
This themed venue is large and authentic enough to attract custom from home and abroad, thanks to realistic prices, decent beer choices and regular events. There is a restaurant and an adjacent hotel should the need arise.

Orient Express

Teslina 10 (01 48 10 548). **Open** 9am-11pm daily. **No credit cards**. **Map** p72 D3 ⑯
Set in the narrow shape of a railway carriage, this tasteful recreation of the famous train is decked out with black-and-white photographs of glamorous passengers in its heyday. French-language signage, shiny copper and a bottle-green colour scheme add to the illusion. No themed drinks but a wide range of spirits may celebrate your arrival or departure.

Runa

Opatička 5 (091 948 9976 mobile). **Open** 9am-1am Mon-Fri; 5pm-1am Sat, Sun. **No credit cards**. **Map** p72 D1 ⑰
Dark but cosy heavy metal bar by Parliament in the Upper Town. The music is loud, but not too loud, echoing around the wooden floor and brick walls covered with paintings of HR Giger and sundry album covers. The pinball and table-football table suit the place, as do light and dark Krušovice and Velebitsko beers – and the affordable prices.

ZAGREB

Eli's Caffe.

ZAGREB

Sedmica.

★ Sedmica
Kačićeva 7a (01 48 46 689). **Open** 8am-11pm
daily. **No credit cards. Map** p72 B3 ⑱
Cult bar Sedmica attracts an arty clientele to its
busy, two-storey space. The entrance is below an
unobtrusive Guinness sign above a residential doorway. Long, thin marble tables provide a place to
prop, otherwise you can join the boho crew on the
wrought-iron mezzanine.
▶ *Sedmica can be a difficult place to spot;
the best way of finding it is to look out for
the Guinness sign.*

★ Spunk
Hrvatske bratske zajednice (01 61 51 528). **Tram**
13 to Lisinski. **Open** 7am-midnight Mon-Wed;
7am-3am Thur-Sat; 6pm-midnight Sun. **Credit**
MC, V. **Map** p73 E6 ⑲
Set by the National Library, Spunk is a coffee-break
bar for students by day, and a garage-rock hangout
for savvy musos by night. Atmosphere is helped
along by the visual and aural backdrop of Igor
Hofbauer's murals and rare punk B-sides.

Yaxx
Pavla Hatza 16 (01 48 39 020/www.yaxx.hr).
Open 9am-midnight daily. **Credit** AmEx, DC,
MC, V. **Map** p73 F4 ⑳
Not everyone is here to see the match but Yaxx is
one of the best spots in town to watch it – staff do
their best to meet the most obscure request. The bar,
like the restaurant here, is run by handball star
Vlado Sola, who hasn't shied away from adorning
the entrance with artefacts relating to himself, his
team-mates and fellow Croatian Olympians.

MUSIC & NIGHTLIFE
Aquarius
*Aleja Matije Ljubeka (01 36 40 231/www.
aquarius.hr).* *Tram 17 to Horvati.* **Open**
Café 9am-9pm daily. *Club* 10pm-6am daily.
No credit cards.
This highly professional Jarun lakeside club pio-
neered many of the firsts in Zagreb, including the
one for electronic music. Opened in 1992, this 1,300-
capacity two-floor venue is still ahead of the field.
Fridays are sacrosanct, Blackout Lounge seeing the
dancefloor and huge covered terrace jammed with
young things getting down to commercial hip hop
and R&B. Aquarius can also turn itself into a mid-
sized concert hall. A separate club, A2, was incorporated into the same building in 2008.
▶ *In summer, Aquarius opens its beach club at
Novalja on Pag; see p186.*

Best
Jarunska cesta 5 (01 30 11 943/www.thebest.hr).
Trams 14 & 17 to Savski Most. **Open** 10pm-7am
Fri, Sat. **No credit cards.**
This is the closest Zagreb gets to a mega-club, with
mainstream events and lots of glitz. The music,
house, techno and disco, is commercial, though you
might catch a new local DJ talent on the decks. A
takeover by the people behind Byblos in Poreč in
December 2008 should set Best on a new direction.

Boogaloo
*OTV Dom, Vukovarska 68 (01 63 13 021/
www.boogaloo.hr).* *Tram 13 to Miramarksa.*
Open Call for details. **No credit cards.**

Boogaloo is a 1,000-capacity DJ club and live venue in the OTV Dom building, scene of seminal shows by Laibach and Einstürzende Neubauten in the '80s. A recent change of promoters sees electronic music programmed here for Fridays, rock on Saturdays.

BP Club

Teslina 7 (01 48 14 444/www.bpclub.hr). **Open** 10am-2am Mon-Sat; 5pm-2am Sun. **No credit cards.**
BP is Zagreb's most prestigious jazz club, managed by vibraphonist Boško Petrović. The basement bar is lined with pictures of the stars (Art Farmer, Joe Pass and Ronnie Scott among them) who have played its tiny stage in the corner. It hosts two festivals: Springtime Jazz Fever in late March and Hrvatski Jazz Sabor in early October.
▶ *BP no longer has a monopoly on live jazz in the city – check out Jazz Club; see p88.*

Funk Club

Tkalčićeva 52 (no phone). **Open** 9am-1am daily. **No credit cards.**
Although it might see a standard café-bar by day, by night the Funk Club starts hopping. Spontaneous interaction sparks around the horseshoe bar, while thumping beats rise from the cellar. Down a spiral staircase, in a basement with stone vaulted ceilings, DJs spin catchy house, jazz and broken beats to a dance-happy crowd.

★ Gallery

Matije Ljubeka (091 113 32 21 mobile). Tram 17 to Horvati. **Open** 10am-1am Mon-Wed, Sun; 10am-4am Thur-Sat. **Credit** DC, MC, V.

The Hacienda crew from Vodice opened this club by Lake Jarun. DJs who have starred on the coast – Ian Pooley, David Guetta, David Morales – have all performed here too. Exclusivity is maintained by a tight control on ticket numbers, and the dress code is pretty strict. Inside is sassy rather than swanky, with intimate tent-like booths, and a real sense of fun amid the glitz and bling.

Global

Pavla Hatza 14 (01 48 14 878/www.global clubzg.hr). **Open** *Cafe & shop* 8pm-2am Mon, Tue, Sun. *Club* 8pm-4am Wed-Sat. **No credit cards.**
The first and so far only dedicated gay club in Zagreb attracts a mixed crowd. A café and sex shop by day, it's usually a very busy spot after dark, with three bars, a VIP lounge, a dancefloor and a dark room. A programme of strippers and queer movie nights is part of the build-up to the big event of the week, Saturday Night Fever.

Jabuka

Jabukovac 28 (01 48 34 397). **Open** 9pm-2am Fri, Sat. **No credit cards.**
Everyone in Zagreb knows the Apple, where a generation danced and, sometimes, found romance 20 years ago. This Tuškanac club still offers the sounds of those long-gone 1980s in its modest dance room, while the older revellers gather around the crowded bar and back courtyard.
▶ *Launched at a similar time, also in hilly greenery north of the centre, Saloon (Tuškanac 1A, www.saloon.hr) has recently introduced Logic as an electronic dance spot within the club.*

Aquarius.

KSET.

ZAGREB

Jazz Club

Gundulićeva 11 (091 664 9498 mobile). **Open** 8pm-1am daily. **No credit cards.**

This newbie challenges BP Club's jazz hegemony with a nightly agenda of live sounds, in a handy downtown cellar location.

★ KSET

Unska 3 (01 61 29 999/www.kset.org). Tram 13 to Miramarska. **Open** 8pm-midnight Mon-Fri; 9pm-3am Sat. **No credit cards.**

Adventurous venue for live music, the 400-capacity KSET is an oasis for underground, punk and sundry stylistically diverse artists. At least one night a week, generally at weekends, the speakers are given over to electronic music, often drum 'n' bass.

Ritz Club

Petrijnska 4 (099 660 7182 mobile). **Open** from 7pm daily. **Credit** MC, V.

This tasteful post-work hangout offers cabaret and jazz sounds to a classy clientele. Open until the early hours depending on numbers.

Route 66

Paromlinska 47 (01 61 18 737). Tram 13 to Lisinski. **Open** 9am-1am daily. **No credit cards.**

Zagreb's rock bar par excellence, Route 66 features live music, pool tables and sought-after Velebitsko beer. Photos of Bill Wyman and some guy from AC/DC mark their respective visits, sealing the venue's reputation as a hangout for musicians. Country bands also regularly perform covers.

Shamballa

Passage Cibona (099 721 7777 mobile/www. shamballa.hr). Tram 3, 9, 12 to Tehnički muzej. **Open** 9pm-late daily. **No credit cards.**

Dennis Ferrer opened Shamballa in October 2008 and this distinctly upscale nightspot proceeded to award itself the ungrammatical tagline of 'The Absolute Clubbing'. The clubbers duly came to see what was happening, but the difficult part of the business is now for Shamballa to keep a chic, moneyed crowd coming back to the student quarter.

Sirup

Donje Svetice 40 (091 945 0037/http://sirup club.com). Tram 2, 3, 13 to Donje Svetice. **Open** 9pm-late daily. **No credit cards.**

The team behind the open-air, left-field Porat club in Dalmatia are behind this new venture, opened towards the end of 2008. An adventurous DJ agenda has been promised – dubstep spinner MC Nomad is a recent booking.

★ Tvornica

Šubićeva 2 (01 46 5 5 007/www.tvornica-kulture.hr). Trams 1 & 17 to Šubićeva. **Open** *Café* 8am-10pm daily. *Club* 10pm-4am daily. **No credit cards.**

Tvornica is the best mid-sized venue in town. This is due in no small part to the club's superb pedigree; it's run by the man who was responsible for the legendary Kulušic way back when. With a capacity of 1,500, its gig list has included the likes of Henry Rollins, David Byrne and the MC5. World music is also often scheduled here.

SHOPPING

Mall culture has taken over Zagreb. Of the dozen centres around the city, the **Centar Kaptol** (Nova Ves 11, www.centarkaptol.hr), past the Cathedral, is the most exclusive, with Hugo Boss and Marks & Spencer. More fashion stores and cosmetic boutiques can be found at the **Importanne Centar** and **Importanne Galleria** (Starčevićev trg 10; Ibierov trg 10; for both, www.importanne.hr).

Frankopanska is the exclusive shopping street. Here you find Lacoste, Diesel, Gaultier, Galliano and Moschino. **Ilica** is the traditional hub of Zagreb's shopping scene. Today the little shopfronts of its two-storey houses contain Mango, Lush and local fashion stores **Image Haddad** (No.6, 01 48 31 035) and **Heruc Galerija** (No.26, 01 48 33 569) beside shops unchanged since Tito's day.

In terms of creative designers, **I-GLE** is the flagship outlet for locals Martina Vrdoljak Ranilović and Nataša Mihaljčišin, who also stock their menswear at **Victor**, Croatia's first concept store; and at **Sheriff & Cherry**, an exciting urban fashion boutique. **Kathy Balogh** (Radićeva 22, 01 48 13 290; open 8am-noon, 4-7pm Mon-Fri, 9am-2pm Sat) is avant-garde of the old school, but reliably challenging. **Leonarda L** (Gajeva 9, 01 48 75 045; open 9am-8pm Mon-Fri, 9am-3pm Sat) offers tasteful designs, more boho than bling.

The bric-a-brac market on **Britanski trg** is an ideal way to spend a long Sunday morning. For a flea market, **Hreljić** in Novi Zagreb runs on Sundays. Leave yourself half a day to get there by bus and rummage through the mountains of junk. Back in town, both the flower market on **Preradovićev trg** and the main **Dolac** produce market (*see p90* **Profile**) off Jelačić are excellent. If you're looking for Croatian products as presents, try **Natura Croatica** or **Bornstein** (Kaptol 19, 01 48 12 361), a wine cellar in Kaptol stocking local gourmet items.

For English-language books and magazines, **Algoritam** (Gajeva 1, 01 48 18 672; open 8am-9pm Mon-Fri, 8am-3pm Sat) is well stocked and right by Jelačić.

Dolac
Dolac. **Open** 6am-2pm Mon-Fri; 6am-3pm Sat; 6am-2pm Sun. **No credit cards**.
Zagreb's main daily market. *See p90* **Profile**.

I-GLE
Dežmanov prolaz 4 (01 48 46 508/www.i-gle.com). **Open** 9am-8pm Mon-Fri; 9am-3pm Sat. **Credit** AmEx, DC, MC, V.
This shop window for Martina Vrdoljak Ranilović and Nataša Mihaljčišin offers striking designs for men and women, some in manifold layers, others with bizarre colour combinations. Their label enjoys cult status in Zagreb, where they make clothes for theatre productions.

Natura Croatica
Predoravićeva 8 (01 48 55 076/www.natura croatica.com). **Open** 9am-9pm Mon-Fri; 10am-4pm Sat. **Credit** AmEx, DC, MC, V.
Natura Croatica specialises in local olive oils, jams, soaps, pâtés, vinegars, fruit brandies, liqueurs, sweets, honeys and truffle-based preserves. This is the most central branch of a mini-chain.

Sheriff & Cherry
Medvedgradska 3 (01 46 66 082/www.sheriffand cherry.com). **Open** noon-8pm Mon-Fri; 11am-3pm Sat. **Credit** AmEx, DC, MC, V.
This urban style store is the brainchild of Rovinj-born Mauro, responsible for introducing Paul & Joe, Juan Antonio López and Jordi Labanda to Croatia. Here, brands such as Y-3, Schwipe, Trainerspotter and Nudie are set at fair prices while downstairs is limited-edition Adidas gear. New to S&C is the revival of Yugo-era training shoe Startas. *Photo p92.*

Victor
Kralja Držislava 10 (01 45 72 921/www.victor.hr). **Open** 10am-8pm Mon-Fri; 9am-3pm Sat. **Credit** AmEx, DC, MC, V.
Croatia's first concept store is spread over three floors, offering exclusive, quirky and sought-after products under one smartly designed roof. The womenswear (ground floor) and menswear (first

Britanski trg market.

ZAGREB

Profile Dolac Market

Zagreb's most popular living landmark.

Overlooking the main square and in the shadow of the Cathedral, is Zagreb's most precious resource: the Dolac. The Dolac ('Market') is more than just a place of trade and transaction. In this fractured capital of Upper and Lower towns, the Dolac is a constant, a hub of classless social interaction, a weathervane of the local economy and Zagreb's connection with the villages around it, even with distant Dalmatia. Traders' voices are either distinctly urban ('*Kaj*?'), provincial or come from the deepest south. Surrounding the square are little bars and eateries offering *gableci*, cheap late-morning lunches. From 7am, seven days a week, the Dolac is a-buzz until the early afternoon.

After considering several locations, the city fathers had a main market built between Kaptol and Tkalčićeva, Zagreb's most atmospheric thoroughfare. Opened in 1930, it comprised a raised open square lined with stalls of fruit, vegetables and eggs. At street level was an indoor market for meat and dairy traders. In 1933, a fish market, based on the one in Trieste, was set up alongside. This layout remains in place today, with the addition of mezzanine in the indoor section and the recent bright reconstruction of the Ribarnica, the fish market. Florists now occupy the top level, where the Dolac meets Opatinova.

Entering from the street, you walk through the main hall of mainly bakers and butchers. Certain ones stand out. Pekara Dinara from Sesvete is so renowned there are queues outside their two downtown outlets; Dubravice is also reputable. There is even a Kruh naš svagdanji…, 'Give us this day...'. Of the butchers, Pešun-Pešun is a quality purveyor of sausages from Dugo Selo, Leka Crijeva I Zacinj allows you to make your own from the pig's intestines they provide. To the right is a separate area for Mliječni Proizvodi, the dairy producers – for many locals reason alone to visit.

Sir i vrhnje, cream cheese, sold by the plastic cup (bring your own bowl or bag), with a sprinkle of salt and paprika, perhaps a few diced onions, some *kružnjak* cornbread and, at a stretch, spots of *špek* ham or slices of dried sausage, comprise the definitive Zagreb staple. The typical producer, name and address placed on each stall, is a friendly woman of a certain age: the *kumica*. A cross between 'trader' and 'godmother', the *kumica* is a

ZAGREB

much-loved figure of legend. Shoppers have their own favourite; a statue stands to one at the market entrance.

At the back of the main hall are red buckets heaped with sauerkraut. Up stairs you'll find poultry and game, with frozen goods (octopus, cod) in between, and two bars – the Zagorka and the Zalogajnica Tomislav – at each end, the latter where traders lay into cheap *čobanac* goulash after a hard morning's work.

A few drinks to the good, others may congregate in the Buffet Jelsa, a stand-alone *ćevapi* bar for rowdy post-work sing-songs at the back of the open square. Around it, stalls proffer souvenirs, Tito-era ladies' hats and lace. Wooden cabins sell olive oil, best put to use on the fish on offer in the Ribarnica, with pretty mosaics depicting seafood on their walls. You won't find fresh fish on Mondays or when the Jugo or Bora winds blow, and out of season much of what is on offer has been farmed.

Much of what's on offer is also available, fried or grilled to perfection, next door at the wonderful Amfora café-restaurant. Sit on the terrace with a plate of grilled sardines and a glass of wine – there's a 30kn daily menu – and you can observe the open-air market in action. Traders from Zagorje and Dalmatia offer cabbages, *blitva* and other local vegetables; little bundles of mixed veg (*grinzaig*) are ideal for soups. A kuna hike in price of this culinary essential is as fair an indication of the local economy as, say, any interest rate cut by the Bank of England.

Venturing deeper into the market you'll find beans, pumpkins, honey, vinegar and nuts, with dried figs, sun-dried tomatoes and olives near the back, and mushrooms towards the front. Here, you'll also find the Rubelj grill and pizzeria, with a terrace; at the back, overlooking it all, stands the renowned Kerempuh restaurant (*see p81*), which is supplied by the traders below.

MORE MARKETS
For bric a brac, the Sunday morning market on **Britanski trg**, off Ilica, is always popular.

For junk and sundry second-hand artefacts, a flea market runs at weekends on **Hrelić** in Novi Zagreb.

Time Out Croatia **91**

Sherriff & Cherry. *See p89.*

floor) sections feature the best Croatian names, plus Patrick Cox, Yohji Yamamoto and Comme des Garçons. A delicatessen in the basement contains Croatian products (jams, olive oils, bottles of rakija). The top-floor café is worth the visit alone.

WHERE TO STAY

Arcotel Allegra
Branimirova 29 (01 46 96 000/fax 01 46 96 096/www.arcotel.at). **Rates** €160-€175 double. **Credit** AmEx, DC, MC, V. **Map** p73 F5 ❶
Zagreb's first designer hotel, owned by an Austrian chain, has 151 uncluttered rooms with good sound-proofing, pine furniture, funky fabrics and DVD players. The top floor has a sauna and gym, and lovely views from the roof.

Best Western Hotel Astoria
Petrinjska 71 (01 48 08 900/910/fax 01 48 17 053/www.bestwestern.com). **Rates** €120-€155 double. **Credit** AmEx, DC, MC, V. **Map** p73 E/F4 ❷
The Best Western group bought this 1932 hotel between the train station and Jelačić and, after a complete floor-to-ceiling makeover, unveiled it in 2005. A lobby of wood panelling and marble floors leads to red-carpeted hallways lined by replicas of Croatian masterpieces. Rooms range from smallish twins to spacious executives and suites with window-paned sliding doors.

Buzzbackpackers
Babulićeva 1B (01 23 20 267/www.buzzbackpackers.com). Trams 4 & 19 to Heinzelova. **Rates** *Dorm bed* from 125kn; 450kn double. **Credit** AmEx, DC, MC, V. **Map** p73 H3 ❸

Modern and well equipped hostel in the city centre offers a dorm rooms and private ones. TV lounge, kitchen, washing machine and no curfew.

Hotel Antunović
Zagrebačka avenija 100A (01 20 41 111/fax 01 20 41 119/www.hotelantunovic.com). **Rates** €120-€160 double. **Credit** AmEx, DC, MC, V. **Map** p72 A5 ❹
Opened in 2006, this cylindrical-shaped business hotel has made a big splash thanks to its top-floor panoramic bar Vertigo, the first of its kind in the city. Facial and body treatments are available at the three-sauna spa and there's a restaurant (Argante), a bistro (Gabrijela) and a lobby bar (Bulle).

Hotel Aristos
Cebini 33 (01 66 95 900/fax 01 66 95 902/www.hotelaristos.hr). **Rates** €150-€200 double. **Credit** AmEx, DC, MC, V. **Map** p73 H6 ❺
In the Buzin Business Park near the airport, this stylish four-star of 70 rooms and seven suites suits the traveller on expenses. Two congress halls, a modem in every room and the Gallant restaurant, help smooth the process of trade and transaction.
▶ *For other lodging within easy reach of the airport, try the Hotel Stella; see p93.*

Hotel Central
Branimirova 3 (01 48 41 122/40 555/fax 01 48 41 304/www.hotel-central.hr). **Rates** €100 double. **Credit** AmEx, DC, MC, V. **Map** p73 E5 ❻
The cheapest place to stay near the train station. The bland four-storey building contains a pokey lobby and 79 basic clean rooms, some with showers, some with bathtubs. The larger courtyard-facing rooms on the top floors are quiet with leafy views.

▶ *For a little more class a short walk away, the Arcotel Allegra is Zagreb's first boutique hotel; see p92.*

Hotel Dubrovnik

Gajeva 1 (01 48 63 500/501/fax 01 48 63 506/ www.hotel-dubrovnik.hr). **Rates** €150-€170 double. **Credit** AmEx, DC, MC, V. **Map** p73 E3 ❼

Watch Zagreb's daily action unroll from this four-star hotel located off the main square, comprising two six-storey buildings. The older, which dates from 1929, has a spruced-up façade; the younger is a 1980s glass extravaganza. Inside, 258 en-suite rooms come in different shapes and sizes – book a Jelačić-facing one in the old building, ideally in a corner with lots of windows.

Hotel Laguna

Kranjčevićeva 29 (01 30 47 000/fax 01 30 47 077/www.hotel-laguna.hr). Tram 12 to Tehnički muzej. **Rates** €90 double. **Credit** AmEx, DC, MC, V **Map** p72 A6 ❽

For all its design modesty, the three-star Hotel Laguna is a handy little option, particularly as it's only three stops on the tram from the station. The hotel has a sauna, gym and internet access.

Hotel Palace

Trg JJ Strossmayera 10 (01 48 14 611/fax 01 48 11 357/www.palace.hr). **Rates** €130-€160 double. **Credit** AmEx, DC, MC, V. **Map** p73 E4 ❾

A grand Secessionist mansion houses Zagreb's first hotel, now entering into its second century in business (it opened in 1907). Despite the time that's elapsed, it's still an elegant property, catering to the moneyed and the famous. All 123 rooms, three suites and two semi-suites mix art-nouveau decor and contemporary amenities. For minimal noise and the best views of Sljeme, book a courtyard-facing room.

Hotel Stella

Nadinska 27 (01 53 93 600/fax 01 53 93 603/ www.stella.hr). **Rates** *from* €65 double. **Credit** AmEx, DC, MC, V. **Map** p73 H6 ❿

Opened in 2007, the contemporary Stella is another newbie within easy reach of Zagreb airport. A comfortable three-star with 43 rooms, it appears on many generic hotel-booking websites, ideal for business visitors on a bit of a budget.

Pansion Jägerhorn

Ilica 14 (01 48 33 877/30 161/fax 01 48 33 573/www.hotel-pansion-jaegerhorn.hr). **Rates** €100 double. **Credit** AmEx, DC, MC, V. **Map** p72 D3 ⓫

This intimate little spot in a passage at the Jelačić end of Ilica comprises eight smallish and standard rooms on the top floor of a heritage building. The leafy Upper Town is close by.

★ Regent Esplanade

Mihanovićeva 1 (01 45 66 021/fax 01 45 66 050/ www.regenthotels.com). **Rates** €150-€225 double. **Credit** AmEx, DC, MC, V. **Map** p73 E5 ⓬

Fabulous luxury and top-notch service are the name of the game at this art nouveau gem by the station. Since it opened in 1925 to cater to the *Orient Express*, the Esplanade has hosted royalty and movie stars. After a complete refurbishment, it reopened in 2004. Stylish rooms range in size and configuration, but all come with heated floors, goose-down bedding, mist-free mirrors and fancy toiletries in the marble bathrooms. The chef at Zinfandel's restaurant conjures up modern Med classics, while Le Bistro does the best *štrukli* in town. There's a terrace for drinks and outdoor movies in summer, a casino and a gym.

▶ *The same management team has recently made its first foray into Dubrovnik; see p302.*

Sheraton Zagreb Hotel

Kneza Borne 2 (01 45 53 535/fax 01 45 53 035/ www.sheraton.com). **Rates** €140-€200 double. **Credit** AmEx, DC, MC, V. **Map** p73 F4 ⓭

International comfort is available at this unsurprisingly classy business and conference hotel in the Lower Town: marble bathrooms in all 306 rooms and suites, heated indoor pool, massage treatments.

▶ *The Four Points Sheraton in the business quarter (Trg Sportova 9, 01 36 58 333) is the shiny blue-glass tower you see for miles around.*

ZAGREB

Hotel Dubrovnik.

Westin Zagreb

Kršnjavoga 1 (01 48 92 000/fax 01 48 92 001/ www.westin.com/zagreb). **Rates** *from* €150 double. **Credit** AmEx, DC, MC, V. **Map** p72 C4 ⓮

A central mid-range option, the Westin has a contemporary feel, with spacious, well-equipped bathrooms. Facilities include a gym, sauna and solarium, a heated indoor pool and the hotel bar, Diana.

GETTING THERE

From the airport

Zagreb's Pleso **airport** is 17km (10.5 miles) south-east of the city centre. Buses (30mins journey time, 30kn) run to Zagreb bus station every half-hour from 7am-8pm daily, then after each flight arrival. To Pleso from the bus station, buses run every half-hour, 4.30am-9am Mon-Fri (from 4am Sat, Sun), then 10am, 11am, then every half-hour until 8pm. A taxi should cost about 250kn.

By train

Zagreb main station, Glavni kolodvor, is at the southern fringe of the Lower Town, connected by trams Nos.6 and 13 with the main square of Jelačić, 15 minutes' walk away. There are direct links with Munich, Vienna and Budapest, and one overnight service from Paris requires only one change, in Munich. Inland, Zagreb has a direct service with Split, Rijeka and the larger towns in Continental Croatia – but the local network is slow and infrequent.

By bus

Bus services from around continental Europe arrive at Zagreb's bus station also on the No.6 (and No.2) lines three tram stops away. The website www.akz.hr gives details of the many inter-city routes out of Zagreb – Croatia's buses are far more frequent than its trains. The fastest service from Split is just under five hours.

By car

Via the Euro Tunnel, Cologne, Salzburg and Maribor in Slovenia, Zagreb is a 1,600-km drive from London. The quickest journey would take 16 hours, more than 13 of it motorway. Be aware that Zagreb is a parking nightmare once you arrive.

GETTING AROUND

Zagreb runs by **tram**. Some 16 routes cross the city, most passing through the main square of Jelačić. A ticket costs 8kn from a newsstand (stamp on board) or 10kn from the driver. It is valid for 90 minutes if travelling in one direction. A day ticket is 25kn. There is also a four-line network of night trams (16kn/20kn).

INSIDE TRACK SLJEME

Zagreb has become a major destination on the international ski circuit thanks to the recent and significant development of nearby Sljeme. A short drive from the city, this **mountain retreat** is both a family day out and a ski centre equal to many in the Alps. This is where future four-time Olympic champion Janica Kostelić learned her sport, her success and influence persuading the local authorities to invest in its expansion. From 2005, Sljeme has hosted events in the World Cup programme, later complemented by the popular Snow Queen women's event. And it's not only professionals who practise winter sports here – amateurs of all ages can enjoy night skiing, sledging and snowboarding. The price of ski passes is kept reasonable and those wishing to stay over will find a new four-star apartment hotel nearby. For more details, see www.sljeme.hr.

Tariffs and network maps are available at www.zet.hr. **Buses** serve outlying areas, many setting off from the ranks on the suburban side of the train station. Ticket tariffs are the same. **Taxis** are picked up from ranks around town, including the station and just off Jelačić. The standard rate is 25kn plus 7kn per kilometre, hiked up 20 per cent 10pm-5am, Sundays and holidays. Luggage is charged at 5kn per piece. Call 01 66 00 671 or 970.

RESOURCES

Hospital
Šalata 2 (94).

Internet
Sublink Internet Centar *Teslina 12 (01 48 11 329/www.sublink.hr).* **Open** 9am-10pm Mon-Sat; 3-10pm Sun.

Police
Petrinjska 30 (92).

Post office
Branimirova 4 (01 48 40 340). **Open** 24hrs Mon-Sat; 1pm-midnight Sun.

Tourist information
Zagreb tourist office *Trg bana Jelačića 11 (01 48 14 051/www.zagreb-touristinfo.hr).* **Open** *Mid June-Aug* 8.30am-10pm Mon-Fri, 9am-5pm Sat; 10am-2pm Sun. *Sept-mid June* 8.30am-8pm Mon-Fri; 9am-5pm Sat; 10am-2pm Sun.

ZAGREB

Continental Croatia

Continental Croatia

Wheatfields, vineyards and burgeoning urban hubs.

Croatia is not only about its celebrated coast. The large swathe of land to the north, between Istria and the borders of Slovenia, Hungary, Bosnia and Serbia, contains more than just the capital, Zagreb; the fertile plans of Slavonia are home to a quarter of Croatia's population. The region has a continental climate of freezing winters and scorching summers, and shares the Pannonian love of roast pork, stuffed peppers and young wine.

Its capital is **Osijek**, the only university town in Slavonia, with a vibrant urban scene, galleries, theatres and nightspots. **Slavonski Brod** is the second city and makes for a good base for exploring the hills, forests and vineyards of central Slavonia. The small town of **Djakovo** has preserved the scale and feel of its 19th-century heyday, when it was home to the enlightened Bishop Strossmayer – the surrounding countryside is still dominated by its towering, neo-Gothic cathedral. Further east is the area most affected by the Yugoslav war. Although life is slowly returning to normal, you still see burned-out villages and, off the beaten track, signs warning of uncleared minefields. Towns include pretty **Ilok** and its wine cellars, the railway hub of **Vinkovci** and ruined **Vukovar** and its war memorial.

Immediately north of Zagreb is **Hrvatsko Zagorje**, a region of castles and picturesque villages. Hugging up against it is **Varaždin**, whose namesake county town is the other urban hub of the north, whose Baroque surroundings host some of Croatia's most important cultural festivals.

OSIJEK

The main town of the Slavonia and Baranja region, **Osijek** is set on the right bank of the Drava, near its mouth into the Danube. Tree-lined avenues of pastel Secessionist mansions meld incongruously with a young weekend party scene, anchored by the cobblestone fortress of **Tvrdja**. Filled with cafés, nightclubs, top-notch restaurants and students, Osijek is a welcome surprise for those here to explore the nearby castles and the **Kopački rit** nature reserve (*see p46*). As more businessmen and tourists arrive – a budget air link with the UK should be in place by the summer of 2009 – new places are opening and old ones expanding. Long-time hotel favourite **Waldinger** has opened a high-end restaurant; at Tvrdja, **Kod Ruže** is a newbie with trappings of rustic Slavonia but a menu that'll make a city slicker smile.

Sightseeing

Slavonia's regional hub was founded on the ruins of the Roman town of Mursa – located on the right bank of the river Drava, close to its confluence with the Danube. The town thrived in medieval times, but was sacked and destroyed by Ottoman soldiers in 1526. During a century and a half of Turkish rule, the city was remodelled in an oriental style, and famously had an 8km (five-mile) long wooden bridge out into the marshes, celebrated as one of the wonders of the world, but burned down by Croatian noble Nikola Zrinski in 1664.

In 1687 the city was occupied by the Habsburgs, who built a mighty fortress and erased all architectural remains of the Ottoman period. The Tvrdja complex combined administrative and military functions, and was the heart of the town during its 18th-century

INSIDE TRACK
NATURE BREAKS

Continental Croatia contains two of the country's most celebrated national parks and nature reserves: Plitvice and Kopački rit. Plitvice, a natural wonder of waterfalls, lakes and steep mountains, is about three hours from Zagreb. Kopački rit, close to Osijek, comprises 23,000 hectares (57 acres) of wetlands, home to over 200 species of birds. For more details, *see p44*.

revival. Its **Holy Trinity Square** was bounded on the north by an imposing Military Command, on the west by the building of the Main Guard, and on the east by the Magistrates' Office, now the **Museum of Slavonia** (Trg svetog trojstva 6, 031 250 730; 8am-2pm Tue-Fri, 10am-1pm Sat, Sun; 15kn), housing a motley collection of local oddities.

In 1809, Osijek was granted the title of Free Royal City and the city became a thriving multicultural metropolis with trade and cultural links to Budapest. **Europska avenija** is a broad tree-lined boulevard in Habsburg style and contains well preserved art nouveau townhouses – particularly Nos.12 and 22. Opposite is **Osijek Art Gallery** (Galerija likovnih umjetnosti; Europska avenija 9, 031 251 280; 10am-6pm Tue-Fri, 10am-1pm Sat,

Sun; 10kn), with works by Adolf Waldinger (1843-1904), who died poor but is now rated one of Slavonia's greatest landscape painters.

The centre of the Upper Town is **Trg Ante Starčevića**, a nice square criss-crossed by tram lines, full of shops and cafés, and marked by the 90-metre tower of the **Church of Sts Peter & Paul** (known as the **Cathedral**). Other architectural sites include the Moorish-style **Croatian National Theatre**, founded in 1907, and the Baroque **Church of St James** (1727) on **Kapucinska**, a street also notable for its busts of historic personalities. There's a riverside promenade that leads to the Tvrdja citadel, and a dramatic pedestrian suspension bridge over the Drava. On the other side of the river are the city zoo and the recreational centre **Copacabana**, with pools and a sandy beach.

During the Yugoslav war, Osijek avoided heavy destruction despite being on the frontline. Just over the rive,r minefields are marked with yellow signs. De-mining is slow, dangerous and not 100 per cent guaranteed.

The **Nature Park of Kopački rit**, a few kilometres north-east of Osijek, comprises wetlands that are home to 260 species of birds. *See p46*.

Where to eat

Alas
Reisnerova 12A (031 202 311). **Open** 10am-11pm daily. **Credit** AmEx, DC, MC, V. **Map** p99 B3 ❶

Kod Ruže.

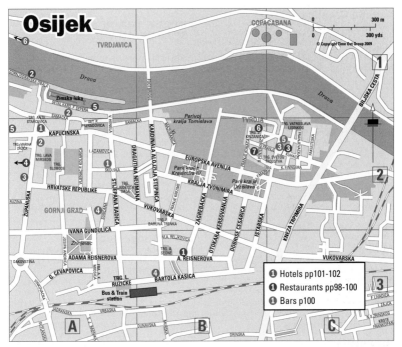

Osijek

❶ Hotels pp101-102
❶ Restaurants pp98-100
❶ Bars p100

Alas, in the local dialect, is not a lament but actually means 'fisherman'. So it's not surprising that the speciality of the house is *perkelt od soma*, a heaty fish stew with huge pieces of catfish in a spicy paprika sauce. Book at weekends.

▶ *For stew of a Hungarian variety, try the Madjarska retfala (Šandor Peterfija 32, 031 302 243), whose iš-fiš paprikaš is made with cockerel.*

Galija
Gornjodravska obala (031 283 500). **Open** 10am-11pm daily. **Credit** AmEx, DC, MC, V. **Map** p99 A1 ❷
This smart-looking spot on a riverboat is hidden away to the left after walking from the main square

---

**INSIDE TRACK
SLAVONIAN CUISINE**

Slavonia has more in common with Hungary than Dalmatia when it comes to cuisine. Its signature dish, *fiš paprikaš*, is a spicy fish stew similar to its Magyar cousin. River fish such as carp, pike and catfish are typical ingredients. *Cobanac* is a meaty stew not unlike goulash while *kulen* is the local spicy salami.

---

to the Drava. Net drapes on the ceiling, black wooden chairs with stylish upholstery and plenty of space make it popular for business meetings. The Galija is essentially a steakhouse but with plenty of other options as well.

★ Kod Ruže
Franjo Kuhac 25 (031 206 066). **Open** 9am-midnight Mon-Thur; 9am-1am Fri, Sat; 10am-4pm Sun. **Credit** AmEx, DC, MC, V. **Map** p99 C2 ❸
Right in the very heart of Tvrdja, Ruža was originally a house purchased for 900 Hungarian forints in 1758. Today, the restaurant, which opened in 2007, is the best place in town for food, atmosphere and overall evening-on-the-town mojo. Grab a seat on the cobblestone terrace in the back or inside where the cobbles join with wooden floors, heavy wooden tables and leather chairs – all tastefully commingled with Ottoman-esque designs in the padded booths, old portraits on the walls and thick candles burning on tables next to baskets of walnuts. Order the grilled deer stuffed with carrots, frogs' legs or perch fillet and listen to the traditional band play a sort of Slavonian mariachi for the room. Tables go quickly at weekends.

▶ *There are a number of bars on the south side of Holy Trinity Square that are good for a pre- or post-meal drink; General von Becker's has historic resonance.*

Laguna Croatica

Dubrovačka 13 (031 369 203). **Open**
10am-10pm daily. **Credit** AmEx, DC, MC, V.
Map p99 A2 ❹
Traditional Croatian restaurant decked out in wood
and stone, with a focus on Dalmatian and freshwater fish dishes. The dining area of this popular
hideaway is quite small, so booking is advised.

Lumiere

*Šetalište Kardinala F Šepera (099 473 6833
mobile)*. **Open** 8am-midnight daily. **Credit**
AmEx, DC, MC, V. **Map** p99 A1 ❺
Opened in October 2008, this lounge bar and restaurant are under the same ownership as Waldinger so
you can rely on a touch of class. Attached to Osijek's
retro cinema, Lumiere offers food and drink every
day with live music at weekends. Decor comprises
light wood and cream-cushioned chairs and stools,
and black-and-white showbiz photos; the menu features fish, meat, pasta and Oriental dishes.

Muller

Trg J Križanica 9 (031 204 770). **Open**
10am-11pm daily. **Credit** AmEx, DC, MC, V.
Map p99 B2 ❻
Reliable restaurant in the Tvrdja area that caters
more to visitors than locals. The menu features
grilled rump steak, fried *smudj* (perch) and the full
range of Croatian specialities.

Slavonska kuća

Kamila Firinger 26 (031 369 955). **Open**
9am-11pm Mon-Sat. **Credit** AmEx, DC, MC, V.
Map p99 B2 ❼
A favourite with the locals, this restaurant is a good
place to savour regional specialities in a self-con-
sciously Slavonian atmosphere.

Where to drink

Amsterdam

Radićeva 18 (no phone). **Open** 7.30am-11pm
daily. **No credit cards. Map** p99 A2 ❶
One of the most appealing of the student bars along
Radićeva, this basement joint is all dark wood and
even darker rock. Once you make it down the stairs
out of the sun, you may not find yourself stumbling
up into the night for many pleasurable hours.

Mala Kavana

Županijska 2 (no phone). **Open** 6.30am-11pm
Mon-Sat; 8am-11pm Sun. **No credit cards.**
Map p99 A2 ❷
The kind of solid Eastern European café you would
expect in the main square. Inside is tastefully kitsch,
with black leather chairs and burgundy taffeta curtains, and views outside to the Cathedral and surrounding Secessionist buildings.
▶ *For more classic coffeehouse atmosphere,
try the café in the Hotel Central; see p101.*

**INSIDE TRACK
SLAVONIAN WINES**

Slavonia is renowned for its wines,
particularly whites such as Graševina,
Riesling and Pinot Blanc. Several
companies open their cellars to the
public. The most prominent, **Kutjevo**
(034 255 041, www.kutjevo.com), based
at the village of the same name north of
Slavonski Brod, attracts 15,000 visitors a
year to its 800-year-old wine cellar. Lunch
is also provided. **Zdjelarević**, 20km (12.5
miles) from Slavonski Brod in Brodski
Stupnik, is Croatia's first wine hotel (035
427 775, www.zdjelarevic.hr). Guests can
enjoy the fruits of the family vineyard,
regional dishes and comfortable lodging.

★ Old Bridge Pub

Franje Kuhaca 4 (031 211 611). **Open**
7.30am-2am Mon-Thur, Sun; 8am-4am Fri, Sat.
No credit cards. Map p99 C2 ❸
A busy Tvrdja bar, with the global appeal of
Guinness logos, smoked-glass windows and brown-
leather armchairs, attracting business types,
assorted bohemians and ale aficionados. The fun
takes place on three floors. The bottom is a disco,
the middle is a pub and upstairs is a country-club
restaurant of sorts with orange padded leather
chairs. Dishes include grilled lamb, steak sandwiches and trout.

S Co Bar

Sunčana 8 (no phone). **Open** 8am-4pm
8pm-midnight Mon-Sat. **No credit cards.**
Map p99 A2 ❹
As Voodoo, this first-floor dive was an original alternative spot. Now it delights in groovy murals, high
stools, low sofas and arty hits for the cultural mob.

St Patrick's Pub

Franje Kuhaca 15 (031 205 202). **Open**
7am-midnight Mon-Wed; 7am-1am Thur-Sat;
9.30am-midnight Sun. **No credit cards.**
Map p99 C2 ❺
On the main square, St Patrick's is not awash just
with students like its neighbours – and it's often the
busiest place here. Chelsea memorabilia adds a personal touch, otherwise it's pub business as usual.

Nightlife

★ Bastion

Trg V Lisinskog (no phone). **Open** 7.30pm-
3.30am Tue, Wed; 9pm-5am Thur, Fri; 9pm-6am
Sat. **No credit cards.**
Once a café and now an all-night club next to the
river, Bastion – located in an old brick building – is

the newest hotspot in town. It has bars upstairs on a balcony and next to the ground-level dance floor. The interior is a slick mix of clean white and coloured lights. Giant projections play across the back wall as an all-age group mimics the moves and parties to hip hop, house and the like.

Club Q

Franje Kuhaca 15 (031 210 330). **Open** 8am-11pm Mon-Wed; 9am-5am Thur, Fri; 7pm-6am Sat; 7-11pm Sun. **No credit cards.**
Club Q is the biggest club in the bar hub, with DJs and regular live music, and occasionally the dreaded turbofolk. But one of the attractions of the place is that the hedonistic young regulars who frequent the place would be happy with anything, frankly.

Tufna

Franje Kuhaca 10 (031 215 020). **Open** 8am-midnight Mon-Wed; 10pm-4am Thur; 10pm-5am Fri; 10pm-6am Sat. **No credit cards.**
One of the livelier dance venues in town, a stone's throw from the bar hub in Tvrdja. Pop anthems blast on three dance floors and DJs probe the boundaries of local techno in the basement.

Where to stay

Hotel Central

Trg Ante Starčevića 6 (031 283 399/fax 031 283 891/www.hotel-central-os.hr). **Rates** 514kn double. **Credit** AmEx, DC, MC, V. **Map** p99 A2 ❶

A comfortable mid-priced option on the main square, the Central has a stylish foyer and 39 rather more standard rooms. The café preserves the atmosphere of the typical coffeehouse that was an important institution of social and cultural life from the late 1800s to World War II.

★ Hotel Osijek

Šamačka 4 (031 230 333/fax 031 230 444/www.hotelosijek.hr). **Rates** 950kn double. **Credit** AmEx, DC, MC, V. **Map** p99 A1 ❷
This Yugoslav-era hotel has been given a complete makeover, turning it into one of the most luxurious hotels in Slavonia, with staff displaying an attentiveness and attention to detail to match. It has one of the best locations in the city, on the riverside promenade, with great views of the Old Town and across the Drava. The best panorama is enjoyed from the jacuzzi in the 14th-floor spa centre, which also includes a gym and multiple saunas.

★ Hotel Waldinger

Županijska 8 (031 250 450/fax 031 250 453/www.waldinger.hr). **Rates** 950kn double. **Credit** AmEx, DC, MC, V. **Map** p99 A2 ❸
This four-star seeks to recreate the Habsburg era. Named after the famous local 19th-century painter, the hotel is a listed building and fine example of Secessionist architecture. As well as the 16 rooms in the hotel, which all come with high ceilings and bathtubs, the Waldinger also has a three-star pension with more budget-minded prices and a parlour-like café facing main street. A new restaurant upped

CONTINENTAL CROATIA

Hotel Osijek.

the already good facilities in 2007 and another is planned for 2009, as well as a wine cellar offering regional tipples. The current menu includes duck breast fillet in an oriental sauce and rabbit in white wine, partaken in art-nouveau surroundings with columns and chandeliers.

Kn Mursa

Bartola Kačića 2A (tel/fax 031 224 900). **Rates** 520kn double. **Credit** AmEx, MC, V. **Map** p99 B3 **4**

Overlooking the station and owned by the railway company, this hotel is in many ways stuck in a time warp, but still provides some of the best-value accommodation to be found in town. Many of the otherwise dingy rooms have excellent views of the city from their small balconies.

★ Villa Sveti Rok

Sv Rok 13 (031 310 490/fax 031 310 499/ www.villa-sveti-rok.hr). **Rates** 885kn double. **Credit** AmEx, DC, MC, V. **Map** p99 A2 **5**

A four-star boutique near the main square, Villa Sveti Rok is something of a home from home. Its seven rooms are tastefully finished with wooden floors, flat-screen TVs and WiFi. Each has its own colour scheme and all are decorated with light and happy artwork. Some balconies overlook the private back garden where guests can take breakfast; the bathrooms feature futuristic massage showers. The owners, the Junučić family, augment the bright atmosphere and you'll find a beauty salon next door.

Zoo Hotel

Sjevernodravska obala, Tvrdjavica (031 229 922/fax 031229 911/www.zoo-hotel.com). **Rates** 490kn single; 690kn-750kn double. **Credit** AmEx, DC, MC, V. **Map** p99 A1 **6**

Drive round over the bridge or take the chain ferry from the city centre across the Drava, and you'll find Osijek's newest hotel by the city zoo. That sets the theme of the decor: imitation animal-skin finishings blend with the minimalist furniture. Functional looking from its pastel-green boxy exterior, Zoo Hotel delivers on its four stars, albeit in the slightly clinical way that goes with new, purpose-built hotels. Its restaurant is a great place to sample good traditional game dishes and take in a peaceful view of the river. And, of course, it's handy for the zoo too.

Getting there & around

Osijek's modest **Klisa airport** (www.osijek-airport.hr) is 20km from town. An Intercity **train** from **Zagreb** takes just over three hours, and there are frequent **bus** connections with the capital. The bus and train **stations** are south of the city centre, ten minutes' walk away, on the No.2 **tram** route. Tram No.1 links with the Tvrdja. Tickets (7kn) are sold at newspaper kiosks. For a **taxi**, call 031 200 100.

Resources

Hospital
Josipa Huttlera 4 (031 511 511).

Internet
Lorenza Jagera 24 (031 212 313).

Police
Trg Lavoslava Ružička 1 (031 237 112).

Post office
Kardinala A Stepinca 17 (031 253 869).

Tourist information
Osijek Tourist Office *Županijska 2 (031 203 755/www.tzosijek.hr).* **Open** *Summer* 7am-8pm Mon-Fri; 8am-noon Sat, Sun. *Winter* 7am-4pm Mon-Fri; 8am-noon Sat.

SLAVONSKI BROD

Situated at the ancient crossroads between the Pannonian plain and Bosnia, halfway on the motorway between Zagreb and Belgrade, the fate of Slavonski Brod has owed a lot to shifting borders. Following the liberation of the region from Turkish rule in 1691, this ancient river crossing point (*brod*) was chosen as the location for an Austrian military garrison and an important Franciscan monastery. With the incorporation of Bosnia into the Austrian empire and the building of a strategic railway bridge, the fortunes of the city took a turn for the better. The late 1800s was marked by the building of grand merchants' houses on one of the largest public squares in the country.

In the second half of the 20th century the town was transformed according to Socialist urban planning after its destruction by Allied bombing, and it became a centre of heavy industry. From 1991 the city has again sat on an international border, that between Croatia and Bosnia, weathering the rapid decline of its heavy industry through an influx of thousands of business-minded refugees from Bosnia. Locals brave the customs officers on the bridge to stock up on cheap cigarettes, alcohol and petrol in Bosanski Brod.

The main site of historical interest in town is the **Fortress**, which until the mid 1990s was in the hands of the military. It has since been restored and integrated into the city, and is now the home to two schools, the Town Hall and the **Ružić Art Gallery** (Brod Fortress, 035 411 510; 10am-2pm, 4-7pm Mon-Fri, 10am-2pm Sat-Sun; 10kn). This sizeable gallery is primarily a depot for the Ružić collection, which is made up of more than 400 works by the mid-twentieth century sculptor Branko Ružić and his contemporaries.

**INSIDE TRACK
FARMERS' MARKET**

Slavonski Brod's city market, or
Tržnica, is one of the liveliest in the
region and a direct outlet for farmers from
the surrounding countryside to sell their
home-grown vegetables, eggs, sausages,
chickens, and the traditional cheese and
cream. The covered area houses dairy
products, butchers and fishmongers; the
outside rows of concrete tables heave
with fresh fruit and vegetables.

The **Franciscan monastery**, like the
Fortress dating back to the early 18th century,
has an impressive Baroque church and
atmospheric cloisters. Sunday morning services
are an important civic ritual, followed up with
a visit to the café-lined Sava embankment.
Opposite the monastery, the **Regional
Museum of Brodsko Posavlje** (Starčevićeva
40, 035 447 415; 9am-7pm daily) is the place to
see anything from exquisite Slavonian folk
handicrafts to hunting paraphernalia and
bizarre local archaeological finds. In the
courtyard of the museum, **Galerija Balen**
(035 448 403, www.galerijabalen.net; 5-8pm
Mon-Fri) is a noted art gallery with a clued-up
mix of Croatian painters and international stars.

Where to eat

For dining, try the regional specialities in
the **Slavonski Podrum** (A Štampara 1, 035
444 856), a wood-panelled cellar, especially
the grilled fish from the Sava. **Pizzeria Uno**
(Nikole Zrinskog 7, 035 442 107) offers reliable
pizzas from a wood-fired oven and Slavonian
specialities from *grah* stew to grilled liver.

Where to drink & nightlife

Kazalište Kavana/Hlapić (Trg Stjepana
Miletića 12) is in the building of the Socialist-era
Modernist theatre-and-library complex, with
high ceilings, comfortable sofas and careful
service. The terrace looks out over the Sava.
The bar scene revolves around the riverside
promenade, Šetalište braće Radić. Earlier on,
Moulinarij (No.19) is ideal for local Ledo ice-
cream and strong coffee with mint chocolates
amid a quiet, chatty atmosphere. The walls are
decorated with photographs of pre-World War
II Slavonski Brod. Later on, try **Green Park** or
the **Iguana**, whose live iguana died from smoke
inhalation. Much later on, head to Drunk Street,
Starčevićeva. Here **Alfa** (No.19, 035 233 800)
is a good place to start the night and **TNT**

(No.1, no phone) a fine place to finish it.
Mention must be made of dive bar **Rupe** (Trg
Ivane Brlić-Mažuranić 5, 035 410 010) and the
lounge bar on the same square, **Navigator**
(No.8, 098 341 541 mobile). Don't miss **Snoopy**
(Mažuranićeva 10), the hangout for the boho
crowd. At this bamboo-clad haunt of local
wastrels, drop-outs and general malingerers,
the music does not falter from the path of ex-
Yugo cult rock and Anglo-Saxon indie faves.

Where to stay

The main hotel in town is the **Savus** (Ante
Starčevića 2A, 035 405 888; 850kn double),
ideally located on the main square. It is
Slavonski Brod's first four-star, with modern
and comfortable rooms, and a marble-filled
café and restaurant. Overlooking the Sava, the
Rezidencija Uno (Šetalište braće Radića 6,
035 415 000, www.uno-brod.hr; 600kn double)
offers individually furnished rooms with plenty
of character in a renovated townhouse.
The new family run **Hotel Central** (Petra
Krešimira IV 45, 035 492 030; 250kn single,
580kn double) is just that, 15 comfortable
rooms right in town, with a decent breakfast
and free broadband WiFi throughout.
In the cheaper bracket, **Lotos** (Trg Ivane
Brlić-Mažuranić 10, 035 405 555; 400kn double)
is a guesthouse, bar, restaurant, pizzeria and
ice-cream shop rolled into one, on the main
square. The **Magnus Rooms** (JJ Strossmajera
46, 035 436 536; 180kn double) are respectable
private lodgings within reach of the market.

Getting there

Regular **trains** from **Zagreb** (2.5hrs) serve
Slavonski Brod – the **station** is a short walk
from the centre. The **bus station** next door
accommodates frequent services from the
capital (3hrs). Buses from **Osijek** take 2hrs,
from **Djakovo** 1hr 15mins.

Resources

Tourist information
Slavonski Brod Tourist Office *Trg Pobjede
30 (035 445 765/www.tzgsb.hr).* **Open** *Summer*
7am-9pm Mon-Sat. *Winter* 7am-7.30pm Mon-Sat.

DJAKOVO

Djakovo preserves the feel of a small
Slavonian market town, with the added
attractions of an impressive cathedral, a strong
wine-making tradition, and the opportunity to
visit the **Lipizzan stud farm**. **St. Peter's
Cathedral** is Djakovo's landmark, visible for
miles from whichever direction you approach

INSIDE TRACK
ORIENT EXPRESS

The **Orient Express** may be associated with Istanbul, but Agatha Christie's fictional murder on board took place between Vinkovci and Slavonski Brod. Christie describes the night train leaving Belgrade for Zagreb, stopping at Vinkovci then being trapped in snow before 'Brod'. During that time, Mr Ratchett was stabbed 12 times. Christie did the journey herself, staying at the famous Esplanade railway hotel in Zagreb. Today, the night train takes 40 minutes between Vinkovci and Slavonski Brod on its journey from Belgrade to Salzburg, via Zagreb.

the town. It's the most important religious building not only in Djakovo, but in Slavonia. The cathedral was built between 1866 and 1882 by the cultural and political activist (and bishop of Djakovo) Josip Juraj Strossmayer. The town has a Strossmayer Monument, a Strossmayer Square, a Strossmayer Museum, and a well kept and shaded Strossmayer Garden behind the cathedral, where folkloric performances are staged in summer.

Djakovo is well known in Croatia as a centre for the breeding of Lipizzan horses, unusual in that when they are young they are dark grey, but gradually become completely white. The history of the stud farm can be traced back to the 13th century, but it was not until 1806 that the Lipizzan horses arrived in the wake of the Napoleonic invasion. The **Djakovo Paddock** (Augusta Šenoe 45, 031 813 286, www.ergela-djakovo.hr) is set in rolling green fields full of wild flowers in summer. Visitors can wander freely around the stables.

Near the stud farm, **Sokak** (Šenoe 40, 031 820 332) is a restaurant done out like a small street, as its name implies, and features a daily changing menu with local specialities. Other options include **Slavonska kuća** (Štarčevića 134, 031 822 336), an atmospheric cellar with a focus on game dishes and fine local white wines. The **Zelena Laguna** hotel (Stjepana Radića 17, 031 821 634) and the **Djakovo** (Nikola Tesle 52, 031 840 570, www.hotel-djakovo.hr), a three-star, provide lodging.

Hourly **buses** run to Djakovo from **Osijek** (45mins); every two hours from Zagreb (4.5hrs).

VINKOVCI

Vinkovci is a small, typical Slavonian town set on the banks of the river Bosut. It's elongated and devoid of elevation but enlivened

by a Baroque centre, main square, park and a parish church built in 1777.

The town's heritage is not only architectural, however. As Cibalae, it was populated by the Romans and was the birthplace of two emperors, Valens and Valentinian I. In the 11th century the Slavs renamed the place Sv Ilija. After the Turks, the Austrians ruled. And after industrialisation, Vinkovci became a major railway junction.

The composer of the Croatian national anthem, Josip Runjanin, was born here. Today the most important event in the calendar is **Vinkovačke jeseni** ('Vinkovci Autumn'), a traditional folk fête held each September.

Where to eat

The best-known restaurant in town is **Lamut** (Ulica kralja Zvonimira 23, 032 332 588), which offers local specialities such as pork shank in sauerkraut. **Prkos** (Ulica Stjepana Radića 27, 098 1663 3918 mobile) goes to considerable lengths to provide authentic food from a century ago: game in mushroom sauce, a variety of sausages (*kulin, švargle* and *kravavice*) and stews (particularly venison and fish). It also makes its own bread on the premises. **Marabú** (Glagoljaška 8, 098 901 3753 mobile) and **Mystique** (Ulica kralja Zvonimira 32, no phone) are two ethnically themed cafés that stand out from the norm.

Where to stay

The town has three main hotels. The **Cibalia** (Ulica Ante Starčićeva 51, 032 339 222, www.hotel-cibalia.com, 600kn) opened in 2000, a standard three-star near the bus and train stations. The oldest (and biggest) is the **Slavonija** (Duga Ulica 1, 032 342 555, www.son-ugo-cor.com, 375kn), with boxy rooms. The **Gem** (Ulica kralja Zvonimira 120, 032 367 911, www.hotelgem.hr, 440kn) is unusual in that it has two indoor tennis courts, as well as a sauna and billiard room.

Getting there

Vinkovci is one of the few places in Croatia where the **train** is quicker than the **bus** – 3hrs from **Zagreb** as opposed to 4-5hrs by bus. Buses run every hour between **Vinkovci** and **Vukovar** (50mins).

Resources

Tourist information
Vinkovci Tourist Office *Trg Bana Josipa Šokčevića 3 (032 334 653/www.tz-vinkovci.hr).* **Open** 8am-3pm Mon-Fri; 8am-1pm Sat.

Vukovar War Memorial.

VUKOVAR

The memory of war still weighs heavily on the city of **Vukovar**. Despite the many millions of euros spent on reconstructing the town, which was completely devastated during an 87-day siege at the hands of the Serbian military in 1991, there are still many tell-tale signs of the city's grim history. Apart from hushed groups on sombre bus tours, the centre of town still feels deserted and unloved, with few attractions to merit a long stay. There is, though, a nice walk along the bank of the Danube from the ruins of the **Eltz Manor** to the oasis of the luxurious **Hotel Lav**. This, and July's newly inaugurated **Vukovar Film Festival** (www.vukovarfilmfestival.com) are the most positive things to have happened since the war.

There are, of course, plenty of memorials to the suffering endured by the civilian population during the occupation and the heroism of the city's 2,000 resistance fighters. Key sights include the famous **Water Tower**, which was peppered with bulletholes during the siege and played a cameo role in several films about the war. Climb up the hill to the **Franciscan Monastery** for an instructive view of the half-restored Baroque town centre, while in the entrance to the church itself, there's an eerie memorial, made up of a pile of human bones and skulls, to the human tragedy that accompanied the architectural destruction.

Vukovar was always a mixed city and, in former times, a beautiful one. After the Turks retreated in the 1600s, Germans, Jews, Serbs, Ukrainians and Hungarians flooded in. A German entrepreneurial family by the name of Eltz developed it as a craft and trading centre. Their palace is the one damaged by the river. By the 1900s Vukovar's Baroque façades were home to a thriving bourgeois community, with significant Ruthene and Slovak citizens too. When the Yugoslav war started, Vukovar was still a centre for manufacturing, mainly tyres.

Vukovar was the scene of some of the most notorious war crimes of the Balkan conflict. In recent years, a memorial complex has opened in **Ovčara** outside town to remember the approximately 200 people who were taken from the local hospital by Serbian paramilitaries to a discretely located dairy farm and massacred on November 20 1991. One of the storage hangars in the Ovčara farm was used as a transit camp for prisoners, and is now the site of a hi-tech memorial house, with alternating photos of the victims around the dark walls, and a swirling vortex in the centre. A kilometre or so further along the road there's a dirt track leading to an isolated ravine where the shooting actually took place and a mass grave marked with a grey obelisk and sculpted dove.

Vukovar holds a particular place in the Croatian psyche. Its bravery under siege means that its name is chanted whenever the national football team play; the anniversary of its surrender is marked with sombre programmes on the radio. A visit here can still be a shocking experience but one not without reward.

The main restaurant in town is **Vrške** (Parobrodksa 3, 032 441 788), one of the few buildings to have survived 1991 completely unscathed. A simple place with a terrace on the Danube, it offers a diverse range of freshwater fish. The most popular dish is pike-perch prepared in croquettes with a pinch of beer inside. Meat dishes are prepared on a wood-fired grill. Other specialities include *Vučedolski uštipak*, a fritter of ground meat with bacon and cheese, and grilled hamburger with goat's cheese. Vukovar's four-star hotel, **Lav** (*see below*), on the opposite bank, houses an equally swish restaurant, with local delicacies such as smoked pork sausage (*kulin*), fried frogs' legs, venison stew (*čobanac*), plus local cheese (*Vukovarski podlivani sir*) for dessert. Some 100 Slavonian wines are available.

The **Danielle Bar** (Ulica Marija Jurić Zagorke 6, 032 410 387), in the neighbourhood of Mitnica, has a music programme of house and ambient. The first bar to open after the war was **Ferrari** (Ulica dr Franje Tudjmana 5, 032 442 500), now with weekend parties. The only disco is **Quo Vadis** (Ulica bana Josipa Jelačića 98, 098 311

204 mobile), a multi-floored venue, one half café, one half nightclub with DJ decks.

The **Hotel Lav** ('Lion') opened in 2005 – or rather reopened in 2005, as the first hotel to open in town was the Lav in 1840. It was a Socialist-style building until 1991. The current model (Ulica Josipa Jurja Strossmayera 18, 032 445 100, www.hotel-lav.hr, 900kn) is a smart business hotel. It has a restaurant (*see above*), and fine cakes in its riverside cafe. The two-star **Dunav** (Trg republike Hrvatske 1, 032 441 285, 420kn), which housed journalists during the 1991 siege, is still in operation. It has 56 simple rooms, all en-suite.

Getting there & around

There is a one direct train service a day to Vukovar from **Zagreb** (4hrs) via **Slavonski Brod** (1hr 20mins). Regular buses run from **Vinkovci** (50mins) and **Osijek** (45mins).

Resources

Tourist information
Vukovar Tourist Office *Ulica Josipa Jurja Strossmayera 15 (032 442 889).* **Open** 8am-3pm Mon-Fri; 8am-1pm Sat.

ILOK

Ilok is the easternmost town in Croatia and is attractively situated on a hill overlooking the Danube. The old town is surrounded by picturesque brick walls dating from the Middle Ages when Ilok blossomed as a religious and trade centre. Within the city walls, fortified with towers and bastions, are historical sites connected by a park, from **Odescalchi Castle** on one side to the **Franciscan church & monastery** on the other.

Odeschalchi is one of the largest Baroque buildings in Croatia, constructed on the ruins of a medieval one by an Italian aristocratic family put in charge of the town after their influential relative Pope Innocent XI ended the Turkish occupation. The Odeschalchis are famous for setting up wine cellars at the castle and encouraging the planting of vineyards in the surrounding hills. The family left Ilok in 1945 and now resides near Rome. The two-storey palace is a protected cultural site and currently partly under restoration but the cellars can still be visited, the palace restaurant is open, and there's a magnificent view of the Danube.

The Franciscan Monastery preserves the impressive library and cell of St Ivan Capistran, the patron saint of Ilok and its most colourful historical figure. Capistran was born in Italy in 1386, and presided as a judge before joining the Franciscan Order to undertake missionary work

across Europe. He preached in favour of the Holy War against the Turks and helped to defend Belgrade against the Ottoman advance in 1456, which as a consequence postponed the fall of Slavonia for another 70 years. Capistran died and was buried in Ilok, and is pictured over the main altar in the church. The painting shows him in a monk's habit and with a crusaders' flag leading the defenders of Belgrade, perhap ironic given recent history.

Remains of the 100-year Turkish rule include a hammam in the fortifications and a turbe or Ottoman mausoleum, both rarities in Croatia. The **Museum of the City of Ilok** (Trg sv Ivana Kapistrana, 032 590 065) is located in Kurija Brnjaković while the castle is being restored. It does not have a permanent display but runs temporary exhibitions.

Many visit Ilok for its walks, cycle routes – and wine cellars. Almost every street has at least one winery and there is an easy route to a dozen cellars. Highlights include the old Ilok cellars established by the Odescalchi family in heart of town. The wine varieties on offer include Graševina, Chardonnay, Pinot Blanc and Silvanac, and, among the reds, Cabernet Sauvignon and Frankovka. Ilok is also famous for its golden-coloured and aromatic Traminac.

You can also dine at the **Odescalchi Castle** (Šetalište M Barbarića 5, 032 590 126), in suitably traditional surroundings. If you prefer a view, the **Hotel Dunav** (J Benešića 62, 032 596 500, www.hoteldunavilok.com) enjoys an

Ilok.

enviable setting perched up on the riverbank. The **Captain's House** (Dunavska 6, 032 518 168) on the riverbank, signposted from the main road near the village of Sarengrad, belonged to a figure of Danube lore; all passenger boats would honk in salute as they passed him. Today in his place is a restaurant serving home-made fish and meat dishes, accompanied by superb Ilok wine. They rent out traditional Danube boats and fishing gear, are welcoming to children, and offer the option of horse riding.

To stay somewhere cheaper, the **Pansion Comfort Masarini** (Stjepana Radića 4, 032 590 050) has single rooms for 100kn and doubles for 150kn. The **Izvor Života** (Benešićeva 12, 098 270 813 mobile) is a family house with simple rooms (140kn per person) plus unusual extras like rides in a traditional horse and cart, and house champagne.

Getting there

Ilok is only served by **buses**. The daily stopping service from **Zagreb** takes eight hours; the fast one via **Slavonski Brod** (3hrs), **Vinkovci** (1hr) and **Vukovar** (45mins) takes five-and-a-half hours.

Resources

Tourist information
Ilok Tourist Office *Trg Nikole Iločkog 2 (032 590 020/www.turizammilok.hr)*. **Open** 9am-noon Mon-Fri.

HRVATSKO ZAGORJE

The closest trip from Zagreb is to **Hrvatsko Zagorje**, squeezed up between the capital and Slovenia. Amid the picturesque villages and vineyards, its main attractions are the castles of **Trakošćan** and **Veliki Tabor**, Tito's home village of **Kumrovec** and **Varaždin**.

If heading for Trakošćan don't miss the lovely town of **Krapina** (www.krapina.com), with one of the world's richest Neanderthal sites boasting fossil remnants of Homo sapiens.

Up by the Slovenian border is the fairy-tale castle of Trakošćan (www.trakoscan.hr; May-Sept 9am-6pm daily, Oct-Apr 9am-4pm daily; 20kn), some 80km (50 miles) north of Zagreb. Perched on a small hill fronted by a picture-perfect lake, Trakošćan is a 19th-century neo-Gothic version of the medieval original, complete with turrets, a drawbridge and a landscaped park. The living quarters of the castle's last owners, Count Drašković and his family, are open as a museum, with furniture from different periods (Baroque, Rococo and Biedermeier), family portraits and antique weapons dating back to the 15th century.

More impressive and less crowded is the UNESCO-protected hilltop castle of Veliki Tabor, 40km (25 miles) north-west of Zagreb (www.veliki-tabor.hr; Apr-Sept 10am-5pm daily, Oct-Mar 9am-3pm daily; 20kn). This golden, pentagonal fortification dates back to the 12th century, with four semicircular towers added in the 15th. The three-level maze of galleries around the central courtyard contains knight armours, antique rifles and curios such as an 1883 chandelier from a transatlantic steamboat and the skull of Veronika Desinić, a peasant girl who, according to legend, was drowned and bricked up in the castle wall for falling in love with the castle owner's son. The castle hosts events from medieval battles to falcon hunting tournaments. Nearby, every July the Tuhelj thermal baths stage a **film festival** with DJ parties (www.taborfilmfestival.com). With the best view of the castle from the opposite hilltop, and traditional Zagorje specialities made with cottage cheese, **Grešna Gorica** (049 343 001, www.gresna-gorica.com) is a rustic restaurant also steeped in the Desinić legend. Its name means the Hill of Sin.

Another highlight is the open-air museum of Kumrovec, a village best known as the birthplace of Josip 'Tito' Broz. The **Old Village Museum** (www.mdc.hr/kumrovec; Apr-Sept 9am-7pm daily, Oct-Mar 9am-4pm daily; 20kn) shows the core of a reconstructed village, with peasant houses, farmsteads and the house where Tito was born.

Klanjec, a pretty little town by the Slovene border, contains the **Antun Augustinčić Gallery** (www.mdc.hr/augustincic; Apr-Sept 9am-5pm daily, Oct-Mar 9am-3pm Tue-Sun; 20kn); three exhibition rooms offer a chronological look at the career of this prolific sculptor. Look out for a replica of his most celebrated work, *Peace*; the original stands outside the UN building in New York.

Getting there & around

Due to the sporadic and unreliable public transport to and around **Zagorje**, a day trip from **Zagreb** to the castles and villages is only viable with a car or as part of a tour. Consult **Event Tours** (www.event.hr) or **Mystik Tours** (www.mystik-tours.hr) for details. For more information on Croatian castles and museums, visit www.mdc.hr.

VARAŽDIN

Varaždin is the cultural, economic and administrative centre of Hrvatsko Zagorje. It's a pretty, Baroque city, its skyline punctured by church towers, and its centre lined with pleasant parks and gardens. It celebrates its

Varaždin Castle.

800th anniversary in 2009, and to mark this, Varaždin is renovating its **National Theatre**, hosting the world handball championships and increasing the profile of its many cultural festivals. In 2008 the town's **Radar Festival** played host to Bob Dylan.

Historically, Varaždin was a fortress town, a stronghold against Turkish raids. It passed through the hands of several owners, including the aristocratic Erdődy family, until 1925. For a brief time in the 18th century, it was the capital of Croatia, hosting the Parliament (Sabor) and the Royal Croatian Council.

The city's pedestrianised Baroque centre has a noble feel about it. The 14th-century **Castle** (042 210 339, www.mdc.hr/varazdin; summer 10am-5pm Tue-Sun, winter 10am-3pm Tue-Sun; 20kn) houses the **City Museum**, with displays of arms, local crafts and furniture. **Varaždin Cathedral** (Pavlinska 5), built in 1647, is distinguished by its Baroque entrance and 18th-century altar. In between castle and cathedral, the **Town Hall**, built in 1523, hosts the changing of the guard every Saturday.

Where to eat

To dine in historic surroundings, head for the **Zlatna Guska** (Jurja Habdelića 4, 042 213 393), in the basement of the 350-year-old Zakmardy Palace. Both decor and dishes have historic themes. It's set in parkland by the National Theatre. In less ornate surroundings, **Cimplet** (Braće Radić 102, 042 206 101) serves veal steaks and freshwater fish, the chef using modern takes on traditional dishes. Among the many spots for pasta and pizza that you're bound to pass, the **Angelus** (A Stepinca 3, 042 303 868) is a typical example.

Where to drink

Daytime café culture thrives along **Gajeva** and around the open squares. In the evenings, options include **Aquamarin** (Gajeva 1, 042 311 868), with DJ events and drinks promotions. Proclaiming itself as 'Varaždin's first lounge bar', **Mea Culpa** (Ivana Padovca 1, 042 300 868) has a pleasantly modern interior and broad drinks menu. Across the square stands **Soho** (Trg Miljenka Stančića 1), which fancies itself as *the* place to be after dark.

Where to stay

Two hotels opened recently. Near the train station, the well priced **Varaždin** (Kolodvorska 19, 042 290 720, www.hotelvarazdin.com) comprises 27 neat rooms. The city-centre **Istra** (Ivana Kukuljevića 6, 042 659 659, www.istra-hotel.hr; 860kn-990kn double), inaugurated in 1911, has been completely renovated and is now a smart four-star with a restaurant. The **Pension Maltar** (Prešernova 1, 042 311 100, www.maltar.hr; 235kn-295kn single, 435kn-465kn double) is a popular option close to town.

Getting there & around

Buses from **Zagreb** (1hr 45mins) leave almost hourly. Regular **trains** take 2hrs 15mins.

Resources

Tourist information
Varaždin Tourist Office *Ivana Padovca 3 (042 210 987/www.tourism-varazdin.hr).* **Open** *Apr-Oct* 8am-6pm Mon-Fri; 9am-1pm Sat. *Nov-Mar* 8am-4pm Mon-Fri.

Istria

Istria.
See p111.

Istria

A magic triangle of truffles, wine and bucolic bliss.

Istria feels separate from the rest of Croatia. Christened 'Terra Magica' by the Romans, this small, triangular peninsula was Italian until World War II. Istria has its own, celebrated gastronomy, its own wines and olive oils. Nothing is ever far away, and inland is every bit as beautiful as the coast. You can spend the day at the coastal resorts of **Rovinj**, **Poreč** or **Novigrad** and dine luxuriously in the main town of **Pula**. Inland is dotted with timeless hilltop villages, **Grožnjan**, **Motovun**, **Hum**, and restaurants Italians cross the border to

savour. Oddities such as Tito's island menagerie of **Brijuni** or Mussolini's purpose-built mining village of **Raša**, make a fortnight here a varied and attractive proposition.

PULA

Pula is as urban as Istria gets. Although it's not the county town of Istria – that honour rests with **Pazin** – it is indisputably the region's commercial centre and home to almost half its population. For shopping, art or arrival by air, Pula is the place. What the town lacks in terms of attractive waterfront it more than makes up for in terms of antiquities.

The original **Roman Forum** remains the major meeting point with cafés offering outdoor tables. While the **amphitheatre**, locally known as the 'arena', continues to host events, Pula hopes to develop itself as a major cultural destination. Plans have been proposed to create a 'cultural ring' which would intersperse new, contemporary venues with the town's existing historical sites. There's even talk of establishing a Museum of Contemporary Art.

The city's sprawling waterfront includes a port handling close to one million tons of cargo every year, a marina for yachters, a forested stretch of beach with a promenade and, outside the centre, resorts, built in the 1960s and '70s in **Verudela** and neighbouring **Medulin**.

Pula amphitheatre.

ISTRIA

INSIDE TRACK
JAMES JOYCE

Not everyone falls for Pula. Former resident James Joyce hated it. He wintered here immediately after eloping with Nora Barnacle in 1904, writing desperate letters home comparing the place to Siberia. The house where he taught, near the Golden Gate, is now a café, the **Uliks** (Ulysses).

Sightseeing

As a mark of just how important the city was to the Romans, note that they built their sixth-largest amphitheatre here. Pula became a Roman colony a century after they first arrived in 177 BC. It produced wine and olive oil, and by the time of Augustus from 63 BC 'Pietas Iulia' was a thriving urban centre with a forum, temples and city walls.

Between Augustus and the Austrians, Pula diminished to a minor port of a few hundred citizens. The Habsburgs made 'Pola' their naval hub and centre for shipbuilding at the end of the 19th century. After passing into Italian hands, Pula was heavily bombed by the Allies in World War II, then industrialised again under Tito. Package tourism came in the 1970s.

Now slowly reviving, Pula is one of those rare coastal towns where life goes on in winter.

Sightseeing

The must-see attraction is, of course, the already mentioned **amphitheatre** (Flavijevska, 052 219 028; open summer 8am-7pm daily, winter 9am-5pm daily; 20kn). Set a short walk north of the city centre, its outer walls are remarkably preserved, and a wonderful backdrop for the film festival and big-name concerts that take place here every summer. Inside, however, is a bit of a mess of green plastic seating and clumps of stone, the view at the top of the sloping interior a disappointing one of the grass verge running to the harbour and crane after crane beyond. But you do get a sense of the gladiatorial contests held here until AD 400, particularly when you go down to the corridors on the sea-facing side where the lions were kept. Through a long tunnel lined with Roman masonry, you'll now find a few displays about olive oil production and a rather detailed map of Via Flavia, which connected Pula with Trieste. Outside is a modest souvenir shop with the same opening hours as the arena.

The second of the Roman attractions stands at the south-east entrance to the town centre. The **Arch of the Sergians**, or **Golden Gate**, was built in 30 BC. Its most notable aspects are the reliefs of grapes and winged victories on the inner façade. Passing through the arch and past the statue of James Joyce, marking where the author taught in 1904-05, you walk down the Roman-era high street, the Sergijevaca. It leads

Forum.

to the heart of Pula, the Roman **mosaic** and **Forum**, and **Temple of Augustus**. The mosaic dates to the second century AD and has geometric motifs representing the twins Amphion and Zethos. Alongside is the Forum, still the main square, today lined with cafés, the Town Hall, tourist office and, lining the far side, the six classical Corinthian columns of the

Temple of Augustus. Inside is a modest collection of Roman finds (052 218 689; open summer only, 9am-3pm daily; 10kn).

Pula's main two religious buildings, the Gothic-style **Franciscan Church** and the **cathedral**, a Renaissance façade built on a Roman temple, are set near the Forum, below the centrepiece **Fortress** (Kaštel).

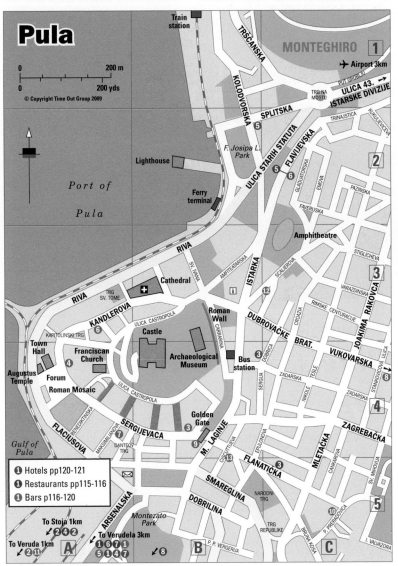

Pula

0   200 m
0   200 yds
© Copyright Time Out Group 2009

Train station

MONTEGHIRO 1

✈ Airport 3km

TRŠĆANSKA

KOLODVORSKA

SPLITSKA

PUT GROBLJA
TRG NA MOSTU
ULICA 43.
ISTARSKE DIVIZIJE

TRINAJSTICA

KUKULJEVIĆEVA

F. Josipa L. Park

ULICA STARIH STATUTA

FLAVIJEVSKA

GLADIATORSKA

EMONIA

PAZINSKA

2

Lighthouse

FAVERIJSKA

Port of Pula

Ferry terminal

Amphitheatre

STIGLICHEVA

RIVA

SV. IVANA

AMFITEATARSKA

ISTARKA

SCALIEROVA

VARAZDINSKA

3

RIVA

TRG SV. TOME

Cathedral

i

CROAZIA

RIMSKE CENTURACIJE

DUBROVAČKE

JOAKIMA RAKOVCA

KANDLEROVA

KAPITOLINSKI TRG

ULICA CASTROPOLA

Castle

Roman Wall

CARRARINA

BRAT.

VUKOVARSKA

Town Hall

Franciscan Church

Archaeological Museum

Bus station

DOBRICA

SERGIJA

ZADARSKA

NIKOLE TESLE

STANKOVIĆEVA ULICA

8

Augustus Temple

Forum

Roman Mosaic

ULICA CASTROPOLA

ZADARSKA

4

FLACIUSOVA

BENEDIKTINSKA

MAKSIMIJANOVA

SERGIJEVACA

Golden Gate

M. LAGINJE

CISCUTTIJEVA

EPULONOVA

FLANATIČKA

ZAGREBAČKA

MLETAČKA

CANKAROVA

SV. MIHOVILA

Gulf of Pula

DANTEOV TRG

❶ Hotels pp120-121
❶ Restaurants pp115-116
❶ Bars p116-120

SMAREGLINA

NARODNI TRG

DOBRILINA

Montezato Park

P. P. VERGERIJA

TRG REPUBLIKE

P. PRERADOVICA

BRUNA KOSA

10

5

I. VALVAZORA

To Stoja 1km
❷❹❷

To Verudela 3km

To Veruda 1km
❷❶⓫

A

❶❻❼❶
❺❶❹❼

❽

B

C

ISTRIA

Where the moment lasts

CROATIA | ROVINJ – VRSAR

Hotels & Resorts

Enter a world of comfort, service and style in Maistra hotels, magnificently situated in the wonderful and picturesque Mediterranean towns of Rovinj and Vrsar. The outstanding services, distinctive character of Croatian hospitality and superb facilities blend with the relaxed natural and unique historical environment making our hotels & resorts an ideal choice for leisure, short breaks, active holidays, Wellness & Spa or business.

maistra
ROVINJ-VRSAR

Tel: +385 (0)52 800 250
e-mail: info@maistra.hr
www.maistra.com

INSIDE TRACK
ITALIAN ISTRIA

From the early 1800s to World War II, Italian was Istria's official language. After Benito Mussolini came to power in 1922, many aspects of Croatian life were frowned upon or banned. Even today, many of the older locals still speak Italian, place names have an Italian equivalent and street signs are often dual language. After World War II, Tito saw the peninsula and key ports of Pula and Trieste as spoils of war. Trieste was controlled by the Americans as Zone A; Zone B inland was under Yugoslav authority. In 1954, the London Memorandum assigned Zone A to Italy and Zone B to Yugoslavia. A mass exodus to Italy then ensued. Tito attracted other Yugoslavs to the region by developing a tourist industry here in the 1960s.

Neither contain much of enormous interest. The Fortress, originally the Roman Capitol, was built by the Venetians in the 17th century; it houses the **Istrian Historical Museum** (Gradinski uspon 6, 052 211 566; open summer 8am-8pm daily, winter 9am-5pm daily; 10kn). Towards the old Roman wall is the worthwhile **Archaeological Museum of Istria**.

Anything else of interest lies south of the city centre, on or off the main Veruda road leading to the hotel hub and best beaches of Verudela. Halfway to the two nearest beaches, at Stoja and Valsaline, is the ornate, verdant **Naval Cemetery**, built by the Habsburgs, the perfect spot for a stroll on a hot summer's afternoon.

Archaelogical Museum of Istria

Carrarina 3 (052 218 603/www.mdc.hr/pula). Open *Summer* 9am-8pm Mon-Sat; 10am-3pm Sun. *Winter* 9am-2pm Mon-Fri. **Admission** 10kn. **No credit cards. Map** p113 B4.
Many of the best local Illyrian and Roman finds have been put on display at the Archaeological Museum of Istria, a three-storey traditional exhibition with good English-language documentation. You'll find jewellery, coins and weapons from Roman and medieval times, ceramics and fossils from pre-history, plus mosaics and sarcophagi. New finds mean that the halls are extended every so often.

Where to eat

Borghese

Monte Paradiso 21 (052 392 111). Open 11am-midnight daily. **Credit** AmEx, DC, MC, V. **Map** p113 A5 ❶

Reputable fish and seafood restaurant in Verudela with prices to match. Starched white tablecloths and napkins await the diner in an interior embellished with natural light. The fish is fresh and finely prepared, but don't miss out on the recommended starter of mixed salad with fruits de mer and speciality main dish of scampi ravioli.

Gina

Stoja 23 (052 387 943). Open 11am-11pm daily. **Credit** AmEx, DC, MC, V. **Map** p113 A5 ❷
Stone walls, polished wood and an Istrian-style fireplace create a cosy space for a family-run restaurant, where guests, and the food, get special attention. Along with fish and hearty meat dishes, the Istrian-style menu features seafood and pasta combinations, like ravioli stuffed with crab. The pasta and bread, are own-made. There's a qualified sommelier on the staff, and the wine list features about 60 mostly local choices, including many from Istria. Located just uphill from the seaside Lungomare promenade, near the forested peninsula of Stoja.

Kantina

Flanatička 16 (052 214 054). Open 8am-midnight daily. **Credit** AmEx, DC, MC, V. **Map** p113 C5 ❸
Hidden behind the main market, this lovely terrace restaurant serves Istrian delicacies in a converted Habsburg villa. The decor is contemporary, as is the careful presentation of the food. Truffles feature heavily, either with steak or, more traditionally, with *fuži*, Istrian pasta twists. There are plenty of greens, rocket particularly, some 40 types of wine and the cake selection is outstanding.

Milan

Stoja 4 (052 300 200/www.milan1967.hr). Open *Summer* 11am-midnight daily. *Winter* 11am-midnight Mon-Sat. **Credit** AmEx, DC, MC, V. **Map** p113 A5 ❹
One of the top three restaurants in town is set in a modern three-star hotel by the Naval Cemetery – both are friendly and family-run but the ground-floor restaurant is the biggest attraction. A display case heaves with riches fresh from the sea, duly listed on a long main menu. Most dishes are reasonably priced considering the quality on offer. Shellfish come in all types, although risotto portions are (in Croatian terms) quite small. Frog's legs with polenta is a speciality. For wine, you're literally spoilt for choice, as the cellar here has 700 examples, running up to 1,000kn a bottle. Let the waiter advise.

Scaletta

Flavijevska 26 (052 541 599). Open *Summer* 10.30am-11pm daily. *Winter* 10.30am-11pm Mon-Sat. **Credit** AmEx, DC, MC, V. **Map** p113 C2 ❺
Scaletta is two venues in one, a pavilion on one side of the main road up from the amphitheatre, and a dinky little dining room on the other, where you'll

ISTRIA

find its charming hotel, round the corner up a slight incline. Scaletta is a splendid option for its location – and its kitchen. A risotto Scaletta with fruits de mer is delicately seasoned with saffron and sprinkled with raisins. Steak comes with white truffles, lobster with Istrian noodles, *rezanci*. Malvazija and other Istrian tipples are the customary accompaniments, although you can order up an Erdinger wheat beer – Scaletta is German-owned.

▶ *For details on staying at the Scaletta, see p121.*

★ Valsabbion
Pješčana uvala IX/26 (052 218 033/www.valsabbion. net). **Open** *Feb-Dec* 10am-midnight daily. Closed Jan. **Credit** AmEx, DC, MC, V. **Map** p113 A5 ⑥

The best table in town and certainly one of the top five in Croatia. Attached to the high-quality hotel of the same name, Valsabbion comprises two dozen tables, half on a bay-view terrace under a bright white canopy, half in a tasteful, art deco interior of refined pastel colours. The food more than equals this establishment's international reputation, inventive and satisfying. If money is not an issue (how often do you dine at Valsabbion?), try the tasting menu of ten gourmet creations, perhaps truffle carpaccio or wild asparagus, all wonderfully presented. À la carte, locally sourced Kvarner Bay shrimps or Premantura crabs are teased with touches of greenery. The wine list is 200 strong.

▶ *For lodging information, see p121.*

Vela Nera
Pješčana uvala (052 219 209/www.velanera.hr). **Open** 8am-midnight daily. **Credit** AmEx, DC, MC, V. **Map** p113 A5 ⑦

Incongruously set next to a supermarket, but with a terrace overlooking the pretty Marina Veruda, this is Pula's second-most notable restaurant. Its modern, spacious interior is a refreshing change from the starched-white formal approach common elsewhere in town. Informal, too, are some of the combinations

adventurously thrown together. The salmon and whisky carpaccio as a cold starter, for example, or the peaches and champagne mingled with scampi in the house risotto. Dining partners can dip into the house fish platter or meat version. More than 100 wines to choose from too.

Vodnjanka
D Vitezića 4 (052 210 655). **Open** *Summer* 9am-11pm Mon-Sat. *Winter* 9am-5pm Mon-Sat. **No credit cards**. **Map** p113 B5 ⑧

This family-run restaurant is off the main drag, close to Rojc, popular with Pula's cultural movers and shakers. Note the waiter's multicoloured goatee. The food is great, based on traditional Istrian cuisine with lots of fresh fish and game. The must-try is the house aperitif: three herbal brandies, layered in a single glass and topped off with a lid of ice with a hole in the middle. Be prepared to wait at the bar if you're just dropping in.

Where to drink

Kn Bunarina
Verudela 9 (052 222 978). **Open** *Summer* 9am-midnight daily. *Winter* 9am- 9pm daily. **No credit cards**. **Map** p113 A5 ①

This local fishermen's bar is sited on the jetty of Bunarina. In high season tables cover every square inch as customers watch the boats or wait for a ferry to Fratarsko island. It serves food in season too.

Cabahia
Širolina 4 (no phone). **Open** 10am-midnight Mon-Sat; noon-midnight Sun. **No credit cards**. **Map** p113 A5 ②

Great spot for a summer evening, this, in the bar hub halfway between town and Verudela. A light Latin American theme runs through the leafy front garden and jumble-sale back room bar – Café do Brasil sacks, a Che Guevara flag and cocktail – although the beer is Slovenian Laško.

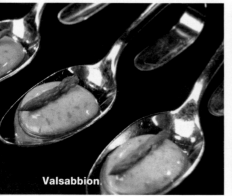

Valsabbion.

Caffè Uliks

Trg Portarata 1 (052 219 158). **Open**
6.30am-10pm daily. **No credit cards**. Map
p113 B4 ❸
The statue outside gives it away. A century ago
James Joyce taught at a school in this building by
the Roman arch. He and his eloper are also honoured
with a Joyce cocktail (Jameson's, Martini Bianco and
Krašokova pear) and a Nora of Bailey's, Bacardi and
cream. Other Irish drinks include bottled Guinness
and Kilkenny (and tasty Irish coffee) in this otherwise standard bar in a pedestrianised square.

Cvajner

Forum 2 (052 216 502). **Open** 8am-11pm daily.
No credit cards. Map p113 A4 ❹
Or to give it its official title, the Kunstkafe-Cvajner.
Either way, it's a splendid bar for the main square of
a tourist-swamped historic Roman town centre. Part
gallery, part junkshop, the Cvajner is bohemian in
appearance but not gratuitously so. Unmatching furniture, sculptures and an old carriage are placed
around a spacious, high-ceilinged interior where parts
of an old wall are dated AD 1928. Bottles of Chimay
and dark Laško complement the standard cocktails,
best partaken on the Forum terrace. *Photo p120.*

★ E&D

Verudela 22 (052 894 2105). **Open** *Summer*
9am-2am daily. *Winter* 9am-midnight daily.
No credit cards. Map p113 A5 ❺
Here you sit in a sculpted hilltop garden, with a
small pool and several levels of terrace seating,
enjoying fine views of the sea below while sipping
sunset cocktails or morning coffee. Located above
the Lungomare promenade, near a cluster of resort
hotels, this stunning café, spread amid greenery, can
get hopping from happy hour onward. In summer,
a full seafood menu at reasonable prices means you
don't have to decide whether to eat or drink. DJs spin
lounge and dance music on summer evenings. It's a
60kn taxi from town and worth every lipa.

Epidemija

Kandlerova 12 (no phone). **Open** 6am-midnight
Mon-Fri; 8am-midnight Sat, Sun. **No credit
cards**. Map p113 A3 ❻
The Union Pivo sign outside says 'Coco'. Ignore it.
The beer is Laško, the place is Epidemija and local
media types have been meeting here in a fug of cig-
arette smoke since it opened in 2004. By the cathedral, beneath the Fortress, it's a strange find but a
popular one for those in the know.

Mushroom Pub

Prolaz kod Zdenca 4 (052 210 686). **Open**
Summer 7am-2am daily. *Winter* 7am-midnight.
No credit cards. Map p113 A4 ❼
A mixture of alternative types, eternal students and
Hajduk Split fans keeps this charming terrace and
bar on an picturesque old-town square buzzing with

INSIDE TRACK VODNJAN

Vodnjan, 11km (seven miles) north of
Pula (bus No.22, 20mins), houses the
biggest church in Istria, **St Blaise** (052
511 420, open summer 9am-7pm Mon-
Sat, 2-7pm Sun, winter by reservation
only). Its main attraction lies in an area
curtained off behind the altar: mummified
bodies of three saints brought here from
Venice. There is a 35kn charge to see
them. There are also hundreds of saintly
relics in the sacristy (30kn).

a friendly vibe until late. It's a good place to catch
the game on TV or warm up before the clubs start
hopping– if you ever make it out of the bar, that is.

Old Friends

Vukovarska 33 (098 275 989 mobile). **Open**
7am-midnight Mon-Fri; 8am-midnight Sat;
10am-midnight Sun. **No credit cards**.
Map p113 C4 ❽
As the name suggests, this funky little pub, with a
baby grand piano suspended over the bar and a
colourful aquarium underneath it, started as a gath-
ering place for a group of friends. Those friends'
friends heard about it, and now there's a queue outside on Friday and Saturday nights. Squeeze in then
you can, as it's the ideal place to mingle with locals
in a sociable mood. Cool mix of eclectic music supplied by the charming and fun-loving bar staff, and
by DJs at weekends.

Opola Bistro

Trg Portarata 6 (052 210 322). **Open** *Summer*
8am-2am daily; *Winter* 8am-midnight daily.
No credit cards. Map p113 B4 ❾
On the first floor of a modern shopping centre downtown, this fashionable cocktail bar and restaurant is
a favourite spot for chilling out or starting a night on
the town. A decent seafood menu can be perused from
the balcony terrace, with its a view of the Golden Gate
arch and a busy square. A pleasing mix of new music
is supplemented with lounge DJs on weekend nights.
It's also a good call for breakfast or a snacky lunch.

P14

Preradovićeva 14 (052 382 987). **Open**
5pm-midnight daily. **No credit cards**.
Map p113 C5 ❿
Jozo Ćurković's wonderful little alternative haunt at
the far end of Flanatička attracts an arty clientele
for impromptu stand-up performances and one-off
events. Centrepieced by a snake-shaped bar table,
decorated with mushrooms and a lit-up globe, P14
is an address like no other downtown bar. Dark
Laško on draught and plenty of Istrian spirits from
the bar propped up by friendly regulars.

ISTRIA

Profile Brijuni: Tito's Xanadu

The islands in the sun that provided a home from home to politicians and tycoons.

The Brijuni archipelago lies off Istria's west coast, a 15-minute boat journey from Fažana, just north of Pula. Most of the 14 islands are off-limits to the public. Luckily, there is so much to see on the other two you're unlikely to feel hard done by.

Veliki Brijuni is the largest of the islands and contains the vast majority of its treasures. Beautiful and vaguely surreal – English country estate meets Jurassic Park – it consists of hectares of well-maintained, green parkland surrounded by the dazzling Adriatic and planted up with avenues of prehistoric-looking pines. This is where you'll find a golf course, a bird sanctuary, botanical gardens, the zoo and safari park, three museums and the main archaeological sites. A map of the islands is posted at its harbour – including details of where to find the dinosaur footprints that dot the island's shoreline.

The oldest remains of human habitation date from 3,000 BC. Built in the bay of Javorika, this Neolithic settlement is only one small part of over 40 hectares (100 acres) of archaeological sites contained on the islands. After 177 BC the Romans built villas and facilities for processing olive oil and the manufacture of amphorae. The last of their olive trees, dating from AD 400, still flourish on the main island. The largest Roman complex is sited in the bay of Verige. This impressive development includes a series of temples, thermal baths and a fish pond. It also included a working harbour that remained in use well into the sixth century.

Byzantium added fortified walls to the main Roman complexes, although these were breached in 788 by Frankish King Carlo the Great, who built his palace on the south-eastern corner of Verige, using the existing Roman sanitation and central heating.

In 1312, an outbreak of bubonic plague wiped out the population, so when the Venetians claimed the islands in 1331 there was no one there to resist. During this time, the area became marshy and a haven for mosquitoes. Brijuni had to wait until 1893 before it was rescued from its malaria-infested stupor, after Austrian steel magnate Paul Kupelwieser bought it as real estate. His dream was to create an English-style country park.

Renowned microbiologist Robert Koch was Kupelwieser's facilitator. In 1900 Koch was about to begin experiments into the eradication of malaria in Tuscany. The Austrian read about this in the newspapers and immediately contacted Koch, suggesting he carry out his preliminary research on Brijuni. It was a stroke of genius – and an unqualified success. In 1905 Koch was awarded the Nobel Prize for medicine. He had also succeeded in isolating the cholera and tuberculosis

bacteria. A carved monument erected in his honour stands by the harbour in Veliki Brijuni.

Kupelwieser excavated the archaeological treasures. He built villas, planted trees and landscaped gardens; he built continental Europe's first 18-hole golf course and he even established a zoo. In fact, Kupelwieser had created his own Xanadu but he died in 1918. Brijuni later passed into the hands of Mussolini's Italy.

After the war, the Brijuni archipelago, along with the rest of Istria, became part of Tito's Yugoslavia. The leader used Brijuni as his base, conducting diplomacy with the Non-Aligned Movement and inviting the world's rich and famous to his idyllic playground. As you step onto Veliki Brijuni's quayside you are following in the footsteps of Haile Selassie, Queen Elizabeth II, JFK, Sophia Loren – anyone who was anyone in the 1960s. You can see them documented in the 'Josip Broz Tito on Brijuni' exhibition housed in the main museum. Another, 'From the Memory of an Old Austrian', celebrates the vision and achievements of Kupelwieser.

Tito was regularly presented with exotic animals. As a result, the zoo on Veliki Brijuni continued to expand. You can still see many of the animals, including Indira Gandhi's elephants Sony and Lanka. Those who died were stuffed and placed in Brijuni's Natural History Museum, part of a three-museum complex near the harbour. There's a Tito exhibition next door.

The Brijuni National Park offices are on the quayside at Fažana. Here, you can book excursions plus yachting, golf and diving expeditions. The organised tour passes Veliki Brijuni's sights on a little train with an accompanying guide. It takes about four hours including the sea crossing from Fažana. Independent travellers can hire a bike or a little electric buggy. Lodging at a seaside villa here can be arranged via 052 521 367, www.brijuni.hr.

Cvajner. *See p117.*

ISTRIA

Podroom

Buducinova 16 (no phone). **Open** 9am-1am daily.
No credit cards. Map p113 A5 ⓫
One of the main candidate for taking the title for best
bar in Pula, the Podroom makes good use of its leafy
garden with a stone waterfall, plonking a bar in the
middle of it and seats all around. Inside, however, is
a bit of a mess – a picture of a woman with a fried
egg, a sign saying 'Harley Davidson Motorcycle
Club' – but a friendly, clubby vibe wins the day.
Plenty of 40kn cocktails too.

Rock Café

Scalierova 8 (052 210 975). **Open** *Summer*
8am-2am daily. *Winter* 8am-midnight daily.
No credit cards. Map p113 C3 ⓬
Aerosmith, Elvis, Boston, the Beastie Boys, prog and
metal classics rock the speakers of this 15-year-old
institution, a large two-room bar near the amphitheatre, dressed up in dark wood, old posters, music
memorabilia and murals with subjects like Jim
Morrison. A boisterous young crowd of locals neck
beers from the bottle, shoot pool, cruise the long bar
or roomy booths and sometimes break into dance.
Mirko, the enthusiastic owner, hosts Friday gigs,
jazz, blues and rock, mostly from Croatian combos.

Scandal Express

Ciscuttijeva 15 (052 212 106). **Open** 7am-
midnight Mon-Fri; 7am-2pm, 6pm-midnight Sat;
8am-2pm, 6pm-midnight Sun. **No credit cards.**
Map p113 B4 ⓭
Scandal Express is a tiny, smoky dive where the
local bohemians meet. You'll find it near the theatre
at the Giardini end of Flanatička. There's no room
whatsoever around the bar, so the regulars tend to
hug the corners by the entrance or, more usually,
spill out on to the narrow street.

Where to stay

Hotel Histria

Verudela (052 590 000/fax 052 214 175/
www.arenaturist.hr). **Rates** €180-€318 double.
Credit AmEx, DC, MC, V. **Map** p113 A5 ❶
Hotel Histria is a landmark four-star in the area,
commanding a view of Verudela Bay from the bank
facing the Valsabbion. All 240 simply furnished
rooms have sea-facing balconies. Facilities include
a circular outdoor pool, a heated indoor one – both
with seawater – a sauna, gym and disco, and there
are some 20 tennis courts and other sports pitches
nearby. It also has a casino and conference centre.
Although somewhat pricey considering the prosaic
nature of the rooms, the hotel's half-board rates are
a snip at €5 over the price of a room.

Hotel Milan

Stoja 4 (052 210 200/fax 052 210 500/
www.milan1967.hr). **Rates** 550kn-590kn single;
720kn-850kn double. **Credit** AmEx, DC, MC, V.
Map p113 A5 ❷
Situated by the Naval Cemetery before you get to
the Stoja headland, the Milan is best known for its
quality restaurant. Its dozen three-star rooms are
clean and comfortable, and within easy reach of the
modest beach at Valkane Bay.
▶ *For more details on dining here at one of the*
best restaurants in town, see p115.

Kn Hotel Omir

Sergija Dobrića 6 (052 210 614/fax 052 213
944). **Rates** 450kn single; 600kn double. **Credit**
AmEx, DC, MC, V. **Map** p113 B/C4 ❸
The Hotel Omir is a handy cheapie in the centre of
town, a Socialist-style guesthouse with old furnishings and light fittings, and a wonderfully weird

breakfast room that's decked out with art and an aquarium. There are 19 blissfully quiet rooms and a pizzeria downstairs.

▶ *If the Omir is full, then the Galija round the corner (052 383 802, www.hotel-galija-pula.hr) is in the same price bracket.*

Hotel Palma

Verudela (052 590 000/fax 052 214 175/www. arenaturist.hr). **Rates** €60-€122 double. **Credit** AmEx, DC, MC, V. **Map** p113 B5 ❹
The three-star Palma shares some of the facilities of the nearby Histria, particularly the 20 tennis courts. Guests have the use of three outdoor pools, one with a water slide, and a bowling alley. Rooms have balconies, although the hotel faces inwards away from the sea. Attractive half-board rates only add €3 to the price of a double. The Palma is open year round.

Kn Hotel Riviera

Splitska 1 (052 211 166/fax 052 219 117/www. arenaturist.hr). **Rates** €64-€84 double. **Credit** AmEx, DC, MC, V. **Map** p113 B2 ❺
Classic old Habsburg hotel whose grand façade and marble lobby belie the fact that its 65 rooms need renovation. It's in the Arena Turist hotel group, so, hopefully, this won't be too long in coming. In the meantime, it's a handy base if you're just in by train – the station is five minutes away – and want to see the amphitheatre and a few sights around town.

Hotel Scaletta

Flavijevska 26 (052 541 599/fax 052 540 285/ www.hotel-scaletta.com). **Rates** €55-€68 single; €84-€99 double. **Credit** AmEx, DC, MC, V. **Map** p113 C2 ❻
Conveniently located, German-run hotel and restaurant a short walk from the station from the amphitheatre. The dozen rooms (ten doubles, two singles) are all simple and comfortable, and a decent breakfast is included in the price.

Valsabbion

Pješčana uvala IX/26 (052 218 033/fax 052 222 991/www.valsabbion.net). **Rates** €178-€258 double. **Credit** AmEx, DC, MC, V. **Map** p113 B5 ❼
Ten immaculately conceived rooms comprise the hotel accommodation at the high-class restaurant Valsabbion. Half have sea-view balconies, but all are equipped with fine taste. Of the the rooms, six are doubles, with the remaining four providing suites of varying levels of space and refinement. The buffet breakfast is outstanding, although check to make sure the price is included in the rates when you're staying as this changes during the year. You could opt to pay more – about double the room rate – but include in the price a four-course dinner at one of Istria's finest restaurants. There's also a panoramic pool, fitness facilities and various beauty treatments.
▶ *For more details on dining here, see p116.*

Getting there & around

Pula **airport** (052 530 105, www.airport-pula.com) is six kilometres (3.5 miles) north-east of the city centre. A taxi from the airport costs about 200kn.

In summer there is a twice-weekly **fast-boat** ferry service connecting Pula with **Rimini** and **Venice**. You can find details at www.find-croatia.com/ferries-croatia. The only service within Croatia is a **car ferry** between **Zadar**, **Mali Lošinj** and Pula, from mid June to early September. It leaves Zadar five times a week at 6.30am, returning from Pula mid afternoon. The journey time is eight hours, foot passenger fare for Zadar–Pula about €15. For details see www.losinjska-plovidba.hr/Ljetni.htm.

The **train** station is north on Kolodvorska, which is about a ten-minute walk from the centre of town. A service from **Zagreb** runs four times a day, journey time about seven hours, with a bus between **Rijeka** and **Lupoglav**. There is also a daily service with **Ljubljana** (4hrs).

Pula has two **bus stations**, one in the city centre at Istarska, the other north-east of the Roman amphitheatre at Trg Istarske Brigade (052 502 997). There are daily international services from **Trieste** and **Venice** and a summer one from **Milan**. There are buses every hour from Zagreb and regular ones from the main towns in Istria. Details are at www.pulainfo.hr/en/autobus.asp. Bus firm **Pulapromet** (www.pulapromet.hr) runs services to **Vodnjan**, **Premantura** and **Medulin** as well as ones within town. Buses for **Stoja** (No.1) and **Verudela** (Nos.2a and 3a) leave every 20 minutes (15mins). Nearly all stop at both stations in town. There is a **taxi** office by the Roman wall at Carrarina (052 223 228, 098 715 230 mobile).

INSIDE TRACK NIGHTLIFE

With downtown closing early, nightlife is limited to trendy bars in Veruda and mainstream clubs north-east of the centre. The best is **Aruba** (Šijanska cesta 1), with a bar outdoors and packed two-room disco inside. The more intimate and central **Mimosa** (Vukovarska 13, 098 963 6171 mobile) is a busy rock bar with a stage for local acts in the back room. **Club Uljanik** (Dobrilina 2, 098 285 969 mobile, www.clubuljanik.hr) by the harbour has a good pedigree of alternative bands and DJ nights, as does **Rojc** (Gajeva, www.rojcnet.hr).

ISTRIA

Resources

Tourist information
Pula Tourist Office *Forum 3 (052 219 197/
www.pulainfo.hr)*. **Open** 8am-8pm Mon-Sat;
9am-8pm Sun.

MEDULIN

Medulin is Pula's playground. With 70km
of indented coastline and the region's one
and only sandy beach, this southern tip of the
peninsula is Istria's most heavily developed
tourist destination. Much was built for the mass
markets of the 1970s but if watersports and
family-based beach activities are what you're
after, then head south 7km from Pula.

Sightseeing

Medulin, the main town and administrative
centre, combines with nearby **Pomer**,
Premantura, **Ližnjan** and **Banjole** to
comprise the **Medulin Riviera**. Still a working
fishing port, the old centre of Medulin remains
quaint and picturesque with alleyways winding
between tall, Venetian-style buildings and a
central piazza housing the tourist information
office, post office and the **Church of St
Agnes**. There's a slightly hair-raising one-
way system to help negotiate traffic through
the maze of impossibly narrow streets.

Medulin prides itself on its sports facilities.
There are eight tennis courts right on the
shore; three volleyball courts; six grass
football pitches; track and field facilities, and
mapped-out cycling routes. Add to this six
diving schools, two equestrian centres and a
sports centre for parasailing, water-skiing, jet-
skiing, beach canoeing and sea kayaking, and
you can see why Medulin is a popular training
destination for European athletes. Sailing and
windsurfing are also popular pastimes. Centres
include **Shark Diving** (Autokamp Meduline,
052 894 274, www.diving-shark.hr),
Premantura Windsurfing at the Hotel
Belvedere (Stupice, 091 512 3646 mobile) and,
for horse riding, **Ranch Lunge** (Fucane 9, 052
576 106, www.ranchlunge.com) in Medulin.

Medulin's long, sandy beach, **Bijeca**,
includes waterslides and is a magnet for young
families. Many head for the islands of **Ceja**
and **Levan** in Medulin Bay, reached by regular
ferry. Other small islands are served by water
taxis, if you prefer more secluded sunbathing.

Until recently, Premantura was a sleepy little
fishing village. Sat opposite Medulin, a far cry
from the busy beaches across the water, its little
coves offer secluded, if rocky, access to the sea,
its shady pines protection from the midday sun.
Such splendour could not go unnoticed and

Medulin.

pretty soon there was a private building
boom. Although the tiny centre remains largely
unchanged, Premantura has burgeoned around
its outskirts with modern holiday apartments
and hacienda-type private houses.

In the village are the usual amenities plus a
tall, stone belltower which stands alone, right
in the centre, acting as an unmarked mini-
roundabout. Premantura is also the gateway to
Kamenjak, the protected tip of southern Istria.

Where to eat

★ Batelina
Čimulje 25, Banjole (052 573 767). **Open**
5-11pm daily. **No credit cards**.
Batelina is generally acknowledged to be one of the
best fish restaurants in Istria – reserve days in
advance. If you're dropping in on spec, do so early.
The owner is a professional fisherman and the menu
depends entirely on what he and his friends managed
to land that morning, don't expect a set menu. It's a
small venue with only 26 covers, with seats outside
in summer. Try the mixed marinated fish as a starter,
small portions of half-a-dozen types including crab,
sardines and tuna. A three-course meal, with wine,
will cost about 450kn a head. No lunchtime service.

Kn Konoba Ankora
Selo 144, Premantura (052 575 642). **Open**
10am-10pm daily. **No credit cards**.
The only konoba in Premantura to serve cheap
cooked daily lunches, this place fills with the locals
all year round. It's cheap and cheerful, with a large
terrace complete with a barbecue and old anchors.

▶ *Another cheap place to eat, and right on the harbour, is the Konoba Mi/erija (Brajdine 106, 052 526 711).*

Konoba Stare Užance

Premantura 127A (052 575 163). **Open** 5-11pm daily. **No credit cards.**

Inside an old stone house in Premantura, a young couple pamper a few lucky guests every evening. With only four tables indoors and precious few more in the garden, making a reservation is essential if you want to ensure a place. Sanja and Sandro Frančula strive to give customers the best an Istrian-style konoba can provide. It's an informal restaurant with hearty fare, including truffles with bacon or cheese; local *pršut*; manestra bean soup; and *supa*, a *bukleta* jug of warm red wine, toast, pepper, olive oil and sugar. Fresh seafood includes fish grilled over a fire, cuttlefish and octopus salads.

Where to stay

Hotel Arcus

Burle, Medulin (052 529 100/fax 052 529 101/www.arcus.hr). **Rates** €50-€116. **Credit** MC, V.

This year-round new-build makes a nice change from the usual block. It's smaller in scale, with only 84 rooms, sited right on the seashore opposite Medulin's main promenade. Facilities include an indoor pool, gym, aromatherapy and massage.

Hotel Medulin

Fucane, Medulin (052 572 001/fax 052 576 017/www.arenaturist.hr). **Rates** €90-€163. **Credit** AmEx, DC, MC, V.

Medulin's only four-star has 178 rooms and 12 suites on four floors. The Yugo architecture may not be inspirational but the rooms are big and clean, with air-con throughout. On the sea, 10km from Pula.

Getting there & around

Local **bus** company **Pulapromet** serves **Premantura** and **Medulin** from **Pula**, Nos.25 and 26 leaving roughly every 20 minutes. Call 052 223 228 for a local **taxi**.

INSIDE TRACK
LOCAL LODGING

Medulin's accommodation comprises small, private flats and large, 1970s resort complexes, reflecting the cheap and cheerful mass tourism focus. Be aware that, being so close, Pula and Medulin are considered interchangeable when it comes to hotels, so if you want to stay in Medulin, check the address.

Resources

Tourist information

Medulin Tourist Office *Centar 223 (052 577 145/www.istria-medulin.com).* **Open** *Summer* 8am-9pm daily. *Winter* 8am-4pm Mon-Fri.

ROVINJ

Perhaps the showiest resort settlement in Istria, **Rovinj** manages to maintain a meticulously cared-for old quarter and extensive tourist amenities without feeling fake or overdone. The natural setting is stunning: a harbour nicknamed 'the cradle of the sea' by ancient mariners because the archipelago of islands, stretching from here to **Vrsar**, ensured calm, untroubled waters. The man-made structures in the Old Town are also attractive: tightly clustered old houses, painted in cheery Venetian reds and Habsburg pastels, connected by cobbled streets barely wider than a footpath.

Sightseeing

These attractions, combined with shaded, rocky beaches, have been bringing in groups of tourists since 1845, when a steamship line from Trieste stopped here. And yet tourism has not overwhelmed Rovinj or closed the local fishing trade, which still brings fresh catches to its excellent restaurants. Traditions are celebrated – hence the recently opened multi-media museum dedicated to the local *batana* fishing boat, Batana House. Rather than overdevelop, Rovinj has sought to retain its old charm – a charm for which tourists pay a premium. This is one of Croatia's nicer, and pricier, resort towns.

Before World War II, this was an Italian resort, and the large Italian community, which includes many restaurateurs, encourage an emphasis on fine dining and good living. Rovinj has been settled since at least the seventh century, when it was an island centred around a low, cone-shaped hill sticking out of the sea. The populace overflowed to the mainland, and in 1763 Habsburg engineers attached Rovinj Island to the rest of Croatia, turning it into a peninsula. The hill still defines the shape of the mostly car-free Old Town, and an easy stroll up the spiralling road to the top affords views of surreal beauty.

Sightseeing

Some of the best panoramic views are from the **Cathedral of St Euphemia** (10am-2pm, 3-6pm daily), which caps the hilltop. This Baroque structure was built in 1736 to house the remains of Euphemia, a virgin martyr, who

ISTRIA

INSIDE TRACK NIGHTLIFE

In high season, the Medulin Riviera is party central. The harbour Riva is full of people, bar terraces fill and locals prepare for a night at one of the big discos: **Joy** in Premantura; **Dali**, or the **Imperial** (Fucane 72, 098 193 8984 mobile, www.disco-imperial.com) in Medulin.

was fed to the lions by Emperor Diocletian around 304. Legend says her massive stone coffin disappeared from Constantinople and miraculously floated ashore in Rovinj, providing a fishing town with a catch from heaven and a patron saint. St Euphemia's tomb and relics can be seen inside the cathedral.

Other sights worth spotting in town are the open-air **market** and the **City Museum** (Trg maršala Tita 11, 052 816 720, www.muzej-rovinj.com; open summer 9am-noon, 7-10pm Tue-Sun, winter 9am-1pm Tue-Sat; 15kn), next to the **Balbi Arch**, the original town gate. The museum has some historical exhibits as well as contemporary art. Rovinj has a reputation as a home for artists – and galleries. **Grisia**, a stone-paved thoroughfare leading up to the cathedral, is packed with galleries and ateliers, selling crafts, kitsch and amateur seascapes. In summer, most spill on to the pavement. Every August, in a festival of outdoor shows, anyone selling art can set up shop here.

Batana House

Obala P Budičina 2 (052 805 266/www.batana. org). **Open** *June-Sept* 10am-3pm, 5-10pm daily. *Oct-Dec, Mar-May* 10am-1pm, 3-5 pm daily. Closed Jan, Feb. **No credit cards**.

This is surely the Mediterranean's first multimedia museum dedicated to a fishing boat. The vessel in question is the *batana*, the traditional wooden boat of the Rovinj region. Still very much in use today, the *batana* is a living symbol of Rovinj culture. A modern exhibition, the museum uses film, music and interactive exhibits. It provides a taste of the local lifestyle with guides in traditional costumes and creative workshops where you can try your hand at making fishing nets or demijohns.

Where to eat

Amorfa

Obala Alda Rismondo 23 (052 816 663). **Open** 11am-midnight daily. **Credit** AmEx, DC, MC, V.

The Amorfa, right on the harbourside, is one of the pricier places in town. The slick service and the decor, which includes an indoor goldfish pond and a nicely appointed terrace decked in white tablecloths, help make your meal more of an event. The

dishes include hearty portions of excellently prepared seafood standards, along with a few special items, like salted sea bass.

▶ *For something rather cheaper to eat, try Toni (Driovier 3, 052 815 303), a mid-range, checked-tablecloth joint.*

★ Blu

Val de Lesso 9 (052 811 265). **Open** *Summer* noon-10pm daily. **Credit** AmEx, MC, V.

Starter, swim, main, swim, dessert, swim. Yes, Blu has a great location, best enjoyed over a long, long lunch. Always among locals, tourists in the know and day-trippers from Zagreb. Peruse the menu over a glass of Malvazija and home-made thin pizza-style bread with rosemary, sea salt and award-winning olive oil produced a few miles away. Food is sensibly fish and seafood-based and ranges from a simple seafood spaghetti for a very reasonable 70kn through to scallops with truffles and polenta, or sea bass with caviar and saffron. Simple roast fish with potatoes is also available and great shared among a table of four. Prices are less than you'd imagine considering the quality and view across the sea to Rovinj's Old Town. Inside, evening dining is a little more formal, around an old Roman garden. *Photo p126.*

Calisona

Trg na mostu 4 (052 815 313). **Open** 8am-midnight daily. **Credit** AmEx, MC, V.

Just beyond the Balbi Arch is a small square where a large awning covers a relaxing terrace serving sophisticated seafood. Along with Istrian standards like fetuccine with truffle, lobster with tagliatelle and succulent fresh grilled fish, there are creative offerings such as squid stuffed with scampi, Dalmatian-style octopus salad, and sole in Chardonnay. Meat includes steak, a grilled platter for two and *ražnjici*, a spiced Balkan-style pork kebab.

★ Enoteca Al Gastaldo

Iza Kasarne 14 (052 814 109). **Open** 11am-3pm, 6-11pm daily. **No credit cards**.

INSIDE TRACK BEACHES

In town, there is a small busy beach area in front of the Hotel Rovinj. For the pine-forested beaches on the fringes, you'll need sandals to wade on the jagged shore, but the lack of sand means the sea is incredibly clear, great for snorkelling or diving. Head south of town, past the marina and the Hotel Park, to the area of Monte Mulini and the wooded peninsula of Zlatni Rt. The walk along the water is a little more than a kilometre from town. There is a cluster of resorts here, but it's uphill, so the beaches are mostly quiet.

Excellent seafood is served amid a cosy, romantic clutter of antiques and old paintings, around an Istrian-style fireplace used for cooking. This friendly, family-run restaurant on a quiet corner of the Old Town is not the cheapest, but it's perfect for that special meal. Fresh shellfish, sole, quality catch of the day and lobster are dressed in superior sauces, made from ingredients like truffles, or a simple-but-sublime mix of garlic and basil with top-quality olive oil. Istrian specialities include fine seafood pastas, meat dishes baked in a clay oven and sausages.

Giannino
Augusto Ferri 38 (052 813 402). **Open** 11am-3pm, 6-11pm daily. **Credit** AmEx, DC.
Popular restaurant by the Old Town draws repeat customers with its Italian cuisine. The menu is dominated by fresh catches from Rovinj's fishermen, but the sauces, and the pastas, have an Italian influence. Seafood and pasta meet in great dishes like noodles *mare monti* or rigatoni with lobster, a very Istrian recipe. Local ingredients get shown off in tempting offerings like sole with truffles.

★ La Puntulina
Sv Križa 38 (052 813 186). **Open** noon-3pm, 6pm-midnight daily. *Cocktail bar* 6pm-2am daily. **No credit cards**.
Perched on a drop above the sea, this family-run establishment puts a gourmet Italian touch into local cuisine. La Puntulina starts with the same fresh

---

INSIDE TRACK ISLAND HOPS

The most popular excursions are to nearby **St Katarina Island** and dazzling **Crveni otok** (Red Island), both a short hop by taxi boat from the main harbour. Each has a hotel but offers enough secluded cover to warrant the 10kn-20kn return journey.

---

ingredients sold around town, but here dishes stand out through creative sauces and a careful mix of flavours. The fish fillet Puntulina, with a delicately spiced tomato sauce, the scallops in brandy, the local squid in polenta and the fish carpaccio all provide exciting ways to enjoy fresh seafood. Get the table nearest the window for a sea view and afterwards go downstairs to the cocktail bar, with a stunning secluded terrace on the sea.

Trattoria Dream
Joakima Rakovca 18 (052 830 613). **Open** 11.30am-10pm daily. **Credit** AmEx, DC, MC, V.
On a bustling Old Town side street just in from the harbour, this place tries very hard, and mostly succeeds. The food is good, the service is friendly, but prices are not cheap, especially for wine. The pretty interior, with a working fireplace and a skylight, has charming furniture. There is an impressive variety

ISTRIA

Rovinj.

INSIDE TRACK
ROVINJ MARKET

Trg Valdibora hosts a hectic open-air market (open 7am-4pm daily) selling the day's catch and local produce. The array of fresh seafood is almost reason enough to go self-catering. Browsing is great fun and there are plenty of items you can take with you: home-made grappa, wine and lavender oil. By 1pm, many fresh-food vendors go, leaving souvenir shops hawking knick-knacks made from shells, Croatian-flag beach towels, paintings, postcards and other non-essentials.

of seafood, including salted sea bass, salmon, tuna and frogfish, and all is cooked with care. The fresh bass is remarkably tender, with a delicate flavour.

Veli Jože
Sv Križa 1 (052 816 337). **Open** 10am-1pm daily. **Credit** AmEx, DC, MC, V.
Istrian-style dishes flavour the menu of this quaint spot near the harbour with a high-ceilinged interior crammed with antiques and seagoing kitsch. There is seating for 50 on a pavement terrace. Specialities include shellfish lasagne, crab with truffles, cod in white wine and baked lamb with potatoes.
▶ *Another harbour cheapie is Neptun (Joakima Rakovca 10, 052 816 086), rustic and friendly.*

Where to drink

★ Caffè Cinema
Trg Brodogradili 16 (no phone). **Open** 7am-midnight Mon-Fri, Sun; 7am-1am Sat. **No credit cards**.
A trendy terrace adds a touch of class to this busy corner of the harbour and draws a sizeable, mixed crowd. The spacious, dramatic black-and-white interior is dedicated to great films, with stills from old classics and a life-sized Alfred Hitchcock doing his cameo in the bathroom mirror. Behind the long bar is an oversized clock and, most often, a smiling face. Music, ranging from pop to electronic to hip hop, generally has a fast beat. A fun spot.

Valentino
Sv Križa 28 (052 830 683). **Open** 11am-1am daily. **No credit cards**.
Pricey cocktail bar at the end of the harbour has fab outdoor seating on a terrace a few feet over the sea. Step off the street, lose the crowds and commune with nature, your cocktail and your companion.

Viecia Batana
Trg maršala Tita (091 539 9172 mobile). **Open** 7am-1am daily. **No credit cards**.

Popular with locals for breakfast or the early evening drink, this bar's terrace has a sunny southern exposure facing the busy harbourside square by the Hotel Adriatic and the sea beyond. Although the neighbouring bars share the view, they're never quite as full. Your coffee may take a minute longer, but it will arrive with a smile.

Zanzibar
Obala Pina Budičina (052 813 206). **Open** 11am-1am daily. **No credit cards**.
Big, loungey wicker chairs with bright red cushions surround low drinking tables on the terrace of this popular cocktail bar near a busy section of the harbour. At happy hour, tables fill with people here to gawp at people or the gorgeous sunsets over the sea. Inside, the DJs encourage you to hang around for the rest of the night, a pricey proposition with cocktails running at 60kn plus.

Nightlife

Monvi Entertainment Centre
Luja Adamovića, Monvi, south of the marina at the resort area (052 545 117/www.monvi center.com). **Open** *Summer* 11am-4am daily. *Winter* see website.
This large complex has several bars, a pizzeria, a Mexican restaurant, an amphitheatre for live music, and a huge, air-conditioned dancefloor packed with young tourists and locals all year. This has become a major stop for touring bands or DJs, and on summer

Blu. *See p124.*

nights the club can get some serious talent – on the decks and on the dancefloor. The collection of bars can feel a bit shopping mallish, but as the evening wears on, there's a sense of security in knowing there are about a half-a-dozen places to slip away for a drink and a chat. The club is south of town, near the big resort hotels but far enough away for everything to go on all night.

Where to stay

Hotel Adriatic

Obala Pina Budičina 2 (052 815 088/fax 052 813 573/www.maistra.hr). **Closed** mid Oct-Mar. **Rates** €65-€108 single; €188-€288 double. **Credit** AmEx, DC, MC, V.

Simple three-star on the harbour lets 27 rooms in a central location for mid-range rates. Although it's the oldest hotel in town, built a century ago, the large, basic rooms are in good shape. The hotel's pleasant terrace café is one of many along the busy harbour. The noise from here can be a bit of a problem in sea-view rooms, but this is a great place for couples and anyone looking for fun in town.

★ Hotel Istria

Sv Andrea (052 802 500/fax 052 813 484/ www.maistra.hr). **Closed** Jan-mid Mar. **Rates** €57-€108 single; €170-€264 double. **Credit** AmEx, DC, MC, V.

Many high-end hotels today in Croatia have spa facilities – none occupies a whole island. St Andrew's, referred to as Crveni otok, or Red Island, houses this four-star hotel complex of 376 rooms (plus 50 at the nearby Park Hotel), four restaurants, three bars and three pools. A beach is within 50 metres, while activities include yachting, windsurfing and football on a real pitch. As for the spa, there's relaxation and recharge massages, whirlpools indoor and out, Turkish and Finnish saunas and Kneipp baths. All is set amid lush greenery, the interior imbued with relaxing scents and colours.

★ Hotel Monte Mulini

A Smareglia (052 636 000/fax 052 636 001/ www.maistra.hr). **Rates** €310-€646 double. **Credit** AmEx, DC, MC, V.

INSIDE TRACK GAY ROVINJ

Although Rovinj's gay bar and separate gay disco closed in 2007, the town is still known as a gay-friendly destination. The nude beaches at **Polari Bay** and adjacent **Cape Eve**, 3km (two miles) south of town, have a reputation as a meeting place and are ideal for casual socialising. The 13 small islands here have thick forests surrounded by beach.

INSIDE TRACK BAR HOPS

The cafés at the north-west end of Rovinj harbour, such as the cocktail bar in **La Puntulina**, **Valentino** or the **Zanzibar**, are great places for sundowners. After dark, the best bar crawl is in the tiny streets at the bend of Obala Alda Rismondo and in Joakima Rakovca, a little street near the harbour; don't miss **Buzz** (No.5), **Hannibal** (No.36) or the **Rock Café** Roxy (No.15). **Rio** (Obala Alda Rismondo 13) provides the ideal bookend to a night out.

The big hotel opening in Medulin during the 2008 season was this five-star makeover, with two gourmet restaurants and 119 rooms (including ten suites) reconfigured and refurbished by top designers. All the rooms, which are fitted with bespoke furniture, have balconies – the Hotel Monte Mulini brushes up to a rocky beach with natural shade from nearby greenery so there's something to look out onto from your balcony. The comprehensive sports facilities include four indoor clay tennis courts, a basketball court, a bowling alley and gym. There are pools indoor and out, plus a spa and all the massage and beauty treatments imaginable.

★ Hotel Villa Angelo d'Oro

Via Švalba 38-42 (052 840 502/fax 052 840 111/www.rovinj.at). **Closed** Sept-mid Mar. **Rates** €85-€136 single; €138-€242 double. **Credit** AmEx, DC, MC, V.

Rovinj's other five-star is in a beautifully restored old building on the site of a 17th-century bishop's palace. The location, along a narrow, winding stone-paved street halfway up the hill that defines Rovinj's Old Town, is both quiet and central. The lobby, the museum-quality stairway and the individually styled rooms all ooze antique opulence. The garden café, hidden from the street by ancient stone walls, and the sheltered rooftop loggia, with its beautiful sea views, provide stunning sanctuary. The 'wellness area' includes a sauna, jacuzzi and solarium. It has a superb seafood restaurant worth visiting even if you're not staying and a wine cellar where you can arrange tastings. Only 24 rooms, so book early.

Getting there & around

There are regular **bus** services from **Zagreb** and **Pula**, which is the site of the nearest airport. The bus station is at **Trg na Lokri**, a short walk east of the Old Town. For a **taxi**, call 052 811 100.

From late June to mid September, Tirrenia (www.tirrenia.it) runs a fast boat from **Trieste** every day but Monday at 8am (3-4hrs). Three times a week it continues to Brijuni.

ISTRIA

Profile Touring Istria's Top Tables

The best places to eat are often tucked away off the beaten track.

Inland Istria is a haven for gastrophiles. Some of the most inventive cuisine in Croatia is to be had in a one-horse town where a particular chef has decided to set up shop and create to his heart's content.

A classic example is **Konoba Morgan** near Buje, up in the north-west corner of Istria near the Slovene border. It's not signposted, but you take the main road out of Buje, then a track on the left-hand side about 1km (half a mile) before Brtonigla. Morgan (Bracanija 1,052 774 520; closed mid Sept-mid Oct; open mid Oct-mid Sept 11am-10pm daily) is often busy with Italians who travel to eat here on a regular basis. Marko Morgan, the young restaurateur, produces excellent but simple dishes based on authentic Istrian recipes. The top-quality ingredients are all sourced locally and attention to detail predominates. The process involves the whole family, Morgan senior hunting the wide selection of game, mother and sister working in the kitchen. Specialities include home-made polenta with game (rabbit, pheasant, wild boar, venison or quail); pasta stuffed with chestnut purée; and *krestine*, red pasta filled with white, cockerel meat. Morgan also places great emphasis on blending the right wine with the right food. The restaurant has some of the region's finest vintages including almost-forgotten varieties like Plavina and Hrvatica.

Morgan is pleasingly unpretentious. After hours, he might play piano for his guests, perhaps on the large, covered terrace. The view is relaxing although the surroundings are somewhat ramshackle. Note the dilapidated farm building with its Communist red star

From the top: Zigante, Konoba Morgan, Konoba Morgan, Vrh, Konoba Astarea.

still precariously perched on top of the roof.

As for his name, it's not uncommon in this part of Istria. Legend has it that the infamous pirate Captain Henry Morgan hid from his pursuers in the Limski Kanal and was happy to fraternise with the womenfolk.

A short drive away, **San Rocco** (Srednja ulica 2, 052 725 000, www.san-rocco.hr) in Brtoniglia is a hotel and restaurant. For lodging, you won't do better – the San Rocco has won Best Small Hotel in Croatia two years running, in 2007 and 2008. A dozen beautifully furnished rooms are ranged around a spa, two pools, a wine shop, wine cellar and, best of all, a restaurant. It's the perfect base for any gastronomic tour. You can enjoy a massage, swim, then tuck into superb fish and truffle-flavoured dishes prepared with San Rocco's own-made olive oil. Proximity to the sea means that the fish here is wonderfully fresh – meat often dominates menus further inland. Accompanying wines will be carefully chosen – Brtoniglia is known as the City of Wine.

If San Rocco provides a satisifying if formal dining experience, more modest but entirely pleasurable meals can be had in the same locality, at Anton Kernjus and family's **Konoba Astarea** (Ronkova 9, 052 774 384). The fish soup here is outstanding and the meat is cooked over an open fire in the corner. There are *peka* dishes too, this slow-cooking method known as *ripnja* in Italian-influenced Istria. Anton is happy to talk you through the menu.

Mention must also be made of the famous **Zigante** truffle restaurant in Livade near Motovun (052 664 302, www.zigantetartufi.com), where white-gloved staff serve a moneyed clientele in a spot made famous by the discovery of the world's biggest truffle in 1999.

For something somewhat less showy, **Marino**, halfway between Momjan and Buje (Kremenje 96B, 052 779 047, www.konoba-marino-kremenje.hr, closed Tue, Jan, no credit cards) is run by Marino Markezić. Also a leading wine producer – his family winery Kabola has been in operation since 1891 – Markezić is an aficionado of the Slow Food movement. His small, superbly conceived menu takes full advantage of the area's fresh produce. Autumn brings game and the pungent white truffles for which Istria is famous – they even garnish the signature

warm, chocolate cake at the close of the meal. If you're here out of season, Marino's head chef Marko Rastović produces excellent dishes using the preserved variety.

Finally, **Vrh** (052 667 123, closed Mon, no credit cards) near Buzet provides classic Istrian cuisine of a consistently high quality. The menu includes standards such as gnocchi with game goulash or truffles, steak with truffles, as well as home-made sausages. There are pleasant surprises, such as pasta *fuži* fillings of forest mushrooms and wild asparagus. The nettle paté is particularly good too. Host Nevio Petohlep produces the house wine, including Malvasija Frizante, a bubbly variety with a Napoleonic legend attached to it. Vrh is signposted 2km (1.25 miles) down the road from Motovun to Butoniga – take the left-hand turn.

MANESTRA
If you're after a hearty soup, plump for *manestra*. *Manestra* used to be passed from house to house to ensure that the whole village shared in the dish.

ISTRIA

Resources

Tourist information

Rovinj Tourist Office *Obala P Budičina 12 (052 811 566).* **Open** *mid June-mid Sept* 8am-9pm daily; *mid Sept-mid June* 8am-3pm Mon Sat.

VRSAR

Vrsar is like Istria in miniature: a medieval hill-top town perched above a stunning natural harbour with its own mini-archipelago of islands and sited at the mouth of the beautiful **Limski kanal**. This is the Istrian town that Casanova fell in love with and you can understand why. In its historical heyday, Vrsar was influential as seat of the Poreč bishopric.

Right at the top of the town is the 12th-century Romanesque **Bishop's Palace**. Largely unspoiled, Vrsar's Venetian-style architecture lines a maze of narrow streets – reminiscent of Istria's inland towns such as Motovun. This is the main residential area and, although there's lots to see you will find only one café-bar, **Papilion** (Porečka 2, 052 441 892) and even this is closed in winter. Intimate and atmospheric, this is where locals recommend taking a first date. Failing that, it's a great place for soaking up historical vibes. Nearly all the social action takes place down below on the main waterfront, Obala maršala Tita, site of the larger restaurants and bars.

Vrsar has a different feel to its larger neighbours. The natural landscape is more in evidence and the atmosphere more genteel and less frenetic. For action, you usually head to Rovinj or Poreč.

INSIDE TRACK
LIMSKI KANAL

One of Istria's most dramatic natural phenomena, the Limski kanal drives a narrow 10km sliver of sea into the peninsula. Densely forested cliffs rise straight up to a height of 150m, with calm, green water below. As a protected area, sailing in the kanal is restricted but you can take private guided boat trips from Rovinj or Vrsar. Operators in Vrsar harbour provide two-hour trips of around 100kn per head. There are five-hour excursions with a picnic which also take in the islands – cost around 180kn. Check with **Excursions Mikela** (091 5769 382 mobile, www.vitontours.hu). There's a viewing platform by the main road.

Vrsar, therefore, has dug up something different. **Montraker** is a large, abandoned stone quarry on the main beach at the edge of town. Already known for its sculpture summer schools, this site stages an ongoing beach party throughout the season. With no cars or permanently built structures here, nightlife is laid on in a stunning location without impinging on the natural landscape or the peace of the town. 2008 was Montraker's first season – making it worth checking out for 2009.

Where to eat

Fančita

Dalmatinska 38 (052 441 019). **Open** *May-Oct* noon-11pm daily. **No credit cards**.
Vrsar has plenty of pizzerias to choose from but Fančita was voted one of the top five in Istria. The main eating space is the large, roofed terrace which makes up for its lack of sea views with plenty of rustic knick-knacks. Inside the traditional wood-fired oven is the main draw. This is a relaxed, family-run restaurant. There's a full menu featuring plenty of traditional Istrian dishes plus a good local wine list.

Kn Istarska konoba

Koštar 1 (052 444 599). **Open** *Summer* 11.30am-11.30pm daily. *Winter* 4-11pm Mon, Wed-Fri; noon-11pm Sat, Sun. **No credit cards**.
Istarska konoba is great fun and the perfect place to bring the kids. Zoran, your host, is a professional magician. Once a body-building champion in former Yugoslavia, Zoran started using magic tricks as part of his performances. He entertains his guests directly at their tables. There's no extra charge – it's all part of the service. He levitates, he pulls rabbits out of thin air, that kind of thing. Always phone ahead, though – Zoran often gets booked. Magic aside, the food is quality regional fare at reasonable prices.

★ Trošt

Obala maršala Tita 1A (052 445 197). **Open** 10am-midnight daily. **Credit** AmEx, DC, MC, V.
It's easy to be put off by the 1970s exterior or the steep flight of steps leading up to this first-floor location, but don't be. This is easily the best restaurant in Vrsar. The large terrace has a wonderful view out over the harbour. Inside there are two dining areas. The smaller room has an open fireplace – employed in the cooking of some dishes – wooden beams and rustic walls. The second space is rather more formal, with sliding glass doors that open out onto the terrace in summer. The high quality of both the food and the service is happily accompanied by reasonable prices, some 200kn for an average meal. Unsurprisingly, the menu majors on fresh fish and seafood – house specialities include sea bass in salt and fish baked with potatoes under hot ashes. Booking is essential.

Vrsar.

Where to drink

Al Porto
Obala maršala Tita 33 (052 441 001). **Open**
6am-1am daily. **No credit cards.**
Al Porto is part ice-cream parlour, part cake shop
and part café-bar. It offers 48 different types of ice-
cream (plus six diabetic choices) and a mind-bog-
gling array of sundaes, complete with paper
umbrellas and lashings of whipped cream. The
decor is upmarket rustic with comfy tub chairs and
low tables. The terrace is right on the quayside
where the fishing boats moor – a prime location during 'Fishermen's Fests' – and the main reason it
opens so early in the morning. If the weather is bad
don't be surprised to see the place filled with card-
playing sea salts.

Buba
Dalmatinska 8 (no phone). **Open** *July, Aug*
7am-2am daily. *Sept-June* 7am-midnight daily.
No credit cards.
Buba is Croatian for 'bug' – there's half a VW bee-
tle suspended over the entrance. You'll find the
remainder inside, along with Hajduk Split shirts,
biking memorabilia and, weirdly, ancient terracotta
amphorae. This local hangout is buzzing even out
of season – in summer there's also a DJ in residence
at weekends. The music is eclectic and the clientele
young. Also, during the summer, Buba pitches an
additional tent by Nives.

Marinero
Obala maršala Tita 9 (no phone). **Open** *July,*
Aug 7am-2am daily. *Sept-June* 7am-midnight
daily. **No credit cards.**
This atmospheric bar gives a whole new meaning
to the term 'watering hole'. Sited in an old *cisterna*,
its vaulted ceilings and stone columns are offset with
funky wall murals and nautical paraphernalia.
Cocktails are the big thing here. House special

Marinero combines white rum, Curaçao and Red
Bull. The beer drinkers aren't left out – you can try
a Moscow Mule (lager & lime with vodka) or Dream
of Beer (white rum, lager & champagne). There's a
small terrace and in summer Marinero pitches an
extra tent on the other side of the harbour, by Nives.

Nives
Obala maršala Tita 23A (no phone). **Open**
July, Aug 7am-2am daily. *Sept-June* 7am-
midnight daily. **No credit cards.**
Although this building is Yugo concrete naff and the
venue small, Nives is Vrsar's focal bar in summer.
The town's only internet café, it also boasts Vrsar's
only pool table. Space is limited so there's a real risk
of being cued in the back while catching up on your
emails. Much of the action takes place outside on the
harbourfront and the large grass area nearby. Buba
and Marinero pitch tents here and suddenly space
doesn't seem so much of an issue.

INSIDE TRACK VIKING

Near Vrsar, the dramatic landscape
of the Limski kanal looks so much like a
Scandinavian fjord that director Jack
Cardiff filmed Viking drama *The Long
Ships* there in 1963, starring Nordic-
looking Richard Widmark. In his honour,
locals opened a restaurant, **Viking** (052
448 223, closed Jan, Feb), a superb fish
restaurant with huge plate-glass windows
and an outdoor terrace affording
uninterrupted views of Limski's green
waters. Oysters are the house speciality,
as is lobster *buzara*-style on a bed of
pasta. Viking also excels in white-fleshed
sea-fish such as sea bass, dentex, john
dory, gilthead and grouper.

ISTRIA

Where to stay

Hotel Pineta
*Vrsar (052 441 150/fax 052 441 150/www.
maistra.hr)*. **Rates** €52-€90. **Credit** AmEx,
DC, MC, V.
This three-star hotel is sited on a slight hill at the
edge of a pine forest – hence the name. Billed as
Vrsar's most luxurious hotel, the Pineta is functional
but its semi-circular format is quite funky – and you
have good views over Vrsar Bay. There is air-conditioning throughout and an indoor pool, spa facilities and a conference room which can accommodate
80 people. Pineta offers 95 rooms and four suites. It's
open all year round.

Koversada FKK
*Koversada Biesička, Vrsar (052 441 171/
www.maistra.hr)*. **Closed** Nov-Apr. **Rates**
vary. **Credit** AmEx, DC, MC, V.
If you'd rather holiday *au naturel* then head for one
of the world's largest nudist colonies, housing up to
7,000 guests and more at a large campsite. At the
other end of the scale, Koversada offers 119 four-
star, self-contained, two-person apartments. This
self-contained holiday 'town' is right on the beach
and offers naturists all they could wish for. Istria has
a long tradition of nudism but Koversada is the original and probably still the best resort. Its undis-
putable claim to fame is having been the one and
only destination of its kind behind the Iron Curtain
– Koversarda opened in 1961.

POREA

At first it can be hard to see the grandeur of
Poreč for the tourists. Hoards of visitors fill the
treasured sixth-century **Basilica**, the ancient
square built by Romans and the scores of
restaurants, cafés and one-price-fits-all package
hotels. Restaurant staff attempt to pull you in

INSIDE TRACK BEACHES

Either side of town, walkways follow
the coast, past rocky or pebbly beaches.
Some stretches of shore are reserved
for residents of a nearby resort, but most
are open – and packed. The stroll south,
towards Plava Laguna and Zelena
Laguna, can be the most rewarding. If
you continue south of the Hotel Delfin, the
beaches are rocky but somewhat more
private. For even more privacy, take a
taxi boat (every 30mins, 7am-11pm daily,
12kn) over to Sv Nikola from the harbour.
Here you'll find pine-shaded paved and
pebble beaches, notably the circular
Oliva near the Fortuna Island Hotel.

Euphrasian Basilica.

for a meal in the pestrianised Old Town, and
tacky souvenir shops cram the 2,000 year old
stone-paved thoroughfare of **Decumanus**. But
if you can see past the crowds, you can take in
a lot of history. Decumanus, the square called
Trg Marafor, and the ruins of the **temples
of Neptune and Mars**, are evidence of the
Roman occupation. The harbour contains
reminders of Venetian dominance until the
18th century, when Poreč was ruled by
Napoleon and then the Habsburgs. The
Venetians also built a town wall in the 15th
century, which stretched from the harbourside
Round Tower, now occupied by a bar, to the
inland **Pentagonal Tower**, now a restaurant.
    Most of the resort hotels are outside town, on
a green strip where pine forests run up to the
beach, **Plava Laguna** and **Zelena Laguna**,
linked by an open-air tourist train.

Euphrasian Basilica & Bishop's Palace
Sv Eleuterija (052 431 635). **Open** 10am-5pm
daily. **Admission** *Church* free. *Belfry* 10kn.
Museum 10kn. **No credit cards**.
The basilica, built in the sixth century by Bishop
Euphrasius, is an important surviving example of
Byzantine art. The surrounding complex offers
impressive sights too – you can absorb the best in 20
minutes or linger for a couple of hours. The main
attractions are the wonderfully preserved gold-gilt
and mother-of-pearl mosaics, which shine with a
brightness that belies their age. The largest and most
stunning is in the apse, above and behind the altar,
depicting a procession of saints and angels around
the Virgin Mary holding the baby Jesus. Euphrasius
built his three-nave basilica on the foundation of a
fifth-century church. Mosaics from earlier churches

are still visible in the floor of the northern nave. Alongside is an eight-sided baptistery, and beyond a belfry, which you can climb for a view of the seaside and the surroundings. Next to the church is the former Bishop's Palace housing a museum that contains mosaics gathered from earlier churches.

► *If you're hungry after a morning's sightseeing, try the Rialto (Ljudevita Gaja 3), which is behind the Bishop's Palace.*

Where to eat

Dvi Murve
Grožnjanska 17 (052 434 115/www.dvimurve. hr). **Open** *Feb-Dec* noon-11pm daily. **Credit** AmEx, DC, MC, V.
Outside the more touristy part of town is a popular konoba with a large, pleasantly shaded terrace with a busy grill in one corner. They cook up fine seafood, including the standards and local specialities such as sea bass baked in salt and lobster in spaghetti. This is also a good place to stray away from the standards and opt for traditional Istrian dishes such as stew with dried lamb, goulash and noodles, wild game or a plate of grilled meats.

► *If you've just arrived at Poreč bus station and need sustenance, the Istra (Bože Milanovića 30, 052 434 636) serves honest local fare.*

Peterokutna kula
Decumanus 1 (052 451 378). **Open** noon-midnight daily. **Credit** AmEx, DC, MC, V.
In a pentagonal tower built in 1447, near the entryway to the Old Town, this restaurant offers indoor and outdoor seating in nicely restored spaces. As a 170-seater, it's clearly touristy, but the cuisine is designed to show off the best of Istria, with truffles appearing in several dishes, including steak.

► *In another of Poreč's historic towers is a bar with a view: the Torre Rotonda (Narodni trg 3A).*

★ Sveti Nikola
Obala Maršala Tita 23 (052 423 018/www. svnikola.com). **Open** *Mar-Dec* noon-midnight daily. **Credit** AmEx, DC, MC, V.
A winning combination of location, superb cuisine and elegant ambience have helped Sveti Nikola build

INSIDE TRACK
ITALY BY BOAT

Venezia Lines (www.venezialines.com) run day trips to Venice, stopping at Pula, Rovinj and Rabac. Tickets include a one-hour guided tour of Venice. The journey time is a just over two hours each way, with a five-hour stay in Venice. **Tirrenia** (www.tirrenia.it) also run a fast boat to Trieste (3hrs).

a reputation as one of the top tables in Poreč. The terrace is right on the harbour, the meticulously designed interior has great sea views and the food features creative interpretations of Istrian classics. The fish carpaccio appetiser is an unusual and tempting mix of scampi, frogfish and octopus. The meat carpaccio comes with truffle, parmesan and ruccola. Fancy mains include fish fillet with asparagus and black truffles, lobster and steak. A sommelier sees to the rotating wine list.

Ulixes
Decumanus 2 (052 451 132). **Open** noon-midnight daily. **Credit** AmEx, DC, MC, V.
Step off crowded Decumanus, down a few steps, and into a cool, cavernous old stone room, charmingly cluttered with antiques and old shipping paraphernalia. The garden behind, in a secluded courtyard, is equally attractive. The speciality is the Istrian version of 'surf and turf': seafood and truffles. Surf includes calamari, octopus salad and fresh fish, and less common varieties like ray and sole. Truffles can be had in pasta or as part of various starters such as sheep's cheese or carpaccio. There are usually some interesting daily specials.

Zlatna Ribica
N Tesle 21 (052 452 272). **Open** noon-3pm, 7-11pm daily. **Credit** AmEx, DC, MC, V.
Stroll along the water, away from the crowds downtown, for stand-out seafood served in a pine-shaded sea-side terrace on the beach of the Pical resort, with a great view of the Old Town across the water of Uvala Peskerija bay. The kitchen does a great job with the limited number of offerings, and the short menu includes less common dishes, like oysters, crab salad and scallops. Meat options include steak with pasta and truffles. Fast, friendly service.

Where to drink

Atelier
Obala Maršala Tita 3A (052 428 880). **Open** 10am-2am daily. **No credit cards**.
Sited next to a flight of steep steps, this popular bar is tucked away behind the sea front. It's a contemporary venue known for its exhibitions and live music events. Those fake zebra-skin sofas look so much better after a couple of beers.

► *Also slick is the Caffè Bar C&D at No.12, open from 8am for coffee and cocktails.*

Comitium Cocktail Bar
Marafor 15 (no phone). **Open** 11am-2am Mon-Thur, Sun; 5pm-2am Fri, Sat. **No credit cards.**
A garish, oversized sandwich board nearby alerts the passing tourists to a beautiful garden bar amid the Roman ruins of Marafor. Cocktails, cold Bavaria on tap and a classy, polished wood and marble interior set this place off from the nearby competition.

ISTRIA

ISTRIA

INSIDE TRACK
DRINKING TIPS

The focus on family tourism means that cafés here cater to a tamer crowd looking for ice-cream or a post-dinner cocktail. Trg Marafor has several terrace bars, including **Mango Mambo**, a cocktail bar with a slightly hipper vibe. In the resorts, the discos can feel part of a package tour. The best spot is **Colonia Iulia Parentium** (Gradsko Kupalište), both a bar and a dance club.

Epoca
Obala maršala Tita 24 (no phone). **Open** 8am-2am daily. **No credit cards**.
Good music, friendly staff and a sociable buzz sets this place apart from the other harbourside bars. Near the tip of the peninsula that holds the Old Town, at the beginning of the busy strip of cafés and restaurants, Epoca offers a spacious indoor bar and sea views. Dancing has been known to break out in the evening, though the crowd you'll be schmoozing with will be mostly fellow travellers. Good cocktails.

Lapidarij
Sveta Maura 10 (052 431 595). **Open** noon-midnight daily. **No credit cards**.
Within the City Museum's garden is a pleasant courtyard bar that provides sanctuary from the crowds in the Old Town. It hosts concerts, particularly Wednesday's jazz residency, bringing the best practitioners of all its various forms – from swing to acid jazz – into Poreč for jam sessions.

Mozart Caffè
Rade Končara 1B (052 432 317). **Open** 6am-2am daily. **No credit cards**.
This terrace and bar really shouldn't be the busiest location in town. Not only is it set behind the bus station and Hotel Poreč, separated from the marina by a small park, they play dubious Italian pop on the stereo and the fashion channel on the TV. But it's strangely popular and always packed with a loud young crowd that includes many locals – a welcome respite from the tourist hordes.

Yesterday
Park Olge Ban 2 (098 190 662 mobile). **Open** *Summer* 7am-1am daily. *Winter* 7am-11pm daily. **No credit cards**.
A Beatles theme bar, run by the son of an Oldham-born fan who gave Paul McCartney a loveheart necklace backstage in 1965. Two years later, Jackie Carnihan met a hotel receptionist while on holiday here, got married and had two children. Macca couldn't have written it better. Unplugged local acts play on Fridays.

Nightlife

Byblos
Zelena Laguna (091 113 3221 mobile). **Open** *June-Sept* Mon-Sat. **No credit cards**.
Opened in 2007, this is the club that Istria has been waiting for. Quality sound system, quality cocktails and a quality agenda – David Guetta, Deep Dish and Roger Sanchez, for example. Mario Lucchi designed the 4,000sq m interior, mainly black-and-white, simple but effective, with a beach lounge bar too. Ladies' night is Mondays, international DJs Fridays. You'll find it near the Hotel Delfin.

Where to stay

Kn Hotel Delfin
Zelena Laguna (052 414 000/fax 052 451 658/www.plavalaguna.hr). **Closed** Nov-Mar. **Rates** €23-€43 single; €50-€96 double. **Credit** AmEx, DC, MC, V.
This low-frills resort offers a decent budget option for families. The huge complex, has 800 rooms on a hilltop in a pretty pine-forested peninsula. The rooms are small and plain, but reasonably cool in the pine-shaded building despite the lack of air-conditioning. Pebble and less crowded rocky beaches nearby are quite separate from the rest of Zelena Laguna. There's a sports centre next door plus an outdoor pool with saltwater.
▶ *Plavi Laguna also have a couple of four-star resort hotels here – see website for details.*

Hotel Hostin
Rade Končara 4 (052 408 800/fax 052 408 857/www.hostin.hr). **Rates** €41-€89 single; €52-€126 double. **Credit** AmEx, DC, MC, V.
The Hostin chain only has one hotel in Poreč, and it offers competitive luxury at decent prices. The modern but attractive resort complex, surrounded by pines, is next to the marina by a strip of seaside greenery that holds all the resorts. Amenities include pool, sauna, whirlpool, steam room, gym and nearby pebble beach. Diving, boat and bike rentals nearby.

Hotel Poreč
Rade Končara 1 (tel/fax 052 451 811/www.hotel porec.com). **Rates** €42-€66 single; €58-€100 double. **Credit** AmEx, DC, MC V.
This blocky concrete building with 54 rooms is close to the bus station and a small park by the marina. Of all the hotels in town, this is furthest from the holidaymaker bustle. All the comfortable rooms have balconies, although the views are a little mundane – and there's no air-conditioning.

Getting there & around

The nearest airports are in **Pula** and **Trieste**, Italy. Half a dozen services a day run to Poreč **bus station** (Rade Končara 1, 052 432 153) from each main town in Istria, and Zagreb. There is a taxi stand at the bus station or call 052 432 465 or 052 438 347, 098 209 675 mobile.

Resources

Tourist information

Poreč Tourist Office *Zagrebačka 9 (052 451 293/www.istra.com/porec).* **Open** 8am-10pm daily.

NOVIGRAD

Novigrad can seem like a humble resort town by Istrian standards. It's neither as posh as Rovinj nor as packed as Poreč, but that's precisely why this can be a charming location for a relaxing time by the sea. The emphasis here is on quality, from the five-star **Hotel Nautica**, with its own marina, to the deservedly reputable restaurants in the small harbour. Instead of being crammed with tourist businesses, the seaward tip of the Old Town peninsula has a shaded park and a waterside walkway. Still, for a community of fewer than 3,000 people, Novigrad finds room for a surprising number of decent bars, hotels and restaurants. The more modern part of town stretches less than a kilometre east, as far as the bus station and a small hotel complex.

Sightseeing

The Old Town around the harbour offers fine food, good bar crawling and the **Museum Lapidarium**, specifically built to house Roman remains. The Old Town is connected with the marina and other facilities via the pleasant seaside promenade of Rivarella.

Novigrad was called Cittanova by the Venetians, who graced the town with most of its elegant historical sights. The Venetian-style campanile beside **St Pelagius**, a Baroque 18th-century church built on the foundations of a medieval basilica, rises over the modest network of streets. Here in the main square, **Veliki trg**, and the main street of **Velika ulica**, stands a landmark Venetian loggia, containing the **Town Hall**. North of town at Karpinjan, near the new marina, is the **Rigo Palace**, built in 1760. As well as a gallery with contemporary exhibitions, it contains a permanent display of ancient tombstones and Byzantine fragments.

Gallery Rigo

Velika ulica 5 (052 757 790/www.galerija-rigo.hr). **Open** varies. **Admission** free.
One of Istria's most important independent galleries has a fast-moving programme of challenging, contemporary exhibitions throughout the year.

Museum Lapidarium

Veliki trg 8A (052 726 582/www.muzej-lapidarium.hr). **Open** *Summer* 10am-1pm, 6-10pm Tue-Sun. *Winter* 10am-1pm, 5-7pm Tue-Sun. **Admission** 10kn; 5kn reductions; free under-14s. **No credit cards**.
Istria's first purpose-built museum is a first-class example of successfully siting modern architecture within the context of an old town. Lapidarium was built to house Roman architectural remains, dating from the first century AD, discovered in the locality.

Novigrad.

INSIDE TRACK BAR HOPS

Half-a-dozen decent bars dot the town centre. You could make a little bar hop from the Vitriol, to Aquarius, K Ribaru and Lite, ending up opposite the Hotel Cittar at the chaotic late-night Delfin or grungy Ara. Discos are found in high season at the hotel complex on the eastern outskirts of town.

Superbly exhibited, this small museum sets a world-class standard in Istria. As well as temporary exhibitions, the Lapidarium accommodates a display of pieces and items collated from Novigrad's Romanesque churches.

Višnjan Observatory

Istarska 5, Višnjan (052 449 212). **Open** by appointment.

Equidistant from Novigrad and Poreč, famous for discovering more than 1,400 minor planets over the last decade, Višnjan is one of the world's most prolific astronomical discovery sites. The team here are currently constructing a new observatory nearby, called Tican, which will house a one-metre telescope. The Višnjan Observatory is also involved in educational projects, run by students and volunteers.

Where to eat

★ Damir i Ornella

Zidine 5 (052 758 134). **Open** noon-3pm, 6.30-11.30pm Tue-Sun. **Credit** AmEx, DC, V.

Commonly acknowledged to be the best place in town, this 28-seat diner is worth booking at least a day ahead. Signposted on Velika ulica, it's set in a narrow sidestreet near the seafront. Inside, a simple bare-brick interior is a comfortable setting for raw fish and shrimp specialities. The grilled lobster is excellent too. Desserts include a popular kiwi flan.

Konoba Čok

Sv Antona 2 (052 757 643). **Open** noon-3pm, 6-11pm daily. **Credit** AmEx, DC, MC, V.

On an enclosed front terrace by a roundabout on the edge of the Old Town, a board reads: 'Welcome from Family Jugovac'. While his son Viljan runs the kitchen, Sergio takes care of guests and the wide range of Istrian wines on offer. This simple, well-run seafood eaterie is indeed a welcome treat, with fresh sea bream, sea perch and sole , lobster, and all kinds of shellfish including oysters. Truffles decorate the steak and pasta starters, and meals are generally bookended by a complimentary fruit brandy.

Mandrać

Mandrać 6 (052 757 369). **Open** noon-3pm, 6-11pm daily. **Credit** AmEx, DC, V.

The walls of Mandrać's backroom are covered in gastronomic awards and even though there are seats for 200 diners, it's best to reserve in summer. Fresh fish and grilled meats are well presented on warmed plates, garnished according to the friendly advice offered by the waiter. Despite the high standard of service and preparation, prices are reasonable.

▶ *Traditional Sidro (052 757 601) is next door.*

Where to drink

Cocktail Bar Code

Gradska Vrata 20A (092 801 037). **Open** 8am-midnight Mon-Thur, Sun; 8am-2am Fri, Sat. **No credit cards.**

This slick, urban, black-and-white cocktail lounge seems incongruous among the more low-key cafés of Novigrad, but it works. House music blares from the speakers while silenced hip-hop videos flash on a wide screen. The bartender is ready to give a showy shake to 23 basic types of cocktail, averaging around 40kn each and served in pretty generous portions. There are DJs on Saturdays.

Kavana Ogledala

Gradska vrata 24 (no phone). **Open** 8am-midnight daily. **No credit cards.**

Also known as Caffè degli Specchi, this is nothing like the grand coffeehouse of the same name in Trieste. It's a simple café serving frothy coffee and gooey cakes whose character and colour change on a Sunday afternoon. Then it transforms into the local branch of the AC Milan fan club; its modest interior is decked out in red and black and buoyant with an unthreatening sense of celebration.

Little Caffè

Gradska vrata 15 (098 939 7573 mobile). **Open** 8am-midnight Mon-Thur; 8am-1am Fri, Sat. **No credit cards.**

A young, professional crowd hangs out in this swish café in the heart of Novigrad. A little art on the walls, a decent choice of whiskies and Istrian bitters, Guinness and Kilkenny by the bottle, it's a cut above most bars in the Old Town. Could do with a touch of music, a shortcoming in these parts.

★ Vitriol

Ribarnička 6 (052 758 270). **Open** 8am-midnight daily. **No credit cards.**

INSIDE TRACK RESORT DIGS

Novigrad's limited stock of mid-range accommodation is filled out by the provision of season-only resort hotels on the edge of town, past the bus station. Check www.laguna-novigrad.hr for details of the Maestral and the Laguna.

Vitriol is the best bar in Novigrad. With a terrace lapped by the sea and overlooking the setting sun, the place is trendy enough to appeal to weekending Italians without losing its young, lively, local character. Concoctions have a distinct Italian flavour (Negroni, Garibaldi) but include a zingy Novigrad Beach of gin, Campari and orange juice. Local wines are chalked up on a board outside, beers include Kriek and Kilkenny and there are enough hot drinks to fill an entire menu.

Where to stay

★ Hotel Cittar
Prolaz Venecija 1 (052 757 737/fax 052 757 340). **Rates** €88-€122 double. **Credit** AmEx, DC, MC, V.

Its exterior built into a section of Venetian wall in the city centre, the Cittar is one of the best mid-range hotels in Istria. Run by a small, friendly team under Sergio Cittar, it contains 14 rooms with smooth, varnished floors, comfortable, big beds and capacious baths. A breakfast of warm croissants, meats and cheeses is taken in the sunny conservatory at the front. Half-board is offered in summer, when it's best to reserve at least a week in advance.

★ Hotel Nautica
Sv Antona 15 (052 600 400/fax 052 600 490/www.nauticahotels.com). **Rates** €95-€211 single; €132-€262 double. **Credit** AmEx, DC, MC, V.

Istria's first five-star hotel, opened in 2006, the Nautica is uncompromisingly modern. The spacious, sumptuous complex has an ongoing nautical flavour. The bespoke, dark wood, leather and brass furniture is styled after on-board outfittings – it even extends to the ship's wheel bedheads. With an excellent restaurant, large lounge bar, indoor pool and spa, it's a welcome addition to Istria's rapidly improving hotel stock. For those on sailing holidays, the ship-to-shore facilities could not be better.

Kn Torci 18
Torci 34 (052 757 799/fax 052 757 174/www.torci18.hr). **Closed** Oct-Apr. **Rates** €50-€80 double. **No credit cards.**

Djurdja and Lino Beletić run this sturdy three-star pension and restaurant in the centre of town with a dozen clean, comfortable rooms, some overlooking a courtyard.
▶ *The restaurant here is a destination in its own right for well priced, local standards.*

Resources

Tourist information
Novigrad tourist office *Porporella 1 (052 757 075/www.istra.com/novigrad).* **Open** *Summer* 8am-8pm daily. *Winter* 8am-3pm Mon-Fri; 8am-1pm Sat.

Getting there & around

Novigrad is poorly served by public transport. There are only four buses a day from **Zagreb** and **Pula**. It might be quicker to get to **Poreč** and change for a more regular service between the two towns 18km (11 miles) apart. The bus station is a ten-minute walk outside town. For a taxi, call 052 757 224, 098 806 349 mobile.

GROŽNJAN

With 23 galleries and plenty of studios, the tiny town of **Grožnjan** is now known as the 'Town of Artists'. Nearly wiped off the map not once but twice, Grožnjan is a place with an instinct for survival.

Sightseeing

Grožnjan is one of Istria's prettiest medieval hilltop towns, 228 metres above sea level. Its position provides spectacular views, the Adriatic coast to the west and the dramatic landscape of the glorious Mirna Valley to the east. The northern region of Istria is rich with these ancient, Italianate settlements. What sets Grožnjan apart is that this town feels loved, alive and cared for. Amazing when you

Grožnjan.

consider that, just 40 years ago, it lay derelict and deserted – and not for the first time.

In 1630 bubonic plague almost wiped it out. The Venetian republic set about revitalising the municipality. Tradesmen and artisans settled in the town itself. Grožnjan grew and prospered. In 1902 Austrians built the Paranzana Railway, opening up new markets in Koper and Trieste.

After World War II, this part of Istria was assigned to Tito's Yugoslavia. Some two-thirds of north-west Istria emigrated to Italy. In Grožnjan only 20 souls remained. Gradually, local artists began using the empty buildings as studio space and by 1965 it was formally declared a 'Town of Artists'. Grožnjan's street signs are hand-painted ceramics, rather than state-manufactured enamel; the colours of the shutters are subtle but just right; there are ancient-looking stone seats perfectly sited for enjoying the view; and everywhere you look, there's a gallery. There's a perfect little town square and outside the town loggia on balmy, summer evenings are recitals by operatic tenors or noodling jazzers, all performing as part of the **Grožnjan Musical Summer** (www.hgm.hr).

The town has managed to come full circle. Today's artists and crafts-people link back to the tradesmen and artisans of the 17th century. The spirit of Grožnjan continues – beautiful, creative and very much alive.

Where to eat & drink

The main restaurant in town is the **Bastia** (1. Svibanja 1, 052 776 370), under the church tower. Fabulous local dishes include home-made sausage, rumpsteak with truffles and pasta *fuži* with wild game. **Art'A** (Trg corner 3) is a suitably arty café with a panoramic terrace and is open all year round.

Where to stay

The only hotel in town is the **Pintur**, closed between January and March, and always full at festival time. Otherwise, this guesthouse (M Gorjana 9, 052 731 055) of four rooms is most accommodating. A short drive away, the nearby **Radanić Hotel** (052 776 353, 091 783 3772 mobile), run by the old local Italian-speaking gentleman of the same name, is a friendly, cheap, traditional guesthouse.

Getting there & around

There is no public transport to Grožnjan. Your only option is to take the **Buzet-Buje** bus and ask the driver to drop you off at **Bijele Zemlje**, and walk the 3km uphill from there. Usually locals will pick you up when you're coming up or down the hill.

Resources

Tourist information

Grožnjan Tourist Office *Umberta Gorjana 3 (052 776 131/www.groznjan-grisignana.hr).*

MOTOVUN

Motovun – Montona to the Romans – is one of the most beautiful and best preserved of Istria's medieval hilltop settlements. These days it's best known for its Film Festival, which transforms this otherwise sleepy town into a cultural and party hub for one week every summer.

Motovun is sited on the summit of a 277-metre (910-foot) hill in the middle of the Mirna Valley, surrounded by truffle-rich forest. When the original prehistoric settlement was founded, it would have been surrounded by water. In those days the estuary stretched right up to the 'Gates of Buzet' at the head of the valley. It was down this ancient inlet that Jason and his Argonauts are supposed to have fled after having captured the Golden Fleece.

Sightseeing

In its day, Motovun was the communications hub for all of inland Istria. From its strategic position, it controlled the merchant routes that wound across the valley floor on the way to the coast. In 1278 Motovun came under the rule of Venice, a major outpost on its border with the Austrian empire. Although depopulated as a result of the Italian exodus after World War II, a new wave of inhabitants – many of them artists and writers – has set up home here in recent times. The result is the Motovun Film Festival, started in 1999.

> ### INSIDE TRACK
> ### MOTOVUN FILM FESTIVAL
>
> Motovun Film Festival is central Istria's cultural highlight. For five days in late July, the town is transformed into a party hub, occasionally patronised by famous names, a cross between Sundance and Glastonbury. The festival presents some 80 documentaries, features and shorts. The top prize is the Propeller of Motovun. Other awards include From A to A, for the best regional film from Albania to Austria. Screenings are scheduled from 10am to midnight, followed by live music until 3am. A campsite is set up at the bottom of the hill but many sleep in their cars. See www.motovunfilmfestival.com.

Motovun.

Non-residents are banned from driving the town's narrow cobbled streets – there's a car park at the bottom of the hill.

Motovun's two sets of fortified walls divide the town into three sections – the higher you climb, the older it gets. As you wend your way upwards, past rather dilapidated, 16th- and 17th-century Venetian-style houses, you pass several small shops, offering wine, truffles and local grappa.

As the road levels it passes through the main city gate dating from the 15th century. Its walls are hung with Roman tombstones taken from the cemetery of **Karojba**, a village 5km (3 miles) away on the road to Pazin. Within the gate is a museum of antique weaponry. The entrance is on the far side of the gate. Also here is the town's art gallery. Next door is a small café whose terrace is sited on the other side of the street, against the first set of fortified walls. Sitting here you have a clear view to the Adriatic. Just in case, a telescope has been thoughtfully provided. There's a cashpoint opposite, the only one in the area.

A few steps further, facing the town loggia, is the 13th-century gate into the original heart of Motovun. This walkway is particularly steep and slippery – use the handrail. This entrance houses a small restaurant, **Pod Voltum**. From the archway you walk on to the main square. Dominated by a magnificent 13th-century belltower, the piazza is sited over a huge *cisterna*, or water collection pit, which used to supply the town. You can still see the 14th-

century well. Next to the tower is the baroque **Church of St Stephen** and, opposite, a Renaissance palace citadel, housing the local cinema. The piazza also houses Motovun's only hotel, the **Kaštel**. It's at this point that all the climbing pays off. Stroll along the original 13th-century walls and a 360-degree panoramic view reveals the whole of inland Istria before you.

Where to eat

Kn Konoba Dolina

Gradinje 59/1, Livade (052 664 091). **Open** noon-10pm Mon, Wed-Sun. **No credit cards**.

A short drive from Motovun (head into Livade and take a right at the only roundabout) Dolina is a perfect example of fantastic, simple local food in a simple, local place. Many Italians drive down for the night. It's slightly off the beaten track, not touristy or flash – and all the better for it. It's also incredibly good value. The secret is the quality of the fresh ingredients: huge plates of meaty porcini mushrooms served with olive oil; *fuži* with truffles, squid with chips, cabbage salad, beans. Dolina gets busy with locals sat around wooden tables, repeat guests and chattering eldery Italian ladies from the nearby spa. There's half-a-dozen tables outside too. If you lived here you would be a regular.

▶ *Livade is best known for the Žigante truffle restaurant – see p128* **Profile**.

Konoba Mondo

Barbacan 1 (052 681 791). **Open** varies. **No credit cards**.

Taken over by the sweet couple who run the Caffè Bar Montona Gallery, the Mondo has kept its attractive lay-out, with tables on the terrace and in the basement; kept its trusted staff to run the place; and kept its loyal client base whose favoured establishment features extensive use of local produce.

INSIDE TRACK
LOCAL BOUTIQUES

Motovun has several small, independent boutiques specialising in truffles, wines, olive oils, jewellery and souvenirs. Two merit individual mention: **Motovun Gallery** on Borgo is run by Zagreb-born Renata who uses her contacts in the arts and crafts scene to display a contemporary selection of paintings, sculpture, jewellery and crockery from the ground floor of her family home. **Atelier M**, on the other side of the hill at Gradiziol 11 (052 681 560), is run by Eni, whose atmospheric photographs of inland Istria are sold framed and unframed in a variety of sizes. Hand-printed T-shirts are also available.

Pod Voltum

Šetalište V Nazora (052 681 923). **Open**
Summer noon-11pm daily. *Winter* noon-11pm
Mon-Tue, Thur-Sun. **No credit cards**.
'Under the Arch', by the old city gate, serves a selection of honest, regional fare, including truffles, and
can always be relied upon to have a fire blazing in
winter. A rare non-smoking establishment.

Porte Pontone

*Ponte Porton, Kostanjica (052 776 395/
www.ponte-porton.hr).* **Open** 11am-11pm
Mon, Wed-Sun. **No credit cards**.
Set in an old house and recently refurbished, Ponte
Pontone sits on the road between Grožnjan and
Motovun, on the Mirna towards the sea. It's a little
pricier than most konobas but the menu is a little
more varied and imaginative than most – fish
options are rare in inland Istria. Outside there's half-
a-dozen tables lit by fluorescent strips; inside the two
rooms vary in their formality. Dragan is the local
and talented chef. The presentation is more fancy
than rustic – food (great chunky chips) comes on
square black plates. You can also stop off for a beer
and there are rooms to rent upstairs.

Kn Propeler Pizzeria

Jozef Ressler 8 (052 903 2666). **Open** *Mar-Nov*
10am-11pm daily. **Closed** Dec-Feb. **No credit
cards**.
Opened just before the 2008 Film Festival, this spot
offers some welcome variety to Motovun's dining
options, which tend to be centred on the truffle. At
the top of the Old Town, it dispenses a steady stream
of thin-based pizzas and interesting salads to visitors and locals. Prices are very good value – a mid-
morning snack of mozzarella, basil and tomato
panini (warmed in the pizza oven) is 12kn. The owners are a mix of local and London-trained, so pizzas
feature organic spicy rocket, with chunks of parmesan and chilli oil. The truffle does make an appearance and is a surprisingly good topping. Salads
include roasted red peppers with local sheep's
cheese. In the evening, it fills with locals knocking
back the Favorits. The only negative is the single
oven – if you're in a big group expect a slight delay
and enjoy the view.

INSIDE TRACK KINO BAUER

Kino Bauer is a cosy gem of a cinema
that closed with the arrival of DVDs.
Recently a group of foreigners based
in Motovun has started screening films
here, from children's to art-house, often
in English or with English subtitles. Check
local noticeboards to see what's on –
entry is free. The movie theatre is behind
an unmarked door in the main square.

Where to drink

Caffè Bar Montona Gallery

Trg Josefa Ressela 2 (052 681 524). **Open**
8am-midnight daily. **No credit cards**.
Run by friendly local couple Claudio and Lela, this
relaxed café is set on top of the hill, with beautiful
views of the Mirna valley laid out below. If you can,
try and get here when the sun is setting. Tables are
lined up on the terrace outside, and there's a scatter-
ing of furniture within for long winter nights. Being
the only proper bar in town – in fact, almost the only
bar up here – it attracts locals of every stripe, can-
ing the *biska* and arguing about nothing at all. The
next day, it's all forgotten.

Where to stay

Kaštel

*Trg Andrea Antico 7 (052 681 607/fax 052
681 652/www.hotel-kastel-motovun.hr).* **Rates**
€43-€49 single; €70-€83 double. **Credit** AmEx,
DC, MC, V.
Behind the bright red façade of Motovun's only hotel
are 28 spacious three-star rooms set around little
patios. Some have balconies. Attractive half-board
rates are available at the in-house restaurant, offering game, truffles and Istrian specialities in a chest-
nut-shaded garden or renovated dining room.
▶ *Rooms are also available upstairs at the Porte
Pontone restaurant; see above.*

Getting there & around

The infrequent **bus** from the transport hub
of **Pazin** takes 45 minutes to get to Motovun.
The twice-daily **Pula-Buzet** line also drops
off at Motovun, as does the **Zagreb-Buzet**
bus service.

Resources

Tourist information

Motovun Tourist Office *Trg Andrea Antico 1
(052 681 758).*

HUM

Wrapped around by its thick, medieval
walls, **Hum** is billed as the smallest town in
the world. To qualify as a bona fide town, a
settlement must contain a school, a church, a
post office, a town hall and a pub. Squeeze in a
dozen houses and that's Hum. Traditionally it's
been home to just two families, with the priest
also the publican.

But things are changing. As you wander
round the town's single, circular street, be
careful not to trip over any building rubble.
People have cottoned on to Hum's charm and
slowly the town is coming to life.

**INSIDE TRACK
ROA ACCORDION FESTIVAL**

Hum lies near Roč, famous for its
Accordion Festival on the second Sunday
of May. The festival is a celebration of the
diatonic accordion or *trieština*, a unique
five-tone instrument quite unlike the
octave-based accordion of Bavarian
bierkellers. *Trieština* players were a dying
breed when the Roč festival began in
1989. That May, 16 players gathered in the
town square. The following year they were
joined by a handful of amateurs, and so
on, until the big bash of today.

Sightseeing

As you pass through the town's massive, metal
doors you enter a cave-like antechamber hewn
straight out of the rock. Above is the Town
Hall. On the walls are stone tablets inscribed in
ancient Glagolitic, a Slavic script for which
Hum is famous. Ahead is the main square; to
the left is the ludicrously large **Church of the
Exalted and Blessed Virgin Mary** with
its magnificent crenellated belltower. The
consecration chapel of **Sv Jeronima** in the
graveyard houses 12th-century frescoes
covered with Glagolitic graffiti.

Left is a Lilliputian house with a picturesque
loggia. This is the main street – the only street.
A small gallery signed 'Imela' is the source of
Hum's second claim to fame: *biska*, grappa
flavoured with mistletoe – made from the
leaves rather than the poisonous berries. It's
either bright green or golden brown in colour,
depending on whether fresh or dried leaves
have been used.

Further up the street is the **Hum Museum**
(052 662 596, open summer 11am-5pm daily),
which is really a souvenir shop but with a small
collection of old Istrian furniture and artefacts
to justify its name. You can also buy Glagolitic
alphabet charts.

Where to eat

Finish the circuit of the town and step out of
the main gate and into Hum's single restaurant,
only open at weekends: the **Konoba Hum**
(052 660 005, open 11am-11pm Sat-Sun) has a
covered terrace with a beautiful view down into
the valley – this is the perfect setting to share
a *bukaleta* (drinking jug) of traditional Istrian
supa. Clearly invented by a peasant with no
food in the house, this speciality consists of
red wine topped off with warm, toasted bread
liberally sprinkled with olive oil.

Getting there & around

Hum is 5km (3 miles) from the main **Buzet-
Lupoglav** road. There is no public transport
but coach tours can be booked throughout the
summer from most tourist offices in Istria.

LABIN

The only major town on Istria's wild east coast,
Labin is something of a law unto itself. Sited
on a high peak, 3km (two miles) from the sea,
Labin is said to have been founded by Celts in
the fourth century. They christened it 'Albona'
or 'Alvona' ('town on a hill') and this ancient
name is still in use. A century later the Romans
recorded the presence of unruly pirates. The
local Matija Vlačić was a leading European
religious reformer alongside Martin Luther. In
recent history, Labin's miners revolted against
Mussolini and declared an independent
republic. Labin has always had attitude.

Sightseeing

With a population of 10,000, Labin is an
economic centre – the plain beneath the Old
Town sprawls with a thriving residential
and business community. Technically known
as 'Podlabin' ('Under Labin'), this is where
Mussolini built his two new towns to house
local miners. You can see a reconstructed
shaft at Labin's excellent museum.

As you ascend the steep, cobbled hill up to
the old town you pass by the beautiful villas
built to house the white-collar workers. Passing
through the first city gate you enter the main
square – still **Titov trg** – with its brightly-
painted buildings and Venetian loggia. This
is the town's social hub dominated by the
landmark **Velo** café, restaurant and
nightspot. The terrace packs in summer.

Labin has a vibrant arts scene and the
majority of talent is home grown, artists
preferring to stay here. As you continue
uphill, through the second gate, and explore
the old town you pass galleries, studios and
workshops. **Municipal Gradska Galerija
Labin** (Ulica 1.maja 5, 052 852 464) provides an

INSIDE TRACK LOCAL DIGS

The bulk of the hotel stock in the area
is located in Rabac, a town set up for
tourists. If you'd really rather stay in
Labin, then check if private rooms might
be available from the information point
set up between Easter and October at
Titov trg 10 (052 852 399).

agenda of contemporary exhibitions, opposite the **Labin Museum** (Ulica 1. maja, 052 852 477). These and other public spaces are commandeered for the annual **Labin Art Republic** (www.labin.hr) series of arts events in July and August. Initiated in 2003, it stages live shows, exhibitions, and ad hoc street entertainment. The event is usually themed. Studios open their doors and visitors are given access to private and public collections.

Don't miss the sculpture park, **Mediterranean Sculpture Symposium** (**MKS**; 052 852 464) in nearby **Dubrova**. Look out for the large, green glass cube, due to be the visitors' centre. International residencies take place each year. Artists provide contributions to a pathway continuously being added to.

Back to the old town, **Šetalište San Marco** is a terrace on the old city walls providing an unbroken vista out over the Kvarner Bay. Locals claim that the shallow depth of the sea here, only 80 metres, encourages growth of a specific plankton, and thus outstanding seafood. If you carry on walking to the top of the town, the whole of eastern Istria is laid out before you. Within immediate view, sited on a spectacular sea cove 3km (two miles) down the hill, is Labin's counterpart port of **Rabac**.

Where to eat & drink

Gostionica Kvarner

Šetalište San Marco (052 852 336). **Open** 10am-10pm daily. **Credit** MC, V.
Fabulous view, fabulous food, all produced locally; what more could you want? It's also the best-sited restaurant in Labin, the terrace seating on Šetalište San Marco with stunning views out over the Kvarner Bay. There's a large, wide-ranging menu, including an Istrian hot plate of small portions of local specialities such as tagliatelli with chicken, *fuži* pasta with beef and gnocchi with wild boar. The must-try is *krafi*, shaped like ravioli, pasta sweetened with raisins, rum and sugar and stuffed with four types of local cheese. In summer the restaurant grills fish and meat on the terrace.

Velo

Titov Trg 12, Labin (052 852 745). **Open** varies. **No credit cards**.
Three venues in one, all busy, all year round. In the basement, a comfortable, half-trendy, half-rustic restaurant boasts glowing terracotta walls, plenty of artwork and a traditional open fire in winter. The food is typical Istrian fare (no pizzas, despite what the sign says) at very reasonable prices – no wonder artists fill the place. Above, the café and its terrace throng in summer. The Rock Café nightspot occupies the first floor. Look out also for the Spider Café Bar opposite, another good late-hour drinking haunt, with DJs in summer.

Getting there & around/Resources

See p143.

RABAC

If Labin is strong on culture, **Rabac** provides all the summer fun. As you travel down spectacular hairpin bends towards Rabac Bay, the small town comes into view like something straight off the French Riviera. The steep hillside is crowded with brightly-painted houses – nearly all offering vacation apartments – and, at the bottom, is the holiday village of Rabac. Seaside gentrification is already underway. The Valamar Bellevue has upped its status to four stars; the boutique Villa Annette opened in 2006. Away from the beach fun, you can explore the nature trails, one leading to the **Tears of St Lucia**, a natural spring that is reputed to heal your eyes if you wash them with the water. You are also close to the ferry terminal at **Brestova**, for access to **Cres** and **Lošinj**, and their sandy beaches.

Where to eat & drink

Nostromo

Obala maršala Tita 7 (052 872 601/www. nostromo.hr). **Open** 11am-11pm daily. **Credit** AmEx, DC, MC, V.
Nostromo has a large, roofed terrace where you can enjoy your meal looking out over Maslinica beach in Rabac Bay. Understandably, the menu majors on fish and seafood specialities – although not exclusively – and there's a reasonable range of local wines. Nostromo also rents out rooms and apartments.

Where to stay

Hotel Amphora

Rabac (052 872 222/fax 052 873 345/www. hotel-amphora.hr). **Rates** €58-€124. **Credit** AmEx, DC, MC, V.

INSIDE TRACK
RABAC SUMMER FESTIVAL

The main event here is the **Rabac Summer Festival** of electronic music on Giradella Beach (www.rabacsummer festival.com), an all-weekend biggie. In 2007, 8,000 came to enjoy John Digweed, Dave Clarke, Desyn Masiello and others. It attracts an international crowd – many tickets are sold in Italy and Slovenia. For dance music here outside of festival time, head for the mainstream **Andrea** disco or **Tropic** beach bar-club.

Velo.

If you want to be right in the thick of things, then the Hotel Amfora, Rabac's most central hotel, is the one to book. Only 30 metres from the seafront, and renovated in 2003, it has air-conditioning, a summer terrace and small pool. Half the 52 rooms have a sea view. Open year round.

Valamar Bellevue Hotel & Residence

Rabac (052 465 200/fax 052 872 561/www. valamar.com). **Closed** Nov-Mar. **Rates** €60-€202 double; €34-€118 single. **Credit** AmEx, DC, MC, V.
This newly-renovated, four-star under the Valamar umbrella is sited on the beach just north of Rabac, connected to town by a little train. It comprises 155 rooms, 16 luxury ones in separate villas, two pools, one for kids, and plenty of family entertainment all summer. It's all spanking new and the prices, all half-board, are reasonable.

★ Villa Annette

Raška 24, Rabac (052 884 222/fax 052 884 225/www.villaannette.hr). **Closed** Jan-Mar. **Rates** €85-€159. **Credit** AmEx, DC, MC, V.
Villa Annette is a stunningly modern boutique hotel overlooking Rabac Bay. The decor is terrific, with plenty of well-placed art work and the 12 suites are well designed, with space and character. Villa Annette boasts an infinity pool with views out to islands of Cres and Lošinj, a great slow-food restaurant, and the cost is not exorbitant, considering the quality of the accommodation. There are various suite options – the prices quoted above are for a couple or three people in the smallest one.

Getting there & around

Don't let the 3km of steep hill between **Labin** and **Rabac** put you off because there's a frequent daily **bus** service, running from 6am to 10pm every day. A timetable is available from the tourist office. Local **taxi** firms include Jasmin (098 916 1863 mobile) and Ivanić (098 226 960 mobile).

Resources

Tourist information
Labin-Rabac Tourist Information *A Negri 20 (052 855 560/www.rabac-labin.com).* **Open** 7am-3pm Mon-Fri.

INSIDE TRACK
REZERVAT LIBURNA

South of Raša on the way to Pula is one of Istria's most popular attractions: the **Rezervat Liburna donkey sanctuary** (052 857 706, 091 521 1232 mobile, www.rezervatliburna.hr). Here Ivica Perko is attempting to preserve local Mediterranean breeds, many of which are now virtually extinct. The group roams free for the most part, protected by a river that cuts through the middle. A modest museum is filled with interesting objects, and there's a nature trail.

The SEA VIEWS
The CONVENIENCE
The CHOICE
The ELEGANCE
The INDIVIDUALITY

LIBURNIA RIVIERA HOTELS
OPATIJA/CROATIA

The only place to be.

We understand that different hotels are required for different occasions.
Our portfolio of hotels can cater for all your needs.

Liburnia riviera hotels invite you to enjoy a carefree stay

www.liburnia.hr • www.liburnia.biz • www.visitopatija.net • 00385 51 710 444

Kvarner

Pag.
See p185.

Kvarner & Islands

Croatia's biggest islands are offset by a Habsburg gem.

Nature really comes to the fore in Kvarner. Although the main islands of **Krk**, **Lošinj** and **Rab** have long been developed for tourism, around them nature – in the form of hilly terrain, the Bura wind and havens for dolphins and griffon vultures – contrasts with the easy pleasures of Dalmatia. **Cres**, in particular, is relatively untouched. Away from the DJ scene at Zrće, **Pag** also feels bare and isolated. Although Pag doesn't officially belong to Kvarner – this long, arid island is administratively divided between the mainland and Zadar – it is included

in this section as it is closely connected with the other islands in the gulf. Easy transport links are one of the area's boons – both Krk and Pag have bridges to continental Croatia and most ferry hops are short and frequent.

On the mainland, the two main towns are chalk and cheese. For much of its past, the gritty port of **Rijeka** didn't belong to Croatia at all, but to Italy and Hungary. Next door, **Opatija** had its glory days in the late 19th century. Here, the Habsburgs built ornate villas and grand spa hotels, many of which can still be checked in to – at a price. Further on, **Lovran** offers quality seafront dining.

RIJEKA

As you pass through on the way to the ferry boat that will take you to your holiday resort, it's easy to miss out on **Rijeka**. This working port city, Croatia's third largest with a population of 150,000, has no beaches and its busy harbour is lined with tall loading cranes that look like droopy-headed dinosaur skeletons. Ugly Socialist-era high-rises loom over the town from the hills above, while the Old Town architecture consists of squat, bulky Habsburg constructions.

But Rijeka has a fascinating history, quality restaurants and a kicking nightlife. The fact that it's one of the few spots on the coast that doesn't need to cater to tourists means that visitors are not subjected to the commercial overkill felt elsewhere on the Adriatic – you'll be dining, drinking and dancing with locals.

About the city

Founded by the Romans, and Habsburg from the 1400s, Rijeka fell under Hungarian control in the late 1700s. The landlocked Magyars built

a new harbour, Baroque landmarks and sundry industries, including the world's first torpedo. Much of the city had been destroyed by a devastating earthquake in 1750, so that most monuments predating this date were wiped out; hence the consistently Baroque look you'll observe in Rijeka's Old Town.

> ### INSIDE TRACK RISJNAK
>
> Some 40km (25 miles) north-east of Rijeka stretches the thick, steep forest of the **Risnjak National Park**, centred by the 1,528-metre- high (5,013-foot) mountain of the same name. Here reside bears, wolves, lynx and chamois. Without a car, the park is tricky to reach. There are several buses to Delnice (1hr 15mins); the shuttle bus to the park's office and entry point of Crni Lug (Bijela Vodica 48, Crni Lug, 051 836 133, www.risnjak.hr, open 7am-10pm daily, 30kn) leaves late afternoon. Agencies in Rijeka also provide excursions.

Capuchin Church.

Fiume, as Rijeka is still known to Hungarians, had no indigenous Magyar population. When their legitimacy was challenged in 1868, the Hungarians switched papers on Emperor Franz Josef at the signing ceremony, and a majority Slav population endured 50 more years of rule from Budapest. As a result of the indignation expressed in the influential local newspaper *Riječki Novi List*, displaced Dalmatian intellectuals stirred up a groundswell of opinion which resulted in the Declaration of Fiume 1905, a call for a united land of South Slavs. It failed but it helped spread the notion of 'Yugoslavia', one that would come to fruition after World War I.

With the collapse of the Habsburg Empire after the war, the Hungarian Governor fled his magnificent palace, and in marched Italian patriot, pilot and poet Gabriele D'Annunzio with 200 soldiers to proclaim 'Fiume' as Italian and his own state. Mussolini's men took Rijeka a year later, the Germans in 1943. Rijeka industrialised under Tito, rusted in the 1990s, but recent developments – the motorway from Zagreb, the road bridge from the nearest airport on Krk island – may see a change in fortunes. The Gateway Project, signed with the World Bank for 300 million euros, will see the Rijeka waterfront transformed in ten years, with a brand new passenger terminal, nautical centre and marina.

Sightseeing

The main **Korzo** runs parallel to the embankment **Riva**. A few Baroque façades (including the remake of the original medieval **City Tower**) fade behind modern shops and cafés. A short walk west is the main bus station, backdropped by the bizarre, two-level **Capuchin Church**. Further to the west is the train station, which provides a useful direct service to Zagreb. Beyond is Opatija, easily reached by the regular bus service. To the east, the Korzo ends at the local bus station (from where the services to Opatija set off) and the so-called **Dead Canal**, which is now pretty and pedestrianised rather than morbid. Its nearby continuation, the Rječina, is the division between Rijeka and the former separate areas of **Sušak** and **Trsat**. Between the wars, this was the border between Italy and newly founded state of Yugoslavia.

Spending a few hours on the hilltop around **Trsat Castle** can be a pleasant way of passing the afternoon, but if you don't have much time, you can turn left from the canal at Titov trg into Žrtava fašima to find several mildly diverting attractions.

First up is **St Vitus' Church** (Grivica 11, 051 330 897; open 9am-noon, 5-7pm daily), which is topped by a Baroque rotunda, a Venetian-inspired creation from the 1600s.

Rijeka

- ❶ Hotels p156
- ❶ Restaurants pp151-152
- ❶ Bars pp152-155

Train station

Bus station

Capucin Church

Modern & Contemporary Art Museum

Municipal Museum

Natural History Museum

History & Maritime Museum

State archives Rijeka

Palace of Justice

St Vitus' Church

Roman Arch

Old Town Hall

Church of St Jerome

Church of the Assumption

City Tower

Orthodox Church of St Nicholas

Croatian National Theatre

Main Market

Kazališni Park

Nicole Hosta Park

Nazora Park

RIVA

Harbour

Rječina

Mrtvi Kanal

Trsat 2km

1.5km

FRANE RAČKI

ŠETALIŠTE

ANDRIJE

FIUMARA

IVANA ZAJCA

RIVA BODULI

KREŠIMIROVA

© Copyright Time Out Group 2009

100 m
100 yds

Across the street and a few doors down is the quirky new computer museum, **Club Peek&Poke** (Ivana Grohovca 2, 091 780 5 709 mobile, www.peekpoke.hr; open 5-8pm Mon-Fri; 10am-2pm Sat; 10kn). Children can play with still-functioning versions of the machines their parents worked on a dozen or more years ago, and marvel at how primitive they were.

St Vitus' Church stands at the edge of the Old Town. Just above it rises the stately **Governor's Palace**, commanding a view of the sea; from here, D'Annunzio would have seen the battleship sent from Rome in 1920 to force his capitulation. Exhibits belonging to the **History & Maritime Museum** here (Muzejski trg 1, 051 213 578; open 9am-8pm Tue-Fri, 9am-1pm Sat; admission 10kn) are overshadowed by Alajos Hauszmann's sumptuous state rooms. Next door, the **City Museum** (Muzejski trg 1/1, 051 336 711; open 10am-1pm, 5-8pm Mon-Fri, 10am-1pm Sat; 20kn) contains modest exhibitions in a two-floor space. Overlooking these two buildings is the **Natural History Museum** (Lorenzov prolaz 1, 051 553 669; open 9am-7pm Mon-Sat, 9am-3pm Sun; 10kn), with an aquarium and botanical garden outside.

Spinal Frana Supila leads towards Trg republike Hrvatske, which contains the **University Library**, accommodating Rijeka's internationally renowned **Modern & Contemporary Art Museum** and its collection of Glagolitic scripts. Temporary exhibitions feature Croatia's leading artists.

★ Modern & Contemporary Art Museum

Dolac 1/II (051 334 280/www.mmsu.hr). **Open** 10am-1pm; 6-9pm Tue-Sun. **Admission** free. **Map** p149 C2.

Founded in 1948, this is the largest provincial museum of its kind in Croatia. Spreading over the second floor of the University Library, the Modern & Contemporary Art Museum holds a large, permanent collection of works by prominent Croatian artists and stages regular exhibitions as well as an International Biennale of Drawings. On the ground floor is a permanent collection of Glagolitic scripts, including examples of the fist printed books in Croatia.

Trsat Castle

Petra Zrinskoga (no phone). **Open** *Apr-Nov* 9am-midnight daily. *Dec, Feb, Mar* 9am-3pm daily. Closed Jan. **Admission** free. *Tours* 15kn. **No credit cards**.

Visit this fort for the panoramic view alone, best enjoyed from the Gradina terrace café beneath the Nugent mausoleum. Irish-born Austro-Hungarian naval commander Laval Nugent-Westmeath fought Napoleon and rebuilt this medieval Frankopan fortress to house his family and his art collection, the latter no longer open. The mausoleum is worth a look in, if only for the bad press it gives Nugent's daughter, the 'evil and eccentric' Countess Ana. Down back towards the No.1 bus terminal, you pass Our Lady of Trsat Church and the small Franciscan monastery.

▶ *Decent dining and drinking options nearby include the Sabrage Café and Trsatika restaurant; see p155 and p152.*

Trsat Castle.

MIR JUNAKA

Feral

Matije Gupca 5B (051 212 274). **Open**
9am-11pm Mon-Sat. **Credit** MC, V. **Map**
p149 E3 **1**
Feral is a handy little downtown restaurant specialising in seafood, with a few meaty options too.
Cooked frog with potatoes and kale is one of the
more unusual of these, otherwise the menu features
the standard white sea fish and scampi. Mozzarella
salad makes a nice change from seafood, Löwenbräu
beer something different from the stock Istrian
wines. The front terrace is open in summer.

Konoba Blato

Titov Trg 8C (051 336 970). **Open** 6.30am-
11pm Mon-Sat. **No credit cards**. **Map**
p149 F1 **2**
In a sturdy wood-and-tile cellar on the pedestrianised square where the two main canals meet,
Konoba Blato is a small, dimly-lit eatery that makes
home-style seafood and hearty meat dishes in a
pleasant family atmosphere. The fish is always fresh
and well prepared, as is the octopus salad to accompany it. There are only half-a-dozen tables, busy during work breaks, and the tiny bar has a few stools,
nearly all occupied by locals.

Kn Konoba Fiume

Vatroslava Lisinskog 15B (051 312 108). **Open**
6am-6pm Mon-Fri; 6am-3pm Sat; 6am-2pm Sun.
Closed 1st 2wks Aug. **No credit cards**. **Map**
p149 D4 **3**
Some 30 yards from the main market, near the port
and the Korzo stands the stone-walled, brick-arched,
high-ceilinged Fiume. Drop in for its daily offering
of grilled ray, mackerel, sardines, tuna, squid,
goulash, boiled beef, veal in sauce and, a special
treat, cod stew on Fridays. Simple meals, cooked in
the local way, are based on the freshest seasonal
ingredients from the nearby market. Decent local
wines, affordable prices and a warm welcome from
black-haired Nena, a big fan of the The Big O, make
you feel at home.

Kn Konoba Nebuloza

Titov trg 2b (051 372 294). **Open** 11am-
midnight Mon-Sat. **Credit** AmEx, DC, MC, V.
Map p149 F1 **4**
A friendly little restaurant next to the Rječina Canal
provides perfectly prepared fresh seafood at reasonable prices in a comfortable atmosphere. They serve
a lot of the fish others do, but the menu here lets you
know when it has been farmed instead of caught
wild. House-special starters include smoked tuna,
and goulash or lamb stew with local *šurlice* noodles.
Meat eaters get a choice of toppings, like truffle
sauce or rosemary and caper for their steaks, thick
and juicy. The amicable waiters will not only show
you the catch of the day, but tell you what's fresh-

Municipium.

est – even if it's something less expensive, like calamari. The side room has big windows with a great
view of the canal below.

★ Municipium

Trg Riječke rezolucije 5 (051 213 000). **Open**
10am-11pm Mon-Sat. **Credit** AmEx, DC, MC, V.
Map p149 D2 **5**
Municipium is set in a grand Habsburg-era building, tucked away in a quiet courtyard right in the
centre of town. Door staff greet you at the entrance
– decorum is all. The menu is vast and fish-oriented,
most of it priced in the 300kn/kg range, very reasonable considering the quality of service, presentation
and the fare itself. Courgettes, wild asparagus and
other greens get a look-in and the wine list runs to
150 (mainly Croatian) varieties. If you're going to
splash out, do it here.

Pizza Delfino

Trg Jurja Klovića (051 336 736/www.delfino.hr).
Open 8am-11pm, Mon-Tue; 8am-midnight Fri;
noon-midnight Sat; noon-11pm Sun. **Credit** MC.
Map p149 D2 **6**

INSIDE TRACK KUKURIKU

North-west of Rijeka, in the old town of
Kastav, the **Kukuriku** (Trg Matka Laginje
1A, 051 691 417, www.kukuriku.hr)
makes regular appearances in national
gastronomic guides for its seasonal slow
food, superb wines and the panoramic
views from its terrace.

KVARNER & ISLANDS

Capitano.

Perhaps the best pie in town, this pizzeria was spun off from the deservedly popular Delfino in Lovran, and it's packed nightly with locals. The terrace looks out on to a pretty and secluded Old-Town square, which lies just uphill from the Korzo, while an interior of long wooden benches and tables is generally taken over by big families or noisy groups of drinkers. It's a lively place. There are 16 types of pizza, with generous, fresh toppings. It may help to book ahead, but you can usually find a spot – if you don't mind sharing your table.

Tapas Bar
Pavla Rittera Vitezovica 5 (051 315 313). **Open** 7am-10pm Mon-Sat. **Credit** AmEx, DC, MC, V. **Map** p149 E2 **7**
On a small Old-Town street off Pavlinski trg, this popular new spot offers snappy service to diners seated on tall stools at high counter-like tables. Dishes come in *ración*-sized portions, each about 30kn-35kn, so you can make an affordable meal out of several dishes, or order the daily meat or fish menu, three dishes and dessert for 100kn-130kn. Attention to detail stands out: octopus terrine is sliced thin, served on rocket with parmesan shavings and balsamic sauce, garnished with moist sun-dried tomato. Triple fish comprises perfectly grilled sea bass, shrimp and calamari, with rich roulades of spinach.

★ Trsatika
Šetalište J Rakovca 33 (051 217 455). **Open** 11am-11pm Mon, Tue, Thur-Sun. **Credit** MC, V. **Map** p149 F1 **8**

Fabulously located up in Trsat, this part pizzeria, part grill offers high-grade versions of renowned standards, with a terrace view to boot. Specialities include roast suckling pig, grilled, roasted or boiled lamb, *šurlice* pasta and goulash from Krk, and roast veal knuckle. A rustic oven in the corner turns out large, cheap pizzas in two sizes, the house Trsatika with ham, mussels, scampi and cheese coming in at under 40kn. If you have a day in Rijeka, set aside a couple of hours here.

Zlatna Školjka
Kružna 12a (051 213 782). **Open** 11am-11pm Mon-Sat. **Credit** AmEx, DC, MC, V. **Map** p149 C2 **9**
With a good location and a reputation as one of the best places in town, this busy cellar restaurant can charge higher prices than most. Along with the usual seafood offerings, appetisers include fish carpaccio with capers, and marinated salmon. The day's fish is displayed on ice, and includes a wide selection of molluscs. The hefty salads can work as a small meal, followed by a number of cheeses. Snappy service adds to a pleasant atmosphere.
▶ *The same management runs a great pizzeria, the Bracera (Kružna 12), which can be found just down the alleyway.*

Where to drink

Belgian Beer Café Brasserie
Trg republike Hrvatske 2 (051 212 148). **Open** 6am-1am Mon-Thur, Sun; 6am-2am Fri, Sat. **Credit** MC, V. **Map** p149 C3 **1**

Genuine brasserie atmosphere to this place, set so close to the harbour you can see ships passing from the handful of tables outside. Inside is wooden, with Flemish inscriptions on the walls and almost authentic *pissoirs*. The Belgian dishes are hearty and the selection of compatriot brews improved of late.

★ Capitano

Adamićeva 3 (051 213 399). **Open** 7am-4am daily. **Credit** MC, V. **Map** p149 C3 ②

Beautiful old-style bar in a sumptuously large indoor-outdoor space right on the harbour attracts a young, fashionable crowd. The dark wood and marble interior, with a huge old-fashioned mirror behind the bar, has expensive-looking decor and pleasant gallery seating. The indoor back terrace is inside a shopping centre, where DJs spin for dancers at weekends. The real terrace, out front facing the harbour, is one of the nicer ones in Rijeka. Relax in wicker while you watch crowds and boats go past.

Česka Pivnica

Titov trg (098 928 1800 mobile). **Open** 10am-midnight daily Mon-Sat. **Credit** MC, V. **Map** p149 F1 ③

In this big, rustic L-shaped cellar that is now a Czech beer hall they serve draught Pilsner Urquell, Kozel and several types of Czech Budweiser, including dark; they also stock many bottled beers and all the standard hard stuff. Prices are good: a small glass is 7kn, regular 10kn and pints 15kn. It's also great for breakfast, the food on offer beer absorbent, predominantly meaty and in large part traditional Czech, like *bramborak*, a big turkey cutlet inside an even bigger potato pancake.

El Rio

Jadranski Trg (051 214 428/099 265 0720 mobile). **Open** 7am-1am Mon-Wed; 7am-5am Thur-Sat; 9am-1am Sun. **No credit cards**. **Map** p149 C2 ④

The outdoor seating and general buzz around the popular El Rio dominates the square at the western end of the Korzo, just in from the sea. Daytimes, this is the place to people watch and be watched. By night it fills with a young crowd on the make, and towards the weekend it's a heaving club. The lush interior, the arched brick ceilings, the brisk waitstaff

and the well dressed clientele create a classy atmosphere, at least superficially. The cocktail menu features 20 choices, DJs spin on late weekend nights. ▶ *Along the Korzo, the Mali Café (No.18, 051 335 606) is a relaxed, pre-club spot.*

Karolina

Gat Karoline Riječke (051 330 909). **Open** 6am-midnight Mon-Thur, Sun; 6am-2am Fri; 6am-4am Sat. **Credit** MC, V. **Map** p149C/D3 ⑤

A slick, modern glass-enclosed structure, sitting all by itself on a pier in the main harbour, houses an upmarket bar that draws a mix of yuppies, tourists, hipsters and hard-drinking barflies. The bar's terrace is on the sea; inside is a carefully designed, dimly lit space, with high tables and tall stools in the middle of the bar area, and lower chairs with zebra-striped cushions at the two ends. The darkness releases inhibitions, and the techno and trance music inspires a good time. DJs and dancing at weekends.

Kosi Toranj

Put Vele Crkve 1 (051 336 214). **Open** 7am-midnight Mon-Sat. **Credit** MC, V. **Map** p149 E2 ⑥

Kosi Toranj has a winning terrace, on a small hidden square with an aged leaning tower that gives the establishment its name. The interior is an attractive needle-shaped room, with two long glass walls, big art and low, lounge seating. DJs spin deep house and electronic music on party nights, but the turntable is well handled by the cheerful bar staff, who tend toward interesting and eclectic. Hungarian trip hop, anyone?

Opium Buddha Bar

Riva 12A (051 336 397). **Open** 7am-3am Mon-Wed; 7am-5am Thur-Sun. **No credit cards**. **Map** p149 C3 ⑦

This unusual venue has an iguana in one corner and, in the other, a gold-painted Buddha. A fun, young crowd fills the big space in between with loud conversation and quiet smooching. There are DJs and dancing at weekends, and the rest of the music selected is eclectic and usually reliably good. The terrace covers a large stretch of the Riva facing harbour, in Rijeka's bar central.

Kn Ri

Brodokomerc Forum, Riva (051 311 019). **Open** 8am-11pm daily. **No credit cards**. **Map** p149 D3 ⑧

If you're sitting on the upper harbourfront terrace of the Ri, chances are you've got a ship to catch. There she is, right in front of you, gleaming white and blue, while your waitress (slowly) brings out a dirt-cheap cold beer for you to raise a glass to adventures ahead. Ri itself remains trapped in a Socialist time-warp, with the decor, the furniture and the service, unchanged since Tito's day. But hey, rather this than any global chain café at twice the price.

INSIDE TRACK CLUB BARS

Venues like **Capitano**, **El Rio** and **Karolina** operate as semi-clubs, with late opening, DJs and due attention given to cocktails. Some of the boats nearby also double up as late-night places of entertainment. Wander the Riva after midnight and you'll find you have dozens of drinking and dancing options.

KVARNER & ISLANDS

Profile Rijeka Carnival

It might not be as big as Rio's, but it's older.

Croatia's biggest carnival takes place in Rijeka, a colourful procession of thousands on the Sunday before Shrove Tuesday.

The Mardi Gras tradition here dates back centuries, when it was a festival to welcome the coming of spring and scare off any lurking Turks. Then as now, masks were elaborate and ugly, and evil spirits were sent packing by local menfolk dressed in animal skins and huge, clanging cowbells: the *zvončari*. Always up for a spot of costumed fun, the Habsburgs revived the concept in the late 1800s, before Rijeka got tangled up in too much political torment to entertain street parties. In 1982 three masked groups walked down a Korzo of bemused onlookers. Since then, numbers grew every year, so that by 2001 4,000 took part in the parades. For the 25th anniversary event in 2007, it was nearer to 100,000. No wonder locals call it the 'fifth season' – after spring, summer, autumn and winter.

Rijeka Carnival (www.ri-karneval.com.hr) runs over four days in January and February. Depending on when Shrove Tuesday falls, the Queen's Pageant usually takes place on the third Friday in January, followed by the Zvončari Parade, which takes place the next day. By tradition, the bell-ringers clang their instruments and move in steps according to their village of origin. Then, thirteen days before Shrove Tuesday, on the Saturday lunchtime, the Children's Parade runs through the streets of town. The big event, however, is the International Carnival Parade, which begins at noon on the following Sunday. It usually takes the whole afternoon for floats to pass down the main streets before celebrations into the night at stalls and tents set up around the canal.

Tour companies such as Adriatica put together all-in packages for visitors – check www.adriatica.net for details.

River Pub
Frana Supila 12 (051 213 406). **Open** 7am-2am
Mon-Wed; 10am-4am Thur-Sat; 6pm-2am Sun.
No credit cards. Map p149 D2 🟢
Beautifully upholstered furniture sits on an old tiled
floor, while a sturdy bar counter holds up taps of
Bass, Caffrey's, Guinness and Kilkenny. The framed
photographs from around Istria are a nice touch, old
regional maps too, with a few busts of Irish writers.
Set behind a big, wooden, unsignposted door facing
Optani opticians, halfway down from the museums.

Sabrage
Petra Zrinskog 2 (091 793 1536 mobile).
Open 7am-midnight daily. **No credit cards.**
Map p149 F1 🔟
Up in Trsat, this lovely spot is well stocked and well
staffed. Along with classic cocktails and long drinks,
there's a long wine list, a Tinto Reserva hiding
among the Zlatni Plavac and Dingač. Whiskies, such
as 14-year-old Oban and ten-year-old Talisker, can
be sipped in an elegantly carved wooden interior
decorated with portraits of famous locals. There are
nice hot chocolates served too.

Nightlife

Kn Dva Lava
Ante Starčićeva 8 (051 332 390). **Open**
8am-11pm Mon-Wed; 8am-3am Thur-Sat.
No credit cards.
The Two Lions comprises two cramped storeys of
edgy flirting in a sci-fi film set. The music veers from
the mainstream, cocktails are dangerously cheap,
and local youth eye their potential catches from the
lounge bar/viewing platform upstairs. No fee unless
a name act is programmed.
▶ *For pre-club drinks, try the downtown
Charlie Bar (Trg Ivana Koblera, 051 315 053)
by the City Gate.*

Indigo
Stara Vrata/Trg Ivana Koblera (051 315 174).
Open 8am-midnight Mon-Wed; 8am-4am Thur-
Sat. **No credit cards.**
This trendy new place tries very hard – and in the
main succeeds. The food – fish, meats and pasta – is
passable, but Indigo is more of a bar-club, suited for
weekend nights when they pack in crowds for big-
name DJs from Croatia and sometimes abroad. Even
when there are no DJs, you can count on recherché
hip hop, trance and electronica coming out of the
speakers. The interior is striking: kind of retro-futur-
istic with lots of red plastic, a glass floor and neon
arching round doorways. Attractive terrace too.

★ Palach Club
Kružna 6 (051 215 063). **Open** 9am-11pm Mon-
Fri; 5pm-1am Sat; 5-11pm Sun. **No credit cards.**
Turn off the Korzo and you're on a gritty, graffiti-
adorned sidestreet, where teenagers with punk hair-

cuts loiter by the entrance. Inside, the Palach spreads
out across a ground-floor complex with several
rooms dedicated to either dancing, art display or
tables for drinking and chatting. Decor varies from
shiny industrial to an all-black dance hall. The café
is open all day. By early evening the place begins to
fill up with students, slackers and other party animals, chatting by the main bar, dancing to DJs or
watching live bands from Croatia and Europe.

★ Nina 2
RI-2 Luka (no phone). **Open** 9am-3am Mon-Thur,
Sun; 9am-5am Fri, Sat. **No credit cards.**
Once a dodgy casino, this spacious boat has been
converted into one of the most popular dance spots
in town. No more gun searches at the door; now the
whole operation oozes class, from the slick staff to
the fancy mist sprayers that cool the outdoor areas.
Live bands play and DJs spin a range of danceable
music, from disco to Latin to electronica, for a mostly
young crowd who boogie in a big room with a great
bar on the middle floor of the boat. Get out on deck,
and into the fresh air, for conversation and lounging. Three bars keep drinks flowing.

Phanas Pub
Ivana Zajca 9 (051 312 377). **Open** 7am-
1am Mon-Wed; 7am-3am Thur-Sat. **No
credit cards.**
Down at the harbourfront, this place is best experienced late at night, when a two-floor wooden pub
with maritime knick-knacks is thick with hormones,
pinging around the room to a commercial dance and
rock soundtrack. However, it can get very busy late
on and become difficult to get inside. Guinness,
Kilkenny and Stella, wines and cheap cocktails complement the standard Ožujsko, but the drinks here
are secondary to the eye-contact action around the
three-deep long bar counter.

Stereo Dvorana
Strossmayerova 1 (www.zabava.hr). **Closed**
June-Aug. **Open** Sept-May 8am-4am Wed-Sat;
4pm-1am Sun. **No credit cards.**
This big, dark club and concert space lies in the
heart of town, behind the Neboder Hotel. Over the
school year, it attracts the bigger name DJs and live
bands passing through, showcasing underground

**INSIDE TRACK
RIJEKA CARNIVAL PLANS**

If you're coming here for the Carnival
in February, make sure you book your
accommodation early. Rijeka's already
limited hotel stock fills up fast, and you
might find it a handy option to stay in
nearby Opatija – if that's not booked
up as well.

---

sounds, house and breakbeat. Opening hours are sporadic – often it will keep going until after dawn, and sometimes it might be open for special events on Mondays or Tuesdays.

Where to stay

Continental
Šetalište Andrije Kačića-Miošiča 1 (051 372 008/fax 051 372 009/www.jadran-hoteli.hr). **Rates** €61 single; €77 double. **Credit** AmEx, DC, MC, V. **Map** p149 F2 ❶

It looks grander than it is, but at these prices in the centre of town, overlooking the canal and with a pretty terrace internet café on its doorstep, you can't really complain. Last renovated in 1989, a century after it opened, the Continental offers convenience rather than comfort in its 38 rooms. Brown was all the rage in 1989, apparently. Prices reflect a slight rise in June 2008.

★ Grand Hotel Bonavia
Dolac 4 (051 357 100/fax 051 335 969/ www.bonavia.hr). **Rates** €99-€131 single; €122-€161 double. **Credit** AmEx, DC, MC, V. **Map** p149 C2 ❷

Rijeka's classiest option, in the Adriatic Luxury Hotels group. In the heart of town, this is a modern business hotel, with a new spa centre and gym; sauna cabins and massage and beauty treatments are also a recent introduction. The 120 rooms are tastefully done out, the in-house Bonavia Classic restaurant is one of the best in town, and the terrace café overlooks the city.

★ Jadran
Šetalište XIII Divizije 46 (051 216 600/fax 051 216 458/www.jadran-hoteli.hr). **Rates** €92-€108 single; €109-€128 double. **Credit** AmEx, DC, MC, V. **Map** p149 F3 ❸

Completely renovated in 2005, the seafront Jadran has also hiked its prices considerably. The 66 rooms are nicely fitted, but you're paying for the location. Set by Rijeka's first stretch of swimmable sea, with its own stop on the No.2 bus route east of town in Pećine, the Jadran ('Adriatic') has been a spot for bathing and relaxation since it opened in 1914. There's a price supplement for sea-facing rooms. Half- and full-board deals also available.

INSIDE TRACK
JADRAN HOTELS

The main local lodging group is **Jadran Hotels** (www.jadran-hoteli.hr), who have five properties in Rijeka and the vicinity. Check the website for off-season bargains – their two out-of-town locations are attractively cheap.

▶ *If you'd like seafront relaxation but can't afford to pay top dollar, the Lucija Kostrena (Kostrenskih boraca 2/2, 051 289 004) in the same group is less than half the price, 1.5km away in Kostrena.*

Kn Neboder
Strossmayerova 1 (051 373 538/fax 051 373 551/www.jadran-hoteli.hr). **Rates** €61-€66 single; €76-€82 double. **Credit** AmEx, DC, MC, V. **Map** p149 F1/2 ❹

If you're looking for a cheapie in town and the Continental is full, you'll have to come here, to the appropriately named 14-floor 'Skyscraper' by the flyover. After renovation in 2008, the Neboder jumped from two- to three-star status, with an underground car park and café. The wonderful Socialist-era lobby has, rather sadly, been replaced by something more modern – while the rooms remain adequate. This is still a medium-range hotel with prices to match – for the moment.

Kn Youth Hostel Rijeka
Šetalište XIII Divizije 23 (051 406 420/ www.hfhs.hr). **Rates** €15.50-€17.60 dorm bed; €37.80-€41.80 double. **No credit cards.** **Map** p149 F3 ❺

Opened in 2006, the former Villa Kozulič has been transformed into a modern, 60-bed youth hostel, the first one in town. Well sited in Pećine, east of town by the sea on the No.2 bus route from the train and bus stations, the YHA offers standard dorm beds and three comfortably equipped double rooms in the attic, a snip for the price and location. Open all year, it has a TV room, internet and a kitchen.

Getting there & around

Rijeka airport (051 842 040, www.rijeka-airport.hr) is on the northern tip of the island of Krk, near Omišalj, 25km (15.5 miles) south of town. An Autorolej bus meets the weekly arrivals (45mins, 30kn). Its terminus is the suburban bus station near the canal in the city centre. **Taxis** should have a set fee of 160kn, but many can charge at least 300kn.

Rijeka is Croatia's biggest transport hub and biggest port. Jadrolinija **catamarans** serve Cres and Mali Lošinj, and Rab and Novalja. The main **coastal ferry** runs once a day in summer, twice a week in winter, between Rijeka and **Stari Grad (Hvar)**, **Korčula** and **Dubrovnik**. The main office of **Jadrolinija** (051 211 444, www.jadrolinija.hr, open 7am-6pm Mon-Fri, 8am-2.30pm Sat, noon-3pm Sun) is by the harbour at Riva 16. The **harbour** is right in town, near the **national bus station** just west of the Korzo, on Trg Žabica. There are hourly buses from Zagreb (3hrs 30mins) and regular ones from Split (8hrs 30mins) and Zadar (4hrs 30mins).

Neboder.

The **train station** is further west from the national bus station. There are four trains a day from Zagreb (the journey time is around four hours), and there are daily services from Ljubljana, Vienna, Munich and Budapest. For Pula, a bus runs as far as Lupoglav and is then met by a train.

You should only need to use the **city bus** network if you're going to Trsat (No.1) or Pećine (No.2) – the centre is compact. Tickets are 10kn for these zone 1 destinations. The **No.32 bus** for **Opatija** (25mins, 14kn) leaves every 20 minutes from the suburban station by the canal, passing the train station.

For a **taxi** call 051 332 893.

Resources

Tourist information
Rijeka Tourist Office *Korzo 33 (051 335 882/www.tz-rijeka.hr)*. **Open** *Mid June-mid Sept* 8am-8pm Mon-Sat; 9am-2pm Sun. *Mid Sept-mid June* 8am-8pm Mon-Sat; 9am-2pm Sun.

OPATIJA

The grand villas surrounded by palm groves and regal century-old hotels lining the steep wooded shoreline speak of **Opatija**'s pedigree as a resort destination. With its recent crop of high-end restaurants, competitive cluster of four- and five-star hotels and gorgeous old palm-shaded villas converted into luxury accommodation, Opatija seems ready to offer

every comfort to today's visitors too. All is as it should be – this town was made for the most demanding tourists.

Sightseeing

In the late 19th century, when the Austro-Hungarian empire reached its apex, the Habsburgs made this town of dazzling vistas and rocky beaches one of the hottest spots in Europe. Opatija was the place where royalty took their holidays and Isadora Duncan took her lovers.

Drawn by its royal associations, wealthy socialites built Secessionist and neo-classical mansions on the rocks above the sea, or stayed in hotels of imperial elegance. Unlike most Croatian resorts, where a tourism infrastructure was added on to an already existing settlement, Opatija's Old Town was purpose-built for tourists – rich ones.

Before 1844, Opatija was nothing but a fishing village with 35 houses and a church. Higinio von Scarpa then built opulent **Villa**

INSIDE TRACK NAME GAME

Villa Angiolina, the Opatija mansion that is credited with starting tourism in Croatia in 1844, was built next to an old abbey. Opatija means 'Abbey' in Croatian, which is where the town's name comes from.

Opatija.

Angolina, named after his wife, and surrounded it with a menagerie, an exotic garden and influential guests. The villa, with its neo-classical interior featuring trompe l'oeil frescoes, now hosts jazz and classical concerts, as well as exhibitions.

The property was bought in the 1880s by the chief of the regional railway board. Spotting a business opportunity, he soon began promoting Opatija as an overland getaway destination for a certain class of European, catered for by the opulent hotels that were being built at the same time. An accent on health tourism – spa baths and vigorous walks along the Lungomare – kept this clement resort busy year-round. Mahler, Puccini and Chekhov were among the visitors.

This legacy lingers in the stunning architecture, Viennese-style coffeehouses and Central European atmosphere, which are kept alive by the large number of Austrian tourists. Pricey Opatija has traditionally drawn wealthy, conservative visitors, who prefer seaside strolls to raucous nightlife. But there is a local young contingent, coming from Rijeka and elsewhere along the coast, who keep the late-night bars and the town's disco busy. And the modern-day counterparts of fin-de-siècle spa establishments in the shape of 'Wellness' and boutique hotels are opening along the riviera, attracting a trend-conscious clientele. Meanwhile, few other Croatian towns can boast the gastronomic quality offered by adventurous young chefs who have made Opatija and neighbouring

Volosko their base – Dubrovnik can't hold a candle to Opatija as far as contemporary cuisine is concerned.

The resort is deliberately arranged on a steep hill facing the sea, offering fine views of the Bay of Kvarner. Further vistas and several beaches can be found along a 12-kilometre-long shaded promenade, along the rocky coast: the Lungomare. Stretches of rocky beach are fronted by towering villas, some of them abandoned and others converted into luxury hotels. Further along stretch the quieter, pebbly shores of Ičići and **Lovran**, before Medveja, with its own attractive shingle beach.

Where to eat

Bevanda
Zert 8 (051 712 772/www.bevanda.hr). **Open** 12.30-11.30pm daily. **Credit** AmEx, DC, MC, V.
Sumptuous seafood is served under a regal-looking glass atrium that covers a seaside terrace on the promenade in Opatija's Lido, near Villa Angolina. A good variety of fresh fish is prepared simply but expertly, making this one of the better places in a town full of top-quality seafood. The restaurant also has a large, well-decorated interior, although the glass-roofed terrace is a magical place to sit – try and reserve your table here.

★ Bistro Yacht Club
Zert 1 (051 272 345/www.yacht-club-opatija.com). **Open** 9am-1am daily. **Credit** AmEx, DC, MC, V.
Non-sailors can be pampered at this superb seafood restaurant on the water at Opatija's marina. The kitchen handles all the basics expertly, while throwing in a superb codfish pâté that you spread on a hearty light-brown toast; baked octopus; monkfish parisienne; and fine white fish grilled *al forno* in wine. The smart interior, done in cheerful light blue, and the relaxed but deferential waiters, make you feel like you have a 60-footer floating somewhere nearby. Recommended.

Hotel Miramar Restaurant
Ive Kaline 11 (051 280 000/www.hotel-miramar. info). **Open** 12.30-11.30pm daily. **Credit** AmEx, DC, MC, V.

INSIDE TRACK **EASY REACH**

Opatija is located in the Bay of Kvarner at the point where the Mediterranean reaches most deeply into the European continent, making this a convenient drive for many in Central Europe. The town is less than 500km (300 miles) from Munich, Vienna or Milan.

Profile Gourmet Volosko

Eating by the dock of the bay.

A 15-minute seaside stroll from the centre of Opatija takes you past stunning vistas to the edge of Volosko and a tiny harbour where fishing boats bob in the chop of Kvarner Bay. There is only room for three businesses here: the lively **Caffe Bar Kon-Tiki** (*see p161*) and two of the more unusual and creative restaurants in Croatia. The 100-plus-year-old Plavi Plodrum and fresh upstart Le Mandrać both seek to provide the most compelling gourmet dishes using the best fish and other seasonal ingredients. The clear winner of this competition is the dining public.

Plavi Podrum (*see p160*), the oldest restaurant in the Opatija Riviera, is run by Daniella Kramarić, an award-winning sommelier backed up by a cellar holding about 300 types of wine. The stock is 60-70 percent Croatian, but most other wine countries are well represented.

The wine also gets into the food, like the first item on a five-course, 440kn, degustation menu: 'tuna sea ham on a black-truffle cream with black Hawaiian salt and lemon-Merlot 2006 coronica sorbetto'. The meal also comes with a soft flavourful black bread, made with cuttlefish ink. While the Plavi Podrum was always a source of excellent fresh seafood, the haute-cuisine bent of the current menu seems to have been encouraged, at least in part, by the arrival of the neighbour, **Le Mandrać** (*see p160*), just a few years ago.

Deniz Zembo is the chef and his wife Alma is maitre D' at Le Mandrać, where the freshest ingredients are combined creatively and served in a strikingly modern but tasteful glassed-in terrace. With a cuisine he describes as

'Mediterranean and light French cooking with traditional food', chef Zembo turns the treasures of the Adriatic into delightful dishes. Cold orange-and-carrot soup is served with home-smoked Kvarner octopus; sashimi or the fresh shellfish of the day is done in moules marinieres style, with lemon foam, a solid sauce, and Istrian ham with parsley and lemon.

The degustation menu at Le Mandrać changes daily, and consists of 15 small courses, meant to be consumed over several leisurely hours. A different wine is recommended with each course, and Le Mandrać is able to draw on its own well-stocked cellar. However, Le Mandrać doesn't stray too far from its Croatian roots. Even the decor manages to stand out among the neighbouring canvas awnings and still blend well with the antiquity of the village square.

Volosko is also home to other fine eateries, like the **Amfora** (Črnikovica 4, 051 701 222), a highly respected traditional seafood restaurant that has also been adding some gourmet touches and boasts a lovely terrace looking on to the sea. The **Konoba Ribarnica** (A Stangera 5, 051 701 483) is a more rustic, affordable option.

WIND-SURFING
Volosko is also known as one of Croatia's great windsurfing spots – you can ride the waves at Volosko harbour itself before heading off for your gourmet meal.

KVARNER & ISLANDS

Sveti Jakov.

At a serene turning point in the promenade, this resort hotel's restaurant serves fine seafood on a seaview terrace. The kitchen uses good local ingredients, like truffles, available with fillet of beef or with *fuži*, pasta twists. The house grilled fish, mixed fish, sea bass and calamari are all well prepared. You can also order an à la carte menu, and receive the meal that hotel guests get for the price of their room.

★ Le Mandrać

Obala Frana Supila 10, Volosko (051 701 357/ www.lemandrac.com). **Open** 11am-midnight daily. **Credit** AmEx, DC, MC, V.
Classy and inventive establishment in the gastronomic enclave of Volosko, 2km (1.25 miles) from Opatija, employs local ingredients to create nouvelle-style cuisine and fusion recipes. *See p159* **Profile**.
▶ *For a choice of aperitifs and a sunset view, pop into the Caffè Kon-Tiki; see p161.*

Mali Raj

Obala maršala Tita 191 (051 704 074). **Open** noon-midnight daily. **Credit** MC, V.
Down the main road, some three kilometres from the town, Mali Raj is in the neighbouring village of Ičići – an appetite-building seaside stroll along the Lungomare. Secluded in a cool, woody section of the promenade, on the bottom floor of a tiny, pricey pension, Mali Raj provides one of the prettiest terraces and best meals in a town that is full of great food and great views. The service is swift, friendly and professionally unobtrusive. They push the top-quality white fish – the fresh, succulent sea bass is worth

the price. Alternatively, you can splash out on lobster or scallops here with confidence or get equal pleasure from the satisfactory steaks.
▶ *If you enjoyed this, another great meal in a beautiful villa can be ordered at the Restaurant Ariston (see below).*

Sveti Jakov

Hotel Milenij, Sv Jakov Park, Obala maršala Tita 109 (051 202 000/www.ugohoteli.hr). **Open** noon-midnight daily. **Credit** AmEx, DC, MC, V.
The restaurant of the five-star Hotel Milenij is set in a villa dated 1866, where respiratory specialist Dr Julius Glax worked. A noble arched portico covers half the restaurant's terrace in the park. Inside, the decor beams with Baroque opulence. Sveti Jakov's capable kitchen does wonderful things with fresh seafood, like octopus salad served in wine sauce or catch of the day, an assortment of fresh fish brought out on a plate for detailed discussions and selection. Special menus contain meatier, central European dishes designed to recreate the Habsburg era.
▶ *For details on the Hotel Milenij; see p163.*

★ Plavi Podrum

Obala Frana Supila 12, Volosko (051 701 233). **Open** noon-midnight daily. **Credit** AmEx, DC, MC, V.
A great seafood restaurant has added gourmet touches to its cuisine, helping make Volosko a gastronomic destination. *See p159* **Profile**.

Restaurant Ariston

Hotel Villa Ariston, Šetalište maršala Tita 179 (051 271 379). **Open** 4-11pm daily. **Credit** AmEx, DC, MC, V.
The sumptuous dining room and shaded garden of an old villa converted into a hotel are the settings for superior seafood dinners. These are augmented with fancier fare, like fillet of *branzino* stuffed with scampi, monkfish in white wine or tuna in a rosemary-tinged Mediterranean sauce. Deferential waiters also offer a complimentary appetiser of petit fours with fish stuffing. You can sit under your own small gazebo or on the upper terrace for a commanding view of the sea.
▶ *Excellent seafood in an attractive, al fresco location can also be enjoyed at Vongola (Šetalište maršala Tita 113, 051 711 854), nearer to town.*

Where to drink

Café Wagner

Obala maršala Tita 109 (051 202 071). **Open** 7am-midnight daily. **Credit** MC, V.
A Viennese-style café invoking Opatija's Habsburg heritage with its creamy cakes, it gets mobbed for 4pm coffee time. Superior central European desserts are prepared with seasonal local ingredients. The quality of the espressos, cappuccinos and other brews stands up to the cakes. *See p161* **Inside Track**.

★ Caffè Kon-Tiki
Obala Frana Supila 12, Volosko (051 701 661).
Open 8am-midnight daily. **No credit cards.**
Right between Volosko's two gourmet restaurants, is this great seaside terrace for before- or after-dinner drinks. The Kon-Tiki is busy all day with a good mix of locals and visitors enjoying Croatian beer on tap for 18kn a pint, bottled varieties including Guinness, or one of the 70 types of cocktails. The gorgeous harbour view and convivial atmosphere are compelling reasons to hang around and watch the sun set over the distant hills of Istria.

Caffè Bar Leonardo
Obala maršala Tita 129 (no phone). **Open**
8am-midnight daily. **No credit cards.**
As the road slopes east of town, this fine terrace and triangular-shaped bar has a commanding view of the bay and a casual, comfortable feel that encourage you to hang around on the low, well-cushioned chairs. No cocktails, but decent coffees, and the standard beers, wines and spirits. A fine place to refresh and recuperate in the thick of things.

Choco Bar
Obala maršala Tita 94 (051 603 562). **Open**
8am-midnight daily. **Credit** AmEx, MC, V.
Classic Croatian chocolatiers Kraš have opened this palace of decadence, somewhat disguised as a café, on Opatija's main drag. Along with their elaborate sweets, tantalisingly displayed under glass in the glitzy interior, they also serve cakes, mousse and cocktails, which are all made of chocolate, plus the hot drink variety. Excellent coffee is also available.

INSIDE TRACK
GOOEY DELIGHTS

Mid afternoon is cake time in Opatija. Along with well known temples to confectionery such as **Café Wagner** *(see p160)* and the **Grand Café** *(see below),* the **Café Palme** (Obala maršala Tita 108, 051 706 300) in the Hotel Bristol offers sticky treats on a terrace lined with palm trees. Live jazz plays in the evening.

The pretty covered terrace, with modern decorative touches, is a nice place to relax and watch the busy boulevard go by.
► *To explore more of Opatija's gooey side, see above* **Inside Track**.

Grand Café
Obala maršala Tita 85 (051 295 001). **Open**
7am-10pm daily. **Credit** AmEx, DC, MC, V.
This Viennese-style coffeeshop offers cakes, ice-cream sundaes, good coffee, fancy teas, eight types of cocktail and most other types of booze. They also make their own chocolate sweets and pralines, which you can buy for immediate consumption or in a mixed box to take away. *See above* **Inside Track**.

Hemingway
Zert 2 (051 711 205/www.hemingway.hr). **Open**
7am-2am Mon-Thur, Sun; 7am-5am Fri, Sat.
Credit MC, V.

Café Wagner

KVARNER & ISLANDS

This slick seaside space of several bars and two small dancefloors is the main local spot to drink and party. After sundown it heaves with fun-seeking holidaymakers looking to mingle over Opatija's best cocktails. Plush, low chairs make it hard to leave the covered terrace, with its view of the marina on one side and the open sea on the other. The dancefloors are serviced by DJs and gratuitous go-go dancers. A recently added restaurant serves until 2am.

▶ *If things get too hectic here, hop over to late-opening Galija (Zert 3, 051 272 242) opposite.*

Kavana Coretto

Obala maršala Tita 119 (no phone). **Open** 7am-11pm Mon-Thur, Sun; 7am-midnight Fri, Sat. **No credit cards.**

This cocktail bar is on a terrace raised above the downtown beach, in a busy section of the promenade. Lounge in a swinging chair or sink into a low, cushiony couch, listen to clubby music and take in passers-by and the sea vistas. It's easy to start a night in the Coretto, where happy hour buzzes on for several, but by the time midnight comes, you'll have to head to the later bars.

▶ *For more cocktails on the same promenade, try the bar at the chic Design Hotel Astoria; see below.*

★ Monokini

Obala maršala Tita 96 (051 703 888). **Open** 7am-2am daily. **No credit cards.**

The main contemporary bar attracts a younger, more bohemian crowd. Friendly staff give enthusiastic service, even though things can get hectic later on. The bar, on the main road through the heart of town, comes with arty decor that includes changing exhibitions by Croatian artists. CDs range from techno to rock. Internet café at the back.

Nightlife

Disco Seven Lounge Bar

Obala maršala Tita 125 (099 477 7000 mobile). **Closed** Winter. **Open** *Summer* 11pm-6am Thur-Sat. **No credit cards.**

This two-year-old disco, run by the Hemingway along the promenade, is the first club to open here in ages, and one of the few places still busy after 2am. There's a seaside terrace above, and more outdoor seating at ground level, by the entrance. The dancefloor is indoors, DJs spinning house, disco and weekend classics.

▶ *Warm up with a sea view and great cocktails at Hemingway; see p161.*

Where to stay

Beller

Poljanska cesta 12, Ičići (051 704 101/091 791 6842 mobile/fax 051 704 296/www.beller.hr). **Rates** *Apartment* €70-€120. **Credit** AmEx, DC, MC, V.

Seven comfortable apartments set in a four-star villa a short way down the Lungomare from Opatija near the ACI marina at Ičići. Properties can be hired out by the night or, except in summer, by the month (€600-€700). All come with a private terrace, internet facilities and air-conditioning, and private parking is a boon for traffic-swamped Opatija. Units accommodate two people comfortably, four easily, and are a short walk from the sea and a sports centre with tennis courts.

★ Design Hotel Astoria

Obala maršala Tita 174 (tel/fax 051 706 350/www.hotel-astoria.hr). **Rates** €65-€85 single; €93-€137 double. **Credit** AmEx, DC, MC, V.

This hotel, built in 1904, was stylishly renovated in 2006, a slick, modern interior in a classic old building creating a splash on Opatija's seaside. The bar is a destination in its own right. The 50 rooms, done up in natural tones and striking furnishings, all come equipped with flat-screen satellite TVs, air-conditioning and high-speed internet access. Despite all this, this chic four-star has quite reasonable rates – at least for the time being.

Grand Hotel 4 opatijska cvijeta

VC Ermina 6 (051 278 007/fax 051 295 001/www.milenijhoteli.hr). **Rates** €65-€82 single; €90-€164 double. **Credit** AmEx, DC, MC, V.

A villa that once belonged to the noble Eszterházys has been combined with a fin-de-siècle hotel and renovated to form a campus of four striking, pastel-coloured buildings amid pretty shaded lawns. It stretches uphill from the marina, a boon for the majority of the 262 rooms with balconies. There are also indoor and outdoor pools, a spa, gym and restaurant. You'll certainly feel pampered.

★ Grand Hotel Adriatic

Obala maršala Tita 200 (051 719 000/fax 051 719 025/www.hotel-adriatic.hr). **Rates** €90-€110 single; €125-€175 double. **Credit** AmEx, DC, MC, V.

This new spa- and sport-oriented four-star on the seafront also contains a casino and convention cen-

INSIDE TRACK
SEA TREATMENTS

Doctors who realised the health benefits of seawater and seawater derivatives invented thalassotherapia – Opatija is still home to a medical institution based around this therapy. It is now a centre for medical research and for provision of seawater-based treatments for cardiology, rheumatism and psychiatric conditions. See www.thalassotherapia-opatija.hr for details.

tre. Pride of place goes to the top-floor health area: heated seawater pool; Finnish sauna; Turkish bath, plus a dozen massage and bath units. Outside, the expansive terrace gives a view of the Kvarner Bay. The Adriatic offers two outdoor tennis courts and can arrange climbing and hikes around National Parks. The 300-room complex comprises two hotel buildings; guests in the cheaper Adriatic II three-star also have access to the spa and pool.

Hotel Agava

Obala maršala Tita 89 (051 278 100/fax 051 278 007/www.milenijhoteli.hr). **Rates** €71-€89 single; €110-€196 double. **Credit** AmEx, DC, MC, V.

This villa, built in 1896, was renovated in 2006 to make a 76-room four-star hotel in a luxurious setting near the sea and the pretty Angolina Park. The rooms are stunning – polished wood floors, period-style furnishings, air-conditioning and internet. Little extras, such as international newspapers delivered to your door, and laundry and room service available from 6am to 10pm, offer that special touch.

▶ *Guests can also use the gym and swimming pools at sister hotel, the Grand Hotel 4 opatijska cvijeta; see p162.*

★ Hotel Ambasador

F Peršića 1 (051 710 444/fax 051 271 503/ www.liburnia.hr). **Rates** €83-€108 single; €134-€176 double. **Credit** AmEx, DC, MC, V.

The latest accommodation in the local Liburnia fleet, the Ambasador is an impressive, five-star spa hotel of ten floors, 180 rooms, a private beach and best of all, the Five Elements Wellness Centre. Over two floors, this involves saunas, an indoor heated seawater pool, an eight-person whirlpool, a children's pool, massage showers and treatments based on the Five Elements principle. Throw in the Hortenzia summer garden restaurant, the Palma bar and Manhattan cocktail bar, and you have a very tidy year-round operation indeed.

▶ *This five-star spa hotel is attached to the cheaper, four-star Villa Ambassador – same contact details. Guests may also use the Five Elements spa centre in the adjoining hotel.*

Hotel Kvarner

P Tomašića 1-4 (tel/fax 051 271 202/ www.liburnia.hr). **Rates** €60-€75 single; €100-€150 double. **Credit** AmEx, DC, MC, V.

Croatia's first luxury hotel on the Adriatic, the Kvarner, right on the promenade, is still an imposing imperial presence in the heart of Opatija. Some of the sheen has come off since its glory days, which is why this revered institution is now one of the better bargains in town. Fans of grandeur will love the majestic size of the Crystal Ballroom, the ornate hotel lobby and the splendid seaside terrace beyond it. The rooms themselves are large, furnished in antique style but do not have modern conveniences

INSIDE TRACK
CHEAP STAYS

Not everyone who comes to Opatija can afford the five-star spa luxury the town thrives on. Two- and three-star hotels are few and far between, so the solution is to take a private room. Local agencies such as **Atlas** (Obala maršala Tita 116, 051 271 033, www.atlas-croatia.com) and **Da Riva** (Obala maršala Tita 170, 051 272 990, www. da-riva.com) can book rooms for you.

like air-conditioning. Prices are a little higher for the sea-view rooms, but worth it, as these are usually larger. With restaurant, bar and terrace café, there are plenty of good places to lounge, plus there are massage treatments, a sauna and an indoor pool. The grounds include an outdoor pool surrounded by a patio and steps leading down to the hotel beach.

▶ *For more contemporary spa treatments, sister Hotel Ambassador is a five-star treat; see above.*

Hotel Milenij

Obala maršala Tita 109 (051 202 000/fax 051 278 007/www.milenijhoteli.hr). **Rates** €86-€106 single; €100-€162 double. **Credit** AmEx, DC, MC, V.

A newly renovated villa from the late 1800s and an adjacent modern building, offer some of Opatija's fanciest and certainly most expensive accommodation – though the Milenij can seem like it's struggling to deserve its five-star status. The rooms are tastefully decorated and kept in impeccable shape, but they're small. All are air-conditioned, with internet connections and fluffy bathrobes. Luxuries include a pool with a retractable glass roof, 24-hour room service and a spa centre.

▶ *Although half-board deals here only include a buffet-style service, the outstanding Sveti Jakov, which is attached to the hotel, is well worth the outlay; see p160.*

Hotel Miramar

Ive Kaline 11 (051 280 000/fax 051 280 028/ www.hotel-miramar.info). **Rates** €70-€135 single; €120-€320 double. **Credit** AmEx, DC, MC, V.

The 1876 Villa Neptune has been superbly renovated and expanded to include three guest villas, creating a full-service resort hotel with its own rocky beach. Stylish, comfortable and air-conditioned rooms have their own balcony or terrace. There's a spa with a heated pool, whirlpool, saunas, steam room and beauty treatments. Cross the footbridge from the Lungomare for the private fenced-in beach.

▶ *The terrace restaurant here is a destination in its own right; see p158.*

KVARNER & ISLANDS

Hotel Mozart

Obala maršala Tita 138 (051 718 260/fax 051 271 877/www.hotel-mozart.hr). **Rates** €85-€120 single; €120-€178 double. **Credit** AmEx, DC, MC, V.

Of all the refitted fin-de-siècle confections on Opatija's shore, perhaps the Mozart is most true to the genre. Behind a striking façade of art-nouveau curves and sea-facing balconies, 26 rooms of equal style echo the grandeur of the period. There's enough room for a cosmetic studio and piano bar, and meals can be taken in a pretty courtyard. If you're not bothered about state-of-the-art, but happy to pay for luxury, this is the place for you.

Kn Villa Ariston

Obala maršala Tita 179 (tel/fax 051 271 319/ fax 051 271 877/www.villa-ariston.hr). **Rates** €48-€65 single; €82-€110 double. **Credit** AmEx, DC, MC, V.

A short walk along a beautiful wooded section of the seaside Lungomare takes you to a majestic restored villa with a masterpiece of a garden, a great restaurant and caring service, all at reasonable prices. The tall yellow exterior of the old mansion is striking, and the lobby oozes old-time luxury. The rooms run from suites with polished wood floors to comfortable doubles or singles. In all, there are only 22 beds, which means you can always find a quiet place in the beautiful green grounds. The villa is an affordable three-star, because it lacks a spa centre and other such luxuries – but it sure feels grand.

▶ *For more details of the outstanding restaurant here; see p160.*

Getting there & around

Bus No.32 runs every 20 minutes from **Rijeka** suburban bus station, by the canal, to Opatija – the journey takes 25 minutes and costs 14kn. It also stops at Rijeka train station on the way. From Opatija, the service leaves for Rijeka from the slight incline by the bus information office.

Resources

Tourist information

Opatija Tourist Office *Obala maršala Tita 101 (051 271 310/www.opatija-tourism.hr).* **Open** *June-Sept* 8am-9pm Mon-Sat; 6-9pm Sun. *Sept-June* 8am-3pm Mon-Fri; 8am-2pm Sat.

LOVRAN

Arranged along the foot of sheltering Mount Učka, and set on a rise above the sea that provides some astonishingly beautiful views, **Lovran** is an ancient settlement with a centuries-old town centre and Habsburg-era villas dotted along a lush, green seaside promenade. The town is smaller and feels more exclusive than Opatija, its neighbour about five kilometres (three miles) away. But despite this there's still plenty of life here, taking it easy on the pebbly beaches and or getting busy in the jumping bars, which get packed with a generally younger crowd. And, as with other towns along the Lungomare promenade, Lovran's collection of superb restaurants is sufficient reason to visit.

About the city

Lovran, with a population of 5,000, wasn't always the small fry in Kvarner. A busy settlement since at least the seventh century, 'Lauriana' was named after its many laurel trees. In the 12th century, the Arab writer and geographer Al-Idrisi said: 'Lovran is a large and progressive city, which has ships always ready, and shipbuilders always employed'. Along with shipbuilding, Lovran traded locally grown cherries, peaches and their well-known sweet chestnuts, called marrons, celebrated with their own festival in October.

Lovran was ruled by the counts of Istria until the 15th century, when Austrians took over. It remained under Austrian rule until the Habsburg empire fell apart at the end of World War I.

Modern tourism came here in the late 1800s, as the wooden sailing ships that had employed Lovran's builders were being replaced by steam vessels built elsewhere. Following the lead of Opatija, which was becoming well-known as a destination for holidaymakers seeking a healthy climate, Lovran shifted its economy toward tourism. Many luxury villas went up by the sea, mostly along the main road of Šetalište maršala Tita and the Lungomare promenade.

Today, many villas have been restored into superior forms of accommodation, offering relative seclusion by the sea, with four-star extras. Even if you don't check in, it's worth checking out the grand exteriors of these old mansions while taking in amazing sea vistas on the shaded Lungomare.

INSIDE TRACK MOUNT UČKA

Mount Učka Nature Park stretches inland from Lovran. Its highest peak, 1,401-metre tall Mount Vojak, is topped by an old tower that offers stunning views of Croatian islands and the Italian Alps. The park has 50 hiking paths and eight mountain-bike trails. Contact the park office at Liganj 42 (051 293 753/ www.pp-ucka.hr).

Lungomare promenade.

Sightseeing

The Old Town of Lovran is perched above
the harbour. It's easiest to access through the
Eastern City Gate, **Stubica**, which faces the
sea. Inside is a quaint asymmetrical clutter of
streets, courtyards and old houses centred
around **St. George's Square** (Trg sv Jurja).
The square is dominated by **St. George's
Church**, built in the 12th century and
reconstructed in the 15th, when local artists
added Gothic frescoes. The church was
enlarged in the 17th century; Baroque chapels
were added and the bell tower was attached to
the rest of the structure. Both the square and
the church are named after the town's patron
saint, a likeness of whom can be seen slaying a
dragon in one of the decorative doorway arches
in the old town. With the exception of the **Old
Town Tower**, diagonally facing the church,
the medieval fortifications are gone, most built
over with houses. Left unprotected, the Old
Town has been invaded by tourists.

Beaches

There are two good beaches in town.
Kvarner beach is on a bend in the Lungomare
promenade, past the Old Town in the Opatija
direction. This is a terraced concrete beach,
usually the busier one in town, with simple
food and decent drinks available from the
snack bar/café. **Plaža Peharovo**, in the other
direction, toward Medveja, is right next to the
No.32 bus terminus in Lovran, along the main

drag of Šetalište maršala Tita. This is a pretty,
well-shaded pebbly beach, with its own snack
bar, surrounded by tall woods on three sides.
   Probably the best beach around is **Medveja**,
a large pebbly crescent, a ten-minute walk
south from Lovran on the main drag. All along
the Lungomare promenade, there are spots
where you can get down to rocky beaches. If
you can handle the rocks (bring flip-flops), you
can usually find a quiet patch to call your own.

Where to eat

Konoba Marun
Stari Grad 52 (098 192 8462 mobile). **Open**
noon-1am daily. **No credit cards**.
There's no fish, but plenty of the cuisine from inland
Istria in this small indoor tavern-restaurant in the
Old Town. Istrian *fuži* pasta is prepared with beef
and parmesan or truffles, also served in risotto or
with steak. Other pastas include small but delicious
portions of own-made meat ravioli, served with courgette and camembert or gorgonzola sauce. You'll get

---

**INSIDE TRACK
COVER CHARGES**

Prices around Lovran are generally
reasonable but there is an annoying
tendency among local restaurants to
follow the Italian lead and to charge a
cover of 5kn or more per diner. Make
sure you check this before you order.

---

equal satisfaction from the meaty mains, such as steaks, lamb chops and veal. Good meat starters include *pršut* Istrian ham or *kulen*, a spicy salami.

▶ *For seafood close by, try the pricier Lovranska Vrata (Stari Grad 94, 051 291 050), right on St George's Square.*

★ Pizza Delfino

26. Divizije 4 (051 293 293/www.delfino.hr). **Open** 11am-midnight daily. **Credit** AmEx, DC, MC, V.

A short uphill walk from the harbour takes you to a restaurant with a spacious interior containing kitsch murals, a beautiful garden offering glimpses of the sea below and some of the best pizzas in Kvarner. The deservedly popular Delfino lists 16 types of pizza, and nine feature ham. The limited variety isn't a problem as the superb sauce, thick melted cheese and thin hard crust underneath are all so good. Pastas, lasagnes and grilled meats are also available.

▶ *Delfino has a branch in Rijeka, also with quality pizzas – Trg Jurja Klovića, 051 336 736.*

Restoran Knezgrad

Trg Slobode 12 (051 291 838). **Open** 11am-11pm daily. **Credit** AmEx, MC, V.

Slip away from the crowds for good seafood on a terrace facing a pretty little park, at the edge of the Old Town. Along with standard appetisers like *pršut* ham and a delicately seasoned octopus salad, they offer goulash with dumplings and pasta with scampi in cream sauce. A good choice of top-quality fish, shellfish and calamari includes langouste lobster. Steak, liver and grilled meat round out the rather large menu. Service is friendly and unobtrusive.

★ Restoran Najade

Šetalište maršala Tita 69 (051 291 866). **Open** 11am-1am daily. **Credit** MC, V.

With superb seafood, a great terrace at sea level below most of the town, and reasonable prices despite the 7kn-per-diner cover charge, the Najade is a contender for best meal in Lovran. The wide selection of fresh fish includes less common offerings like sole, monkfish and turbot; crustaceans include scallops and lobster, served grilled, or stewed *buzara* style. The mixed fish platter is a great way to get what's freshest. Meat eaters can get châteaubriand for two or Balkan-style grill. They have about 30 white wines and 25 reds, mostly Croatian. The relaxed waiters might even break into song between tables.

Where to drink

Buffet Stubica

Stari Grad 25 (051 293 412). **Open** 7am-10pm daily. **No credit cards.**

In front of the Stubica doorway leading to the Old Town, on a terrace with a great view down to the harbour and sea below, locals gather for beery con-

versation and philosophising. There is food here, too, but the main attraction is affordable alcohol and a chummy crowd, which convenes early, for breakfast beers, and tends to linger through the day.

▶ *If you're after something more substantial, the Konoba Marun is a good nearby bet; see p165.*

★ Caffè Bar Orange

Šetalište maršala Tita 57 (098 924 3265 mobile). **Open** 8am-2am daily. **No credit cards.**

The gorgeous view from the terrace – on a low bluff just above the sea, along the Lungomare – is reason enough to come here. Add in funky decor, friendly local regulars, a sweetly sarcastic barmaid and a soundtrack from rock to R&B, and you have a winning bar. A young crowd filters in and out of Caffè Bar Orange all day, and by nightfall the place has usually become quite lively. The interior features pebble paths on the floor, leopard- and zebra-patterned furniture and raised bathroom tiles over the toilet urging customers to 'sit please relax'. Parties ratchet up when students come back and the bar hosts DJs and dancing.

Kn Caffè Bar Guc

Šetalište maršala Tita 63 (no phone). **Open** 10am-2am daily. **No credit cards.**

Right on the harbour, below the rest of town, an amicable young staff runs a comfortable terrace bar with a good mix of music. Drinks are cheap, with a *travorica* herb grappa going for 8kn and 28 types of cocktails available for between 15kn and 35kn. The place only opened in summer 2008, but it has already begun to pick up a regular crowd, many of them students or at that age. There are DJs and live music, and closing time can be delayed until first light. During the daytime, Caffè Bar Gruc is a gorgeous setting for a quiet cup of coffee.

Gradska Kavana

Šetalište maršala Tita 41(051 294 444). **Open** 7am-midnight daily. **Credit** AmEx, MC, V.

On the main street, this Habsburg-era cafe brings a little bit of old Vienna to Lovran. The fancy Baroque-style interior and classy-looking terrace provide a perfect setting for gooey cakes, ice-cream, and good coffee. There are more than 50 cocktails, most rea-

INSIDE TRACK
DRAGA DI LOVANA

For a gastronomic experience and picturesque outing, take a taxi for ten minutes to the family-run hotel **Draga di Lovrana** (Lovranska draga 1, 051 277 689, www.dragadilovrana.hr/onama.php), high over Lovran near the top of Mount Učka. Expect great fresh fish and commanding sea vistas.

sonably priced at 25kn-35kn. The speciality is an ice-cream cocktail: your choice from seven flavours, vodka, Triple Sec, grenadine and sugar. There's an à la carte restaurant around the side.

Lovranski Pub

Šetalište maršala Tita 41(051 293 237). **Open** 7am-2am daily. **No credit cards.**

This old-style, dimly lit wood and brick interior, with taps dispensing Guinness and decent beers, is done up like a classic pub. But the big back garden, fenced in by greenery and shaded by umbrellas and baby palm trees, is far too idyllic to belong to an ordinary bar. There's even a children's playground in one corner. In the evenings, when the bar draws a sizeable crowd of locals and visitors, there are DJs or live music acts. Hopheads may appreciate the beer plate, a tray with 16 foamy glasses. The kitchen opens at noon, serving pizzas and sandwiches.

▶ *If the children get bored in the playground, treat them to a cake or ice-cream in the Gradska Kavana upstairs; see p166.*

Where to stay

Excelsior Hotel

Šetalište maršala Tita 15 (051 292 233/fax 051 271 503/www.liburnia.hr). **Rates** €80-€155 double. **Credit** AmEx, DC, MC, V.

Lovran's biggest hotel is a modern ten-storey four-star with 177 rooms, an indoor and outdoor pool, a restaurant, nearby tennis courts and its own concrete beach a short walk away from the town's concrete beach. It's the classic resort hotel experience but a comfortable choice if you want all your needs seen to in one place.

▶ *For something cheaper nearby, the three-star Bristol (No.27, 051 291 022) is another Liburnia with the same website details.*

★ Hotel Park

Šetalište maršala Tita 60 (051 706 200/fax 051 293 791/www.hotelparklovran.hr). **Rates** €53-€96 single; €86-€152 double. **Credit** AmEx, DC, MC, V.

With a commanding position at a bend in the main road, next to the Old Town and above the harbour, the four-star Park is as central as you can get. The pretty old structure is new inside, restored in 2005. The priciest rooms face the sea; the others face the forest behind the hotel. There is a small indoor pool, a gym and a jacuzzi – a sauna and beauty treatments are planned. The helpful staff, and extras, like laundry service or a choice of 200 newspapers, provide a classy touch.

Hotel Lovran

Šetalište maršala Tita 19/2 (051 706 200/ fax 051 291 222/fax 051 292 467/www.hotel-lovran.hr). **Rates** €31-€68 single; €52-€126 double. **Credit** AmEx, DC, MC, V.

INSIDE TRACK
LUXURY VILLAS

Lovran's lodging speciality is high-end conversion of historic villas. Some, like the **Villa Astra** (Viktora Cara Emina 11, 051 294 400, www.lovranske-vile.com), have a spa and top-class restaurant. Nearby at No.3, the **Villa Magnolia** (051 294 897, www.villa-magnolia.info) retains its Habsburg grandeur. On Šetalište maršala Tita, the **Villa Vera** (No.5, 051 294 120, www.hotel-villavera.hr) and the **Villa Eugenia** (No.34, 051 294 800, www.eto.hr) are also luxury options.

Two old villas, last renovated in 2003, have been converted into one medium-sized three-star hotel, with 53 moderately-priced rooms, near the centre of Lovran. Those with air-conditioning facing the sea are more expensive. There is a bar, a restaurant and a tavern on the premises, as well as a concrete hotel beach, and tennis courts nearby. Could be an affordable way to fit the family into an old villa.

Kn Pansion Stanger

Šetalište maršala Tita 128 (051 291 154/ www.pansion-stanger.com/uk). **Rates** €20-€48 single; €36-€66 double. **Credit** AmEx, DC, MC, V.

Among the cheaper and simpler local lodging options, this modern bed-and-breakfast is located along the sea, about a kilometre from the centre of Lovran towards Medveja and its fine beaches. The 21 rooms are in decent condition; each has a bathroom, a fridge and a balcony. All in all, it's a good base for an affordable seaside getaway.

Getting there & around

Bus No.32 runs every 20 minutes from **Rijeka** suburban bus station, via Opatija. The journey takes half an hour and costs 15kn. Lovran is at the end of the line.

Resources

Tourist information

Lovran Tourist Office *Šetalište maršala Tita 63 (051 291 740/www.tz-lovran.hr).* **Open** *Summer* 9am-9pm daily.

KRK

As you travel the high altitude motorway bridge from the mainland to **Krk**, past mind-blowing vistas of steep stony hills and sea, you can feel a dramatic change in your surroundings. Across the bridge is Croatia's

Crikvenica. See p172.

largest and most populous island, a region unto itself, boasting a widely varied grouping of attractive resort towns. There's big busy **Krk town**, with its bustling bars and other tourist businesses. (You can get donkey rides around town and have your name written in rice or imprinted on a custom number plate.) Near the southern tip of the island is popular **Baška**, whose famous Blue Flag sandy beach is, at nearly 2km, one of the largest on the coast. **Vrbnik** is quieter, and the place to go for gastronomic delights. **Malinska**, is also a relatively quiet getaway with a good gastronomic scene – perhaps the island's best. Although Krk town is probably the top all-around place for drinking, Malinska is becoming a nightlife hub, with two of the island's three late-night clubs. **Omišalj**, one of the towns closest to the mainland bridge, is the home of Rijeka's airport.

Sightseeing

Krk's tradition of tourism goes back as far as almost anywhere on the coast – they were issuing picture postcards here as far back as 1866. After being inhabited by Liburnians, Illyrians, Romans and Croats, Krk was ruled by powerful medieval dukes, the Frankopans, who once held half of modern-day Croatia. Krk town's walls date to pre-Roman times, and the oldest of the towers in that wall, the square one at **Trg Kamplin**, was built in 1191. The best-preserved historical site, the three-nave **Cathedral of the Assumption** (Trg sv Kvirina, open 9.30am-1pm, 5-7pm daily), built on the site of an early Christian basilica, dates from the early 1200s, with a bell tower from the 16th to 18th centuries. The **Kaštel**, with a cylindrical tower, is Venetian, as are the three city gates and the rest of the wall. The Old Town's squares and main thoroughfare of **JJ**

Strossmayera, now lined with souvenir shops and fast-food outlets, throng with tourists all summer long.

Nearby is **Punat**, where a beautiful bay shelters a large harbour. In the middle is the islet of **Košljun**, home to a 15th-century Franciscan monastery with a religious treasury.

Tourists also pack Baška in the south, Krk island's other main attraction. Its sandy shore, beach towel to beach towel in high season, begins on the western end of the harbour. You walk to it via a busy, café-lined promenade – in summer you'll be walking two or three abreast. The beaches of Krk town, sandy but crowded, are north-west past the harbour. Further on are quieter, more rocky ones. Malinska boasts well groomed beaches a seaside stroll west of the harbour. To escape the crowds, keep walking towards Porat to find rockier ones.

Baška Aquarium

Na Vodici 2 (051 860 171/www.silotourist.com/ aquarium_english.htm). **Open** 9am-10pm daily. **Admission** 30kn; 15kn reductions. **No credit cards.**
Located below ground in a building near the bus station, the recently opened Baška Aquarium has 20 tanks containing more than 100 species of fish, as well as one of the richest collections of shellfish and snails in Croatia.

Where to eat

★ Bistro Trattoria Franica

Ribarska 39, Baška (051 860 023). **Open** 11am-midnight daily. **No credit cards**.
The raised terrace by the bustling harbour is not the only asset here – Franica offers some of the better food on tourist-swamped Baška. Italian specialities are not all that can be recommended; the seafood menu includes two types of fish platter for two, plus scallops, tuna steak and mackerel. Local delights,

concocted with seasonal ingredients, include a hearty goulash with potatoes Krk-style, and a roasted octopus so rich and filling that, were it not for the taste, you would swear it was beef. There are seats in the beautiful interior if the terrace is full.

Cicibela

Emila Geistlicher 38, Baška (051 856 013). **Open** *Jan-Oct* 10am-midnight daily. Closed Nov, Dec. **Credit** AmEx, DC, MC, V.

Amid the long line of venues on Baška beach, Cicibela, run by the jolly Bogdesić family, stands out for its cookery. You can opt for lobster or one of many seafood-pasta combinations: squid in its own ink or scampi with spaghetti. There's no outdoor seating but tables by the window have sea views.

▶ *For quality seafood and steak, the summer-only Lantino at No.30 (051 856 484) is a handy and reliable option.*

Frankopan

Trg Svetog Kvirna, Krk town (051 221 437). **Open** *Jan-Oct* 10am-11pm daily. Closed Nov, Dec. **Credit** AmEx, DC, MC, V.

This terrace restaurant under the belltower of the cathedral, in a pretty part of the Old Town, serves fine seafood, pizzas and schnitzels to a steady stream of tourists. Appetisers include regional specials such as *pršut*, Pag cheese and Istrian truffles. Stand-out main dish is langoustine lobster. While the food and location are great, waitstaff can be overwhelmed in peak season – set aside plenty of time and you won't be disappointed.

Konoba Corsaro

Obala Hrvatske mornarice 2, Krk town (051 220 084). **Open** 11am-2am daily. **No credit cards**.

Of the several accommodating restaurants on Krk town's harbour, this is the more spacious, with 120 seats, 90 on the terrace. It also has the more attractive decor and attentive waiters. Along with the classic seafood offerings – catch of the day and the platter for two are fine choices – they offer *šurlice* with goulash, and a decent steak with truffles.

▶ *The Konoba Šime (051 220 042) and the recently upgraded restaurant at the Hotel Marina (see p171) are also recommended choices nearby.*

INSIDE TRACK BURA WIND

Whatever travel plans you have may be affected by the *Bura* wind, which blasts down through the mountain passes above the gulf. When it roars, the Krk bridge (linking to the region's only airport, now a budget air destination from the UK) is forced to close and no boats can go out.

★ Konoba Nino

Lina Bolmarčića, Malinska (051 859 011). **Open** 7am-11pm daily. **No credit cards**.

Serious seafood is served in a casual atmosphere at this roofed-over terrace cluttered with maritime kitsch in a shady spot steps from Malinska's downtown beach. Nino attracts summer regulars, who gab with the friendly waitstaff and linger over wine long after lunch is done. The fare consists of excellent preparations of the typical Kvarner offerings, plus fancier scallops and lobster, and the prices are reasonable: the fish mix for one, variable according to that day's catch, comprises three varieties with potatoes for 90kn. They also do steaks, a mixed Balkan grill and other meat dishes. A brunch of cheese, ham and bread is served before 11am.

★ Portić

Portić 10, Malinska (no phone). **Open** *Apr-Sept* noon-midnight daily. Closed Oct-Mar. **No credit cards**.

The appetiser of bread with fish spread plonked down before your order arrives hints that dinner at Portić will be a treat – and it is. Starters such as spaghetti with mussels or the fish soup swimming with shrimp, stand out. The fish is cooked perfectly, and served to your terrace table lapped by the sea. The place is popular and at times service here can be harried but never less than courteous.

Restoran Galeb

Emila Geistlicher, Baška (051 860 071/091 201 3726 mobile). **Open** 9am-midnight daily. **Credit** AmEx, DC, MC, V.

One of the classier restaurants on a waterside promenade full of snack bars, the Galeb offers great fish in a cool, blue, covered terrace overlooking Baška beach. The menu also features meat, like steaks and grilled *pleškavica*, but the exceptional variety of seafood is the main attraction. Try the mixed shellfish platter, with scallops, oysters, mussels and clams. Unusual starters include smoked sea-bass fillet in horseradish sauce, scampi cocktail or green tagliatelle with fruits de mer. There are fancy mains, like lobster, grilled or stewed *buzara* style, or house-style, golden-browned from the oven.

Where to drink

Casa di Frangiapane

Šetalište sv Bernardina, Krk town (091 229 4602 mobile). **Open** *Apr-Sept* 8am-midnight daily. Closed Oct-Mar. **No credit cards**.

The former Casa di Padrone is now the house of Frangiapane, but not much else has changed. This harbourside café bustles day and night with a young, party crowd, squeezed into an enclosed terrace overlooking the dock and a two-floor indoor space. After dark, DJs play party tunes for summer abandonment. Cocktails clutter an extensive menu but plump for something simple and enjoy.

KVARNER & ISLANDS

Kn Estivo Pub

Zvonimirova, Baška (no phone). **Open** 9am-2am daily. **No credit cards**.

In a courtyard off Baška's main drag, above the harbour, is a charming covered garden, prettier than your local back home but still aspiring to be a pub. With cheap beer (7kn-14kn), affordable cocktails (six varieties) and relaxed service, this new spot is seeking to beat the nearby competition – there is also occasional acoustic music.

▶ *For cocktails in a more basic setting, the summer-only Havana (Palada 11) and Caffè Bar Sun & Fun (Palada 4) near the ferry pier are other Baška favourites.*

Pub Tiffany

A Stepinca, Krk town (no phone). **Open** Apr-Sept 8am-1am daily. Closed Oct-Mar. **No credit cards**.

Half-a-dozen large tables, shared with strangers, and a stunning terrace enjoy gorgeous sea views atop a stretch of Old Town fortification. This place gets packed after dark, when rock and disco hits mingle with the animated conversation of the young visitors. It's also popular during the day.

Tajana

JJ Strossmayera, Krk town (no phone). **Open** Apr-Sept 9am-midnight daily. Closed Oct-Mar. **No credit cards**.

Even with an Old Town setting and rather over-the-top decor (note the poker table ceiling), the Tajana still manages to feel like a local. The big, marble-covered bar counter, the pool table and fruit machines all create a comfortable environment for regulars and visitors to step off the busy tourist thoroughfare to chat and nod their heads to a nice mix of alternative rock and dance tunes. A DJ booth is manned at weekends but the dance space is limited – most sip and natter.

Volsonis

Vela Placa 8, Krk town (no phone). **Open** 8am-3am daily. **No credit cards**.

A doorway in the Old Town wall opens to the gorgeous garden terrace of this party hub, also a cavernous two-floor indoor club. It is often the liveliest bar in Krk, with drinkers packing in from early evening. The garden has a great bar, which serves cocktails until 2am but go inside for DJs from Italy and Croatia, live music and later drinking.

▶ *To carry the night on, nip next door to the Jungle disco; see p171.*

Nightlife

Club Boa

Dubašljanska 76, Malinska (051 858 770/ 091 517 9991 mobile/www.clubboa.com). **Open** June-Sept 11pm-5am daily. Closed Oct-May. **No credit cards**.

A downtown cellar done up in black, with a genuine boa inside a terrarium, draws a young crowd for local DJs and guests playing commercial electronica

Vrbnik. *See p168.*

and techno-based dance music. Opened in 2006, this is Malinska's second club and helps add to the buzz started with the Crossroad on the edge of town.

Discothèque Crossroad
Sv Vid, Malinska (051 859 960/www.crossroad-discotheque.com). **Open** *June-Sept* 11pm-5am daily. Closed Oct-May. **No credit cards.**
At an intersection a ten-minute taxi ride from Malinska harbour and 12km (eight miles) from Krk town, the island's biggest disco has indoor and outdoor dancefloors where local DJs and occasional foreign spinners provide commercial dance tunes for a sizeable young crowd. There are live shows by big Croatian bands in peak season. Watch out for flyers – you might catch a stint by Jeff Mills, a go-go girl competition or an R&B, funk or hip-hop night.
▶ *To arrange a taxi, call 091 252 6785 or 098 258 502, both mobile numbers, and agree a fee.*

Jungle
Stjepana Radića, Krk town (051 221 503). **Open** *May-Sept* 9pm-5am daily. Closed Oct-Apr. **No credit cards.**
A typical summer disco in the heart of Krk's Old Town pumps out mainstream pop and disco classics for lighthearted holidaymakers. Guest DJs from around Europe break up the regular beat on odd nights. The crowd is predominantly young but because there are few other places around, there is a little more age range than in most Croatian clubs. Open on sporadic weekends in winter.

Where to stay

★ Atrium Residence Baška
Emila Geistlicher 38, Baška (051 656 111/fax 051 856 880/www.hotelibaska.hr). **Open** Apr-Oct. Closed Nov-Mar. **Rates** €78-€196 double. *Apartments* €108-€492. **Credit** AmEx, DC, MC, V.
Opened in 2008, this is the most luxurious lodging in Baška. It's as close as you can get to the water without swimming in it, but entry is at the rear, offering a sense of privacy and exclusivity. Rooms facing the sea have five stars and higher prices. This is a 'residence', not a hotel; even the ordinary rooms feel special. Most units are fixed up as studio apartments or suites, with kitchenettes and varying degrees of luxury. The best have more than 100sq m of space, in-room saunas and outdoor jacuzzis on spacious private balconies where you lounge four storeys above the beach.
▶ *The same group have several properties here – guests at the nearby cheaper Corinthia/Zvonimir (same contact details) have use of tennis courts.*

Kn Hostel Krk
Dr Dinka Vitezića 32, Krk town (tel/fax 051 220 212/099 502 002 mobile/www.hostel-krk.hr). **Rates** 194kn-264kn double. **Credit** AmEx, DC, MC, V.

INSIDE TRACK
LOCAL TREATS
Krk is most known for *šurlice*, thin tubes of pasta eaten with goulash or lamb stew. The local white wine, Vrbnička, is best tried in situ in its hilltop village of Vrbnik, where the rustic **Konoba Nada** (Glavaca 22, 051 857 065) runs wine tours.

In a tangle of Old-Town streets, this clean and comfortable 60-bed hostel offers five doubles among its five dorm-room options. An in-house pizzeria and safe parking are additional attractions. Ideal (and cheap) if you're spending most of the time outdoors.
▶ *For something a little more classy without having to pay top dollar, the Hotel Bor (Dražica 5, 051 220 200, www.hotelbor.hr) offers proximity to the beach without package-tourist hassle.*

Kn Hotel Kanajt
Kanajt 5, Punat (051 654 340/fax 051 654 341/www.kanajt.hr). **Rates** €50-€80 single; €70-€150 double. **Credit** AmEx, DC, MC, V.
This noteworthy, family-run three-star offers 20 rooms within easy reach of Krk town but closer to the quieter activity of pretty Punat. Overlooking the marina, the Kanajt was once a 16th-century summer retreat for local bishops, and calm is still the order of the day. The warm welcome here (and equally warm bathrooms) invariably encourage repeat custom.

★ Hotel Marina
Obala Hrvatske mornarice, Krk town (051 221 128/fax 051 221 357/www.hotelikrk.hr). **Rates** €104-€143 single; €160-€220 double. **Credit** AmEx, DC, MC, V.
After renovation in 2007 and 2008, the Marina shot from a two-star to a four-star, with ten luxury units on three floors, in the centre of the action. The hotel entrance is near the harbour but rooms have air-con and you can shut out the noise. All rooms have a sea view; the pricier ones their own terrace. The restaurant is on a seaside terrace, with prices to match.
▶ *In the same group, the Dražica (Ružmarinska 6, 051 655 755) is a big three-star with outdoor pools, tennis courts and kids' activities.*

Kn Hotel Tamaris
Emila Geistlicher 34, Baška (051 864 200/fax 051 864 222/www.hotelibaska.hr). **Open** Apr-Nov. Closed Dec-Mar. **Rates** €36-€85 single; €60-€142 double. **Credit** AmEx, DC, MC, V.
Set right on Baška beach, this modest three-star provides 15 doubles, 15 apartments and a large, panoramic terrace to take in the view. The rooms are standard-issue but spring and autumn rates are reasonable, particularly if you go for the half-board option for an extra five euros a head.

INSIDE TRACK
MALINSKA DIGS

In Malinska, the **Malin** (Kralja Tomislava 23, 051 850 234, www.hotelmalin.com) and **Pinia** (Porat 31, 051 866 333, www. hotel-pinia.hr) offer sporty relaxation, the Pinia getting a four-star spa makeover in 2008. The **Adria** (Obala 40, 051 859 131, www.hotel-adria.com.hr) provides basic lodging at reasonable prices, by Malinska beach.

Getting there & around

The **airport** by **Omišalj** on the northern tip of Krk serves **Rijeka** on the mainland. At present there is no public transport to Krk town, 20km (12 miles) away – a taxi (098 369 730 mobile) should cost 300kn. Regular **buses** run from **Rijeka** (1hr 20mins) to **Krk town**, via **Malinska** and then down to **Baška**. A couple a day come from **Zagreb**. **Ferries** hop between **Valbiska** and **Merag** on **Cres** (30mins), and **Baška** and **Lopar** on **Rab** (50mins). In high season only, there is a regular service between **Crikvenica** on the mainland and **Šilo** on Krk's north-eastern tip (30mins).

Resources

Tourist information

Krk Island Tourist Office *Trg sv Kvirina 1, Krk town (051 221 359/www.krk.hr).* **Open** 8am-3pm Mon-Fri.
Krk Town Tourist Office *Obala Hrvatske mornarice, Krk town (051 220 226/www.tz-krk.hr).* **Open** 9am-9pm daily.

RAB

With its remote beaches, lush forests and main town full of jumping bars, **Rab** island can offer wildlife or a wild time. The Romans were so smitten with **Rab town** Emperor Octavian Augustus gave it municipal status in the 1st century BC. The main square is still called **Trg Municipium**, but the town's well known skyline of four bell towers came after the Romans, in medieval times, and many of its architectural treasures were shaped by that era.
The island has two faces. The south-west corner is lush and green; the north-western end barren and rocky. The whole island, the busiest of the Kvarner string, offers any number of jaw-dropping views. Visitors head through the pine woods for the remote sandy beaches on **Lopar**, a peninsula on northern Rab, while the party crowd heads south for the bars and bustle of

Rab town. Other attractions on the island include stunning beaches in **Kampor** and **Pudarica**, and sprawling parklands with pine and oak forests in **Kalifront** and **Dundovo**.

Sightseeing

Illyrians settled on Rab in 350BC, followed by Greeks and Romans, then the Venetians, before two waves of plague hit in the 15th century. Venice allowed refugees to come in and run local businesses and the island was developed for tourism from the late 19th century. A long history of receiving holidaymakers means that Rab has an extensive tourist infrastructure of established bars and restaurants, and staff who take pride in their work.
Rab town is on a skinny peninsula that sticks out parallel to the mainland, bounded within city walls, distinguished by those four church towers. Three main streets – Upper, Middle and Lower – are interlinked with tiny lanes. The town is also divided into the oldest quarter, **Kaldanac**, at the far south-eastern end, and **Varoš**, with elegant Gothic and Renaissance buildings. The historic core is accessed by focal **Trg sv Kristofera**. The **Church of St Mary the Great** (open 10am-1pm, 7.30-10pm daily) has the biggest of Rab's four towers. The church itself, consecrated in 1176, is quite plain with later Renaissance touches. You can climb the campanile for superb views.
The oldest belltower is neighbouring **St Andrew's**, a mix of Renaissance and Baroque styles. Further inland on the hillcrest, the **Church of St Justine** contains a modest collection of sacred art, while the fourth tower belongs to the **Church of St John**. Not much survives aside from the tower but you can climb it for great views. This hilltop row of churches sits above an Old Town that drops straight down to the sea. Stairs cut into it lead down to the water. Inland from the old walled town, where the peninsula meets the mainland, there is a beautiful park called **Komrčar**, with paths winding around heavily wooded hills and emptying out onto the crowded beaches.
Unlike Rab town, most of Lopar is new. Its centre – a school, a church, the post office opposite and a few shops – consists of one street and addresses are given as one number. Few come to Lopar for its services – Central Europeans (you'll see German, Czech and Hungarian on most menus) still descend in droves for its beaches alone.
In Rab town, the crowded town beach is reached through Komrčar park. For more wild swimming, catch a boat in the harbour for a short trip to **Frankj**, a nearby peninsula with pretty rocky beaches. **Paradise Beach** in Lopar, the best known on Rab, is at the heart

of the tourist settlement, and buses to Lopar stop here. It's a big, pretty beach, where the sand slopes gently into the water, safe for kids.

Where to eat

Astoria
Trg Municipium Arba, Rab town (051 774 844/www.astoria-rab.com). **Open** *May-Nov* noon-3pm, 6-11pm daily. Closed Dec-Apr.
Credit AmEx, DC, MC, V.
Attached to a small, family-run apartment hotel is this professional restaurant. With fine food, considerate service and an attractive upstairs terrace, overlooking the main square and harbour, this is one of the best choices in town. Top-quality monkfish and bass lead a dependable line-up of seafood, but there are steaks and vegetarian offerings too. Snappy table settings add a touch of class.
▶ *For post-meal drinks on the same main square, the San Antonio Club (No.4, 051 724 145, www.sanantonio-club.com) shares terrace space with the adjoining Velum to provide cocktails and party sounds until 1am.*

Fortuna
Lopar 573, Lopar (051 775 387). **Open** noon-midnight daily. **No credit cards.**
Uphill from the beach and across from the Hotel Lopar stretches this beautifully sculpted terrace, where palm trees grow from a tiled floor, providing a sought-after shaded spot for pleasant meals in an attractive, casual atmosphere. Fortuna has the usual seafood offerings, plus mackerel, hake and sole – lobsters are ordered a day in advance. Check the chalkboard for specials, written up in German.

INSIDE TRACK NATURISM

Rab became one of Europe's first naturist resorts after King Edward VIII swam naked here with Wallis Simpson. Around the peninsula are about 20 beaches. Follow the shoreline – the path is not always clearly marked. The biggest and best known is Sahara. Without a boat, the easiest way to Sahara and other remote beaches is to go to where the Lopar road passes the San Marino hotel settlement and follow the signs for trails through the woods.

★ Gostionica Feral
Lopar 69, Lopar (051 775 288). **Open** noon-3pm, 5pm midnight daily. **No credit cards.**
Near Lopar's ferry slip on the main road is a pretty porch/terrace, covered with vines that appear to have been growing since Gostionica Feral first opened as a restaurant all the way back in 1971. Though the atmosphere in this family-run establishment is relaxed, food and service are taken seriously. The speciality is lobster how you like, top-quality white fish or calamari Feral-style, ie stuffed with fruits de mer, potatoes and local green *blitva*. Book a day ahead for fish stew old-fisherman style or suckling pig on a spit.

Gostionica Labirint
Srednja ulica, Rab town (051 771 145). **Open** 11.30am-2pm, 5.30pm midnight daily. **No credit cards.**

Church of St John.

Distinctive dishes are served in this Old Town spot with a warm, rustic indoors and a split-level roof terrace – though the only view is other rooftops. Local specialities include Rab-style fish soup with good-size chunks of fish, mussels, a scampi, potatoes and rice in hearty broth; and 'fish prepared in the manner of a good housewife of Rab', ie baked. Look out too for fillet of shark, and langouste lobster, grilled or broiled. Most is flame-grilled downstairs.

▶ *Other rustic, traditional treats are on offer at the Konoba Rab (Kneza Branimirova 3, 051 725 666), also in Rab town – in particular lamb, veal or chicken slow-cooked under a baking lid.*

Kn Laguna

Lopar 544, Lopar (no phone). **Open** *Summer* 11am-11pm daily. **No credit cards**.
Located steps from the entrance to Paradise Beach, this large eaterie with a bright, airy interior and spacious, tree-shaded terrace, offers decent seafood and good service in a no-frills atmosphere. The calamari, scampi, sea bass and mussels are all straight from the Adriatic and deftly prepared; the delicate, flaky mackerel, roasted with fresh rosemary, is sublime. Pizzas and meat options keep many families happy.

▶ *More local fare is provided at San Lorenzo (Lopar 571, 775 004), opposite the San Marino hotel complex – spit-roasted pork is a speciality.*

Santa Maria

D Dokule, Rab town (051 724 196). **Open** 10am-11pm midnight daily. **Credit** AmEx, DC, MC, V.
In the Old Town, around the corner from the main square, the Santa Maria creates an impression with its pretty interior of rough stone walls and gorgeous sea views. Little wonder that this was a palace 200 years ago. Lovely outdoor seating also faces the har-

KVARNER & ISLANDS

INSIDE TRACK
LOCAL PRODUCE

Natura Rab (Trg Municipium Arba, 051 721 927, www.natura-rab.hr) in Rab town offers locally produced honey and by-products, candles, marmalade and aromatic oils.

bour. Thankfully, the food does justice to the beautiful setting: excellent scampi and seafood; steaks and stews. A little pricier than the competition but reasonable all the same.

▶ *The management here have recently opened a drinkerie next door, with a Columbus theme – the 1492 Cocktail Bar; see below.*

Where to drink

Kn 1492 Cocktail Bar

D Dokule, Rab town (051 724 196). **Open** 10am-1am daily. **Credit** AmEx, DC, MC, V.
Next door's Santa Maria restaurant is behind this slick cocktail bar with great service and music ranging from Latin to electronic. The name and decor continue the restaurant's Columbus theme. There are over 50 cocktails on offer, frozen, champagne-based and sours, averaging at 45kn. During happy hour from 6pm, several go for 30kn.

▶ *For a sunset view and cocktails in Rab town, the Banova Vila Beach Bar (Šetalište fra Odorika Badurine) is the ideal spot, open until 3am.*

Amadeus Pub

Biskupa Draga 25, Rab town (091 573 4531 mobile). **Open** 6pm-2am daily. **No credit cards**.

Lopar beach.
See p172.

Dylan, Hendrix, Black Sabbath and sundry rockers are blasted through the speakers in this fun and friendly rock-dive bar. It's on a narrow Old Town street, one in from the harbour, so the outdoor seating doesn't have a view; the interior is cheery, with fitting memorabilia on the wall. The up-for-a-party server is a rock enthusiast, and also your DJ.

Banova Vila Beach Bar
Šetalište fra Odorika Badurine, Rab town (099 442 038 mobile). **Open** 6pm-2am daily. **No credit cards**.
On the seaside walkway beneath the spot where Komrčar Park meets the Old Town, Banova Vila may not be paradise but get the right sunset with the right someone, and this little beachside bar will be damn close. A thatched roof and 25 types of cocktails (30kn) help things along nicely. Everyone, the staff included, seems young and good-looking, and you can sip drinks by the sea until 3am.

Caffè Biser
Srednja ulica, Rab town (no phone). **Open** 9am-midnight daily. **No credit cards**.
Beside Trg Sv Kristofor, where Rab's Old Town begins to bustle with bar life, this attractive café boasts a spacious, shaded terrace, a pleasant interior and a small gem of a courtyard at the back. It's a fine place for a daytime coffee or to kick off an evening's bar crawl. Generous, reasonably priced drinks snappily served are an added incentive.

Le Journal
Donja ulica 10, Rab town (091 529 9608 mobile). **Open** 10am-midnight daily. **No credit cards**.
A landmark disco for nearly three decades from 1978, this venue hung up its dancing shoes to become a café-bar. DJs can still be expected – the owner says that Le Journal will just cater more to the day-long street traffic from passing tourists rather than the late-night crowd. Located in a street full of bars and restaurants, Le J always picked up on the buzz from nearby – particularly Forum. Now the crowd is feeding back the other way.
▶ *The summer-only Forum at 9A (098 872 664 mobile) is a busy, dimly-lit bar alongside.*

Nightlife

Santos Beach Club
Pudarica beach, Barbat (051 724 145). **Open** mid July-early Sept early until last guest daily. Closed Mid Sept-mid July. **No credit cards**.
Catch one of the hourly buses from 10pm from Rab town for the 10-km (six-mile) trip to Pudarica beach by Barbat, and a decadent outdoor dance experience. Hundreds of punters, plus the occasional go-go dancer, shimmy on the pebble beach to house and disco hits. There are also gigs by local bands. SBC has a thatch-shaded lounge, a beach volleyball court and a small pool for those who show up (and pose)

by day. Modelled after the beach clubs on nearby Pag, the Santos may not be original but it can guarantee you a busy party most nights in high season.

Vox
Obala P Krešimira, Rab town (no phone). **Open** *Summer* 8am-3pm, 5pm-2am daily. Closed Winter. **No credit cards**.
It's hard to miss the Vox, slap in the middle of the harbour, inside a piece of city wall in the Old Town. As the bars around close, Vox and its decent-sized dance space fills with a fun-loving crowd, ready to party to commercial dance tunes. The staff are up for a party too and the volume of holidaymakers should guarantee an entertaining evening. By day, the terrace comes into its own for relaxed coffees.

Where to stay

★ Hotel Arbiana
Obala P Krešimira 12, Rab town (051 775 900/fax 051 775 929/www.arbianahotel.com). **Rates** €70-€110 single; €110-€200 double. **Credit** AmEx, MC, V.
Set in a lovely old villa, the Arbiana, with 28 rooms, provides comfortable lodging in an elegant setting – and the only real four-star option on Rab. The building, opened in 1924 as the Hotel Bristol and renovated in 2006, is at the tip of the peninsula that holds Rab's Old Town. It's near everything but away from the busiest part of the harbour. Most rooms have balconies overlooking the harbour-side walkway and the sea beyond. All are spacious and decorated with classic, antique-style furniture and big, cushy chairs. Also beautifully furnished are the two bars and the notable restaurant, the San Marino.

Kn Hotel Epario
Lopar 456A, Lopar (051 777 500/fax 051 777 510/www.epario.net). **Rates** €34-€48 single; €54-€92 double. **Credit** AmEx, V.
This newly built, comfortable spot provides 28 small and functional rooms, with air-con, a stone's throw from Lopar's main beach. There is also an exercise room, a playroom and a small restaurant – decent, affordale and by the sea. Dinners are included for an extra five euros a head.
▶ *If the Epario is booked up, the resort complex opposite, the Hotel Village San Marino (051 775 144, www.imperial.hr), should have capacity.*

Hotel Imperial
Palit, J Barakovića, Rab town (051 724 522/fax 051 724 117/www.imperial.hr). **Rates** €51-€68 single; €78-€118 double. **Credit** AmEx, MC, V.
An imposing five-storey Mediterranean-style building, the Imperial is set inside a seaside park which connects Rab Old Town with its nearest beaches. This three-star was one of Rab's first hotels, built a century ago, but its 134 rooms are newly renovated, each with air-conditioning and standard fittings.

The grounds contain three tennis courts, a goofy golf course and terrace cafés. There is public car parking nearby. Given the convenience, the Imperial works out to be one of the better deals in town.

Kn Hotel Istra

Markantun de Dominisa, Rab town (051 724 276/fax 051 724 050/www.hotel-istra.hr). **Rates** €42-€59 single; €64-€98 double. **Credit** AmEx, MC, V.

This old building of 100 rooms, with tiny bathrooms and no air-con, provides a budget option in a central location. No frills but this pretty structure stays cool on summer evenings and has a terrace café.

Kn Rab Hoteli

Obala P Krešimira 4, Rab town (051 602 000/ fax 051 602 899/www.rabhotel.com). **Rates** €40-€78 single; €55-€135 double. **Credit** AmEx, MC, V.

With a modern building tastefully incorporated into the old city wall, this hotel has the most central location in town. And as the same facility has gone from the four-star Ros Maris to the current renamed three star, the Rab Hoteli has dropped in price, making it an attractive bargain. They still provide a pool, sauna, jacuzzi, gym, beauty treatments and massages, restaurant and two bars. And they still have close to 140 rooms, renovated in 2004 with modern fittings and air-con. You may not miss the star at all, or much of the action in Rab's Old Town.

Getting there & around

Regular ferries run from litoral **Jablanac** (30mins) to Rab's southern tip at **Mišnjak**. A summer one links with **Baška** on **Krk**. Buses from Mišnjak go via Rab town to Lopar. In summer a daily **catamaran** runs from **Rijeka** (2hrs), then to **Novalja** on Pag (50mins). Three daily buses run from Rijeka to Rab town (3hrs 30mins), two from Zagreb (6hrs).

Resources

Tourist information

Rab Tourist Office *Trg Municipium Arba 8, Rab town (051 771 111/www.tzg-rab.hr).* **Open** *Summer* 8am-10pm daily. *Winter* 10am-2am Mon-Sat.

CRES

Cres is one of the largest and least developed of Croatia's islands – 3,000 residents live in ancient settlements dotted around 400 sq km of wild rugged landscape. Tourists come here for low-frills holidays near beautiful beaches, or to enjoy the stunning and rare wildlife.

If your idea of wildlife is partying, Cres may not be what you're looking for. But the capital

Cres town provides good tourist amenities and a nice place to holiday; the rest of the island offers interesting opportunities to get away from the crowds.

Sightseeing

Cres is long enough to have two distinct landscapes, verdant in the north, known as **Tramuntana**, barren to the south. The north contains the two settlements of **Beli** – home to the **Caput Insulae Eco Centre**, which works to protect rare resident birds – and the commercial centre of Cres town. There, fishing boats bob in the café-lined harbour, behind which serpentine, car-free streets weave between attractively austere and fading pastel buildings. Cres town dates back at least a couple of millennia, and the island itself has been inhabited since the Palaeolithic era. It was successively ruled by Romans, Byzantines and the first independent Croatians around 822. The Venetians took over the island for about 400 years, beginning around the tenth century, and put up the older remaining landmarks in Cres town. Of particular note is the **Church of Our Lady of Snow**, in the heart of town, dating from the 16th century with a bell tower from the 18th. This can be found by going from the main harbour-side square of Frane Petrića, through an old gate adorned with the town clock.

If you continue west from Cres town's harbour, you'll reach the Lungomare seaside promenade that leads to the town's pebbly beach, a long attractive stretch, served by snack bars and restaurants. Taking the Lungomare in the opposite direction will get you to the town marina, and beyond that to a beautiful natural seaside walk along the wide bay of Cres town.

The southern part of Cres island has the former regional capital of **Osor**. As a major trading port, 'Apsorus' was the largest Roman town on the Croatian Adriatic after Pula. Since then, Osor has been in permanent decline, although its **Archaelogical Museum** (open 10am-noon, 7-9pm daily, 10kn) shows that medieval Osor was still sizeable.

In between north and south are the ancient villages of **Lubenice** and **Valun**, both with attractive beaches; and **Martinšćica**, which is

---

INSIDE TRACK CHEAP DIGS

Rab town has a range in lodgings; Lopar tends towards the low-frills. Here, two- to four-storey garden homes have flats for rent to tourists. Check with the **Lopar Tourist Office** (051 775 508, www.lopar.com) for details.

Cres.

a small tourist development that is centred around a 16th century monastery and a good, although pebbly, beach. Lubenice offers an insight into island life as it once was. This 4,000-year-old settlement is home to 20 ageing souls and crumbling stone buildings, including a Romanesque chapel used as storage space by a local family. On the jagged coast, a series of secluded pebble coves are reached by a steep footpath leading through the underbrush. Nearby Valun is a charming fishing village whose parish church contains the **Valun Tablet**. Its inscription from the 11th century is an early example of the ancient local tongue of Glagolitic.

The middle of Cres island is also home to rich natural life, characterised by the presence of at least 140 griffon vultures, protected here since 1986. In the middle of the island, freshwater **Lake Vrana**, its surface above sea level, its depths below the sea bottom, supplies both Cres and Lošinj, and is strictly off-limits to visitors. **Porozina** at the northern tip is the main point of entry from the little port of **Brestova**, on the Istria-Kvarner border.

Caput Insulae Eco Centre

Beli (www.supovi.hr). Open Summer 9am-7pm daily.
This nature reserve and volunteer centre protects and monitors a colony of some 70 pairs of rare griffon vultures, who make their homes on the cliffs nearby. Set up by Dr Goran Sušić in a school built between the wars, the Eco Centre is also a base for nature trails through Tramuntana, an area of honey buzzards, peregrines and other rare birds, as well as 1,500 types of plants. You'll find documentation and an English-language exhibition at the centre itself.

Where to eat

★ Adria Grill

Zazid 5, Cres town (051 571 520). **Open** *Summer* noon-3pm, 5pm-midnight daily. Closed Winter. **Credit** AmEx, DC, MC, V.
Fresh, superbly prepared fish and meat are served in a romantic courtyard, behind tall walls near Cres town harbour. Shade is provided by an olive tree, a fig tree and grape vines, crammed into the Adria's cosy courtyard garden, where conscientious and efficient servers tend ten tables. The menu features the recommended Cres calamari, bigger and juicier than the average squid, and scallops and lobsters, as well as steak, veal and Balkan-style grilled meats.
► *To dine on the harbour itself, the no-frills Regatta Bufe (Varozina 5, 051 571 452, open Apr-Sept) offers quality fish and grilled meats.*

Konoba Bonaca

Ulica Crekog Statuca, Cres town (051 572 215). **Open** *Summer* 6pm-midnight daily. Closed Winter. **No credit cards**.
This simple but satisfying restaurant is linked to the fish market next door, guaranteeing a good supply of fresh ingredients. They also offer meat: two types of steak and delicious Cres lamb. There is no outdoor seating, but the interior is old-fashioned and cosy, done up stone and wood, and permeated with a delicate aroma of fish being grilled over coals. *Photo p180.*

Restaurant Santa Lucia

Lungomare Svetog Mikule 4, Cres town (051 573 222). **Open** *Easter-Sept* 9am-11pm daily. Closed Oct-Easter. **Credit** DC, MC, V.
This waterside spot at the end of the harbour on the way to the seaside promenade is slightly pricier than most others, but worth it. Seafood is handled superbly, whether it's the lobster served to order, the octopus baked in a *peka* dish or the simple fish soup adorned with a tasty scampi. Truffles show up as an appetiser with cheese, served with *fuži* noodles

---

INSIDE TRACK CRES LAMB

To enjoy renowned Cres lamb and other delicacies, try **Toš Juna** in Valun (051 525 084, open Apr-Oct 10am-11pm daily), in an old olive mill. **Mali Raj** (Vidovići 11, 098 715 856 mobile, open summer 7-11pm daily) is a family-run konoba in Vidovići, 2km from Martinšćica. On Lubenice's main square, **Lubenička loža** (051 840 427) offers local cheeses and *pršut* ham, and views across to St Ivan Bay. Up the hill, **Konoba Hibernicia** (Lubenice 17, 051 840 422, open Apr-Oct 11am-11pm daily) specialises in lamb cooked in the traditional way.

KVARNER & ISLANDS

Profile Spearfishing

You thought Ernest Hemingway was tough? Think again.

Lošinj is a major centre for spearfishing. Top exponents of this lonesome and mildly dangerous activity are using the waters around here to take this once primitive sport to new levels. A European Cup takes place every year in Lošinj just before New Year and in 2010 Lošinj will have the honour of hosting the World Cup – much as it did in 1957.

So what is spearfishing?

The sport comes more naturally to those who live near the sea. Their fathers or grandfathers were probably fishermen. Now with a more stable job on the mainland, for the spear fishermen, this is the best way to maintain contact with their heritage. They gather in clubs on many Croatian islands, caring for the preservation of marine life and promoting this beautiful sport. Spear fishermen account for less than one per cent of the national catch. National and regional competitions provide the chance to examine the sea's health.

Spear fisherman can hold their breath for more than five minutes and operate at depths of 30 or 40 metres. A diver must be in tip-top condition and physically relaxed to keep his heart at a slow 40 to 50 beats per minute. Shallow-water blackouts can be fatal. It is essential for the diver to know his limitations.

According to 26-year-old Croatian Daniel Gospić, the current European champion, the best zones are around the outer islands, the rich waters from Cres to Dugi Otok, and around south Dalmatia. Gospić grew up in Lo?inj, 20 metres from the sea, and made his first bow and spear himself. He began winning trophies as a teenager. Today, his hunting limits are at 38 metres deep. 'Competitions are pure adrenalin, with no time to be meditative like in recreational

GOING UP
Diving is Croatia's fastest-growing sport – there are now more than 100 clubs dotted down the coast, many in spectacular locations. See www.prodiving.hr.

hunting,' he says. 'You must perform hundreds of deep and quick dives in four hours with hunters on your back the whole time. It's like an underwater battlefield. On the second day of the European Championships in Spain in 2007, the visibility was barely one metre and you could only shoot when the fish was practically looking at you straight in the eyes. That day I somehow managed to catch caught 27 kilos.'

Gospić recommends spear fishing in spring and autumn when the sea is calm and fish less nervous. 'Over the last ten years the fish have learned to recognise us as predators and escape. We need to dive deeper. For recreational spear fishing, you must not push yourself to the limit and not get frustrated if you don't catch that much at first.'

A free-diving course is the first step in becoming a spear fisherman. Instructors train beginners in what happens to their bodies when diving without equipment – you must always listen to the signs your body sends you.

The Croatian sea is a giant aquarium. Dangerous and poisonous spices include the marbled electric ray; the eagle ray; the moray; the streaked weever and the large scaled scorpion fish. Spear fishermen must obtain permission to hunt from any official fishing or diving club (www.hssrm.hr). Licences are waterproof and you must carry one with you at all times. Membership (50kn) of a diving association is also obligatory. A day pass is 50kn with other ones available for three days (150kn), a week (300kn) and one month (700kn). The daily catch limit is five kilos. Do not keep bottles of compressed air for scuba diving together with a

spear gun on your boat. Certain species can only be hunted in season – see www.efsa.hr ('slovo zakona'). You cannot fish near beaches or swimmers, in or near marinas, in national parks and other protected areas. You must mark your area with a safety buoy for craft to give you a 50-metre leeway. In 2007, a powerboat killed spear fisherman Darko Kulić near the island Žirje, now commemorated with a floating sculpture. You may hunt from dusk to dawn but not with underwater lamps. They are easily seen in any case, and are strictly forbidden. And, finally, never dive alone. Recommended spearfishing spots can be found at www.submania.hr.

or on the steak. There is also Cres lamb on the grill. The open-air tables, covered terrace and large, decorative indoor room are tended by friendly servers.
▶ *Another quality location on the same strip is Borova Šumica (No.17, 051 571 891), with a shady, split-level terrace by the beach. It doubles up as a karaoke and cocktail spot at night.*

Where to drink

Caffè Arsan
Cons 4, Cres town (051 571 259). **Open** *Mar-Sept* 6.30am-2am daily. Closed Oct-Feb. **No credit cards.**
This late-running bar has seating right on the harbour, and a cluster of tables on a pretty rear terrace on the Old Town square of Trg Arsan. With-it young servers provide cocktails and other tipples to a partying crowd who gets more raucous after dark. Music tends toward dance and electronic sounds.
▶ *Next door, the Burin (No.2, 051 572 010, www.burin.hr) has harbourside tables, a rock soundtrack and an array of cheap cocktails.*

Caffè Bar Astoria
Šetalište XX Travnja 1, Cres town (051 571 556). **Open** *Mar-Sept* 7am-2am daily. Closed Oct-Feb. **No credit cards.**
A good variety of rock, techno and soul music, and a nice garden, set this place off from the competition on the nearby harbour. While the garden fills with a youngish crowd, there's a mix of ages and nationalities inside, where there's a pool table. The 16 varieties of cocktail are reasonably priced at around 30kn.

Where to stay

Kn Hotel Kimen
Melin I/16, Cres town (051 573 305/fax 051 573 002/www.hotel-kimen.com). **Rates** €24-€67 single; €40-€84 double. **Credit** AmEx, MC, V.
The two-star Kimen offers a total of 223 affordable, basic rooms in three buildings situated inside a big wooded campus right in the middle of Cres town's long beach. The 1970s-style main building, has the slightly more expensive, recently renovated ones, with bathrooms, balconies and air-conditioning. Sports facilities are nearby.

★ Hotel Zlatni Lav
Martinšćica 18D, Martinšćica (051 574 020/ fax 051 574 070/www.hotel-zlatni-lav.com). **Rates** €32-€69 single; €50-€112 double. **Credit** AmEx, MC, V.
Cres island's nicest hotel, the small three-star Golden Lion, is set above the bay of Martinšćica, a tiny seaside village that boasts a fine gravel beach. The hotel offers five larger suites and 25 doubles with air-conditioning and showers. The pricier rooms have their own balconies and sea views. The restaurant, serving seafood, lamb and brick-oven pizza, is handy in this small town with limited amenities. Nothing fancy, but all the basic comforts.

Kn Kovačine
Melin I/20, Cres town (051 573 150/fax 051 571 086/www.camp-kovacine.com). **Rates** €56-€86 double. *Camping* €4.60-€8.40; *mobile homes* €40-€109. **Credit** MC, V.

Konoba Bonaca. *See p177.*

INSIDE TRACK
CHEAP ROOMS

In Cres town, contact **Josip Cule**
(Zagrebačka 22, 051 572 254, 098
864 895 mobile), **Valdarke** (Melin II/33,
051 319 027, www.cres-travel.com) or
Cresanka (Varozina 25, 051 571 161,
www.cresanka.hr) for private rooms.
The **Villa Rivijera** (Lungomare sv Mikule
12, 051 571 161) also has cheap, basic
hostel lodging in an old villa.

Perhaps the best location in Cres town, the wooded area along the lengthy, attractive town beach has been given over to a campsite. Those with trailers or tents should find all the comforts they're used to. Mobile homes have toilets, showers and kitchens and sleep up to four; a house, near the tip of the campsite, has 13 double rooms, with bathrooms, air-conditioning, TV and minibar.

▶ *The same company run Rooms Cres (Riva Creskih kapetana 10, 051 571 161), simple, clean lodgings right on the harbour.*

Getting there & around

Two ferries hop to Cres: from **Brestova** on the Istrian mainland to **Porozina**; and from **Valbiska** on **Krk** to **Merag**. Both run every hour or so and take 30 minutes. In summer a daily catamaran links with **Rijeka** (1hr 20mins) and **Mali Lošinj**, all going into Cres town, some to **Martinšćica**. At least five buses a day run between Cres town and Mali Lošinj, two linking with **Zagreb**. Summer weekdays, some six buses a day run between **Cres town** and **Osor**, significantly fewer at weekends and in winter. Transport to north Cres is scarce. There is a **taxi** rank at **Cres town bus station** (Zazid 4, 051 571 664, 098 947 5592 mobile).

Resources

Tourist information
Cres Tourist Office *Cons 10, Cres town (051 571 535/www.tzg-cres.hr).* **Open** *Summer* 9am-10pm daily.

LOŠINJ

Near the southernmost end of Kvarner Bay, **Lošinj** island's beautiful rocky coast and pristine waters attract dolphins, spearfishers and tourists, who first started arriving en masse in the late 1800s, after Emperor Franz Josef and Prince Franz Ferdinand first came.

The island caters to the needs of its many visitors with stand-out restaurants, fun bars and a range of accommodation, from rooming houses to boutique hotels. Although it's the smaller island, Lošinj has far more tourist amenities than relatively undeveloped Cres.

About the island

Cres and Lošinj used to be one island until the ancient Liburni tribe, here before the Romans, dug a canal at Osor. The canal, now spanned by a bridge, was dug to shorten the passage for ships following the old Amber Route, which connected the Baltic Sea to Ancient Egypt. Ships would later become very important to Lošinj. Although the island was sparsely populated until the 13th century, it developed into a centre of shipping and shipbuilding and was a leading regional maritime power by the 19th century.

The reinvigorating effects of its sea breezes, clean water and 2,600 hours of annual sunshine, earned Lošinj an official designation as a health resort in 1892. Habsburg royalty followed and now tourism is the island's main industry.

Most activity centres around two towns with misleading labels. **Mali Lošinj**, 'Small Lošinj', is the bigger town, about 4km (2.5 miles) from quaint little **Veli Lošinj**, 'Great Lošinj'.

Sightseeing

Mali Lošinj, the largest island town in the Adriatic with a population of 7,000, is situated around a long wide harbour, lined with Habsburg-era façades that face one another across the water. Strolling the broad walkway from one end of the harbour to the other takes about 20 minutes, but try to give yourself more time. It's a beautiful waterside, filled with great restaurants and bars. Lively **Trg Republike Hrvatske** is the big square at the crotch of the harbour. Pop into the **Art Collections** (Vladimira Gortana 35, 051 231 173; open summer 10am-1pm, 7-10pm daily; winter 10am-noon, 7-9pm daily) for modern Croatian and 17th- and 18th-century Italian works.

There are good beaches near Mali Lošinj, including the popular rocky and pebbly stretches in wooded Čikat, just on the other side of a hill from the harbour.

Neighbouring Veli Lošinj is centred around a small harbour surrounded by steep hills. On one rise right on the harbour is boxy pink **Church of St Anthony**, which contains seven Baroque altars and works by Vivarini and other Italian masters. The sinners hang out down below, in a bustling clutch of good bars and restaurants. On another hill above the harbour is a crenulated Venetian tower, built as a fortification in 1455 and now used for art exhibitions. It currently has a replica of the statue of Apoxyomenos, a 6-foot-four-inch bronze, apparently jettisoned from a storm-tossed Roman vessel in the beginning of the first century and found off Lošinj in 1999. The original is being restored, but is due to return for permanent display in Mali Lošinj by 2010. The bronze depiction of a nude athlete scraping oil from his body has quickly become something of a mascot for the island, and you'll see his picture and name everywhere.

Walk along a ridge above the town's beach to reach Veli Lošinj's other harbour, tiny **Rovensko**, which manages to squeeze in three great restaurants and a pebbly beach.

Veli Lošinj is also home to the **Marine Education Centre**, dedicated to dolphin studies. The exceptionally pure water around the island is home to a colony of dolphins, which you can see (but not touch) by booking excursion boats from Veli Lošinj. Spearfishing and apnoea fishing – where divers have no air tank but just hold their breath – have a long tradition here; there's a European Cup held just before new year. A statue of a diver stands near Trg Republike Hrvatske.

Marine Education Centre

Kaštel 24, Veli Lošinj (051 604 666/www. blue-world.org). **Open** 9am-1pm, 6-8pm daily. **Admission** 10kn; 7kn concs. **No credit cards**. This centre, based around the dolphin colony off Veli Lošinj, teaches about the wildlife of the Croatian coast and the importance of protecting it. Visitors are shown a short documentary film about dolphins and the Adriatic (with English subtitles), dioramas, posters and computer graphics. Volunteers can

INSIDE TRACK
BEST BEACHES

A short walk from the north-west corner of Mali Lošinj harbour is a verdant peninsula containing Slatina, Čikat and Dražica, where the jagged coast, with several small inlets, is lined with resort hotels and tree-shaded beaches. The strong Bora wind makes them popular with windsurfers. The nudist beach is in the southern-most end of this stretch, just past the Hotel Vespera. Veli Lošinj has a nice little pebbly beach at Rovenska. Between the downtown harbour and Rovenska are rocky spots for bathing.

spend longer periods here, working with wildlife. The MEC does not run dolphin trips but can recommend local boat companies who do. They are also at pains to point out that at no time should visitors touch the dolphins when out on the water.

Where to eat

★ Bora Bar Trattoria/Tartufferia

Rovenska 3, Veli Lošinj (051 867 544/www. borabar.com). **Closed** Nov-Mar. **Open** *Apr-Oct* 10am-midnight daily. **Credit** AmEx, DC, MC, V. The heart of the gastro enclave of Rovenska bay is this charming and idiosyncratic establishment run by chef Marco Sasso. Born in Pisa, Sasso was one of the first truffle dealers in the US until he opened La

Lošinj

Tartufferia, a Hoboken restaurant ranked among the top five in New Jersey. Then he met his Croatian partner and came here to open this place. Sasso gets the fungus fresh from Istria and applies it in starters, such as tuna carpaccio with marinated celery roots and truffles. Many ingredients come fresh from the sea on which the terrace is perched – scampi, served with a subtle Grand Marnier sauce. Desserts include own-made panna cotta or chocolate mousse. The menu changes according to which ingredients are available fresh. The atmosphere is enhanced by Sasso, who pops out of the kitchen to chat with the many return visitors, and to play his didgeridoo. *Photo 185.*

Konoba Odyssey

Velopin 14, Mali Lošinj (051 231 893). **Open** 11am-2pm, 6-11pm daily. **No credit cards**.
Sit on a wooden terrace by torchlight over the water, on the Premuda side of Mali Lošinj harbour, and enjoy hearty portions of simple seafood dishes prepared flawlessly. They also serve good meat dishes: steak; chicken and Balkan-style lamb preparations.

Konoba-Pizzeria Bukaleta

Del Conte Giovanni, Mali Lošinj (098 258 415/098 170 8155 both mobile). **Open** 10am-11pm daily. **Credit** AmEx, DC, MC, V.
The hulking brick oven here turns out the kind of pizzas that would pass muster across the water in Italy: a perfectly molten mix of cheese and sauce atop a thin, crispy crust. Despite the casual feel of this place, with a rustic interior, reasonable prices and a relaxed awning-covered terrace on a square in the Old Town, attention is paid to detail. Each table gets a Peugeot pepper grinder, the pizza comes with a sharp, heavy stainless steel knife, the servers are not only friendly but also fast, and the food has been fussed over. They also do fair risottos, pastas, seafood (tuna steak, several styles of calamari, anchovies) and beefsteak, chicken and veal.

Konoba Ribarska Koliba

Obala maršala Tita, Veli Lošinj (051 236 235). **Closed** Nov-Mar. **Open** *Apr-Oct* 9am-midnight daily. **No credit cards**.
One of the fancier restaurants on Veli Lošinj's little harbour, the only one on the same side as St Anthony's Church, the Koliba is also one of the more expensive places to eat here, especially after you pay the 5kn-per-head cover. The food is worth it. Rarer offerings include a tasty shark steak with a delicately garlicky sauce, a brodetto tomato-based fish stew, and baked fish. Calamari can be had fried, grilled or stuffed with seafood, and lobster comes grilled or with spaghetti. Along with the usual steaks, meats also include lamb on a spit.

Restaurant Baracuda

Priko 31, Mali Lošinj (051 233 309/091 223 1613 mobile). **Closed** Nov-Mar. **Open** *Apr-Oct* 10am-midnight. **Credit** AmEx, DC, MC, V.

This popular restaurant on Mali Lošinj harbour, visible from the upstairs terrace, is a sure bet for seafood. Choose from a menu that changes according to what's fresh – this is a safe place to splash out on lobster, served on a bed of spaghetti. Steak or lamb are also available. The front terrace is hidden from passers-by with huge palm trees.
▶ *Nearby, the Priko is a handy terrace bar for pre- or late post-dinner drinks; see p184.*

Restoran Marina

Privlaka, Mali Lošinj (051 231 232). **Open** 8am-11pm daily. **Credit** AmEx, DC, MC, V.
You wouldn't wander into this simple looking terrace restaurant at the foot of the Privlaka bridge, with retro-Socialist design touches and a view of boats in dry dock, unless you happened to be at the marina. But yachters in the know come here to swap stories and sailing tips while enjoying outstanding meals and first-class service. A grill on the terrace produces wonderful aromas and fantastic fresh fish, while the kitchen keeps busy turning out thin-sliced octopus salad and top-quality roast lobster.

Where to drink

Caffè Bar Nautica

Vladimira Gortana 77, Mali Lošinj (no phone). **Open** 7am-1am daily. **No credit cards**.
Though the bar is one street inland, the Nautica's awning-covered terrace is right on the water, and it's one of the busiest in a string of outdoor cafés in the narrow crotch of Mali Lošinj harbour. An efficient waitstaff serves cocktails, local brandies, ice-cream and toasted sandwiches in a great spot for watching people and the water.
▶ *Moby Dick at No.38 (051 231 228) is the latest one to stay open on the harbour strip, at 2am.*

Kn Caffè Bar Riva

Obala maršala Tita 36, Veli Lošinj (no phone). **Open** 9am-10pm daily. **No credit cards**.
This bar, which lies in the heart of Veli Lošinj's small harbour, opposite St Anthony's Church, has two faces: a sunny terrace jutting out into the sea has tables under big umbrellas; while a pub-like interior is cool and dark, with a whiff of too many spilled drinks. Surrounded by sports trophies, a TV shows any football match that happens to be on. Either milieu is comfortable and the prices are among the cheapest in town.

Caffè Buffet Balun

G Garibaldija 11, Mali Lošinj (no phone). **Open** 11am-11pm daily. **No credit cards**.
Offering a different, smokier atmosphere than other terrace bars around Trg Republike Hrvatske, this sports dive frequented by locals is a great place to watch a game. Grilled meats, calamari and other snacks are also available. Harbourside outdoor tables are served by a friendly, seen-it-all crew.

KVARNER & ISLANDS

**INSIDE TRACK
WATERFRONT BARS**

In Mali Lošinj, action is focused on Trg Republike Hrvatske. Bars on the eastern half, around Nautica, seem fancier. On the western half, around Pritko, are rock bars, like **Konoba Catacomba** (Del Conte Giovanni 1, 051 231 888), which features local garage bands of varying quality. **Villa Anna** (Velopin 31, 051 233 223, www.vila-ana.hr) has a night bar that stays open until 5am in summer. A boat docked nearby, the *Marina*, hosts parties, with occasional belly dancing.

Kn Caffè Bar Saturn

Obala maršala Tita 1, Veli Lošinj (051 236 102). **Open** 8am-10pm daily. **Credit** MC, V.

Caffè Bar Saturn is a funky little bar in front of the cheapish Pansion Saturn, with wild, predominantly red walls and out-there decor, that attracts a crowd of young locals and budget guests. Sessions tend to begin in the early afternoon here. It's a perfect place to gaze over the sunny harbour, with a shaded terrace and benches facing the water, spectator-style. The decent range of drinks includes 25 types of cocktail at reasonable prices.

Priko

Priko 2, Mali Lošinj (051 231 185). **Open** May-Oct 8am-2am daily. *Oct-May* 8am-midnight daily. **No credit cards**.

A handy terrace bar near the middle of the harbour draws a sizeable crowd of coffee sippers in the morning, and beer and cocktail swillers by afternoon. In the evening, the music turns toward a mix of dance, pop and rock, and the crowd grows younger. Priko is casual, and an excellent place to go if you'd like to strike up a conversation with a stranger. They list 70 types of cocktail, most running somewhere in 40kn-50kn price range.

Where to stay

Kn Guest House Helios

Čikat, Mali Lošinj (051 232 124/fax 051 231 904/www.losinj-hotels.com). **Open** June-Sept. Closed Oct-May **Rates** €31-€46 single; €42-€76 double. **Credit** AmEx, MC, V.

In a pine forest by the sea, Guest House Helios is a big 1970s-style structure, with 128 singles and 60 bungalows; it's basic but well located. There's no air-conditioning, and the cheapest rooms don't have their own bathroom, but the hotel, just 2km from the centre of Mali Lošinj, is next to a rocky beach, with a sandy one for children nearby and a gravel one a short walk away. Tennis courts, hiking paths and mini golf are all close at hand.

★ Hotel Apoksiomen

Riva Lošinjskih kapetana 1, Mali Lošinj (051 520 820/www.apoksiomen.com). **Open** Mar-Oct. Closed Nov-Feb. **Rates** €70-€110 single; €100-€165 double. **Credit** AmEx, DC, MC, V.

This small four-star hotel is one of the more chic addresses on the island. A boutique hotel with a great location near the centre of the harbour in Mali Lošinj, the Apoksiomen has 24 tasteful and unusual rooms, decorated with original paintings by name Croatian artists. All rooms are air-conditioned, and most have harbour views. The à la carte restaurant has a waterside terrace, and you can have the food delivered to your room.

Hotel Aurora

Sunčana uvala, Dražica, Mali Lošinj (051 231 324/fax 051 231 904/www.losinj-hotels.com). **Open** May-Oct. Closed Nov-Apr. **Rates** €50-€95 single; €80-€170 double. **Credit** AmEx, DC, MC, V.

Renovated in 2008 and, at which time it was upgraded to a four star, this modern, luxury resort hotel in a wooded campus shares a beautiful and busy stretch of beach with its partner resort, the neighbouring Hotel Vespera. Don't expect to be alone, as the Aurora has 393 rooms and restaurant space for 700. They seek to provide all you need, so you don't have to venture to the centre of Mali Lošinj a half-hour stroll away. There are indoor and outdoor pools, a two-floor spa, a terrace bar, tennis and hiking – and a host of extras.

▶ *Neighbouring Vespera (051 231 304) has also had a recent upgrade, incorporating a three-level pool complex leading down to the sea.*

Kn Hotel Punta

Šestavina, Veli Lošinj (051 662 000/fax 051 231 904/www.losinj-hotels.com). **Open** Apr-Oct. Closed Nov-Mar. **Rates** €40-€67 single; €60-€114 double. **Credit** AmEx, DC, MC, V.

This sprawling, Socialist-era resort hotel is situated by a rocky beach, in a shaded campus at the tip of the bay that contains Veli Lošinj's harbour. The expansive 1970s style building provides plenty of family recreation with indoor and outdoor pools, tennis courts nearby and a spa, with entertainment for children and adults.

★ Mare Mare Suites

Riva Lošinjskih kapetana 36, Mali Lošinj (051 232 010/098 946 9217 mobile/www.mare-mare.com). **Rates** €80-€120 single; €100-€140 double. **Credit** AmEx, DC, MC, V.

At the start of the Old Town section of Mali Lošinj harbour, this four-star boutique with 16 beds in six units creates a friendly but exclusive atmosphere. Rooms and suites are done up in a colourful and cheery decor, while the rooftop terrace has gorgeous views, a jacuzzi and a champagne bar – sip, soak and gawp away. There's a spa and cocktail bar too.

Bora Bar Trattoria/Tartufferia.
See p182.

Kn Pansion Saturn

Obala maršala Tita 1, Veli Lošinj (051 236 102/www.val-losinj.hr). **Rates** €24-€36 single; €48-€72 double. **Credit** AmEx, DC, MC, V.
Central, cheap and truly cheerful. Situated in a bright red building that lies right on Veli Lošinj harbour, the Saturn has nine simple but tasteful rooms, four of which are air-conditioned. The bar downstairs is recommended. Restaurants, the beach, and most everything else in town, is nearby. The whole building was renovated in 2005.
▶ *If full, another bargain place to stay in Veli Lošinj is Villa San (051 236 219), an old villa by the harbour.*

Getting there & around

In summer, a daily **catamaran** links with **Rijeka** (1hr 20mins) and **Mali Lošinj**, going on to **Cres town**. At least seven **buses** a day run between Cres town and Mali Lošinj; two link with **Zagreb**. From mid June to the start of September a car ferry runs daily to Mali Lošinj from **Zadar**, as well as a catamaran from **Pula**.

INSIDE TRACK
CHEAPER DIGS

In Mali Lošinj, smaller villas and pensions include the more remote **Favorita** (Sunčana uvala, 051 520 640, www. villafavorita.hr) and harbourside three-star **Villa Anna** (Velopin 31, 051 233 223, www.vila-ana.hr). Between these facilities, rooms and apartments can be found at **Lošinjska Plovidba** (Riva lošinjskih kapetana 8, 051 233 040, www.lostur.net) and **Sanmar Priko** 24 (051 238 293, www.sanmar.hr).

Resources

Tourist information

Lošinj Tourist Office *Riva Lošinjskih kapetana 29, Mali Lošinj (051 231 547/www. tz-malilosinj.hr).* **Open** 8am-8pm daily.

PAG

Approaching Pag by a regular 20-minute ferry hop from the mainland, you may be forgiven for thinking that you've landed on the moon. The east coast is a bleak, forbidding landscape of stark white and barren limestone karst blown bare by the Bura wind, set into stark relief by the blue expanse of sea and sky. When it's hot, it's baking. The upside is the food produced here under such harsh conditions: outstanding lamb and the most famous cheese in all Croatia, *paški sir*.

About the island

Pag is thin and 64km (40 miles) long, made up of two parallel mountain ranges. Settlements are mainly sleepy fishing villages, with two towns, **Novalja** and **Pag town**. Novalja is a resort town that's become party central. **Zrće** beach, a short bus ride away, is the biggest club hub in Croatia. Families have also discovered the safe, shallow beaches around Novalja, where the pebbles are easy on young feet. Excellent beaches can be found at either end of Novalja's harbour. The town has Roman origins, and there's even a famous underground aqueduct, as well an arts centre, but most visitors come here for the beach, the party, or ideally both.

By contrast, the administrative and commercial centre of Pag town exudes cultural heritage. Narrow, fortified medieval streets

KVARNER & ISLANDS

INSIDE TRACK PAKLENICA

At Pag's south-eastern tip a spectacular road bridge leads to the **Paklenica National Park** (023 369 155, www.paklenica.hr), ideal for casual hikers and hillwalkers. It is most famous for the canyons of Velika and Mala Paklenica.

weave beneath a 15th-century Gothic **cathedral** and the sun beats hard off the white stone pavement as ladies painstakingly stitch Pag lace in doorways and alleys. Daily life proceeds at a crawl. From the bars and restaurants of the old harbour, the sea gives way through a series of dykes into saltpans, in use for 600 years.

The island retains much of its tradition. It has been populated since prehistory, was fortified by the Romans and became a salt-producing centre under Venice from 1403. Across the bay, near Pag town's beaches, clusters of modern apartment buildings and crumbling Tito-era hotels sit incongruously. Even historic Pag town has had to succumb to tack, as the posters advertising pole-dancing and mud wrestling seem to show.

The south-west part of Pag is a little greener, covered mainly in sage brush and maquis with sheltered valleys that grow vines and olives. There are also more beaches, which are mainly pebbles, in sheltered coves, some of which can

Pag cathedral.

only be reached by taking precipitous tracks. The 24km (15-mile) peninsula leading to the island's western tip at **Lun** is worth the trip out. **Jakišnica** is a picturesque fishing village on this peninsula, off the beaten track but with excellent fish restaurants and the newest lodging on the island: the swanky, four-star **Luna Hotel**.

Where to eat

★ Boškinac

Novalja Škopljanksa 20 (053 663 500/091 663 5001 mobile/www.boskinac.com). **Open** noon-midnight daily. **Credit** AmEx, DC, MC, V.
Hands down the nicest place to wine and dine on Pag, with a superb hotel.
▶ *For details of all there is to offer at Boškinac, including accommodation; see p187.*

Konoba Bile

Jurja Dalmatinca 35, Pag town (023 611 127). **Open** 11.30am-11pm daily. **No credit cards**.
This atmospheric little stone-walled cellar is the place to go to try the local wines, hams and cheeses. Served with a smile but with little fuss, the chatty regulars enjoying the informal grazing as much as you. Close to the church, this is an ideal spot for a late, light lunch after a morning spent at the beach.

Moby Dick

Obala Petra Krešimira IV, Novalja (053 662 488). **Open** noon-midnight daily. **Credit** AmEx, DC, MC, V.
This enormous restaurant around the harbour has an equally expansive terrace dotted with shady palm trees and sun umbrellas, surrounded by a stone fence. There's also a comfortable, airy interior. The standard types of seafood are prepared fresh off the boat, with pizza, Pag cheese and Dalmatian *pršut* also readily available. There are decent local wines too. Moby Dick is big and busy, but despite this the service doesn't slack.

★ Na Tale

Stjepana Radića 2, Pag town (023 611 194). **Open** noon-11pm daily. **Credit** AmEx, DC, MC, V.
The top table in Pag town, overlooking the bay at the edge of the seafront, the food matching the wonderful location. The seafood is another attraction, the fresh white meat of the catch of the day brought out by superb sauces. Octopus lasagne and Pag lamb are other specialities, best enjoyed away from the burning sun in the shaded courtyard.

Starac i More

Braće Radic, Novalja (053 662 423). **Open** noon-midnight daily. **Credit** AmEx, DC, MC, V.
In a street just off the harbour, this pretty old stone building with a nice, enclosed terrace is usually rec-

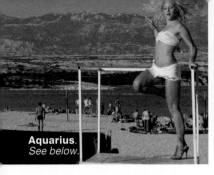
Aquarius.
See below.

ommended by locals for its seafood. It's certainly a good place to splash out on a mixed platter, heaped with scampi, complemented by a wide choice of local wines. Relaxed, friendly and efficient.

Where to drink

Amazona
Trg Loža, Novalja (no phone). **Open** 7am-2am daily. **No credit cards.**
The name could well refer to the smart waitresses but this is by far the the coolest, liveliest bar on a square full of them. It also tends to close last, soaking up guests from neighbouring venues by the evening's end. Tourists missing more substantial brews can call up a Guinness or Kilkenny on tap. There's a small, heavily decorated indoor space and several tables jammed on to the terrace, shared by several bars. You can expect decent cocktails here and, if so required, ice-cream.

Kaštel
Trg Loža, Novalja (no phone). **Open** 6.30am-1am daily. **No credit cards.**
Another stand-out location surrounded by bars, the Kaštel comprises a tiny indoor space and a few terrace tables but its big cocktails are the best on the square. While the traffic shifts from bar to bar, there's usually a reliably happening crowd here. The same management run the restaurant next door.

El Faro
Trg Loža, Novalja (no phone). **Open** 6am-2am daily. **No credit cards.**
Although standing by the ferry slip in the harbour and thus separated from the other bars on the square, El Faro still feels central and loads of fun. The cosy bar inside a small, stucco-and-glass structure, along with shaded outdoor tables, offer eye-popping vistas of the pier and sea beyond. As dance and rock tunes play, El Faro fills with the pre-disco crowd. The buzz keeps up until way past midnight.

Nightlife

Cocomo
Obala Petra Krešimira IV 9, Novalja (www. cocomoclub.com). **Open** *Apr-Sept* 9am-4am daily. **No credit cards.**

On the harbour, this jungle-themed club is a safe bet. Downstairs you'll find a large enclosed terrace that lies opposite an indoor dancefloor. Upstairs is an all-indoor dance space. Both host DJs and live music, and are serviced by five different bars, staffed by professional cocktail shakers kitted out in the appropriate attire. Decadence breaks out amid the life-sized stuffed tigers and zebra-striped bar stools. This is the best dancing downtown and ideal if you're just after a late, lively bar.

Where to stay

★ Boškinac
Novalja Škopljanksa 20, Pag island (053 663 500/fax 053 663 501/091 663 5001 mobile/ www.boskinac.com). **Rates** €80-€110 single; €120-€210 double. **Credit** AmEx, DC, MC, V.
By a field near Novalja, this four-star hotel and restaurant is the nicest place to dine and lodge on Pag island. Set in bucolic surroundings, on grounds containing their own vineyards, owners Mirela and Boris put classic Croatian flavours, modern design and top service to the fore. Dishes in the restaurant, which with its cascading stone terraces and an informal *konoba* filled with hanging hams below is worth visiting in its own right, showcase traditional and home-grown cuisine. The dozen rooms and suites, each named after local variety of flora, are individually decorated in soft, seasonal Mediterranean colours, with expansive views of the surrounding pine woods, olive groves and vineyards. Boškinac also lays on gastronomic and wine weekends, horse-riding and other activities.

> ## INSIDE TRACK ZRĆE
>
> Zrće beach near Novalja is the Croatian Ibiza. The three key clubs are the **Kalypso**, the **Papaya** and **Aquarius**, all open-air and stretched out on the white, pebbly beach. Most are near 24-hour operations, offering sports activities and poolside drinking by day, and partying through the night. It's a huge industry – as commercial as most of the music played.

INSIDE TRACK
PAG FLAVOURS

The flavours on the Pag dinner table are influenced by the arid, saline environment. Inhabited by more sheep than humans, Pag lamb is deeply flavoured with the aromatic herbs sheep consume, as is the trademark Pag cheese (*paški sir*). Pag fish has a particular flavour, due to the lower oxygen levels in the highly saline waters. Accompanied by a bottle of local Žutica dry white wine and a digestif of *travarica* herb brandy, the Pag culinary experience is complete.

Kn Hotel Liburnija

Ulica hrvatskih mornara, Novalja (tel/fax 053 661 328/www.turno.hr). **Open** June-Aug. Closed Early Sept-May. **Rates** €34-€62 single; €45-€83 double. **Credit** AmEx, DC, MC, V.

A modern building facing the centre of town from across the harbour houses a simple two-star on a popular sand-and-pebble beach. The rooms are small, basic (there's no air-conditioning) but eminently affordable. The location is a ten-minute walk from the heart of Novalja, which is thankfully far enough away to escape the noise of partygoers. Slightly less crowded beaches are close by.
► *The same group also run the summer-only Hotel Loža at Trg Loža 1 (051 661 313), equally cheap and right in party central.*

Hotel Plaža

Marka Marulića 14, Pag town (023 600 855/ 091 563 1097 mobile/fax 023 600 201/ www.plaza-croatia.com). **Open** Mid June-mid Sept. Closed mid Sept-mid June. **Rates** €100-€144 double. **Credit** AmEx, DC, MC, V.

This relatively modern four-star provides views across the bay to the Old Town, as well as 23 well appointed doubles and six apartments. All have access to the pool, gym, sauna and spa – and there is a cocktail bar and restaurant on-site too.

Hotel Tony

Dubrovačka 39, Pag town (tel/fax 023 611 370/ www.hotel-tony.com). **Open** June-Sept. Closed Oct-May. **Rates** €70-€100 double. **Credit** AmEx, DC, MC, V.

Hotel Tony's 20 spacious rooms just north-east of Pag Old Town provide relaxation and a handy stretch of beach nearby. There's no need to go into Pag if you're feeling lazy – the Tony has its own restaurant, and half-board rates are more than reasonable. You will have to book early though, as this is a popular getaway and only open for four months of the year. Staff are happy to help with boat hire and WiFi is also provided on every balcony.

★ Luna Hotel

Jakišnica (053 654 700/fax 053 654 754/www. luna-hotel.hr). Open Mid Mar-Sept. Closed Oct-mid Mar. **Rates** €78-€186 double. **Credit** AmEx, DC, MC, V.

The newest hotel on Pag is a 20-minute drive from Novalja, and is a much needed quality option with two pools (including one for children), a spa centre, lounge bar and restaurant. It is also right on the water, on the northern tip of the island, a short drive from the ferry port of Žigljen with its regular connection to the mainland. Most of the 93 rooms, divided into three categories, face the sea. All have internet access. The Luna stays open for six months, longer than other hotels on the island. Standard rooms out of high season are a bargain.

Getting there & around

The easiest hop to Pag is the hourly **ferry** from **Prizna** on the mainland to **Žigljen** (20mins) on Pag's north-eastern tip, 5km (3 miles) north of Novalja. Twice daily buses between **Rijeka** and **Zadar** call at both **Novalja** and **Pag town**, the only public transport link (30mins) between the two. There's a taxi stand (098 282 872 mobile) at the ferry port in Novalja.

In summer a daily Jadrolinija **catamaran** runs in the morning from Novalja to **Rijeka** (2hrs 30mins), turning round at Rijeka in the afternoon. It also passes by **Rab town**, so it's possible to hop from Rab town to Novalja (50 mins) in the afternoon, and go from Novalja to Rab in the morning. Pag town is an hour from **Zadar**, three hours from **Rijeka** and five hours from **Zagreb** – there are five **buses** a day from the capital.

Resources

Tourist information
Pag Town Tourist Office *Od Špitale 2 (023 611 286/www.pag-tourism.hr).* **Open** *Summer* 8am-8pm daily. *Winter* 9am-noon Mon-Fri.
Novalja Tourist Office *Trg Brščić 1 (023 661 404/www.tz-novalja.hr).* **Open** *Summer* 9am-6pm daily.

INSIDE TRACK
FAMILY VILLAS

The **Villa Olea** (023 697 439, www.villa olea.hr) is a fine example of the kind of family-run apartment accommodation springing up on Pag. It's in the quiet fishing village of Šimuni, 10km (six miles) from Pag town and offers full board in six air-conditioned two- or three-bedroomed apartments.

Zadar & Šibenik

**Lavender
Bed Bar.**
See p210.

Zadar & Šibenik

Zadar & Šibenik

Clubbing hubs, historic treasures and astounding natural beauty.

Zadar and **Šibenik**, the key towns of northern Dalmatia, are lesser known to foreigners than Split or Dubrovnik. Yet they offer as much history, natural beauty and, particularly in the case of Zadar, entertainment, as either. Until recently, the lack of international transport links has meant that much here is only known to those in Croatia – Šibenik is still isolated as far as planes, trains or boats are concerned. Zadar is firmly on the map, mainly thanks to the success of Brit-run bar and DJ terrace The Garden, and its annual summer music festival.

The Zadar archipelago and the 140 islands that make up the **Kornati National Park** are reason alone to visit the region; the nearby island of **Murter** gives easiest access, connected by bridge to the mainland. The cathedral city of Šibenik is the gateway to the other great natural attraction of the area, **Krka National Park**, now with a new hi-tech Visitor Centre. Picture-postcard **Primošten** and the fishing village of **Tribunj** offer relative tranquillity in contrast to the bustling and developed tourist towns of **Vodice** and **Biograd**.

ZADAR

There seems to be no stopping **Zadar**, the main city of northern Dalmatia. It's not just the number of projects that have been realised in recent years but the innovation and vision behind them: the **Garden** and offshoots; the landmark public installations of **Nikola Bašić**; and the **Arsenal**, an arts centre like no other in Croatia. Nearby stands a newly opened four-star city-centre hotel, the **Bastion**, while Garden stablemate **Barbarella's** is sited at Petrčane, where Croatia's biggest music festival takes place. Next door to that, Falkensteiner's huge **Punta Skala Resort** complex should open in summer 2009. Back in Zadar, a new museum (of antique glassware) is being built, while the landmark Maraska building is destined to become a top-quality hotel. Zadar hasn't had it this good since it was a busy resort a century or more ago.

Stuck out on a peninsula halfway between Split and Rijeka, Zadar was isolated from the mainland for significant chunks of the 20th century. Italian (Zara) between the wars, and having suffered severe Allied bombing during World War II, Zadar became part of Tito's Yugoslavia until 1991. Under serious threat

by Serbian forces for four years, Zadar was cut off from Zagreb completely for 14 months during the Yugoslav War.

Zadar's isolation has given it a distinctive local culture. It is perhaps most identified with the cherry liqueur Maraschino – you'll see the sign of the local producers, Maraska, all over town (*see p199* **Viva Maraska!**). The town is also known for its sunsets, which even managed to draw Alfred Hitchcock here for one day in 1964. His portrait can still be seen around town and he provided inspiration for the Nikola Bašić's 'Greeting To The Sun' installation. The famous red sunset, and prime space atop the Venetian city walls attracted the UK crew to plant the Garden club there, accessed, if so desired, by rowboat from the mainland to this busy peninsula.

Everything takes place in this criss-cross of streets on a tongue of land some 600 metres (1,968 feet) long and 300 metres (985 feet) wide, encircled by the fortifications, with scenic embankments below and the sea beyond. Cars are only allowed as far as these quays; locals scurry about their business in the narrow downtown streets. To reach the mainland, pedestrians either have to walk as far as the narrow section of channel at Foša, halfway to

INSIDE TRACK
ZADAR ARCHIPELAGO

For real relaxation, take a catamaran or boat from Zadar to the relatively unspoilt archipelago nearby. An island hop might require an overnight stay but the reward is sandy seafloors and dramatic scenery. Most routes are run by Jadrolinija and take about 90 minutes. The hydrofoil to Sali on Dugi otok is run by **Mia** (40mins, 20kn, www.miatours.hr). With 200 islands and islets, the possibilities are complex and none has much by way of transport once you arrive. The largest is Dugi otok, Long Island, 50km (31 miles) long in fact. Its intricate, coastline hides many coves and beaches accessible only by boat.

St Donat's Church.

the bus and train stations away to the east; cross the busy footbridge enclosing the border of the marina of Jazine; or, as people have been doing for centuries, pay the ferryman to take them over the water.

The most central point of entry is by boat, with the three ferry points dotted on the north embankment below the Venetian fortifications.

Sightseeing

The Romans built Iadera, the peninsula, with a regulated street pattern, four gates and a forum – much of which you will still see today. Part of the old Roman Forum forms focal square **Zeleni trg**; sundry sections of stone pillar peter out towards the south quay of Obala kralja Petra Krešimira IV. On and adjacent to Zeleni trg are Zadar's four main sights: **St Donat's Church**; the **Cathedral**; the **Archaelogical Museum**, and **St Mary's Church & Treasury**. The extraordinary Byzantine treats of the Treasury are the absolute don't miss.

Alongside the Forum runs the spinal street of Široka, linking the new cultural hub of Three Wells (Trg tri bunara) to historic Five Wells (Trg pet bunara) at each extremity of the city centre. Around the edge of the city, the south embankment was once the chic side of town, with a pier for fast passenger ships and four-storey buildings in the classic, Habsburg mould. Much was built with Maraska money, the local manufacturers grown rich from liquor sales. Here the Hotel Bristol and its namesake coffeehouse were landmarks, even when the Italians moved in and renamed them Excelsior. The quay was almost completely destroyed by Allied bombing. All that remained was the hotel, renamed the Zagreb and still the subject of a long-running saga to rebuild it.

Focus has shifted to the north shore. As if by way of announcing it, as you turn the south-west corner of the quay to head north, bizarre noises greet you, sounding not unlike the Clangers sighing for want of soup. Thirty-five organ pipes emit unworldly tones through holes bored into the smooth, new paving stones, their size and velocity determined by the waves of the sea. The eccentric **Sea Organ**, inaugurated in 2005, was designed by Nikola Bašić and built in nearby Murter. Come here after dark and you'll be greeted by a stunning light show following the rhythms of the Sea Organ in a similarly unworldly display. The **'Greeting To The Sun'**, designed by the same architect, comprises 300 multi-layered glass plates in a circle, synchronised with the same wave energy. Beneath the glass are solar modules that spring into life at sunset to simulate our solar system. Around the glass is a metal ring

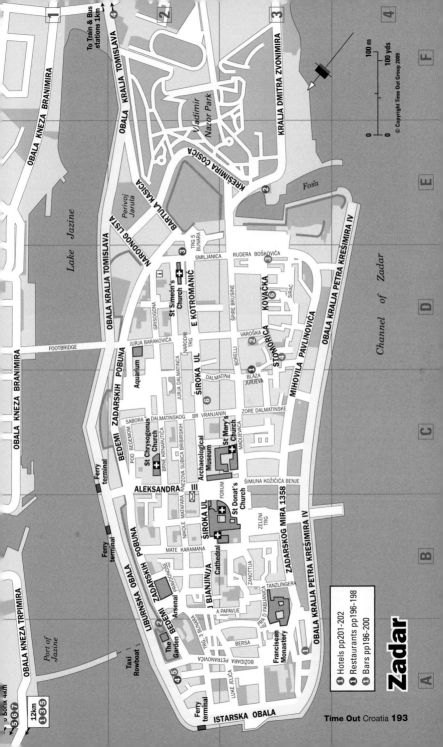

Zadar

- ① Hotels pp201-202
- ① Restaurants pp196-198
- ① Bars pp196-200

Time Out Croatia **193**

© Copyright Time Out Group 2009

100 m
100 yds

To Train & Bus stations 1km

OBALA KNEZA BRANIMIRA

OBALA KRALJA TOMISLAVA

Lake Jazine

NARODNOG LISTA

BARTULA KAŠIĆA

KREŠIMIRA ĆOSIĆA

KRALJA DMITRA ZVONIMIRA

Vladimir Nazor Park

Perivoj Jarula

FOOTBRIDGE

OBALA KRALJA TOMISLAVA

Foša

Channel of Zadar

OBALA KRALJA PETRA KREŠIMIRA IV

BEDEMI ZADARSKIH POBUNA

OBALA KNEZA BRANIMIRA

Aquarium

JURJA BARAKOVIĆA

GRISOGONA

St Simeon's Church
E KOTROMANIĆ

TRG 5 BUNARA

SMILJANICA

RUDERA BOŠKOVIĆA

ŠPIRE BRUSINE

SIRAC

KOVAČKA

STOMORICA

Varoška

NARODNI TRG

DALMATINA

ŠIROKA UL

JURJA DALMATINCA

BORELLI

BLAŽA JURJEVA

MIHOVILA PAVLINOVIĆA

POD BEDEMOM

SABORA

St Chrysogonus' Church

DALMATINSKOG

BRNE KRNARUTIĆA

KNEZOVA ŠUBIĆA BRIBIRSKIH

BR VRANJANIN

ZORE DALMATINSKE

Archaeological Museum

St Mary's Church

MADIJEVACA

OBALA KRALJA PETRA KREŠIMIRA IV

ALEKSANDRA III

Ferry terminal

Ferry terminal

NIKOLE MATAFARA

MATE KARAMANA

ŠIROKA UL

FORUM

St Donat's Church

ŠIMUNA KOŽIČIĆA BENJE

ZELENI TRG

ZADARSKOG MIRA 1358

LIBURNSKA OBALA

BEDEMI ZADARSKIH POBUNA

ZADARSKA OBALA

I BJANJIN/JA

PRANDONOŠE

Cathedral

ZANOTTIJA

TANZLINGERA

A PAPAVIJE

FRA D FABIJANICA

BERSA

TRG 3 BUNARA

The Garden
Arsenal

BOŽIDARA PETRANOVIĆA

Franciscan Monastery

LUKE JELIĆA

Taxi Rowboat

Port of Jazine

OBALA KNEZA TRPIMIRA

To Borik 4km

12km

Ferry terminal

ISTARSKA OBALA

Zadar.

ZADAR & ŠIBENIK

inscribed with local details from a medieval
calendar originating from Zadar but now
kept in Oxford. *See p195* **Profile**.

Further round you find the three ferry
terminals including a new cruiser pier; one of
Croatia's biggest and best morning markets;
and the **Port Gate**, one of two Renaissance-
era stone entrances to town that carry the
carved Lion of Venice (*photo p197*).

The eastern end of the Old Town is centred
on **Narodni trg**, surrounded by the **Guard
House** and **City Loggia**, both original
Renaissance structures that were built by the
Venetians. The former is now rediscovering
its role as the **Ethnographic Museum**, the
exhibits slowly returning after wartime storage;

the latter is an art gallery. Nearby is **St
Simeon's Church** (Trg Šime Budinića, 023
211 705, open summer 8am-noon, 4-7pm daily,
winter 8am-noon daily), which is named after
Zadar's patron saint. It houses the ornate Silver
Casket of St Simeon, commissioned by
Elizabeth of Hungary in 1377.

Here, around Five Wells, is the Venetian
Land Gate, the narrow channel of Foša and
the little warrens of the old Varoš quarter,
including curving, bar-lined Stomorica.

Archaeological Museum

Trg Opatice Čike (023 250 516). **Open** *July, Aug*
9am-1pm, 5-9pm Mon-Sat. *May, June, Sept* 9am-
1pm, 5-7pm Mon-Sat. *Oct-Apr* 9am-2pm Mon-Fri;
9am-1pm Sat. **Admission** 10kn. **No credit
cards. Map** p193 C2.
Founded in 1832 but since rehoused in a modern
building by the Forum, this museum and its 100,000
artefacts are arranged on three floors. At the top is
a prehistoric section of ceramics and weaponry;
below is a Roman and Liburnian floor, including a
model of how the Forum would have looked; and the
Middle Ages are displayed on the ground floor, with
bizarre local gravestones.

St Donat's Church

Zeleni trg. **Open** *Summer* 9am-10pm daily.
Admission 10kn. **No credit cards. Map**
p193 B3.
No longer a place of worship but the unusual cylin-
der shapes of this Byzantine church are an emblem
of Zadar. Built at the beginning of the ninth century,
in the pre-Romanesque period, its interior is a sim-

INSIDE TRACK NIN

A trip to Nin, 45 minutes from Zadar
by bus, gives you the option of a morning
poking around old churches and an
afternoon at the sandy beach 15 minutes'
walk north of town. Nin is a historic,
fortified town set on a small island in
a lagoon. An old Roman settlement, it
was the residence of the first Croatian
kings, as a look around its excellent
Archaeological Museum (023 264
160, open summer 9am-10pm Mon-Sat,
winter 9am-noon Mon-Sat) will illustrate.
The tiny **Church of the Holy Cross** is
the oldest in Croatia.

Profile Nikola Bašić

The artist who made Zadar the place to visit.

No Croatian artist has had an effect on his immediate environment as much as Nikola Bašić. Creator of Zadar's two most prominent and contemporary pieces of public artwork, the *Sea Organ* and *Greeting to the Sun*, it is Bašić who has most helped push Zadar into *Vogue* magazine's top 25 worldwide places to visit. And he's not finished yet. His 1246 project involves a commemorative stone for each of Croatia's 1,246 islets and islands, part of a new concept of tourist development that blends natural and cultural heritage.

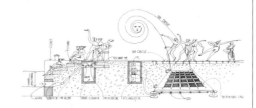

Born in Murter in 1946, Bašić studied architecture in Sarajevo, returning to his native Zadar region ten years later. His professor, Zlatko Ugljen, was a significant influence, as was an island childhood. Murter's two marinas – Hramina and Betina – are Bašić designs, as are several churches, convents and buildings around Croatia. Bašić is also proud of the stage he created for Pope John Paul II's visit to Zadar in 2003 – but it is the *Sea Organ* and *Greeting to the Sun* that have really broken the mould.

When commissioned to revive the embankment, Bašić took his inspiration from Zadar's sunsets and the sound of waves on the shore. Resisting the conventional approach, he wanted the space to be a 'kaleidoscope of metaphors', an appreciation of the true spirit of Zadar. Though there's modern technology involved in *Greeting to the Sun*, the *Sea Organ* could have been engineered centuries ago; for Bašić, it is more man-enhanced natural phenomenon than man-made installation.

Bašić overcame initial local resistance, and technical and budgetary challenges, to create a unique soundscape. The same waves power the equally remarkable *Greeting to the Sun*, a series of multi-layered glass panels designed to simulate the solar system. Bašić has finished his commission. Now the city has to complete its own brief and open a ferry and passenger port, and a hotel.

Meawhile Bašić will retire to his idyllic islet of Gangaro to 'catch cuttlefish and dry figs'.

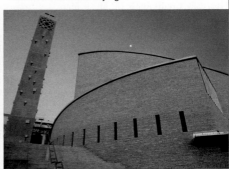

ple, high-ceilinged space with exceptional acoustics for musical events such as the 'Strings Only' evenings, for which the church is used today

St Mary's Church & Treasury

Trg Opatice Čike (023 250 496). **Open** *Church* 8am-noon, 5-8pm daily. *Treasury* 10am-12.30pm, 6-7pm Mon-Fri; 10am-12.30pm Sat. **Admission** 20kn. **No credit cards**. **Map** p193 C3.

The jewel in Zadar's crown is the church of this Benedictine convent, a 16th-century remake of an early Romanesque one dating back to 1066. The bell-tower, restored after Allied damage, also dates to this early period. The nuns were responsible for curating the stunning treasures next door, known as the Gold and Silver of Zadar (Zlato i Srebro Zadra). Set over two floors, the Treasury houses Zadar's finest ecclesiastical artefacts, finely carved, ornate examples of Byzantine craft and religious Venetian art from the 16th century. Saints' limbs are enclosed in sumptuous gold and silver reliquaries, icons, crucifixes, and everything is beautifully presented and illuminated. The collection spans 1,000 years, until the 18th century.

Zadar Cathedral

Trg Sv Stošije. **Open** *Summer* 8am-6pm daily. *Winter* 8am-12.30pm daily. *Campanile Summer* 9am-8pm daily. **Admission** *Campanile* 10kn. **No credit cards**. **Map** p193 B2/3.

The Cathedral of St Anastasia (Katedrala Sv Stošije), beside St Donat's, is the largest cathedral in Dalmatia and was built in late Romanesque style during the 12th and 13th centuries. Decorative friezes and delicate stonework depict birds, animals and religious figures, although many visitors enter to climb the bell tower for the fabulous view of Zadar. The campanile, partially built in the second half of the 15th century, was completed in 1894 to the design of English architect TG Jackson.

Where to eat

Dva Ribara

Blaža Jurjeva 1 (023 213 445). **Open** 10am-11pm daily. **Credit** AmEx, DC, MC, V. **Map** p193 C/D3 ❶

A restyled minimalist interior, with a glass-encased, stainless-steel kitchen and wood-fired pizza oven, provides modernity and increased capacity for Dva Ribara – but at the expense of much of its former terrace. The heavy leather menu in four languages reminds you of the old-school tradition, similar to its sister operation Foša. This one is firmly downtown, adjacent to the bar quarter of Stomorica. Despite the name, the Two Fishermen, meat is the order of the day here, the signature dishes being hulking carnivorous platters for two.

▶ *If you'd rather eat traditional dishes in tradtional surroundings, stablemate Foša has kept its looks; see below.*

Kn Foša

Kralja Dmitra Zvonimira 2 (023 314 421). **Open** noon-midnight daily. **Credit** AmEx, DC, MC, V. **Map** p193 E3 ❷

This well established, old-school fish restaurant stands in and is named after the narrow channel by the city walls. Its stone square of terrace sits atop the waters with a fine view to sea – it's as if you were dining on a public square but without the bustle. All the standard white fish and shellfish are served, either with traditional local green *blitva* and potatoes, or as part of a seafood risotto or pasta dish. Service is also charmingly old-school and the prices are reasonable too.

▶ *For even cheaper local dishes, Ljepotica (Obala kneza Branimira, 023 311 288) near the pedestrian bridge is as homely as can be.*

Kn Konoba Skoblar

Trg Petra Zoranića (023 213 236). **Open** 7am-midnight Mon-Sat; 7.30am-10pm Sun. **Credit** AmEx, DC, MC, V. **Map** p193 D2 ❸

Konoba Skoblar, a traditional tavern between St Simeon's Church and Five Wells, is named after an old football player who then passed the establishment on to his cousin. It fills around *marenda* time at elevenish, locals snacking on salted anchovies or octopus salad while mulling over the fate of the popular local basketball team. Skoblar does full lunches and dinners too, and in summer the meat offerings are reduced to leave kitchen space for plenty of fish and shellfish dishes – there are at least three kinds of shells in the black risotto. Sweet desserts are the house speciality here, either kalelarga cheesecake or Sv Stošija, a cherry cake made with Maraska, the local fruit liqueur (*see p199* **Viva Maraska!**).

★ Kornat

Liburnska obala 6 (023 254 501). **Open** 11am-11pm daily. **Credit** AmEx, DC, MC, V. **Map** p193 A2 ❹

A good candidate for best restaurant in town. By the ferry port adjacent to the Maya bar, the Kornat is classy enough to have a cloakroom, refined enough to have a superb selection of Croatian wines but relaxed enough to avoid giving a stuffy dining experience. The bottles are on display around a bright, modern interior, its 20 tables ably manned by equally bright, fluent-English staff. Although prices are much as elsewhere in town, the ingredients are not: truffles are used in sauces to garnish the standout monkfish, dry porcini mushrooms to help flavour the steak. Specialities include black risotto and the chocolate cake.

★ Lungo Mare

Obala kneza Trpimira 23 (023 331 533/091 169 2335 mobile). **Open** 10am-midnight daily. **Credit** AmEx, DC, MC, V. **Map** p193 A1 ❺

This loveliest restaurant terrace in Zadar overlooks the sunset on Draženica Bay, a 15-minute walk from

Port Gate. *See p194.*

Arsenal. *See p200.*

town. Inside is beautifully tiled, with a little art, and a decor that is more modern than the traditional, neat waiting staff would suggest. Lungo Mare is equally appreciated for its fresh seafood and meat dishes, such as the house fish plate or pork fillet, stuffed with scampi, cheese or *pršut* and mushrooms. The wine list, possibly the best in town, runs into three figures and includes a few French and Italian names among the classic Croatian ones. Do try the house cheesecake.

Niko

Obala kneza Domagoja 9 (023 337 888). **Open** 11am-midnight daily. **Credit** AmEx, DC, MC, V. **Map** p193 A1 ➏
One of the first restaurants to be privatised in former Yugoslavia, Niko is not too pretty from the outside, but houses one of the most popular kitchens in Zadar – almost an institution. Set near Marina Borik on Puntamika's southernmost headland, Niko contains both a small hotel and a proud restaurant with an extensive choice of wine. Fresh fish arrives daily and is then prepared with carefully selected olive oil over a wood-fire grill. Regulars tend to go for the green tagliatelle with scampi and the tiramisu. A spacious terrace overlooks the sea.
▶ *Rooms at the Niko go for around 1,000kn, with a 150kn discount for payment in cash.*

Where to drink

Café Brazil

Prilaz hrvatske citaonice 1 (no phone). **Open** 9am-midnight daily. **No credit cards**. **Map** p193 A3 ➊

Just tucked in from the newly landscaped embankment, this handy little café offers a view of the sea from its gravel terrace, an ice-cream stall outside in summer and long drinks from 15kn including a Bruce Lee, a 007 James Bond and a Café del Mar of champagne and orange. Bottled Leffe and Hoegaarden, and morning coffees, are served from the sunken bar inside.

Djina

Varoška 2 (no phone). **Open** 8am-11pm daily. **No credit cards**. **Map** p193 D3 ➋
Djina is a great little gallery bar situated just off the main square, done out with bizarre egg-shaped heads designed by Silvijana Dražković. A trendy crowd gathers by day to drink any number of fruit teas, the electronic musical backdrop increasing as the night wears on. There are a couple of chairs on the busy street outside.

Inside

Poljana Pavla Pavlovića, Rudjera Boškovića 6 (023 301 310). **Open** *Summer* 8am-1am daily. *Winter* 8am-midnight Mon-Sat. **No credit cards**. **Map** p193 D3 ➌
Now known as Inside, the former Space Lab is a chilled-out minimalist white space tucked away in a passageway in Zadar's student quarter. Its day begins with breakfasts and speciality teas, taken outside or sipped in the narrow space within. After a daytime of snacks and board games, by the early evening the cocktails are on the go, someone has manned the DJ decks and the regulars arrive, a mixture of people in the local music business, boutique owners and other DJs.

Viva Maraska!

Zadar's local tipple is its most celebrated export.

You could easily be forgiven for thinking you'd arrived at a place called Maraska instead of Zadar. Where the sign 'Zadar' should be at the train station, the word 'Maraska' appears instead. Walk into town, and there are adverts for Maraska around every corner. The stately Maraska building, by the breakwater, is a local landmark (and soon-to-be high-end hotel).

Maraska is everywhere and so is the Maraschino drink for which it's famous. George IV and Queen Victoria sent warships to bring back their favourite tipple and, in 1887, the Prince of Wales, later to become King George VI, made a personal visit to the distillery to collect his. Other famous Maraschino lovers include Napoleon, King Louis XVIII of France, the Tsar of Russia, Casanova, Baudelaire, Alfred Hitchcock and many of the passengers on the *Titanic*. In 2005, Maraska's Maraschino became available in the Vatican.

The Dalmatian sour cherry, marasca, probably originated from around the Caspian Sea and Anatolia. It is the key ingredient of this prized fruity and aromatic liqueur, aged in special oak casks. The leaves and stalks play their part too; the stones are set aside for crushing and distilling into kirsch. Thriving in the northern Dalmatian soil, at heights of 200 metres above sea level, and nurtured by the Mediterranean climate, the cherries are richer, sweeter and fleshier than any other, exceptionally high in fruit content and full of minerals. The recipe for Maraschino was created in the 16th century in the Dominican monastery of Zadar and named Rosolj, derived from the Latin *ros solis*, or 'sunny dew'. Even now, it is still presented in bottles encased in hand-woven reed, each requiring 20 minutes' work by the local women who sit in a circle in the raffia room.

Commercial distillation started in the 17th century

and developed in the 18th. As capital of Dalmatia, 'Zara' received foreign dignitaries such as Girolamo Luxardo of Sardinia. His wife perfected the liqueur at home and, in 1821, Girolamo established the first Luxardo distillery. In 1913, the third generation of Luxardos built a new modern distillery. This is today's magnificent Maraska building, destined to become a luxury hotel.

After World War II, Giorgio was the only surviving brother of the fourth generation of Luxardos, he restarted the business in Italy with a distillery in the Veneto. In Zadar, the business was nationalised, then privatised and recently passed into the hands of the Bosnia-based Mepas Group.

Maraska's swinging fortunes have impacted on the local economy. Just before the Yugoslav War, annual production averaged 5,000 tons, with 90 per cent of the end product exported. It was also the largest employer in town. Cherries were the third largest crop in the region after olives and grapes. Heavy bombardment destroyed much of it, but the recovery has been swift and the company has established some 100,000 new plants in the fertile plains of Zemunik, near Zadar airport.

ZADAR & ŠIBENIK

▶ *As an alternative during the day, the Coffee Lounge, which is in the same passageway (No.6, 023 318 870), is equally popular with the local student crowd.*

Kantun

Stomorica 5 (no phone). **Open** 7am-midnight Mon-Fri; 8am-2pm, 6pm-midnight Sat. **No credit cards. Map** p193 D3 ❹

Most characterful venue in bar-lined Stomorica, Kantun is a little grunge, a little underground, filled with cig smoke and student drinkers, observed by a large portrait of the poet Tin.

▶ *If Kantun is too busy or too smoky, the adjacent Lotus is almost as much fun. For something more intimate, try Rio, which is round the corner at Putevac 5.*

Maya Pub

Liburnska obala 6 (023 251 716). **Open** 7am-3am Mon-Sat; 10am-3pm Sun. **No credit cards. Map** p193 A2 ❺

Maya Pub is an ethno-themed hangout by the ferry terminal, with a quayside terrace. Eastern, mostly Balinese, decor in a big space that accommodates some of the most popular local bands on a stage set up to one side. Most of the time it's DJ sounds and it's not a bad place for a quiet pint of Guinness or Kilkenny of an afternoon.

Viaz

Široka (no phone). **Open** 7am-midnight daily. **No credit cards. Map** p193 C2 ❻

Electronic sounds boom around the two floors of this bar on Zadar's main downtown street. It's a weird design, some stones under glass by the main entrance, boxy furniture all in orange and green, but draws in attractive young people. Although it has no street number, you'll find it opposite a busy court-yard bar, named the Kale Larga after the familiar name for Široka.

Music & nightlife

Arsenal

Trg Tri bunara 1 (023 253 833/www. arsenalzadar.com). **Open** 7am-3am daily. **Credit** MC, V.

Set in a huge renovated 18th-century warehouse, Arsenal is unique in Croatia, in size, ambience and the sheer variety of events and attractions. These include a gallery, cocktail bar and new à la carte restaurant upstairs. The spacious stage hosts world music, *klapa*, name DJs and local bands. The sound is superb and there's a show of some kind most evenings. Additional features include a tourist information centre and agency; independent local fashion designer group Fashion.Hr, and a wine store. Tables between the stage and the bar allow for lounging, sipping and snacking from the extensive menu – the space is cleared for gigs and dancing. *Photo p198.*

INSIDE TRACK
MAINSTREAM CLUBS

For all Zadar's new cachet, many youngsters are happy to stick to their local haunts. Year-round **City Club Forum** (Marka Marulića, 091 300 0064) is a small, popular place by Jazine, playing house and hip hop, while **Gotham** (Marka Oreškovića 1, 023 200 289) is a Batman-themed entertainment complex by the Nova Banka tower. Locals also go to **Caffe Maraschino** (Kneza Branimira, 023 211 250), east of the footbridge on the mainland, or head to the big-name clubs near Primošten, Vodic and at Zrće, Novalja on Pag.

Barbarella's

Punta Radman put 8, Petrčane (www.the gardenfestival.eu). **Open** according to progamme. **No credit cards.**

The Garden crew, who sited their annual festival in these verdant grounds, have gone on to make a more permanent venue out of it. Originally built in 1973, the retro, snail-shaped main building, known to locals as the Maxi Bar, has been classily re-styled as Barbarella's Discotheque, in honour of the Birmingham club that hosted the finest bands way back when. May 2008 saw the opening of Barbarella's circular Beach Bar, which is spectacularly located on a small peninsula on the sea front. Improvements to the main building include air-conditioning and a Funktion One sound system.

▶ *The people who run the Garden Festival are also responsible for the Garden (see below).*

Garden

Liburnska obala 6 (023 364 739/www.the gardenzadar.com). **Open** *Late May-late Sept* 10am-1am daily. **No credit cards.**

Superbly located UK-owned outdoor lounge bar and club features quality live music and name DJs all summer, weather permitting. The Garden centres around a vast panoramic terrace now with private cabanas replacing the minimalist furniture and beds, amid established trees and great views. By day, locals and (mainly UK) tourists relax, read the papers and watch passing ships. By night there's a full agenda, with tapas and finger food. Well chosen local wines and well priced cocktails are the order of the day – Croatian and Belgian beers are equally good value too. The Garden is one of the most important things to have happened to Zadar in recent years, and the team behind it, UB40 drummer James Brown and music producer Nick Colgan, have not rested on their laurels.

▶ *The owners of the Garden are also in charge at Barbarella's (see above).*

Where to stay

★ Falkensteiner Punta Skala Resort

Punta Skala (+43 1 605 4020/www.falkensteiner. com). **Open** Summer 2009. **Rates** *Diadora per person full-board* €85-€209. *Spa Iadera* €170-€350 single; €180-€360 double. **Credit** AmEx, DC, MC, V. **Map** p193 A1 **❶**

The first phase of this massive project near Petrčane, 12 km (seven miles) west of Zadar, includes a five- and four-star hotel, the largest spa facilities in Croatia, a village with shops and restaurants, apartments and sports facilities. The resort area is surrounded by sea and beaches, and there's a full programme of entertainment for kids and grown-ups. Phase two will see a new bar and discotheque in the village, on top of the fish restaurant, pizzeria and ice-cream parlour. The four-star Diadora is designed to be the last word in family holidays. Its 250 family-suite apartments, most with sea views, accommodate two adults and two kids, entertained at Falky Land, an indoor children's adventure park and Falky Game Heaven: kindergarten, cinema and disco. The five-star flagship Spa Iadera comprises 210 rooms, most with a sea view, with every treatment imaginable in the spa area.

▶ *For more details of children's activities here and around Dalmatia, see p56.*

★ Hotel Bastion

Bedemi zadarskih pobuna (023 494 950/fax 023 494 951/www.hotel-bastion.hr). **Rates** 810kn-1,170kn single; 940kn-1,380kn double. **Credit** AmEx, DC, MC, V. **Map** p193 A2 **❷**

Zadar has been waiting a long time for a good city-centre hotel and Hotel Bastion, which opened in June 2008, thankfully doesn't disappoint. Slovene architect Jani Vosel has blended old and new with flair. It's a four-star boutique, with 23 rooms and five apartments, a video conferencing room, restaurant, bar, small cardio-vascular gym and spa (100kn). The original stone is featured throughout, including in the spa, where the edge of the stone floor marks the boundary of the 13th-century fortress Kaštel on which the hotel is built. Inside and out you'll find the original stone catapult balls used to defend it. The 60-cover restaurant focuses on Med-style slow food – the owner has a fish shop in the market. There's plenty of parking space (70kn) and windows sound-proofed against the noise of The Garden nearby and crowds milling outside the Arsenal.

Hotel Club Funimation Borik

Majstora Radovana 7 (023 206 100/fax 023 332 065/www.falkensteiner.com). **Rates** €82-€177 single; €114-€236 double. **Credit** AmEx, DC, MC, V. **Map** p193 A1 **❸**

The big attraction of this four-star family hotel – apart from its year-round availability – is the Acquapura spa complex. This comprises four areas:

Hotel Bastion.

a spa with thalasso seawater treatments; a steam and dry sauna; indoor and heated outdoor pools, plus one for kids; and a gym. The thalasso area contains 16 treatment rooms alone. The Funimation puts on children's events all summer; also included in the price are windsurfing, tennis and volleyball – plus three daily buffet meals. You pay extra for courses in diving and sailing. Club Funimation includes the formerly separate Hotel Adriana Select, restyled as the Garden Wing Adriana. This recently built part of the resort, with its own pool area and easy access to the sea, is quieter.

▶ *The Falkensteiner has another major, child-friendly actitivy and spa hotel complex opening in 2009 – the Falkensteiner Punta Skala Resort; see above.*

Hotel Kolovare

Bože Peričića 14 (023 203 200/fax 023 203 300/www.hotel-kolovare-zadar.htnet.hr). **Rates** €75-€120 single; €105-€165 double. **Credit** AmEx, DC, MC, V. **Map** p193 F2 **❹**

This is a recently upgraded classic Socialist-era hotel, on the edge of the city centre towards the bus station. The Kolovare is surprisingly large, 230 rooms, a third of them singles for the passing domestic business crowd. Opening on to the beach, it also has an outdoor pool and a gym, but rooms are pretty bland.

▶ *For a classier kind of city-centre hotel, head for the recently opened Bastion; see above.*

Hotel President

Vladana Desnice 16 (023 333 696/www.hotel-president.hr). **Rates** €125-€168 single; €140-€222 double. **Credit** AmEx, DC, MC, V. **Map** p193 A1 **❺**

ZADAR & ŠIBENIK

Self-styled classy four-star in the Borik area, where much is made of the decorative aesthetic, the porcelain dishes and cherrywood furniture. Whether it's all in good taste is another matter – the Vivaldi restaurant has glass table dividers etched with the score from the *Four Seasons*. Still, there's 24hr room service and all rooms have balconies.

Kn Hotel Venera
Šime Ljubića 4a (023 214 098/www.hotel-venera-zd.hr). **Rates** 300kn-450kn single; 360kn-450kn double. **No credit cards.**
Map p193 D3 ⑥
A modest cheapie in a narrow side street of the bar quarter of Stomorica. A dozen small rooms over a travel agents have been renovated to incorporate a little shower and twin beds for simple, clean comfort. Singles have to pay the double room rate in high season. It's also referred to as the Jović Guesthouse and is convenient if you're spending a night in Zadar.

Villa Hrešć
Obala kneza Trpimira 28 (023 337 570/fax 023 334 336/www.villa-hresc.hr). **Rates** €60-€86 single; €90-€160 double. **Credit** AmEx, DC, MC, V. **Map** p193 A1 ⑦
Overlooking Maestral Bay, a ten-minute walk from town, this is by far the best mid-range option for comfort in Zadar. The suites are suitable for two to four guests, six at a push for a nominal extra fee. More like condominiums, they comprise a living room, kitchenette, dining room, bedroom and modern bathroom with marble washbasin, all capacious, all immaculately furnished – and all overlooking the sea. The larger ones have a terrace, with the biggest the size of half a football pitch. The view, which is shared by those in the outdoor pool, is striking. Patris runs a decent terrace restaurant here too.

Getting there & around

Croatia Airlines buses (25kn, 15mins) meet domestic arrivals to Zadar **airport**, 8km (5 miles) south-east of town at Zemunik Donji and run to the bus station before terminating at the northern ferry quay by the Old Town. Buses are scheduled to set off from the same points 60-80 minutes before each Croatia Airlines departure – other passengers should take the nearest service to their flight, or take a taxi (170kn-220kn).

Ferries serving Rijeka and Dubrovnik, and the islands in the Zadar archipelago, dock at the same northern quay.

There are buses almost hourly from Zagreb (5hrs), Rijeka (4.5hrs) and Split (3.5hrs) to Zadar. A modest train service links with Knin (2.5hrs) and the InterCity line between Zagreb and Split. Zadar **bus** and **train** stations are next to each other 1.5km (a mile) east of the Old Town centre, a 15-minute walk.

Buses Nos.2 and 4 run to the ferry terminals, bus No.5 goes to Puntamika and Borik via the modern centre of town. Tickets are 6kn, pay on board. For a **taxi**, call 023 251 400.

Resources

Tourist information
Zadar Tourist Office *Ilije Smiljanića 5 (023 212 222/www.zadar.hr)*. **Open** *Summer* 8am-midnight daily. *Winter* 8am-8pm daily.

UGLJAN

The most accessible island from Zadar is Ugljan, with hourly boats to the largest village of Preko (20mins), which is so close that it feels like part of the city. Pick a quiet weekday to swim around here. Pronounced 'oog-lee-an', this 52-km long, green island is separated from the mainland by the narrow Zadar channel and connected by bridge to its less populated neighbour, Pašman.

Ugljan takes its name from the Croatian word ulje, 'olive' – the island is covered with more than 200,000 olive trees. The crop has been harvested here for more than 2,000 years and, along with fishing, remains central to the local economy and culture. The olive trees are also responsible for Ugljan's unique position as a private island. Each local family owns one of the hundreds of orchards that cover the largely unpopulated western slopes. With so many small, private plots, land purchase is rendered all but impossible.

Two new marinas may, however, go some way towards changing the lie of the land. First the **Olive Island Marina** in Sutomicica (023 335 809, www.oliveislandmarina.com) has been given permission to develop a resort area there; and **Preko Marina** (023 286 169, www.marinapreko.com), which is close to the ferry port, opened for business in 2008, with a user-friendly system for booking into berths and an environmentally friendly approach to dealing with nautical waste.

Large areas of Ugljan can be explored by a network of paths for hikers and bikers, and campers are also well served, with several large sites situated on the flatter, northern part of the island.

So far lacking chic hotels, swanky bars or cool nightlife, Ugljan often passes under the radar when people talk about Croatian islands. People don't come here to be seen or because it's fashionable. Life goes on at a slow pace with little fuss and the friendly locals expect visitors to take it or leave it. Tourists and Zadar residents come to enjoy the simple things in life in an unhurried, uncontrived way, on an island with a distinctive Mediterranean feel.

Ugljan.

Sightseeing

The regular 30-minute Zadar-Preko ferry
serves the island. Two buses are synchronised
with the arrival of the inbound ferry and fork
both north and south on the one main road
that connects the villages spaced along the
populated eastern side. Exploring the island by
bike or on foot is made simple by the excellent
network of clearly marked routes – pick up a
map from the tourist offices in Preko, **Kali** or
Kukljica. However, drivers should be wary,
as the tracks are narrow. If you're wondering
about the worth of slogging along a hiking trail
in the daytime heat, it's worth knowing that
remote and barely visited swimming spots are
usually the reward for carrying on. A hike
to **Mount St Michael** is recommended,
especially if you can arrive before sunset.
A moderate 265 metres, the summit is
occupied by the remains of a 13th-century
Venetian fort and a communications centre.
The 360-degree views of Ugljan and the
surrounding islands are extraordinary.

Preko town is a brisk walk from the port
and makes a good base for exploring. Bikes
can be hired from the tourist office (023 286
108, www.ugljan-pasman.com) and mopeds
from private companies in the area. It has a
good swimming beach, although a better
swimming spot can be found on the tiny island
of **Galevac**. A few metres offshore, accessible
by taxi boat, this lovely island is home to a
15th-century Franciscan monastery.

Pretty Kali is a short drive from Preko with
a couple of spots to eat and drink. Kukljica,
further south, offers boat trips to Kornati, a
market and good fish restaurants. The holiday
village of Zelena gives it a resort atmosphere.

Where to eat, drink & stay

In Preko, waterfront **Ivo** (Mul 3, 023 286
390; closed Jan, Feb) is the biggest restaurant,
serving an excellent house fish stew. To the
north, **Ugljan village** consists of nine hamlets.
Fishermen sing over end-of-day drinks by the
harbour. The **Ritam** beach bar on the south
side of the harbour has waterside seating and
stays open late.

There are only two hotels on the island:
improved two-star **Preko** (023 373 547) and
the standard **Hotel Ugljan** (023 288 004,
www.hotel-ugljan.com), each named after
the community in which it resides. The **Vila
Zdenko Lukin** (023 281 607, 098 9 517 659
mobile) on the road between Preko and Kali
has large rooms and apartments, most
overlooking the sea, for very reasonable
rates. Zdenko, the friendly owner, runs
trips to the nearby Kornati islands.

TRIBUNJ

In 2002, **Tribunj** was a quiet fishing village
with a great big unfinished concrete building
and several fishing boats. The building is now
part of an extremely smart marina filled with
posh yachts; the fishing boats remain in the
outer part. Back then, year-round **Restaurant
Tople** seemed too formal; its owner has just
sold his small hotel accommodation, **Villa
Diana**, to a Russian owner with grand
upmarket plans.

Yet for those in the know, Tribunj is a gem
of a destination. The old town is on a tiny oval
island, connected to the mainland by a small
stone bridge. Most of the north-east side of the
island faces the marina; on the south-west side

ZADAR & ŠIBENIK

INSIDE TRACK
TRIBUNJ DONKEYS

Tribunj is also a village of animal lovers with an annual donkey race and a sanctuary for more unfortunate donkeys on the nearby island of Logorun.

are bars, cafés and municipal boat moorings. By the bridge are the tourist office (summer 8am-1pm, 5-9pm Mon-Sat, 8am-noon Sun) and post office. Restaurants are scattered all around the area, both on and off the island. As if that's not enough, the more cosmoplitan tourist town of **Vodice** is a lovely 40-minute walk away linked by a blue-flag beach; the tranquil area of **Sovlje**, with its secluded beach and wonderfully located restaurant **Plava Val**, is also nearby.

Where to eat, drink & stay

Plavi Val (098 337 154 mobile, www.plavi-val.com) offers all the Dalmatian favourite fish and meat dishes, with prices only slightly higher than the norm – look at the setting. Tribunj also has seven apartments to let and provides a free taxi service to diners within a ten-mile radius. In the Old Town, **Konoba Simun** (091 523 6004 mobile, closed Oct-mid Apr) is lovely inside and out, perhaps verging on the snooty. Expect to pay 500kn per kilo of lobster sailor-style and 60kn for mussels *buzara*. Lyrics from a song by local singer Arsen Dedić opens the arty menu. The understated **Konoba Palma** (Jurjevgradska 21, 098 869 667, 098 612 517, both mobiles, closed Oct-mid Apr) has Slavonian owners who return to a ranch in winter to prepare the smoked ham and spicy *kulen* sausage. Both are delicious, the smoked ham discernibly different from its Dalmatian cousin dried in the Bora wind. Prices are reasonable.

On the same marina road, the **Movie Resort Hotels & Apartments** (www.themovieresort.com) is a stylish hotel with an adequate beach and a film-themed interior. Drive past the marina and it's just past the Restaurant Tople and the last pier. The nearby Villa Diana has only just come under Russian ownership and there are plans to refurbish all 15 rooms to take it upmarket from its current, harsh, two-star status. A website is also promised.

KORNATI

The Kornati archipelago has qualities that make it unique. It is made up of 140 islands and islets in an area only 35km (22 miles)

long and 14km (8.5 miles) wide. Between the long, thin island of **Kornat**, which faces the coast, and the chain of islands on the other side, there is a stretch of water naturally protected from the open sea, with dozens of safe bays to drop anchor. Once you pass through one of the two narrow gates to the north and south, you leave the worst of the waves behind, and enter a strange, other-worldly environment, with barren-looking, treeless hills all around.

The islands on the inside of the national park seem deserted. You might sight the occasional sheep, or a small votive chapel, built by a grateful sailor saved from a storm by the natural barrier of the islands, otherwise there's little sign of human habitation. It's a very meditative and minimal landscape, unlike any other island chain in the Adriatic. When you enter Kornati, you know you've arrived somewhere completely different.

Whether you have your own yacht, or come on one of the many tour boats offering day trips around the national park, you will also get to experience the outer side of the archipelago. The contrast between the calm inner space of Kornati and the wild world of the open sea is unmistakable, not least in the geomorphology of the exposed rocks. Sheer cliffs offer spectacular scenes and dramatic sounds, from crashing waves to the echo of the human voice. The seaward side of the island of **Mana** is the most impressive; boats can come right up close to the 100-metre (328-foot) cliffs that stretch for 1.5 km (1 mile). If the sea is not too rough, the outer edge of Kornati is a great place to swim and snorkel, with much marine life just below the the surface of the rocky shoreline.

The area was struck by a series of disasters in 2007. At the end of August, what seemed at first like an insignificant fire broke out on Kornat and 12 young local firemen perished while trying to tackle it, one of the worst tragedies in recent Croatian history. Below the surface, a killer algae threatened some of the bays; above ground, a terrible drought almost wiped out the indigenous Kornati sheep, necessitating emergency action by the Croatian Navy to ship drinking water to the island, but not soon enough to save 1,300 of them. A series of earthquakes also had their epicentre in and around Kornati thoughout that hot, hot summer.

National Park status, which was awarded to the area in 1980, should allow the natural world of Kornati, both above and below the sea, to recover. A few centuries back the islands were reputedly covered with oak trees – now even most of the soil has gone, leaving a thorny, stony environment, where the largest surviving wild animals are frogs, lizards, snakes and birds. The wildest part of the park is in the far south, where a 500-metre (1,640-foot) exclusion zone has been declared around the islet of **Purara**, to allow the development of natural life. One hopeful sign is a colony of dolphins that lives between Kornati and the mainland and manages to co-exist with the fishermen, thrilling lucky visitors who get a leaping dolphin escort across the straits.

Sightseeing

Although signposts at the motorway exit for **Murter** suggest it's an easy journey from there to Kornati, visiting the national park is more complicated in practice. There is no ferry or public transport, and no way to get around the islands without a boat. There are also very few accommodation options in Kornati; most overnight visitors stay on their own yachts. If you have an international captain's licence, then you can rent your own sea-borne transport –

INSIDE TRACK
FEAST OF KORNATI

Kornati comes to life on the first Sunday in July for the Feast of Kornati, when an armada of boats and yachts from all over Dalmatia converges on the church of Our Lady of Tarac on Kornat for a celebration led by the bishop. The tiny bay by the church gets crammed with boats and worshippers jump from deck to deck to reach the shore.

otherwise the only way to reach the park is on a tour. The best are the ones offered by the fishermen of Murter. Tourist boats also leave from **Vodice**, **Pirovac** and **Šibenik**.

Visitors pay a day fee, 40kn for excursion tourists, 80kn for yachtsmen and guests. Recreational fishing permits are 150kn per day.

With your own boat the ideal place to enter Kornati is through the straits of **Opat**, between the south side of Kornat and **Smokvica**. You will be accosted by park rangers on speedboats, who sell you an entrance ticket. There are reception centres on the islands of **Ravni Žakan** and in the village of **Vruje**. Overnight mooring is possible in a dozen bays in the park, mostly at floating moorings marked by red buoys. Among the best bays for overnighting are Lavsa, Levrnaka and Ravni Žakan. There is also a marina on the island of **Piškera**, which is only open in the summer months.

The nearest departure points for an excursion to Kornati are on the island of **Murter** (*see p206*). If you take a stroll along the harbours of **Jezera** or Murter town, you'll see several boats offering day trips to Kornati – there'll probably be someone standing with a clipboard trying to sell tickets. All these trips offer a similar sort of deal, including entry to the national park, a journey around the most impressive natural sights, the chance to swim, and a fish barbecue washed down with a couple of glasses of the local red. Most of the vessels are converted fishing boats, and many of them convert back during the winter months, when the surly tourist guides return – perhaps gratefully – to their true profession.

ZADAR & ŠIBENIK

Kornati.

Where to eat & stay

There are around 20 restaurants in Kornati, most of which offer excellent fresh fish, as well as the islands' traditional aromatic lamb. Most of the visitors find a spot on the jetty, or anchor in the bay, and the restaurants cater to the upmarket sailing crowd rather than the day-trippers.

Party-minded **Konoba Idro** (Lavsa Bay) has plenty of buoys, a long jetty and very good scampi. For the fabulous **Restoran Piccolo** in Smokvica Bay, turn left as you enter Kornati through the strait of Opata. The full range of Dalmatian specialities include scampi, calamari, lobster and first-class fish on the grill. The Piccolo runs on solar energy so there's no distracting hum or noisome fumes from a poorly serviced diesel electricity generator. The **Restoran Piškera** on the island of the same name has a longer season than the summer-only options – find it opposite the only marina in the national park. Their chef prepares the freshest, locally caught fish for the many returning guests.

Apart from staying on a private yacht, the only other options in the national park are the small campsite on the island of **Levrnaka**, or renting one of the few inhabitable stone houses on the islands. You can arrange this through one of the tourist agencies in **Murter town** (*see below*). As there is no public transport to the islands, your hosts will take you to the cottage by boat, and leave you there for an agreed period of time – take ample food and drink. This popular kind of tourism is touted locally as 'Robinson Crusoe'.

Resources

Kornati National Park (www.kornati.hr) has two reception centres: **Ravni Žakan** and **Vruje**. The main office is in **Murter town** (Butina 2, 022 435 740).

MURTER

You won't find many gems of Dalmatian medieval architecture on **Murter**, but there are, however, breathtaking views of Kornati, a gentle landscape and a criss-cross of tempting paths leading to secluded bays and beaches. It is also easily accessible, and has picturesque villages which quietly carry on with their own business apart from the tourist trade. In many ways it's a family and activity-oriented island, and is one of the main centres on the Adriatic for sailing, diving and big game fishing, as well as the more usual pastime of lying on the beach. Murter is ideally placed for exploring the countless islands of Central Dalmatia, and is the closest departure point for the Kornati National Park. The island can also serve as a base for exploring the well-preserved medieval cities of **Šibenik** and **Zadar**, as well as the national parks of **Krka** and **Velebit**.

Traditionally, the villages on the island have quite distinct local identities, with **Jezera** known as the main fishing village; **Betina** as the place where traditional ship building still goes on, and Murter as the home of the slightly-aristocratic owners of the uninhabited islands of Kornati. All the towns and villages on the island are linked by one road, and are easily accessible by frequent bus services, interrupted

Porat. *See p207.*

INSIDE TRACK PORAT

The least commercial club in the region is also the most talked about: the **Porat**. To find it, drive 2km out of Pirovac on the Magistrala towards Zadar, then take a track on your left and look for glowing olive trees. Set in a forgotten grove, this open-air venue was set up as a counterpart to the glitzy superclubs nearby. Clued-up party-goers dance on two floors surrounded by trees individually illuminated in different colours. The management team has recently also moved into Zagreb.

twice a day for half-an-hour at 9am and 5pm, when the bridge at **Tisno** is raised to allow sailing boats to pass.

The town of Murter is the biggest settlement on the island, famous for its sandy beach **Slanica** and buzzing restaurants and cafés. A short walk up hill from the crowded centre takes you to the **Ghetto**, with its maze of steep side streets and traditional architecture. Betina is a very picturesque stone town set on a hill, and has circular streets that offer enjoyable walks up to the village church. If you're lucky, the local priest will let you scramble up the church tower for an amazing view of the island. The craftsmen of Betina still practise the ancient art of boatbuilding, making the island's distinctive *gajeta* fishing boats with lucky painted eyes. The centre of Betina, with its square full of cafés, is a good place to watch local teams play waterpolo in the sea of the old port as older residents concentrate on a game of bowls. Jezera is the island's best kept secret, missed by many of the tourists who rush on to Murter and Betina. This village is where most of the island's fishermen reside, as its bay provides the nearest safe harbour to the open sea. Around sunset, fishermen head back to harbour. Although it's tempting to join the crowd jostling by the boats to buy fresh fish, a more reliable option is to get up early and head to the market behind the tourist office.

Beaches

You don't need more than a mountain bike to reach any number of secluded beaches and bays around the island. A favourite is **Koromašna Bay**, signposted from Jezera, which has a small half-island with an unbeatable sea view. **Slanica** is a fair walk from Murter town, but it's one of the best beaches on the island, and much better than the downtown alternative. It has an amazingly turquoise sea, its shallowness

ideal for games of frisbee and general fooling about in the water. It can get very crowded in mid-summer, with noisy cafés and pizzerias, so get there early, or walk through the campsite to the next bay, which has similar characteristics but is virtually undiscovered.

At **Jezera** the municipal beach is a simple concrete and pebble affair, but there's a little beach bar and a fabulous view of the islands. Continue walking along the beach to find your own peaceful spot under the shade of an olive tree and watch the fishing boats and yachts come in and out of Jezera harbour. There is also a waterslide and rentable paddle boats.

Where to eat & drink

Bubizzeria Zameo ih vjetar
Hrvatskih Vladara 5, Murter town (022 435 304). **Open** *Apr-Nov* noon-2pm, 5pm-midnight daily. Closed Dec-Mar. **Credit** AmEx, DC, MC. V.
At this elegantly designed modern restaurant, it's hard to resist the *bubizza* or 'sister of the pizza,' topped with roasted vegetables such as courgette and artichoke. This is also a good place to try a range of unusual starters and main courses, from baked octopus to chickpea salad. The restaurant belongs to the family of the architect Bašić, famous for creating the Sea Organ of Zadar, so open your eyes for interesting details. *See p195* **Profile**.

Gallileo
Obala Sv Ivana 31, Jezera. **Open** *Summer* 10am-2am daily. **No credit cards**.
Usually the noisiest bar on the harbour, this blue neon bar is a favourite with local young fishermen and the summer party crowd. On a lively night, locals go in for cheap brandy chasers or just don't bother with beer at all. The trail from here leads up to the Zenit nightclub at the car wash, and from there on it can only be downhill.

Konoba Broščica
Put Broščica, Tisno (022 438 361). **Open** 7am-1am Mon-Sat; noon-1am Sun. **Credit** AmEx, DC.
If you're looking for good, ordinary Dalmatian food and snacks – calamari, grilled meats, pancakes for dessert – then this is a fine option. It has a cosy stone and wood interior and is popular with locals. It's also a good pizzeria and delivers to Tisno and Jezera.

Konoba Kandela
Obala Sv Ivana, Jezera (022 438 267). **Open** 11am-2pm, 5-11pm daily. Closed Oct-Apr. **Credit** AmEx, DC, MC, V.
This restaurant is on the posher end of the scale and has a lot of regular guests, so in the season it tends to fill up fast – reservation is advisable. They serve all the classic Dalmatian specialities, with excellent scampi *buzara* and a tasty vegetable risotto as a side dish to grilled fish or meat.

ZADAR & ŠIBENIK

Konoba Leut

Ribarska 7, Jezera (022 438 346). **Open**
noon-midnight daily. **No credit cards.**
Just behind the harbour, in an authentic fisherman's
street, the Konoba Leut provides significantly better value meals than the restaurants on the bay. Its
signature dish is a fish platter for two, or the simple
oslić fillet with *blitva*: hake with kale and potatoes.
Service is friendly but slow, while the fish is fresh
and locally caught.

Tic Tac

Hrokešina 5, Murter town (098 278 494).
Open *Apr-Sept* noon-2pm, 3pm-midnight daily.
Closed Oct-Mar. **Credit** AmEx, DC, MC, V.
As this is one of the most famous restaurants on the
Adriatic, it can be hard to find a table in high season. Tic Tac is tucked down an alleyway that leads
straight to the sea, with tables all the way along. The
restaurant became famous for offering sushi dishes
as an alternative to traditional Dalmatian fare.
Highly recommended is its *brodetto* with monkfish
and the imaginative starters, although not every
dish seems to work as well as these.

Tony's

Obala Sv Ivana, Jezera (no phone). **Open**
Apr-Sept 8am-1am daily. Closed Oct-Mar.
No credit cards.
If you happen to be here when the sport fishermen
come back, you may see a large tuna strung up. If
you're interested in catching one yourself, ask at the
bar as Tony runs most of the boats moored at the
jetty. Otherwise, just turn up for drinks at the closest café to the beach.

Nightlife

Čigradja

Put Škole 1, Čigradja Bay (no phone). **Open**
Summer 8pm-4am days vary. **No credit cards.**
This café on Murter town beach is known for occasional parties and club nights, which are always well
advertised on billboards stuck up around the island.
Čigradja caters mainly for more mature musical
tastes, with jazz and blues predominating, but the
guest DJ nights also make the most of a great seaside setting. This is the logical late night option if
you're based in Murter town.

Where to stay

Camp Slanica

Slanica Bay (022 445 255). **Closed** 16 Nov-14
May. **Rates** €4/person; €3.60/tent; €2.70/car.
No credit cards.
In the middle of a pine-tree forest, Camp Slanica is
also just a stone's throw from Slanica beach, which
is less crowded than Lučica beach and the half island
of Školjić. The camp has two restaurants, a supermarket and tennis courts.

Hotel Borovnik

Trg dr Sime Vlasica 3, Tisno (022 439 265).
Rates €45-€70 double. **No credit cards.**
This hotel overlooks the bridge to the island in
Tisno. The Borovnik has been recently renovated,
and it has a restaurant and small outdoor pool. The
hotel is popular with larger groups.

Kn Hotel Colentum

Butina 2, Murter town (022 431 111).
Rates €30-€70 double. **No credit cards.**
This 200-bed hotel in Slanica Bay is in an excellent
location if your priority is to be first on the beach in
the morning. For Murter town it's a bit of a trek.

Jezera Lovišća

Jezera Lovišća (022 439 600/www.jezera-
kornati.hr). **Rates** €8/person; €6/tent.
Credit AmEx, DC, MC, V.
This is the biggest campsite and apartment village
on the island, a short walk from Tisno and Jezera.
Set in its own bay, it has tennis courts, a diving centre, restaurant and shop. Aqua aerobics are
announced at regular intervals. It's at the start of a
pleasant bike-friendly walk on the old road to Betina.

★ Kosirina

Kosirina Bay (022 435 268). **Rates** €4/person;
€4/tent. **No credit cards.**
Probably the most beautiful campsite here, in a spot
where no one passes without stopping for stunning
views of the Kornati archipelago, clearest when the
Bura blows. There are unspoilt inlets and rocky out-
crops easily reached on foot. Basic facilities.
▶ *The same management run the nearby Plitka*
Vala site (022 435 218), close to Betina.

Say Adriatic

ACI Marina, Jezera (022 439 300). **Rates**
apartment €55-€105. **No credit cards.**
Say Adriatic is a newly built, upmarket hotel 50
metres (165 feet) from the Jezera Marina, family-
friendly as can be, with a kids' playground, pool and
a large car park. It was recently chosen as a weekend retreat for two dozen ambassadors from the
Zagreb diplomatic corps.

Getting there & around

Buses go to Murter town from **Šibenik** (1hr)
and **Vodice** (30mins) about every 2hrs. There
are two daily buses from **Zadar** (2hrs). The bus
serving the main road along the island is pretty
frequent and fares are nominal.

Resources

Tourist information

Murter Tourist Office *Trg Rudina (022 434*
995/www.tzo-murter.hr). **Open** *July, Aug* 8am-
10pm daily. *Sept-June* 8am-noon Mon-Fri.

BIOGRAD

Biograd na moru (Biograd-On-Sea), the biggest town between Zadar and Šibenik, is a lively seaside tourist spot and an excellent base from which to embark on a family holiday. In medieval times, it was the coronation site for Hungarian kings but was demolished by the Venetians in 1125, and again in 1646, in the retreat from the Turks. What little remains of its once royal heritage includes the **Church of St Anastasia**, built in the remains of the crown cathedral in 1761; the early Romanesque **Church of St Anthony**, reconstructed and used for art exhibitions in summer, and the 11th-century ruins of **St John the Evangelist's Basilica**.

Biograd's location is its major asset and makes a good base for exploring the nearby Kornati Islands. Pašman, joined to Ugljan by a road bridge, is a 15-minute ferry trip; Zadar and Šibenik are either side, and **Vransko Jezero**, Croatia's largest lake, is next door. **Krka National Park** is a half-hour drive away and, with the mountains stepping back from the coast for a while, it's good cycling country.

The centre lies on a small peninsula and is packed with bars and restaurants. Another clutch of bars is crammed into the street at the head of the peninsula, by the ferry terminal, where you'll find the small **Regional Museum** (Krešimirova obala 22, 023 383 721) featuring treasures recovered from a 16th-century Venetian galley that sank off the islet of Gnalić, in the Pašman Canal.

Head along the car-free seafront promenade past the Ilirija hotels and you come to the Olympic pool area and **Dražica** beach. Further on, past the extensive tennis centre, you'll arrive at **Soline**'s sandy beach with bars galore. Walk away from the peninsula in the other direction, past Marina Kornati, and you'll find another long beach, a couple of campsites and yet more bars and restaurants.

Where to eat & drink

A handful of venues are open all year, including the **Marina Kornati Restaurant** (Šetalište kneza Branimira 1, 023 384 505) offering anything from full-blown formal dining to a quick snack; **Konoba Barba** (Frankopanska 2, 023 383 087; *photo p210*), a characterful, good value locals' haunt that majors on fish, especially sardines; **Casa Vecchia** (Kralj Koloman 30, 023 383 220), a service-oriented pizzeria in a converted stone house with a delightful walled terrace; and **Carpymore** (Kralja Tvrtka 10, 091 300 2009 mobile, www.carpymore.hr), a Dalmatian pub (no food) in a large, tastefully renovated stone building, with live music most Thursdays and Fridays. **Konoba Bazilika** (Ulica Sv Ivan 5, 023 384 451) is a cosy new restaurant, tucked away by the Basilica ruins, with an innovative menu that includes vegetarian dishes, salt-cod pâté, main-meal salads and aromatic fig pancakes. **Konoba Cotonum** (Josipa bana Jelačića 2, 091 520 6338 mobile) is newly refurbished with a Roman theme and lovely courtyard.

Lavender Bed Bar.
See p210.

Konoba Barba. *See p209.*

ZADAR & ŠIBENIK

Summer highlights include **Šangulin Kavana & Bar** (Kraljice Jelene 3, 023 385 150), a crisp, chic seafront spot that offers toast, croissants and ices; and **Lavender Bed Bar** (Hotel Adriatic, Tina Ujevića 4, 023 290 700), where you can sip your cocktail from the comfort of a lilac-coloured bed surrounded by greenery and sea views (*photo p209*).

Nightlife

Poco Loco (Dražica beach, no phone) is the beach bar for partying Caribbean style – many of its cocktails are sold by the metre. Hotel Adriatic's pool complex has a live band or DJ at weekends but many locals head to **La Habana** (091 353 7332 mobile), a short taxi ride to the small village of Sv Filip i Jakov. Here there's a large terrace and beach bar, cocktails, pizzas by the slice and Cuban accoutrements.

Where to stay

Biograd's hotels are mostly of the package holiday style but the three hotels in the **Ilirija Group** (Tina Ujevića 4-7, 023 383 556, www.ilirijabiograd.com), **Kornati**, **Ilirija** and **Adriatic**, deliver contemporary facilities. The Ilirija has a top-floor spa. There are two new family-run hotels: the **Palma** (Vlaha Bukovca 3, 023 384 463, www.hotelpalma.com.hr) and **Villa Mai Mare** (Marina Drižića 5, 023 38 43 58, www.maimare.hr). Both are a five-minute walk from the beach and offer good value modern comforts.

Getting there & around

The **bus station** (023 383 022) in the centre of the peninsula, has regular services to **Zadar** and **Šibenik**. **Ferries** to **Tkon** on Pašman run at least hourly in the summer. Rent a boat from the small marina outside the Ilirija Group hotels to explore around 150 islands and islets within a two-hour reach.

Resources

Tourist information
Biograd Tourist Office *Trg hrvatskih velikana 2 (023 385 382/www.tzg-biograd.hr).* **Open** *Summer* 8am-9pm Mon-Fri. *Winter* 8am-3pm Mon-Fri.

VODICE

Vodice, 11 kilometres (seven miles) west of Šibenik, is a lively and established tourist centre. The town derived its name from the abundance of fresh water wells in the area and exported drinking water up to the end of the 19th century. Architecturally, there's not a lot to show for the Turkish and Venetian days, with the stones from the city's defensive walls and towers used to build houses. However, the **Coric Tower**, built from Brač stone by a rich Šibenik family, dates back to 1646; the tiny gothic **Church of St Cross**, built in 1402, is now used for summer exhibitions, and the **Parish Church of St Cross** is the work of Šibenik baroque builder Ivan Skok, built between 1746 to 1749. The relatively new **Aquarium** (obala Matice Hrvatska 33, 098 214 634 mobile; admission 20kn) is by the main square.

West of town is the Punta Peninsula with the tall **Hotel Punta**, set in pine woods, and a number of concrete piered beaches. There are more beaches along the four-kilometre (2.5-mile) coastal path to **Tribunj**, with its beach bars and ice-cream shops.

Where to eat & drink

There's no shortage of choice in Vodice and years of tourism have led to menus that are more varied than elsewhere in Dalmatia. **Arausa** (Trg Dr Franje Tumana, 022 443 152, open Apr-Sep) is a traditional Dalmatian restaurant with an expansive sea-facing terrace, plenty of ambience and a wide menu choice. New **Rustica** (Pamukovića 5, 098 883 528 mobile) provides reasonably priced Dalmatian food in traditional surroundings. Quietly chic **Pizzeria Spalato** (Obala V Nazora 14, 022 441 414), on the seafront, is good value and serves more than pizzas. **Santa Maria** (Pamukovića 9, 022 443 319; *photo p212*), the oldest restaurant in Vodice, is known for its quirky interior.

Located by the war memorial, **Café Dalmatino** (Obala V Nazora 18, 022 440 240) is a great bar for all weathers; watch the ferries go by or lounge on the sofas. **Caffè Bar Lanterna** (Obala V Nazora 13, 022 443 230) serves prize-winning home-made ices and a selection of cakes either outside or in a bright, bold interior. **Makina's** (Ive Juričev Cote 20, 022 440 015) is at once a smart traditional indoor *konoba*, an expansive restaurant terrace and, nearer the sea, an outdoor bar and disco mecca for youngsters in summer.

Nightlife

Vodice can boast one of Croatia's most successful nightclubs, **Hacienda** (*photo p212*) and, in its wake, the more commercially oriented **Exit**, now joined by **Opium** one floor below. Commonly acknowledged to be the best summer club in Croatia, Hacienda (Magistrala,

INSIDE TRACK
HOPS FROM VODICE

The untouched islands of **Prvić** and **Zlarin** are a short ferry ride from Vodice – or finish the ferry trip in Šibenik (total journey time 85 mins). Ferries run from Vodice to Šibenik, via these two islands, twice a day off-season and up to five times a day in summer.

www.hacienda.hr; open summer only) is the closest Croatia gets to a superclub. A powerful laser beams out for 50km (31 miles), pointing to the spot where 2,000 clubbers come together from Split to Zadar on several dancefloors. DJs here have included David Guetta, Martin Solveig and Ian Pooley; the club management also has another elite venue, the Gallery, in Zagreb.

If you head on to the Magistrala back into Vodice, at the marina you'll find one of the most promoted clubs on the coast: Exit (Obala J I Cota, Marina, Vodice; open summer only). Quite small, with a two-floor interior, it's commercial but fun on its night. A broad terrace overlooks the bobbing boats, the music is pretty standard and there's a pizza kitchen if you get hungry. Exit hasn't got a website, but you can't miss its posters all the way along the coast. Opium (www.opium-club.com), opened in 2007, can be found below Exit.

The **Hookah Bar** (Plava plaža, www.hookah-bar.com; open summer only; *photo p212*), in front of Hotel Punta, is a luxurious oriental-styled lounge bar with resident DJ and guests; a second bar in the same style is in the grounds of Hotel Olympia. The **Caffè Bar Virada** (obala Matice Hrvatske 16) has DJs and live bands all year round but only at weekends in winter.

Where to stay

Most lodging is in the form of large, package-type hotels or apartment accommodation in the resort area just east of town. **Hotel Imperial** (Ulica Vatroslava Lisinskog 2, 022 454 454, www.rivijera.hr) is probably the biggest and most expensive of the three-star resort hotels. **Hotel Olympia** (Ljudevita Gaja, 022 452 452 www.olympiavodice.hr, open mid Mar-Nov) earned a fourth star with improvements inside and out, including entertainment for children. **Hotel Orion** (Stablinac 2, 022 442 861) is a good value three star on the main road. **Hotel Punta** (Grgura Ninskog 1, 022 451 451, www.hotelivodice.hr) is a modern, smart, four-star close to town with its own pine woods and beach. Most rooms have uninterrupted sea views and the spa facilities include indoor and outdoor pools, a VIP room for couples and a medical centre offering dental treatment and cosmetic surgery.

Getting there & around

A **bus** to Vodice takes 90 minutess from **Split**, one hour from **Zadar** and 15 minutes from **Šibenik**. Buses run at least once an hour. Vodice **bus station** is behind the marina buildings east of the town centre. Many local tour agencies will arrange transfers by minibus to Zadar or Split airports.

Santa Maria; Hacienda; Hookah Bar. For all, see p211.

Resources

Tourist information

Vodice Tourist Office *Obala Vladimira Nazora (022 443 888, www.vodice.hr).* **Open** *Summer* 8am-10pm Mon-Sat; 9am-5pm Sun. *Winter* 8am-3pm Mon-Fri.

ŠIBENIK

Šibenik finally seems to be springing to life. Like Zadar, it took a hammering in the recent war, and is still recovering, but change is in the air for the whole area. It's always had the potential to become the kind of destination it's smartening itself up to be. The sprawling industrial suburbs, a reminder of its industrial past and significance as a port, camouflage a delightful **Old Town**. Alleyways and stone steps threaten to lead nowhere but are full of surprises – historic churches and atmospheric squares are tucked around almost every corner, and the golden globe of the unmissable **Cathedral of St Jacob** pops up in the distance, over the rooftops, when you least expect it.

Šibenik also has three new assets: the superbly located and upmarket **Konoba Pelegrini**, which also uses the newly revamped terrace displaying Šibenik's ancient four wells; the recently restored **Medieval Mediterranean Garden of St Lawrence's Monastery**, which is now complete with café and restaurant; and a new shopping centre, CityLife, a short walk west of the Old Town. The already busy promenade lined with bars and restaurants thrives during the summer, overlooked by the ancient network of crumbling fortresses atop the city, guarding the entrance to the Krka estuary that leads to the town from the open sea.

The biggest drag on the pace of tourist development is the poor hotel stock with only one, somewhat jaded, hotel in town. That should change as **NCP** (www.ncp.hr) continue to expand their existing marina and peripheral facilities in the Mandalina area. **Marina Mandalina** already has some of the best berthing and refit/repair facilities for superyachts in Croatia – and now NCP has announced a partnership with international marina developers IGY to provide Croatia's first dedicated marina for superyachts alone, expected to be open for the 2009 season, with an upscale resort area to follow. The plan includes two luxury hotels, villas, a business centre and shopping zone. In the meantime, there are good lodging options just outside Šibenik, and a couple of even better ones on the nearby unspoilt islands of **Krapanj**, **Zlarin** and **Prvić**.

Dubrava Sokolarski Centar.

Šibenik is also handy for the **Krka National Park** (*see p45*); **Etnoland** discovery park; the **Dubrava Sokolarski Centar** (*see p47*) for falconry – and the key nightspots of the Hacienda in Vodice and Aurora in Primošten.

Sightseeing

First mentioned in 1066 by King Petar Krešimir IV, Šibenik is one of the few Adriatic towns with a Croatian rather than Greco-Roman heritage. Despite Byzantine, Austro-Hungarian and French occupation, it was Venetian rule (1412-1797) and the Ottoman presence that left the deepest imprint. Most buildings in the historic centre, including the star attraction, the Cathedral of St Jacob, date from this era.

Down an alley beside the Cathedral is the **City Museum** (Gradska vrata 3, 022 213 880), occupying what, under the Venetians, was the Duke's Palace, residence and office of the prince. The large permanent collection is in storage while the main museum is closed and undergoing extensive refurbishment works. When it reopens in summer 2009, the permanent exhibition will cover the history of Šibenik from pre-historic times to the present day. Meanwhile, there are a number of temporary exhibitions which can be accessed from the museum's entrance on the Riva promenade.

Šibenik.

South of the Cathedral and main square, the 15th-century Gothic **St Barbara's** church hosts the **Museum of Sacred Art** (Kralja Tomislava 19, open 9.30am-noon, 4-7pm Mon-Fri, 9.30am-noon Sat, 7kn, closed Oct-May). It's a modest collection spanning the 14th to 17th centuries, with religious paintings, polyptychs, ancient manuscripts, wood engravings and silver and gold objects.

After three further churches on Zagrebačka, the road slopes steeply to emerge at **St Anne's Fortress** (open dawn-sunset, 10kn). Built during Venetian rule as protection from the Turks, this now decrepit structure rises on the site of an earlier stronghold. Nothing impresses so much as the rooftop and the view across the estuary to the surrounding islands.

★ Cathedral of St Jacob
Trg Republike Hrvatske (022 214 899). **Open** *July-Aug* 8.30am-8pm Mon-Sat; 1-8pm Sun. *Sept-June* 9am-6.30pm Mon-Sat; 1-6.30pm Sun. **Admission** free.
Gothic and Renaissance fuse beautifully in this monumental three-aisled basilica. Hampered by plague and fire, it took over 100 years to build, with the work overseen by a series of architects, most notably the Zadar-born Juraj Dalmatinac and his successor Nikola Fiorentinac. The cathedral was eventually consecrated in 1555. An Ivan Meštrović statue of Dalmatinac stands outside the main entrance. Inside, the features of note include the octagonal cupola; the stunningly ornamented baptistery with a vaulted ceiling displaying angels and cherubs; and an external wall frieze that manages to span all three apses. This features 74 sculpted stone faces of prominent Šibenik citizens, allegedly those who refused to contribute funds. In the war of 1991, the unique vaulted roof of interlocking stone slabs was badly damaged and it took a team of international experts to rebuild it.

Etnoland
Postolarsko 6, Drniš (099 220 0200 mobile/ www.dalmati.com). **Open** *Easter-Oct* noon-6pm daily. **Admission** 35kn; 18kn reductions; free under-6s. *Tours* (with lunch) 109kn-299kn. **No credit cards**.

INSIDE TRACK
REMOTE LUXURY

A five-minute boat trip from nearby Brodarica – site of the renowned restaurant Zlatna Ribica – is Croatia's lowest lying and smallest inhabited island, Krapanj. The island traditionally thrived on sponge harvesting and its main, fabulous hotel is built on the site of the old sponge co-operative. **Spongiola** (Obala I Krapanj, Brodarica, 022 348 900, www.spongiola. com) has been fitted out to high standards with an indoor pool, gym and sauna. It specialises in diving trips, water sports and excursions – there's also a small beach in front. It's a charter flotilla base in summer so things can get busy every other weekend on changeover day. Ask at the Zlatna Ribica restaurant for someone to ferry you over.

This new and ambitious theme park illustrating the traditional Dalmatian way of life is a short drive from Šibenik in the village of Pakovo Selo on the road to Drniš. Unassuming on the outside, its carefully designed 15,000 square metres allow you to experience exactly what life was like in Dalmatia before the age of electricity. Although individual visitors are welcome, you will only scratch the surface unless you join an organised tour, lasting three-and-a-half hours including lunch. *Photo p216.*

Medieval Mediterranean Garden of St Lawrence's Monastery
Information office *Trg Republike Hrvatske 4 (022 212 515/www.cromovens.hr).* **Open** *May-Sept* 9am-7pm daily. *Mar, Apr, Oct* 9am-4pm daily. Winter varies. **Admission** free.
Opened in 2007, fully restored after a century of neglect, the garden of the St Lawrence monastery complex is the only one of its kind in Croatia and rare in Europe. The restoration was completed by award-winning landscape architect Dragutin Kiš and follows an established pattern: pathways designed in a cross, a water feature, four areas filled with medicinal plants and herbs, roses, capers, and a section devoted to several different coloured varieties of thyme. The modern café and restaurant sit within it and educational and tourist events include the torch-lit 'Medieval Evening in Dalmatia', with a traditional three-course meal served by staff in medieval costume to the sounds of Dalmatian music.

Where to eat

No.4/Četvorka
Trg Dinka Zavorovića 1 (022 217 517). **Open** 8am-11pm Mon-Thur, Sun; 8am-1am Fri, Sat. **No credit cards.**
Meat is the name of the game at this steakhouse on a small square right off Zagrebačka, where a young bunch munches on pepper, cheese or truffle steaks, or one of the gnocchi or lasagne dishes. In the mornings, it's a café; at night, a cocktail bar. The terrace is a pleasant and shady place, embellished by a mural of a braying donkey, and there are two cosy bars up a steep flight of stone stairs. On the second floor is an intimate, four-tabled, wooden-roofed balcony with commanding views of the square and its Gothic-Renaissance church.

★ Barun
Podsolarska 24 (022 350 666). **Open** *Summer* 11am-11pm daily. *Winter* 11am-11pm Mon-Sat. **Credit** AmEx, DC, MC, V.
Some 4km (2.5 miles) out of town, on the road that leads to the Solaris hotel resort, Barun is a favourite place for a business lunch when you want to impress your guests. The first-floor restaurant has a fantastic view over cultivated fields and the Šibenik archipelago. The greeting can be a little frosty but the interior is as classy as the view – antique chairs,

smart tablecloths and plenty of greenery. Established for over 20 years, Barun has a menu best described as upmarket traditional. A popular choice is steak: châteaubriand for two or *biftek café de paris*. There are also eight apartments for rent.

★ Gradska Vijećnica
Trg Republike Hrvatske 3 (022 213 605). **Open** 9am-midnight daily. **Credit** AmEx, DC, MC, V.
Set in the former Venetian town hall, from which it takes its name, the GV makes use of its nine arches and splendid terrace view of St Jacob's Cathedral to provide a superb setting for sampling the best of the local cuisine at prices just above average. In winter, dine inside a small restaurant with a big mirror and crisp white tablecloths – the sort of place you'd take your parents to lunch. A great place for a fish-based *marenda*, or late-morning snack.
▶ *For cheaper domestic dishes nearby, try the Konoba Dalmatino (Fra Nicole Ružića, 091 542 4808 mobile) in a small square off the main one.*

★ Pelegrini
Jurja Dalmatinca 1 (022 213 701/www. pelegrini.hr). **Open** 8am-midnight daily. **Credit** AmEx, DC, MC, V.
Set on the roof terrace of the currently closed Bunari Museum, the Pelegrini offers a view across the estuary – in the café, customers perched on bar stools

Cathedral of St Jacob.

Etnoland. *See p214.*

can gaze at the Cathedral framed by the glass doors. Unveiled in June 2007, the Pelegrini opened all its terrace, including a children's play area, in June 2008. The menu is refreshingly different and in wine-bar style. Choose from a selection of cheeses (goat's, sheep's and cow's milk), smoked meats or salamis for hors d'oeuvres, then either snack on salty fish pie, lean bacon pie, pilchards or snails, or brunch on bacon and egg, and fresh orange juice. The mains menu includes ravioli Pelegrini (ricotta and prawns), tuna alla Šibenik, and summer risotto (courgette, chilli, lean bacon and gorgonzola. Salads, soups and a novel range of desserts finish off the meal. The house wine is good value; choice ones include Plavac Mali Grgić and a Barolo 1999.

Peškarija

Obala palih omladinaca (022 217 797). **Open** 11am-11pm daily. **Credit** AmEx, DC, MC, V.
Walk through an atmospheric stone passageway and you reach a terrace under the hillside of the Old Town, with a couple of tables and benches set in greenery. To look at the water instead of the pink decor inside, sit in the glass-enclosed loggia in the back. Quality fish and meat options include standards and offbeat dishes such as fried shark, Dalmatian frog's legs and Mexican paella with chicken, veal and vegetables. Save space for the baked ice-cream in breadcrumbs.

Tinel

Trg pučkih kapetana 1 (022 331 815). **Open** *Summer* noon-3pm, 6.30-11pm Mon-Sat. **Credit** AmEx, DC, MC, V.
Sample well-prepared regional mainstays served with creativity at this stylish little spot on a small square across from St Chrysogonus' church, the town's oldest. On a hot day, reserve a table on the tree-shaded stone terrace. The narrow townhouse offers two-floor seating inside an elegant but cramped interior with seashell-themed paintings and plenty of ambience. Specialities include *pašticada* (beef, bacon and gnocchi in a wine-and-vinegar sauce) and ray fish fillet with rocket, courgettes and tomato sauce. Dried figs in wine are the best dessert choice.

Uzorita

Bana Jelačića 58 (022 213 660/www.uzorita.com). **Open** 11am-1am daily. **Credit** AmEx, DC, MC, V.
A local favourite in Šubićevac, a 20-minute walk from the Old Town, Uzorita has been dishing out some of the area's best Dalmatian food since 1898. The cool patio features a lovely open hearth and vine-covered seating. The glass-enclosed interior has exposed stone walls and an old-fashioned fireplace. Try the seafood kebabs or the mussels harvested from the restaurant's own farm.

INSIDE TRACK
DOWNTOWN DRINKING
& NEARBY NIGHTSPOTS

In town, bar tables lining seafront Obala Prvoboraca fill with pre-clubbers until they head off to the main venues nearby. Šibenik is the ideal base to explore Croatia's best-known nightspots: **Hacienda** (*see p211*); **Aurora** (*see p218*); **Exit** (*see p211*), and the more underground **Porat** (*see p207*).

★ Zlatna Ribica

Krapanjskih Spužvara 46, Brodarica (022 350 695/www.zlatna-ribica.hr). **Open** 11am-11pm daily. **Credit** AmEx, DC, MC, V.

It may have lost some of its cachet but this gourmet institution still provides consistent excellence in the seafood arena. Since 1961 it's been drawing locals with its fabulously fresh daily catch. Now tourists have discovered it, too; there's a private dock for yachters, an information desk and apartments to rent. The yellow-painted covered terrace has a scenic view to the island of Krapanj, while the interior comes with kitschy floral decor. The meal starts with a customary bread basket and home-made fish pâté, followed by your pick of fish from the big platter at the entrance. If in doubt, order the excellent gilthead sea bream or sea bass with *blitva* or the fish platter for two. Worth the 8-km (5-mile) taxi ride.

Nightlife

Inside Club

Bioci (no phone). **Open** 7am-midnight Mon-Wed, Sun; 7am-1am Thur; 7am-4am Fri, Sat. **No credit cards**.

This popular venue, only just out of town, has been designed for its dual role as a café by day and a club by night. The main area includes a large island bar with two smaller spillover ones at each end. The VIP lounge and bar at the back, separated by a beaded curtain, is a feast of leopard-skin cushions and sofas. Elsewhere, the heavy gilt-edged mirrors, relief paintings and net drapes blend well, assisted by plenty

of candlelight. Outside there's decking and comfortable seating but the view of the main road is not what you're after. Music is mainstream party dance sounds. It's on the main road towards Split out of Šibenik – look on the right for a set of traffic lights next to a big car park.

Where to stay

Hotel Jadran

Obala dr Franje Tudjmana 52 (022 212 644/ fax 022 212 480/www.rivijera.hr). **Rates** 660kn-780kn double. **Credit** AmEx, DC, MC, V.

Aching for renovation and pricy with it, Šibenik's sole hotel occupies an unseemly four-floor building on the waterfront. After negotiating the lobby, you'll find the small rooms have equally miniature tubs in the en-suite bathrooms but no air-conditioning or balconies. Request a sea-facing room, the same price as the others. Nice views from the terrace café too.

Hotel Panorama

Šibenski most (022 213 398/fax 022 213 111/ www.hotel-panorama.hr). **Rates** €63-€105 double. **Credit** AmEx, DC, MC, V.

Fab views of the Krka estuary are the main draw of this 1970s concrete-and-glass cube by the Šibenik Bridge, 4km (2.5 miles) west of town. The former motel has a marble-floored lobby with a vaguely nautical theme extending to its series of blue-carpeted rooms. These en-suite units are on the dark side but all come with air-conditioning, balconies and cherry-wood furniture. For the best panoramas,

Pelegrini. *See p215.*

ZADAR & ŠIBENIK

INSIDE TRACK SOLARIS

A large hotel complex 6km (3.5 miles) south of town, the **Solaris** (Hotelsko naselje, 022 361 007, www.solaris.hr, closed Nov-Mar), set in pine forest, is a handy local accommodation option. Expect to pay around 150 euros for a double, full board.

pick one of the eight south-facing rooms – or dine in the terrace café-restaurant. Entertainment is provided by a new gym, the mini football pitch and bungee jumping from the bridge. Regular buses ply the route; a taxi charges about 100kn.

Getting there & around

Šibenik is two hours from **Split** and one and a half hours from **Zadar** by hourly **bus**. **Knin** is one hour 20 minutes, linking with the InterCity train between Zagreb and Split. Šibenik **bus station** is near the ferry terminal at Obala Hrvatske mornarice, just south of the town centre. There are currently no mainline ferry services into Šibenik, only services to the nearby islands.

Resources

Tourist information
Šibenik Tourist Office *Obala Dr Franje Tudjmana 5 (022 214 411/www.sibenik-tourism.hr).* **Open** *May-Oct* 8am-8pm daily. *Nov-Apr* 8am-2pm Mon-Fri.

ZLARIN & PRVIĆ

A short ferry hop from Šibenik are the lovely islands of **Zlarin** and **Prvić**. A landscape of olive groves and vineyards is dotted with typical Dalmatian fishing villages and fringed with quiet pebble and rock beaches. A couple of restaurants, hotels – including a stunner, **Maestral** – and an occasional apartment rental reveal recent signs of tourist development.

Zlarin is half-an-hour by ferry, its sleepy bay village featuring a 15th-century church, a single hotel-restaurant, the Koralj (Zlarinska obala 17, 022 553 621, www.4lionszlarin.com), and shops selling coral, the ancient local trade all but fading out. A further 15-minute boat ride takes you to Prvić Luka, the main village on the island of Prvić. Here you'll find one of the most stylish hotels on any Adriatic island, the Hotel Maestral (Rodina 1, 022 448 300, www.hotelmaestral.com), a 19th-century schoolhouse on the main village square, where 12 air-conditioned, mostly sea-facing rooms

combine sleek contemporary decor with typical local elements such as exposed stone walls and green wooden shutters. The house restaurant, **Val**, serves excellent Med fare on a waterfront terrace. From here, a scenic path leads northwest to the picture-perfect village, Šepurine. Were it not for the classy **Ribarski Dvor** restaurant, it would feel frozen in time.

In high season, five ferries connect Šibenik to the islands from Monday to Saturday, and two on Sundays. Off-season, boats are less frequent. Allow 25 minutes for Zlarin and 40 for Prvić.

PRIMOŠTEN

Primošten, 28km (17 miles) south-east of Šibenik, is a languid little seaside town. Despite its lack of tourist attractions – or tourists, come to that – this half-island is a decent spot for a couple of days' unwinding. Fragrant pines back its pretty beaches, hilltop restaurants offer fresh seafood and stunning views, and seafront cafés fill with locals. Younger visitors don't come for any of this: they come to Primošten for the **Aurora**, one of the best (and certainly the best located) club in Croatia, and similar nightspots within an easy drive.

Primošten's car-free core is set on a small picturesque island linked to the mainland by a short causeway. Winding alleys lined with green-shuttered stone houses lead uphill to the **Church of St George**. From the small church cemetery of this 1485 edifice, stellar sunset views stretch to the open sea and the seven islets that front the coastline. A promenade around the Old Town features a mix of nicely restored stone mansions and their modern concrete counterparts.

North of here, the **Raduća peninsula** contains pine forests, pebbly beaches and Primošten's only hotel, the **Zora**. Raduća and the Old Town are linked by the Mala Raduća cove. Beyond, a hinterland still scarred by a major fire in 2007 contains rolling vineyards and 30-odd hamlets. The most famous and most visited of them is the village of **Primošten Burnji**, where locals make red Babić wine.

Where to eat & drink

Kn Konoba Jerko
Crnica 1 (022 570 280). **Open** *Easter-Oct* 8pm-midnight daily. **Credit** AmEx, DC, MC, V. A great location, this. Pick a table by the beach for great sunsets over the bay between the Old Town and the Raduća peninsula or sit in the shady green terrace on the other side of the building, near the tiny church. All the standard Dalmatian fish and steak dishes are on offer and there's also a budget meal of the day. Under new management in 2009 but the style is expected to remain the same.

Primošten

▶ *Not only is the food good, but the Konoba Jerko is a great place to stay; see p220.*

★ Konoba Papec

Splitska 9 (no phone). **Open** *Summer* 7pm-midnight daily. **No credit cards**.
Don't miss the pre-dinner samples of local specialties at this rustic tavern in one of Primošten's oldest and most photographed townhouses. A small, dark interior with thick stone walls is decorated with traditional costumes and wine-making equipment. Outside, wooden benches and wine-barrel tables provide lovely seafront seating. The friendly owner, born in the house, brings out reasonably priced bite-size portions of goat's cheese soaked in olive oil, *prosciutto* and olives, paired with a glass of Babić wine or a shot of *rakija*, all own-made in the local villages.

Restaurant Kamenar

Trg biskupa J Arnerića 5 (022 570 889/www. restaurant-kamenar.com). **Open** *Easter-Dec* 9am-1am daily. **Credit** AmEx, MC, V.
Mulberry and acacia trees shade the terrace of this pair of renovated stone houses facing the Old Town gates. The pricey menu runs the full gamut of seafood mainstays. Just name your fish – sea bass, grouper, John Dory, bream – and it will come to you fresh and delicious. House specialities include steak in scampi sauce and anglerfish in lemon. Of the two

INSIDE TRACK
DOWNTOWN DRINKING

Before club time, young partygoers hit the dozen café-bars lining the Mala Raduća seafront. Crowds spill out on to the street and venues merge, but popular spots include **Popaj**, at the town entrance, and **Nautica**, a few steps down the seafront towards the Old Town.

dining rooms, pick the one in the back with family bric-a-brac: black-and-white snapshots, an old radio and aerial photos of Primošten from the 1960s.
▶ *There are some excellent rooms to stay in here; see p220.*

Restoran Panorama

Ribarska 26 (022 570 011). **Open** *Summer* noon-2pm, 6pm-midnight daily. **No credit cards**.
Gorgeous sea vistas complement a well-executed repertoire of Adriatic seafood at this addition to Primošten's terrace dining scene. Right below the church, it's often less crowded than its hilltop neighbours, and better for a romantic sunset meal. Forget the tiny, nondescript interior and grab a white wooden bench outside, by a small swimming pool. The monkfish fillet is nicely prepared and the mixed fish platter for two great value. Recommended.
▶ *If all the outdoor seating is taken, walk around the island until the you see the signs for Babilon and Galeb, both summer-only restaurants atop a long set of steps with great views.*

Nightlife

Admiral, Marina Frapa

Uvala Soline, Rogoznica (www.marinafrapa.hr). **Open** *May-mid Sept* 11pm-4am daily. **No credit cards**.
Marina Frapa is Croatia's classiest marina, with quality apartments and entertainment in a big complex within easy walking distance of Rogoznica, a short drive from Primošten. Its nightclub, Admiral, shed its risqué image after being taken back into direct management. Now locals join the sailing visitors who moor up overnight here. With space for 500, Admiral stages a live act each night, with dancers and resident MC DJOJ; bartenders juggle bottles and throw fire. Performers warm up around the pool around 9pm if you fancy a pre-show cocktail, and there's a light display by the fountain.

Aurora

Magistrala (098 668 502 mobile/www.aurora club.hr). **Open** *June-Sept* 8pm-4am daily. **No credit cards.**

Set 2km (1.25 miles) south of town, Aurora was opened just as war was breaking out in May 1991. It has spanned many trends in dance music and hosted almost all known domestic DJ, plus international names. The first floor, containing a cocktail bar, steakhouse, pizzeria and pool tables, is open during the day, and after 11pm the second level swings into action: three dancefloors, an open-air palm-fringed area, six bars, pool and a chill-out lounge zone, all open till 4am. Resident DJ Pero is well connected and attracts the likes of Carl Cox, Laurent Garnier, Roger Sanchez, David Morales and John Digweed. National pop stars are also a regular feature. Expect foam parties, retro nights, R&B and hip hop, and a crowd of anything up to 3,500.

Legends Pub

Don Ive Šarića (022 570 277). **Open** *Summer* 7am-4am daily. *Winter* midnight-4am. **No credit cards.**

Just outside the town centre, Legends is housed in a large old building, revamped to an Irish theme. Opened in December 2008, it should appeal to older locals and mainstream expats with a musical agenda of *klapa* and golden oldies.

Where to stay

★ Hotel Zora

Raduća (022 570 048/fax 022 571 120/ www.zora-hotel.com). **Open** Apr-Oct. **Rates** €61-€185 single; €86-€262 double. **Credit** AmEx, DC, MC, V.

This complex of nine interlinked low-rise buildings, set in pine forest, has modern decorative touches. Marble floors, stylish armchairs and shiny columns dress the lobby. The café-bar offers a lovely sea-facing terrace, while rooms, though small, come with balconies, pine floors and colourful wall prints; most have superb views. The glass-domed seaside heated pool area has underground treatment rooms and a roof that opens when the sun's out or stays closed if you want to swim under the stars. The herbal garden is a nice touch too. There's entertainment for kids plus sports and excursions.

Kn Kamenar

Trg Biskupa J Arnerića 5 (tel/fax 022 571 889/www.restaurant-kamenar.com). **Open** Mar-Nov. **Rates** €25 single; €40 double. **No credit cards.**

This is the most old-world charm you can get for your money in Primošten, in a 150-year-old stone building at the entrance to the Old Town. Above the restaurant of the same name (*see p219*) is a family-run collection of seven small but pleasant rooms with pine-wood floors. The communal balcony has

lovely views of the surrounding rooftops, all very intimate and informal. Prices include a modest breakfast at the restaurant.

★ Kn Konoba Jerko

Crnica 1 (022 570 380/www.apartmani-jerko). **Rates** *Apartment* €50-€80. **Credit** AmEx, DC, MC, V.

Jerko is open all year round, though the restaurant (*see p218*) is closed in winter and has been sub-let to new managers. Run by an enterprising and charming young couple who have lovingly restored this family house in arguably the best location in town, the four identical apartments on the first floor are individually accessed from the external stairs, overlooking the terraced restaurant area. Each air-conditioned unit has a double bedroom, a lounge with a convertible sofa, a shower/toilet, kitchen area and a dining room looking out over the sea. Sadly no balconies but the beach is just in front of you.

Villa Koša

Bana Jelačića 4 (022 570 365/www.villa-kosa.htnet. hr). **Rates** €49-€54 double. **No credit cards.**

A ten-minute walk east of the Old Town, this duo of garish pink-yellow buildings has a string of modern suites inside and a pebble beach just in front. Units vary in size and layout – some have kitchens and separate living room areas – but all come with natural light, a balcony or loggia. Great views of the old town. Air-conditioning is charged as an extra.

Villa Silvija

Rupe 24 (022 570 533/fax 022 571 720/www. hotelsilvija.com). **Open** May-Oct. **Rates** €45-€82 double. **Credit** AmEx, DC, MC, V.

For unobstructed sea and Old Town views, book one of the 11 well-equipped suites inside this white modern structure, which is just a ten-minute walk uphill from the busy main road. Don't expect villa-like luxury, but you can count on balconies, kitchenettes, separate bedrooms and air-conditioning in most of the units. The floor plans do differ – some bathrooms are on the small side – but the decor is standard 1970s chintz. There's a cleaning fee slapped onto the bill at the end, usually around 120kn.

Getting there & around

Primošten is an easy hop from near northern neighbour Šibenik. **Buses** leave every couple of hours and take 25 minutes. Once in Primošten, walking is the only option.

Resources

Tourist information

Primošten Tourist Office *Trg biskupa J Arnerića 2 (022 571 111/www.tz-primosten.hr)*. **Open** *June-Oct* 8am-10pm daily. *Nov-May* 8am-noon Mon-Fri.

Split

Split.
See p223.

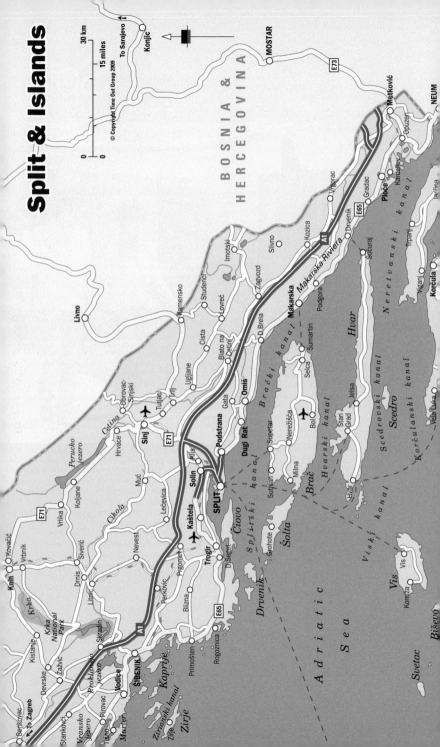

Split & Islands

Dalmatia's hub allows easy hops to Croatia's most sought-after islands.

Every summer, thousands flock to **Split**, the departure point for the key islands of **Brač**, **Hvar** and **Vis**. More are also taking time to explore Croatia's second city, packing the revamped Riva promenade and narrow passages of the adjoining ruined Roman palace, the centrepiece of this busy port. Past the pricey café terraces of the Riva, a regular traffic of car ferries, catamarans and fast boats glide or whizz to the islands: family-friendly Brač with its famous beach of Zlatni Rat; party-centric, Hvar, darling of the yachting crowd; and the more remote Vis, equally up for fun in a more rough-and-ready fashion.

Back on the mainland, **Trogir** and, to a lesser extent, **Kaštela**, make best use of their proximity to Split airport to fill with seasonal visitors. To the south of Split, **Omiš** and **Dugi Rat** will soon benefit from the opening of a major marina resort, taking the limelight away from the traditional package tourism of the hotel-lined **Makarska Riviera**. There, a key spa hotel and a revived nightlife scene may lure the more discerning visitor to this maligned stretch halfway to Dubrovnik.

Split

The de facto capital and main transport hub of Dalmatia is trying to attract tourists in its own right. A long-term plan to transform this city, an industrial centre under Tito, has begun with a makeover of the **Riva** promenade and the opening of half-a-dozen attractive hotels – almost half-a-dozen more than you would have found here ten years ago.

If all goes to plan, most of the bay will become a hotel complex and conference centre,

causing the train and bus stations to be relocated from their convenient spots near the ferry port. Meanwhile, property, rent and rates have gone through the roof. Ultimately, though, it comes down to coffee, Split's source of energy and social glue. Many locals are now taking their languid daily dose at cafés behind the overpriced Riva, within the Roman palace itself – a sign of the times if ever there was one.

SIGHTSEEING

Split's real attraction is not pedestrianised promenades or luxury lodging. Split's USP sits behind the Riva; the grand gutted shell of Roman Emperor **Diocletian's Palace**, a 30,000sq m maze, the atmospheric ruin where you will be spending most of your time. Away from it, you'll find historic relics from the same era at the **Archaeological Museum** and, most of all, the **Ivan Meštrović Gallery**, in the villa designed by the sculptor himself.

The Roman palace & around

Some 1,700 years on, the Emperor Diocletian would still recognise his palace – or the shell of it, at least. This vast, rectangular complex fell

INSIDE TRACK SPLIT CARD

The **Split Card**, available from the tourist office and travel agencies, is valid for 72 hours. It costs five euros, unless you can prove that you are staying in registered local accommodation for at least three nights, in which case it is free. The Split Card allows free entry to city museums, 50 per cent discounts to galleries, plus reductions at certain shops and restaurants, and for certain car hire or excursions. See www.visitsplit.com.

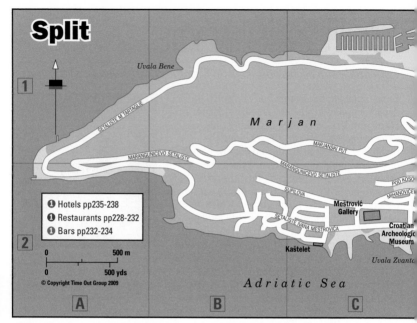

into disuse in the sixth century, 300 years after its construction as a grand home by the locally born leader of the Imperial Guard, who retired here in AD 305 and spent the last few years of his life gardening. In AD 614 refugees flooded in from nearby Salona (today's Solin) and locals have been eking out a living in its manifold alcoves and alleyways ever since. Today its two-metre-thick (seven-foot) walls hide any number of shops, bars and businesses. Kids play football under groaning washing lines, cats scamper into dark recesses and palpitating Dalmatian pop music blares from decrepit windowsills. Local bar culture thrives. You're bound to get lost but this is half the fun.

Wandering aimlessly around the palace is one of Split's essential experiences. There is no ticket office or protocol – you just stroll in. Four gates guard its main entrances: Golden, Silver, Iron and Bronze. The latter gives access, through the basement of Diocletian's old Central Hall, now filled with souvenir and craft stalls, to the Riva.

Amid the chaos, added to over the centuries, two landmarks stand out: the courtyard of **Peristil**, a major crossing point, and, beside it, the **Katedral Sveti Duje**. Once the site of Diocletian's mausoleum, and still guarded by a granite sphinx from ancient Egypt, this octagonal building was converted into a church by the refugees from Salona. Through the

INSIDE TRACK
PALACE DESIGN

The urban layout of **Diocletian's Palace** was meticulously studied by Scottish architect Robert Adam 250 years ago, who correctly felt that its Roman symmetry would be of benefit to European design. His resultant publication influenced the Georgian look of Bath, Bristol and London.

Middle Ages, it was given finely carved doors, an equally beautiful pulpit and eventually a belltower offering a panoramic view of the palace. The climb (5kn) can be quite dizzying, so only try it if you have a head for heights.

In the north-east corner of the palace, the **Split City Museum** (Papalić Palace, Papalićeva 1, 021 360 171) is worth visiting for the 15th-century Gothic building itself rather than sundry paintings and weaponry within.

By the time Split was part of the Venetian empire, the population had long since spread outside the palace walls. Split's role as the main access point for trade in fast boats between Venice and the East – thus avoiding the pirate-infested waters further north – helped the local economy prosper. A short period of French rule

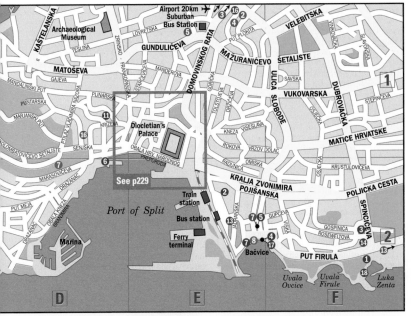

Split & Islands map

- Archaeological Museum
- Diocletian's Palace
- See p229
- Port of Split
- Marina
- Train station
- Bus station
- Ferry terminal
- Bačvice
- Airport 20km
- Suburban Bus Station
- Uvala Ovcice
- Uvala Firule
- Luka Zenta

Diocletian's Palace.

SPLIT & ISLANDS

saw rapid urban development, such as the landscaping of the waterfront embankment below the arches that once enclosed Diocletian's living quarters. The **Riva**, now officially known as the Obala hrvatskog narodnog preporoda, is Split's main drag. Its recent and slightly gaudy makeover has not pleased everybody however.

The palace is fringed by two prominent statues by Dalmatian sculptor Ivan Meštrović: one of literary scholar Marko Marulić in Trg braće Radić in the south-west corner, the other of medieval bishop Grgur Ninski by the Golden Gate. To the east, the Silver Gate was only discovered accidentally after Italian bombs in 1941 shattered a later outer wall. Just beyond, the city's main produce market runs daily. Beyond that, past the nearby train and bus stations, and harbour opposite, over the rail tracks is the city beach and modest leisure complex of **Bačvice**. You can walk from the Roman palace to Bačvice in 15 minutes.

On the other, western side the palace, the busy **fish market** is found in a little square alongside Kraj Sv Marije. Adjacent runs Marmontova, another Napoleonic introduction, a smart(ish) pedestrianised avenue, Split's main shopping street and location of the French Institute. At the top stands the stern edifice of the **Croatian National Theatre**.

Away from the palace

On the other side of the National Theatre stands the **Archaeological Museum** (Zrinsko-Frankopanska 25, 021 318 720,

open summer 9am-1pm, 5-8pm Tue-Fri, 9am-1pm Sat, Sun, winter 9am-2pm Tue-Fri, 9am-1pm Sat, Sun, 20kn). Key historical finds from the nearby Roman capital of Salona are the main reasons to visit the exhibitions here: mosaics, sarcophagi and such like. A short walk north-west takes you to Stari plac, the old ground of local football club Hajduk Split. Although the pitch is now used for rugby, the bars here fill with football fans whenever Hajduk or national team Croatia are playing at the main Poljud stadium another ten minutes further up Zrinsko-Frankopanska.

Two further cultural attractions are set within reasonably easy reach. The most rewarding is **Ivan Meštrović**'s own **Gallery** (Setalište Ivana Meštrovića 46, 021 340 800, open summer 9am-9pm Tue-Sat, noon-9pm Sun, winter 9am-4pm Tue-Sat, 10am-3pm Sun, 20kn), a neo-classical villa built by the sculptor himself in 1931. Although he only lived here for two years before fleeing the Italian invasion, Meštrović was able to use it both as a workshop and exhibition space. Today its two floors and garden contain around 100 of his works, some of a patriotic nature, some sensual. Nearby, **Kaštelet** at No.39 (same admission ticket) accommodates his religious carvings. The beach below, Zvončac, is less well known but has a couple of decent bars on it.

Most, though, prefer Bačvice to the east. Beyond it, the waterfront developments at **Firula** and **Zenta** contain key restaurants, mainstream nightspots and the tennis centre where Goran Ivanišević first played.

Riva.

Profile Picigin

Split is the spiritual home of Croatia's native summer sport.

For most visitors, Split's city beach of Bačvice is a modest affair – a half-moon of shingly sand a short walk from the main harbour, a couple of showers, a little greenery and shallow sea just right for the kids. But to locals, Bačvice is Wembley, the home and temple of the city's best loved sport: picigin.

As much an art form as a pastime, picigin is something like volleyball in water, but with a much smaller ball, no net and usually no points. Here it is played according to the classic rules: five players and a bald tennis ball, or *balun*. Traditionally non-competitive, the aim of the game is to keep the ball out of the water for as long as possible. To this end, players bat it between each other with the palm of either hand. The artistry comes in keeping the ball dry. A dazzling leap or dive to keep the *balun* on its journey should score well – if scores are being kept.

Bačvice makes a perfect picigin pitch for two main reasons. Firstly its sandy, gently sloping, shallow beach allows for optimum acrobatic performance while minimising the risk of injury. Ideally, for speed and a cushioned fall, the water should be just above the ankles and well below the knees. Just as importantly, it is lined with a number of bars and cafés, so that players can strut their stuff to a relaxed and appreciative audience, ie females. No more peacock sport was ever invented.

Non-competitive its origins may be but picigin is being taken increasingly seriously by its aficionados. Associations and competitions are growing up around it, not least the New Year's Day's dive-off for die-hards. Off-season, you'll recognise seasoned and serious players by a distinctive limp caused by repeated injuries to their big toe. In summer, any picigin player worth his salt will be wearing the obligatory figure-hugging Speedos.

Other picigin pitches include the beaches at Sunj on Lopud near Dubrovnik; Medulin, on the southern tip of Istria, and Baška on Krk. It is even played inland, on the banks of the Drava river in Osijek, as far as you can get from Bačvice without being in Hungary.

AFTER MATCH DRINKS
Bačvice is the perfect place to chill out after a hard day's picigin, with bars such as the Žbirac and the Tropic Club Equador acting as the players' home away from home.

WHERE TO EAT

Bekan

Ivana pl Zajca (021 389 400). **Open** 10am-midnight daily. **Credit** AmEx, DC, MC, V. **Map** p225 F2 ❶

A taxi journey or 20-minute walk from the centre, the Bekan is highly regarded. Traditional in decor and kitchen, it is set in the Zenta centre overlooking the water. Superior versions of Dalmatian seafood faves, or the house special of shrimp cream soup, are best enjoyed on the expansive terrace.

▶ *If you're looking for a pre- or post-meal cocktail, the chic Lemon Bar is right nearby; see p234.*

★ Bistro Black Cat

Segvićeva 1 (021 490 284). **Open** *Summer* 8am-11pm Mon-Sat. *Winter* 9.30am-11pm Mon-Sat. **Credit** AmEx, MC, DC, V. **Map** p225 E2 ❷

A five-minute walk from the Riva, this affordable, foreigner-friendly find offers English breakfasts, curries, chilli con carne and copious salads with fresh seasonal ingredients and top dressings. Home-made desserts include cheesecake, fruit crumble, American pancakes and an unmissable chocolate brownie sundae. The filled croissants and wraps make ideal beach snacks; cocktails include natural ingredients and not sickly syrups. The covered terrace is heated in winter.

Boban

Hektorovićeva 49 (021 543 300/098 205 575 mobile). **Open** 10am-midnight daily. **Credit** AmEx, DC, MC , V. **Map** p225 F2 ❸

INSIDE TRACK DIOKLECIJAN

Part restaurant, part bar, this humble landmark has been serving locals with cheap dinners and strong drinks for longer than most regulars can remember – it even has its own nickname, Tri Volte. Signposted in yellow ('Grill') around the palace, **Dioklecijan** (Dosud 9/Alješina, 021 346 683) spreads over a square of pavement just inside the sea-facing palace walls. The food may be modest but the view is wonderful.

Opened in 1973 and thoroughly praised ever since in Croatia's top gastronomic guides, Boban is tucked among residential buildings a steep walk up from Firule. If you don't know how to get there, the taxi driver will. Specialities include filet mignon in red-wine-and-truffle sauce, and monkfish medallions flamed with cognac and accompanied by a béchamel cream sauce. Expect the best local wines.

Bota Šare

Bačvice (021 488 648/091 175 4484 mobile). **Open** 10am-midnight daily. **Credit** AmEx, DC, MC, V. **Map** p225 F2 ❹

At this traditional venue, the menu contains the proud claim that almost everything you eat is grown, caught or produced within 1,000 metres of your table. A giant boat acts as a bar and an open ice chest brims with fresh fish. Prices are more than

Enoteka Terra.

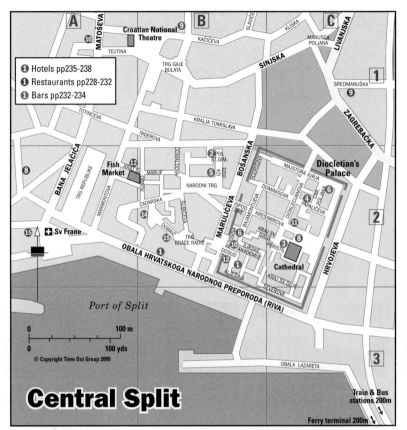

© Copyright Time Out Group 2009

Central Split

Train & Bus
stations 200m

Ferry terminal 200m

SPLIT & ISLANDS

fair, and even the Bota seafood platter with lobster is affordable. The Dalmatian singers are laid on for the locals, not the tourists.

▶ *Stellon is more contemporary; see p232.*

Bruna
Hotel Park, Hatzeov perivoj 3 (021 406 425). **Open** 6.30am-midnight daily. **Credit** AmEx, DC, MC, V. **Map** p225 E2 ⑤
The Bruna was named after a wealthy benefactor who patronised the hotel during the lean war years. They can rustle you up a breakfast of eggs cooked to order, and later an evening meal accompanied by piano, sax and violin on a palm-fringed terrace. Asparagus, Beaujolais or truffles appear in season and guest chefs spice up special events.

Kn Buffet Fife
Trumbićeva obala 11 (021 345 223). **Open** 7am-midnight daily. **No credit cards. Map** p225 D1/2 ⑥

Seadogs and backpackers tuck into Split's cheapest local delights at the far end of the Riva. Pan-fried fish is refreshingly priced by the portion rather than per kilo. You'll also find meat dishes such as tongue, tripe and *pašticada* stew.

★ Enoteka Terra
Prilaž braće Kaliterna 6 (021 314 800). **Open** 10am-midnight Mon-Sat; 11am-midnight Sun. **Credit** AmEx, MC, DC, V. **Map** p225 E2 ⑦
In the rustic basement of a century-old building behind Bačvice beach, this is both an upscale eaterie and wine boutique. You can pair local reds and whites with your fish fillet in truffles and wine, or beefsteak in a dried-plum-and-honey sauce. Boss Jaksa can tell you about the wine tastings.

★ Konoba Hvaranin
Ban Mladenova 9 (091 767 5891 mobile). **Open** 11.30am-midnight daily. **No credit cards. Map** p229 A2 ⑧

Discover the city from your back pocket

Essential for your weekend break, 25 top cities available.

POCKET SIZED *from £6.99*

**TIME OUT GUIDES
WRITTEN BY
LOCAL EXPERTS**
visit timeout.com/shop

Once a bland café, the Radovanis' Hvaranin is one of the liveliest of Split's traditional venues. With mum and dad in the kitchen and son behind the bar, this is a second home for many journalists and writers whose books sit on the shelves. Everything is simple, home-made and delicious. Specials include *gregada* fish stew Hvar-style, and white risotto with mussels. Don't miss the traditional dessert, *rožata* crème caramel. Seating is limited so book ahead.

Kn Konoba Kod Jože

Sredmanuška 4 (021 347 397). **Open** 10am-midnight Mon-Fri; noon-midnight Sat, Sun.
Credit AmEx, DC, MC, V. **Map** p229 C1 **❾**
Jože's friendly Tavern is central but slightly off the beaten track – head out of the Golden Gate, over the park and Sredmanuška opposite, up a slight incline. Splendid local food at reasonable prices awaits. After a tasty starter of Dalmatian ham or one of eight soups, choose your fish from the tray of the day's catch, to be prepared simply but satisfyingly as you observe adjacent street life from the terrace.

Le Monde

Plinarska 6 (021 322 264/www.lemonde.hr). **Open** 7am-midnight daily. **Credit** AmEx, DC, MC, V. **Map** p229 A1 **❿**
Also known as Kavana-Bistro Anika, Le Monde's downtown restaurant is tucked behind the National Theatre. It's a warren of rooms and terraces, where classy Dalmatian dishes are served. Your attentive waiters will also recommend the special of the day.
► *If you enjoyed the food at this venue, Le Monde has two others in the city, one in Marjan, one in Firule – check the website for details.*

Kn Makrovega

Leština 2 (021 394 440/www.makrovega.hr). **Open** 9am-6pm Mon-Fri; 9am-5pm Sat. **No credit cards. Map** p225 D1 **⓫**
Good news for veggies, who will need to check the map on the website to find this place, at the far end of a residential courtyard near Marmontova. The interior is sharp, minimalist and a little feng shui. The food is varied and the portions are generous. The changing daily menu comes with or without soup, and in two forms, macrobiotic or vegetarian. It's no smoking throughout and a dry ship.
► *For meat-free delights with booze, the nearby Šperun is laden with fresh veg; see below.*

Noštromo

Kraj Sv Marije 10 (091 405 6666 mobile). **Open** 11am-11pm daily. **No credit cards. Map** p229 A2 **⓬**
Two eateries sit by Split's open-air fish market. This one is smart, smart enough to charge serious prices for good Dalmatian wines and well-presented meals. Amid the tasteful artwork, locals treat each other or celebrate birthdays over a fish platter for two, as fresh as you'll find anywhere.

INSIDE TRACK TRADICIJA

If you're strolling round the place and fancy something sweet, **Tradicija** (Bosanska 2, 021 361 070) is Split's oldest and most revered cake shop. Gooey desserts, elaborate biscuits and local varieties of pastry, they're all here. Sadly closed on Sundays.

► *For those on a budget, the neighbouring Zlatna Ribica bar can provide a plate of squid and glass of beer for less than 50kn.*

Kn Ostarija u Vidjakovi

Prilaž braće Kaliterna 8 (021 489 106). **Open** 11am-midnight Mon-Sat; 11am-11pm Sun.
Credit AmEx, MC, DC, V. **Map** p225 E2 **⓭**
Between the port and Bačvice, Ostarija u Vidjakovi is a homely konoba that offers simple relaxation. Pictures of Split throughout its history hang beside old Hajduk ones. Tasty, well priced food keeps locals happy: peppers stuffed with mincemeat and rice, *pastičada* stew and fish served in the Dalmatian way with *blitva* greens. *Photo p232.*
► *For budget food nearer the Riva, head for the Buffet Fife; see p229.*

Kn Pimpinella

Spinčićeva 2A (021 389 606/091 121 3014 mobile). **Open** 11am-midnight daily.
No credit cards. Map p225 F2 **⓮**
The unashamedly modest Pimpinella prides itself on its steak or fish prepared on a charcoal grill, its black risotto with shellfish, its *gregada* fish stew and its octopus or veal *peka* slowly cooked with potatoes under a baking bell. A small front terrace contains a couple of tables in the shade.
► *If you're at the Zenta Marina and feel like splashing out, go to nearby Bekan; see p228.*

★ Šperun

Šperun 3 (021 346 999). **Open** 9am-11pm daily. **Credit** AmEx, MC, DC, V. **Map** p229 A2 **⓯**
This great little Dalmatian buffet stands just behind Sv Frane church near the Riva. In the neat and rustic interior, you'll find a table groaning with Adriatic goodies – little fish, fresh vegetables, olive oils and so on. Prices here are completely reasonable – even for a blue fish mixed grill, grilled tuna fish with capers or oven-roasted sea bream with olives. Marinated cheese and octopus salad feature among the many starters.

Kn Stare Grede

Domovinskog rata 46 (021 485 501). **Open** 8am-midnight Mon-Sat; noon-midnight Sun.
Credit AmEx, MC, DC, V. **Map** p225 E1 **⓰**

SPLIT & ISLANDS

Ostarija u Vidjakovi.
See p231.

On the main road near the Art Hotel, this spot would be easy to miss. The enthusiastic chef buys his steaks daily and serves them up with a variety of sauces: pepper; truffle; mushroom and gorgonzola. The accompanying chips are equally excellent. It gets busy with locals at weekends, so book or get there before 7.30pm. Occasional live folk music too.

Stellon

Bačvice (021 489 200/www.stellon-split.com).
Open 8am-midnight Mon-Thur, Sun; 8am-1am Fri, Sat. **Credit** AmEx, MC, V. **Map** p225 F2 ⑰
Named after a founder of local football club Hajduk, this chic spot is owned by ex-star Goran Vučević. It's a fine place for a drink, to dine out, or simply to be seen. Overlooking Bačvice, the terrace is divided between bar and restaurant. Modestly described as a pizzeria, the latter offers grilled fish (sea bream, angler), gnocchi with truffles, and so on. Book at weekends when you're passing by during the day.

Velo Misto

Šetalište Kalafata (021 388 777). **Open** 10am-midnight Mon-Fri; noon-midnight Sat, Sun. **Credit** AmEx, DC, MC, V. **Map** p225 F2 ⑱
Overlooking Zenta Marina, this modern restaurant is as expansive as its menu yet still has queues on Saturday nights in winter. The walls display the work of a keen photographer and outside there's a bare terrace looking out over the boats. Food includes pizzas at good prices, a fish platter for two and a stellar salmon in caper-and-rosemary sauce.
▶ *If this is full, there are plenty of nearby options, including the Bekan; see p228.*

WHERE TO DRINK

★ Academia Ghetto Club

Dosud 10 (021 346 879/091 566 7000 mobile).
Open 10am-1am daily. **No credit cards**.
Map p229 B2 ❶
The most bohemian of the bars in the palace, the AGC comprises a front courtyard, a small bar leading to a muralled main room with a vaguely erotic theme ('Welcome to the House of Love'), and an upstairs gallery, open according to event. Arty locals mingle with tourists happy to hear reliably good music. It forms one end of the narrow, stepped Dosud bar run, passing by Fluid opposite and finishing at Puls – or vice versa.

INSIDE TRACK
PALACE BAR HUBS

The palace is a dark warren of bars, most of which you'll never find again without taking a ball of string. Two hubs might make your bar crawl easier. One is along Majstora Jurja by the northern wall, where you'll find the somewhat neat **Porta**, **Teak** and **Kala** bars, plus a few others. Just in from the Riva, across the square of Trg braće Radić and the green awning of the **Shook Café**, **Puls**, **Fluid** and the **Academia Ghetto Club** encourage drinkers up on the stepped thoroughfare of Dosud.

▶ *For a similarly arty bar in the other corner of the palace, there's Ave at Rodrigina 4 (021 322 627).*

★ Bifora
Bernardov prilaz/Poljana stare Gimnazije (no phone). **Open** 6pm-midnight daily. **No credit cards**. **Map** p229 B2 ❷
Another of the palace bars you really want to find again, this DJ den is set on an unmapped square just behind Iza Lože and the youngsters at Gaga. Bifora brings a giggly clientele to a dim space whose mural depicts red-spotted mushrooms and grinning pixies. Alternatively, get a table on the deserted square.
▶ *If it's cocktails rather than DJ sounds you're after, Gaga (Iza Lože 5) serves cheap ones round the corner.*

Luxor
Kraj sv Ivana 11 (no phone). **Open** 9am-midnight daily. **No credit cards**. **Map** p229 C2 ❸
The somewhat grandiose Luxor offers a vague Egyptian theme, tied in with the sphinx statue outside on Peristil. One of the biggest and most prominent bars in the palace – a more adventurous management might use the space more wisely.

Planet Jazz
Poljana Grgura Ninskoga 3 (no phone). **Open** noon-midnight daily. **No credit cards**. **Map** p229 C2 ❹
Seemingly, this cubbyhole of a palace bar has little to recommend it above the others, until you find a table on the terrace, enjoy the jazzy, clubby sounds emerging from within and realise there's probably no place you'd rather be right now. There's not much of a view – generally people's washing, in fact – but it's captivating nonetheless.

★ Po Bota
Subićeva 2 (098 215 379 mobile). **Open** 6pm-1am Mon-Sat. **No credit cards**. **Map** p229 B2 ❺
Tiny Po Bota is tucked away to the left of the Milesi Palace on Trg braće Radić with its back up against the sea – there's just enough room for a couple of tables, fish motifs on a bare-brick wall, a corner of bar counter and a tap of Stare Brno. An in-the-know crowd does the rest.

Red Room
Carrarina poljana 4 (021 459 231). **Open** 9am-midnight Mon-Thur; 9am-1am Fri, Sat. **No credit cards**. **Map** p229 C2 ❻
Opposite a wall of football graffiti in a crumbling square in the north-east corner of the palace, the Red Room is primarily a pre-club DJ bar and chill-out zone. By day, young couples intertwine on fat cushions in the exotic interior.
▶ *Another worthwhile pre-club DJ bar is 4 i Po Sobe (Dubrovačka 49, 021 382 277), best accessed by taxi.*

★ Vidilica
Nazarov prilaz 1 (021 394 480). **Open** 8am-11.30pm daily. **No credit cards**. **Map** p225 D2 ❼

Luxor.

SPLIT & ISLANDS

INSIDE TRACK
TOP TERRACE

For a hike, the best terrace in town and a little history, go to the far end of the Riva away from the port. Take the little street on the right, Solurat, just before the **Buffet Fife** (*see p229*). About 100 metres along, on the right, rise 231 stone steps. Climb them and you reach Vidilica, and its wonderful terrace view over Split Bay. Next to it is a Jewish cemetery established in 1575, and one of the oldest and largest in Europe. The Vidilica building, still with a Hebrew inscription, used to be the Ceremonial Hall of the cemetery.

No terrace offers a better view than this. From Vidilica you can see the whole of Split laid out before you – and the islands beyond – all from atop Marjan peninsula. The bar contains blown-up sepia postcards of pre-war Split scenes but most of the patrons immediately grab an outside table. Parents should note that there is a steep drop, but children are kept safe by the stone wall guarding it. Just don't let the kids try out their climbing skills.

★ Žbirac

Bačvice (www.zbirac.hr). **Open** 7am-midnight Mon-Fri; 7am-1am Fri, Sat. **No credit cards**. **Map** p225 E2 ❽

The best of the Bačvice bars, this one is a small detached terrace right on the beach whose popularity is due to a slightly more clued-up clientele than the young locals on the pull in the main complex. The little touches make it, too – the framed old colour photographs of the same Bačvice view you're gawping at, the comical picture of fat blokes playing football on the menu cover. A nice buzz.

▶ *Once this closes, walk round the beach to the Tropic Club Equador and adjoining open-air disco; see p235.*

MUSIC & NIGHTLIFE

Hemingway Bar Split

Osmih Mediteranskih igara 3-5 (091 211 995 mobile/www.hemingway.hr/split). **Open** 10am-4am daily. **Credit** AmEx, DC, MC, V.

Upmarket chain Hemingway has taken over the long-established Tribu, down by the sea near the Poljud stadium. As well as a new name, the venue has had a complete makeover. A large central bar is complemented by an equally large and chic interior, plus an outdoor area. It's a huge space to fill, but HBS packs in trendy young things every night – the brand, established in Zagreb, Opatija and elsewhere, is also known for its quality cocktails.

▶ *If you're looking for something of a different scale and in a different style, the popular Sing Sing (Poljudsko šetalište, 099 477 2336 mobile) is set under the seats of the Poljud stadium itself.*

★ Jungla (Hula Hula)

Šetalište Ivana Meštrovića (098 745 557 mobile). **Open** 8am-midnight Thur; 8am-6am Fri, Sat. **No credit cards**.

At the city end of Ivana Meštrovića, near the ACI Marina, this prominent and newly renovated terrace bar offers plenty of space for relaxation after a day at Zvončac beach. Families and couples gather over evening drinks on the terrace. After dark, the team from underground crew Murall has recently moved in, taking its chances here with rock and underground techno music, and house DJs such as Craig Walsh and Nathan Coles.

▶ *Two minutes' walk from Jungla is Obojena Svjetlost, so close that you can flit between venues; see below.*

Kocka

Savska (021 540 537/www.kocka.hr). **Open** Oct-June according to schedule. **Credit** AmEx, DC, MC, V.

If you want to catch a non-mainsteam DJ or live act, this intimate club is where five local music associations hold their gigs. A young, savvy crowd gathers for punk, electro, drum 'n' bass or techno. Entry fees are nominal or none at all. Closed in summer.

Lemon Bar

Šetalište Kalafata (no phone). **Open** 7am-3am Mon-Thur, Sun; 7am-4am Fri, Sat. **Credit** AmEx, DC, MC, V.

Open all day but busier at night, the trendy Lemon Bar attracts the RTL TV crowd and local celebrities. Cream-cushioned rattan sofas and high stools surround a large, island bar. The mosaic tiled snakeskin walls, animal skins and baby banana plants provide a tropical theme. Two terraces, one above the other, overlook Zenta Marina – this is a place to see and be seen.

Masters

Osejačka (021 536 983). **Open** Oct-June 9pm-6am Sat. **No credit cards**.

This is the mainstream club everyone heads to, especially now that it only runs on Saturdays. Local pop singers, folk acts and DJs keep the crowd happy from October to June, after which the scene moves to the seaside. Near the Gripe sports centre.

Obojena Svjetlost

Šetalište Ivana Meštrovića 35 (021 358 280). **Open** noon-3am daily. **No credit cards**.

The wide terrace of this disco-bar is right on Kasuni beach, on a quieter stretch of seafront below the Meštrović Gallery – look out for the green Zlatorog beer sign on the main road above. Palm trees and wicker chairs create an idyllic tableau; inside, Coloured Light puts on DJs and regular live music, an open-air attraction in summer. It's a handy alternative to Bačvice and fairly central too.

O'Hara Music Club

Uvala Zenta 3 (098 364 262 mobile). **Open** 9am-3am Tue-Thur, Sun; 9am-4am Fri, Sat. **No credit cards.**
On the waterfront at Zenta, unpretentious O'Hara's attracts locals and tourists with a wide variety of music – anything from reggae to Dalmatian folk. Two floors, a summer terrace and outside bar allow plenty of space to dance or relax.

Puls

Buvinina 1 (no phone). **Open** 10am-1am daily. **No credit cards.**
Just follow the noise round the corner from the green awnings of the Shook Café by the statue on Trg braće Radić. Puls is a well-established two-storey party bar, its young custom spilling out on to the alleyway that bookends the mini bar run of this Dosud intersection. Always packed, its downstairs bar is a smoky hangout for drinkers, while upstairs offers a little dancing and eye-contact games.
▶ *To warm up with something more alternative, the Academia Ghetto Club is at the other end of the Dosud passageway; see p232.*

Treće poluvrijeme (Kuka)

Zrinsko-Frankopanska 17 (no phone). **Open** 10am-midnight Mon-Thur, Sun; 9pm-6am Fri Sat. **No credit cards.**
If it's past the palace closing time of 1am and you're still thirsty, head to this small bar behind the National Theatre near the old football ground – everyone else does. The 'Third Half' is also handy for post-match relaxation – rock, pop and house sounds will keep you out of mischief until dawn.

Tropic Club Equador

Bačvice (no phone). **Open** 10am-2am daily. **No credit cards.**
Occupying a sweeping first-floor terrace that juts out over the Adriatic, the Equador is a refreshingly unglitzy café /nightspot. By day it's the ideal place for a post-beach beer and to watch the sun go down.

INSIDE TRACK
CLUB INFORMATION

For details of clubbing and music events in and around Split, check www.clubbing-scene.com. For mainstream information, get listings brochures *Splitski Navigator* or *Scena* from tourist bureaus. Flyers can be found at the **Bifora** (*see p233*), **Planet Jazz** (*see p233*) and **Žbirac** (*see p234*).

By night it becomes a disco bar, crowds milling around each bar counter and finding floor space to dance near the half-moon of starlit patio.
▶ *When the TCE closes, everyone drifts to the adjoining open-air Bačvice bar which keeps serving long after you should have gone home.*

Vanilla

Baženi Poljud, Poljudsko šetalište (021 381 283). **Open** 9am-3am Mon-Thur; 9am-4am Fri, Sat. **No credit cards.**
Adjoining the Hemingway in the beachside sports complex, Vanilla is the kind of place that Croatians call 'fancy' – which means it sells drinks with umbrellas in them to a well-dressed young crowd. As a pre-club disco bar, Vanilla does a job, although in reality it's just some wicker furniture overlooking the swimming pool, and a little clubby music.

WHERE TO STAY

Adriana

Obala hrvatskog narodnog preporoda 8 (021 340 000/www.hotel-adriana.hr). **Rates** 550kn-650kn single; 750kn-900kn double. **Credit** AmEx, DC, MC, V. **Map** p229 B2 ❶
The 14 well-priced three-star rooms above this waterfront restaurant offer a simple, comfortable stay within an easy walk of the harbour. Some are quite small – choose if you can. Terrace breakfast is included in the price.
▶ *The Adriana is a pizzeria in its own right, also selling seafood and grill dishes.*

Art Hotel

Ulica Slobode 41 (021 302 302/fax 021 302 300/www.arthotel.hr). **Rates** €103-€111 single; €117-€160 double. **Credit** AmEx, DC, MC, V. **Map** p225 E1 ❷
Opened in 2005 in a tastefully renovated factory building, the four-star Art Hotel provides 36 spacious rooms, all with large beds, and modern facilities including a gym, although the planned sauna and pool now won't happen.
▶ *As the Art Hotel has no restaurant, walk five minutes to the Stare Grede for quality steaks and seafood dishes; see p231.*

★ Atrium Hotel

Brodarica, Domovinskog rata 49A (021 453 510/fax 021 473 539/www.hotel-atrium.hr). **Rates** €165-€185 single; €205-€260 double. **Credit** AmEx, DC, MC, V. **Map** p225 E1 ❸
Near the Art Hotel, the sleek Atrium is set in the new Brodarica complex of shops and offices. Behind a dark-glass exterior (look out for the remains of a Roman aqueduct in the lobby gallery), a seven-floor interior contains 99 large rooms and two suites, all done out in wood and marble. The panoramic top-floor Comfort Zone offers superior saunas (infra-red and Finnish), pool, jacuzzi and gym.

INSIDE TRACK
PRIVATE ROOMS

As you come into Split by boat or by bus, you will be assailed by old ladies offering you a private room. Agree a price, follow her to the lodging – if you're walking there, it shouldn't be too far from the centre – and a cheap bedroom will be yours. If you'd rather not take pot luck, then the **Turist Buro** on the Riva (no.12, 021 347 100; open summer 8am-9pm Mon-Fri, 8am-8pm Sat, 8am-1pm Sun; winter 8.30am-8pm Mon-Fri, 8.30am-1pm Sat) can arrange a slightly dearer one for you. Pay the fee at the desk for the key and a photocopied map.

Dalmatian Villas

Croatian office *Kralja Zvonimira 8 (021 340 680/www.dalmatinskevile.hr)*. UK office *(01536 791 340/www.croatian-coastal-accommodations.com)*. **Rates** €245-€420/ week double; €350-€1,032/week apartment. **No credit cards**.
These tastefully refurbished, stone villas, which are situated a short walk from the main market, can accommodate up to 56 people at any one time. Sleeping from two to eight people, with all the usual facilities, Dalmatian Villas also has a few double rooms priced by the week – single days are available but expect to pay a premium.
▶ *If you're happy with your stay here and are heading out to the islands, Dalmatian Villas also has a luxury villa on Brač. See the website for further details.*

Kn Hotel Consul

Tršćanska 34 (021 340 130/fax 021 340 133/ www.hotel-consul.net). **Rates** 620kn-650kn single; 850kn-920kn double. **Credit** MC, V. **Map** p225 E1 ❹
A handy little hotel this, a 15-minute walk north of the palace, with 15 rooms and four suites that are well furnished and equipped. There's a nice big terrace, too, and half- and full-board rates are available at reasonable supplements. It's quickly booked out, so phone well in advance.
▶ *If this is full and you're happy to pay a little extra, the Globo is a short taxi ride away; see below.*

Hotel Globo

Lovretksa 18 (021 481 111/fax 021 481 118/ www.hotelglobo.com). **Rates** €107-€120 single; €119-€169 double. **Credit** AmEx, DC, MC, V. **Map** p225 E1 ❺
Renovated in 2007, with ongoing and substantial investment in continuous refurbishment, this smart, modern four-star is located north of the palace, a 15-minute walk from the Riva. It's geared towards the business community, hence the recently added conference room, and particularly helpful staff.

Kn Hotel Jupiter

Grabovćeva širina 1 (tel/fax 021 344 801/ www.hotel-jupiter.info). **Closed** Mid Nov-mid Mar. **Rates** 200kn-250kn per person. **No credit cards**. **Map** p229 B2 ❻
Opened in 2004, this basic hostel-type pension offers 13 clean rooms with showers in the corridors. Rooms are spacious enough for two people but couples will have to push the single beds together. No breakfast, no frills, but located right in the palace – look out for the black-and-yellow Jupiter pizzeria sign behind Buvinina. The hotel is opposite, across a quiet inner courtyard square.

★ Hotel Park

Hatzoev perivoj 3 (021 406 400/fax 021 406 401/www.hotelpark-split.hr). **Rates** €113-€137 single; €143-€189 double. **Credit** AmEx, DC, MC, V. **Map** p225 E2 ❼
A well-appointed four-star in quiet grounds behind Bačvice beach, the Park combines 85 years of tradition with most modern facilities – no internet in the 54 rooms as yet. Two suites in an elegant villa have been given a stylish makeover. Guests can sip cocktails on the tranquil terrace before dining at Bruna.
▶ *The Park offers one of Split's best hotel restaurants, the Bruna; see p229.*

Hotel Peristil

Poljana kraljice Jelene 5 (021 329 070/fax 021 329 088/www.hotelperistil.com). **Rates** €95-€135 single; €120-€162 double. **Credit** AmEx, MC, V. **Map** p229 C2 ❽
This modern hotel in the palace now has a terrace restaurant, the Tifani, overlooking the Peristil. It's a three-star establishment, with nine simple, comfortable doubles and three singles, all reasonable for the price and the location. The rooms are artfully decorated with wooden floors and taffeta curtains, and contain flat-screen TVs.
▶ *New to the palace in the same price range, the Marmont is a short walk away; see p238.*

INSIDE TRACK NEW IN 2009

2009 sees two major hotel re-openings. First, the **Hotel Split** (put Trstenika 19, 021 303 111, www.hotelsplit.hr), past Firule, becomes Split's first Radisson hotel, with all the trimmings. Then the **Hotel Marjan** (obala Kneza Branimira 8, 021 302 211, www.hotel-marjan.com), once the city's finest lodging, will be able to show off its long-awaited revamp.

Le Méridien Grand Hotel Lav. *See p238.*

Hotel President

Starčevićeva 1 (021 305 222/fax 021 305 225/
www.hotelpresident.hr). **Rates** €120-€200 single;
€156-€228 double. **Credit** AmEx, MC, V. **Map**
p229 B1 **9**

Behind the National Theatre, this four-star establishment is one of Split's best kept secrets. Superbly
finished in period style, the hotel has 63 rooms of
varying size and ten suites that all come with
jacuzzis and the latest in mod cons. It's classy, spacious and centrally located.

▶ *The owners will open a new hotel in Solin,*
outside Split, in 2009 – the five-star riverside
Regina promises all the style of its sister. See
the website for details.

Hotel Slavija

Buvinina 2 (021 323 840/fax 021 323 868/
www.hotelslavija.com). **Rates** 650kn-890kn
single; 790kn-1,150kn double. **Credit** MC, V.
Map p229 B2 **10**

Modernisation has seen all 25 recently refurnished
rooms fitted with showers and a TV, and by late
2009 there will be a lift and a restaurant serving for
all meals. However, the rooms overlooking the bar-
lined alleyway outside still have the noise of Split's
nightlife drifting up until 1am at least. For years this
was the only lodging option in the palace – classier
or cheaper ones now abound.

Hotel Vestibul Palace

Iza Vestibula 4 (021 329 329/fax 021 329 333/
www.vestibulpalace.com). **Rates** €120-€190
single; €210-€260 double. **Credit** AmEx, DC,
MC, V. **Map** p229 C2 **11**

Set in a little building adjoining the open-roofed
vestibule in the palace, this seven-room boutique
hotel is swish – but perhaps not swish enough to justify the €200-plus outlay. Rooms do have nice decorative touches, such as natural brick, but the
building simply isn't big enough to allow for any
additional facilities.

▶ *The same management team has opened a*
new lodging at Villa Dobrić, which is close to
the palace; see p238.

Kn Kaštel

Mihovilova širina 5 (021 343 912/www.kastel
split.com). **Rates** €40-€70 single; €55-€90
double. **Credit** AmEx, DC, MC, V. **Map**
p229 B2 **12**

Little-known three-star in the palace, at the end of a
narrow alleyway near the Shook Café. Built in 1896
as a private home, it was converted into a hotel in
2005, and refurnished in 2008. The ten rooms are
simple, clean and the best value for small groups of
palace-bound party-goers.

▶ *If this is full, the nearby Hotel Jupiter can*
provide lodging with few frills; see p236.

SPLIT & ISLANDS

INSIDE TRACK
JOKER CENTRE

The new **Joker Centre** in Brodarica near the Atrium Hotel is more than just a mall – although it does have four floors of retail space and many high-street chains. Its top-floor Sky Bar is one of Split's most popular spots while the Broadway Kina cinema shows most movies in original English-language versions.

★ Le Méridien Grand Hotel Lav

Grljevačka 2A, Podstrana (021 500 500/ fax 021 500 705/www.lemeridien.com/split). **Rates** from €115. **Credit** AmEx, DC, MC, V. **Map** p225 F2 ⑬

Set 6km (nine miles) from town at Podstrana, Le Méridien finally fills the gap in Split's hotel provisions for a proper, top-of-the-range five-star establishment. Arrive by water taxi from the airport, take a dip in the infinity pool, luxuriate in the wine or truffle therapies of the Diocletian spa, or just gaze at the superyachts in the marina from the terrace. A casino, nightclub and sunken champagne bar provide more mischievous entertainment. *Photo p237.*
▶ *For a spa break of comparable quality, try the Hotel Horizont down the coast in Baška Voda; see p248.*

Marmont Hotel

Zadarska 13 (021 308 060/fax 021 308 070/ www.marmonthotel.com). **Rates** €125-€178 single; €198-€250 double. **Credit** AmEx, DC, MC, V. **Map** p229 B2 ⑭

This swish new city-centre four-star, close to the palace, comprises 21 rooms, a presidential suite and a roof terrace. Original exposed stone, wooden floors and minimalist style characterise the common areas – classy walnut furniture and free WiFi feature in the large guestrooms.

Villa Dobrić

Dobrić VII (021 308 000/fax 021 308 008/ www.vestibulpalace.com/dobric). **Rates** €120-€170 single; €140-€240 double. **Credit** AmEx, DC, MC, V. **Map** p229 B2 ⑮

The Dobrić, under the same ownership as the Hotel Vestibul Palace, opened in 2008. Two guestrooms occupy the first floor, two junior suites sit above. The original stone walls and the lobby bar (with inside and outside terraces) display style you would expect from the Vestibul stable.

Kn Villa Varoš

Miljenka Smoje 1 (tel/fax021 483 469/091 469 681 mobile/www.villavaros.hr). **Rates** 400kn-800kn double. **Credit** AmEx, DC, MC, V. **Map** p225 D1 ⑯

Tucked away in the venerable Varoš neighbourhood close to the palace, this is one of the best options for price and comfort. The rooms are new, simply and properly finished, with satellite TV and air-conditioning. There are also three apartments with spacious living areas. The owner, Joanne, a Croat from New York, also owns the building housing the restaurant Leut round the corner, where guests can have breakfast for a nominal extra.

GETTING THERE

From the airport

Split airport is 20km (12.5 miles) north-west of town between Kaštela and Trogir. A Croatia Airlines bus is usually waiting (30kn, 30min journey time) when planes arrive. If you're flying back on Croatia Airlines, its buses depart 90 minutes before each flight from the stop by the Jadrolinija kiosks at the harbour end of the Riva. For other airlines, check bus times at the Croatia Airlines office on the Riva or phone 021 203 119 – there's no timetable at the stop. If no buses coincide with your flight, then you must take a taxi or city bus No.37 from bay No.3 or No.4 at the suburban station at the corner of Domovinskog rata and Gundulićeva. Buy a ticket from the station kiosk and stamp on board. The bus (every 20-30mins from 4am-11.30pm) goes to Trogir – the stop by the airport is not named as such, so keep a look out. A taxi either way costs 250kn-300kn.

By train

There are four InterCity trains a day from Zagreb, journey time five hours. The station is on the Riva side of the bus station, diagonally opposite the port, with left-luggage facilities.

By bus

Frequent buses run from Zagreb (five hours journey time) and Dubrovnik (four-and-a-half

INSIDE TRACK
EASY PARKING

To avoid your illegally parked car being towed away by the local *pauk* ('spider'), you can pay and monitor your parking fee by text message from your mobile phone. Just send your registration number (no spaces) to the number marked on the nearest blue box, remembering to add the international code (+385) from a non-Croatian phone. A text reminder warns if you need to add more time. You can also pay and display with coins. Getting your car back from the pound at Pujanke (021 376 848) costs around 350kn.

hours journey time) – remember to keep your passport handy from Dubrovnik as part of the journey goes through Bosnia.

By boat

Split is a major port, with frequent services from Rijeka in the north, and Ancona in Italy. Tickets and timetable information are available at the harbour terminal or the Jadrolinija and adjacent Split Tours kiosks at the Riva end of the harbourfront.

By car

With the new motorway, Split is a four-hour, 400-km drive from Zagreb down the A1. You'll pay just over 20 euros in toll fees.

GETTING AROUND

Walking is the only practical way to get around the town centre. To go to the hilly peninsula of Marjan or beyond Bačvice, take a city bus (9kn on board, 7kn from a kiosk) from either end of the Riva at Trg republike or Zagrebačka by the market. Taxis such as Radio Taxi (970) or Taxi Riva (021 347 777) are parked at either end of the Riva.

Hops to the islands of Hvar, Brač and Vis require a couple of hours and a nominal foot passenger fare of around 30kn. The ferry terminal is a short walk from the Riva, a large building you can't miss diagonally opposite the bus station. Catamarans and hydrofoils leave from the Riva, behind a building surrounded by cafés on the main waterfront. Tickets and information are available at the harbour terminal or the Jadrolinija and Split Tours kiosks at the Riva end of the harbourfront.

RESOURCES

Hospital
Spinčeva 1 (021 556 111).

Internet
Dencall *Obala Kneza Domagoja (021 345 014/www.dencall.com).* **Open** *Summer* 8am-11pm daily. *Winter* 9am-8pm daily.

Police station
Trg hrvatske bratske zajednice 9 (021 307 022).

Post office
Obala Kneza Domagoja 3. **Open** 7am-9pm Mon-Sat.

Tourist information
Split Tourist Office *Peristil (021 345 606/www.visitsplit.com).* **Open** *Summer* 9am-8pm Mon-Sat; 9am-1pm Sun. *Winter* 9am-5pm Mon-Fri.

Around Split

TROGIR

Trogir was first settled by Greeks from Vis in 300 BC. Listed as a UNESCO World Heritage Site, the **Old Town** reflects the influences of subsequent Roman, Hungarian, Venetian, French and Austrian rule. Its walled medieval centre is a warren of narrow cobbled streets, radiating from the cathedral square of **Trg Ivana Pavla II**, flanked by a wide seafront promenade, the **Riva**. In summer, the harbour wall is lined with luxury yachts and tripper boats and the lively summer festival has entertainment on offer most evenings.

The Old Town stands on an islet, separated from the mainland by a man-made canal, and linked by another road bridge to **Čiovo** island. It's a fine setting but the two single-lane bridges will be choked all summer until a new bridge is built further east. Trogir's marina, with a cluster of bars and restaurants around it, lies on Čiovo. Just over Čiovo bridge are a couple of hotels, including, to the left, the recently opened four-star **Hotel Palace**. By the mainland bridge is the bus station and the ever-busy, open-all-hours market.

Entering from the mainland, you pass through the baroque **Land Gate**, guarded by a statue of local patron St John of Trogir. Here also is the **Town Museum** (Gradska vrata 4, 021 881 406). Set in the Garagnin Palace, it's a low-key display of archaeology, books, antique clothes and documents, but the courtyard is lovely and often used for klapa concerts in the summer. *See p244* **Profile**.

Ahead stands the 15th-century Venetian Čipiko Palace, built for a rich Croatian family who then spread their wealth in Kaštela. Alongside, the three-naved **Cathedral of St Lawrence** (Trg Ivana Pavla II, 021 881 426) took 300 years to build and is famed for the magnificent western portal, built in 1240. The 47-metre-high **Bell Tower** affords magnificent views of the town and surrounds. Past it are the

INSIDE TRACK BEAT THE CROWDS

Trogir is good for an out-of-season visit – most of the good hotels and the best restaurants stay open all year round. In high season it can be pretty packed but neighbouring Seget (Donji and Vranjica) offers respite from the crowds and decent restaurants. Try **Barba** (Hrvatskih Žrtava 42, Seget Donji, 021 884 880) or **Astoria** (Seget Vranjica, 021 798 270).

INSIDE TRACK BEACH TRIPS

Čiovo has a string of good pebbly beaches, busy in summer when the apartment trade booms. A morning ferry from the Riva goes to Drvenik Veli and Mali islands, coming back early evening (not Fridays). Krknjaši Bay, on the east side of Drvenik Veli, is a remote pebble beach with the clearest of water and a summer-only seafood konoba, **Krknjaši** (021 893 073). Lodging is also available.

Town Hall, the **Loggia** and **Clock Tower**. The Loggia, with its Renaissance reliefs and sculptures, dates back to the 14th century though was lovingly restored in the late 19th. Exiting the Old Town via the Sea Gate, and turning right on the Riva, you come to medieval **Kamerlengo Castle**, now used as an open-air cinema and events stage with a tower that offers more great views. The town walls once connected the castle to **St Mark's Tower**, at the other end of the lush football pitch. Unlike the crumbling castle, St Mark's has been painstakingly restored and the open top floor is now a café; the interior has been given over to a small museum of Dalmatian music. Turn left from the Sea Gate towards the bridge and you pass the 16th-century loggia that used to house the fish market, which has since moved to the mainland side of town.

Where to eat

Čelica

Čiovo-Lučica (021 882 3440). **Open** *Summer* 11am-midnight daily. *Winter* 4pm-midnight. **No credit cards**.

In an unlikely but delightful piece of recycling, an old wooden car ferry is now a restaurant, decked out with fishing gear and nets – its bar was the captain's bridge and the car platform provides the spacious dining area. The menu is extensive, the prices reasonable and you can normally expect a complementary fish pâté starter. Walk over the bridge to Čiovo, turn right and it's on the right just before the marina.

★ Fontana

Obrov 1 (021 885 744/www.fontana-trogir.com). **Open** 7am-midnight daily. **Credit** V.

Fontana has a large terrace with a sea view, nestled between a school and a church, just in from the Riva. Neatly decked out inside, with cushioned benches to match the pine tables, it serves quality traditional Dalmatian fish and meat. Prices are slightly above average but portions are ample and the view lovely. Popular for special occasions and business lunches.
▶ *For something similar but cheaper, Alka (Augustina Kazotića 15, 021 881 856; open Apr-Oct) is almost next door.*

Kamerlengo

Vukovarska 2 (021 884 772). **Open** 9am-midnight daily. **Credit** DC, MC, V.

Of the more upmarket restaurants in the Old Town, Kamerlengo is the one that visitors seem to return

Trogir.

Kamerlengo Castle.

to. The terrace, with its charcoal oven, set between the stone walls of the building, provides a great setting in which to sample the Dalmatian treats – barbecued fish is the speciality.

▶ *For Dalmatian treats with all the trimmings such as folk costumes and live music, Pašike (Sinjska, 021 885 186) is a popular spot.*

Pizzeria Mirkec
Budislavićeva 15 (021 883 062). **Open** 8am-11pm daily. **Credit** MC, V.
Mirkec's summer terrace provides a prime spot on the Riva to enjoy the tasty, good-value pizzas and pastas on offers. In the colder months, diners can climb the stairs for cosy indoor seating or use the halfway house just before the restaurant entrance. The experienced waiters are friendly and efficient.

★ Škrapa
Hrvatskih Mučenika 9 (021 885 313). **Open** *Summer* noon-11pm daily. *Winter* noon-11pm Mon-Sat. **No credit cards**.

**INSIDE TRACK
SUNSET DINING**

For a rustic dinner over a perfect sunset, drive to the summer-only **Konoba Duga** (091 582 8666 mobile). A bumpy track leads from the west part of Čiovo to the south side. Once there, you'll find a lovely terraced beach and a stone building with a restaurant in it. The freshest grilled fish and meat accompany the view. The food is pricier than in town but worth every lipa.

Delightful staff, a cosy ambience and artistic table decorations tipify Škrapa. The restaurant is the home of honest, grilled Dalmatian food, provided at fair prices to locals and visitors alike The house *rakija* brandy comes round on a little tray with a bicycle bell. Seating is inside and out.

Where to drink & nightlife

The busy bars on the **Riva** and the **Cathedral Square** often have live acts playing during the summer. **Big Daddy's** and **Padre** are the first ones you find from the main road and they share a large open-air stage behind them. They're the focal point for summer nightlife until they close at around midnight. People then either pile into taxis for **Hacienda** (*see p255*), or head for the open-air club **Stone Age**, which is in Plano, about 8km (12 miles) from the centre. The more secluded **Radovanov trg**, behind the Cathedral, has bars with terraces for a quieter aperitif – try the secluded **Galion** or the more adventurous **Smokvica**. If you're staying in Trogir later on, by the Land Gate as you arrive from the mainland bridge is busy late-opening lounge bar **Martinino** (Hrvatskih Mučenika 2). **Monaco** is a big disco bar, just to the right as you walk over the bridge to Čiovo; **Dijamant** (Lučića 8) opens at weekends from 9pm.

Where to stay

Kn Concordia
Obala bana Berislavića 22 (021 885 400/fax 021 885 401/www.concordia-hotel.net). **Rates** 400kn-450kn single; 550kn-680kn double. **Credit** AmEx, MC.

SPLIT & ISLANDS

Set behind a 300-year-old façade, on the Riva near Kamerlengo Castle, 14 rooms provide value for money. The larger sea-facing ones have balconies.

Hotel Jadran
Hrvatskih žrtava 147, Seget Donji (021 800 500/fax 021 800 697/www.hotel-jadran.com). **Rates** €65-€95 single; €112-€150 double. **Credit** AmEx, MC, V.
Recently refurbished, this child-friendly spot has 12 family rooms out of 140, most with a sea-view – kids get a discount. There's an open-air pool, gym and sauna. It's a bus ride or half-an-hour walk from Trogir.

★ Hotel Palace
Put Gradine (021 685 555/fax 021 685 550/ www.hotel-palace.net). **Rates** 590kn-890kn single; 790kn-1090kn double. **Credit** AmEx, DC, MC, V.
The four-star Palace opened its doors in July 2008 and hopes to have its spa and polyclinic ready for 2009. Over the bridge on Čiovo, a ten-minute walk from the centre, the Palace has 20 rooms, all with balconies, some with sea views. Four separate apartments include two huge ones. Disabled rooms and ample parking are welcome rarities and there is a bar and restaurant too.
▶ *For class at cheaper prices, the four-star Villa Meri (Splitska 1, 021 882 555, www. villa-meri.com) has six rooms at €120 and an apartment with a roof-top terrace.*

Vila Sikaa
Obala kralja Zvonimira 13 (021 881 223/fax 021 885 149/www.vila-sikaa-r.com). **Rates** 520kn-800kn single; 550kn-850kn double. **Credit** AmEx, DC, MC, V
Sharing the same archway entrance as the Atlas travel office, just over the bridge from the Old Town to Čiovo, this modern and well equipped four-star is popular with business travellers. Comfortable rooms have sizes dependent on budget, while all can enjoy the sunny internet café area and aperitif bar.

Getting there

From **Split airport**, the regular No.37 bus runs to Trogir every 20 minutes (10kn). A taxi will cost about 150kn. Between June and September, a private **ferry** runs four times a day from Split to Slatine on Čiovo (journey time one hour, 30kn). Check with **Atlas Trogir** (obala kralja Zvonimira 10, 021 881 374, www.atlas-trogir.hr) for times or 091 727 1244 mobile.

Resources

Tourist information
Trogir Tourist Office *Trg Ivana Pavla II/1 (021 800 401/www.trogir.hr).* **Open** *Summer* 8am-7pm Mon-Fri; 8am-3pm Sat. *Winter* 7.30am-3pm Mon-Fri; 7.30am-3pm 1st & 3rd Sat/mth.

KAŠTELA
The seven villages of **Kaštela**, which are located on the back road from Split airport, remain one of Dalmatia's best kept secrets. Turn off towards the sea and, in a very short space of time, you'll uncover, from west to east: Kaštel Štafelić, Novi, Stari, Lukšić, Kambelovac, Gomilica and Sućurac. The No. 37 bus between Trogir and Split links all the villages and the sea quality is generally at it's best to the west.

The Kaštels are so named because each has at least one castle, built for the Croatian nobility in the 15th and 16th centuries. Koriolan Čipiko was amongst the first of the Trogir gentry to move out to Kaštela, in 1481. His village became Kaštel Stari ('Old Castle') to differentiate it from the parvenues (his nephew Pavao) who moved to Kaštel Novi ('New Castle') a few years later.

Wide promenades hide decent restaurants and bars. The sweeping Kaštela bay, with its clutch of harbours and beaches, provides an idyllic location for a leisurely afternoon's stroll. The old stone houses, many of which are now renovated, in the characterful village centres, were built close together to maximise the protection afforded by their castles. **Kaštel Lukšić** is the focal point with a handful of trendy bars at its centre. Here, inside the castle itself, is the **Kaštela tourist office** (Dvorac Vitturi, Brce 1, 021 227 933, www.kaštela-info.hr). Kastel Štafilić claims to have the only castle which was never actually conquered by the Turks and one of the oldest olive trees in the world, still going at 1,500-plus years. The prettiest castle, in Kaštel Gomilica, was built by Benedictine nuns.

Where to eat

Baletna Škola (Kaštel Kambelovac, 021 220 208), on the site of an old ballet school, is a locals' favourite with a diverse but essentially traditional Dalmatian menu. The huge tree-shaded terrace faces the sea and there's as much room again inside. It's hard to beat **Konoba Intrada** (Obala kralja Tomislava, Kaštel Novi, 021 231 301) for atmosphere, value for money across the menu, and great pizzas. **Odmor** (021 220 263), on the north side of the main Kaštela road, just east of a big block of flats and supermarket in Kambelovac, has a surprisingly secluded terrace, great chips and low prices. **Bimbijana** (Marina Kaštela, Kaštel Gomilica, 021 222 780) is a spacious traditional restaurant and large terrace serving hearty snacks and mains to hungry sailors. These and others are open all year round, though the promenades fill in summer with seasonal spots.

Kaštela

Where to drink

Kaštela is an ideal place to go for a bar crawl. Start in Štafilić at the secluded modest beach-fronted bar **Nehaj**, which is a favourite with windsurfers. Following the delightful smells emanating from the bakery next door, weave your way, hopefully not too unsteadily, towards Novi and Stari via **Gabine**, where there is live music most summer weekends. After the more genteel **Imaš** in Novi's small square, head for any of Stari's seafront bars. For the less energetic, wander around Lukšić and pick one of the wicker-chaired cafés by the castle; or **Bugsy's**, which lies just to the east, with a twin terrace and a large interior full of prohibition-era memorabilia.

Where to stay

The best bet is probably three-star **Hotel Villa Zarko** (Obala kralja Tomislava 7A, Kaštel Lukšić, 021 228 160, www.villa-zarko.com). It's on the edge of Lukšić, with 16 rooms, a terrace restaurant-bar and a tree-lined beach (shingle and concrete) mostly to itself. **Hotel Resnik** (Resnik, Kaštel Štafilić, 021 798 001, www.resnik-hotel.hr, open 15 Apr-15 Oct), by the airport in a huge pine-wooded campus with its own beach, is due for a major facelift. For now, expect faded, package-era bargain accommodation. Keep an eye on the **Hotel Palace** (Obala kralja Tomislava, Kaštel Stari), a grand piece of beach-fronted 1920s' architecture on the road to modernisation – but currently closed. For comfortable, budget accommodation, **Sveti Jure** (Obala kralja Tomislava, Kaštel Novi, 021 232 759, www.svjure.com) or **Motel Tamaris** (Kralja Tomislava 38, Kaštel Kambelovac, 021 206 222) will oblige. Three-star **Villa Kristalia** (Bijačka, Kaštel Štafilić, 021 234 920) is popular with French families and has its own outdoor pool. There's plenty of modern apartment accommodation, particularly in Štafilić.

OMIŠ & DUGI RAT

Past Split, towards Makarska, the area around **Omiš** and **Dugi Rat** has yet to claim Makarska's riviera status but should be next on the list. Aside from Omiš itself, it is mostly a collection of small villages that developed inland, around the olive groves and vineyards that first brought people here, and then descended towards the sea as tourism and industry took over from agriculture. Omiš, now probably best known for its annual klapa music festival (see p244 **Profile**) is stunningly photogenic. Craggy mountains rise up directly behind the old stone houses, alleyways and squares that make up its compact centre, and around the mouth of the river Cetina, popular for rafting trips and climbing. Perched on the

Profile Klapa

An unplugged folk genre goes electric.

You won't find many forms of music that can hold a rapturous football stadium of 15,000 people as easily as a table of four in a village taverna. Once the clichéd domain of tourist restaurants in holiday resorts down the Adriatic coast, *klapa* is breaking out to entertain big crowds across Croatia – Croatian crowds.

A kind of mournful Adriatic barbershop, much like fado in Portugal, *klapa* is unique to Croatia. Native aficionados are hoping to follow Georgia and Sardinia by having it placed on the UNESCO Living Heritage list alongside more tangible gems such as Diocletian's Palace in Split and Šibenik Cathedral.

True *klapa* is multi-part harmony singing, traditionally by an unaccompanied all-male group. The first tenor leads with a simple melody and the second tenors, baritones and basses follow in close harmony. Lyrics are about love, the sea, the homeland, tales of loss capable of bringing grown men to tears.

Though adopted throughout Croatia, Dalmatia is the home of *klapa*, particularly the town of Omiš, which set up the first *klapa* festival in 1967. Now in July, the festival (www.fdk.hr) hosts over 80 groups with all-female groups now accepted. In Split, the annual concert at the football stadium attracts 15,000, though instruments are now key to broadening *klapa*'s appeal to a younger audience.

Klapa Libar is also part of its contemporary face. Originally from different groups, these six innovative young musicians had their epiphany in 2007 when they entertained VIP diners at a yacht-racing event in Split. Emboldened by a few drinks, bored of singing the same old *klapa* songs at weddings and funerals, they decided to liven things up a little. Mixing *klapa* with rock music, they made a big splash and soon afterwards a CD, with *klapa* versions of Croatian ballads and rock standards, from Bad Company to the Eurythmics. To download two of their tracks, link to www.livingstone-magazine.com/libar.

Joško Caleta, working on klapa's UNESCO accession, has mixed feelings about its new popular form. 'Pure *klapa* spontaneously derives from friendship and fun, and was never something driven by money,' he complains.

It's a familiar dilemma, but hopefully there's room for both. Meanwhile, no Dalmatian holiday is complete without a bunch of sturdy locals breaking out into traditional song.

KLAPA SITES
In July and August, klapa features in summer festivals at most Dalmatian towns and villages; see: www.fdk.hr. www.klapa-trogir.com has info in English, some lyrics and a free MP3 download.

INSIDE TRACK SOPARNIK

The inhabitants of Poljica's two-dozen settlements celebrate its history ever year with the traditional Soparnik, a vast pancake cooked on hot coals, filled with local *blitva* greens, garlic and a few secret ingredients. These are produced in cooking contests from village to village over the summer, to be carried on people's heads as part of the festivities.

mountaintops, as the river gorge meets the sea, the remains of medieval defences built by the counts of Kačić and Bribir gave a safe haven for the pirates of Omiš. West of Omiš is Dugi Rat with its collection of beaches, cafés, bars and pizzerias. Its centrepiece will be the **Korenat Point Resort**, set to open partly in 2012.

Around these two centres, along the coast, is a collection of holiday settlements, some with stunning beaches, but many still making the transition from the package tourism of old: large pink-and-white boxy hotels and a plethora of apartment accommodation of various appeal. Inland, the Republic of Poljica ('Small Fields') stood from the 11th century to the beginning of the 19th, and was regularly fought over for its important geographical position. Present-day locals of the 20-plus settlements are still uncovering relics from its heyday.

Dugi Rat.

Where to eat

Kod Mije
Lokva Rogoznica/Ruskamen (021 870 193). **Open** 10am-11pm daily. **Credit** AmEx, DC, MC, V.
After the turn-off to Hotel Ruskamen from Dugi Rat, the coast road invisible from its raised terrace, Kod Mije offers a huge menu of 170 dishes – oysters, omelettes, steaks, roast lamb and fish platters.

Konoba Bracera
Glavica, Duće (021 735 444). **Open** 11am-midnight daily. **Credit** AmEx, DC, MC, V.
A stepped terrace off the main road provides a fine setting for summer dining, overlooking pine woods and a secluded pebble beach. Around a dark-wood interior, huge models of traditional sailboats adorn the rafters separating the ground floor from the gallery dining area. The extensive menu has a couple of surprises, such as spiny lobster, house-style. More traditionally, there's lamb ribs, grilled fish and meat and *peka* dishes.

Where to drink & nightlife

For cooling lunchtime drinks watching the rafters, the restaurants on the south bank of the Cetina, try **Kaštil Slanica**, about 4km (2.5 miles) upstream and **Radmanove Mlinice** (for both: 021 862 073) just further. The former has folklore evenings on Wednesdays in July and August. For a spectacular view, the rooftop terrace bar of **Villa Dvor** (*see p246*) is hard to beat. In Omiš, July's annual Klapa festival sees venues in the small squares of the Old Town fill in turn with music. *See p244* **Profile**.

Where to stay

Hotel Plaža
Trg kralja Tomislava 6, Omiš (021 755 260/ fax 021 755 261/www.hotelplaza.hr). **Rates** €76-€164 double. **Credit** AmEx, DC, MC, V.
Opened in 2007, the centrally located Plaža overlooks Omiš' long, sandy beach. Most of the 36 rooms

INSIDE TRACK BEACHES

The river Cetina endows this area with sandy beaches, one in Omiš town centre, and quality clear water. Heading east, there are a number of good pebble beaches, including **Brzet** and **Ruskamen**, backed by pine trees but dominated by Socialist-era hotels. The beaches around **Dugi Rat** are great for families with plenty of cafés and entertainment – just east is one of the longest.

INSIDE TRACK
UPSCALE TOURISM

Korenat Point Resort (www.korenat point.com), in Dugi Rat, is the focus for the region's plans to grab a share of the upmarket tourism market. This 21-hectare site will house a five-star, 200-bed hotel and 350-berth marina. The first phase should be complete by 2012.

and five apartments have sea-view balconies. A small spa contains a Finnish sauna and 'special adventure showers'. Note that in summer, this four-star sells to foreign agencies and individuals wanting to stay need to book for a minimum stay of a week. In the quieter winter, the restaurant terrace becomes a modest skating rink.

Villa Dvor

Mosorska 13, Omiš (021 863 444/fax 021 863 452/www.hotel-villadvor.hr). **Rates** 560kn-750kn single; 800kn-960kn double. **Credit** AmEx, DC, MC, V.

High on the cliffs over the Cetina, reached by more than 100, well-lit, stone steps, this completely renovated and partially rebuilt conversion of a family house provides guests with a spectacular setting and quality facilities. Its somewhat harsh three-star status is largely down to the size of the rooms and balconies – so you're getting a bargain. Inside is modern and tasteful, with attractive furnishings. There's a cosy indoor restaurant and bar in the unlikely event that you've had enough of the views from bar on the roof-top terrace. Beyond beckons the open sea. It's a 20-minute walk from town but there's ample parking for those who don't want to do that climb.

▶ *Villa Dvor is a good base for river rafting – most of the agencies are on the nearby banks of the Cetina.*

Getting there

Local buses run regularly from Split – allow 30 minutes for the journey.

Resources

Tourist information

Omiļ Tourist Office *Trg kneza Miroslava (021 861 350/www.tz-omis.hr).* **Open** *Summer* 8am-8pm Mon-Fri; 8am-noon Sat. *Winter* 8am-3pm Mon-Fri.
Dugi Rat Tourist Office *Poljika cesta 133 (021 735 244/www.tz-dugirat.hr).* **Open** *Summer* 7am-2pm Mon-Fri; 7am-1pm Sat. *Winter* 7am-2pm Mon-Fri.

MAKARSKA RIVIERA

Riding south on the main coastal road from Split to Dubrovnik, just past Omiš, a big blue sign announces: '**Makarska Riviera**'. Thus begins the 60 kilometre (37 miles) stretch of mainly purpose-built hotels with the nightlife hub of **Makarska** in the middle. Few historic monuments survived the Turkish occupation of the 1500s or the earthquake of 1962, a decade after which a decision was taken to turn this section of the coast – some of it quite pretty,

Villa Dvor.

SPLIT & ISLANDS

INSIDE TRACK
LOCAL BEACHES

Although Makarska is one long riviera, Croatian holidaymakers are quite fussy when it comes to where they swim. For them, the most attractive pebble beach is at Brela, approached through pine trees close to the centre; while the longest is at Tučepi. Other lovely stretches include the one 3km south of Makarska; the coves between Drvenik and Zaostrog; and the beach between Brist and Gradac.

with palm fringed pebble beaches – over to package tourism. Though some of the hotels are still quite bland, some have been improved to four-star standard – the Russian-owned **Hotel Horizont**, in **Baška Voda**, is probably the best spa hotel in the country.

Every few kilometres from Brela to Gradac along the dangerous coast road, the welcome/farewell sign posts pop up in quick succession: **Brela**, revered by locals, Baška Voda, Makarska, **Tučepi**, **Podgora**, **Drvenik** (*photo p248*), **Zaostrog**, **Brist** and **Gradac**.

The islands of Brač, Hvar (both connected to the coast by ferry) and Pelješac come into jaw-dropping view to your right. To your left rises the constant, imposing, grey façade of the **Biokovo** mountain range, site of the nature park. If you do find a tranquil spot, the natural backdrop is stunning in both directions. Nearby is Bosnia, its underwhelming coastal resort of **Neum** and, a short drive away, the old Ottoman town of **Mostar**.

Note that the majority of bars, restaurants and hotels on the Riviera are seasonal – all the venues listed run between late spring and early autumn, unless otherwise stated.

Where to eat

Nearly all Makarska Riviera tourist hotels have restaurants – off-season half board rates can be attractive. Notable stand-alone venues include the upscale **Jeny** at Gornji Tučepi 49 (021 623 704) near Tučepi and **Jež** (Petra Kreimira IV 90, 021 611 741) in Makarska town, where you'll also find **Stari mlin** (Prvosvibanjska 43, 021 611 509). **Rajski vrt** (Obala kneza Domagoja 44, 091 582 6956 mobile) in Brela is a good find near the Hotel Soline.

Where to drink & nightlife

Makarska town is the best place to be and one of Croatia's top party destinations. During the evening, head behind the waterfront to bar-

lined Lištun, for **Bety** (No.1, 021 612 185) and the **Pink Panter** (No.2, no phone). If you're more fussy about your cocktails, then the **Pineta** (091 541 5157 mobile) in Gradac, at the furthest southern tip of the Riviera, does better ones than most. You're best to stay in Makarska town, all the same.

Much of the fun there centres around the **Buba Beach Bar** (www.bubabeachbar.com), which provides an enthusiastic crowd with after-beach parties, international guest DJs and dancing till dawn, and it remains the most popular hangout by day as well. **Club Deep** (Osejava peninsula, 098 320 055 mobile), located in a cave, remains a focal point, though **Peter Pan** (Fra Jure Radića), at the former Opera club near the football stadium, is the new place to see and be seen in. Live music bands and guest DJs like Ian Pooley and Latin Prince help to fill an open-air space for 1,500 punters and VIPs. **Popeye** (Mala obala) is a commercial discotheque downtown and **Grotta** (Sv Petar, 091 569 4657 mobile) is also a club located in a cave.

Where to stay

Aparthotel Milenij

Šetalište kralja Petra Krešimira IV 5, Baška Voda (021 620 644/404/fax 021 620 399/ www.hotel-milenij.com). **Rates** vary. **Credit** AmEx, DC, MC, V.
The Aparthotel Milenij has 27 four-star apartments spread over five floors, from small to spacious. There's 24-hour room service, a restaurant, two cocktail bars (one on the beach), a TV lounge with a pool table, gym, sauna, outdoor pool and an underground garage. Popular with UK tour operators.
▶ *If this is booked up in high season, for an aparthotel of similar quality nearby, the Tamaris in Tučepi (Slatina 2, 021 678 222, www.hotel-tamaris.hr) has 40 sea-view apartments.*

INSIDE TRACK
BIOKOVO NATURE PARK

Parallel for much of the Makarska coast is the Biokovo mountain ridge, which forms the protected **Biokovo Nature Park** (www.biokovo.com). This unspoiled stretch of pine, scrub and stone attracts experienced hikers and climbers. Although its highest peak, Sveti Jure, stands immediately above Makarska town, a five-hour climb away, always go prepared and check the weather forecast for the day at the tourist office. The stunning view from the top, though, is worth all the effort.

Drvenik.

Bacchus

Obala sv Nikole 89, Baška Voda (021 695 190/fax 021 679 150/www.hotel-bacchus.hr). **Rates** *Per person half-board* from €100. **Credit** AmEx, DC, MC, V.

Near the beach and the centre of Baška Voda, the Bacchus is a renovated four-star establishment whose rooms, suites and apartments contain king-size beds. Rates vary wildly; April and October are half the price of July. On site are a restaurant with a sea-facing terrace, an indoor pool and a sauna.

Berulia

Frankopanska, Brela (021 603 599/fax 021 619 005/www.bluesunhotels.com). **Rates** vary; see website or phone for details. **Credit** AmEx, DC, MC, V.

Now in the dozen-strong local BlueSun group of hotels, the Berulia has had a significant upgrade to earn it four-star status. Set in pine trees opposite three other stablemates, it has an indoor pool, sauna

INSIDE TRACK
HOTEL RATES

Nearly all establishments on the Makarska Riviera offer attractive half-board deals with prices set per person – an individual traveller can stay for bargain rates in May or September, with pool, sauna and other leisure facilities thrown in. On the down side, many venues also levy an extra 30 per cent for stays of less than three nights.

and gym. Other activities provided on site include minigolf, bowling and table tennis, and there are tennis courts available nearby.

▶ *Also in the BlueSun group, the award-winning Afrodita in Tučepi provides quality facilities by a Blue-Flag beach. See website for details.*

Hotel Horizont

Stjepana Radića 2, Baška Voda (021 604 555/ fax 021 604 923/www.hoteli-baskavoda.hr). **Rates** *Half-board* €104-€214 double. **Credit** AmEx, DC, MC, V.

Hotel Horizont is the flagship of the Russian-owned Hoteli Baška Voda Group, where Russian opulence, contemporary design and spacious modern facilities extend to the labyrinthine spa complex. There you'll have a huge range of treatments at your disposal, as well as an old-school Russian masseur. Most of the 202-plus rooms, spread over five floors, have sea views, and there's a choice of restaurants including Matrioshka with its Russian specialities.

★ Kn Hotel Porin

Marineta 2, Makarska town (021 613 744/ fax 021 613 688/www.hotel-porin.hr). **Open** all year. **Rates** 550kn-750kn double. **Credit** AmEx, DC, MC, V.

Lovely, central three-star in a late 19th-century Renaissance-style palace-cum-fortress, once used as the town library. Renovated into a hotel in 2002, this palace offers two dozen beds in seven rooms, with one two-floored apartment. It's right by the sea, it has terraces either side and a panoramic one on the roof – and in high season, it's affected by noise from the bars immediately downstairs. Come before the crowds or flop here after a nearby barhop.

Meteor

Kralja Petra Krešimira IV, Makarska town (021 615 344/fax 021 611 419/www.hoteli-makarska.hr). **Rates** from €75 double. **Open** all year. **Credit** AmEx, DC, MC, V.

Reopened in 2006, this Socialist-era ziggurat has now become a four-star hotel – international football clubs use it in the winter time so you know the facilities must be top rate. It has a spa, pools outdoor and in, two restaurants and the Tropicana disco. The rooms vary from boxy singles to quite spacious doubles with a terrace.

★ Park Hotel

Kralja Petra Krešimira IV, Makarska town (021 608 200/fax 021 608 202/www.park hotel.hr). **Rates** 744kn-1,694kn double. **Credit** AmEx, MC, V.

Opened in 2007, this chic, modern four-star, has a spa, gym, pools indoor and out, a restaurant and cocktail bar. The see-through lift and room numbers dyed into the carpets add individuality. Good views, plenty of space in most rooms and luxurious suites also give it that extra edge. It shares a long, pine-shaded beach with the Meteor (*see above*).

★ Kn Riva

Slakovac, Brist (021 695 598/www.hotel-riva.brist.hr). **Rates** *from* €50 double. **Credit** MC, V.

A lovely little place this, its loggia-style restaurant terrace lapped by a relatively secluded stretch of the Adriatic, below the balconies of each of its neat, rooms. The half-board rates here are absolute bargains, out of season, when the only sound you will hear is the occasional fishing boat. Ask about weekly rates, too – sometimes they offer seven nights for the price of six. The Riva is a short stroll downhill from the Zvijezda Mora bar, which is right by the southbound Brist bus stop, an easy beach walk from Gradac.

Villa Andrea

Kamena 46, Tučepi (021 623 008/098 356 71 mobile/fax 021 695 259/www.villa-andrea. info). **Rates** *from* €40 single; *from* €65 double. **Credit** MC, V.

Opened in 2005, the Villa Andrea trying to lift itself above the norm for the Makarska coast without pricing itself out of the market. To this end, its 16 rooms are comfortable and well-furnished, the terrace restaurant is convivial and 24-hour reception is a rarity at these prices. Parking facilities too.

Getting there & around

The riviera is served almost hourly by buses between **Split** and **Dubrovnik**, all year round. Makarska town is 75mins from Split (about 40kn) and three hours from Dubrovnik (just over 100kn). For short hops down the riviera,

simply flag down a passing bus at the bus shelter on the coast road with the town's name on it and pay the nominal fee once on board.

Resources

Tourist information

Each resort on the riviera (www.makarska-riviera.com) has its own modest tourist office: **Brela** (021 618 337, www.brela.hr); **Baška Voda** (021 620 713, www.baskavoda.com); **Makarska** (Obala Kralja Tomislava 16, 021 612 002, www.makarska.hr); **Tučepi** (021 623 100, www.tucepi.com); **Zaostrog** (021 697 511); and **Gradac** (021 697 511, www.gradac.hr)

BRAČ

Despite being one of the closest islands to the mainland – less than an hour by catamaran – and prime candidate for the most popular, **Brač** gives you the option to carouse with the hordes or be lost in solitude. In many ways, Brač is Croatia's everyisland. In **Bol**, it has a town where you can grab a lively cocktail and head to the island's postcard shot, the country's most famous beach, **Zlatni Rat**, windsurfing central. From Bol you can trek to the area's highest peak, the 778-metre **Vidova Gora**, or investigate remote and traditional villages, where donkeys still work the rugged landscape to transport grasses, grapes and olives.

And, because Brač is so close to Split, you can do it in a day trip. A bus or hire-car ride from the northern entry port of **Supetar** – the other main tourist centre and family-friendly

---

INSIDE TRACK
SUMMER SPORTS

Thanks to its location, Brač is a windsurfing and kite-surfing centre. Between the end of May and the start of August a strong afternoon Maestral wind from the west creates ideal conditions. Clubs along Bol beach include **Big Blue Sport** near the Hotel Borak (Podan Glavice 2, 021 635 614, 098 497 080 mobile, www.big-blue-sport.hr), for windsurfing and sea kayaking, and the main kite-surfing centre, **Yellow Cat** (098 288 581 mobile, www.zutimacak.hr/kite) near Zlatni Rat. Both teach beginners. Diving can be arranged at **Orca Sport** (021 740 625, www.orca-sport.com) – the best spots are between Bol and Milna. For a week in mid July, Sutivan on the north coast hosts the **Extreme Sports Festival** (www.vankaregule.com).

Gently Does It

Ispod peke – slow food the Dalmatian way.

Ispod peka is a classic feature on Dalmatian menus. Diners are requested to order it at least a day in advance, and ideally for at least four people. So what is this strange dish that you can't just order up and devour? *Ispod peke*, literally 'under the bell', is a way of slow cooking under a dome-shaped lid.

When Dalmatian mothers discovered their city cousins using ovens, this time of cooking bell was adopted as the country way to bake meat – and the successor to boiling food or roasting it on the spit. The age of electricity came relatively late to rural Croatia but still the popularity of this old cooking method survives.

Traditionally in winter, the wood fire would be prepared on a stone slab in the most multifunctional area of the house – the place to get warm over a chat – and above the fire would be an array of meats in the course of being smoked. Chickens and turkeys were early *peka* favourites but, with the advent of refrigeration and the first butchers, small cuts of lamb and veal were added to the repertoire. Cooking *ispod peke* is also credited as being the first appetising Dalmatian way of cooking octopus.

Polite but knowing smiles will greet you when you ask for the secret of a good *peka* – everyone has their own tips and special ingredients. Know thy *peka* also applies to the dome under which the meat is cooked. The fragile clay *pekas* were eventually replaced, in the early 20th century, with more robust iron ones – but no two ever produce quite the same result, although the distinctive succulent meat, delicious potatoes and all-round juicy flavours are unique to this type of cooking. Once the wood has turned into burning ashes on the hot stone slab, the iron bell is covered with the ashes and the contents start slowly cooking at a temperature of around 230 degrees centigrade, which goes down to about 170 degrees when cooked.

There are endless discussions about whether to turn the meat and when. The practicalities are that with so many factors having an input into the cooking temperature, you can never be sure exactly when it will be perfect. Having a peek inside the peka about 20 minutes before time gives the opportunity to assess the situation and perhaps turn the meat at the same time.

resort with sand-and-pebble beaches and package hotels – goes past pines, olive groves and marble quarries to the southern coast and Bol. When explored, Brač allows travellers to step off the tourist conveyor belt, take a break from the herd and gain a deeper sense of the island and its culture.

Brač, 40km long and 15km wide, is karst rock. This supple white stone has been used by Croatia's finest sculptors. Examples fill the cemetery near Supetar, with tombs of Byzantine and art nouveau fancy created by local Ivan Rendić. His 1900s contemporary Toma Rosandić made the **Petrinović Mausoleum**, the most impressive monument here. The village of Donji Humac, south of Supetar and with views of the nearby quarry, provides an opportunity to observe the stone-carving tradition with a carefree ramble through an authentic settlement. It also contains one of the island's real gastronomic gems: **Kopačina**. Another easy excursion from Supetar is to the ancient hilltop settlement of **Škrip**, where the **Museum of Brač** (021 630 033) in the Radojković Tower contains a Roman relief and artefacts relating to traditional olive cultivation. Further east, **Pučišća** is an oft-overlooked coastal town with a quiet and protected harbour. There you will find the nicest hotel on the island in the boutique **Palace Dešković**.

Supetar is the setting-off point for buses to the old fishing village of **Milna** and the quieter beaches around it. From Bol, the dramatic clifftop **Blaca Hermitage** (091 512 9312 mobile) is a four-hour walk; it contains astronomical instruments, clocks and an atlas

from 1623. On the way you pass **Murvica**, set below the Dragon's Cave, covered with pagan paintings of wild beasts from the 15th century. East of Bol, at **Glavica**, stand the Dominican church and monastery (021 778 000; open May-June, Sept 10am-noon, 5-7pm daily; July, Aug 8am-noon, 5-9pm daily; 10kn), with a museum, which contains prehistoric finds, Greek coins and a Tintoretto.

Behind Bol, Vidova Gora offers its magnificent view of the island and further off across Central Dalmatia. Allow two hours for the walk from the baroque **Church of Our Lady of Carmel** in the centre of Bol – you'll find the **Vladimir Nazor** tavern (021 549 061, 098 225 999 mobile) at the top.

Where to eat

Konoba Gust
Radićeva 14, Bol (021 635 911/098 423 003 mobile). **Open** *Easter-Nov* noon-2am daily. **No credit cards.**
The interior of this rustic konoba off Bol's main square is a collection of weathered green shutters, wine bottles, giant floor plants and wicker lampshades under a wooden-beamed ceiling. Tables spread outside and line the foyer, done up with traditional farm equipment and pictures of celebrities. The homely atmosphere brings folks in but it's the food, as they say, which brings them back. The *gregada* – a stew of boiled fish, scampi, shells, potatoes, onions and herbs – is the speciality. There are also lovely steaks, lobster spaghetti and veal served over rice with a tomato, cream and cheese sauce – plus a wonderful selection of top-end reds and whites.

SPLIT & ISLANDS

Konoba Gust.

Konoba Mlin

Ante Starčevićeva 11, Bol (021 635 376).
Open *May-Oct* 5pm-midnight daily. **Credit**
MC, V.

This romantic old mill, used as recently as 1900, is
east of Bol's main harbour and has a secluded, tree-
shaded terrace above the sea. The tiered terraces are
great places to take in the sunset and enjoy the fabulous fish, which sizzle on an outdoor grill. The
menu also offers good meat dishes and thinly sliced
Dalmatian ham as an appetiser.

★ Konoba Tomić

*Gornji Humac (021 647 228/www.konoba
tomic.com).* **Open** *May-Oct* 5pm-midnight daily.
No credit cards.

This legendary konoba stands in the 800-year-old
house of the Michieli-Tomić family, whose wines
and brandies are sold all over Croatia. Practically
everything that you'll be served is hand-made on the
property, from the *pršut* ham to the lamb, plus, of
course, the wine and varied fruit spirits. If you are
there in the autumn, you may be lucky enough to
watch the family make wine the old-fashioned way,
using a hand-turned press. You can visit the farm,
too. Prices are reasonable for the quality and authen-
ticity. Succulent octopus is prepared *ispod peke*,
under a cooking bell with hot coals. Order this, and
your table, in advance. Tomić is near the airport,
north-east of Bol.

★ Kopačina

*Donji Humac (021 647 707/098 689 760
mobile).* **Open** 10am-midnight daily. **Credit**
AmEx, DC, MC, V.

If not the best restaurant on the island, certainly it
has no rivals in the realm of lamb, which is served
with a Forrest Gump-like dedication and in every
way imaginable. There's lamb soup, lamb on the
spit, boiled lamb, lamb chops, lamb steak, lamb pâté
and the local favourite: lamb under the *peka*. The
clientele includes well-heeled tourists pointed here
by locals and workmen still dusty from the nearby
marble quarry, visible from the restaurant's multi-
levelled and shaded terrace. Above, on an open-air
and wooden-roofed stone patio, you'll find owner Ivo
working the grill and the mechanised spit, which
turns with a bike chain. Beyond is an expansive, renovated indoor dining room. But back to the lamb. In
July and August there's a lamb buffet (170kn) and
guests can try every variety mentioned above plus
lamb liver, local cheese, salted anchovies and lentil
soup with smoked ham. Don't leave without trying
the *vitalac*, although this is probably best tried in the
absence of vegetarians as it consists of lamb liver
wrapped in the intestines of a lamb which has just
drunk milk. It's an island speciality.

Nono Ban

Gornji Humac (021 647 233/www.nonoban.com).
Open noon-midnight daily. **No credit cards.**

This attractive restaurant is run by Jakša Versalović
by the Supetar-Bol road, in a nice natural setting.
With a fine view of Bol 10km away, and its own car
park, the Nono Ban is also popular because of its
healthy food. The menu may be typically Dalmatian
but here they catch their own fish and produce their
own wine, brandies, cheese and meat products:
chicken; ostrich; lamb; veal and smoked ham.

Punta

*Punta 1, Supetar (021 631 507/www.vila
punta.com).* **Open** *Apr-Nov* 8.30am-midnight
daily. **Credit** AmEx, DC, MC, V.

On a secluded point right on the beach and away
from the busy harbour terraces, this big house is a
great place to grab a seaside table for breakfast,
lunch or dinner. Watch windsurfers cavort as you
choose from a konoba-style menu with a wider-than-
average range of fresh fish, including John Dory,
grouper and mussels. Meat lovers can devour the
usual Balkan grilled classics and there are vegetarian options among the pizzas. Rooms for rent too.

Restoran Gumonca

Mirca, Supetar (021 630 237). **Open**
noon-midnight daily. **No credit cards.**

Mirca is a tranquil little place some 3km from
Supetar towards Sutivan. Its old centre feels like
some forgotten village where time has stopped –
nearby Gumonca Cove with its beach and small
dock for fishing boats is Mirca's real hub. Here the
Restoran Gumonca has a long-standing reputation
based on its à la carte menu of seafood specialities.
You can also find traditional Dalmatian meat dishes.
The terrace overlooking the sea is surrounded by
rose bushes, shaded by grapevine and oleander,
while the separate smaller one of the adjacent bar
gives out over the bay.

Restoran Lovrečina

Postira (021 784 528/098 264 319 mobile).
Open noon-midnight daily. **No credit cards.**

Lovrečina is located in a beautiful wooded and
sandy little bay east of Postira. Its name derives
from Sveti Lovre, St Lawrence, the old church here
whose walls can still be seen. Later in the 11th century, this was probably the site of a Benedictine
monastery. The menu offers free-range lamb, tripe,
dolce garbo sweet-and-sour lamb livers, lamb prepared under a baking bell, octopus, sardines, fritule
sweet fritters and *kroštule* – knotted sweet desserts.

Ribarska kućica

*Ante Starčevića, Bol (021 635 033/098 938
0989 mobile/www.ribarska-kucica.com).* **Open**
June-Oct 10am-midnight daily. **No credit cards.**

A beautiful old house on a rocky walkway offers
views of a cosy cove beach and the sea. Each of the
terraces has tables. It's pricey, but if you're going to
have lobster on Brač, it should be here. There's an
adventurous selection of sauces and side dishes.

Bathing On Brač

Shifting sands and bare-all beaches make Braă a holiday fave.

Zlatni Rat is the reason why many visit Brač and certainly why they visit Bol. The Golden Cape is the money shot in every tourist brochure. To reach it, walk west from the harbour where buses and ferries drop you off, until you reach Put Zlatnog Rata, the promenade, a shaded walkway through a pine forest that follows a rise above the beach. The resort hotels are uphill from the promenade, among the pines, and the coast is below. The first big swimming area you come to is Potočine beach, about a kilometre (half a mile) outside town. This pretty cove with small, roundish pebbles draws windsurfers and sunbathers and is packed tight during the high season.

Further on is Zlatni Rat, altogether some 30 minutes from Bol, whose 500-metre-long finger of fine shingle sticks into the sea like a natural pier. It is constantly in motion, its shape shifting with the tides. High waves and gentle winds combine to create ideal conditions for swimming and windsurfing, especially on the westward side, where the waves come from the

open Adriatic. The water is shallow and the seabed relatively smooth – equally ideal for kids. For more privacy, head west, past the nudist beach of Paklina, beyond which the coast gets rockier and you'll need to swim with sandals.

Further is a secluded location with few other bathers. There is also a small cove with a beach of sand and small pebbles a short walk east of the harbour, right before the Dominican monastery. This is close to town and can fill with bathers.

If you're staying in Supetar, just west of the harbour, still in the middle of town, is a sizeable child-friendly fine-pebble beach that draws scores of bathers from the nearby resorts. If you follow the beachside path west, past the park on a small peninsula, you find more smooth pebbly beaches. If you don't mind a rocky coast, put on a pair of swimming sandals and continue west for another couple of kilometres, along a tall stone wall. Here, you'll find isolated spots where you can sunbathe on flat rocks and swim, right next to an aromatic pine forest.

Vinotoka

Jobova 6, Supetar (021 630 969/098 207 447 mobile). **Open** noon-midnight daily. **Credit** AmEx, DC, MC, V.

This tranquil old building on a steep street offers authentic Dalmatian food, primarily from the sea. The family has a fishing boat and produces its own olive oil and wines, red and white. The dining is housed in two rooms, one newly refurbished in modern style but with elements of traditional Dalmatia, like the wooden boat in the centre. There's also a new, more expansive menu to match: smoked tuna with olives and lemon, for example; and a larger list of top wines.

Where to drink

Caffè Bar Marina

Porat, Supetar (091 153 8130 mobile). **Open** *Summer* 7am-2am daily. *Winter* 7am-midnight daily. **No credit cards**.

The Marina has a small terrace on the harbour with an outdoor cocktail bar and a large, elegant bar indoors. After dining, a lively crowd of fun seekers comes here for a quality cocktail or a shot of local grappa. There's techno, pop and Croatian music and a lively staff, while warm local regulars give the place a lived-in feel.

Caffè Bar Pjerin

Put Vele Luke, Supetar (021 630 082). **Open** 6.30am-2am daily. **No credit cards**.

Mainly locals frequent Pjerin, where neon pulls you in off the strip. The music is a mix of disco, hip hop and Croatian. The young staff is charming, if sometimes lost. You'll find it near the corner of 1.Svibnja.

> ### INSIDE TRACK
> ### BRAČ BAR TIPS
>
> Bar staff on Brač don't like to interrupt a good party so places often stay open well past their stated closing times. Most, though, close in winter or open for much shorter hours. In Supetar, **Put Vele Luke** – the small street that starts near the town's beach – is the main drag for drinking and nightlife. In Bol, most of the action is down by the harbour.

Caffè Ben Quick

Vlačića, Supetar (021 631 541). **Open** 7am-2am daily. **No credit cards**.

Between the port and the Vele Luke area, this is the choice of locals who care to have a quiet cocktail – like a B52 or Banana Colada – or mixed drink on the terrace covered by a terracotta roof. Plop down in one of the cane chairs under the old stone house, sip on a cold one on the tile-floored patio, listen to relaxed pop tunes over the speakers and drink in the sunset views across the harbour.

Cocktail Bar Bolero

Put Zlatnog Rata, Bol (no phone). **Open** *May-Oct* 8am-1am daily. **No credit cards**.

At a scenic high point on the promenade, plush wicker chairs and sofas and meditative world music tempt you to this pine-shaded terrace cocktail bar to admire the view of windsurfers and Hvar beyond. It gets a good crowd by late afternoon and stays lively.

Veradero Cocktail Bar.

Pivnica Moby Dick

Loža 13, Bol (021 635 281). **Open** noon-midnight daily. **No credit cards.**
Downstairs is an open-air, multi-terraced and stone-columned affair, with sea views. The bar inside has stone archways, a pool table and a boat hanging from above; the cavernous feel is livened by reggae. Upstairs, over the harbour and Sv Ante chapel, there's a rooftop restaurant serving octopus salad, steak and grilled tuna.

Nightlife

Hacienda

Selca (no phone). **Open** *Summer* midnight-dawn Thur-Sat. **No credit cards.**
Between Selca and Gornji Humac, this hacienda-style spot offers seclusion and a distinctly flexible approach to nocturnal time-keeping. A young crowd jigs to house music, often until dawn, among the olive trees in the open air.

Summer Club Luna

Sv Roka, Supetar (www.summerclubluna.com). **Open** *end June-Sept* 7am-dawn daily. **No credit cards.**
On the road to Bol, this open-air newbie won plenty of friends when it started operations in 2008. The owners, who run the café and traditional restaurant, crank it up at night with DJs thumping house, techno and hip hop well into the morning. The entry price of 40kn-80kn means you dance under the stars and atop stone terraces beside scantily dressed show-girls, while disco balls swirl a light show across the dark, Dalmatian sky.

Veradero Cocktail Bar

Frane Radića, Bol (no phone). **Open** *May-Oct* 8am-2am daily. **No credit cards.**
Right in the main square, this fully open-air cocktail bar features comfy wicker chairs scattered on a stone patio and between pine trees that grow through the floor. By day, prerequisite palm-frond umbrellas shade tables filled with coffee drinkers and there are soft Latino grooves. By night, a DJ lays down tunes from a stand with the venue name spelled out in giant wooden letters and dancing on the tables becomes positively de rigueur. Ask for a signature Mojito, Daiquiri or Long Island Ice Tea. For football matches, all eyes will be glued to the flat screen TV by the DJ perch.

XXL

Put Vele Luke, Supetar (021 630 699). **Open** 10am-2am Mon-Thur, Sun; 10am-5am Fri-Sat. **No credit cards.**
Head downstairs to enter this large dark bar and dancefloor. Foreign and talented local DJs attract a young, energetic set who come here to seriously shake it. The same management runs Space Fun, a cocktail fiesta spot on the beach.

Where to stay

Hotel Elaphusa

Put Zlatnog Rata, Bol (021 306 200/fax 021 635 477/www.bluesunhotels.com). **Rates** *Half-board* €84-€196 double. **Credit** AmEx, DC, MC, V.
Recently renovated and upgraded to a four-star, this hotel, which is situated amid the pine trees just off the walkway to Zlatni Rat, is the best of the BlueSun group. Its 300 rooms and six suites are fairly standard but they are, however, spacious, with wooden floors, and half have sea views from their terraces. The facility has pools both indoor and out, a rock-terraced sunbathing area, a whirlpool, a children's pool, a gym and ball games. There's a good spa centre, plus a restaurant with theme dinners. Throw in disco bar Ela and disco bowling, and it's perfectly possible to never leave the hotel grounds.
▶ *Cheaper nearby BlueSun hotels include the Riu Borak (021 306 202) and Riu Bonaca (021 306 269).*

Hotel Kaštil

Frane Radića 1, Bol (021 635 995/fax 021 635 997/www.kastil.hr). **Open** mid-Mar-Oct. Closed Nov-mid Mar. **Rates** €66-€142 double. **Credit** AmEx, DC, MC, V.
Thirty-two rooms, renovated for 2008, are set inside a pretty old stone building with its back right on the harbour. It also contains the restaurant Vusio, pizzeria Topolino and the Varadero cocktail bar. Many rooms have a sea view but above the terrace restaurant and busy harbour, so noise might be an issue. Others may prefer to go straight from last drinks on the waterside home to bed.

★ Hotel Palace Dešković

Pučišća 16 (021 778 240/fax 021 778 256/www.palace-deskovic.com). **Open** Apr-Nov. Closed Dec-Mar. **Rates** €124-€186 single; €166-€248 double. **Credit** AmEx, DC, MC, V.
By far the nicest option on Brač. Hotel Palace Dešković comes with all of the contemporary accoutrements, WiFi, heated bathroom floors and massage bathtubs. But the 13 rooms also come with history – the hotel is older than the town's church next door. As its name implies, this four-star is a renovated palace. A registered cultural monument, it has been in the family since its construction in 1467. On the outside, the Renaissance feel has held pretty steady. Inside, thanks to dedicated owner, Ružica, each spacious room is unique, with antique furniture and beds. In No.6, Secessionist furniture sits atop woven oriental rugs. Adorning the walls of the seven suites and six double rooms are Ružica's paintings. At street level, the restaurant is also four-star, with dishes like angler fish wrapped in bacon. Out back, a leafy, walled garden is perfect for breakfast or relaxing after investigating beautiful little town-hugging Pučišća Bay.

Kn Pansion Palute

Put Pašika 16, Supetar (021 631 730/fax 021 631 541). **Rates** 190kn-220kn single; 320kn-380kn double. **Credit** AmEx, V.

This comfortable family-run pension has a loyal following, with parking, internet and 12 affordable en-suite rooms equipped with air-con. The staff is pleasant, English-speaking and helpful. There are half-board packages, too, in the decent restaurant.

Villa Giardino

Novi put 2, Bol (021 635 286/fax 021 635 566). **Open** mid May-mid Oct. Closed mid Oct-mid May. **Rates** €89-€98 double. **No credit cards.**

This family-run old villa is usually booked-up in high season – but bag one of the 14 rooms and you'll be a guest in someone's mansion. The interior is meticulously arranged yet comfortably renovated, with antiques furnishing many rooms, which have air-con, ceiling fans and heating. Reserve No.4 and slumber in the bed Emperor Franz Joseph slept in on a visit in 1875. Breakfast is served on the front terrace and there's a lovely garden at the back. Note the rave reviews in the visitors' book.

Waterman Resort

Put Vele Luke 4, Supetar (021 640 155/fax 021 631 130/www.watermanresorts.com). **Open** Mar-Nov. Closed Dec-Feb. **Rates** €48-€112 single; €84-€144 double. **Credit** AmEx, DC, MC, V.

This package-tourist complex of 566 units and rooms for 1,500 people, is composed of several hotels under the same management team near the main beaches in Supetar. Shared facilities include a spa and sports centre.

Getting there & around

Brač is one of the few Adriatic islands to have its own **airport** (021 631 370, 021 648 615, www.airport-brac.hr), 15km (9.5 miles) north-east of Bol. A minibus meets arrivals and takes passengers (30kn) to Bol. For Supetar, a taxi (098 264 741 mobile, 098 781 377 mobile) costs 300kn.

Supetar is the island's main port. Jadrolinija (021 631 357, www.jadrolinija.hr) runs 14 **ferries** a day from Split (25kn, 1hr) and Split Tours (021 352 481, www.splittours.hr) runs another six. A car costs about 200kn. From Supetar **buses** (021 631 122) run to most other destinations on Brač – in summer there are five a day to Bol or Milna. The bus station is located just east of the ferry port.

In summer Jadrolinija runs a daily **catamaran** (25kn, 50mins) from Split to Bol. It links Bol with Jelsa on Hvar (20mins). SEM Marina (021 325 533, www.sem-marina.hr) runs a catamaran from Split to Milna, and then on to Bol – price about 85kn. Two ferries a day (30kn, 30mins) shuttle between Makarska on the mainland and Sumartin on the far east cape of Brač. Two buses a day run from Sumartin to Supetar – sadly neither linking with the afternoon ferry.

Resources

Tourist information

Bol Tourist Office *Porat bolskih Pomoraca (021 635 638/www.bol.hr).* **Open** *June-Aug* 8.30am-10pm daily. *Sept-May* 8.30am-3pm Mon-Fri.

Supetar Tourist Office *Porat 1 (021 630 551/www.supetar.hr).* **Open** *June-Sept* 8am-10pm daily. *May, Oct* 8am-4pm Mon-Sat. *Nov-Apr* 8am-4pm Mon-Fri.

HVAR

By now, it's no secret that **Hvar** is, outside of Dubrovnik, the epicentre of the Dalmatian travel industry. Holidaymakers come to around the yachts lined along the harbour of the namesake capital and among the revellers forking out more than top dollar (in Croatian terms) to party into the night. And there's no reason to believe that this will change any time soon. The recent major overhaul of all the key hotels here in the **Sunčani Hvar** chain completes the picture.

The hub of it all is **Hvar town** harbour. In high season this pretty, petite Venetian capital of 3,000 locals on the island's south-west tip overflows with 30,000 visitors every day. They swarm the attractive waterfront and adjoining main square, **Pjaca**, doing coffee, the nearby market and the modest selection of sights by morning, the beach by day and the bars by night. Prices now match those of fashionable hotspots elsewhere on the Med. Sunčani Hvar's **Amfora Hotel** broke new ground when it opened in the summer of 2008, its conference centre containing an outdoor meeting area and cascading pool area lined by bars, restaurants and gardens. Another new property, the

---

**INSIDE TRACK
AT YOUR SERVICE**

Sunčani Hvar hotels offer a tailor-made service to guests and non-guests alike. The Hvar Experience Programme provides transfers, by yacht or car, from the mainland or around the island, as well as handling booking and reservations. Details are available at the front desk of any of their hotels: contact concierge@suncanihvar.com or visit www.suncanihvar.com.

Hvar.

independent boutique **Hotel Park**, provides a welcome bit of competition.

Other spots on this lavender-covered island, a thin strip extending east for 60km to the isolated port of **Sućuraj**, have started to emerge as quieter, yet no less interesting options – most notably **Jelsa** and **Stari Grad**. In both, old neighbourhoods with stone houses, ornate colonnaded balconies and winding pedestrian promenades, polished by centuries of travellers, take top billing over discos. In Jelsa's serpentine alleyways, for instance, quality eateries – able to focus on a smaller handful of tourists – have sprouted up to offer the standard with a flurry of improv. In Stari Grad, a burgeoning café-and-gallery vibe fits well with the low-key attitudes. There's a sense in each town that, except for a few mad weeks, it's just you, the locals and ancient stone decor.

Sightseeing

Stari Grad is also the point of entry for car ferries from Split. It was here that Greeks from Paros settled in 385 BC and named it Pharos – later bastardised to 'Hvar'. Invading Venetians then shifted the centre of power (and the name) to the west coast port of today's Hvar town. While the Venetians were building their capital, the island became the hub of a Croatian cultural renaissance.

Today, the most prominent sight in Stari Grad is the summer retreat of 16th-century poet Petar Hektorović, the **Tvrdalj** (021 765 068; open June-Sept 10am-1pm, 6-8pm daily, 10kn),

known for its inscribed walls, gardens and fishpond. Nearby, a 15th-century **Dominican monastery** houses a **museum** (open summer 10am-noon, 4-7.30pm Mon-Sat; 10kn) containing other Hektorović artefacts, Greek gravestones and a Tintoretto, *The Mourning of Christ*, claimed to feature Hektorović himself. More Greek, Roman and maritime items are on display at the **Bianchini Palace** (021 765 910; open summer 10am-noon, 7-9pm daily; 10kn) by the Tvrdalj.

Hektorović never saw his Tvrdalj finished. As a preliminary to the crucial naval Battle of Lepanto near Corfu in 1571, the Turks attacked Stari Grad, Jelsa and Hvar town.

The Venetians rebuilt the capital you see today in the early 1600s. It is centrepieced by Pjaca, or Trg sv Stjepana, the rectangular main square lined with shops and restaurants, framed by the harbour and **Arsenal** at one end, the market and **St Stephen's Church** at the other. This also features a treasury (open summer 10am-noon, 5-7pm daily; winter 10am-noon daily; 10kn) containing two late Renaissance paintings. The Arsenal is used as a contemporary art gallery. Above stands the **Venetian Citadel** (Španjola, 021 718 936; open summer 8am-midnight daily; 15kn), with a display of Greek and Roman finds, and a fine view from the ramparts.

AROUND HVAR

Public transport on Hvar can be, at best, inconvenient. The easiest way to explore its secluded coves and seldom-visited villages is

Stari Grad.

by using a hire car, a bicycle or scooter. In
Hvar town, **Navigare** (021 718 721, 098 727
070 mobile) on the main square hire scooters,
boats and cars, as do **Luka Rent** (021 742 946,
091 591 7111 mobile) at the harbour.

Zvir (Križna Luka, 021 741 415, www.
jkzvir.hr) is a renowned sailing club. Marinas
include **Adriatic Croatia International
Vrboska** (021 774 018, m.vrboska@aci-club.hr)
and the **ACI Marina** in Palmižana (021
744 995, m.palmizana@aci-club.hr). Diving
is best organised at the **Diving Center
Jurgovan** (021 742 490, 098 321 229 mobile,
www.divecenter-hvar.com) by the Hotel
Amfora, a short walk around the harbour
away from the action.

For sea kayaking, sailing tuition, hiking,
climbing or a combination package including
all of the above, **Hvar Adventure** (021 717
813, 098 978 4143, www.hvar-adventure.com)
just off the harbour behind the theatre, is the
best outfit of several offering services on the
island. The north coast between Jelsa, Vrboska
and Stari Grad is ideally suited to cycling.

In nearly every case, you need to be prepared
to walk beyond the crowds to get to the great
beaches. But for those with less time to make
the hike, each of the main settlements has its
own modest beach: Hvar town has one just
down from the harbour near the **Dalmacija
Hotel**; Stari Grad has beaches lining each side
of the bay, the southern one towards **Borić** less
crowded; and Jelsa has child-friendly **Mina**.
Other bathing areas near Jelsa include
Grebišce, 1.5km (one mile) away, containing
bar-restaurant **Corni Petar**.

Taxi boats run to the **Glavica** peninsula
and the nudist beach on nearby **Zečevo** island.
On the undeveloped south coast, **Zavala**,
Dubovica and **Sveta Nedjelja** are secluded
spots and a relatively cheap taxi journey from
any of the main coast towns. A 45-minute hike
east of Hvar town (before reaching Milna) is
rewarded with the crystal-clean, white-stoned
Mekičevića Bay frequented by naturists and
otherwise known as Robinson's Beach – so
called because of the restaurant of the same
name there. Boat taxis also run to the beaches
of the **Pakleni Islands**, in particular the sandy
one at **Palmižana** (*see p262* **Profile**). Naturists
gather at the nearest island to Hvar town,
Jerolim, and **Stipanska** on nearby
Marinkovac.

Where to eat

Kn Alviz
*Dolac, Hvar town (021 742 797/098 286 443
mobile). Open Easter-mid Oct 6pm-midnight
daily. Mid Oct-Easter 6pm-midnight Fri, Sat.*
Credit AmEx, DC, MC, V.

INSIDE TRACK GRODA

The alley running parallel to Hvar town
main square, from St Stephen's Church
to the harbour, named after Hvar's
greatest figure from history, Petar
Hektorović, is known by all as Groda.
From top to tail, Groda is lined with
restaurants – **Luna, Macondo, Paradise
Garden** – so if one is full or doesn't have
the terrace seat you're after, try another.
In high season it can get as crowded
as the harbourfront, so be prepared to
push through the crowds.

Something of an upscale pizza and pasta joint
beyond Hvar town's car park and bus station, Alviz
also serves first-class fish and risotto with shrimp
and-curry sauce. Find a table on the back patio
under the 80-year-old grapevine that winds its way
above your head and still provides grapes, used by
the family for the restaurant's fruit, wine, dessert
wine and grappa.

★ Antika
*Donja Kola, Stari Grad (021 765 479/098
171 7491 mobile). Open Feb-Nov noon-3pm,
6pm-1am daily.* **No credit cards.**
The heart of a growing funky scene in Stari Grad,
Antika is part traditional, part laid-back modern.
A hodgepodge of dining-room furniture crowds
pine floors upstairs and stone tiles below; candle-
sticks overflow with years of accumulated
coloured wax under wooden beam ceilings; and
plaster walls with framed photos and faded paintings fill a house that was built in 1566. Outdoor
tables line the alley and piazza round the corner.
The food veers from grilled fish fare without
subjecting you to pizza. Starters include tuna
carpaccio and chicken breast salad; mains (45kn-
85kn) shark in a sour cream and chive sauce, and
cooked-to-order steak in a garlic, green pepper or
stroganoff sauce. Opposite, Antika's café-bar
plays Creedence and Zim, and serves cocktails
(24kn-32kn); White Russians are the speciality.
Pull up a converted tractor seat downstairs or have
the friendly staff pulley up your drink to the
breezy terrace as you lounge on the faded orange
cushion of a brown wicker couch.

Eremitaž
*Priko, Stari Grad (021 766 067/091 542 8395
mobile). Open Mid Apr-mid Oct noon-3pm,
7pm-midnight daily.* **Credit** AmEx, DC, MC, V.
This 15th-century sea-view stone house between the
harbour and the tourist hotels offers well-made, reasonably priced Dalmatian standards on a pretty,
shaded front terrace. The building used to house
sick sailors in quarantine.

Huljić

Banski Dolac, Jelsa (021 761 409). **Open** *June-mid Sept* 6pm-midnight daily. **No credit cards.**
Huljić is a real find. Guests are looked after over reds and whites made by owner Teo Huljić before a meal at the four-storey collection of terraces that is the restaurant proper. The design theme is handcrafted sturdy: wood and stone on stone tiles. An old wine press sits in the corner as world music wafts. The bar centrepiecing the restaurant has a terracotta roof and a tree sprouting through it. The philosophy, according to Teo, is part Dalmatian and part New Age. Example: grilled tuna with fruit sauce of figs, melon, wine and herbs. The home-made pesto and pine nuts pasta is a must. Booking advised in summer.
▶ *If you can't get a table, nearby Nono (021 761 933), run by the genial Ivo, has the freshest fish and superb steaks.*

Humac

Humac (091 523 9463 mobile). **Open** *Summer* noon-10pm daily. **No credit cards.**
In a deserted village of the same name surrounded by lavender fields some 8km (5 miles) east of Jelsa, signposted on the bumpy main road to Sućuraj, this traditional konoba serves all the classic Dalmatian specialities by candlelight on an open flame. This is no gimmick – as well as no inhabitants, Humac has no electricity.

Kn Jurin Podrum

Donja kola, Stari Grad (021 765 804). **Open** *Summer* noon-2.30pm, 6pm-midnight daily. **Credit** AmEx, DC, MC, V.
Set in the tangle of streets in Stari Grad old town, this is a fine local bistro to suit all budgets. There's seating outdoors and a picture of Tito on the wall inside, under the beams and Christmas lights. To match the changing artwork, the food philosophy is also slightly different: as well as the usual shellfish in sauces you'll find interesting diversions such as octopus and courgette spaghetti.

★ Luna

Petra Hektorovića, Groda, Hvar town (021 741 400/098 748 695 mobile). **Open** *May-Sept* noon-midnight daily. *Sept-Apr* noon-3pm, 6pm-midnight daily. **Credit** AmEx, DC, V.
A lovely dining experience, partly thanks to the starlit roof terrace (accessed via the 'stairway to heaven') and the brightly painted dining room with walls adorned with driftwood – and partly thanks to an adventurous and well-priced menu. The dumplings in a mushroom and truffle sauce and flat pasta with clams, olive oil, garlic, white wine and parsley are wonderful. And there's not a customer – those who can afford it – who hasn't raved over the Lobster Lunatic: lobster in tomato, white wine and brandy sauce (490kn/kg). Tomas and the buzzy staff in neat blue uniforms provide patter and a tasty gratis pâté starter with warm toast. *Photo 262.*

▶ *If the terrace is full and but you're still looking to dine al fresco, try the Paradise Garden (021 741 310) at the church end of Groda.*

★ Konoba Menego

Petra Hektorovića, Groda, Hvar town (021 742 036/091 722 9773 mobile/www.menego.hr). **Open** *Apr-Nov* 11.30am-2pm, 5pm-midnight daily. **Credit** MC, V.
This place is as close to traditional as downtown Hvar can get: candles in old holders; ham legs hanging from the ceiling of a stone restaurant; oars everywhere; ropes, nets, goatskins and farm implements; wicker lampshades above the wooden tables and serious looking ancestors in black-and-white photos. The menus are strapped to tools. Try the offerings equivalent to Croatian tapas: appetiser portions of vegetables from the family's garden on the nearby Pakleni Islands; meats and cheeses from Pag and Drnis; and solid local wine and olive oil to accompany. Reserve in July and August.

Macondo

Petra Hektorovića, Groda, Hvar town (021 742 850). **Open** *Apr-Oct* noon-2pm, 6.30pm-midnight Mon-Sat; 6.30pm-midnight Sun. **Credit** AmEx, DC, MC, V.
You'll be lucky to grab a table here, at the harbour end of Groda – but the interior is homely enough, with a fireplace and modern art on display. The grilled fish, though pricey, is awfully good. Regulars swear by it, phoning owner Niksa Barišić ahead of time during the day to see what's fresh for them later on. Fishermen come every day to let Niksa plan his menu. Don't be frightened to go out on a limb and try the Big Mama steak: stuffed with cheese, ham and olives. A typical Dalmatian dessert might be too much, so there are home-made sweets for sale by the front door which you can take home as souvenirs.

Maestral

Hotel Amfora, Amfora Bay, Hvar town (021 750 300/www.suncanihvar.com). **Open** *June-Sept* 11am-midnight daily. **Credit** AmEx, DC, MC, V.
The white tent and teakwood deck of this open-air yacht restaurant attached to the Hotel Amfora offer quality grilled Dalmatian dining in atmospheric surroundings. Fresh fish, fine wines and, in the evenings, klapa singers, provide a relaxing, grown-up finale to a day at the beach nearby – plus shade at lunchtime.

★ Robinson

Mekičevića Bay (091 383 5160 mobile/www. robinson-hvar.hr). **Open** *June-mid Sept* 11am-nightfall daily. **No credit cards.**
About a 45-minute trek from Hvar town toward Milna on a path along the sea, Robinson – without electricity or water (hence the name) – sits on a secluded bay prized by sailboats. (If you would prefer not to walk, call Domagoj, the owner, chef and

Hvar.

waiter. He will set you up with a boat.) After you get to the restaurant put in your order then take a swim in water even bluer than usual because the beach stones are bleached white. Nude bathers throw on a T-shirt when Domagoj calls for lunch and a beer under a thatched roof. Specialities of the hut include grilled fish, lobster, lamb, grilled squid, octopus salad and green tagliatelle with shrimp. What he doesn't catch or grow is boated over every day.

Roots

Riva, Hvar town (021 750 750/www. suncanihvar.com). **Open** 11am-midnight daily. **Credit** AmEx, DC, MC, V.
Providing real destination dining right on Hvar town harbour, this is the signature restaurant of the Hotel Riva. Chef Steven Pieters and his team push the boat out where adventurous cuisine is concerned, with as much of the produce as possible locally sourced, and cooked with an adventurous, contemporary twist. Try the meats in house marinades, or the fish, caught that day, which is prepared with imaginative accompaniments and sauces. There are special seasonal menus.

San Marco

Hotel Palace, Trg sv Stjepana, Hvar town (021 750 750/www.suncanihvar.com). **Open** *June-Sept* 11am-midnight daily. **Credit** AmEx, DC, MC, V.
The flagship restaurant of the oldest hotel on Hvar, the Palace, is in keeping with the historic character of its surroundings. The fare on offer is typically Dalmatian – fish grills, seafood delicacies and succulent meat dishes – served while a live band and singer accompany with jazz and blues standards.

Turan

Jelsa (021 761 441/098 957 5269 mobile). **Open** *mid Apr-mid Oct* 5pm-midnight daily. **Credit** AmEx, DC, MC, V.
At the back of Jelsa old town and up a leafy (and nameless) incline, keep an eye out for Turan, the restaurant's new name, and Dominko, its former name, and that of the company that owns it. The venue is one and the same. It's worth exploring for the friendly staff and the fabulous terrace for summer dining. Host Martin prides himself on *peka* specialities (*see also p250* **Gently Does It**), producing succulent meats and lobster from under the traditional coal-covered bell-shaped metal lid – and his flambé desserts.

Val Marina

Hotel Adriana, Fabrika, Hvar town (021 750 750/suncanihvar.com). **Open** 11am-midnight daily. **Credit** AmEx, DC, MC, V.
Set in the lobby of the Hotel Adriana, this chic Med fish restaurant and bar provide quality dining and drinking with a harbourfront location. Steven Pieters and his team come up with classy inventions to suit the setting, underpinned by locally harvested seafood and fine domestic wines. The stand-out selection on the menu is the five-course Dalmatian Blue featuring a main of Mljet lobster medallion atop an olive bruschetta.

Yakša

Petra Hektorovića, Groda, Hvar town (091 277 0770 mobile/www.yaksa.com). **Open** *Summer* 10am-4pm, 7pm-1am daily. *Winter* noon-2pm, 6-11pm daily. **Credit** AmEx, MC, V.

Luna. *See p260.*

Profile Palmižana

Go back to nature at this unusually plush retreat.

When locals in Hvar town say they are going to the beach, they don't mean the modest spots by the harbour. They take a quick taxi boat to the Pakleni Islands, to relax, naked if they feel like it, amid the smell of fragrant pines, uninhibited in uninhabited nature. Facilities are equally bare, with one stellar exception: **Palmižana**.

Set in a natural harbour on the north-east coast of the main island of Veliki Otok (also known as Sv Klement), Palmižana flourished thanks to botanist Eugen Meneghello, who created a unique garden of rare, exotic species here. The compound opened up for tourism as early as 1906. His son Giorgio-Toto and daughter-in-law Dagmar

then built a holiday complex around it: the **Pansion Meneghello**.

Regardless of Hvar's hotel expansion, Meneghello (*see p268*) will remain a premier place to stay, eat or just visit when you're in the vicinity. Dagmar is still the grande dame of the property and runs the show along with her three children. But the surroundings are just the half of it.

On the grounds are fashion shows and a constant string of art openings by young and established artists alike. There is also a stellar restaurant, serving high-end gastro delights made from fresh, local ingredients. A two-minute walk toward the water brings you to another top-end dining experience, Toto's, run, appropriately enough, by Dagmar's son Toto.

Art workshops, courses in diving, fishing, sailing, as well as sandy beaches and classical concerts, are all close at hand, as is the nightlife of Hvar town, a boat taxi away (15kn, 30 mins). Book a spot in one of the Meneghello's 14 stone bungalows well in advance.

HOLIDAY COOKING
Cookery classes here have recently been conducted by the best in the business, TV chef Ana Ugarković, formerly of Zagreb's Kerempuh, who learned her trade in England.

Yakša is a place to impress, somewhere for a romantic candlelit dinner, somewhere to be seen. It can seem pricey but, if the occasion is right, it gives you reason to forget the expense and enjoy. The food here is exquisite and tables sit under the stars in the narrow cobbled street. The menu changes with season. Adriatic lobster is grilled with herbs and served with salad and thick, quartered Yakša fries; beefsteak with local aromatic herbs. If you have to wait for a table, Yakša has its own bar courtyard just around the corner.

Zlatna Školjka

Petra Hektorovića, Groda, Hvar town (098 168 8797 mobile). **Open** *May-Oct* noon-3pm, 7pm-midnight daily. **No credit cards.**
Billing itself as a slow food restaurant, the Golden Shell at the church end of Hektorovića, does a number of welcome inventive dishes along with Dalmatian standards. Varieties of lamb stew are a house speciality as well as cheeses in olive oils, eaten on a simple shaded terrace with unpretentious checked tablecloths. Owner Ivo also offers a challenge menu: four-course and you just say whether you want the food from land or sea.

Zorače

Uvala Zorače (021 745 638). **Open** *Summer* 11am-11pm daily. **Credit** MC, V.
Run by the Barišić family, this konoba in Zorače, which is 6km (3.5 miles) from Hvar town, is set in a small, quiet bay, making it a great place to escape the hectic high season. Food is typical, local and good. Fresh fish and meat are slow-cooked in the traditional way under the bell. If you reserve the best outside table, which is on top of the cliff and ideal for a sunset beverage, order your food in advance. Zorače feels like going round to a friend's house for dinner – relaxed and friendly, no bad thing when Hvar is so rapidly going upmarket.

Where to drink

Batana

Vagonj, Stari Grad (021 766 018). **Open** *Summer* 8am-1am daily. **No credit cards.**
Opened by a father-and-son team of former sailors, this is something between being a konoba and a wine bar. Set in an open-air courtyard, it is a marvel of innovation and indicative of Stari Grad itself: a combination of island self-reliance and gourmet taste. A glass of red Ivan Dolac Plavac Barrique goes nicely with the *pršut* and cheese plate; sea salad sits perfect beside the stone basins and the old wine press. This is a great place to come after dinner to sip on a dessert wine or a glass of cherry brandy. Ask about the stone model boat in the corner.

BB Club

Hotel Riva, Hvar town (021 750 750). **Open** 11am-1am daily. **Credit** AmEx, DC, MC, V.

In tune with Hvar town's new cosmopolitianism, the BB Club appeals to the party-minded fraternity whose yachts gently rock in the harbour outside. A DJ spins on the waterfront terrace while mixologists fix quality cocktails – note the Hvar Rose Martini of vodka, Vermouth, grenadine and orange bitters.

Colonnade Beach Bar

Bonj les Bains, Amfora bay (021 750 750). **Open** *Summer* 11am-2am daily. **Credit** AmEx, DC, MC, V.
A palm beach club in the classic mould, the Colonnade suits the Riviera chic of its location, Bonj les Bains beach. It's not only the champagne cocktails, there's quality dining to be had too.
▶ *For something similarly chic après-beach, the Splash Bar under the same management is just opposite.*

Hula Hula Beach Bar

Majerovića, Hvar town (no phone). **Open** *mid May-late Sept* 9am-9pm daily. **No credit cards.**
This is the place for in-the-know locals up for daytime partying and après-beach relaxing. The spot is a short walk round the coast from the Hotel Amfora on a reasonably isolated jut of coastland called Majerovića. The decor is Bali-meets-Adriatic with comfy wooden recliners, fringed umbrellas and a wooden bar. The owner, Wolf, has lived all over the world and has brought his own concepts to Hvar. While lounging with a Piña Colada or Margarita, listening to the soulful tunes and watching the sunset – in one of the few spots in town where it actually disappears into the sea – you can order a meal from the bar's adjoining sister restaurant, Bubba Gump: big salads with chicken, Thai chicken curry or the snack tower of chicken wings, chips, grilled vegetables, mixed salad and dips, a real communal pig-out.

Kavana Pjaca

Trg sv Stjepana, Hvar town (021 741 868). **Open** *Summer* 7am-3am daily. *Winter* 7am-11pm daily. **No credit cards.**
An expanse of wicker chairs occupies a right-angle of flagstone at the harbour end of the main square, the perfect spot to check email on the free WiFi and enjoy a full breakfast of bacon, eggs and croissants. In the afternoon, Pjaca can provide delicious sandwiches such as the Niçoise and, in the evening, Campari, local wines and proper whiskies.

Kiva Bar

Fabrika, Hvar town (no phone). **Open** *Summer* 9pm-2.30am daily. *Winter* 9am-2.30am Fri, Sat. **No credit cards.**
Viva la Kiva! When all around is wicker and swizzle sticks, old Kiva is an honest-to-goodness bar. It says so on the wall ('It's A Bar!') and is as good as its word, playing old rock and roll faves, and funk and jazz tunes in a loud, intimate, stone room. True, it also displays the lyrics to 'Imagine', a cheap toy

Villa Verde.
See p266.

guitar and peace signs, unforgivable trespasses any-where else – but with music this good and drinking this serious, they must be having us on. Set on the far quay near the Hotel Palace.

Libido
Jelsa waterfront (no phone). **Open** *Summer* 6pm-2am daily. **No credit cards**.
This is a Jelsa cornerstone, located where the beach meets the harbour, above Gringo's pizzeria, under the same umbrella – look for the giant 'wine & cock-tail bar' sign. Bohemian artwork, beaded candleholders, African masks and panoramic seaside views provide the backdrop for jigging to clubby music and sipping on seriously strong cocktails such as the 'Kick in the Balls': rum, melon liqueur, coconut, orange juice and cream.
▶ *Alongside Libido, Dgigibaoo is a great, late DJ haunt.*

Loco Bar
Trg sv Stjepana, Hvar town (no phone). **Open** *Summer* 9am-3am daily. *Winter* 8am-midnight daily. **No credit cards**.
The first thing Zoran, Loco's owner, will tell you is that Loco has the best coffee in town. It's definitely the least expensive – and it *is* good. This is one of the few places in town that doesn't automatically raise its prices every season. Consequently, the locals drink here. A great place to relax before sub-merging into or emerging from the crowded Hvar alleys, it's one of several bars lining the main square. Upstairs, in the classic old stone and wood interior, Zoran's paintings are on display and for sale in his atelier. Outside, the striped lounge furniture, a

happy and funky assortment of music and better than decent mixed drinks make this one of the brighter spots in the locality.

Pršuta Tri Wine Bar
Petra Hektorovića, Groda, Hvar town (098 969 6193 mobile). **Open** *Summer* 6pm-2.30am daily. **No credit cards**.
Pršuta is a sanctuary when Groda is groaning elbow-to-elbow in high season. Affable owner Vidan, a veteran of the last war, won't hesitate to discuss history and/or the culinary specialities of Croatia. Wooden beamed ceilings and antique fur-niture surround sofas, *pršut* ham hangs from the ceiling. A glass of top quality red (30kn-70kn), such as a Zlatan Plavac Grand Cru, goes perfectly with a plate of Croatian sheep's cheese or whatever Vidan decides to bring out and share with the room. It's not uncommon for perfect strangers to become friends and sample each other's tipples. The wine cabinet contains a '47 Bourgogne, and there is, at any given moment, more than 1,000 euros of wine open behind the bar – and a guitar in the corner for anyone who feels the inclination.

Sports Bar
Hotel Delfin, Hvar town (021 741 168). **Open** 11am-1am daily. **Credit** AmEx, DC, MC, V.
Shoot pool, spin table football, sip Beck's, see the match on TV and sink classic bar food at this pop-ular venue, the only one of its kind on the island.

Tarentela
Pjaca, Jelsa (no phone). **Open** *Summer* 8am-2pm, 4pm-2am daily. **No credit cards**.

SPLIT & ISLANDS

Riva. *See p268.*

On the main square, this Jelsa institution has a plain interior, and a wide terrace where the action takes place. Named after the local snub-nosed lizard, Tarentela has generated a gang of regulars over five years, a fine collection of CDs and peppy staff – crazy Mario and the crew – overseen by progressive bar owner Dominic. Chilled by day, cool for cocktails at sundown and absolutely ideal pre-club.

Top Sky Bar & Terrace
Hotel Adriana, Hvar town (021 750 200).
Open 11am-2am daily. **Credit** AmEx, DC, MC, V.
With a wraparound view of Hvar town, the harbour and Pakleni islands beyond, The Top offers quality cocktails and sea-facing massages atop the Adriana Hotel. Multi-level terraces provide visual contrast to the stunning blue view.

Villa Verde
Jelsa waterfront (no phone). **Open** *Summer* 7pm-2am daily. **No credit cards**.
Under bar chief Ivana Gamulin, Villa Verde is the liveliest spot away from Hvar town. In a vast garden terrace of pebbles surrounded by palms and oleanders, a crowd of locals and internationals soak in the night air and sip on cocktails (all 40kn) made of fresh ingredients, such as the mint picked on the premises. Designated drivers can still belly up to the bar and order a bevy of milkshakes like the Bomba: banana, peaches, nuts, milk and sugar. As a bartender hand-crushes ice and grinds brown sugar and lime before mixing in cachaça for a signature Caipirinha, a DJ – framed by a red wall, a stone colonnaded banister, and fig trees – blends acid funk on the portico of the one-time private hacienda. Occasional live acts. *Photo p265.*
▶ *If VV appeals, try also Tremendo, a chilled lounge bar which is to be found at the far edge of Jelsa harbour.*

Zimmer Frei
Petra Hektorovića, Groda, Hvar town (098 559 6182 mobile). **Open** *Summer* 8pm-3am daily. *Winter* times vary. **No credit cards**.
Look out for the white cushions spread on a narrow side street near the church opposite the Zlatna Školjka restaurant. In an equally stark interior, owner Jugo runs a tidy ship, having learned his bar trade in Germany. The cocktails are tasty, the signature Zimmer Frei (50kn) of Bacardi, Malibu, grenadine and coconut juice a knockout. It has nice touches, too – the chairs come from Aloha, the first proper bar in Hvar town. Open all year round.

Nightlife

Carpe Diem
Riva, Hvar town (021 742 369/www.carpe-diem-hvar.com). **Open** *Summer* 9am-3am daily. *Winter* 9am-midnight daily. **Credit** MC, V.
Opened in 1999, Carpe Diem is still the line in the sand and the landmark cocktail-swigging hangout of celebs and the yachting fraternity. It's also the perfect place for a daytime coffee, before 'Sunset Grooves' greet the post-beach crowd from 5pm to 8pm. There's a fashion show twice a week. Then DJs kick it at night. Behind a loggia façade, it's surprisingly ordinary inside, with just higher-than-normal prices and standard music for the genre. Its reputation stems from its VIP scene in high season, upon which Hvar hype is fuelled. Its reservation-only policy in August (put your name on the list as you pass by during the day) means that the terrace (and separate bar) operates as a celebrity zone.

Chuara
Jelsa waterfront (091 575 5114 mobile/www.chuara-jelsa.hr). **Open** *Summer* 9am-1pm, 5pm-5am daily. *Winter* 8pm-3am daily. **No credit cards.**
This enclosed courtyard lounge, full of urban flair, gets immediate marks for style – white-cotton chair covers and red lights highlight a billowing white-cotton trellis scattered around giant palms. Chuara's main service to Jelsa is as a pulsating disco, right now in its groove and gaining notoriety. Cocktails like the Beverly Hills Ice Tea (vodka, tequila, gin, white rum, Triple Sec and champagne) flow all night as partygoers move from the patio in to the club and DJ Andy S – a Londoner with Croatian roots – directs the crowd with R&B, hip hop, UK garage and house on a dancefloor surrounded by strings of white lights. On any given night, there's also live music and dancing showgirls.

Digigibaoo
Jelsa waterfront (no phone). **Open** *June-Oct* 9am-5am daily. **No credit cards.**
Located by Libido, where the beach meets the eastern edge of the harbour, this is a mellow terrace for cocktails by day and a vibrant music bar by night. Once the action moves from idyllic sunset to pitch black painted room, DJs rock the place into the wee hours with deep and funky house, hip hop and non-commercial beats. There's occasional live music, too – sometimes jazz. That bear-like guy is owner Niko, as friendly as can be. Order a Blue Lagoon and settle in for a while.

Veneranda
Hvar town (no phone). **Open** *Summer* 10pm-5am daily. **No credit cards.**
Set in a hillside Venetian fortress behind the Hotel Delfin east of Hvar town harbour, the Veneranda is an open-air disco with DJs, and dancers who inevitably end up in the swimming pool around the dance floor. Look out for flyers stuck up around town and be prepared to pay upwards of 100kn to get in at weekends.

Where to stay

Adriana
Hvar town (021 750 200/fax 021 750 201/www.suncanihvar.hr). **Rates** €237-€512 single; €248-€523 double. **Credit** AmEx, DC, MC, V.
This four-star Sunčani makeover overlooking the yacht harbour boasts serious amenities: a big spa complex with all the treatments and programmes (including yoga); a rooftop terrace with heated swimming pools indoor and out; a panoramic bar – and rooms to match.

Amfora
Hvar town (021 750 300/fax 021 750 301/www.suncanihvar.hr). **Rates** €171-€440 single; €182-€451 double. **Credit** AmEx, DC, MC, V.
The Amfora reopened its doors in the summer of 2008 as the most deluxe conference hotel in the region – but it's more than just a conference hotel. Set in pine trees a ten-minute walk from the main square in Hvar town, the Amfora is also a leisure lodging with a private section of beach called Les Bains, and a top-notch seafood restaurant. A cascading pool, landscaped gardens and a spa round out its attractive features.
▶ *For more on the drinking and dining on offer at Amfora, see p260 and p264 for the Maestral and Colonnade Beach Bar.*

Hotel Hvar
Jelsa (021 761 122/fax 021 761 811/www.dalmacija-holiday.com). **Closed** Nov-late Mar. **Rates** €65-€175 double. **Credit** AmEx, DC, MC, V.
The best of the Dalmacija Holiday resort quartet in the same area, Hotel Hvar is a well-equipped three-star establishment. It boasts indoor and outdoor pools, an exercise room and a children's club. All 206 rooms have balconies, with sea and park views. Beaches are a hop away.
▶ *Three more Dalmacija Hotels venues are in Jelsa – see the website for details.*

Hotel Park
Hvar town (021 718 337/fax 021 741 520/www.hotelparkhvar.com). **Rates** €80-€320 double. **Credit** MC, V.
Next to the Palace hotel overlooking the harbour, and served by a cheerful staff, this is an alternative to the Sunčani Hvar chain of hotels. This Baroque building has 14 apartments and one room, all tastefully designed with sleek white couches and modern wooden furniture against exposed stone. All have internet, plasma TVs, massage showers, and views of the sea and Pakleni Islands.

Hotel Podstine

Pod Stine, Hvar town (021 740 400/fax 021 740 499/www.podstine.com). **Closed** Nov-late Mar. **Rates** €99-€282 double. **Credit** AmEx, DC, MC, V.

The family-run Podstine has 52 rooms and is tucked away by its own beach a 15-minute walk down the coast from Hvar town harbour. Prices for sea-view rooms increase gradually from April through to high season, but you'll also be getting a lovely terrace restaurant, spa centre, tennis courts, outdoor swimming pool and any number of rental and excursion options, including the hotel's own yacht. The buffet breakfast is included in the price.

Palace

Trg sv Stjepana, Hvar town (021 741 966/ fax 021 742 420/www.suncanihvar.hr). **Closed** mid Nov-mid Mar. **Rates** €57-€250 single; €76-€257 double. **Credit** AmEx, DC, MC, V

The most historic of the Sunčani Hvar chain, the Palace occupies a section of a Venetian loggia, hence the lovely façade facing the harbour. The oldest hotel on Hvar, it had an upgrade for the 2008 season, with serious renovation to the indoor swimming pool, rooms and sea-view suites. The historic exterior, though, is sacrosanct. *Photo p261.*

Pansion Meneghello

Palmižana, Sv Klement, Pakleni Islands (021 717 270/fax 021 717 268/091 478 3110 mobile/www.palmizana.hr). **Closed** Nov-late Mar. **Rates** per person €30-€70. **Credit** AmEx, DC, MC, V.

Pansion Meneghello is a unique island retreat. It's a relaxing place to stay and, if required, even educative. *See p262* **Profile**.

Pansion Murvica

Sv Roka Jelsa (tel/fax 021 761 405/www. murvica.net). **Rates** 280kn-350kn double. **No credit cards**.

Set behind the bus station, and signposted on the right as you enter town, this comfortable family-run pension consists of three studios (all with a kitchenette) and a double room. Its decent restaurant opens from Easter to Hallowe'en. There's not much of a view but if you prefer character to package hotels, choose the Murvica.

Riva

Riva, Hvar town (021 750 100/fax 021 750 101/www.suncanihvar.hr). **Rates** €143-€528 single; €154-€539 double. **Credit** AmEx, DC, MC, V.

The Riva is a classy but pricey hotel set in a century-old building on Hvar town harbourfront. The 33 rooms over three floors are seriously trendy, with see-through shower doors and artsy Hollywood themes (James Dean or the incomparable Audrey Hepburn, for instance). All have flat-screen TVs and

WiFi. Amenities are dictated by space – there's no room for a fitness centre or a swimming pool – but ample attention has been given to the upscale Roots Mediterranean restaurant and the terrace BB bar, where you can expect tasty cocktails and a summer of regular DJ appearances. *Photo p266.*

▶ *For more on the drinking and dining on offer at the Riva, see p262 and p264 for Roots and the BB Club.*

Vila Irming

Sv Nedelja, near Jelsa (tel/fax 021 745 768/ www.vi.irming.hr) **Closed** Nov-Apr. **Rates** apartments per person €35-€60. **No credit cards**.

A 15-minute boat ride from Hvar town brings you to Sveta Nedjelja, a romantic wine and fishing village at the bottom of Sveti Nikola hill. There are two good restaurants, Tamaris and Bilo Idro, and one shop. The Privoras' detached villa sits in the middle of a sheltered grove, imbued with the pure scent of pine and sea. Hammocks are hung in the garden, sun loungers just below, and there's a pebble beach and marina a minute away. There's also great free-climbing and a deserted lagoon five minutes away. Fire up the barbecue for freshly caught fish. The Privoras are happy to organise everything, including transfers to and from Hvar town.

▶ *Idyllic privacy is not confined to the Irming – Palmižana has it too; see p262 Profile.*

Getting there & around

Car ferries arrive at **Stari Grad**, which lies 16km (ten miles) to the east of Hvar town, where traffic is barred from the centre. Half-a-dozen a day run from **Split** (1hr 45mins, 38kn foot passengers, 250kn car). Ferries running on the main coastal line down from **Rijeka** or up from **Dubrovnik** also call at Stari Grad, as do international lines from **Ancona** and **Pescara** on the Italian coast, run by Jadrolinija, Split Tours and SNAV.

Another regular ferry option from the mainland is at **Drvenik** on the Makarska Riviera to the town of **Sućuraj** (40min, 30kn) on Hvar's eastern tip. Sućuraj is practically isolated as far as local buses are concerned, so make sure you have your own transport or arrange for someone to pick you up.

The fastest way to get to **Hvar town** from Split is by taking the Jadrolinija **hydrofoil** (May-Sept, 50min, 30kn). It leaves late morning from the Split Riva and turns around soon after. The main daily Jadrolinija car ferry from Split to Vela Luka at the far western tip of **Korčula** and **Lastovo** also calls at Hvar town but note that only foot passengers may disembark at this stop. Jelsa is linked from **Bol** on Brač by Jadrolinija catamaran (45mins, 30kn), although it only runs in summer.

Hvar **buses** are suited for getting on and off the island. Incoming and departing ferries to Stari Grad harbour are greeted by buses. About seven a day head from Hvar town to Stari Grad harbour (*trajekt* on timetables) and Stari Grad town (30mins, 20kn), with a couple more on summer weekends. From Stari Grad harbour to Stari Grad town, the bus (7kn) covers the 3km journey before calling at or linking with **Vrboska** and Jelsa.

A taxi between Hvar town and Stari Grad costs around 200kn. Agree on a price with the reliable **Tihi Taxis** (021 741 888, 021 742 902, 098 338 824 mobile) beforehand.

Resources

Tourist information

Hvar Tourist Office *Trg sv Stjepana (021 741 059/www.hvar.hr).* **Open** *June-Oct* 8am-2.30pm, 3.30-10pm daily. *Nov-May* 8am-2pm Mon-Sat.

Jelsa Tourist Office *Mala Banda (021 761 017/www.tzjelsa.hr).* **Open** *Summer* 8am-11pm Mon-Sat; 10am-12.30pm, 7.30-9.30pm Sun. *Winter* 8am-1pm Mon-Fri.

Stari Grad Tourist Office *Obala dr Franje Tudjmana (021 765 763/021 765 231/www.stari-grad-faros.hr).* **Open** *Summer* 8am-10pm Mon-Sat; 9am-1pm, 5-8pm Sun. *Winter* 8am-2pm Mon-Sat.

VIS

Vis island has a special place in the hearts of many Croatians, who consider this a truly unspoiled example of the best of the Dalmatian coast. Its designation as a military base under Tito froze development for more than 40 years, allowing farming and fishing to remain the dominant activities. Today, tourism is taking over this remote island, one of the farthest from the mainland in Croatia. Vis has become a hot destination among those in the know who want a quiet getaway amid a gorgeous patch of clear sea, which provides great fish, swimming and diving.

While the party scene here may not be as raucous as on Hvar, Vis island's gastronomy can compare with any Dalmatian destination. The natives, whose dialect is a Croatian-Venetian hybrid that is incomprehensible to many Croats, take real pride in their unique culture – and cuisine. Local fishermen and farmers provide ingredients for the food, including native specialties like *pogača*, a fish-stuffed bread, while vintners provide indigenous wines, like the red Plavac and the white Vugava.

Traditionally, the farmers and vintners are from around **Vis town**, the main port in the north-east closest to the mainland. Fishing,

INSIDE TRACK VIS BEACHES

Small downtown beaches lie just north of Komiža harbour. Further, near the Hotel Biševo, are busy **Uvala Pod Gospu** and **Bjažičevo**, with small pebbles easy on the feet. South from Komiža is **Kamenica**, a mix of sand and small pebbles with the bar of the Aquarius disco (*see p275*) to hand. In the other direction are the quieter pebble beaches of **Lučica** and **Jurkovica**. Halfway between Komiža and Vis town, **Uvala Stiniva** is reached via a steep downhill trek on foot. On the west side of Vis town harbour, the public beach near the Hotel Issa is popular. On the other side of the bay, past the British Naval Cemetery, there's a good pebble beach at **Grandovac**. Away from the main towns, beaches are only accessible by boat, car or motor scooter. There are inviting sandy ones in the narrow inlet of **Stončica** and near the village of **Milna**, and stony ones south of Milna and along the whole southern coast of the island. These include **Srebrena** near the village of Rukavac, with flat, pale stones and beautiful views

INSIDE TRACK BRITISH VIS

Of all Croatia, remote Vis is the one with the most links with the UK – the British ran the island after Napoleon fell. Just beyond Kut lies a British naval cemetery, with graves of those who fell in the early 1800s, and in World War II. The post-Napoleonic naval commander was Sir William Hoste, after whom the local cricket club, revived after nearly 200 years by an Aussie returnee, is named. Vis was spared the fate of becoming an Adriatic Gibraltar – British rule was only short-lived.

though less intense than it once was, is still centred around the more secluded village of Komiža, on the seaward side of the 17-km (ten-mile) long island. Between these two main settlements are smaller villages, some famous restaurants and wonderful beaches.

Around Vis

Vis town was created through the union of the seaside communities of Luka, the working harbour area, and Kut, the neighbourhood with more food, fun and night-time action. Both sides are relatively quiet during daytime beach hours, and most restaurants only open around 6pm. The marina brings in a sizeable yachting crowd who support a growing number of gourmet restaurants. Students also come here for the great beaches and bars.

Komiža feels slightly more bohemian. This is the place to enjoy an easy-going Mediterranean pace and excellent pebbly beaches. Many of Komiža's serving staff are year-round residents, who tend to be more friendly and casual than summer workers. Despite the relaxed atmosphere, the village has some fancy, formal restaurants, as well as the island's only disco, the beachside **Aquarius**.

Obscure historic remains relate to the island's strategic importance since 500 BC. In Vis town, you can find Greek vessels, Roman baths and Baroque Austrian architecture. After passing to the Italians, in 1944 Vis was used as a base by Tito and his Partisans. It remained a military facility, and off-limits to all foreigners, until 1989. You can visit Tito's cave headquarters, halfway up Mount Hum – ask at any travel agency.

The major historical sights in Vis town are the **Archaeological Museum** in the Austrian fortress, or **Baterija** (021 711 729; open summer 10am-1pm, 5-8pm Tue-Sun; 10kn), with pottery, jewellery and sculpture

from the Greek and Roman eras, including a 400 BC bronze head of a Greek goddess; and, in Kut, **St Cyprian's church**, 18th-century Baroque with a campanile. The main tourist sight in Komiža is the stubby Venetian fortress and tower called **Kaštel**, which is the Fishing Museum (open summer 9am-noon, 6-10pm daily; 10kn), with memorabilia from Komiža's glory days as a busy hub of the industry.

Beyond, the small islet visible from the harbour in Komiža is **Biševo**, home of the popular **Blue Cave**, with its stunning underwater light. The tour there is a pleasant boat journey and includes time on a sandy beach. See p271 **Profile**.

Unspoiled by development, the clear waters off Vis, dotted with shipwrecks, caves and sites of natural or archaeological interest, are perfect for diving. The **Dodoro Diving Centre** (021 711 913, 091 251 2263 mobile, www.dodoro-diving.com) in Vis town and the **Issa Diving Centre** (091 201 2731 mobile, 021 713 651, www.scubadiving.hr), at the Hotel Biševo in Komiža, offer trips and classes. **Adriatic Kayak Tours** (020 312 770, 091 722 0413 mobile, www.adriatickayaktours.com) run week-long sea kayaking trips around Vis, pick-up in Split or Dubrovnik.

Where to eat

Kn Bistro Pol Rogoc
Barnna Ransonnea 5, Komiža (091 171 3018 mobile). **Open** 8am-3pm, 6-11pm daily. **Credit** AmEx, DC, MC, V.
Neven Kuljić, former chef of the deservedly popular Konoba Bako, moved a few streets inland to open his own restaurant in a pretty, shaded courtyard just past the edge of Komiža's Old Town. There's no sea view or fancy frills on offer here, but the garden is pleasant, the seafood can compare with any place in town, and Kuljić makes guests feel at home – and well fed. The seafood is fresh and cooked while you watch on the big wood-fired brick grill at the back of the garden, under the shade of the eponymous 'rogoc' tree. Side dishes, like a delicious bean-and-courgette concoction, derive from the vegetable plot at the front of the garden. It's a little out of the way, but easy enough to find if you follow signs from Škor or the bus stop.

★ Doručak kod Tihane
Obala Sv Jurja, Vis town (021 718 472/091 271 1010 mobile/www.restorantihana.com). **Open** Apr-mid Oct 9am-1pm, 6pm-midnight daily. **Credit** DC, MC, V.
Stone walls and weathered wooden doors frame this tasteful, historic celeb magnet on Vis Town harbour. Its name translates as 'Breakfast at Tihana's' – Tihana herself takes care of the details. The original floor, from when this was Vis' first hotel in 1911,

Profile Biševo Blue Cave

Nature's light show is Vis island's main tourist attraction.

Every day, around midday, a small miracle takes place inside the sombre stone walls of Biševo island's half-submerged Blue Cave. The water in the bottom of the chamber lights up from below, giving off an eerie blue glow.

It's easy to imagine that ancient visitors to the cave might have regarded this as a spiritual place. Nowadays it is the site of regular pilgrimages – by tourists. In summer, between the peak light hours of 11am and 1.30pm, scores of boats take a 10-15 minute float through the cave, allowing passengers to gawp at nature's light show before they head off to a nearby beach.

The Blue Cave is a natural hole carved into rock along the shore of Biševo Island, which is the five-kilometre (three-mile) long chunk of land you'll see on the left, if you look seaward from Komiža. The floor of the Blue Cave is under the sea, and it has an underwater entrance on its seaward side. When the midday sun is right over, the light shines through this submerged entrance, causing a stunning effect. Unfortunately, the cave is usually so full of boats that you can't jump in for

a swim in the magically-lit water. Some scuba centres can take you out on a diving tour of the cave, via the underwater entrance, but you will have to stay submerged, as the boats make surfacing impossible.

Srebrna Tours (Ribarska 4, Komiža, 021 713 668, www. srebrnatours.hr) and most other Komiža travel agencies arrange day trips, around 100kn per head. You leave between 9 and 11am, for the 45-minute boat ride between Komiža and a Biševo island dock, where you'll have time to order drinks from the thatched-roofed bar. A smaller boat picks you up here and takes you on a round-trip tour of the cave.

While it's a long trip for a quick peek at the cave, probably the best part of the day is still to come. In most tours, once the cave touring boat drops you back at the dock, your original boat returns and carries you on to Porat, a secluded sandy beach on the seaward side of Biševo island. There's another thatched-roof snack bar and a decent seafood restaurant, Konoba Porat. You'll have the afternoon to frolic on this lovely beach – you, and your fellow tourists on the boat trip.

HOW TO GET THERE

Apart from the tours, take the boat *Pruga* (021 713 023) from the harbour. It leaves at 8am, costs 25kn one-way and returns at 4.30pm. Or grab a taxi boat from Komiza to Bisevo, walk to the cave entrance and take a little boat from there.

displays turn-of-the-century tiles. Diners can take in the view of the 16th-century Franciscan monastery and the yachts. The food is excellent, a combo of island traditional and experimental – like the orange soup of oranges, carrots and butter. The grilled veal steak is lathered in a sauce of natural Vis honey and almonds. There is, of course, top-quality white fish and lobster. The meal can be rounded off with pancakes, stuffed with fresh orange or lemon jam. As its name suggests, this is one of the few places in town to offer breakfast, French toast with maple syrup, and Illy coffee.

Kantun
Biskupa Mihe Pusića, Vis town (021 711 306/ 091 371 1306 mobile). **Open** 6pm-midnight daily. **No credit cards.**
It's now half a decade since oenophile owner Ivan Ivičević Bakulić created this special place, under a thick ceiling of grape vines in Luka, serving fine indigenous wines. Today, Kantun also serves superb Mediterranean fare. Inside is a modern makeover of a traditional konoba, each table decked with different tablecloths, the low stone ones in the back room surrounded by local art. A jazz soundtrack adds to the bohemian feel, which is made Croatian with the sizzle of lamb or amberjack on an open grill in the middle of the dining room. Reserve a table here or on the patio, and sip an aperitif in the candlelit, vine-covered courtyard. Then get ready for

Konoba Bako.

huge servings of fish soup, ladled from a silver bowl, accompanied by delicious dark bread with fresh herbs and garlic; leave room for dessert, *rožata* crème caramel, carob or chocolate cake.

Karijola
Šetalište Viskog Boja 4, Vis town (021 711 433). **Open** *June, Sept* 5-11pm daily. *July, Aug* noon-late daily. **No credit cards.**
This summer-only pizzeria has an unbeatable location on a raised terrace overlooking the Prirova pensinsula on the walk to Kut, just beyond the church. The pizzas are easily the best to be had on the island and the wine list features local labels such as Roki and Lipanović.

Konoba Bako
Gundulićeva 1, Komiža (021 713 742). **Open** *Summer* 11am-2am daily. *Winter* 5pm-midnight daily. **Credit** AmEx, DC, MC, V.
On a terrace just above the sea, the friendly beachside Bako provides some of the fancier meals in Komiža while exuding a relaxed atmosphere. There is gorgeous beachside seating, the tables intermingled with pine trees and tall lamps. Inside, sit amid ancient Greek and Roman artefacts recovered from the deep by the restaurant's founder, Tonko Borčić Bako, who dived here for decades. A simple menu includes fresh langouste lobsters, grilled, broiled or served in *brodet* Dalmatian stew. You can also opt for grilled grouper, snapper, rockfish and breaded anglerfish, steak or meat-free pasta sauces. Appetisers include octopus in wine sauce and *Komižka pogača*, the local fish-filled bread. They also offer a great selection of Vis vintages.
▶ *For another spectacular view while you're dining in Komiža, try the Bistro Konoba Jasmina (Brig 42, 021 713 138), where spectacular sunset scenery may accompany steak or lobster.*

Konoba Golub
Podselje (098 965 0327 mobile). **Open** *June-Nov* 11am-midnight daily. **No credit cards.**
Located 4km (2.5 miles) behind Vis town on the old road to Komiža, just above the expanse of flat farmland that dominates the centre of the island, Golub is a super little place to enjoy lamb, fish, squid and home-grown vegetables. They also serve their own olive oil, liqueurs and wine. The restaurant is as simple and rustic as the village, which supports a population of 35. Grab a seat on the open-air patio, covered in a terracotta roof and decorated with wine harvesting equipment. Owner Ivica will deliver your food from a giant open grill.

Konoba Jastožera
Gundulićeva 6, Komiža (021 713 859/www. jastozera.com). **Open** *Mid Apr-mid Oct* 5pm-midnight daily. **No credit cards.**
At this old lobster pot-house hoisted above the sea, dining tables are placed on a floor of planks, under

Konoba Vatrica.

which yachters can pole their tenders into the restaurant and rope off next to the cage from where the dinners are plucked. Waiters happily discuss the ingredients, merits and history of every item on the menu – in particular the several tantalising versions of lobster: langouste lobster with spaghetti au gratin; cream soup with lobster, and grilled lobster with four sauces. As well as lobster, there are crabs, clams and fabulous octopus salad appetisers. Also, available are grills, steaks and an extensive selection of domestic wines. Celebs love it – note the pictures of John Malkovich and other notable Croatophiles to have visited. Not cheap, but worth the price. Book well ahead.

Konoba Roki's
Plisko Polje 17 (021 714 004). **Open** *Apr-Oct* noon-late daily. **Credit** AmEx, DC, MC, V.

INSIDE TRACK
FISHERMEN'S FEASTS

Komiža gets busy around the first
Saturday in August for **Ribarska noč**
('Fishermen's Night'), a weekend party
of music and live performances. The **Vis
Regatta**, usually held the third Saturday
in October, is a yacht race and boaters'
party out of Vis town. On the morning
of December 6, Komiža celebrates **St
Nicholas Day** by burning a boat as a
sacrifice to protect fishermen worldwide.

The inland konoba of this celebrated winemaker is one of the must-dos for first-time visitors. Book by calling or dropping into their wine shop near the Bejbi bar (*see p274*) – they will arrange transport here. The taxi to and from the restaurant is free for parties of four or more. Dishes, from *peka* preparations made under a cooking bell to fresh fish served in the traditional island manner, can be enjoyed at a leisurely pace among the olive groves and vineyards. With such hospitality, it would be rude not to wash it all down with Roki's excellent own Plavac (red) or Vugava (white) wines.

Konoba Vatrica
Kralje Krešimirova IV 13, Kut (021 711 574). **Open** *Summer* noon-late daily. **Credit** AmEx, DC, MC, V.
Deservedly popular, this local favourite in Kut sits under a vine-covered terrace on the waterfront. Black cuttlefish risotto, lobster, langoustines and pasta *vongole* are the specialities, with a daily-changing fresh-fish menu. Portions are generous and the atmosphere convivial. The friendly Vatrica family are happy to open up for you in winter as well, should demand require.

Kn Limoncello
M Gupca 10, Vis town (021 711 823/www. horizon-issa.hr). **Open** 6pm-midnight daily.
No credit cards.
This new restaurant adds a touch of class to Luka by serving fine food in a beautiful setting: a lush garden that climbs a hillside, hidden behind a high stone wall and decorated with sculpted hedges, a

huge Greek-style urn, flowering trees and stone walkways, all set one street up from the sea. The fare includes good preparations of Croatian seafood standards, such as the 'first quality' catch of the day, supplemented with meaty options, like rump steak in mushroom and truffle sauce. The atmosphere is romantic, and it all feels very fancy, but the prices are actually quite affordable.

Pojoda
Don Cvjetka Marasovića 8, Kut (021 711 575).
Open *Summer* noon-3pm, 6pm-1am daily. *Winter* 5pm-midnight daily. **Credit** AmEx, DC, MC, V.

Off a street of restaurants in Kut behind a tall stone wall, Pojoda has a nice garden facing a cheerful, half-opened interior done out in modern decor. Within, a busy flame grill produces delicious Dalmatian-style seafood and barbecued meat. The speciality of the house is the *brodetto*: a stew of onions, garlic, white wine, tomatoes, lobster and top-quality fish. Tempting appetisers include octopus salad, seafood cocktail and *pršut* ham, enjoyed with good local wines. Repeat business is generated by the friendly, efficient service. If you can, try and reserve a table upstairs for the view.
▶ *If they don't have the table you want here, the Val at No.1 (021 711 763) can offer skilled gastronomy in a beautiful setting.*

★ Restoran Senko
Mala travna, Komiža (098 352 5803 mobile).
Open noon-midnight daily. **No credit cards.**

Chef-owner Senko Karuza, a Robinson Crusoe character and well-known Croatian writer, puts on a culinary performance for his fortunate few guests, who are treated to an interactive meal that can last several hours and includes discussions of the natural ingredients of Vis. Take a taxi or boat to the remote picturesque cove of Mala travna on the southern part of the island. You'll be served food made from local and organic ingredients: freshly caught fish; home-made wine, olive oil and produce grown nearby. The menu, based on daily supplies, features the traditional dishes of Vis: smoke-cured fish soup *brodettos*, home-cured fish, bean stew with pasta, and fish grilled over olive-wood and vine embers. Given the unique character of the place, it's advisable to book ahead.

Vila Kaliopa
Vladimira Nazora 32, Vis town (021 711 755/ 091 271 1755 mobile). **Open** *Apr-mid Nov* 1-4pm, 5pm-midnight daily. **No credit cards.**

This is where the yachting crowd goes to splash out some of their money. You'll pay a good 300kn per head all-in to enjoy the shade of the palm trees, bamboo and statues in this enclosed garden between Kut and Luka. Attached is the 16th-century mansion of Milanese nobleman Francesco Garibaldi, making the location and food both memorable. The cuisine is

Dalmatian and Goran Pečarević strives to use mainly local ingredients – the menu changes according to what's fresh that day.

Where to drink

★ Caffè Bar Bejbi
Šetalište Stare Isse 9, Komiža (no phone). **Open** 6am-2am daily. **No credit cards.**

A comfortable dive in the working section of the harbour by the docks, Bejbi ('bay-bee') bustles day and night with people who like to drink and gab. The thatched terrace has its own bar and harbour view, and a new, retro-modern mural. Find pool tables, moody jazz and bossa nova in the large indoor bar. Usually one of the last places to close, this is where all the other parties continue. A worthy stop on any serious bar crawl, it can offer quality cocktails and occasional live acts playing funky rock.
▶ *Komiža's main hub for bars is Škor square, where you'll find the Caffè Bar Bane (No.8) and Speed (No.12).*

Caffè Bar Biliba
Korzo 13, Vis town (021 717 475/091 500 4923 mobile). **Open** 7am-11pm daily. **No credit cards.**

This convenient and convivial terrace, next to the Hotel Tamaris, fills Trg Klapovica square, on the sea in Luka. The indoor section is around the corner, and there is more outdoor seating along the steep, pleasantly shaded stone streets of the Old Town. The location and friendly service attract a large local crowd, even during the day, when most other places in Vis are closed or nearly empty. Internet is available in the back, while the widescreen TV is tuned to sports events.

Kn Cocktail Bar Kanarija
Šetalište A Zanelle 5, Vis town (021 711 138).
Open 7am-11pm daily. **No credit cards.**

The Hotel Issa's cocktail bar, near the hotel and its beach, has a large seaside terrace with comfortable low seating of bamboo and white linen. Tall palms provide shade. There are more than 20 cheap cocktails on offer. The place gets busier toward sundown, as young folks leave the beach; but by late evening, there's more partying to be had in Kut.

INSIDE TRACK
LOCAL SPECIALITIES

The local island speciality, *pogača*, is also known as *Viška pogača* or *Komižka pogača*, depending on which town you are in. In both case, it's a square of dough with a filling of fish (ideally sardines), onion, tomatoes and other ingredients, not dissimilar to a focaccia.

Caffe Bar Bejbi.

Corto Maltese Cocktail Bar
Riva 38, Komiža (098 429 307 mobile). **Open** 8am-2am daily. **No credit cards.**
The place to grab a drink among voluble young locals, the Corto Maltese Cocktail Bar is decorated with silhouettes of the cartoon adventurer of the same name. There are outdoor tables between pine trees on the promenade overlooking the sea. Indoors, a dartboard, a bank of red-booth seating and red walls surround a U-shaped bar, from where owner Toni and his crew serve up good cocktails and dispense beer and wine. Later on, as the crowd weeds out, hang around for disco music and order a top-secret Corto Maltese.

Lambik
Pod Ložu 2, Vis town (no phone). **Open** *Summer* 7am-2am daily. **No credit cards.**
This ancient-looking courtyard and grape arbour is one of the more entertaining and idiosyncratic bars on the island, ably run by a charming young brother-and-sister team who enjoy partying with their equally young guests late into the evening. In the 16th-century villa of Croatian poet Hanibal Lučić, drunken singing and snogging take place on the terrace; the big tables under the vines induce conversation; and the indoor bar area encourages mingling and dancing. The bar serves late, and you may be offered home-made grappa. Decent dance music is often provided by local DJs.

▶ *As a warm-up to the late-night activities of offer at Lambik, hit the Caffè Bar Martin on the same square.*

Zadruga
Riva 33, Komiža (021 713 023). **Open** 8am-2am daily. **Credit** MC, V.
The newest, most chic and most expensive place to drink in Komiža is next to the communal press where locals bring their grapes after harvest. To reach it, walk through the big green doors from the Riva and then nip inside, under the sundial, to the bar. You can also hang out in the courtyard. Mixed drinks and wine are served on wooden tables, tastefully scattered amid old wine equipment and under the stars. Mellow rock plays in the background.

Nightlife

Aquarius
Kamenica beach, Komiža (095 902 7701 mobile). **Open** *July, Aug* 24hrs daily. **No credit cards.**
The only place to really party on Vis, Aquarius is an oasis where traditional island life and big-city rave intersect. The husband-and-wife team of Tomislav and Marcela are Split natives who fell in love with Komiža and were determined to bring something special to this quiet fishing town. Projections beam in the sea while foreign acts and DJs turn this beach disco into an all-night jamboree lasting long past the break of day. A younger crowd is peppered with up-for-it boating types and occasional celebrities, who stick around after the music for a reviving coffee while overlooking the waves. The thatched roof bar, canvas sheltered dance floor and low beach furniture help make sure that the lively atmosphere can also be relaxed.

Where to stay

Kn Hotel Biševo
Ribarska 96, Komiža (021 713 144/fax 021 713 098/www.hotel-bisevo.com). **Rates** 240kn-500kn single; 400kn-700kn double. **Credit** AmEx, DC, V.
Komiža's one big hotel is an adequate three-star resort-style complex with 280 beds. Set on the harbourfront, by a busy beach, the modern Biševo has its own parking and recently added air-conditioning to some of the rooms. The key attraction is the on-site spa centre and sand volleyball court. The restaurant serves breakfast included in the price, and decent seafood.

Dionis
M Gupca 1, Vis town (021 711 963/www. dionis.hr). **Rates** €50-€60 double. **Credit** AmEx, MC, V.
This new family-run bed and breakfast in a recently refurbished old building that's located right on the

SPLIT & ISLANDS

harbour in old-town Luka, has eight clean rooms, each with two beds and air-conditioning. The family also run the downstairs pizzeria.

Kn Hotel Issa

A Zanelle 5, Vis town (021 711 124/fax 021 717 740/www.hotelisis.com). **Rates** €46-€97 single; €62-€130 double. **Credit** AmEx, DC, MC, V.
Boxy, modern structure with 256 beds offers low-frills resort-style accommodation. There are tennis and sports courts, and equipment rental, including bikes and diving gear, nearby. It's right next to the town's main downtown beach. Air-conditioning only available in the pricier rooms. Phone, balcony and satellite TV otherwise provided in each.

★ Hotel Paula

Petra Hektorovića 2, Vis town (021 711 362/ www. hotelpaula.com). **Rates** €69 single; €100 double. **Credit** AmEx, DC, MC, V.
This charming, family-run, 35-bed hotel in an old stone building in Kut, is a wonderful option. The 12 rooms have carefully and individually designed interiors, the service is good and there's fine seafood at the lovely walled terrace restaurant. The cosy hotel wine bar across the alley – run by hotel owner Toni – also welcomes guests.

Kn Hotel Tamaris

Obala sv Jurja 30, Vis town (021 711 350/ fax 021 711 349/www.hotelvis.com). **Rates** €40-€90 single; €54-€120 double. **Credit** AmEx, DC, MC, V.
The Tamaris, which is set in an old harbour-side building, is more attractive than its sister Issa. With 54 beds, it's smaller and rather less institutional. All rooms have air-conditioning. There's a decent restaurant with a harbour-facing terrace, where the inclusive breakfast is served.

▶ *Stablemate Issa is less impressive but can offer more sports and activities; see abobe.*

Kuća Visoka

Obala sv Jurja 22, Vis town (UK 07944 315 949/ www.thisisvis.com). **Rates** *weekly* €595-€900 single. **No credit cards**.
This charming, four-storey stone house in Vis town centre has three bedrooms, two bathrooms, a kitchen and an extensive video library. Advance booking on a weekly basis only.

**INSIDE TRACK
PRIVATE ROOMS**

Don't be shy to enquire about rooms from unexpected sources, such as the owners of the fine wine store **Vina Lipanović**, who also run apartments (021 711 837, 091 893 6302 mobile).

Natural Holiday

Salbunara Bay, Biševo (098 173 1673 mobile/ www.bisevo.org). **Closed** Nov-Apr. **Rates** *4-person bungalow* €520. **No credit cards**.
Owners Davor and Lilian Božanić have built a tiny solar- and wind-powered village of bungalows nestled into old wine terraces atop a secluded cove, moments from the sea on Biševo. They prepare dinners with the vegetables they grow and the seafood they catch. It's something of a five-star camping experience, like going into the wild with your own porters, but it should be noted that this is not for people unwilling to face the elements. Shelters of canvas, wood and stone have double beds and the owners relish the opportunity to share experiences with guests and show them around their island.

Villa Nonna & Casa Nonna

Ribarska 50, Komiža (098 380 046 mobile/ www.villa-nonna.com). **Rates** €35-€80 double. *Casa Nonna house* €100-€230. **No credit cards**.
Affordable, comfortable and central digs are available in this aged yet remodelled townhouse one block from Komiža harbour. Villa Nonna has seven apartments (six, plus one suite) for rent, each more distinctive than a hotel room. Kitchenettes allow you to cook up the produce from the market on your doorstep. The tastefully finished wooden interiors and satellite TVs allow you to impress newly met friends. Across a stone garden courtyard from the main house, the new Casa Nonna has just undergone an extensive renovation and now offers four double rooms for groups of up to nine. There's a large dining room and kitchen, satellite T and two bathrooms. Both are popular, so book early.

Resources

Tourist information

Komiža Tourist Office *Riva sv Mikule 2, Komiža (021 713 455/www.tz-vis.hr).* **Open** *Summer* 8am-10pm daily.
Vis town Tourist Office *Šetalište Stare Isse, Vis town (021 717 017/www.tz-vis.hr).* **Open** *Summer* 8am-10pm daily.

Getting there & around

In summer Jadrolinija runs three **ferries** a day from **Split** to **Vis town** (2hrs, 42kn). Out of season, it's daily. Also in high season, Jadrolinija **catamarans** (75mins, 26kn) run the same route. Out of season the sea can be very choppy. Ferries and hydrofoils run from **Ancona** and **Pescara** in summer. It's a 20-minute bus ride from the ferry dock in Vis town to **Komiža** (20kn). For a **taxi**, call Ivo Pečarević on 098 740 315 mobile or call Taxi Frone Trade: 098 932 1623; 091 558 6092; 099 355 1701, all mobile numbers.

Dubrovnik

Buža.
See p292.

Dubrovnik & Islands

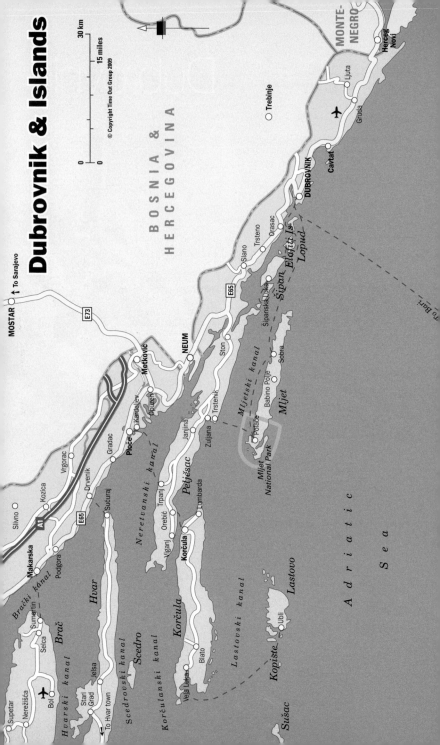

© Copyright Time Out Group 2009

30 km
15 miles
0

To Sarajevo
MOSTAR
MONTE-NEGRO
Herceg Novi
Ljuta
Gruda
Trebinje
Cavtat
DUBROVNIK
Orasac
Trsteno
Slano
Šipanska Luka
Lopud
Šipan Elafiti Is.
Sobra
Babino Polje
Mljet National Park
Pomena
Polače
Mljet
Mljetski kanal
Trstenik
Zuljana
Janjina
Ston
Drače
Trpanj
Vigani
Orebić
Pelješac
Lumbarda
Korčula
Korčula
Blato
Vela Luka
Lastovski kanal
Kopiste
Ubli
Lastovo
Sušac
Adriatic Sea
Scedrovski kanal
Scedro
Korčulanski kanal
Hvar
Sućuraj
Jelsa
Stari Grad
Hvar town
Bol
Nerežišča
Brač
Selca
Sumartin
Supetar
Brački kanal
Hvarski kanal
Makarska
Podgora
Drvenik
Gradac
Vrgorac
Kozica
Silnvo
Ploče
Metković
NEUM
Neretvanski kanal
BOSNIA & HERCEGOVINA
To Bar!
A1
E65
E65
E73

Dubrovnik & Islands

A proudly independent port linked to empty and remote isles.

Strikingly beautiful southern Dalmatia, where Croatia tapers down to Montenegro, has the clearest waters and, in **Dubrovnik**, the lion's share of Croatia's high-end tourist industry. Every year five-star pads with all the trimmings are opened in stunning locations – 2009 is no exception. Yet the celebrated Old Town and pristine sea around it remain intact and open to all. In the north, **Pelješac** is an interesting diversion for windsurfers and wine buffs. In the south, towards the airport, waterfront **Cavtat** is relaxing. The accessible islands of **Korčula** and

Mljet – one a mini-Dubrovnik, the other a wilderness – are holiday destinations in their own right. Little **Lastovo**, halfway out to Italy, feels appealingly lost – just the thing after the hurly-burly of Dubrovnik in high season.

Dubrovnik.

Dubrovnik

Dubrovnik is a one-town tourist industry on its own. As beautiful as the clear blue sea around it, the former centre of the historic, independent Republic of Ragusa invites superlatives and attracts the lion's share of the country's year-round visitors. In fact, when a foreigner thinks of Croatia, the image that likely springs to mind is that of Dubrovnik's proud and pristine fortifications set against the azure background of the Adriatic. The travel brochure covers need little touching up. Anti-clockwise currents running up the coast from Albania mean that the sea is crystal clear here.

As Ragusa, Dubrovnik was a hub of cultural, architectural and scientific achievement, backed by lucrative maritime trading and a progressive urban infrastructure. *See p287* **Profile**. But changing trade routes, and then subjection first to the Napoleonic Code, and then to the Habsburgs, saw Ragusa gradually fade until it reinvented itself under Tito as tourist-friendly Dubrovnik. In 1991 these same tourists watched the news in horror as Dubrovnik was shelled day after day during a six-month siege. Painstakingly rebuilt, it has since entered yet another incarnation, this time one devoted to high-end tourism, most notably where hotels are concerned. Entrepreneurs such as Goran Štrok (*see p300* **Profile**) have upped the ante on luxury lodging – Dubrovnik is now in a similar price bracket to the French Riviera.

DUBROVNIK & ISLANDS

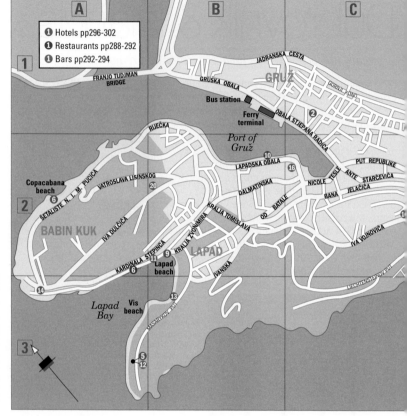

SIGHTSEEING

Where Boškovićeva meets the north flank of
the iconic city walls that encircle Dubrovnik's
Old Town, a map plots the exact points where
the shells fell during the six-month Serb and
Montenegrin bombardment in 1991-92. It looks
like a dartboard. Two out of every three
buildings in the city were damaged. Today,
only the shinier red roof tiles indicate the
brutality the city and its inhabitants endured
during those dark days. Dubrovnik has been
restored to its finest medieval glory and is
fully open for business – as the summer
hordes of tourists testify.

Old Town

Almost everything worth seeing is centred on
the Old Town. To get the best view, and one of
a stupendously clear, blue Adriatic lapping the

rocks below and stretching way beyond, take
the **walking tour** of the city walls (summer
8am-6.30pm daily, winter 9am-3pm daily; 50kn).
Audio-guides (30kn) are available at the main
entrance inside the Pile Gate to the left. An hour
should suffice but take as long as you like.

You'll spend the bulk of your time within
the 15th-century ring of fortifications, in the
small square half-mile (1.3sq km) of gleaming
medieval space bisected by 300-metre-long
(985-foot) Stradun. As you flit between the main
gates of Pile and Ploče, guided by the list of
places on the maroon flags, each venue with its
own logoed white lamp, barkers on every side
street corner call you up to the bland tourist
restaurants on Prijeko. Cats scatter in from the
old harbour, and a cacophony of tour guides
give their spiels. All this is free of traffic until
you reach the bus-choked hub outside the Pile
Gate. Beyond, over the drawbridge, stand the
Lovrijenac Fortress, used for productions of

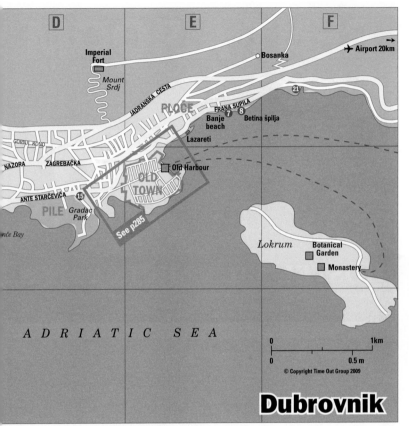

Shakespeare classics during the Summer Festival, and the main road to Gruž and Lapad.

Beyond the Ploče Gate stretches Lazareti beach then a string of luxury hotels. Beside it is the attractive old harbour, where taxi boats set off for the nearby island of **Lokrum**. Just inside the walls is the main square and crossing point of **Luža**, where you'll find the landmark astronomical clock tower (sadly, a modern rebuild of the 1444 original); **Orlando's Column** where all state declarations were read; the smaller of Onofrio's fountains, and a prosaic statue of Shakespeare-era playwright Marin Držić, installed to little celebration in 2008. Few locals greet recent civic initiatives with glee, feeling that their Old Town is being used as a cash cow to the dollar-hungry city authorities. Surrounding Luža are the main historic attractions of the **Rector's Palace**; the **Cathedral** and **Treasury**; the **Sponza Palace**; and the **Dominican monastery**.

Other sights are within easy reach. On the south side of the harbour, round the corner from the Rector's Palace, St John's Fortress (Damjana Jude 2) houses both the **Maritime Museum** (020 426 465, open 9am-2pm Tue-Sun; 15kn) and the **Aquarium** (020 427 937, open summer 9am-9pm daily, winter 9am-1pm Mon-Sat; 15kn). Downstairs is a gloomy collection of tanks containing mainly Adriatic sealife, while upstairs is an attractive collection of ships' models, paintings and photographs detailing Dubrovnik's seafaring history through the Golden Age of Ragusa to the somewhat less glorious modern one.

Walking round from the old harbour, along the rocks fringing the sea-lapped city walls, are spots well-used by bathers and divers. The most popular is by one of the **Buža** bars, where the jagged stones have been planed flat for sunbathers, and metal steps cut into the rock to help you clamber back up.

RENT A ROOM

Vila Micika is one of your best choices for a comfortable and cheap holiday in Dubrovnik! Welcome!

OPEN ALL YEAR

HOSTEL VILA MICIKA ★★★

VILA MICIKA d.o.o. *** Dubrovnik, Mata Vodopića 10, 20000 Dubrovnik, Croatia
Tel/Fax +385 (0)20 437 332, 437 323 www.vilamicika.hr

Your *source* for Dubrovnik's finest private *accommodations.*

Best selection of high-quality, affordable holiday rentals

Online booking and payment

Personalized service

Trusted name in the business

dubrovnikapartmentsource

www.DubrovnikApartmentSource.com
+353 86 167 1222   +385 99 596 3141
contact@DubrovnikApartmentSource.com

Rector's Palace.

INSIDE TRACK
SRDJAN KERA

Former sailor Srdjan Kera has instigated a campaign against politicians selling out his beloved town. His impromtu troupe has staged spoof events around the Old Town, with costumed marchers carrying signs saying '£IBERTA$'. And there's summer's 'Jet Set Glamor', a fake fashion parade for which genuine locals dress up, VIPs are refused entry and tramps allowed in.

Cathedral

Poljana Marina Držića (no phone). **Open** 8am-8pm daily. **Admission** *treasury* 7kn. **No credit cards**. **Map** p285 D3.

The original church, allegedly funded by Richard the Lionheart in recognition of the local hospitality when shipwrecked on Lokrum in the 1190s, was lost to the 1667 earthquake. In its place was built a somewhat bland, baroque affair, free but unenticing to walk around. The main draw is the treasury at one end, a somewhat grotesque collection of holy relics. The arm, skull and lower leg of city patron St Blaise are kept in jewel-encrusted casings; Hungarian King Mátyás Corvinus died before he could receive a somewhat creepy dish and jug.

Dominican Monastery

Sv Dominika 4 (020 321 423). **Open** *Summer* 9am-6pm daily. *Winter* 9am-3pm daily. **Admission** 10kn. **No credit cards**. **Map** p285 E2.

Between the Sponza Palace and the Ploče Gate, this monastery is best known for its late Gothic cloisters and late 15th-century paintings of the Dubrovnik School in the museum. On the walls of the monastery church are a beautiful wooden crucifix by Paolo Veneziano from 1358 and *The Miracle of St Dominic*, a painting by renowned fin-de-siècle artist Vlaho Bukovac from Cavtat.

★ Rector's Palace

Pred Dvorom 3 (020 321 497). **Open** *Summer* 9am-6pm daily. *Winter* 9am-2pm daily. **Admission** 25kn; under-12s 10kn. **No credit cards**. **Map** p285 E3.

The most historic monument in Dubrovnik, the Rector's Palace was rebuilt twice. Firstly, by Onofrio della Cava of fountain fame, was in Venetian-Gothic style, visible in the window design once you ascend the grand staircase to the Rector's living quarters. Thereafter, Florentine Michelozzo Michelozzi was responsible for the loggia façade. On the ground floor, either side of a courtyard, are the prison and courtrooms of the Ragusa Republic, and a separate exhibition of Neolithic-Age finds from Vela Špilja on

In front of the clock tower, the baroque **Church of St Blaise** (open 8am-noon, 5-7pm daily), named after the protector of Dubrovnik through the centuries of trade, torment and tourism, was rebuilt after the 1667 earthquake. Inside, the altar, with a statue of the saint, is the biggest attraction. The stained-glass windows are a modern addition.

On the other side of St Blaise, the adjoining squares of Gundulićeva poljana and Bunićeva poljana are busy day and night. Market stalls cover the pavement in the morning, constant entertainment for diners and coffee drinkers at nearby terraces; bars kick into action after dark.

At the other end of Stradun, by the Pile Gate built in the 15th century, the main drawbridged entrance to the Old Town, stands **Onofrio's Great Fountain**, less ornate than how it looked before the 1667 earthquake. Behind the Franciscan church nearby, the **Franciscan monastery** (020 321 410, 9am-3pm daily; 10kn; *photo p284*), with beautiful cloisters, houses what is claimed to be the world's oldest pharmacy and a museum of religious artefacts.

The main modern attraction is **War Photo Limited**, two floors of conflict photography, of Dubrovnik and other recent clashes. Works by renowned photographers are displayed in temporary exhibitions throughout the summer.

Korčula. Upstairs, where each Rector resided for his month's stint, is a strange assortment of items: sedan chairs, carriages, magistrates' robes and wigs, portraits of local notables and Ivo Rudenjak's beautifully carved bookcase. One curiosity is the clocks, some set at quarter to six, the time in the evening when Napoleon's troops entered in 1806.

★ FREE Sponza Palace

Luža (020 321 032). **Open** 9am-2pm daily. **Admission** free. **Map** p285 D2.

The attractive, 16th-century former customs house and Ragusa mint is used to house the extensive state archives (by appointment only, phone ahead) and temporary exhibitions. Free to enter, a current long-term exhibition has been given space in a small room opposite the ticket office: the Memorial Room of the Dubrovnik Defenders. Covering the terrible 12 months from October 1991 (although keen to point out that isolated attacks continued until the summer of 1995), the exhibition contains portraits of the 300 defenders and civilians who died during the siege and the tattered remnant of the Croatian flag that flew atop strategic Mount Srdj.

★ War Photo Limited

Antuninska 6 (020 322 166/www.warphoto ltd.com). **Open** *June-Sept* 9am-9pm daily. *May, Oct* 10am-4pm Tue-Sat, 10am-2pm Sun. **Admission** 30kn. **No credit cards**. **Map** p285 C2.

Managed by New Zealand war photographer Wade Goddard, who came here in the early 1990s and stayed, this gallery could have easily limited its focus to the city's troubles. However, Goddard soon expanded its remit to exhibit regularly changing

Franciscan monastery. *See p283.*

works by some of the world's leading exponents of this brave art, illustrating flashpoints around the world. The first floor houses the current exhibition; the second shows highlights from previous shows plus images from Yugoslavia in the 1990s. You can also watch slow-paced slide shows on TV screens – none of which is easy viewing. Note that the gallery is open only during the summer. *Photo p286*.

Pile, Ploče, Gruž & Lapad

Ploče is the picturesque stretch of coastline and sliver of land running east from the gate of the same name towards Cavtat and Dubrovnik airport. Until relatively recently, coast and land were pretty much all that was to be found here. Traders would bring their wares over the hillsides by donkey to the Old Town and set up on open ground outside Ploče Gate. The view of Lokrum island, which lounges the length of Ploče, was enjoyed by these passing peasants from Konavle and Bosnia and the handful of nobles who built isolated villas overlooking the sea. However, the siren call of tourism encouraged villa owners to convert their homes and this is now an area of luxury hotels. It is also a hub of culture: one mansion was converted into the **Modern Art Gallery**, while the old quarantine barracks of **Lazareti** is now the DJ spot of the same name. By day

INSIDE TRACK CRUISE SHIPS

If there's one subject that annoys locals more than any other, it is cruise ships. Dubrovnik's authorities see fit to allow in a daily influx of up to ten vessels a day in high season, for the Old Town to be flooded, albeit briefly, with visitors reluctant to part with more than few kuna for a souvenir or two. Everyone complains about it – nothing is done. Such is the volume of traffic that in 2006, two ships locked anchors near the exclusive hotels lining Ploče seafront – high-paying guests had to be briefly evacuated for fear of a crash. A similar plight befell Bermuda, who limited cruise ships to 6,000 passengers a day. The loss in dock revenue was offset by an increase in spending per head around town. Dare Dubrovnik take the risk?

War Photo Limited. *See p284.*

you can lounge on adjoining **Banje** beach, the nearest one to the Old Town, although locals prefer **Sveti Jakov**, a 20-minute walk further along Frana Supila. Each hotel can also offer at least one decent restaurant and most have sea-view terraces.

Pile also overlooks a beach, **Penatur**, which is flanked by the **Lovrijenac** fortress and **Gradac Park**. The former, closed to the public except when it stages open-air performances of Shakespeare in summer, was the look-out post for the Ragusa Republic. It bears the motto, 'Liberty is not for sale, not even for gold', a proud summation of the city's independent spirit and somewhat contradicted by the republic's love of the yellow stuff. In similar vein, high above the hinterland, **Mount Srdj** witnessed brave defensive action by locals in 1991. Until the cablecar link is restored, scaling Srdj is a strenuous, mainly unshaded two-hour climb from the Pile Gate, via Jadranksa cesta. A particular word of warning: don't stray from the footpath as there may still be unexploded missiles on the hillside. At the top is a ruined Napoleonic fort, the hilltop cross you see illuminated at night from town and a breathtaking view. On hot afternoons, don't forget to pack water.

Shortly after Pile, main roads divide. One goes to the main **harbour** and **bus station** at **Gruž**; the other forks off for the twin-headed peninsula of **Lapad** and **Babin Kuk**. Each has been given over to leisure and relaxation, the hilly, verdant landscape sliced by main roads best accessed by Dubrovnik's vintage orange-and-white buses. Hotels dot the twisted shoreline, whose beaches include **Lapad** itself, beneath the

landmark **Hotel Kompas**; and the child-friendly **Copacabana** near the **Hotel Minčeta**, well equipped for water sports.

★ Modern Art Gallery
Frana Supila 23 (020 426 590/www.ugdubrovnik. com). **Open** 10am-8pm Tue-Sun. **Admission** 30kn. **No credit cards**. **Map** p281 E1.
A short walk from the Old Town, the wonderful former Banac Mansion contains four floors and nine rooms of exhibition space, for a permanent collection of 2,000 items (including many by Cavtat-born Vlaho Bukovac) and challenging contemporary shows. This is the only space in town with the scope and the vision to stage such work – it also commands stunning sea views.

INSIDE TRACK
BETINA ŠPILJA

Dubrovnik is surrounded by beaches – tourist-friendly ones such as Lapad and Banje, and ones preferred by locals such as Sveti Jakov and Vila. One little known but easily accessible from the old harbour is Betina špilja, a cave with a fine, white-pebble beach only accessible from the sea. It sits immediately under the Getaldić Mansion, former home of the 16th-century mathematician of the same name, who practised experiments here. Rent a taxi boat from the old port, arrange a pick-up time, take a picnic and the captain's number, and quality, relatively private, beach time can be yours.

Profile Ragusa

The rise and fall of the world's most progressive City State.

For 1,000 years Dubrovnik was the city state of Ragusa, the name given to it by the Italianate refugees who had fled Epidaurum, today's Cavtat, in the seventh century. A wily maritime power run by an enlightened council of local noblemen, Ragusa vied with Venice for Adriatic trade. The sovereignty of La Serenissima here was a short one. Rid of the Venetians by 1358, Ragusa, with its own currency and institutions, quickly blossomed.

The noblemen spoke a local version of Italian and governed a progressive centre of learning and commerce. The lower classes resided on the lower slopes of Mount Srdj and the streets north of Stradun, the dividing line. Although a strict class system was in force, slavery was abolished. There was a public health service, an orphanage, a home for old people, Europe's first pharmacy and an advanced water supply. And all this in the 1400s. Onofrio della Cava's water fountains still stand on Stradun; in 1991 they helped supply besieged residents with water more than 500 years after their installation.

With no royal intrigue, Ragusa thrived. Whenever the Turks threatened, Ragusa paid them off. Citizenship was bestowed upon the skilled and the entrepreneurial, Jews included.

Buildings of marble and stone replaced wooden ones. Ragusa's sailors worked a profitable fleet of 300 ships. Some went with Columbus to the New World in 1492 – ironically, the first step in robbing Ragusa of its riches when Atlantic trade links began to replace Mediterranean ones in importance.

As the economic tide was turning, a great earthquake struck in 1667. The rebuilding programme called for height restrictions in case of further disaster. A century later, Napoleon's forces entered Ragusa in 1806. The republic was abolished.

After Napoleon's defeat, the Habsburgs moved in to control Ragusa until their demise in 1918. During this time, as the local nobility died out, the city was central to the Croatian revival against Vienna. When it became part of the new Yugoslav state, it took its Slav name of Dubrovnik. Ruled from Belgrade, its lack of overland transport links and outdated trades saw economic decline and mass emigration to the Americas. The city claimed by Croatian Fascists, Mussolini, Hitler and Tito's Partisans was a living museum.

ALL IN THE NAME
The Latin name Ragusa derives from the word for precipice, *lausa*, of Greek origin.

DUBROVNIK & ISLANDS

DUBROVNIK & ISLANDS

Around Dubrovnik

The easiest trip is the taxi boat (every 30mins, 15mins journey time, Apr-Oct 9am-7pm daily; 35kn return) from the old harbour to unspoiled **Lokrum**, an island that is big and varied enough to swallow the visiting multitudes even during the high season. Covered in pine trees and dotted with rocky beaches, including a naturist one on the east coast, Lokrum is centrepieced by a ruined Napoleonic fort and botanical gardens (which are still filled with exotic plants and peacocks) set up by the ill-fated Habsburg royal Maximilian. A terrace restaurant is set by the 11th-century Benedictine monastery closed by the French 200 years ago. The monks are said to have left a curse on the island – Maximilian (famously shot by firing squad in Mexico) is one of a dozen notables connected with it who came to a sticky end. It is forbidden to spend the night on Lokrum – no local would want to.

To escape the daytime crowds, take a foot-passenger ferry from the main harbour at Gruž for the three (barely) inhabited of the 14-island Elafiti archipelago: **Koločep**, **Lopud** and **Šipan**. The nearest, Koločep, consists of a couple of modest settlements: Donje Čelo, site of the ferry port and only hotel; and Gornje Čelo, accessible by a pine-shaded footpath. Secluded pebble beaches, some naturist, mark the coastline. To stay over, the three-star **Villa Koločep** (open May-Oct, 020 757 025) or a few private rooms can accommodate. The most developed, but by no means built-up, is Lopud. Dotted with medieval churches, it was popular with local noblemen who built villas on the island, including the Rector, whose summer palace is in ruins. The three-star **Lafodia** hotel complex (open May-Oct, 020 759 022), with a pool, is a short walk from the ferry port. A path near the Grand Hotel, still under long-term reconstruction, leads over the hill to the other side of the island, and the lovely sandy beach of **Šunj** 15 minutes away. It faces Šipan, the largest of the islands, similarly dotted with a few old churches, noblemen's villas, Roman remains and two villages: Šipanska Luka and Sudjuradj. A five-kilometre (three-mile) road through a valley of olive groves links the two. Ferries stop at both. The **Hotel Šipan** (open May-Oct, 020 758 000) overlooks the harbour at Šipanska Luka. Private rooms are plentiful.

Head north from Dubrovnik and you find the village of **Trsteno**, known for its **Arboretum** (020 751 019, open summer 8am-6pm daily, winter 8am-3pm daily, 15kn), 16th-century botanical gardens around a Renaissance villa. The grounds run down to the sea. You either visit as part of an excursion from Dubrovnik or ask the driver to drop you 45 minutes out of

town on the regular service to Split. Between Trsteno and Dubrovnik is **Zaton Mali**, a small fishing village best known for the **Gverović-Orsan** restaurant, one of the best in south Dalmatia (*see p289*).

WHERE TO EAT

Atlas Club Nautika

Brsalje 3 (020 442 526). **Open** *Mid Jan-mid Dec* noon-midnight daily. **Credit** AmEx, DC, MC, V. **Map** p285 B2 ❶
Just outside the Pile Gate, Dubrovnik's most prestigious spot offers two panoramic terraces of starched white-tablecloth formality. To get full value for your holiday blow-out, book sea-view tables Nos.30-38 on the Penatur terrace or Nos.56, 57 or 64 on Lovrijenac. Chef Nikola Ivanišević insists on the freshest fish – shellfish feature in dishes from the Elafiti isles such as Lopud *brodet* with polenta. Budget diners can opt for the light lunch, an Adriatic salad or pasta.
▶ *Under the same management, Proto is almost as classy and inside the City Walls; see p292.*

Defne

Pucić Palace, Od Puča 1 (020 326 200/www.thepucic palace.com). **Open** *May-Oct* 11am-midnight daily. **Credit** AmEx, DC, MC, V. **Map** p285 D3 ❷
Defne occupies the roof terrace of the Old Town's five-star hotel, and is one of its three restaurants. Here, chef Ozgur Donertas puts the accent on flavoursome meat options from Turkey and the Levant as well as maritime ones that come from closer to home. Defne prides itself on its traditional seafood soup with real sea stone.
▶ *In the same hotel, the year-round Café Royale and Razonada wine bar also feature stellar creations by chef Ozgur Donertas.*

INSIDE TRACK
DUBROVNIK
SUMMER FESTIVAL

Celebrating its 60th anniversary in 2009, the **Dubrovnik Summer Festival** is Croatia's most prestigious arts event. High-brow to the point of staid, the Dubrovačke ljetne igre ('Dubrovnik Summer Games') concentrates on faithful renditions of Shakespeare and his local literary counterpart, Marin Držić. Many shows take place at atmospheric, open-air stages set up around the Old Town. Although many events sell out, passing visitors may enjoy the sundry street performances and processions which run for the length of the festival, traditionally July 10 to August 25.

Dubrovački kantun.

★ Dubrovački kantun

*Boškovićeva 5 (020 331 911/091 699 4966
mobile)*. **Open** 10.30am-4pm, 6.30pm-midnight
daily. **Credit** MC, V. **Map** p285 D2 **3**
Andrej Di Leo's cosy restaurant in the heart of the
Old Town is a real treat. Not two minutes from the
tourist traps of Prijeko, the kantun offers healthy
local vegetables, meats and cheeses in a homely
atmosphere. Appetisers are a speciality, of which
we particularly recommend the house platter of
smoked ham, cheeses, anchovies and rocket. Out of
season, try the *pašticada* beef stew. Dalmatian flans
provide a fitting dessert.

★ Gil's Cuisine & Pop Lounge

*Sv Dominika (020 322 222/www.gilsdubrovnik.
com)*. **Open** noon-midnight daily. **Credit** AmEx,
DC, MC, V. **Map** p285 E2 **4**
The big arrival of 2007, Russian-owned Gil's is perfectly located atop the old port. Gilles Camilleri's
fusion menu offers starters such as seashells panna
cotta, and black ravioli with lobster sauce; the
marine-inspired theme is continued with mains such
as mullet and tandoori spices, and black-olive
crusted sea bass with artichokes. Desserts (pineapple ravioli, soft Caribbean chocolate cake) provide
an honorable finale to a fine evening. The wine cellar comprises 6,000 bottles while the terrace bar provides the best cocktails in town. Beg for a booth in
the gun chambers close to the sea.

★ Gverović-Orsan

*Stilkovića 43, Zaton Mali (020 891 267/www.
gverovic-orsan.hr)*. **Open** *Mar-Dec* noon-midnight
Mon-Sat. **Credit** AmEx, MC, V.

In the fishing village of Zaton Mali 7km (4 miles)
north-west of town, this old boathouse was converted
into a restaurant by Niko Gverović in 1966. It is one
of the best in Croatia, beautifully located, reasonably
priced, family-run and a gastronomic winner. Niko
junior runs the place with his mother, Mira, producing the speciality black risotto Orsan: four kinds of
shells and shrimps sautéed in wine and lemon and
mixed with rice soaked in black squid ink. The venue
has its own beach (and shower), so you can take a
dip while your dinner is cooking. *Photo p291.*
▶ *Another classic out-of-town venue is the
Kapetanova Kuća at Mali Ston; see p307.*

Kn Kamenice

*Gundulićeva poljana 8 (020 323 685/020
421 499)*. **Open** *Apr-Oct* 7am-10pm daily.
Nov-Mar 7am-4pm daily. **No credit cards**.
Map p285 D3 **5**
Timeless, traditional and tremendously cheap, this
locals' favourite has hardly changed despite the new
tourist traps around it. A prime site by the market
has not affected prices, decor or staff dress.
Waitresses in mules deliver plates of mussels, squid
and titular oysters in white-tile surroundings. Watch
out for early winter closing times.

★ Levanat

*Šetalište Niki i Meda Pucića (020 435 352/
098 427 794 mobile)*. **Open** *Mar-Oct* 10.30am-
midnight daily. **Credit** MC, V. **Map** p280 A2 **6**
Set in the bay between Lapad and Babin Kuk, the
Levanat is signposted atop four flights of steps from
the main road and on the coastal footpath from
Lapad beach. The trek is well worth the effort.

Make the most of London life

TIME OUT GUIDES
WRITTEN BY
LOCAL EXPERTS
visit timeout.com/shop

Time Out
Guides

Marija Sutić's sassy and flavoursome menu – fried rocket and mozzarella appetiser, prawns garnished with honey and sage – can be savoured by the sea or in a stone, candlelit interior.

▶ *Year-round, try the quality local classics at nearby Komin (Iva Dulčića 136, 020 448 613).*

Kn Lokanda Peskarija

Na Ponti (020 324 750). **Open** 8am-midnight daily. **No credit cards. Map** p285 E3 **⑦**
Everyone's favourite cheapie ensures queues around the old harbour all summer. Nothing fancy here, just good domestic dishes at knockdown prices swiftly served by overworked staff. The management has somewhat overreached itself, placing tables in every available space, but few seem to be complaining.

▶ *Long queues form here on busy summer evenings, but you're almost sure to get a table at adjacent Poklisar or the Taverna Arsenal; see below and p292.*

Nishta

Palmotićeva 5/Prijeko 30 (092 218 8612 mobile). **Open** 6-11pm daily. **Credit** MC, V. **Map** p285 C2 **⑧**
Dubrovnik's first vegetarian restaurant opened in 2008, in the same building as the equally popular Smoothie Bar. Nishta offers miso and gazpacho soups, salads such as the *om* of mixed veg, dried figs and crispy bread, and *tempehritos*, burrito-like treats with tempeh. A fun staff, Laško beer and quality wines by the glass keep the mood bubbly.

▶ *The Dubrovački kantun also has plenty of vegetarian choices; see p289.*

★ Orhan

Od Tabakarije 1 (020 414 183). **Open** 11am-11pm daily. **Credit** MC, V. **Map** p285 A2 **⑨**
Perched between the fortresses of Bokar and Lovrijenac, and with the sea crashing on the rocks below its terrace, Orhan is dramatically located. From his lengthy menu, chef Ivića Miloš might recommend fillet steak in gorgonzola sauce or châteaubriand for two. There's an excellent salad bar with grilled peppers and aubergines, and Grgić heads a decent wine list.

Orsan Yacht Club

Marina Orsan, Ivana pl Zajca 2 (020 435 933). **Open** 9.30am-11pm daily. **Credit** MC, V. **Map** p280 B2 **⑩**
Here in Gruž Bay, a dozen tables sit on a sea-lapped terrace in the shade of a huge pine tree, making for a summer retreat that is enjoyed by cats and regular local diners alike. The Orsan Yacht Club's menu highlights include oyster soup, octopus salad, lobster and Dalmatian rib-eye steak. Wine prices are more than reasonable.

Poklisar

Ribarnica 1 (020 322 176). **Open** 8am-11pm daily. **Credit** AmEx, DC, MC, V. **Map** p285 E2 **⑪**
With its terraces flanking a prominent square by the old harbour, the Poklisar fills up tight in high season. However, prices, given the setting, are reasonable and among the standards is the odd gem: shrimps in saffron sauce or home-made gnocchi with gorgonzola and rocket. Desserts deserve a detour as

Gverović-Orsan. *See p289.*

you arrive from Lokrum: walnut pancakes or wild-fruit parfaits. Get here before the cheesy live music drowns out the lap of the sea.

Porat

Hilton Imperial, Marijana Blažica 2 (020 320 320/www.hilton.com). **Open** 7am-11pm daily. **Credit** AmEx, DC, MC, V. **Map** p285 A1 ⑫
The flagship restaurant of the Hilton can provide local treats – the air-dried, smoked ham and cheese starter, for example – as well as the pan-seared and the rosemary-tinted. The grilled lamb ribs from the lava-stone grill have a rosemary lard crust; the pan-seared tuna has been marinated in lime and rosemary. As you'd expect, it doesn't come cheap but it's worth every lipa if you're after quality. There's decent food available in the lounge bar too.

Proto

Široka 1 (020 323 234). **Open** 11am-11pm daily. **Credit** AmEx, DC, MC, V. **Map** p285 C2 ⑬
From the same family as the upmarket Nautika, the fish-oriented Proto cannot fail to satisfy. As well as squid and lobster in simple, superbly balanced sauces, there's fresh shellfish from nearby Pelješac. The fish soup may be the best in town and you could spend an enjoyable hour over the fish platter for two. There's a fine selection of wines, meal choices for children and Old-Town views from the first-floor terrace. Booking essential.

Taverna Arsenal

Pred Dvorom 1 (020 321 065). **Open** noon-midnight daily. **Credit** AmEx, DC, MC, V. **Map** p285 D3 ⑭
Attached to landmark café graDskavana, this former weaponry occupies a vaulted interior and terrace by the old port. Many domestic wines and *rakija* spirits complement grilled fresh fish (sea bass, swordfish) and top-notch steaks. A smart but unpretentious local clientele parties to live music here on Saturdays.

Tovjerna Sesame

Dante Alighieria (020 412 910). **Open** 8am-11pm daily. **Credit** MC, V. **Map** p281 D2 ⑮
Ideal for mid-priced meals, morning coffees and evening drinks, the Sesame has tables in its front porch, its characterful main bar and its back restaurant, where oyster soup, *Šipan* salad and the house risotto of clams and squid are served.

★ Wanda

Prijeko 8 (098 944 9317 mobile). **Open** *Apr-Nov* 10.30am-1am daily. **Credit** AmEx, DC, MC, V. **Map** p285 D2 ⑯
The wonderful Wanda has breathed life into staid Prijeko, offering top Mediterranean cuisine at reasonable prices. Local Goran Starčić worked in the restaurant industry in Los Angeles before returning to set up in business back home. His team put

together simple, well-conceived dishes using fresh, locally sourced ingredients: soups, appetisers, salads, risottos, and first and second courses. Look out for the seasonal daily specials. Top service too.

WHERE TO DRINK

Buža I

Accessed from Ilije Sarake (no phone). **Open** *Summer* 8am-late daily. **No credit cards**. **Map** p285 D4 ❶
The more haphazard of the two 'Buža' open-air bars, which are cut into the sea-facing rocks, Buža I welcomes sunbathers, divers, drinkers and, more recently, filmgoers. Orson Welles, Jimi Hendrix and others are beamed onto a large screen in this cluster of multi-levelled rocks, planed flat for maritime fun. Dive in, clamber out up the metal steps, order an 18kn Karlovačko beer, and watch a film. It's all behind a doorway marked '8-20' diagonally facing the Ekvinocijo restaurant.

Buža II

Crijevićeva 9 (no phone). **Open** 10am-late daily. **No credit cards**. **Map** p285 C4 ❷
The more well-known of the cliff-face bars. For this one follow signs ('Cold Drinks') by the Jesuit Church and along Od Margarite. A straw roof protects you from the open sun by day; fabulous sunsets ensure that all the tables are full in high season.

Casablanca

Zamanjina 7 (no phone). **Open** 5.30pm-1am daily. **No credit cards**. **Map** p285 D2 ❸
Reasonable candidate for best bar in the Old Town, with tasteful decor and decent sounds. Old film and beer ads brighten the space; posters promote long-forgotten Olympics and pool-table lightshades of coloured glass advertise Coors beer. Cocktails come in creamy or killer varieties, football or music videos are screened and staff buzz about in daft blue shirts with mottos on them. Recommended.

Dubravka 1836

Brsalje (020 426 319). **Open** *Summer* 9am-midnight daily. *Winter* 9am-8.30pm daily. **Credit** MC, V. **Map** p285 B2 ❹
Another makeover job, this time to a landmark café by the Pile Gate. Its interior is now a modernised, sunken room brightened by colourful, sticky cakes and old photos of the trams that terminated here when intellectuals, writers and the chess society were regulars. A spot on the sea-facing terrace is ideal for a glass of Laško and a ham-and-cheese sandwich. Desserts include a *savijačka* of apple or cherry, cake slice and strawberries and cream.

D'Vino

Palmotićeva 4a (020 321 223/www.columis. net/dvino). **Open** 5pm-midnight daily. **No credit cards**. **Map** p285 C2 ❺

Opened in the summer of 2008, Dubrovnik's first wine bar is the brainchild of Canadian Cameron Wilson, who has stocked this small, neat space with more than 100 varieties, at least 80 available by the glass. Every decent Istrian, Slavonian and Dalmatian label is here, plus Italian, Spanish, French, New World and Canadian Pillitteri. Meat and cheese platters (40kn) may accompany.

▶ *If you'd like to buy wine during the day, head for the Vinoteka Dubrovnik; see p296.*

Festival Café
Stradun 28 (020 321 148). **Open** 9am-midnight daily. **Credit** MC, V. **Map** p285 C2 ⑥

This landmark venue on Stradun is pricey even by the standards of Dubrovnik, but it remains popular all the same – everyone meets at the Festival. Breakfasts go for 55kn, dishes of the day 80kn and seasonal mixed drinks 50kn, perhaps a frozen cappuccino with Bailey's. It's got a proper bar counter, a long interior brightened by old Cinzano ads and outdoor seating. Fruit frappés and home-made cakes complete the picture. *Photo p294.*

graDskavana
Luža 2 (020 321 414). **Open** *Summer* 8am-2am daily. *Winter* 8am-11pm daily. **Credit** MC, V. **Map** p285 D3 ⑦

A modern makeover of this vintage coffeehouse has changed its decor (a terrace of neat red-and-blue chairs), its name (silly use of lower case) and drinks. Half-a-dozen cocktails (mojito 60kn, cosmopolitan 55kn) now complement wines by the glass (Pošip 22kn, Malvazija 32kn), cakes, coffees and sandwiches. The clientele hasn't changed a bit – locals of every type and age fill the terrace all day long.

Hemingway Bar
Pred Dvorom (no phone). **Open** noon-1am daily. **Credit** MC, V. **Map** p285 D3 ⑧

Prominent cocktail bar opposite the Rector's Palace offers mixed drinks by the glass or pitcher for four. No real surprises among the long selection, daiquiris and mojitos mixed with Havana 3, a combination of Pernod and Champagne in a Death in the Afternoon, and a pleasant buzz around the bar and terrace.

Libertina
Zlatarska 3 (no phone). **Open** noon-midnight daily. **No credit cards.** **Map** p285 D2 ⑨

This characterful shoebox of a bar is known as 'Luci' after Luci Capurso, owner and ex-member of vintage beat combo Dubrovački Trubaduri. Shying away from his Eurovision Song Contest past, Luci serves the regulars, pleasingly oblivious to the piles of money being made at inferior bars on his doorstep.

Ludwig
Zamanjina 7 (no phone). **Open** noon-midnight daily. **No credit cards.** **Map** p285 D2 ⑩

Even this grunge bar in a Stradun side street has its own dinky little lantern, although you can't see any middle-aged tourists lingering over a pint. Gogol, Mogwai, *Kill Bill* and Hendrix all get a decorative look-in, but it's the hard-living black-clad drinkers hunched around the counter that make the place.

Roxy
Bana Jelačića 9 (no phone). **Open** 10am-1am daily. **No credit cards.** **Map** p280 C2 ⑪

Set on a small stretch lined with party bars, the Roxy is a musos' hangout, with letters from the Beatles Fan Club, an old Animals album and an

Buža II.

original *Penny Lane* 45, all framed and mounted. There's a Seeburg jukebox, too, just for show – chat-level sounds come from the CD player.

Sunset Lounge

Hotel Dubrovnik Palace, Masarykov put 20 (020 430 000/www.dubrovnikpalace.hr). **Open** noon-1am daily. **Credit** AmEx, DC, MC, V. **Map** p280 A3 ⑫

The titular sunset view in full panorama, chic surroundings, a piano player – and happy-hour drinks in the afternoon. Cocktails (60kn) comprise 35 standards, there are specialist Perković brandies (carob, fig, nut) and wines run from a basic 20kn to the best local labels rarely found by the glass. On a clear day you can see Mljet – this is honeymoon material.

Talir

Antuninska 5 (020 323 293). **Open** noon-1am daily. **No credit cards. Map** p285 C2 ⑬

Classic actors' bar in the Old Town, the Talir has had a constant buzz and bonhomie about it since opening in 1983 – just look at the snapshots on the walls. The cosy, wooden interior is packed on summer nights – join the drinkers blocking the stepped passageway outside or get in early and find a seat.

Troubador

Buniceva poljana 2 (020 323 476). **Open** *Summer* 9am-3am daily. *Winter* 5-11pm daily. **No credit cards. Map** p285 D3 ⑭

The most famous bar in town might look like a billboard for T-Mobile, but it's still the lovely old Troubador. Run by Marco, one of the Dubrovački Trubadori, this is a touchstone for the artists, musicians and entertainers of his beat generation. It's also a money-making machine. In summer, the terrace is given over to free jazz concerts and waiters rush between tables packed with tourists.

► *If you're looking for this kind of atmosphere without the crowds, head for Libertina on the other side of Stradun; see p293.*

MUSIC & NIGHTLIFE

Belvedere

Sv Jakov beach, Vlaha Bukovca (no phone/ www.clubpages.net). **Open** *Summer* according to programme. **No credit cards**.

Quite possibly the best DJ nights in Croatia run three times a summer in this ruined congress hotel by Sveti Jakov beach at the far end of Ploče. The setting is as spectacular as the quality of DJs on offer – look out for posters all over town.

► *If you're in town when Belvedere is not running, Lazareti also has quality DJs with a sea view; see p295.*

Capitano

Izmedju Vrta 2 (no phone). **Open** 6pm-4am Wed-Sat. **No credit cards**.

Everyone's favourite pick-up joint, this disco-bar near the Pile Gate is intimate but with room for dancing and opportunity for eye contact.

East-West

Banje beach, Frana Supila (020 412 220/ www.ew-dubrovnik.com). **Open** *Summer* 5pm-3am daily. *Winter* varies. **Credit** MC, V.

A café-restaurant by day, by night East-West is transformed into a clubby beachside cocktail bar.

Festival Café. *See p293.*

The clientele is chic – it's hired for fashion parties – but despite this the place is far from intimidating and the prices are reasonable.

Factory Club
Put Republike (no phone/www.clubpages.net). **Open** according to programme. **No credit cards**.
Opening at the end of October 2008 with a set from DJ Darren Emerson of 'Born Slippy' fame, the Factory gives the local scene a much needed shot in the arm – expect a full agenda in 2009/10.

Latino Club Fuego
Brsalje 11 (020 312 871). **Open** *Summer* 10.30pm-4am daily. *Winter* 10.30pm-4am Thur-Sat. **No credit cards**.
There is little Latin about this last-stop dance-and-drink den, an all-too-easy slide down from the Capitano (*see above*) by the Pile Gate. The nominal entry fee counts towards a first drink.

Lazareti
Lazareti complex, Frana Supila 8 (020 324 633). **Open** according to programme. **No credit cards**.
The best year-round nightspot is set in this old stone ex-quarantine barracks. Pay your 50kn at the gate – more for major events – and head down to an open courtyard under the stars. The main building is at the bottom: a stage for DJ decks and live acts; a dancefloor, and a balcony area with bar. *Photo p296.*

Orlando Klub
Braniteja Dubrovnika 41 (020 312 674/ www.klub-orlando.com). **Open** 5.30pm-late daily. **No credit cards**.
The pierced and the tattoed bowl down from the Pile Gate to a guard hut outside an old hospital complex. Down a path and across a garden strewn with beer cans, they find like-minded souls outside a bemuralled building within which are a stage, DJ decks and side rooms full of recalcitrant teenagers up way past their bedtime: the Orlando Klub.

Revelin Club
Revelin Fort, Sv Dominika (020 322 164/ www.revelinclub.com). **Open** 9.30pm-2am Wed, Thur; 9.30pm-3am Fri, Sat. **No credit cards**. **Map** p285 E1.
This key nightspot is set in the 16th-century fort where the Ragusa senate convened, its terrace and cocktail bar above the old port. Inside is packed with a young, dance-hungry crowd.

SHOPPING

Dubrovačka kuća
Od sv Dominika (020 322 092). **Open** 9am-9.30pm Mon-Sat; 9am-7.30pm Sun. **Credit** AmEx, MC, V. **Map** p285 E2.

Talir.

High-quality treats for sale here include local spirits, sweets, posters, olive oils, regional wines and bath salts. A link with the Museum of Arts and Crafts in Zagreb means beautiful ceramics and glassware at affordable prices.

Eminence Art Workshop
Kunićeva 4 (no phone). **Open** 10am-10pm daily. **Credit** AmEx, DC, MC, V. **Map** p285 D2.
At this tasteful crafts store, Emin sits at a desk carving female figures, African in style but with a Med feel. Jewellery and quirky, colourful hand-painted wooden fish are also on offer.

Gundulićeva poljana market
Gundulićeva poljana (no phone). **Open** 6am-1pm Mon-Sat. **No credit cards**. **Map** p285 D3.
The ideal place to pick up your beach picnic contents is this popular market in the heart of the Old Town. It mainly sells fruit and veg but you'll also find nuts, olive oil, lavender, honey and strong local spirits.

Ivana Bačura
Zlatarska 3 (091 543 1321 mobile/www.ivana bacura.com). **Open** 9.30am-6.30pm Mon-Fri; 9.30am-12.30pm Sat. **Credit** AmEx, DC, MC, V. **Map** p285 D2.
This Zagreb-based designer has a contemporary and personal touch to hand-made jewellery – stylish, simple and quite often silver. Bačura's use of stone is calm – muted reds, greens and blues – and her rings and earrings are nicely understated.

Lazareti. *See p295.*

Ronchi
Lučarica 2 (020 323 699). **Open** 9am-noon,
4-7pm Mon-Fri; 9am-noon Sat. **Credit** AmEx,
DC, MC, V. **Map** p285 D3.
In business since 1858, this hat shop is a local insti-
tution, today run by English-speaking Marina Ronchi
Grabovac. Look out for her classic summer designs.

Vinoteka Dubrovnik
Stradun (020 321 777). **Open** 10am-8pm daily.
Credit AmEx, DC, MC, V. **Map** p285 D2.
Halfway along Stradun, this small shop contains a
decent selection of local and global wines. For a standard bottle to take to the beach, you'll find cheaper
at one of the local groceries outside the Pile Gate.

ARTS & CULTURE

Jadran Cinema
Iza Roka (general information 020 321 425).
Open *Summer* according to programme.
No credit cards. Map p285 B3.
Long-established open-air cinema in the Old Town
with quaint old projecting equipment and wooden
seats – staff hand out cushions as you go in.

Marin Držić Theatre
*Pred Dvorom 3 (020 321 088/www.kazaliste-
dubrovnik.hr).* **Open** according to programme.
Credit MC, V. **Map** p285 D3.
The city's main theatre, which is named after its
most celebrated playwright, Shakespeare contemporary Marin Držić, concentrates on the literary heritage of Dubrovnik. It's also a central venue for
summer's Dubrovnik Festival.

Sloboda Cinema
Luža (general information 020 321 425).
Open According to programme. **No credit
cards. Map** p285 D3.
This year-round cinema right on the main square
shows local and global features. It's also the main
information point for summer's high-profile Libertas
Film Festival.

WHERE TO STAY

Apartments Nives
*Nikole Božđarevića 7 (tel/fax 020 323 181/
098 243 699 mobile/www.dubrovnik-palace.
com).* **Rates** *Summer* €80 apartment. *Winter*
€50 apartment. **No credit cards. Map**
p285 C3 ❶

INSIDE TRACK MARIN DRŽIĆ

Dubrovnik's most renowned hero, with
his own theatre, museum and (recently
unveiled) statue in the Old Town, was not
the noble figure local legend would have
you believe. In fact, this contemporary of
Shakespeare was forced to flee Ragusa
after falling out with the powers-that-be,
living out his days penniless in Italy,
most notably Siena and Venice, where
he died a pauper. Until his plays became
standards, Držić was most remembered
for his nickname, 'The Otter' – the writer
had a thing about wearing fur.

Handy apartments in the Old Town, each with a kitchen, fridge and washing machine. No arguing with the price, especially out of season; the facilities have been improved and the furnishings upgraded.

★ Berkeley Hotel

Andrije Hebranga 116a (020 494 160/fax 020 494 170/www.berkeleyhotel.hr). **Rates** €120-€140 double. **Credit** AmEx, DC, MC, V. **Map** p280 C1 **❷**

Opened in 2007, this lovely aparthotel comprises 20 beautiful suites and one apartment, conceived by ex-Sydney restaurateurs Nick and Marija. All suites have kitchens; long-term stays are also encouraged with overnight stays on one of two yachts. Chef Marija runs the in-house konoba, using steaks the size they used to sizzle in Oz.

Hilton Imperial

Marijana Blažica 2 (020 320 320/fax 020 320 220/http://beta.hilton.co.uk/dubrovnik). **Rates** €200-€400 double. **Credit** AmEx, DC, MC, V. **Map** p285 A1 **❸**

Occupying a grand, fin-de-siècle building near the Pile Gate, the Hilton has location although without the beachside grace of the other five-star venues in town. With its gym and indoor pool open 24 hours, this is a place for execs to convene. Bedrooms are comfortable but unmemorable, many standard ones without sea views. The Porat restaurant (*see p292*), however, is a real winner.

★ Hotel Bellevue

Pera Čingrije 7 (020 330 000/fax 020 330 100/www.hotel-bellevue.hr). **Rates** from €250 double. **Credit** AmEx, DC, MC, V. **Map** p280 C2 **❹**

Opened in February 2007, and reopened in June 2008 after a planning problem, this feat of engineering is the most outlandish project yet by hotelier Goran Štrok (*see p300* **Profile**). The venue, cut into the cliff facing the sea, features the interior design of his wife Renata, using local woods and granite. All the rooms have a sea view, as do the spa and Vapor restaurant. The Nevera restaurant sits on the hotel's very own private beach below.

★ Hotel Dubrovnik Palace

Masarykov put 20 (020 430 000/fax 020 430 100/www.dubrovnikpalace.hr). **Rates** from €200 double. **Credit** AmEx, DC, MC, V. **Map** p280 A3 **❺**

This ten-floor, 308-room luxury hotel reconfigured in 2004 was conceived in 1972, set in woodland paths at the tip of Lapad, in full view of the Elafiti isles. Today this is what everyone sees from their balcony, from the four bars, three restaurants, four pools and gym. New is the tenth-floor sushi bar, Satu.

▶ *Non-guests can still enjoy the knockout view from here by having a drink in the Sunset Lounge; see p294.*

INSIDE TRACK DIVLJA LIGA

Split for football, Zadar for basketball and Dubrovnik for... water polo. To an outsider Croatia's most exclusive destination may not have the sporting tradition of its Dalmatian rivals, but for any local, summer's Wild League tournament is as high-profile as any event in the country. Many expats time their visit around it. Involving ex-professionals and complete novices, this open-sea tourney pits beach team against beach team, veteran against teenager, building up to the grand final in early August in the old harbour. Locals pack the stands built around a three-quarter size regulation water-polo pool; many also moor their boats around it. Although completely amateur, divlja liga generates pride, passion and aggression to warrant a phalanx of TV cameras, also here to film the Croatian celebrities who turn up year after year.

Hotel Dubrovnik President

Iva Dulčića 39 (general information 052 465 000/fax 020 435 622/www.valamar.com). **Rates** €160-€320 double. **Credit** AmEx, DC, MC, V. **Map** p280 A2 **❻**

This leading lodging of the Valamar group has its own section of beach; each of the 181 rooms has a balcony view of the sea and Elafiti Islands beyond. There's an indoor pool, children's entertainment and access to nearby tennis courts.

★ Hotel Excelsior

Frana Supila 12 (020 353 353/fax 020 353 555/www.hotel-excelsior.hr). **Rates** from €250 double. **Credit** AmEx, DC, MC, V. **Map** p281 E1 **❼**

The grand opening of 2008 was the reopening of Dubrovnik's most prestigious hotel, following a 22-million euro refit. Built in 1913, this villa became the Hotel Excelsior in 1930. Royals, writers, movie stars, they all stayed here. Acquired by Goran Štrok (*see p300*) in 2000, it now features four restaurants, three pools, a piano bar and spa. The adjoining Villa Rustica also contains luxury lodging for six.

Hotel Grand Villa Argentina

Frana Supila 14 (020 440 555/fax 020 432 524/www.gva.hr). **Rates** from €200 double. **Credit** AmEx, DC, MC, V. **Map** p281 E1 **❽**

This five-star villa-and-hotel complex has been improved by newly opened Villa Sheherezade, where up to 12 people can relax in opulence for €6,000 a day. The main rates given are for the two

DUBROVNIK & ISLANDS

lovely villas, the Argentina and the Glavić, with a pool, sauna and terrace over a private beach. The Orsula and Hotel Argentina are slightly cheaper.

Hotel Kompas
Šetalište Kralja Zvonimira 56 (020 352 000/ fax 020 435 877/www.hotel-kompas.hr). **Rates** from €90 double. **Credit** AmEx, DC, MC, V. **Map** p280 B2
Now in the Štrok chain, the refitted Kompas and its terrace restaurant dominate Lapad beach. With a sauna, gym, an outdoor pool and indoor one with sea water, the Kompas is still a fair choice for families in the shoulder months. Tennis courts are nearby, the busy pebbly beach steps away. Nearly half the 115 rooms have sea-view balconies.

Hotel Lero
Iva Vojnovića 14 (020 341 333/fax 020 332 133/www.hotel-lero.hr). **Rates** €70-€150 double. **Credit** AmEx, DC, MC, V. **Map** p280 C2 ❿
The Socialist-style Lero is cheap and within easy reach of the Old Town, bus station and ferry terminal at Gruž. Bargain full-board deals are offered year-round. Half the rooms have a sea view.

★ Hotel More
Kardinala Stepinca 33 (020 494 200/fax 020 494 210/www.hotel-more.hr). **Rates** from €150 double. **Credit** AmEx, DC, MC, V. **Map** p280 C2 ⓫
Opened in 2007, this lush, waterfront five-star comprises 34 luxurious rooms and three suites, most with a sea view, an outdoor pool, lounge bar and the top Molteni international restaurant.

Hotel Stari Grad
Od Sigurate 4 (020 321 373/fax 020 321 256/www.hotelstarigrad.com). **Rates** €85-€135 single; €120-€200 double. **Credit** AmEx, DC, MC, V. **Map** p285 C2 ⓬
The dinky Stari Grad is a rare find in the Old Town. The quiet rooms are large enough to accommodate an extra bed (€50) if necessary, and breakfast is served on the fifth-floor roof terrace. The rooms are tasteful but none have a view. Half are singles, making the hotel particularly suitable for the independent visitor here to explore Dubrovnik's treasures.

Hotel Uvala
Masarykov put 6 (020 433 580/fax 020 433 590/www.hotelimaestral.com). **Closed** Nov-Mar. **Rates** €125-€260 double. **Credit** AmEx, DC, MC, V. **Map** p280 B3 ⓭
The newest and only four-star Maestral hotel, the Uvala has a spacious spa centre with full treatments, indoor and outdoor pools, a steam room, sauna and solarium. The other four – Adriatic, Komodor, Splendid and Vis – are resort hotels on the same main road towards the coast at Lapad. Their details are all on this website.

Hotel Grand Villa Argentina. *See p297.*

Importanne Resort
Kardinala Stepinca 31 (020 440 100/fax 020 440 200/www.importanneresort.com). **Rates** from €100 double. **Credit** AmEx, DC, MC, V. **Map** p280 A3 ⓮
Opened in 2007, this complex on the Lapad headland comprises two holiday hotels, the Neptun and the Ariston; and two upscale properties, the Importanne Suites and Villa Elita. The fifth element, and the one that brings the others here in the first place, is a Blue Flag beach and the aromatic pine trees all around. The facilities (massage rooms, hydromassage showers, seawater pools) are second-to-none in Dubrovnik.

★ Karmen Apartments
Bandureva 1 (020 323 433/098 619 282 mobile/www.karmendu.com). **Rates** from €55 apartment. **No credit cards.** **Map** p285 E4 ⓯
Four comfortable year-round apartments at affordable prices not five minutes' walk from the old port. Bohemian touches reflect the past of genial host Marc van Bloemen, whose parents were movers and shakers in the 1960s – that's an original Marcel Marceau self-portrait propped against the wall. Born in London's Troubadour folk club, Marc spent his youth here, and is happy to pass on all years of advice to all-comers. Highly recommended. *Photo p302.*

Kazbek Hotel
Lapadska obala 25 (020 362 900/fax 020 362 909/www.kazbekdubrovnik.com). **Rates** from €350 double. **Credit** AmEx, DC, MC, V. **Map** p280 C2 ⓰
The key new opening of 2008 is this conversion of the villa of the aristocratic Zamanje family (1573) into a five-star hotel of a dozen rooms, one apartment, three restaurants and an outdoor pool with a bar around it. A ten-seat speedboat and yacht are available for guests' use.

Profile Goran Štrok

The man driving Dubrovnik's hotel revolution.

From Tito-era mass tourism to luxury Med destination par excellence – Dubrovnik's transformation has been astonishing, and no-one has done more to achieve it than Goran Štrok. The change has been all the more remarkable considering that most of the top-class hotels this racing-driver-turned-hotelier has reconfigured were either damaged or wrecked by bombing in the early 1990s.

Belgrade-born Štrok studied law at Zagreb University before taking up motor racing in his early twenties, winning seven national titles. Once he retired, Štrok put his experience to use in foreign trade, construction and property development. After successful operations in the UK, Spain and the Far East, Štrok looked to revitalise the tourism industry in his homeland – it was 1994 and Croatia was still very much at war.

Despite the risks, Štrok concentrated on major hotels, starting with the Bonavia in relatively unaffected Rijeka. Croatia's northern port was then a shabby transit town, unused and unloved. Bringing in his wife Renata, an accomplished interior designer, Štrok took five years and 13 million euros to convert a white elephant into the leading business hotel in Croatia, a country which was now emerging from war to re-embrace tourism. Rijeka itself was the hub of a burgeoning international transport network between Italy, Slovenia, Croatia and Budapest.

By the time the revamped Bonavia opened in 2000, Štrok had formed the Wren's Group, renovating prestigious hotel properties in the UK (Windsor, the Cotswolds, Scotland); he now set his sights on Croatia's jewel, Dubrovnik.

The town then had only one five-star, the Excelsior, virtually moribund since Richard and Liz were regulars in the 1960s. Štrok bought it in December 2000. Four months later, he nabbed the ruined Bellevue.

FASHION ŠTROK
Another member of the Štrok family, daughter Vanya, is one half of design duo Gharani Štrok, along with fellow fashion graduate Nargess Gharani.

Within a year, Štrok had the equally devastated Dubrovnik Palace and by 2003, the Hotel Kompas. Four key waterfront venues were now under his control. Štrok could have gone for the easy option, made basic material improvements to each and creamed off the profits. Instead, he sold his operations in Scotland and the Seychelles to pour a fortune into making Dubrovnik the glamorous destination it used to be.

Under the umbrella of newly founded Adriatic Luxury Hotels, Štrok spent 45 million euros to create a five-star conference and spa hotel out of the Dubrovnik Palace. Štrok may have conceived this ten-floor, luxury leisure and conference complex (308 sea-facing rooms and suites; nine bars, restaurants and a nightclub, four pools, spa centre) – and Renata had a hand in much of the interior design – but the original location engineered by Vincek in 1972 needed little improvement. Emerging from dense woodland to the Lapad headland and a floor-to-ceiling view of blue sea, blue sky and the occasional island, on a clear day you can see Mljet. Opened in May 2004, the Dubrovnik Palace ushered in a new era for the city. No longer was Dubrovnik a pitiful place of post-war struggle – this was a chic, high-end, Med destination, along the lines of a Monte Carlo or a Capri. And it was Štrok's vision and business savvy that created it. Hollywood stars, visiting dignitaries, they stayed at the Dubrovnik Palace.

Štrok followed this success with somewhere even more ambitious: the Hotel Bellevue. Here the Štroks really pushed the boat out. What was a two-star ruin became a spectacular five-star spa hotel. Some 24 million euros created 93 rooms

and suites, all hi-tech, all with a sea-view balcony – and all of this cut into a sheer cliff hanging over the Miramare Bay. Below, a private beach and seafront eaterie, the Nevera.

It wasn't to last. After a grand, initial opening on St Blaise's Day, February 2007, the Bellevue was later closed due to planning problems, only to reopen in 2008. During this time, the fashion brand and showcase Zagreb store of Štrok daughter Vanja and fellow UK art & design graduate Nargess Gharani ran into difficulty. The shop closed and with it, the sense of invincibility set around the Štrok family brand.

Early June 2008 proved decisive however. Along with the Bellevue reopening, the Excelsior, extensively renovated to the tune of 22 million euros, unveiled its stunning new design. Maintaining its post-war glamour but adding contemporary touches, the Štroks have created another masterpiece. The stand-alone Villa Rustica restaurant was now a luxury villa. Tito-era elegance at the first hotel in the ALH group – Dubrovnik and the Štroks have come full circle. It remains to be seen whether all this hefty investment can ride out the economic storm.

Karmen Apartments. *See p299.*

★ Pucić Palace
*Od Puča 1 (020 326 200/fax 020 326 323/
www.thepucicpalace.com).* **Rates** €280-€600
double. **Credit** AmEx, DC, MC, V. **Map**
p285 D3 ⑰
A beautiful five-star right in the Old Town, the Pucić
Palace weaves old-world heritage with 21st-century
convenience. Nineteen rooms are individually and
tastefully decorated, with ample beds and sumptuous linens. Large, soundproofed windows allow Old-
Town views – most notably from the Gundulić suite,
overlooking the market square of the same name.
▶ *The summer-only roof-terrace Defne is one of
the best restaurants in town; see p288.*

Regent Dubrovnik
*Na Moru 1, Orašac (099 234 3800 mobile/
fax 020 892 348/www.radissonsas.com).*
To open in the early summer of 2009, the sea-facing
five-star Radisson Regent complements its long-
established sister operation in the capital and adds
another high-end restaurant and cocktail bar to the
city's portfolio. Part of the elite leisure complex Sun
Garden Resort, outside town.

Rixos Libertas
*Liechensteinov put 3 (020 200 000/fax 020 200
020/www.rixos.com).* **Credit** AmEx, DC, MC, V. **Map** p280 C2 ⑱
Opened just before New Year's Eve 2006/07, the
Turkish-owned Rixos was a prime holiday hotel
before the war, bombed in 1991 and reconfigured
with a two-floor spa, two pools and the popular
Golden Sun casino. All five-star, of course.

Vacation Suite Kashe
*Ribarnica 1 (099 219 4385 mobile/
info@dubrovnikapt.com).* **Rates** €140 apartment.
Credit AmEx, DC, MC, V. **Map** p285 E3 ⑲
Right on the old port, this comfortable flat can sleep
four, two bedrooms, two bathrooms, harbour views,
all mod cons and WiFi. An extra two can be put up
at the Studio Bruno downstairs.
▶ *If this apartment happens to be full, try the
Nives, which is equally well located in the Old
Town; see p296.*

Valamar Club Dubrovnik
*Iva Dulčića 18 (general information 052 465
000/fax 020 435 622/www.valamar.com).*
Closed Dec-Mar. **Rates** €85-€340 double.
Credit AmEx, DC, MC, V. **Map** p280 B2 ⑳
The perfect choice for families, the former Minčeta,
near Copacabana beach, has water chutes, banana
rides and pedalos, two pools and a full agenda for
kids. Many rooms have a sea view. It shares tennis
courts, a small football pitch, mini-golf and diving
with the other hotels in the group nearby.
▶ *For a comprehensive selection of the child-
friendly hotels and attractions to be found
around Croatia; see pp56-60.*

Villa Dubrovnik
*Vlaha Bukovaca 6 (020 422 933/fax 020 423
465/www.villa-dubrovnik.hr).* **Closed** until 2010.
Map p281 F1 ㉑
The last of the classic high-end hotels to be over-
hauled, the return of the Villa Dubrovnik should be
the grand opening of 2010.

GETTING THERE

From the airport

Dubrovnik **airport** is 22km (13 miles) south-east of town, down the coast at **Čilipi**. Regular buses (30mins, 35kn) head for town, first stopping near the Pile Gate before going on to the bus station, three kilometres (two miles) west of the Old Town at **Gruž**. From town, buses leave bay Nos.6-8 from Gruž two hours before flights on BA, 90 minutes before those on Croatia Airlines. With another carrier, time your departure around either of these. Buses also stop above the Old Town, immediately beyond Bosanska, to the right of the fire station opposite the shop Okviri Logorio. This is the nearest jump-on point from the centre of town.

A taxi costs about 250kn, which will probably turn out to be nearer to 350kn if you're staying at a hotel on the Lapad or Babin Kuk headland. Call one on 970.

By train

Dubrovnik has no train link. The nearest main station is in Split, four-and-a-half hours away by bus (*see below*).

By bus

Half-a-dozen services arrive daily from Zagreb (ten hours); buses from Split (4.5 hours) are more regular. Remember to keep your passport handy as you pass through Bosnia on the way. For bus websites, *see p316*.

By car

Dubrovnik is a 600-km drive from Zagreb, most of it down the main A1 motorway/E65 coast road; allow at least seven hours. From Split, allow four hours. The motorway is not expected to reach Dubrovnik until 2010 at least.

By boat

All main ferries and catamarans arrive at the main terminal at **Gruž**. The coastal ferry from Bari in southern Italy runs daily in summer, twice a week in winter, leaving around 10pm, arriving in Dubrovnik around 7am the next day, and heading up to Split (ten hours) and then Rijeka (20-24 hours) (Split ten hours).

GETTING AROUND

Libertas city buses link Gruž, Babin Kuk, Lapad and Ploče to the Old Town. Buy a ticket (14kn for two journeys) at any newsstand or in exact change (10kn) from the driver. Gruž is a deceptively long walk to and from town – allow 40 minutes and don't count on easily making it by taxi if you're running late. Although there are cabs aplenty at the Pile Gate, the road to Gruž is always busy and often gridlocked.

Taxis start at 25kn and charge 8kn per km – expect a 50kn-70kn bill for Gruž. Bus Nos.1a, 3 and 8 do the same journey.

RESOURCES

Hospital

Roka Misetica, Lapad (020 431 777).

Internet

Ante Starčevića 7 (020 427 591/www.tz dubrovnik.hr). **Open** *July, Aug* 8am-midnight daily. *June, Sept* 8am-10pm daily. *Oct-May* 9am-9pm Mon-Fri; 9am-7pm Sat.

Police

Ante Starčevića 39 (020 443 739).

Post office

Put republike 32 (020 413 960). **Open** 7am-8pm Mon-Fri; 8am-4pm Sat; 8am-noon Sun.

Tourist information

Dubrovnik Tourist Office *Ante Starčevića 7 (020 427 591/www.tzdubrovnik.hr).* **Open** *Summer* 8am-8pm daily. *Winter* 9am-4pm Mon-Fri; 9am-1pm Sat.

Around Dubrovnik

CAVTAT

Down the coast from Dubrovnik, **Cavtat** is an easy day trip, either by bus No.10 or boat from the old harbour. The southernmost resort in Croatia, Cavtat is built on the old Greek and Roman settlement of Epidaurum, which was sacked by invading barbarian tribes in the seventh century. Refugees flooded to Ragusa and built Dubrovnik.

Attracting holidaymakers here began in the early 1900s. Proximity to Dubrovnik airport means that their modern-day counterparts can breeze in, plot up at their friends' yacht lining the pretty, palm-fringed Riva promenade, and breeze out again – for relaxation and a bit of history, this is a Dubrovnik in miniature without the hassle.

The Riva also contains one of the town's leading attractions, the **Baltazar Bogišić Collection** (478 556; open 9.30am-1.30pm Mon-Sat; 15kn), housed in the former Rector's Palace, its garden dotted with Roman-era stones. Within are rows of books from the library of this prominent collector of the late 19th century, plus a large painting of the Cavtat Carnival from the same era by local realist painter **Vlaho Bukovac**, whose works bring thousands here every year.

His own **gallery**, stands in a sidestreet just off the Riva (Bukovčeva 5, 020 478 646; open summer 9am-1pm, 5-9pm daily, winter 9am-1pm daily; 15kn), and presents a comprehensive overview of this prolific artist. Another key sight is the **Račić Mausoleum** (020 478 646; summer 10am-noon, 6-8pm Mon-Sat, 10am-noon Sun), set on the hilltop tip of the peninsula – follow the path from the prosaic **Monastery of Our Lady of the Snow**, at the other end of the Riva from the Baltazar Bogišić Collection. Built in 1921, the mausoleum is one of the most famous works by Croatia's greatest sculptor, Ivan Meštrović, a mix of styles including Greek, Byzantine and Egyptian. The view alone is worth the climb.

The sea here is particularly clear. Just outside Cavtat is the Hotel Epidaurus, linked to one of Croatia's best diving centres, **Epidaurum** (020 471 386, 098 427 550 mobile, www.epidaurum-diving-cavtat.hr). Roman ruins and sunken ships line the seabed nearby.

Where to eat & stay

The Riva is lined with bars and eateries but the best table in town is easily the **Taverna Galija** (Vuličevića 1, 020 478 566, www.galija.hr), a classy, imaginative (mainly) seafood restaurant with a prominent sea-view terrace. Its nearest challenger is the **Leut** (Trumbićev put 11, 020 478 477, closed Jan), a fish restaurant with a leafy terrace. For drinks and snacks, **Ancora**

INSIDE TRACK
VLAHO BUKOVAC

Born Biagio Faggioni in Cavtat in 1855, the later Vlaho Bukovac gained his artistic education in Paris, where he developed his penchant for Impressionism and, most notably, Pointillism. He brought these back to Croatia when he was at the forefront of all significant artistic events in the 1890s, including setting up the city's Art Pavilion. Around the turn of the century, he moved back home to Cavtat before a new career in academia in Prague, where he died in 1922. Most known for his nudes, literary and religious scenes, Bukovac was a regular visitor to England, where he had enthusiastic patrons in London, Liverpool and Harrogate. He is considered Croatia's greatest artist of the 19th century.

(Obala Ante Starčevića 22), offers tapas, cheap cocktails and internet access.

Cavtat has a number of classy hotels. First is the six-room **Villa Kvaternik** (Kvarternikova 3, 020 479 800, fax 020 479 808, www.hotelvilla kvaternik.com; €85-€178 double), a tasteful conversion of a 15th-century residence in the heart of the Old Town. The sea-view, five-star **Hotel Croatia** (Frankopanska 10, 020 475 555,

Cavtat.

DUBROVNIK & ISLANDS

Karmela. *See p307.*

DUBROVNIK & ISLANDS

fax 020 478 213, www.hoteli-croatia.hr; €152-€316 double) is a massive, multi-tiered year-round resort hotel with pools, tennis courts and two beaches. In the same group, the **Hotel Supetar** (Obala Ante Starčevića 27, 020 479 833, fax 020 479 858; €78-€141.50 double) is cheaper but well located.

Resources

Tourist information
Cavtat Tourist Office *Tiha 3 (020 479 023/www.tzcavtat-konavle.hr).* **Open** *Summer* 8am-8pm Mon-Sat; 8am-noon Sun. *Winter* 8am-3pm Mon-Fri.

PELJEŠAC

Pelješac is passed over by most visitors to Dubrovnik but locals are drawn to its very lack of tourists, fine wines, long shingle beaches and, most of all, the best mussels and oysters in Croatia. They are farmed at **Ston**, one of the two key destinations on the Pelješac peninsula, which sticks out some 90km (56 miles) towards Korčula. The other is **Orebić**, a resort in its own right, a quick hop and a quieter alternative to Korčula. A windsurfing scene nearby gives it the younger edge that Korčula lacks. One road runs the length of the peninsula, and unless you have a car, your best bet is to head for Ston, where Pelješac meets the mainland, by bus from Dubrovnik, or cross from Korčula to Orebić.

With your own transport, you can drive the 65 kilometres (40 miles) of vineyard-lined road, calling at wine cellars serving the famed Postup and Dingač reds. *See p306.*

Excellent beaches stretch either side of the main road too. On the north side, **Divna**, near the two-house village of Duba, some 6 kilometres (3.5 miles) from Trpanj, is secluded and sandy. **Prapratno**, 3 kilometres (2 miles) west of Ston, is also sandy. On the south side, **Žuljana**, before Trstenik, is a lovely village in a bay where you'll find several beaches. The most beautiful is **Vučine**, which is a 15 minutes' walk south.

INSIDE TRACK
STON OYSTERS

Ston's natural lake-like bay has been home to mussel and oyster farms since Roman times. In summer, locals sell 5kn oysters by the side of the road, and renowned restaurants from here to Dubrovnik feature Ston oysters on their menus. The Ostrea Edulis variety can only be found in Ston. Smaller than its Atlantic counterpart, it is served open on its flat side. The meat is also firmer and more richly flavoured. It is also not cut off from its shell, so don't expect to tip it down your throat.

Ston is really two towns in one, linked by hilltop fortifications. Ston, called Veliki ('Great') to distinguish it from its smaller sister of Mali Ston, has its own historic walls, built to protect the salt pans there. Half the 14th-century towers and walls remain, surviving the earthquake of 1996 that destroyed houses in both towns.

Orebić has package hotels and standard restaurants, but has more to pack into a weekend. A major trading centre until the late 19th century, it contains a cluster of grand villas festooned with greenery, built by retired sea captains. Its main sight is a **Franciscan monastery** (summer 9am-noon, 4-7pm Mon-Sat, 4-7pm Sun; 15kn) on a hilltop 20 minutes' walk from the Hotel Bellevue. Built in the late 15th century, it houses Our Lady of the Angels, an icon said to protect sailors in the Pelješac Channel picturesquely spread down below. Before you reach it, another trail leads to the summit of **Sv Ilija**, with panoramic views from 961 metres (3,153 feet) high.

Wines for All Seasons

Pelješac is Croatia's top terroir for quality reds.

When talk turns to top Croatian reds and Pelješac, the first word is usually 'Dingač'. It refers to a short stretch of seaside land where Plavac Mali grapes grow. Only those harvested in this small area, on the underbelly of the peninsula roughly between the towns of Podobuce and Trstenik, have the right to be called Dingač. The land faces south-west and the Dalmatian sun; the calcified, rocky soil retains the warmth and encourages only the heartiest grapes to grow. The steep hillside means a back-breaking harvest but more sunlight reflected right off the sea. The result is a strong, full-bodied red (usually 14 per cent) with a huge bouquet that resembles the great wines of the genre.

'People think only the French make good wine but our wine here is excellent,' says Goran **Miličić**, whose vineyard (020 742 031), on the edge of Potomje, is the centre of Dingač wine tasting. 'The French have five generations but we are only in our first.'

What local winemakers lack in pedigree, they make up for with the quality of the raw materials. As you drive through the tunnel linking Potomje to Dingač's cliff-like

position, nearly every square metre is stuffed with vines hanging heavy with bunches of grapes. The 400-metre tunnel through the hill, connecting town and grapes, was built by residents with their own money during the Communist era. Growers used to lead donkeys over the hill to fill baskets and go back again. From atop the slope the sea is a straight 300 metres down. But for wine, it would be forbidding. Here, it feels like a gold mine.

At **Dalmatinksa kuća** (020 748 017, 091 531 2595), an open-air terrace restaurant in Borak, at the foot of the Dingač hill, owner Mato Violić – who also runs the **Matusko Vineyard** (020 742 393, 098 428 676) in Potomje – explains that because of the incline, harvesters still rope down the side. Nothing is mechanised. 'The plants must be strong to survive because the soil is poor,' says Violić, president of Pelješac's wine road, opened in 2007, which links 11 vineyards along the peninsula. 'But the land is full of minerals. With the right rain, in May, mid July and early August for the September harvest, you will have good wine.'

Locals come to Orebić and its surroundings for the beaches. The nicest one nearby is **Trstenica**, which is pebbly and sandy, with a few bars and a section for naturists. It's a 20-minute stroll east of the ferry terminal. Boats make regular journeys to the village of **Viganj**, the most popular spot for windsurfing in Croatia apart from Bol on Brač. A north-western afternoon wind makes it an ideal place for intermediate surfers to improve their skills. Beginners are best going out on summer mornings, for the mild wind from the south-east. Campsite **Liberan** (020 719 330, www.liberan-camping.com) rents boards and has a windsurfing school; **Perna** (098 395 807 mobile, www.perna-surf.com), between Viganj and Orebić, specialises in kite-surf. The main diving club, **OreBeach**, outside Orebić (Šetalište Kralja Krešimira 121, 020 713 985, 091 1543 5532 mobile), is a modern centre with a hotel and restaurant.

Viganj also contains three lovely churches. The oldest, the 16th-century **St Liberan** – more a chapel, really – sits right on the main spit of beach that is the windsurfing hub. The other two, **Our Lady of the Rosary** and 18th-century **St Michael's**, are on the way to the most noteworthy historic local point of interest: the Nakovana archaeological site, where there is evidence of life here from the Stone Age.

Where to eat & stay

You can snack at most of the wine cellars (*see p306*). For something more substantial, Mali Ston boasts the best tables. Pick of the bunch is the **Kapetanova Kuća**, a converted villa with a fishermen's theme and modern seafood cuisine courtesy of chef Lidija Kralj. It's not cheap but it'll be a meal to write home about.

It's attached to the **Hotel Ostrea** (020 754 555, fax 020 754 575, www.ostrea.hr, 480kn-730kn). The **Vila Koruna** (020 754 359, fax 020 754 642, www.vilakoruna.cjb.net, 550kn-1,000kn) is also comfortable, with a lovely terrace restaurant. The new **Hotel Indijan** (020 714 555, www.hotelindijan.hr) at Orebić is a lovely, family-run four-star. At Viganj, try the **Karmela** (020 719 097; *photo p305*), the outdoor **Forte** (020 611 187) or the more ramshackle **Bistro Ponta** (020 719 060). Viganj has only one hotel: **Villa Mediterane** (No.224, 020 719 196; open June-Oct; 500kn) at the far end of town. Campsites abound – the best is **Antony Boy** (020 719 330, www.antony-boy.com). Private rooms line the seaside road. Beach bars are equally ubiquitous. **Karmela 2** ('Kah-Duh-Va') is the spiritual heart of Viganj and the only place to go out and let your freak flag fly. DJs and live acts perform in summer – look out for the Karmela surfboard and yellow picket fence.

Ston. *See p305.*

DUBROVNIK & ISLANDS

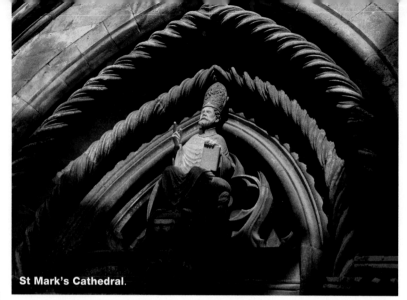

St Mark's Cathedral.

Getting there

Pelješac is served by **bus** from **Dubrovnik**.
Ston is an hour and a half away, Orebić another
hour. Three services a day run the length of the
peninsula, one going over to Korčula two hours
from Ston. There are no other buses.

From Korčula, there are regular **foot
passenger** and **ferry boats** hopping the
30 minutes to Orebić. **Marmo** (020 701 137)
lays on three boats a day between Viganj and
Korčula (14kn). There is a regular **Jadrolinija**
ferry from the transport hub of **Ploče**, just
south of the Makarska Riviera on the mainland,
to **Trpanj** on the north coast of Pelješac.
The crossing lasts 50 minutes. There is also
a frequent service between Sobra on **Mljet**
and Prapratno near Ston.

Resources

Tourist information

Orebić Tourist Office *Trg Mimbelli (020
713 718/www.tz-orebic.com).* **Open** *Summer*
8am-1pm, 4-8pm Mon-Sat. *Winter* 8am-1pm
Mon-Fri.
Ston Tourist Office *Pelješki put 1 (020 754
452/www.tzo-ston.hr).* **Open** *Summer* 9am-1pm,
5-7pm Mon-Sat; 8am-noon Sun. *Winter* 8am-noon
Mon-Sat.

KORČULA

As you approach Korčula from the mainland
nearby, the crowded little houses on the edge of
the island seem to be pushing each other out of
the way to see if you are friend or foe. Holding

them in, a stern medieval fortress centrepieced
by the slim belltower of **St Mark's Cathedral**
stands guard over the narrow Pelješac Channel,
protecting the riches contained on the sixth
largest island in the Croatian Adriatic. So lush
with dark pine forests, vineyards and olive
groves the ancient Greek settlers called it
Korkyra Melaina ('Black Corfu'), Korčula has
managed to avoid the tourist trap tendencies
of its original Greek namesake 480 kilometres
(300 miles) south.

No longer fought over by Turk or Venetian,
Napoleon's troops or Prince-Bishop Petar
Njegoš' Montenegrins, Habsburg Austrians
or Mussolini's Italians, by Partisan or German,
Korčula is one of Dalmatia's most relaxing
getaways, traditionally enjoyed by an older
generation of tourist. The main town of the
same name, set on the north-eastern tip of the
island opposite the Pelješac peninsula, has one
of the best-preserved medieval centres in
Dalmatia. It is the most popular regional
destination after Dubrovnik, with which it
is often compared.

Unlike Dubrovnik, Korčula was governed by
the Venetians, responsible for the layout of the
Old Town, no more than few hundred metres
across. Within the oval walls, streets are laid
out in a herringbone pattern. Those running
west are straight to let in the cool westerly
breeze on burning summer days; those running
east are curved to keep out the chilly winter
Bura wind from the north-east. Those facing
north allowed locals to rush up and quickly
defend the Pelješac Channel.

Equally unlike Dubrovnik, Korčula had not
experienced the upgrading of hotel stock and

INSIDE TRACK MOREŠKA

Korčula's own version of the sword dance, although re-enacted for tourists by the Land Gate in summer, has authentic historic links. Moreška has its origins in Moorish Spain, when battles won by the Christians were celebrated in folk dance and drama. By the time the tradition reached Dalmatia, the Turk was at the door, only to be defeated at the pivotal Battle of Lepanto in 1571. The age-old struggle between good and evil has been dramatised ever since. Here two kings fight over a betrothed princess, their soldiers perform a war dance, swords clash and a brass band blasts out. Each Korčula community has an annual sword-dance festival. In Korčula town, it's July 29 but shows are staged on Thursday evenings in summer.

improvements to the dining options – until 2009. The opening of the five-star **Lešić Dimitri Palace**, refurbishment of the four-star **Marko Polo**, both with restaurants, plus wider variety of dining and drinking options, now give Korčula younger, more upmarket appeal.

Sightseeing

Although Korčula's main claim to fame as the birthplace of Marco Polo may be urban myth, it can offer authentic historic attractions thanks to a medieval building programme begun by one of Polo's contemporaries, ruling Venetian nobleman Count Marsilije Zorzi. Entering the Old Town from the south, you pass through the **Kopnena Vrata** (Land Gate), erected to mark the island's gallant defence against the Turkish navy at the Battle of Lepanto. It leads to the **Punat**, or stone bridge, and the **Veliki Revelin Tower** bearing the Venetian coat of arms. By the gate is a produce market; in summer it is the setting for performances of the Moreška sword dance. Through it is the square of Sv Mihovil, lined with municipal buildings. A small chapel here dedicated to the Miraculous Virgin of the Island was built after Lepanto. Every August 15 a procession runs from the chapel to mark the Virgin's Ascension.

The main street, Ulica Korčulanskog Statuta, leads to St Mark's Cathedral (020 711 049; open Apr-Oct 9am-2pm, 5-7pm daily; 15kn), one of the finest examples of Croatian church architecture and design. Taking three centuries to build, it features several styles, including Gothic, Romanesque and baroque. Most notable is the work by local stonemason Marko Andrijić, responsible for the canopy set on four columns above the altar, or ciborium. Beneath it is the sarcophagus of St Theodore, the protector of Korčula. You can also see here *St Mark with St Bartholomew and St Jerome*, an early work by Tintoretto, whose *Annunciation* also stands in the south nave. Cannonballs and weapons from wars with the Turks are also found here, and a 13th-century icon of the Virgin, prayed to for salvation when the Turks threatened in 1571. Next door, with the same opening hours,

Olive groves near **Vela Luka**.
See p310.

the **Abbey Treasury** contains a collection of Dalmatian art from the 15th and 16th centuries.

Opposite the cathedral, the **Town Museum** (020 711 420; open summer 10am-9pm Mon-Sat; 15kn), set in a 16th-century Venetian palace, contains a copy of the fourth-century Greek tablet from Lumbarda, the earliest evidence of civilisation on the island, Roman ceramics and a reconstruction of a Korčula peasant kitchen.

Korčula's best modern sight stands on the seafront, ten minutes from the cathedral. The **Memorial Collection of Maksimilijan Vanka** (Put Sv Nikole, open summer 9am-noon, 6-9pm daily) shows the art nouveau and Expressionist works by this 20th-century painter and hosts temporary exhibitions by key Croatian artists throughout the summer.

In town, **Banje** beach, by the Hotel Marko Polo, is crowded and not particularly attractive. The nicer, shingle one by the Bon Repos is a trek; locals pack sandy **Luka Korčulanska**, 15 minutes away towards Dominče.

AROUND KORČULA ISLAND

An easy day trip, from Korčula town's smaller east harbour, is the quick, regular taxi boat to **Badija**. This lovely pine-forested island, its 14th-century monastery converted into a residential sports centre, is a haven for deer and naturists. Another option is to take the taxi boat or hourly bus to the early Greek settlement of **Lumbarda**, 6km (3.6 miles)

away. Surrounded by vineyards, Lumbarda is famous for producing the dry, white Grk variety. Nearby are three sandy beaches: modest **Tatinja** to the east; and **Bilin Žal** and **Vela Pržina** on either side of the headland, 15 minutes away. Head south from Lumbarda until you reach a fork – take the left-hand one for rocky Bilin Žal and continue south-east for sandy Vela Pržina. Ask in Korčula town about the buses to Bilin Žal.

To explore the rest of Korčula island, you can rent a boat, car or moped from Rent a Djir (Obala Hrvatskih mornara, 020 711 908, www.korcula-rent.com). There's also an infrequent bus to **Pupnat** on the south shore, with its beautifully clear swimming spot in the bay of **Pupnatska Luka**. Nearby, **Bacva** is another bathing favourite in a secluded bay. The north-shore village of **Račišće** contains what is probably Korčula's best beach, **Vaja**. Walk north of Račišće harbour for 15 minutes to find white pebbles lapped by an indigo sea. Nearby is equally pristine **Samograd**.

Korčula's other hub is **Vela Luka**, the ferry port for Split, Hvar town and Lastovo. There the **Culture Centre** by the Church of St John (020 813 001; open summer 9am-noon, 6-10pm Mon-Sat, 6-10pm Sun, winter 9am-noon Mon-Sat; 15kn) is set in an old school. It has two, rather unexpected, Henry Moore sculptures in its collection and archaeological finds from nearby Vela Špilja (Big Cave), which was inhabited in Neolithic times.

Near Vela Luka, the two small islands of **Proizd** and **Osjak** have clean beaches of white pebbles. Proizd, 30 minutes away by taxi boat (every 2hrs, 30kn) is used by naturists.

Where to eat

Adio Mare

Ulica sv Roka (020 711 253). **Open** *Mid Apr-mid Oct* 6-11.30pm Mon-Sat; 6-11pm Sun. **Credit** AmEx, DC, MC, V.

Around the corner from Marco Polo's house, this most popular of restaurants has queues around the block in high season. As you watch from a high-ceilinged maritime-themed dining room, the cooks in the open-plan kitchen flame-grill your fish or stew your beef in *prošek* (sherry) and prunes, the famous house *pašticada*, served up with sticky gnocchi. *Photo p312.*

★ Gradski Podrum

Trg Antuna/Kaporova, Korčula town (020 711 222). **Open** *Apr-Oct* 11am-2pm, 6-10.30pm daily. **Credit** AmEx, DC, MC, V.

Extensive menu, a terrace on an open square by the Town Hall and St Michael's church, excellent service – there are reasons why the Gradski is just that bit dearer than everywhere else. Try the fish stew with white wine, potatoes and parsley.

INSIDE TRACK MARCO POLO

Korčula's one claim to fame, of being the birthplace of famed traveller Marco Polo, has elements of truth at least. The man who travelled along the Silk Road to Kubla Khan's China was born around 1254, possibly here, perhaps on the mainland in Šibenik, probably in Venice. Polo certainly fought for the Venetians in the famous Battle of Korčula – hence the connection. DePolo is also a family name on Korčula and in Šibenik. Despite the tenuous link, locals in Korčula decided that a 17th-century housed fitted with a watchtower must have been his house – conveniently located on DePolo street, one block behind the island's real main sight, the cathedral. Sadly the islanders have not yet been able to make a proper museum out of it – one has been in the planning stage for years. Meanwhile, tourists have to make do with tacky souvenirs pedelled by poor chaps decked out in Polo gear of medieval breeches and bright floppy hats.

Profile Pločica & Palagruža

Dalmatia's remote lighthouses offer away-from-it-all breaks.

Throughout the 19th century, the ruling Austro-Hungarian monarchy built 48 lighthouses along the Croatian coast. Families were born and raised there – the lighthouse keeper had to be married.

Today, a dozen have been converted into lodgings, providing the visitor with one of Europe's most unusual stays. In the case of Pločica, off Korčula, you can bring up to 14 friends, too. This is the biggest of the ten on the roster of local booking agency adriatica.net, which specialises in unique breaks around Croatia.

Pločica is certainly unique. One of the few of adriatica's venues not to have a lighthouse keeper, there will be nothing but you, the lighthouse and the small island you're both standing on. Fortunately, at least one happens to be beautiful, its land plotted with old fig trees, its waters perfect for diving and fishing. There's a sandy lagoon with shallow waters on the northern side, ideal for children's swimming, and a rocky seabed to the south for divers.

The lighthouse has two three-star apartments, of three and four double rooms each. Choose the bedroom in the north-east corner of the first floor – at dusk, you can see

lighthouse signals from as far away as Hvar and Pelješac. Bring your own provisions and a fishing rod.

From Prigradica on Korčula's north coast 10km (six miles) from Vela Luka, a local picks you up and whisks you off in a speedy dinghy the 15 minutes to Pločica. Price of the transfer both ways is €130 per apartment. An extra 200kn is charged if you want to be fetched from Vela Luka. He will also be within mobile phone reach for any help.

Palagruža, meanwhile, is even more remote. On a clear day, you can see Italy. Only the young and hardy need consider a stay here – the two-hour speedboat journey from Korčula town (€700 return per apartment) may require seasickness tablets. The lighthouse itself is in the middle of the mile-long island – trails lead to pristine beaches. Buy all your groceries in Korčula.

For more details, check www.mediterano.hr, who specialise in lighthouse rentals, or www.adriatica.net (01 241 5611, UK 0207 183 0437). Costs are €15-€20 per person per night depending on the lighthouse.

WITH MOD CONS

Lighthouses aren't all isolated. The child-friendly one at Rt zub, near Porec in Istria, is set by a gentle pebble beach and near tennis courts, playgrounds, supermarket and medical centre. See www.adriatica.net for details.

INSIDE TRACK
LET THEM EAT CAKE

One thing you may notice on a menu here and nowhere else in Croatia is sweet cake. This classic local dessert, under the general heading of *cukarini*, comes in different varieties, such as *prikle* (deep-fried dough with almonds and raisins) and *lumblija* (sweet bread with wine and spices). **Marinero** (*see p313*) have theirs baked in a neighbouring village and delivered daily. If it's just cakes you're after, head to the renowned cakeshop **Cukarin** (Hrvatske bratske zajednice) in a sidestreet in the Old Town.

★ Kanavelić

Ulica Franje Tudjmana 1904, Korčula town (020 711 800). **Open** *May-Nov* 6pm-1am daily. **Credit** AmEx, DC, MC, V.

Until LD opens (*see below*), Kanavelić is the best place to eat in Korčula town. Chandeliers hang below high wooden-beamed ceilings to create historic charm. Recommended dishes include the fish stew – white fish boiled with white wine and olive oil and served around a moat of polenta – and the lobster medallions in tomato sauce served over home-made noodle.

Konoba Belin

Žrnovo Prvo Selo (091 503 9258 mobile/ www.konobabelin.com). **Open** 10am-midnight daily. **No credit cards**.

Just west of Korčula town, Žrnovo is made up of several communities. The first contains Belin, a multi-terraced restaurant, whose food is lovingly prepared and superb. Quality grilled fish, served with local Grk in the open air, turns a summer evening into a memorable occasion.

Konoba Komin

Ulica Don Iva Matijace Opata, Korčula town (020 716 508). **Open** *Summer* noon-3pm, 6pm-midnight daily. *Winter* 5pm-midnight Mon, Wed-Sun. **Credit** DC, MC, V.

Cooked at the old-fashioned fireplace (*komin*) in the centre of the restaurant, the grilled meat and fish at this traditional Dalmatian konoba are hearty and fresh – this is also a great haven out of season.

★ Konoba Mate

No.28, Pupnat (020 717 109). **Open** 11am-2pm, 7-11pm daily. **No credit cards**.

Off the main street in Pupnat is this family-run find. Ingredients are grown on-site. The *pršut* ham comes from the smokehouse behind the terrace; the pastas are hand-rolled and sun-dried, and the meats – lamb and pork – are traditionally cooked under the *peka* lid. The *pašticada*, a slow-cooked roast swimming in plums and sweet wine, is recommended.

LD

Lekšić-Dimitri Palace Korčula, Don Pavle Poše 1-6, Korčula town (020 715 560/www.lesic-dimitri.com). **Open** *from* July 2009.

Befitting its historic, five-star surroundings, the panoramic restaurant of the Lešić-Dimitri Palace Hotel promises to transform the hitherto somewhat staid dining scene of Korčula town. Food will be

Adio Mare. *See p310.*

upscale traditional, with appropriate culinary references to the flavours found along the Silk Road – we are in Marco Polo territory, after all. A top chef will be named as July 2009 approaches.

Marinero
Marka Andrijića 13, Korčula town (020 711 170). **Open** *Apr-Nov* 11am-midnight daily. **Credit** AmEx, DC, MC, V.
In a narrow alley in Korčula Old Town, Marinero offers excellent seafood in an authentic and warm setting. Mother is the chef, her sons catch the daily supply of fish and the local wine flows until the guests start singing too. A favourite is fish cooked *à la gregada* – baked with potatoes and vegetables in a juicy sauce mopped up with hunks of bread. The lighter version, *na lešo*, is fish gently boiled with vegetables to create a delectable and tender meal.

Kn Maslina 2
Plokata 19.Travnja, Korčula town (no phone). **Open** *Apr-Oct* 11am-midnight daily. *Nov-Mar* varies. **No credit cards.**
Every day at this traditional local restaurant, a dozen 30kn dishes are offered to regulars. Favourites include *sočivo* (lentil, chickpea and bean soup); *bakalar* cod stew; home-made macaroni with veal stew, and grilled mackerel. The house white or red is 50kn a litre.

★ More
Lumbarda (020 712 068). **Open** Summer 11am-3pm, 7-11pm daily. **Credit** MC, V.
Feast-sized portions of fine seafood are served on a small terrace covered with thick vines; dangle your toes in the sea before enjoying arguably the best lobster in the Adriatic, with an accompanying order of home-made macaroni in tomato sauce.

Pizzeria Tedeschi
Ulica Don Iva Matijace Opata 26, Korčula town (020 711 586). **Open** *May-mid Oct* 9am-midnight daily. **No credit cards.**

INSIDE TRACK
LIQUID FESTIVAL

The little visited western tip of Korčula island has recently come to life with July's **Liquid Festival**, a weekend of DJ music and visual arts on the island of Proizd, near Vela Luka. Attractively priced (all the profits go to a local association against drug abuse) and beautifully located, Liquid now attracts interest from the UK – although keeping things is very much part of its charm. See www.myspace.com/liquidfestival for details.

This small but well located venue churns out fine pizzas from its wood-stoked oven, and pastas made by the owner's auntie in nearby Žrnovo. Tables have great views of the Old Town walls.

Kn Planjak
Plokata 19.Travnja, Korčula town (020 711 015). **Open** *Summer* 9am-midnight daily. *Winter* 9.30am-10pm daily. **Credit** AmEx, DC, MC, V.
Located on a shaded terrace in a square just behind the market, Planjak is the restaurant to try if you want to tuck into cheap, authentic Balkan grilled meats – go for the 60kn daily menu.

Ranč Maha
Žrnovo-Pupnat road (098 494 389 mobile/ 098 966 7176 mobile). **Open** *Summer* 1-11pm daily. *Winter* 1-11pm Mon-Sat. **No credit cards.**
This ranch-style restaurant, run by the family Marelić, is up in the hills above Korčula town. It's the place to eat *peka*, dishes slow-cooked under smouldering charcoal, ordered in advance. Turning up on spec, try a grilled dish. Home-made grappas provide an aperitif. It's a cosy retreat in winter with a wood-burning fire – call ahead first.

Stupe
Ksenija Raškić, Stupe (098 933 7611 mobile). **Open** *Summer* noon-11pm daily. **No credit cards.**
Stupe island, a short hop from Korčula town, is uninhabited but for this restaurant that serves simple, tasty meals in summer. Arrange a pick-up time with the captain of your taxi boat.

Where to drink

Dos Locos
Šetalište Frana Kršinića 14, Korčula town (091 528 8971 mobile). **Open** *Summer* 7am-2am daily. *Winter* 7am-midnight daily. **No credit cards.**
On the other side of the bus station from the Old Town, wicker-and-bamboo Dos Locos attracts funseekers with DJ beats and music vids.

Fresh
Kod kina Liburne 1, Korčula town (091 799 2086 mobile/www.igotfresh.com). **Open** 9am-11pm daily. **No credit cards.**
Fresh is a backpacker-friendly Canadian-Croatian venture that combines the need for real breakfast (tortilla wraps and smoothies for instance) with after-dark DJ music and cocktails. It's only a kiosk with happy-hour drinks but at least it's somewhere geared to the party crowd.

Marko Polo Mystique Bar
Sv Barbare 3, Korčula town (020 721 5432). **Open** 7am-2am daily. **No credit cards.**

DUBROVNIK & ISLANDS

Massimo Cocktail Bar.

The Marco Polo Mystique Bar is the closest thing Korčula has to a lounge bar offering (relatively) late-night opening, half-decent cocktails and a mix of local and international dishes.

Massimo Cocktail Bar
Kula Zakerjan, Šetalište Petra Kanavelića, Korčula town (020 715 073). **Open** *May-Oct* 6.30pm-2am daily. **No credit cards.**
Set under the turrets of the 15th-century Zakerjan Tower in the northern fortifications, Massimo is accessible by stairs, then ladder. Standard cocktails come to you by pulley as you take in the fine view as far as Pelješac. Be careful about overindulging or it might prove difficult getting down the ladder again afterwards.

Tramonto
Ismaelli 1, Korčula town (091 192 1048 mobile). **Open** *Apr-Oct* 6pm-2am daily. **No credit cards.**
Tramonto's wall-top terrace location and beach-bar vibe make it the perfect spot to sit down for a drawn out sundowner cocktail. Chill-out music and Mojitos that are mixed from mint grown next door attract folks from the super yachts moored out in the channel stretched out below.

Vinum Bonum
Sv Justina, Korčula town (020 715 014). **Open** *Mar-Oct* 9am-10pm daily. **No credit cards.**
Vinum Bonum is the perfect place for local wine and *rakija* grappa – a map even indicates where the labels come from. Regulars, including the occasional Moreška dancer, provide the atmosphere, gossiping away over a plate of *pršut* ham or cheese with the knowledgeable staff.

Where to stay

★ Hotel Feral
Brna (020 832 002/fax 020 832 047/ www.hotel-feral.hr). **Closed** Dec-Mar. **Rates** €70-€140 double. **Credit** AmEx, DC, MC, V.
Renovated in 2005, this hotel has 79 rooms, all with views over the sea and the harbour village of Brna, which is located between Korčula and Vela Luka. The Feral has an outdoor pool, a terrace restaurant and a private beach. The staff can organise kayaking trips, sailing and local excursions.

Hotel Korčula
Obala dr Franje Tudjmana 5, Korčula town (020 711 078/fax 020 711 026/www.htp-korcula.hr). **Closed** Jan-Mar. **Rates** €110-€180 double. **Credit** AmEx, DC, MC, V.
This local landmark was built in 1912 and, sad to say, it shows. Behind the Korčula's pristine, palm-fringed exterior, the 20 shabby rooms have seen better days. Expect old TV sets, no lifts and no air-conditioning. Locals use the café terrace as a meeting place – so should you.

Hotel Marko Polo
Šetalište Frana Kršinića, Korčula town (020 726 100/fax 020 726 300/www.htp-korcula.hr). **Closed** Nov-Mar. **Rates** €130-€220 double. **Credit** AmEx, DC, MC, V.
The four-star, three-floor Marko Polo offers a sea view from most of its 100 rooms. A two-phase renovation, which took the hotel light years ahead of its disappointing surrounding properties, saw new bathrooms fitted, indoor and outdoor pools installed, and a gym and sauna outfitted.

★ Lekšić-Dimitri Palace Korčula
Don Pavle Poše 1-6, Korčula town (020 715 560/
www.lesic-dimitri.com). Open from June 2009.
At last a true quality hotel on Korčula. This five-star
luxury retreat occupies an 18th-century bishop's
palace and five medieval cottages, and comprises six
residences with between one and four bedrooms
each, a high-end spa and top-class restaurant. Open
year-round, the LD should soon attract custom.

Pansion Marinka
Lumbarda (098 344 712 mobile/fax 020 726
300). **Closed** Dec-Apr. **Rates** €40-€60 double.
No credit cards.
With their lodging set among olive trees, across the
street from the sea, owners Frano and Visnja run the
best-value spot on the island. Of the ten simple
rooms, two have balconies. Meals are prepared with
home-grown ingredients – the family's other enter-
prise is Agroturizam Bire, making wine, cheese,
olive oil and an assortment of spirits.

Royal Apartments
Trg Petra Segedina 4, Korčula town (098 184
0444 mobile). **Closed** Nov-May. **Rates** €75-€90
double. **No credit cards.**
Just west of the Old Town, Royal Apartments is a
cluster of five units, the bigger with separate
kitchens and living rooms. Apartments, well marked
with a green awning on the waterside square, are
simple, fairly priced and comfortable.

Getting there

From **Dubrovnik**, a daily **bus** runs to Korčula
town (3hrs, 95kn), ferry price included – part of
the journey is across the water. A **catamaran**
also connects Korčula town with Dubrovnik
(2.5hrs, 55kn) four times a week, and with Split
daily in high season (2hrs, 55kn).

The quickest hop from the mainland for foot
passengers to Korčula town is the boat shuttle
from **Orebić** on **Pelješac** (summer only, Mon-
Fri, every 1-2hrs, 15mins, 15kn). The car ferry
from Orebić lands at **Dominče** (daily every
1-2hrs, 20mins, 10kn) – a shuttle bus takes
you the 2km (1.2 miles) to Korčula town.

The other port is **Vela Luka**. A daily car
ferry docks from Split after calling at Hvar
(3hrs, 50kn). A catamaran arrives from Split
five times a week in summer (2hrs, 35kn).
Between Vela Luka and Korčula town, a bus
runs every one to two hours (80mins, 30kn).

Resources

Information
Korčula Tourist Office *Obala Franje*
Tudjmana (020 715 701/www.korcula.net).
Open *June-mid Oct* 8am-3pm, 4-10pm Mon-Sat;
8am-2pm Sun. *Mid Oct-May* 8am-2pm Mon-Sat.

MLJET

Mljet is the nearest thing to having your own
island. For complete silence, rest and relaxation,
get the catamaran or ferry from Dubrovnik and
leave the world behind.

Mljet is Dalmatia's most southern, most
verdant and, some would argue, most beautiful
isle. More than 70 per cent of this thin, 37km-
long (22-mile) one-road idyll is covered in pine
forest. A third of it is national park. Before Tito
chose Istria's Brijuni as his place for leisure,
luxury and safari animals, Mljet was a prime
candidate for the prestigious role. And though
it never got to accommodate zebras, elephants
and giraffes, Mljet remained a natural escape,
underdeveloped and underpopulated.

According to legend, Odysseus was so
enchanted by Mljet that he stayed here for
seven years. Locals tend to stay for the day,
arriving in someone's boat in the morning,
spending the day cycling and swimming, before
heading back for dinner in Dubrovnik. Tourists
coming with the ferry are plonked at sombre
Sobra, on the north-east coast. Those in the
catamaran go on to the western tip and **Polače**,
named after mildly interesting Roman ruins.
This is your best arrival point, with private
rooms and cycle hire (although there's a steep
hill to start off with). It is 5km (3 miles) to the

Mljet.

new port of **Pomena**, where you'll find the island's only hotel, the **Odisej**, plus more private rooms, cycle hire places and restaurants. The hotel is the island's link with civilisation, boasting a cashpoint and internet access. Note that it closes for the winter.

Halfway between Polače and Pomena is the main ticket office for the national park at **Govedjari**. Kiosks are also dotted elsewhere. If you're spending the night on the island, you do not pay for park entry.

Around the lakes, the little stone-house settlements of Babine Kuće and Soline are nice for a wander. From Veliko Jezera, a hiking path leads to the 253-metre-high (830-foot) high point of Montokuc, allowing fine views of Pelješac and Korčula. Hiking maps of the islands are sold at kiosks in Polače and Pomena. Other sports activities – windsurfing, diving – can be organised from the Hotel Odisej.

The rest of the island contains a few small settlements, centrepieced by the administrative capital of **Babino Polje**, and nothing else but nature. As nearly all tourists hang around the lakes, this is pretty much yours. There's nothing by way of transport or refreshments but the reward is three sandy beaches near **Sapunara**, on Mljet's far eastern tip. The main one can get a little crowded, but the other two, **Podkućica** and the beautiful **Blace**, are quieter, the latter attracting nudists. Locals can find you a private room or there is apartment rental.

On the south coast, a hard walk from Babino Polje or an easy boat excursion from the Hotel Odisej is **Ulysses Cave**, where the nymph Calypos is said to have held Odysseus captive. Seven years stuck in paradise, maybe it was the itch that made him leave.

Mljet National Park

Main office *Pristanište 2, Govedjari (020 744 041/www.np-mljet.hr).* **Open** *Apr-Oct* 24hrs daily. *Nov-Mar* 7am-3pm Mon-Fri. **Admission** *Summer* 90kn; 40kn reductions. *Winter* 60kn; 30kn reductions. **No credit cards.**

Mljet's main draw is this national park covering the western third of the island. Many head first for the salt-water lakes of Veliko and Malo Jezero, linked by a channel of water. Malo Jezero is safe for children and its water is quite warm. Veliko Jezero, on the other hand, is connected to the Adriatic and has tidal flows – make sure you know which way the current is going and don't get swept out. In its centre is the islet of St Mary, with the church of the same name and a 12th-century monastery. An hourly boat links with the little bridge on Malo Jezero or you can hire a small canoe.

Where to eat & stay

Mljet's dining scene is modest but you can find fresh, local dishes at serene lakeside taverns. Note that virtually every establishment closes for the winter, usually by October, to re-open in

Sapunara.

INSIDE TRACK MONGOOSES

As you happily motor or hike your way around Mljet's tree-lined roads, a creature might scuttle past you at top speed: a mongoose. Brought in from India in the early 1900s to rid the island of snakes, mongooses have thrived here ever since. For performing such a useful service – you'll be hard pushed to find a snake anywhere on the island – the mongoose is respected and revered by locals as part of Mljet's singular identity.

the spring. Popular in high season, **Mali Raj** (020 744 115) is a small konoba serving Dalmatian staples with gorgeous views of the lake. **Nine** (020 744 037) is the best of a handful of spots opposite the Hotel Odisej. This is the place to come for fresh lobster, kept in wells outside and fished out at your request. It's a favoured haunt of the yachting fraternity.

Another favourite is the **Melita** (020 744 145), set in the old monastery in the middle of Veliko Jezero, with a terrace by the water. You can eat fish or grilled meat while dipping your toes in the water. Although it's quite out of the way, the **Konoba Barba** (020 746 200) is like dining in somebody's house. Fresh fish and friendly conversation from the old lady are provided in equal measure. It's in the village of **Prožura**, between Sobra and the island's only petrol pumps.

Few tourists bother to stop in the administrative capital of Babino Polje – but this is where you'll find the wonderful, family-run terrace restaurant **Triton** (Sršenovici 43, 020 745 131, 091 205 3531 mobile) and the best bar anywhere on the island, Božo Hadjić's **Komarac** ('Mosquito').

Along with the isolation and pristine beaches of Mljet's eastern tip, you can tuck into fish stew or slow-cooked octopus or goat at the **Stermasi** in Saplunara (098 427 081 mobile, www.stermasi.hr), which also rents out cheap lodging. **Srsen Apartments** (020 747 025/€50 per flat) in Soline stand out because the large limestone house contains sleek, modern flats of a better standard. The balconies have views of the lake and the sea. Private rooms are generally available in Polače and Pomena, although they can be scarce in Sobra. Expect to pay 200kn-250kn for a double. We recommend you phone ahead in high season – you can book at one of Dubrovnik's many travel agencies.

Mljet's only hotel, the **Odisej** (Pomena, 020 744 022, www.hotelodisej.hr; open Easter-Oct) is a three-star establishment, with a bar, restaurant and children's pool. You can expect

to pay €150 in high summer for a double with a sea-view balcony, half that for a basic room in the shoulder season. Staff can lay on a variety of water sports.

Getting there

The **Nona Ana catamaran** leaves Gruž in Dubrovnik every morning for Sobra (about 30kn) then Polače (about 75kn). Allow an hour or so, nearly two for Polače. Some services also call at the Elafiti Islands. It leaves Polače for Gruž late afternoon, and early evening from Sobra. The **car ferry** from Gruž (2hrs, 35kn) runs once a day, generally in the afternoon six days a week, landing at Sobra. It turns around at 6am the next day. The **Dubrovnik-Bari** line calls at Sobra three times a week. There is a regular service to Sobra from Prapratno on Pelješac and in high season from Korčula.

A bus shuttles between Sobra, Polače and Pomena for arrivals and departures of Jadrolinija ferries – but it can be full in high season. There is no other public transport.

You can rent a bike from Polače harbour, the Hotel Odisej or the main ticket office for the national park. **Mini Brum** (020 745 260, 098 285 566 mobile) rents out customised cars from Sobra or offices across the island.

Resources

Tourist information
Mljet Tourist Office *Polače (020 744 086/ www.mljet.hr).* **Open** *Mid June-mid Sept* 8am-noon, 5-8pm Mon-Sat; 9.30-11.30am Sun. *Mid Sept-mid June* 8am-1pm Mon-Fri.

LASTOVO

Located far out in the Adriatic between Croatia and Italy, the small island of **Lastovo** is not an easy destination. Served by a single daily ferry from Split in season, this is a holdover outpost of the Med as it used to be: spare, barren and decidedly untouristy. Its unforgiving isolation, which protected it against pirates, today offers the same respite from the mad march of tourist development sweeping Croatia's coast.

Seemingly cut off from the world by steep cliffs plunging directly into the sea, Lastovo was settled as a safe redoubt against the unending raids of Ushak, Turkish and Genoese pirates. Unlike most Adriatic port towns, Lastovo village is situated beyond the crest of the cliffs, smack in the crater of a dead volcano, its Venetian church spires entirely invisible from the sea. The whole island served as an impregnable defence from sea raiders during the centuries of warfare between the Venetian Republic and Ottoman Empire.

Lastovo.

Lastovo's stormy history has seen it claimed by Venetians, Ragusans, French, British, and eventually Habsburg rulers before being granted to Italy from World War I until 1945 – it was never a part of the Kingdom of Yugoslavia. Mussolini hoped to make Lastovo the site of his ambitious if soft-brained resettlement programme to relocate the poor of overcrowded Naples to a sunny new island home in Dalmatia. Almost all of the Italians were repatriated to Italy after 1945, but the Lastovans still speak a Croatian heavily peppered with Italian words and phrases.

Lastovo was declared a National Nature Park in 2006 but tourists are still precious enough to be greeted with a smile and an invite to a glass of home-brewed *travarica* spirit. Cars pick up pedestrians. Grab a fishing rod and catch your dinner. Swim in a bay all to yourself. Kick off your shoes and really relax. This isn't tourism. This is way-out-thereness, an antidote to the crowds. Think Robinson Crusoe, only with fine wine, seafood risotto and maybe a rented moped.

Lastovo village, at the other end of the island from the port of **Ubli**, is a vertical maze of old stone houses and flower-covered, walled alleys clinging to the inner crater of an extinct volcano. The tiny centre at the top of the hill offers a bar, two markets, tourist information and a restaurant. A path leads down to a small beach at Sv Mihovil.

During the winter carnival, **Poklad**, the cigarette-smoking effigy of a medieval Turk is submitted to various creative indignities while hoisted on a rope 300 metres above the town before being burned by costumed villagers dancing to traditional Moreška music shouting 'UVO! UVO! UVO!'. Obviously, alcohol consumption is deeply involved.

Where to eat & stay

The island has one hotel, the **Ladesta** (Uvala Pasadur, 020 802 100, 098 220 120, www. diving-paradise.net), near Ubli, open May to October. The **Konoba Augusta Insula** (www.augustainsula.com) offers excellent home-made wine and seafood, including delicious lobsters that are seemingly kept by the dock as pets.

Getting there

In season, daily **ferries** to Lastovo from **Split**, **Hvar town** and **Vela Luka** on Korčula arrive at **Ubli**, an undistinguished hamlet and former military base on the south-west coast, where taxis can be found. Moped rental is the best way to see the island.

Resources

Tourist information

Lastovo Tourist Office *Lastovo village (020 801 018/www.lastovo-tz.net)*. **Open** *July-Aug* 8am-2pm, 6-9pm Mon-Sat; 6-9pm Sun. *May, June, Sept* 8am-2pm Mon-Fri.

Directory

Hvar.
See p256.

Getting There & Around

ARRIVING BY AIR

The main international airports are **Dubrovnik**; **Pula**; **Rijeka**; **Split**; **Zadar** and **Zagreb**. **Brač** is used for domestic internal and budget central European services. **Osijek** has also just joined the budget roster. All but Pula have transfers into town.

BY BOAT

Croatia is accessible from Italy by sea. There are a number of routes, the main ones being from Ancona, Pescara and Bari to Split, Hvar and Dubrovnik.

Croatia's main passenger line is **Jadrolinija** (051 666 111, www.jadrolinija.hr). Other companies operating routes between Italy and Croatia are **SNAV** (Ancona to Split; Pescara to Hvar; snav.it); **Split Tours** (Ancona to Split, Stari Grad on Hvar and Vis; www.splittours.hr), and **Venezia Lines** (Venice to Poreč, Pula, Rabac and Rovinj; 052 422 896; www.venezialines.com).

BY RAIL

Croatia has direct train connections with Austria, Bosnia-Hercegovina, Germany, Hungary, Italy, Serbia and Montenegro, Slovenia and Switzerland. The domestic rail network is not very developed, so while Zagreb, Rijeka and Split are linked by train, you cannot get to Dubrovnik.

On the routes it does run, the train service is reasonably efficient and competitively priced. A first-class ticket on the new InterCity service from Zagreb to Split costs around 250kn, second-class 170kn, with three trains a day.

Information on rail links between Croatia and other countries, as well as on internal routes, can be found from **Croatian Railways** (060 333 444, www.hznet.hr).

If you intend visiting Croatia on an Inter-rail pass, you'll need to buy a pass that includes Zone D. See **www.raileurope.co.uk**. Getting to Croatia from London involves three or four changes. To make bookings you will need to call Rail Europe on 08708 371 371 as you can't book this route on the internet.

BY ROAD

The rules of the road are stringent: seat belts must be used front and rear, and using a mobile while driving is forbidden. No under-12s are allowed in the front seat. You must always drive with your lights on. Croatia also has a zero tolerance approach to drink driving, which amounts to no drinking *at all* before getting in your car.

The speed limit is 50km/h (30mph) in built up areas, 90km/h (56mph) outside built up areas, 110km/h (70mph) on major routes designed for motor vehicles, and 130km/h (80mph) on motorways. In the event of an accident, you must contact the police on 92.

English-language traffic reports are given on **radio HR2** throughout the day. Updates are also posted on the website of the **Croatian Automobile Club** (01 464 0800, www.hak.hr), or call for information.

To enter Croatia by car you need a valid driving licence with a photograph, vehicle registration documents and insurance documents (including Green Card).

Car hire

Car hire in Croatia is expensive – about 500kn a day for an average family car. Try and get some quotes online before you travel to avoid any nasty surprises when you arrive. Drivers must be over 21 and must have held their driving licence for at least one year.

Dollar *Croatia: 021 399 000/ www.subrosa.hr.*
Hertz *UK: 0870 844 8844/www. hertz.co.uk. Croatia: 062 727 277/ www.hertz.hr.*
Thrifty *Croatia: 021 398 800/ www.subrosa.hr.*

Petrol stations

Petrol stations are open 7am-7pm, or 10pm in the summer. Some stations in the cities and on international routes are open 24hrs. Stations sell Super 95, Eurosuper 95, Super 98, Super Plus 98, Diesel and Euro Diesel.

BY BUS

Croatia is part of the Eurolines network but journey times can be immense; London to Croatia for example takes more than 36 hours. For more details contact Euroline's UK partner **National Express** (08705 143 219, www.national express.com). For travel from elsewhere in Europe visit **www.eurolines.com**.

Within Croatia, several private companies run frequently between the main towns. The leading one is AutoTrans, **www.autotrans.hr**. An excellent resource is the timetable on the website of Zagreb bus station, **www.akz.hr/En.htm**

TAXIS

Taxis can be found in all towns and resorts. They are not cheap but can be lifeline if you've missed the last bus on an island. A tip is expected.

BY BICYCLE

Cycling isn't big with the locals and the main roads are not particularly cycle friendly. Cycling for tourists is growing, as is mountain biking. Information on bike tracks and mountain biking in central Dalmatia can be found at **www.dalmatia.hr**. Try also **www.findcroatia.com** for a list of links for agencies and websites.

WALKING

Cicerone (www.cicerone.co.uk) publish *Walking in Croatia*, while Sunflower books (www.sunflower books.co.uk), issues hiking guide *Landscapes of Croatia*.

Resources A-Z

TRAVEL ADVICE

For up-to-date information on travel to a specific country – including the latest on safety and security, health issues, local laws and customs – contact your home country government's department of foreign affairs. Most have websites with useful advice for would-be travellers.

AUSTRALIA
www.smartraveller.gov.au

CANADA
www.voyage.gc.ca

NEW ZEALAND
www.safetravel.govt.nz

REPUBLIC OF IRELAND
foreignaffairs.gov.ie

UK
www.fco.gov.uk/travel

USA
www.state.gov/travel

AGE RESTRICTIONS

The age of consent in Croatia is 18. You must be 18 to smoke or drink alcohol.

BUSINESS

Croatia has readily embraced market capitalism. Some of the inefficiencies of the old systsem remain, but Croats are in fact natural-born capitalists.

Personal relationships are important – getting to know each other well over meals or simply coffee goes a long way to ensuring smooth business relations.

There are a number of organisations offering advice and contacts. In Zagreb, there's the **British Croatian Business Network** (01 46 66 440, www.bcbn.org) and the **American Chamber of Commerce** (01 48 36 777, www.amcham.hr). In London a good point of first contact is the **British Croatian Chamber of Commerce** (0208 908 1151, www.britishcroatianchamber.co.uk).

Other sources of information are the subscription-only *Croatia Business Report* (www.croatia businessreport. com) and the book *Doing Business with Croatia* published by Global Market Briefings (www.globalmarketbriefings.com).

CHILDREN

Croatians have a very Mediterranean attitude to children and treat them as little grown-ups. They are generally allowed into restaurants and cafés without any fuss. Croatia may be a major holiday destination, with a clean sea, but be warned that its beaches are mainly stony and children should wear plastic sandals to avoid any sharp rocks or spiky sea urchins. For entertainment, *see pp56-60*.

CUSTOMS

Customs in Croatia has been harmonised with the European Union. Foreign currency can be taken freely in and out of the country, and local currency up to an amount of 15,000kn. You are permitted 200 cigarettes or cigarillos or 50 cigars or 250g of tobacco, and one litre of spirits, two litres of liqueur or dessert or sparkling wine and two litres of table wine. Valuable professional and technical equipment needs to be declared at the border (just to be sure that it leaves with you again and you don't sell it while you're in Croatia).

Anything that might be considered a cultural artefact, art or archaeological finds, can only be exported with the necessary official approval. For more information visit the customs website at www.carina.hr.

DISABLED TRAVELLERS

Croatia is not as enlightened as other countries when it comes to providing facilities for the disabled. That is changing as a result of the large number of people left handicapped by the fighting in the 1990s.

It's vital that prior to travel you make enquiries with your hotel as to whether it has disabled access and facilities – a number of hotels do, but not all.

Savez organizacija invalida Hrvatske *Savska 3, 10000 Zagreb (01 482 9394/www.soih.hr).* The association of organisations of disabled people of Croatia.

DRUGS

Croatia is a transit point for drug smuggling. Penalties for use, possession and trafficking of drugs are severe. Offenders can expect prison sentences and/or large fines. Since the war, Croatia has had to cope with a significant drugs problem among its youth.

ELECTRICITY

Croatia uses a 220V, 50Hz voltage and continental two-pin plugs. Visitors from the UK require an adaptor.

EMBASSIES & CONSULATES

Australian Embassy *Kaptol Centar, Nova Ves 11, Zagreb (01 48 91 200/www.auembassy.hr).* **Open** 8.30am-4.30pm Mon-Fri.

British Embassy *Ivana Lučića 4, Zagreb (01 60 09 100/british.embassyzagreb@fco.gov.uk).* **Open** 8.30am-5pm Mon-Thur; 8.30am-2pm Fri.

British Consulate *Obala Hrvatskog Narodnog Preporoda 10/III, Split (021 346 007/british-consulat-st@st.htnet.hr).*

Canadian Embassy *Prilaz Gjure Deželića 4, Zagreb (01 48 81 200).* **Open** 8am-noon, 1.30-3pm Mon-Fri.

Irish Honorary Consul
Miramarska 23, Zagreb (01 63 10 025/irish. consulate.zg@inet.hr). **Open** 8am-noon, 2-3pm Mon-Fri.
New Zealand Consulate
c/o Hrvatska matica iseljenika, Trg Stjepana Radića 3, Zagreb (01 61 51 382). **Open** 8am-noon, 1.30-3pm Mon-Fri.
US Embassy
Ulica Thomas Jeffersona 2, Zagreb (01 66 12 200/www. usembassy.hr). **Open** 8am-noon, 1.30-3pm Mon-Fri.

EMERGENCIES

In case of an emergency the numbers to call are **92** for the police, **93** for the fire brigade and **94** for an ambulance.

GAY & LESBIAN

Homosexuality was decriminalised in Croatia in 1977, and it is forbidden to discriminate against anyone on the grounds of their sexuality. However, it's only in the last few years that gay and lesbian groups have had any sort of profile and begun to make assertions of their rights – and not without opposition. June's Gay Pride march through Zagreb, established in 2001, was set upon by homophobic protesters a year later. The group **Queer Zagreb** (www.queerzagreb.org) organises a festival of gay art in Zagreb every April, and screenings of gay films every third weekend of the month at the Tuškanać cinema (Tuškanać 1, Zagreb, www.queerzagreb.org/film).

Outside of the capital social mores are far less accepting of unusual behaviour and gay travellers will need to use their discretion.

For an excellent web-based gay guide to Croatia go to **http://travel.gay.hr/en**.

HEALTH

Croatia has a reciprocal medical agreement with the United Kingdom that means – in theory at least – that British passport holders are entitled to free hospital and dental treatment during their stay in Croatia. Even so, we recommend investing in travel insurance because public facilities are not always available and, particularly in the case of an emergency, you may need to go private. The standard of medical care in Croatia is generally good.

Contraception

Condoms are available from pharmacies and groceries.

Dentists & doctors

Pharmacists (*see below*) are usually able to help with minor complaints, but for proper medical care your best bet is to go to the local hospital or emergency unit where a duty doctor can have a look at you. See above for information about medical insurance.

The address and telephone numbers of general hospitals in **Dubrovnik** (*see p303*), **Osijek** (*p102*), **Split** (*see p239*) and **Zagreb** (*see p94*) are given in their relevant chapters in this *Guide*.

Opticians

You will need to pay for optical care. Evey main town centre has at least one optician (*optičar*) and you should be able to get replacement lenses and frames easily. In **Zagreb**, Kraljević (Trg Stjepana Konzula 4, 01 48 19 912) is as good as any.

Pharmacies

Pharmacies are usually open from 8am to 7pm during the week, and until 2pm on Saturdays. In larger towns there will normally be some pharmacies that are open 24hrs. Prescriptions need to be paid for.

STDs, HIV & AIDS

Croatia has one of the lowest rates of HIV/AIDS in Europe. There are ten facilities for free testing in the country. Contact the Ministry of Health on 01 460 7502, www.mzss.hr.

HOTELS

Croatia doesn't do the kind of simple, cheap, two- or three-star, family-run pension that is such a great feature of France, Spain and Portugal. It was a Communist country that had no Western guests (apart from spies and diplomats), then it had package tourism, then it accommodated the business community with luxury hotels whose facilities ticked every box but the one marked 'character'.

Opatija was a five-star resort before there was ever Yugoslavia (those classy Habsburgs!). Dubrovnik was accommodating movie stars while the first package tourists were arriving – and Zagreb has the great railway hotel, the Esplanade – but these are the exceptions. Until around 2003, most of Croatia's hotel stock was bland and functional.

Now that situation is changing – slowly. Starting with Dubrovnik (which has half-a-dozen five-star hotels), Croatia is beginning to realise that a hotel has to offer something special before it can charge Western prices. The tourist board slogan of 'The Mediterranean As It Once Was' still applies to many of the hotel rooms, with their dowdy furnishings and relatively basic facilities. Air-conditioning is not a given. For every Dubrovnik Palace or Pucić Palace (prime contenders for best hotel in Croatia) there are scores of others whose provision for tourists is merely adequate.

Another trap waiting for the independent traveller is the near universal rule of adding surcharges (about 20 per cent) on stays of less than three nights. Quite often the room prices given are for each guest – double it for the price for the pair of you. Many hotels in the main tourist areas (particularly the Makarska Riviera) close between October and April – those in the larger towns tend to stay open. A nominal tourist tax applies throughout.

The real shortfall comes in the mid-range category. There isn't one to speak of. The budget end is equally bereft – which is where the vast network of private rooms comes in. In too many places the accommodation choice for individual travellers is between an overpriced four-star, a multi-storey package hotel or an old lady's front room. The modest handful of hostels (**www.hfhs. com**) do an adequate job. Campsites (autokamp) tend to be fairly basic but cheap, and pitching your tent in the stony soil can be a nightmare. For small groups, many homes are rented out as apartments (apartmeni) and out of high season this can be the ideal, reasonably priced solution.

The most obvious choice for a unique and memorable place to stay is in a lighthouse (*see p311* **Profile**). Some dozen such remote settings have been converted into three-star accommodation units. Villa rental is nowhere near as extensive as it is in, say, Portugal. The exception here is Istria, whose Villas Forum (**www.villasforum. com**) sets the benchmark on how to renovate run-down regional properties in the best local architectural style.

The Croatian tourist board website (**www.croatia.hr**) has a decent accommodation search facility that includes both hotels and private rooms. Website **www.adriatica.net** offers similar facilities.

Note that most local tourist offices will not book a hotel (or private) room for you, but provide you with a list of places and phone numbers. Private travel agencies, set up in all main towns, should be able to accommodate.

ID

Although it's unlikely that you will ever be asked to show it, you are supposed to carry some form of picture ID on your person while in Croatia. Rather than carry around your passport and risk losing it, UK residents are recommended to get the credit-card style photo driving licence.

INSURANCE

Travellers should take out comprehensive travel insurance, especially if you are going to indulge in any risky sports – climbing, skiing, mountain biking – although check the small print first to see if such activities are covered by your policy. If you are going to take expensive equipment make sure that it's also covered. In the event that you need to claim, make sure you get all the relevant paperwork from medical staff or the police.

INTERNET ACCESS

Most towns have a handful of internet cafés and rates are usually reasonable. Wi-Fi is available too, with over 40 hotspots around the country at various hotels, airports and marinas: a list can be found at www.t-mobile.hr. If your laptop is not Wireless Local Area Network-enabled, cards are available from T-Mobile.

LANGUAGE

English is widely spoken, especially by Croats in the tourist industry. Most, if not all, tourist offices will have an English speaker and tourist information material is usually also available in English. Many in Istria and on the coast speak Italian. *See pp326-327.*

LEGAL ADVICE

If you get in trouble with the authorities you should get in touch immediately with your local embassy or consulate (*see p321*) for advice and assistance.

LOST PROPERTY

There are no lost and found offices at stations or airports.

MEDIA

Croatian newspapers and magazines are available from kiosks. The best-selling national daily paper is *Večernji List* followed by *Jutarnji List*. Both are European-owned and follow the line of their publishers. The third best-seller is *Slobodna Dalmacija*, which is a conservative, Dalmatia-based paper with a Zagreb edition.

Sportske Novosti is the main sports daily, carrying the football results from across Europe including the top two divisions in England.

Croatia also has a number of weeklies. The most significant is *Nacional*, which has pulled off some major scoops in recent times. Most notable was an interview with Croat general Ante Gotovina, while he was a fugitive from UN prosecutors. Another weekly, *Globus*, competes with *Nacional* for stories. Other weeklies include the left wing *Feral Tribune* – known for its run ins with the government of Franjo Tudjman. Croatian papers tend to be less prudish than similar mid-range British ones – expect bare flesh to be on display now and then. Pornographic magazines are more openly on display in Croatia than would be expected in Britain.

A surprising number of British and European newspapers and magazines are also available from Tisak kiosks, usually one, sometimes two days late.

Radio

There are some 200 licensed radio stations in Croatia. Of the three main state-run stations, HR1 and HR2 broadcast politics, documentaries, entertainment music and sport. HR3 has a cultural and spiritual agenda. HR1 also carries occasional English-language broadcasts. Some of these are also available on Glas Hrvatska, HRT's external service. There are plenty of commercial alternatives.

Television

There are four main TV stations. HRT1 and HRT2 are state-run and screen news, drama, documentaries and sports programmes. There are also a number of local TV stations.

Croatian TV shows a lot of imported TV series and films from the US and Britain. These are subtitled rather than dubbed.

MONEY

The Croatian kuna (kn) is divided into 100 lipa. Coins are issued in denominations of 10, 20 and 50 lipa, and 1, 2 and 5kn. Notes come in denominations of 10, 20, 50, 100, 200, 500 and 1,000kn. Euros are accepted in the posher hotels, airport bars and some restaurants but the currency in everyday use is the kuna.

Prices in Croatia can roughly be compared to Western Europe. Local goods and those from neighbouring states are a little cheaper; those imported from the West are more expensive. Public transport, cinema and drinking and dining in local places generally cost less here than in the West.

Foreign currency may be exchanged in banks, post offices, most tourist agencies, bureaux de change and at some hotels.

ATMs

ATMs are easy enough to find in main towns but scarcer in the provinces – particularly Istria. Instructions appear in English.

Banks

Banks are usually open 7am-7pm Monday to Friday.

Credit & debit cards

Most hotels, shops and restaurants accept Eurocard, MasterCard, Diners Club, American Express and Visa, as well as debit cards.

NATURAL HAZARDS

There are mosquitoes in Croatia, so it's a good idea to pack repellent. Croatia also has two species of poisonous snake, the horned viper and the common adder. In the unlikely event of being bitten, try not to panic, keep the bitten area as still as possible and get to a hospital immediately.

The only hazard you're likely to see regularly are sea urchins, small spiky black creatures who sit on the rocks just below the water surface of the shore. They are not poisonous but their spikes can be painful. Wear sandals or flip-flops.

OPENING TIMES

Public sector offices and most businesses usually work from 8am to 4pm Monday to Friday. Post offices are open from 7am to 7pm, and generally close at weekends. Shops open from 8am to 8pm weekdays and until 2 or 3pm on Saturdays, although in summer some stay open much longer.

POSTAL SERVICES

Stamps are available from post offices, and from newspaper and tobacco kiosks. Mail across Europe takes less than a week; to the US it's about seven to ten days. Postcards and letters should cost less than 7kn for Europe and around 12kn to the US.

RELIGION

Croatia is 87.8% Roman Catholic (4.4% Orthodox, 0.4% other Christian and 1.3% Muslim). Most towns and villages have a patron saint whose saint's day will be celebrated once a year, usually with a procession followed by feasting and drinking.

SAFETY

Croatia has a low crime rate. Even so, don't be too showy with expensive possessions and don't wander around poorly lit city areas. Follow the same rules that you would at home and you'll be OK.

Foreign women may not appreciate the amount of attention they get from local men, especially those in coastal areas. If it's in danger of crossing the line between flirtatious and harrassment don't be shy of making your displeasure clearly known.

Landmines

Landmines are a problem in the countryside. Look out for signs bearing a skull and crossbones and stay well clear. However, not all minefields are marked and it is definitely not advisable to wander around any abandoned villages or wander across any uncultivated fields. In war-affected areas such as eastern and western Slavonia, the area between Karlovac and Split,

and around Zadar, do not stray away from the main roads or clearly marked footpaths.

SMOKING

Many Croats smoke and it is a far more socially acceptable habit than in the UK or US. No smoking is permitted in public buildings and cinemas, and on public transport. Only a certain number of restaurants, cafés and bars have a no-smoking area. Cigarettes are bought from kiosks marked 'Duhan' (tobacco). Most of the major Western brands are available.

STUDY

If you are looking to study Croatian, many local universities offer summer schools and short courses, including the University of Zagreb (www.croaticum.com.hr). The Croatian Heritage Foundation (01 61 15 116, www.matis.hr) also runs summer schools in conjunction with the university.

In London, the Croatian Language School (020 8948 5771, www.easycroatian.com) runs immersion courses.

University of Osijek *Trg Sv Trojstva 3, HR-31000 Osijek (031 224 102/www.unios.hr).*
University of Rijeka *Trg braće Mažuranića 10, HR-51000 Rijeka (051 406 500/www.uniri.hr).*
University of Split *Livanjska 5, 21000 Split (021 558 222/ www.unist.hr).*
University of Zadar *Ulica Mihovila Pavlinovica, 23000 Zadar (023 200 534/www.unizd.hr).*
University of Zagreb *Trg maršala Tita 14, HR-10000 Zagreb (01 45 64 111/www.unizg.hr).*

TELEPHONES

The dialling code for Croatia is +385. Croatian town and city codes have a zero in front of them that must be left off when calling from overseas.

When calling overseas from Croatia, the prefix 00 is the international access code.

Public phones

Public telephones use cards bought from post offices and kiosks. They come in units ('*impulsa*') from 25 to 500. Units run down fast calling internationally and you need a card of at least 50 *impulsa*, which should cost about 50kn.

It may be more convenient to place a call from a booth set up at most post offices.

Mobile phones

Croatia relies on the mobile. Roaming agreements exist with foreign companies and if you have a roaming facility on your mobile, the only problem should be the hideous expense. Or purchase a local SIM card with a pre-paid subscription; you can usually buy a card with some starter airtime, although you should make sure your mobile is unlocked. A Simpa (T-Mobile) SIM card costs 120kn including 100kn worth of free airtime, although this is added at 20kn after your first call and then 10kn for the next 10 months. If you're only in Croatia for a short while, you may need to buy top-up vouchers at a cost of 50kn or 100kn. For further details visit www.t-mobile.hr.

TIME

Croatia is an hour ahead of GMT and six hours ahead of Eastern Standard Time. The clocks go forward an hour in spring and back an hour in autumn.

TIPPING

Tipping is expected by taxi drivers and waiters in restaurants. Round up bills to the next 10kn-20kn, or by about 10 per cent.

You don't need to tip in pubs and cafés, unless you have received special service and have been there for a while.

TOILETS

Most cafés and bars have toilets – although the staff would probably prefer it if you bought a drink before or after using them. Toilets in train stations, airports and other public areas will sometimes have a lady stationed at the door to collect a user fee of around 2kn – keep a few coins handy on long bus journeys. Universal signs will be placed on the toilet doors to indicate men's and ladies', or look out for *M* (men's) and *Ž* (ladies').

TOURIST INFORMATION

All cities, towns and even a number of villages have tourist information offices. There will usually be at least one person who speaks English. Levels and quality of service are variable. There's also an additional call service **Croatian Angels** (0385 62 999 999) that offers tourist information in English. The website www.croatia.hr is reasonably comprehensive.

Croatian National Tourist Office (UK) *Croatia House, 162-4 Fulham Palace Road, London W6 9ER (020 8563 7979).*
Croatian National Tourist Office (USA) *350 Fifth Avenue, Suite 4003, New York 10118 (212 279 8672).*

TOUR OPERATORS

There are more than 100 tour operators selling all kinds of holidays in Croatia – 15 new ones were set up in 2005 alone. The list below can be no more than a sample. The Croatian National Tourist Office in London (*see above*) has a more extensive register.

adriatica.net (+385 1 24 15 614/www.adriatica.net). Zagreb-based company specialising in lighthouse holidays and trips for special events.
Adventure Company (01420 541 007/www.adventure company.co.uk). Active breaks around Dalmatia: rafting; diving; canoeing; mountain biking and horse riding.
Andante Travels (01722 713 800/www.andantetravels.co.uk). Archaeological tours of Dalmatia including Split, Salona and Brač.
Arblaster & Clarke Wine Tours (01730 893 244/www. winetours.co. uk). Wine tours.
Bond Tours (01372 745 300/ www.bondtours.com). Includes tailor-made trips, apartments, fly drive and adventure tours.
Bosere Travel (0143 834 094/ www.bosmeretravel.co.uk). Specialist trips to Croatia including naturist, diving, painting and trekking.
Hidden Croatia (0871 208 0075/ www.hiddencroatia.com). Breaks and tailor-made holidays.
Holiday Options (0870 0130 450/ www.holidayoptions.co.uk). Large range of holidays in Croatia.
Nautilus Yachting (01732 867 445/www.nautilus-yachting.com). Sailing holidays.
Peng Travel (0845 345 8345/ www.pengtravel.co.uk). Naturist breaks in Istria.
Saga Holidays (0800 300 500/ www.saga.co.uk). Large list of destinations in Croatia.

Sail Croatia (020 7751 9988/0871 733 8686/ www.sailcroatia.net). Specialists in sailing holidays from beginners upwards.
Scuba En Cuba (01895 624 100/www.scuba-en-cuba). Since moved into Croatia, offering diving holidays in Dubrovnik and on Korčula island.
Simply Croatia (020 8541 2214/www.simplytravel.com). Flights from Bristol, London and Manchester to properties in rural Istria, Kvarner and Dalmatia.
Thomson Holidays (0870 060 0847/www.thomson.co.uk). Large range of holidays in Croatia.
Travelsphere (01858 410 818/ www.travelsphere.co.uk). Coach travel.
2 Wheel Treks Cycling (0845 612 6106/www.2wheeltreks.co.uk). Cycling and cruise trips to Istria and Dalmatia.

VISAS

Visitors from the European Union, Canada, USA, Australia and New Zealand do not need a visa if staying in Croatia for less than 90 days. If you're travelling between Split and Dubrovnik, you have to pass a small stretch of coastline around **Neum**, in the territory of Bosnia-Hercegovina. Buses and cars are stopped and identity documents checked. Bosnia-Hercegovina has similar visa requirements to Croatia but it's wise to check beforehand on current regulations.

WEIGHTS & MEASURES

Croatia uses the metric system.

WHEN TO GO

The Adriatic coast benefits from a Mediterranean climate, with hot summers. The average summer temperature is about 25C and in winter 12C. To avoid the crowds go in May or September, when the weather is slightly cooler and hotels are much cheaper.

Public holidays

The following are all national public holidays:
1 Jan New Year's Day; **6 Jan** Epiphany; **Easter Sunday**; **Easter Monday**; **1 May** Labour Day; **Corpus Christi** (movable feast); **22 June** Anti-Fascist Resistance Day; **25 June** Statehood Day; **5 Aug** Victory

Day/National Thanksgiving Day; **15 Aug** Assumption; **8 Oct** Independence Day; **1 Nov** All Saints' Day; **25, 26 Dec** Christmas holidays.

WORKING IN CROATIA

Croatia is a highly desirable place to live and an increasing number of people are settling here and setting up businesses. Aside from tourism, in which you will find a number of expats in sailing and diving clubs, there's also the property sector and the old stand-by of English-language teaching.

Also see the website **www. moj-posao.net** for further opportunities. Although it's aimed primarily at Croats, it's worth a look as you will find bilingual job opportunities posted from international employers, generally based in Zagreb.

Work permits

Working in Croatia requires a work or business permit. To work without one is illegal and can result in a fine or even deportation. To obtain a permit the first port of call is the Croatian Embassy, which in the UK is at 21 Conway Street, London W1T 6BN (020 7387 2022).

Residence permit

A temporary residence permit is required for anyone staying in Croatia for more than three months, whether for work or any other reasons. If you're a long-term tourist, the solution to this might be to nip over the border, have your passport stamped and come back.

If you have a work permit then the temporary residence is available to British citizens for whatever the length of duration of the work permit. Permanent residence can be applied for once you've been in Croatia for five years.

To apply for residence you need a copy of your birth certificate issued within the last three months. The certificate must bear an apostille stamp, which you can only get at the Foreign Office's Legalisation office in London: call 020 7008 1111 for more information. Applicants also need proof of health insurance and a letter confirming that you don't have a criminal record. For more information you can contact the **British Embassy** in Zagreb (*see p321*) or the local department for foreigners at the Croatian Ministry of the Interior.

Vocabulary

The official language of Croatia is Croatian. It has dialects in Dalmatia, Zagreb and Zagorje, and Slavonia, but there is a standardised version used in official documents. Road signs are given in Croatian. In Istria they are often in Italian and Croatian. English is widely spoken in holiday areas but less so in the interior, where if you learn a few phrases, it is likely to be appreciated. For food terms, *see p327* **Decoding the Menu**.

Pronunciation

Croatian is a phonetic language and has no silent letters. For English speakers, the difficulty comes with some of the sibilant consonants, which have different sound to the English ones:

c is 'ts' as in 'hats'
ć is a light 'ch' as 'future'
č is 'ch' as in 'church'
š is a soft 'sh' as in 'shoe'
ž is 'zh' as in 'pleasure'

Other letters are **lj**, as in the 'lli' of million, **nj** as in the 'ny' of canyon and **d**, as in the j of jury. This is often rendered in English as 'dj' (as in Tudjman), a practice we follow in this guide. The Croatian letter j is pronounced as an English 'y'.

Basics

yes *da*
no *ne*
hello/good day *dobar dan*
goodbye *do vidjenja*
hello (on phone) *molim*
hello! (familiar) *bok!*
good morning *dobro jutro*
good evening *dobra večer*
good night *laku noć*
please *molim*
thank you (very much) *vvala (lijepo)*
great/OK *dobro*
I don't know *ne znam*
do you speak English? *govorite li engleski?*
I'm sorry, I don't speak Croatian *Izvinite, ne govorim hrvatski*
I don't understand *ne razumijem*
what's your name? (polite) *kako se zovete?*

what's your name? (familiar) *kako se zoveš?*
my name is… *zovem se…*
excuse me/sorry *oprostite*
where are you from? (polite) *odakle ste?*
where are you from? (familiar) *odakle si?*
when? *kada?*
how much is it? *koliko košta?*
large *veliko*
small *malo*
more *više*
less *manje*
expensive *skupo*
cheap *jeftino*
hot (*food, drink*) *toplo*
cold *hladno*
with/without *sa/bez*
open *otvoreno*
closed *zatvoreno*
can I book a room? *mogu li rezervati sobu?*

Getting around

where is…? *gdje je…?*
where to? *kamo?*
here *ovdje*
there *tamo*
left *levo*
right *desno*
straight on *pravo*
backwards *natrag*
a ticket to… *jednu kartu za...*
single *u jednom pravcu*
return *povratnu kartu*
when does the next bus/ferry/ train leave for…? *kada polazi sljedeći autobus/ trajekt/vlak za…?*
I'm lost *Izgubio same se* (masc)/ *Izgubila sam se* (fem)
how far is it? *koliko je daleko?*
arrival *polazak*
departure *odlazak*
station *kolodvor*
airport *zračna luka*
port *luka*
ferry terminal *trajektna luka*

Booking a room

do you have…? *Imati li vi…?*
reservation *rezervacija*
I have a reservation *Imam rezervaciju*
full board *pansion*
half board *polupansion*
single room *jednokrevetna soba*
double room *dvokrevetna soba*
shower *tuš*
bath *banja/kupanje*

balcony *balkon*
sea view *pogled na more*

Time

In Croatian, half-hours mean half to the next hour, so it may be easier to say *deset i trideset* ('10.30') instead of *pola jedanaest* ('half-to-eleven').

what time is it? *koliko je sati?*
ten o'clock *deset sati*
day *dan*
week *tjedan*
today *danas*
tomorrow *sutra*
yesterday *jučer*
in the morning *ujutro*
in the evening *uveče*
early *rano*
late *kasno*

Numbers

1 *jedan*; 2 *dva*; 3 *tri*; 4 *četiri*; 5 *pet*; 6 *šest*; 7 *sedam*; 8 *osam*; 9 *devet*; 10 *deset*; 11 *jedanaest*; 12 *dvanaest*; 13 *trinaest*; 14 *četrnaest*; 15 *petnaest*; 16 *šesnaest*; 17 *sedamnaest*; 18 *osamnaest*; 19 *devetnaest*; 20 *dvadeset*; 21 *dvadeset i jedan*; 30 *trideset*; 40 *četrdeset*; 50 *pedeset*; 60 *šezdeset*; 70 *sedamdeset*; 80 *osamdeset*; 90 *devedeset*; 100 *sto*; 200 *dvjesta*; 1,000 *tisuća*

Days, months

Monday *ponedjelak*
Tuesday *utorak*
Wednesday *srijeda*
Thursday *četvrtak*
Friday *petak*
Saturday *subota*
Sunday *nedjelja*

January *sljedečanj*
February *veljača*
March *ožujak*
April *travanj*
May *svibanj*
June *lipanj*
July *srpanj*
August *kolovoz*
September *rujan*
October *listopad*
November *studeni*
December *prosinac*

spring *proljeće*
summer *ljeto*
autumn *jesen*
winter *zima*

Decoding the Menu

Useful phrases

are these seats taken?
da li je slobodno?
bon appetit! *dobar tek!*
do you have...? *Imate li...?*
I'm a vegetarian
Ja sam vegetarijanac
I'm diabetic *Ja sam dijabetičar*
I'd like a table for two
molim stol za dvoje
the menu, please
molim vas jelovnik
I didn't order this
nisam ovo naručio
the bill (please) *račun (molim)*

Basics
(osnovno)

ashtray *pepeljara*
bill *račun*
bread *kruh*
cup *šalica*
fork *vilica*
glass *čaša*
knife *nož*
milk *mlijeko*
napkin *ubrus*
oil *ulje*
pepper *biber*
plate *tanjur*
salt *sol*
spoon *žlica*
sugar *šećer*
teaspoon *žličica*
vinegar *ocat*
water *voda*

Meat
(meso)

but leg
ćevapčići/cevapi mincemeat rissoles
čobanec spicy meat stew
govedina beef
grah sa svinjskom koljenicom
   bean soup with pork knuckle
guska goose
gusta juha thick goulash soup
janjetina lamb
jetra liver
koljenica pork knuckle
kunić/zec rabbit
odrezak escalope (usually veal/pork)
panceta bacon
pašticada stew of beef marinated
   in wine
patka duck
piljetina chicken
pljeskavica meat patty
prsa breast
purica/tuka turkey
ražnjići skewered meats

srnetina venison
šunka ham
svinjetina pork
teletina veal
zagrebački odrezak stuffed breaded
   meat chop

Fish / seafood
(riba / plodovi mora)

riba sa roštilja/na žaru
   grilled fish
bakalar dried cod
barbun mullet
brancin sea bass
brodet fish stew
cipal golden grey mullet
crni rižot black risotto (with squid
   ink)
dagnje/mušule/školjke mussels
girice whitebait
hobotnica octopus
jastog lobster
jegulja eel
kamenice/ostrige oysters
kapica clam
kovač john dory
lignje squid
list sole
losos salmon
lubin sea perch
orada gilthead sea bream
oslić hake
pastrva trout
rak crab
šaran carp
sipa cuttlefish
škampi scampi
škrpina sea scorpion
skuša mackerel
štuka pike
trilja red mullet
tuna tuna
žablji kraci frogs' legs
zubatac dentex

Accompaniments
(prilozi)

kruh bread
krumpir potatoes
prženi krumpir chips
riža rice
tjestenina pasta

Salads
(salate)

cikla beetroot
krastavac cucumber
mješana salata mixed salad
rajčica tomato
rokula rocket
zelena salata green (lettuce) salad

Vegetables
(povrće)

cvjetača cauliflower
gljive mushrooms
grašak peas
kuhani kukuruz sweetcorn
leća lentils
mahune green beans
mrkva carrot
paprika pepper
šparoge asparagus
špinat spinach

Fruit & nuts
(voće & orasi)

ananas pineapple
banana banana
dinja melon
jabuka apple
jagoda strawberry
kruška pear
lubenica watermelon
malina raspberry
marelica apricot
naranča orange
orah walnut
šljiva plum
smokva fig
trešnja cherry

Desserts
(deserti)

kolač cake
kremšnita cream cake
kroštule fried pastry twists
palačinke pancakes
rožata crème caramel
sladoled ice-cream
torta gateau

Drinks
(pića)

mineralna voda mineral water
sok (od naranče) (orange) juice
led ice

čaj tea
kava coffee

pivo beer
tamno pivo dark beer
rakija brandy

vino wine
bijelo vino white wine
crno vino red wine
crveno vino rosé wine
penjušac sparkling wine
gemišt spritzer
bevanda wine & water

Further Reference

DIRECTORY

BOOKS

Fiction

Ivo Andrić
The Days of the Consuls
Tales of 19th-century Ottoman-ruled Travnik, by the man both Serbs and Croats claim as their own. Ivo Andrić is best known for his masterpiece *Bridge over the Drina*.

Slavenka Drakulić
As If I Am Not There
Harrowing story of a Bosnian rape victim from the Yugoslav war, by one of Croatia's leading contemporary writers

Branko Franolić
An Historical Survey of Literary Croatian
Offers precisely what it says on the cover.

Miroslav Krleža
The Return of Philip Latinovicz
A classic work, and thus often a set novel in schools, by the acknowledged master of 20th-century Croatian literature.

Miroslav Krleža
The Banquet in Blitva
Satire of Europe in the Age of the Dictators, written in the 1930s.

Dubravka Ugresić
Fording the Stream of Consciousness
The most striking work of this exiled Croatian writer, also known for *In the Jaws of Life*. Ugresić is criticised in Croatia for her neutral stance in the 1990s.

History

Ivo Banać
The National Question in Yugoslavia
In-depth exploration of national identities.

Catherine Bracewell
The Uskoks of Senj
History of the pirate sea-kings of the Adriatic in the 16th century.

Elinor Despalatović
Ljudevit Gaj and the Illyrian Movement
Croatia's national awakening in the turbulent 1830s and 1840s.

Misha Glenny
The Fall of Yugoslavia
Colourful account of how it all ended in carnage, and why, by the BBC's man on the spot.

Ivo Goldstein
Croatia, a History
Goldstein is a Zagreb historian, and he writes here an overview of the country from the earliest times.

Brian Hall
The Impossible Country
Touching travelogue of Hall's journey around Yugoslavia in the build-up to war, 1991.

Robin Harris
Dubrovnik, a History
A recently published coffee-table volume on the Pearl of the Adriatic.

Barbara Jelavich
History of the Balkans
Sets the convoluted history of the region in a broader context.

Allan Little & Laura Silber
The Death of Yugoslavia
Fly-on-the-wall account to accompany the BBC TV series of the break-up of Yugoslavia.

Jasper Ridley
Tito – A biography
A rather sympathetic portrayal of the long-time Communist dictator

Marcus Tanner
Croatia: A Nation Forged in War
From Roman times to today, by the former Balkans correspondent of *The Independent*. It's probably the best general history currently in print.

Mark Thompson
Forging War – The Media in Serbia, Croatia and Bosnia-Hercegovina
Thompson looks in particular at the role played by the local press in manipulating the population. Look out also for Thompson's *A Paper House*, one of the better travelogue histories as Yugoslavia was collapsing.

Travelogue

Michael Donley
Marco Polo's Isle
Impressions from a year spent on Korčula.

Rebecca West
Black Lamb and Grey Falcon: A Journey through Yugoslavia
The benchmark for all Balkan travelogues, the book was actually researched in the late 1930s but its insights remain valid in the same way de Tocqueville's observations on democracy in the US are still worth reading; Rebecca West saw through to the Balkan soul.

Religion

Stella Alexander
The Triple Myth – A Life of Archbishop Alojzije Stepinac
Fair account of the rise and fall of Croatia's war-time primate.

Stella Alexander
Church and State in Yugoslavia Since 1945
Well researched account of confessional relations, written before the killing began again.

WEBSITES

www.croatia.hr
Official tourist website – excellent hotel database.

www.croatia businessreport.com
An English-language website devoted to Croatia's economic and business affairs.

www.croatiafocus.com
Pro-Croatia political articles available in English.

www.croatianworld.net
English-language news articles concerning Croatia.

www.csypn.org.uk
A Britain-based Croatian expat group that organises cultural and social events.

www.dalmatia-cen.com
The Dalmatia Regional Tourist Board's official site.

www.hic.hr
Croatian news in English.

www.hina.hr
Croatian state news agency, with English items.

www.istra.hr
The Istrian Regional Tourist Board's official site.

www.kvarner.hr
The Kvarner Regional Tourist Board's official site.

www.split.hr
The website of the city's municipal authority.

www.titoville.com
A cult site dedicated to the memory of the old leader.

www.visit-croatia.co.uk
A large website devoted to Croatian tourism.

www.zadar.hr
The Zadar Regional Tourist Board's official site.

www.zagreb.hr
The website of the Zagreb municipal authority.

Index A-Z

INDEX

INDEX

Advertisers' Index

Please refer to relevant sections for contact details.

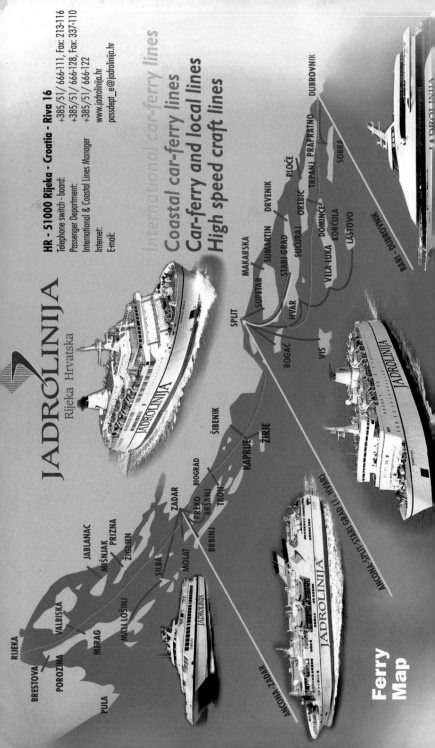

JADROLINIJA
Rijeka Hrvatska

HR - 51000 Rijeka - Croatia - Riva 16
Telephone switch - board: +385/51/ 666·111, Fax: 213·116
Passenger Department: +385/51/ 666·128, Fax: 337·110
International & Coastal Lines Manager   +385/51/ 666·122
Internet: www.jadrolinija.hr
E-mail: passdept_e@jadrolinija.hr

International car-ferry lines

Coastal car-ferry lines
Car-ferry and local lines
High speed craft lines

Ferry Map

RIJEKA
BRESTOVA
POROZINA
VALBISKA
PULA
MERAG
MALI LOŠINJ
SILBA
MOLAT
ŽIGLJEN
PRIZNA
MIŠNJAK
JABLANAC
ZADAR
PREKO
BIOGRAD
BRBINJ
BRŠANJ
TKON
KAPRIJE
ŽIRJE
ŠIBENIK

ANCONA-ZADAR
ANCONA-SPLIT-STARI GRAD (I. HVAR)

SPLIT
ROGAČ
VIS
HVAR
SUPETAR
STARI GRAD
SUMARTIN
DRVENIK
MAKARSKA
PLOČE
OREBIĆ
SUĆURAJ
VELA LUKA
DOMINCE
KORČULA
TRPANJ PRAPRATNO
SOBRA
LASTOVO
DUBROVNIK
BARI - DUBROVNIK